ON THE HISTORY OF
ECONOMIC THOUGHT

BRITISH AND AMERICAN ECONOMIC ESSAYS
A. W. Bob Coats

ON THE HISTORY OF
ECONOMIC THOUGHT
VOLUME I

SOCIOLOGY AND PROFESSIONALIZATION
OF ECONOMICS
VOLUME II

HISTORIOGRAPHY AND METHODOLOGY
OF ECONOMICS
VOLUME III

ON THE HISTORY OF ECONOMIC THOUGHT

BRITISH AND AMERICAN ECONOMIC ESSAYS
VOLUME I

A. W. Bob Coats

London and New York

First published 1992
by Routledge
11 New Fetter Lane, London EC4P 4EE

Simultaneously published in the USA and Canada
by Routledge
a division of Routledge, Chapman and Hall, Inc.
29 West 35th Street, New York, NY 10001

© 1992 A. W. Bob Coats

Typeset in Baskerville by
Falcon Typographic Art Ltd, Fife, Scotland
Printed and bound in Great Britain by
Mackays of Chatham PLC, Chatham, Kent

British Library Cataloguing-in-Publication Data
A catalogue reference for this title is available
from the British Library

ISBN 0–415–06715–4

Library of Congress Cataloging–in–Publication Data
has been applied for

ISBN 0–415–06715–4

To
Louise, Simon and Peter
and, above all,
Sonia

CONTENTS

CONTENTS

Part III Later nineteenth century British economics

Part IV American economics

Part V Recent, general economics

NOTES ON CHAPTERS

All but two of the chapters comprising this volume have been published before. Given below is a listing of sources.

1 Introduction 'First kick up a dust . . .' – previously unpublished.
2 In defence of Heckscher and the idea of mercantilism – *Scandinavian History Economic Review*, vol. II (1958), pp. 73–87.
3 Mercantilism: economic ideas, history, policy – Occasional Paper No. 139, University of Newcastle, NSW, Australia (August 1987).
4 Changing attitudes to labour in the mid-eighteenth century – *Economic History Review*, vol. XI, no. 1 (August 1958), pp. 35–51. Reprinted with an addendum in *Essays in Social History*, M. W. Flinn and T. C. Smart (eds) (Oxford, 1974).
5 Economic thought and poor law policy in the eighteenth century – *Economic History Review*, vol. XIII, no. 1 (August 1960), pp.39–51.
6 The relief of poverty, attitudes to labour, and economic change in England, 1660–1782 – *International Review of Social History*, vol. XXI (1976), pp. 98–115.
7 Adam Smith: the modern re-appraisal – *Renaissance and Modern Studies* (November 1962), pp. 25–48.
8 Adam Smith and the mercantile system – *Essays on Adam Smith*, Andrew S. Skinner and Thomas Wilson (eds) (Oxford: Clarendon Press, 1975), pp. 218–36.
9 The classical economists and the labourer – *Land, Labour and Population in the Industrial Revolution*, E. L. Jones and G. E. Mingay (eds) (London: Edward Arnold, 1967), pp. 100–30.
10 The classical economists, industrialization and poverty – *The Long Debate on Poverty*, Arthur Seldon (ed.) (London: Institute of Economic Affairs, 1972), pp. 143–68.
11 Samuel Hollander's Mill: a review article – *The Manchester School* (September 1987), pp. 310–16.
12 The historist reaction in English political economy, 1870–90 – *Economica* (May 1954), pp.143–53.

ACKNOWLEDGEMENTS

For permission to reproduce the materials in this volume, acknowledgement is due to the following sources: *The Scandinavian History Economic Review* for 'In defence of Heckscher and the idea of mercantilism'; *The Economic History Review* for the following two articles: 'Changing attitudes to labour in the mid-eighteenth century' and 'Economic thought and poor law policy in the eighteenth century'; *International Review of Social History* for 'The relief of poverty, attitudes to labour, and economic change in England, 1660–1782'; *Renaissance and Modern Studies* for 'Adam Smith: the modern reappraisal'; Oxford University Press for 'Adam Smith and the mercantile system' in *Essays on Adam Smith* edited by Andrew S. Skinner and Thomas Wilson; Routledge (formerly Methuen) publishers for 'The classical economists and the labourer', in *Land, Labour and Population in the Industrial Revolution* edited by E. L. Jones and G. E. Mingay; The Institute of Economic Affairs for 'The classical economists, industrialization and poverty' in *The Long Debate on Poverty* edited by Arthur Seldon; *The Manchester School* for 'Samuel Hollander's *Mill*: a review article'; *Economica* for the following three articles: 'The historist reaction in English political economy, 1870–90', 'Alfred Marshall and Richard T. Ely: some unpublished letters' and 'Alfred Marshall and the early development of the London School of Economics: some unpublished letters'; Edward Elgar Publishing Ltd for 'Marshall and ethics' in *Alfred Marshall in Retrospect* edited by Rita McWilliams Tullberg; *The Journal of Law and Economics* for 'Political economy and the tariff reform campaign of 1903' © 1968 by the University of Chicago; Charles Scribner's Sons, an imprint of Macmillan Publishing Company, for 'Economic Thought' from the Encyclopedia of American Economic History; Cambridge University Press and *The Journal of American Studies* for 'Henry Carter Adams: a case study in the emergence of the social sciences in the United States, 1850–1900'; The University of Texas Press for 'Clarence Ayres' place in the history of American economics: an interim assessment'; *The Nebraska Journal of Economics and Business* for 'The current "crisis" in economics in historical perspective'; St Martin's Press and Macmillan Press for 'The revival of subjectivism in economics' in *Beyond Positive Economics* edited by J. Wiseman.

1

INTRODUCTION
'First kick up a dust, ...'

The invitation to prepare an autobiographical introduction to these volumes of essays affords an opportunity to demonstrate the degree of coherence and continuity underlying my various shifts of intellectual interest and attention over the past four decades.

My fascination with the similarities and differences between British and American culture and institutions, dating back to mid-adolescence, has been a unifying motif in my work. It has been nurtured and sustained by frequent transatlantic journeys that have enabled me to study, teach and research in a score or more of American and British universities. In some ways this has been an unsettling as well as a rewarding experience; and the same is true of my reluctance to acquire an unambiguous disciplinary identity, for I have moved, sometimes uneasily, back and forth between economics (mainly in the USA), economic and social history (mainly in Britain) and intellectual history (in both). Periodic forays into economic methodology, historiography, American Studies, the sociology of knowledge and the philosophy of science have given me a particular penchant for Bishop Berkeley's remark that 'those who engage in philosophical debate, first kick up a dust, and then complain that they can't see'.[1] My professional life has, indeed, been a series of dust-kicking episodes, with consequential periodic blurred vision, as well as shifting and uncertain involvements. How far this is attributable to subconscious psychological preferences, and perhaps defences, I cannot say. But it is certainly due in part to the unusual circumstances of my professional initiation.

My academically undistinguished secondary school career in two West London grammar schools (of very uneven quality) was thrice interrupted: by half-time classes, designed to reduce the impact of wartime bombing on teachers and pupils; by a year's employment as a clerk with Middlesex County Council; and, then, after a year in another, far superior, state grammar school, by a premature move to university for one year before

1

being 'called up' for military service. At that time I intended to become a 'sports' master, with teaching as a weak but necessary second string. However, during my initial undergraduate pre-Royal Air Force (RAF) year at Exeter,[2] my aspirations rose somewhat despite – or perhaps because of – the lamentable quality of the economics teaching by a temporary superannuated professor. Little wonder that during the ensuing three-and-a-half years of military service – when I acquired a taste for travel in South Africa and the Middle East, fortunately without running into any serious danger – I determined to abandon economics and switch to English Literature. As a precautionary measure, however, I continued my University of London external degree by correspondence course while in the RAF, studying mainly in the lengthy and tedious gaps between spurts of intensive aircrew training and later, while serving as an intelligence officer in Palestine (as it then was). Most of my reading matter came from the British Council Library in Cairo (Egypt). Eventually I sat my Economic History special papers in Cairo during the intense summer heat. On passing, I applied for a place at the London School of Economics and was accepted, but only on condition that I would take the entire three year undergraduate course. No doubt the university was inundated with similar applications from current and ex-servicemen. Rejecting this offer, I returned to Exeter somewhat reluctantly on my release from the RAF and completed my first degree in eighteen months, (also concurrently passing part of a degree in English, again by correspondence course). Fortunately by this time the teaching at Exeter had been vastly improved, while the intellectual and social atmosphere of the student body was marvellously invigorating, enriched as it was by dozens of mature, worldly wise and highly motivated ex-servicemen and women. This environment was so attractive that I was naturally loath to leave; and in subsequent years I have constantly had to remind myself not to be unduly critical of conventional undergraduates' immaturity. After all, they do grow out of it!

When my degree result proved good enough to qualify me for a postgraduate studentship, I accepted it with alacrity. Unfortunately, the academic conditions at Exeter were far from ideal. I was brusquely informed that there were 'no facilities' for a postgraduate thesis; nor were there any relevant lectures. Consequently, I spent the next two years in unguided, unsupervised reading, and undertaking some limited diploma and undergraduate teaching. From the former I derived a broad, but unselective and somewhat uncritical familiarity with the 'great books' of economics, for I had no one with whom to discuss my ideas and interpretations. From the latter, I derived such enjoyment that I began to view university lecturing as a desirable, albeit distant goal. My initial postgraduate experience, although by no means unique in Britain either then or since, was utterly different from the present day American standardized graduate assembly-line training of economists, with its heavy emphasis on mathematics, econometrics and model building.

My decision to concentrate on the history of economic thought as the best method of remedying the glaring deficiencies of my undergraduate education seems in retrospect distinctly quaint, if not naive, and far removed from the present climate of opinion in which economics graduates display an almost universal disinterest in, even scorn of, the literature of their subject. Thus, this phase of my apprenticeship highlights the change from the older, literary tradition of economics to the current preoccupation with technique.

For my Master's degree, by examination rather than by thesis, I chose a special subject on John Bates Clark, the leading *fin de siècle* American economic theorist, partly as a possible entrée to study in the USA. When I came to take the oral exam this choice seemed to interest my examiners, Marian Bowley and Terence Hutchison, far more than anything I had actually written! They were visibly disappointed to learn that I had no distinctive new insights or discoveries to report, since I had not yet had the opportunity to examine Clark's papers at Columbia University. However, apart from the successful outcome, the oral proved memorable since it gave me my first encounter with Hutchison, who subsequently became a lifelong friend and a major constructive influence on my work.

At about this time I had a remarkable stroke of luck – or, strictly speaking, two strokes – which permanently influenced my subsequent career. From Exeter I had applied, unsuccessfully, for English Speaking Union Fellowships (ESUs) at two of the famous American Ivy League universities. Then, out of the blue came an invitation to be a candidate for a similar ESU Fellowship at the University of Pittsburgh, of which I had never previously heard. At the interview in London my rival was an intelligent, articulate and unusually well dressed young man from the London School of Economics (LSE), obviously a far more prestigious academic institution than Exeter. Assuming he would be selected, I enjoyed a very relaxed interview. Immediately thereafter I was astonished to be informed, unofficially, that I would probably be successful since the other candidate was from the LSE, 'and we don't think they are gentlemen'! Upon my arrival in Pittsburgh, armed with my Fellowship, I recounted this story to the dynamic and efficient organizer of the university's international student reception programme, who was greatly amused. She proceeded to explain that as Pittsburgh had hitherto had ESU Fellows only from Oxbridge for the previous three years, they had specifically asked for candidates from other universities. Thus, a bizarre mixture of strong British anti-LSE and weak American anti-Oxbridge attitudes had combined to open up the new world. So much for the Anglo-American 'special relationship'.

There was one further curious incident before we embarked on our transatlantic adventure. Armed with my ESU Fellowship and Fulbright travel grant I could confidently expect to get a student visa. But as my stipend was obviously inadequate to support two of us, my wife needed an immigrant visa (with the requisite American sponsorship), which would enable her to supplement our income in accordance with the traditional married graduate student system of exploitation. (Oddly enough, the idea that my wife's career might be as important as mine simply did not occur to either of us![3]) At the final stage of the embassy procedure this asymmetry was duly noted by the vice consul who, having heard our explanation, including my intention of staying on for three years in order to get a Ph.D., promptly took her pen and struck out the word 'student' on my documents, substituting 'immigrant'. In later years I have often wondered how many other would-be US immigrants have been granted so swift and painless an adjustment of status.

While I had every reason to expect that the University of Pittsburgh would offer an exhilarating educational experience, in the wider sense of that term, whatever its place in the academic pecking order, I had no idea that it would also prove to be a major watershed in my intellectual development. Once again, chance played a crucial role.

My initiation into the mysteries of American higher education occurred in the 'crypt' of the university's so-called 'Cathedral of Learning', a brash forty-two storey neo-Gothic skyscraper not far from the heart of that large, vibrant American city. This structure was anachronistic enough to disconcert all but the most open or naive of European historical minds. Could it be taken seriously as a monument to American cultural aspirations? Even more directly unsettling was the shock of registration, with its bewildering task of selecting courses from among a virtually infinite array of undergraduate and graduate offerings. Given my limited provincial university experience and the highly structured character of the English degree curriculum, my introduction to the radical differences between the two systems could hardly have been more dramatic. I have been acutely aware of these differences ever since.

At registration I had another major stroke of luck. While scanning the rich cafeteria of course offerings my manifest bewilderment attracted the kindly attention of Bela Gold, Professor of Economics and Research Associate at the university's Bureau of Business Research, who provided helpful guidance. After considerable indecision, I registered for Production Economics and his Research Seminar in Industrial Economics in the first semester, together with Russell Dixon's Institutional Economics, an appropriately American topic that already intrigued me.[4] So impressed was I by Gold's energetically confident, lucid, penetrating but demanding teaching style, that in the second semester I took his Production Economics and his seminar, which focused on Research Methods in the Social Sciences, a virtually uncharted field for me.

Taken as a whole, Gold's courses represented my first totally new and refreshing encounter with an outstanding independent-minded maverick economist, a species both then and now all too seldom encountered in the British university system. If I suffered unduly from complacency, one of our national diseases, it didn't survive for long. Gold's approach to the social sciences was a lasting learning experience. He raised a host of searching and disquieting questions about the nature and significance of economics and the other social science disciplines, many of which I still have not resolved.

Early in our discussions Gold enquired, apparently innocuously, why I proposed to write my Ph.D. dissertation on John Bates Clark. When I replied that the choice seemed fairly obvious, since he was widely recognized as the first American economic theorist of international stature, Gold's unenthusiastic response clearly revealed that he considered Clark neither typical, nor particularly interesting. This led me to reconsider my whole enterprise, since one of my strong, as yet only half-formed, intentions was to explore the possibilities of Anglo-American comparisons. For this purpose Clark evidently would not suffice. So, largely as a result of Gold's prompting, and the stimulus of his wide ranging approach to research methods, I decided to tackle a much more ambitious and characteristically American topic: a study of the protracted series of intense methodological controversies which had been so marked a feature of late nineteenth and early twentieth century American economics. There had been almost no comparable discussions among British economists at the time.[5] Thus I had selected my Ph.D. topic, with Gold's strong support, well before I applied to do further graduate work at Johns Hopkins. Little did I appreciate then, or indeed for some years thereafter, that the quest would take me into a variety of multi-disciplinary, cross-cultural issues, and eventually into the professionalization of economics.

Gold's approach strongly reinforced my predilection for the empirical and policy relevant aspects of economics, as against pure theory, for he effectively combined clear thinking and acute analysis with a healthy scepticism towards orthodox (nowadays termed neo-classical) economics and a profound respect for empirical data. The last of these qualities, unfortunately so rare among latter-day highly trained American economists, naturally appealed to my historian's instincts.

Of course, had I aspired to being an original economic theorist my intellectual deficiencies would soon have become painfully obvious at Johns Hopkins, where my fellow graduates included several who have subsequently had distinguished mainstream careers, including one Nobel Laureate (so far). On the other hand, had I fully committed myself to economic history I might soon have been engulfed and left stranded by the rising tide of cliometrics – as one of those victims wittily depicted as the handloom weavers of an intellectual revolution. As it transpired, despite several decades as a teacher of economic and social history, and almost two as head of an independent university department in the subject, I have always been a somewhat marginal member of that guild, especially with respect to my publications. Even among historians of economics, the disciplinary species with which I have had the closest ties, I have been almost the sole card-carrying economic historian, for the great majority of scholars in the field have started out and formally continued as economists.

Some, of course, are also excellent historians. An unequivocal commitment to economics is obviously less necessary for one who does not regard the history of theory or economic analysis as the Ark of the Covenant. Fortunately, in recent years there has been a rising body of opposition to the unduly narrow, often Whiggish and absolutist approach which dominated the subject for too long. Reading and teaching economic history strengthened my primary interest in the development, dissemination and influence of economic ideas; the interrelationships between economic ideas, events and policies; the historical and institutional (especially educational) context from which they have emerged; and the socio-economic problems to which they have been been addressed.

Where does methodology fit into this pattern? In the autobiography he published in his nineties Richard T. Ely, the controversial first secretary–treasurer of the American Economic Association, claimed that the methodological debates that had accompanied its founding were merely a means to an end, a way of 'breaking the crust' which had settled on American economics.[6] The objective, in other words, was professional rather than purely intellectual. For me, methodology was a means of getting at the differences between British and American economics, and my research evolved into an investigation of the ways in which the discipline has functioned as a potentially important instrument for understanding economic life and shaping economic policy. This pragmatic approach was fully in accordance with Gold's conception of economic research. It eventually became clear that methodological questions, such as 'What is the nature of economics?', 'Is economics a science and if so, what does that mean in epistemological terms?' also had occupational and professional, as well as philosophical and cultural dimensions. However, during my Pittsburgh and Hopkins years, and for some time thereafter, these aspects seemed to be of secondary importance. I was too engrossed in more immediate matters.

After leaving Pittsburgh we had a frustrating, but profoundly mind-expanding drive to California and back, followed by several weeks with relatives in Connecticut before going to Baltimore, a move that almost failed to materialize owing to a departmental administrative error. At Hopkins I entered a far superior, more prestigious and more demanding academic world, and the contrast with Pittsburgh gave me a keen sense of the remarkable heterogeneity of American universities. The Economics Department was of an ideal size[7] – large enough to offer a reasonable range of specialisms, yet small enough to afford abundant opportunities for staff–student interaction and camaraderie – much more so, I soon learned, than in the larger leading graduate schools. It was there that I received my first introduction to serious intellectual peer group discussion and criticism both in the Economics Department's seminars and its journal club, and in A.O. Lovejoy's famous History of Ideas club meetings. Fortunately my age, experience and breadth of education helped to offset my inadequate mathematical and technical capacity, and I still recall with relief and gratitude the generous C grade I received from Carl Christ for my limited performance on the required mathematical economics course. It was in fact a revealing educational experience for, given my grasp of economic theory, I was fully able to understand much of the required textbook, but hopelessly inept when it came to handling the set problems. However, the potential gains in theoretical clarity and precision from mathematical methods were obvious enough, even to me.

The most widely known Hopkins economist during my two-year stay was Fritz Machlup, a distinguished fourth generation Austrian, who single-handedly conducted the required macro, micro and methodology courses. Having quit his native country in the early 1930s to avoid persecution, like so many able Jewish intellectuals, Machlup was a man of strongly pro-European prejudices that obviously predisposed him in my favour.[8] Needless to say, his conception of economic methodology was far more conventional – more formal, logical and abstract – than Gold's, which owed so much to the teachings of his Columbia University mentors, the sociologist Robert Lynd and the great American empiricist, Wesley C. Mitchell. Machlup was extremely sceptical of the reliability of economic data, delighting in demonstrating the errors, anomalies and inconsistencies of official statistics – warnings of subsequent use to me as an economic historian. He was in sympathy, though not uncritically, with Milton Friedman's 'positive' economic methodology, while heavily emphasizing the inadequacies of 'measurement without theory'. Whereas Gold was a pragmatist, less in the strict philosophical than the common sense meaning of that term, Machlup was a committed subjectivist influenced by the works of Lionel Robbins and Felix Kaufmann (which we were expected to assimilate), and Alfred Schütz (whose writings were not, however, included in his monstrous course reading lists). Hutchison, my erstwhile examiner, was forcefully criticized both in class and, soon after I left Hopkins, in a notable confrontation in the 1955 *Southern Economic Journal* which is still reprinted in leading anthologies of economic methodology. Thus, given the combination of influences from Gold, Machlup and Hutchison, and my personal inclination to intellectual non-conformity, it is hardly surprising that I have had difficulty in reaching settled methodological convictions.

Machlup welcomed my choice of dissertation topic; more, I suspect, because he was considering writing a book on methodology and might learn something from my investigations, than because he approved of my mild heterodoxy. He realized that I had an ulterior historical motive in studying methodology, and was intrigued by my protracted and only moderately successful efforts to make sense of the American institutionalists, especially that brilliant idiosyncratic outsider, Thorstein Veblen. Machlup was a careful and conscientious supervisor, with an almost obsessive preoccupation with semantics, which has had a lasting impact on me.[9] Like any good supervisor he set a high standard, and one quickly learned that he had no patience

7

with obscure or sloppy thinking and writing. Nevertheless, he had little or no substantive influence on my research; less so in fact than my other supervisor, George Heberton Evans, the department's wise but overworked chairman.

At the end of my first Hopkins year we spent the summer in London deciding whether to settle permanently in the USA after the completion of my Ph.D. Largely for family reasons we decided against doing so, even though the British academic market seemed far less buoyant than its US counterpart. During that summer I attended a short lecture course at LSE on the British economy, designed for foreigners,[10] and worked on what was to become my first published article – a study of methodological controversy in British economics from 1870 to 90.[11] This marked the beginning of my explicitly comparative investigations. On my return to Baltimore the concluding stages of my graduate education proceeded almost without hitch, apart from a humiliating departmental oral exam which, I subsequently decided, was deliberately designed to take overconfident neophytes down a few pegs. If so, it was entirely successful in my case! By contrast, my Ph.D. oral was a piece of cake, for despite the presence of distinguished professors from several other departments, I clearly knew far more about my somewhat off-beat subject than they did.

My immediate future was easily settled by yet another stroke of good fortune. In my first Hopkins year I both greatly enjoyed and enormously benefited from a series of lectures delivered by a visiting professor, the great British economic historian, T.S. Ashton.[12] This was my first encounter with an outstanding leader in the field,[13] and it left a permanent imprint. Oddly enough, it was only the second course of lectures in the subject I had ever attended, and it proved to be the last! The following year, when an opening appeared for an economic historian at the University of Nottingham, I got the job, most unusually, without an interview. No doubt this was largely because the university's senior economic historian, J.D. Chambers, was a great admirer of Ashton, who had generously supported my application. Little did I imagine that we would be spending the next three decades at Nottingham, apart from occasional leaves of absence in the USA, and one year on the staff of the new University of York (1963–4).

Nottingham in the 1950s proved to be a good base for my continuing education. Economic history was enjoying a boom in Britain, and my two departmental colleagues, David Chambers and Robert Ashton – subsequently the founding Professor of History at the new University of East Anglia – were, in their very different ways, both excellent and congenial. From them I learned more about economic history than ever before, apart from T.S. Ashton's lectures, and in return I occasionally supplied some snippets of elementary economic analysis, about which they were needlessly underconfident. At the end of my first year the formidable external examiner, F.J. Fisher of LSE, neatly pinpointed the differences by describing me aptly, if somewhat disparagingly, as 'that theoretical young man'. I accepted the designation with only mild discomfort, knowing how it would have surprised my Hopkins colleagues. Such was the gulf between economics and conventional British economic history in those innocent, pre-cliometric days.

After spending a considerable time learning some economic history for lecturing purposes, and publishing my first two articles – the one mentioned earlier and a critical analysis of Veblen's methodology based on chapters of my dissertation[14] – I decided to embark on a broad study of the interaction of economic ideas and policy in Britain during the post–1815 period, the heyday of Ricardian political economy. Believing that parliamentary debates constituted a neglected channel of communication between the economists and the public, I began ploughing through numerous volumes of Hansard.[15] But the research results proved meagre relative to the effort involved, though the task left me with a profound and lasting sense of the complexities of the communication process, the dangers of glib oversimplifications about 'influence' and the significant differences between the approaches usually adopted by historians of economic ideas and economic historians.[16] This became yet another of my lifelong intellectual interests.

During the first five years at Nottingham my developing research interests led me to drop my original advanced undergraduate course on 'The Development of the World Economy, 1850–1950' in favour of a broadly based treatment of 'Economic Thought and Policy, 1660–1848', from which eventually emerged a series of articles on topics ranging from late seventeenth century English mercantilism through Adam Smith to studies of economic ideas on labour and the poor law, and the classical economists' views on economic policy.[17] As the students included non-economists from history and my own department, as well as honours economists, there was a continuing but stimulating tension in the task of catering to their various competencies, limitations, needs and interests. Similar, but even more acute pedagogical problems had arisen somewhat earlier when I offered to provide an introductory course in American Economic History as part of the new American Studies programme, for the 'customers' included students with no prior knowledge of economics or, for that matter, American geography, politics, political or constitutional history! This experience helped to shape my broad, eclectic conception of American Economic History, reinforcing my disinclination to become a cliometrician or, indeed, a conventional specialist in any single field or discipline. Thus, personal preferences and institutional needs have broadly operated in harmony.

In 1958 my wife and I returned to the USA with the aid of a Rockefeller Fellowship, which gave me the opportunity to visit the archives of a number of prominent late nineteenth and early twentieth century American economists, with a view to converting my dissertation into a book. However, the experience of re-reading the dissertation during the transatlantic voyage proved disconcerting. My analysis of the methodological controversies seemed reasonable enough, if somewhat superficial and incomplete; but it was almost totally divorced from the broader intellectual, social and cultural context and, indeed, from most other aspects of American economic thought of the period. Such a divorce was in fact fairly typical of the bulk of methodological writing in economics up to that time; and it is only quite recently that serious efforts have been made to undertake close methodological studies of economists' actual practices,[18] or of the interrelationships between economic methodology, intellectual history and the sociology of knowledge.

In my own case, the curious sense of detachment, even alienation, from my first intellectual offspring was substantially reinforced by the experience of archival work, which brought me into intimate contact with my subjects' personal and professional lives. Economists, it seemed, were also human. Moreover, their preoccupation with methodology was by no means as trivial as some commentators had maintained. Nevertheless, there was substantial justification for Ely's claim that the great debate of the 1880s in the United States was in part attributable to the younger, German-trained economists' determination to assert their 'right to exist scientifically' against the incumbent custodians of the ruling orthodoxy.[19] Indeed, as Mary O. Furner has persuasively demonstrated, an essential issue was the profound tension between the rival claims of 'advocacy and objectivity' – the new generation of professional academics' desire to make an impact on American society, while simultaneously benefiting from the protection afforded by science.[20] This tension was especially pronounced among the economists, some of whom were prominent victims in academic freedom cases; but it was also to be found among other American social scientists too, if only because disciplinary boundaries were by no means clear at the time. Thus, the marked difference in the intensity and persistence of methodological controversy among American, as against British economists was evidently due less to epistemological preoccupations than to differences in the two scholarly communities' occupational security and cultural self-assurance. There was also no American counterpart to the British economists' deep-rooted respect for social and intellectual authority and the continuity of doctrinal tradition, which was so conspicuously manifested in the hegemony of the Marshallian paradigm. Several of my later articles have addressed these matters.[21]

In retrospect, four highlights of our Rockefeller year stand out as having exerted a lasting influence on my work: the trip to Austin, Texas, to meet Clarence Ayres, the acknowledged leader of the so-called 'cactus league of dissenting economists' within the institutionalist movement; work on the Henry Carter Adams papers at Ann Arbor, Michigan – surely one of the richest and most revealing archives of any American social scientist; an introductory exploration of the American Economic Association's substantial records at Northwestern University, Evanston, Illinois, with the benign encouragement of the executive secretary, Harold F. Williamson, a leading American economic historian; and meetings at Columbia University with Joseph Dorfman, the doyen of historians of American economics, and Walter

P. Metzger, the outstanding historian of academic freedom and the scholarly profession in the USA. Taken as a whole, the year proved to be enormously fruitful both in personal contacts and in terms of ideas and research possibilities. The wider implications only gradually became apparent, for I was being irresistibly drawn into a combination of intellectual and cultural history, the sociology of science and the professionalization process, much of which had hitherto been entirely overlooked by historians of economics. This explains why I felt inadequately equipped to make substanial progress on my planned book, although I drafted some preliminary chapters.

On my return to the enjoyable, but comparatively humdrum routine of economic and social history teaching at Nottingham, there seemed to be no possibility of effectively pursuing my British and American research interests simultaneously. When I put this to T.S. Ashton, to whom I expressed some concern at my detachment from the mainstream of British economic history, he simply advised me to go my own way – which I probably would have done anyway! But my multiple intellectual schizophrenia, or perhaps mere failure of persistence and consistency, largely explains why my subsequent publications have been in the form of articles rather than the books I intended to write.[22] It also indicates that my primary allegiance, conscious or unconscious, has been to the social science rather than the humanistic historical mode.

Early in 1962, after I had already undertaken to teach in the summer school at Columbia University, I received an entirely unexpected invitation to join the founding faculty at the University of York, one of several brand new institutions inspired by the Robbins Report on Higher Education.[23] As York's opening was to be delayed until 1963, I was able to spend another year in the USA, mainly at the University of Virginia, at Charlottesville, having resisted the temptation to go to Austin where, I suspect, Ayres was hoping to enlist one more disciple. At Charlottesville I learnt more about the sociology of academic life than in any other single year. The unusually able group of economists, with strongly right-wing inclinations, seemed virtually segregated from the rest of the university community, and conscious of being a lone bastion of virtuous economic thinking in an otherwise naughty Keynesian world.[24] Despite the alien intellectual climate, I was nevertheless made very welcome, possibly because it was felt an Englishman could hardly be expected to know better! During that year I renewed my interest in methodology, producing a monograph on *Value Judgments in Economics*, and a short article on 'The origins of the Chicago School(s)', which was an indirect by-product of lively luncheons with my departmental colleagues.[25] There were, however, some disturbing stories from graduate students of the pressures for conformity with the departmental 'line'. How much substance there was in these reports I cannot say, for I had no part in departmental examining other than grading students in my own courses. But they were sufficiently vigorous and reiterated to suggest that libertarianism is not invariably compatible with liberalism, in the correct eighteenth century sense of that term.[26]

York, in its inaugural year (1963–4), was indeed an exhilarating place, having as yet none of the 'dead wood' that seems to be an inescapable, perhaps even essential, ingredient in any organization. There was an almost limitless sense of opportunity, with academic staff from a wide variety of backgrounds, many of whom were determined at all costs to avoid a replication of the defects of the universities whence they had come. These negative views, combined with a generally remarkable enthusiasm and openness to experiment, made for interminable and lively discussions ranging from details of administrative procedure, curricula and future appointments, to fundamental conceptions of the nature and purpose of universities. My early, and possibly ill-advised, return to Nottingham after nine months – as, so I said at the time, a rat who quit before the ship was even fully afloat – was primarily motivated by my decided preference for an independent Department of Economic and Social History, with freedom to collaborate equally with its Economics and History neighbours. My strong personal attachment to David Chambers, who was retiring from Nottingham, was another positive factor. At York it seemed clear that economic history was destined to remain indefinitely as an appendage of economics (as has in fact proved to be the case), with little hope of close collaboration with history. Ironically, as it transpired, the Nottingham situation eventually turned out to be only marginally better in that respect owing to the historians' persistent unwillingness to support any significant degree of curricular integration with economic history, or a full scale joint honours degree. Independence for economic and social history had only recently been achieved there prior to my return, following periods of benevolent subordination, initially to economics and subsequently to history.

Under ideal conditions these organizational dispositions would be merely trivial and boring, with no implications for the way the subject is conceived, taught and researched.[27] But unfortunately, in the 'real' world of academic politics and intellectual tunnel vision this is rarely the case. In the USA since the late 1950s, for example, the influential and welcome – though too often oversold – innovations associated with the so-called 'new' economic history, or cliometrics, could hardly have been conceived, let alone implemented, by scholars trained and located exclusively within history departments. In Britain, on the other hand, the relatively primitive character of the economic historians' theoretical and quantitative equipment meant that the transatlantic influx of new methods and techniques was too often greeted with suspicion, incomprehension and even hostility mingled with apprehension. The slow pace of academic change and the strong resistance to intellectual fashions meant that there was nothing in Britain to match the rapid spread of the American cliometric revolution. Moreover, in the Thatcherite contractionist context of the 1980s economic history's independent departmental status between economics and history (an arrangement unknown in the USA) made it an obvious target for worried administrators misguidedly seeking economies of scale.

Nationally, during that decade, vacant chairs in economic and social history were left unfilled or allowed to lapse; departments withered or were closed down; the number of postgraduate research studentships was severely cut; and academic staff were offered inducements to leave or obliged to merge into the larger communities of economists or historians. Generally speaking, the direct threat to academic freedom was minimal. However, there was certainly pressure for conformity to the new fashion for 'relevant' research; and the climate of opinion – both within the university and outside – was hardly conductive to intellectual vigour. Some of the more enterprising and mobile academic talent departed, while much of the dead wood remained. In sharp contrast to the American academic incentive system, under the new rules promotion to senior positions actually entailed loss of tenure! In Britain, financial exigencies and administrative convenience took priority over academic and scholarly needs and values. The damage to academic morale has been incalculable.

By the time I took early retirement from Nottingham, in December 1982, the fate of my subject locally was sealed. In a move I had already resisted, the defenceless rump of my colleagues was swept into the bowels of the History Department, which had earlier resisted close collaboration; and my chair, the single honours degree and three joint honours degrees all disappeared. Thus my greatest organizational impact on the university was, in a sense, posthumous.

Turning to more strictly intellectual matters, during the late 1960s and early 1970s there was a significant shift in the focus and direction of my research. As already noted, during the early and middle stages of my career, I had been able to ride on the crest of a wave of post-war university expansion and also, in my official capacity as an economic and social historian, to benefit indirectly from the sustained academic and public interest in the problems of long-term economic growth and development.[28] In retrospect, the economists' and historians' collective failure to promote effective interdisciplinary collaborative research on these issues strikes me as one of the major missed intellectual opportunities of the era: a regrettable testimony to the effectiveness of the barriers erected in the process of academic specialization. Towards the end of the 1960s, however, the economic historians' enthusiasm for economic growth was manifestly waning. But by that time a new academic movement appeared, one of much greater significance for me – the revival of research, scholarship and discussion in the history of economic thought. From my standpoint this was indeed a huge, albeit largely unanticipated, windfall.

I have written elsewhere of the nature, timing and reasons for this revival[29] which – to employ growthmanship terminology – was due both to trigger mechanisms and slowly generating forces. With respect to the former, the catalyst was the foundation of the Social Science Research Council (typically, some four decades after its American counterpart), which led to the organization of the first ever British conference on the history of economic thought, held in January 1968, at the University of Sussex.[30] Present at the creation, together with virtually all the leading British scholars in the field, was a seemingly youthful transatlantic envoy from Duke University, Craufurd Goodwin, who boldly announced that he and his colleagues proposed to launch a new specialist journal, *History of Political Economy* (given the acronym HOPE). This clearly suggested that a parallel revival was under way in the USA, with its far greater resources and catchment area. Nevertheless, the British response was predictably ambivalent – pleasure, interest, enthusiasm, tempered with cautious scepticism stemming from a concern that the venture was premature, since a plan to establish a broadly similar British publication had recently foundered for lack of qualitative and quantitative support. Of course, as it transpired, HOPE, under Goodwin's editorship, has more than fulfilled its founders' expectations, helping to make Duke the unchallenged world centre in the field.

Viewed from a longer-term perspective, the revival was attributable to a combination of interlinked ideas and conditions. For example, as a reaction against the post-1945 so-called mathematical–quantitative revolution in economics there was a growing concern that the discipline was becoming excessively narrow and technocratic – a view that is even more widely held now, a quarter century later. The interest in economic growth and development had heightened some economists' awareness of the historical and institutional dimensions of economic change (another matter of growing interest today, albeit in a somewhat different form); and there was also a concurrent philosophical and methodological reaction against the prevailing scientistic and positivistic climate of opinion, not only in economics, but in the social sciences generally. These ideas were soon reinforced by the disintegration of the Keynesian consensus, and the growth of sectarian doctrinal schools, each seeking a respectable historical lineage. (The results of such quests were not always respectable, but they served as a provocation and stimulus to serious scholarly work.) Also conspicuous failures of economic forecasting and policy measures undermined the discipline's scientific reputation, contributing to a crisis of professional self-confidence[31] which inspired various *ad hoc* and scholarly enquiries into the roots of the discipline's predicament. Thus, for several reasons it seems that the historians of economics had, perhaps unwittingly, timed their revival propitiously.

By dint of being at the right place at the right time, I was fortunately able to contribute to the revival in a number of ways: as author of the inaugural article in HOPE, and as a member of its editorial board; as founding editor of the *History of Economic Thought Newsletter*, now in its 48th issue (most of them from other editors); as organizer or co-organizer of a number of the regular annual history of economic thought conferences held in Britain, and the economic thought and policy sessions at the quadrennial International Economic History Congress during the 1970s and early 1980s;[32] and as co-supervisor of a systematic guide to archive sources in economics.[33] More satisfying still, has been the emergence of a national and international network of scholarly colleagues, research students and friends, with the consequential opportunities for global travel. Specialist learned societies have been established in various countries, each with its own bulletin or newsletter. National and international conferences have proliferated, especially in connection with the anniversaries of such luminaries as Smith, Marx, Keynes, Schumpeter, Marshall, *et al.*; and there has been a veritable flood of new books and articles, including the first four volumes in a projected series of more than a dozen 'country' studies of the development of economic ideas.[34] Yet another striking manifestation of the internationalization of the field has been the multi-country project on 'The institutionalization of political economy: Its introduction and acceptance into European, American and British universities'.[35] To the best of my knowledge, there has been no comparable international collaborative study of any other academic discipline.

During the 1970s the principal focus of my own research shifted towards the study of the role of economists in government, a topic hitherto almost entirely overlooked by historians of the discipline. In retrospect this neglect seems extraordinarily myopic, given the striking post-1945 growth in the numbers of economists employed in non-academic positions, both in the public and private sector. Under the conventional division of academic labour such a topic fell somewhere in the interstices between economics, economic history, public administration, and the history and sociology of the scientific professions. Of course there were scholarly and popular writings in all these fields bearing directly or indirectly on the subject; but no one had made this the specific focus of historical research. To me it was simply a logical extension of my long-standing interest in the nature of economics as an academic discipline and profession, and the question of what economists actually 'do' – i.e., the uses to which the economist's knowledge and skills can be put, especially for policy purposes. It was a fairly obvious (but, in my case, long-delayed) step from the epistemological questions underlying my Ph.D. thesis, cited earlier,[36] to issues of pressing importance to business and government personnel officers, such as: 'Why employ economists?'; 'What do economists know, that trained personnel in other fields don't?'; and, above all, 'What can economists contribute to the organization's successful performance?'. Answers to these questions were by no means obvious, as is suggested by the cynic who remarked that by the 1970s in Britain, every minister demanded his own trained economist, just as every medieval monarch had wanted a court jester! Interest in the matter was undoubtedly fostered by the aforementioned 'crisis' in the discipline, and the serious public disagreements within the economists' ranks.[37] However, my own preoccupation with the sociology of economics and the professionalization process antedated the 'crisis', for it had been stimulated by my research on the American Economic Association and the Royal Economic Society.[38] The writings of Hutchison and Sir Alec Cairncross had been additional important sources of insight and encouragement.

When I began this work there was already a voluminous literature on the objectives, successes or failures of various economic policies, the 'influence' (or otherwise) of Keynesian and other doctrines, and an intriguing, slowly accumulating output of publications by ex-government employees or economic advisers reflecting on their experiences. These writings were usually occasional, limited in scope and, often exculpatory – *post hoc* rationalizations of past errors and misdemeanors. Moreover, they generally viewed governmental affairs from a detached, lofty standpoint, as though economists functioned exclusively as participants in, or close to, the highest councils of state, delivering Olympian pronouncements on matters of crucial importance. Evidence that the great majority of economists in government neither operated at those levels or in that way, revealed the need to look more closely at what really went on and how they actually fitted into the complex machinery of government.

Research of this kind would obviously be a large scale and prolonged undertaking, covering a range of issues wide enough to satisfy even my continuing quest for ever expanding intellectual horizons. Fortunately I was able to obtain Social Science Research Council support for work on the vast archival resources in Whitehall, and subsequently, via my friend and future colleague Craufurd Goodwin, substantial Ford Foundation funding for the planning and direction of a multi-country comparative study, which I subsequently edited.[39] Later still, with the help of John Williamson and Margaret de Vries I organized a conference and edited a study of the role of economists in international agencies, yet another wholly uncharted territory.[40]

As might be expected, the pursuit of these enquiries involved trespassing on a number of distinct disciplinary enclaves while addressing such issues as: the supply (i.e., educational sources and training facilities), functions and market for economists; general social and cultural attitudes towards intellectuals, professionals and experts in the countries concerned; the nature of the political system; the structure and functioning of government and bureaucracy; professional solidarity or divisiveness, ethics and standards; and the question of influence. The scholarly repercussions of these studies have been disappointingly limited, although growing gradually. This was partly because they are difficult to undertake, but also because the first study was published simultaneously as a book and as an entire issue of HOPE, and consequently was not widely reviewed. However, there have recently been valuable related or complementary volumes, such as Peter A. Hall's *The Political Power of Economic Ideas*, *Keynesianism Across Nations*

(1989),[41] which distinguishes between economist-centred, state-centred and coalition-centred perspectives, and the collection of studies edited by Mary O. Furner and Barry Supple, *The State and Economic Knowledge. The British and American Experiences* (1990).[42]

It was during this period that I at last began to appreciate more fully the close interconnections between methodology, the sociology of science and professionalism, a process in which Thomas Kuhn's classic, *The Structure of Scientific Revolutions* (1962), was the catalyst. I first encountered the book at Charlottesville, via Ronald Coase, and like many others I was captivated. So great was its impact that my short published discussion of its implications for the history of economics is one of my most widely-cited papers.[43] For a time everybody seemed to be reading (and often attacking) Kuhn – as earlier in economic history, with W.W. Rostow's controversial *The Stages of Economic Growth* (1960) – and discussions resounded with paradigms, anomalies, crises and scientific revolutions juxtaposed against 'normal' science. Of course the fad was exaggerated, but the insights were lasting, especially the prospect of a broader, more comprehensive yet empirically sound perspective on the development of economics.

Underlying all the excitement was a deeper appreciation of the limitations of the positivist conception of science, based on the image of physics, and the opening of science studies to a range of political, social and even religious influences. As Mark Blaug once remarked, a major reason for Kuhn's popularity among social scientists, including economists, was that it involved the demystification of the natural sciences, an almost irresistible species of iconoclasm. For me it has led to a renewed lengthy process of methodological dust-kicking (to cite Berkeley's dictum). An especially fascinating by-product was my contact with Imre Lakatos, Karl Popper's successor at the LSE, a brilliantly imaginative philosopher of science who turned some of us away from Kuhn towards his own, more historically manageable, 'methodology of scientific research programmes' (MSRP). I made two attempts to examine the relationship of MSRP to economics in Lakatos' LSE seminar, and was subsequently one of the privileged participants at the most lavish and intellectually exciting conference I have ever attended, at Nafplion, Greece, in 1974. There was a veritable galaxy of intellectual stars present – including economists, historians of economics, and philosophers and historians of the natural sciences.[44]

As might be expected, my conversion to the Lakatosian approach proved transitory, although as with Kuhn a valuable permanent residue has remained. In this respect my experience has been fairly typical of those economic methodologists who are also primarily historians of economics. While acknowledging the attractions of general intellectual frameworks that help to give shape to 'stubborn and irreducible facts', to use A.N. Whitehead's expression, I have also been conscious of the difficulties involved in attempts to apply these broad explanatory schema to specific historical individuals, events or periods. The theorist's and the historian's interests too often pull in opposite directions. Yet, on the other hand, historians too often rely on implicit, poorly thought out theorizing.

Within the past decade economic methodology has been, and indeed still is, in an unprecedented state of ferment. Positivism – if that blanket term is still permissible – is undoubtedly dead, but no serious successor is in sight. Friedman's 'positive' methodology is still popular among practising economists (most of whom have little or no interest in methodology *per se*), less because of its intellectual merits than because it boosts their self-image as bona fide scientists. Popperian falsificatism – even in its sophisticated form – has been seriously undermined. Various novel doctrines and approaches – such as discourse analysis, rhetoric, hermeneutics and constructivism – now have powerful and energetic advocates, yet are meeting strong resistance. These methodological disagreements add fuel to, but also cut across, the doctrinal divisions that still persist, despite the continuing dominance of the neo-classical mainstream. Thus many of the contentious issues raised during the crisis of twenty years ago remain unresolved.

To some commentators the present state of affairs borders on anarchy. Tolerance has become sheer licence; acceptable scholarly standards have been abandoned; and the barbarians are at the gates. My own reaction is less melodramatic. Under the combined influence of Gold, Machlup, Hutchison, Kuhn, Lakatos and others, I still lack an entirely satisfactory or defensible philosophical position, even after a lengthy period of sampling most of the currently contending approaches. However, I firmly believe there has been progress in economic methodology during my career.[45] The average quality of methodological discussion has risen remarkably in terms of logic, subtlety, philosophical depth, breadth of knowledge and concern for how economists (and other social scientists too) actually go about their business. My own position is eclectic[46] – somewhere in the capacious middle ground that Wade Hands so aptly dubbed 'post-positivist pre-post-modernist'. Also my friend Bruce Caldwell, who has been so valuable a guide, has provided a sound, though by no means sufficient, basis for historical research with his 'critical rationalism' (earlier 'critical pluralism').[47]

In the history of economics generally, as in economic methodology in particular, the range of research activities has widened considerably during the past three decades; and as readers of the foregoing account will appreciate, I have warmly welcomed this trend. It is a manifestation of the process Clifford Geertz termed 'the blurring of genres' – in this instance the overlapping or convergence between the history, philosophy and sociology of science as applied to economics. Among the social sciences, economics has had by far the strongest and most deeply entrenched mainstream tradition. Its proponents have hitherto been extraordinarily skilful in resisting radical change, while at the same time making marginal concessions to innovators, not all of whom have been either radicals or barbarians. As a perennial (but not, I hope, blind) optimist I have participated in methodological controversy more as a keenly interested interpreter than as a committed partisan.[48]

When my full-time teaching and administrative career at Nottingham ended, I taught for six months at Emory University in Atlanta (my second stint there) and then spent the following academic year (1983–4) as a Fellow at the National Humanities Center, in North Carolina. As with the Netherlands Institute for Advanced Studies, at Wassenaar, where I had spent the 1972–3 academic year, the facilities for research, thinking and writing were excellent. In each case the comparative absence of external commitments called for self-discipline in the allocation of time, and I found it difficult to resist the temptations offered by the library services, which gave unrestricted access to the region's scholarly depositories, and free photo-copying of articles. Consequently, I engaged in an orgy of reading, encouraged by contacts with Fellows in other disciplines.

While at the Humanities Center my friend, Neil de Marchi (whose doctoral thesis I had examined, with Hutchison, some years earlier) suggested that I should consider joining the Duke faculty. This was so obviously a 'natural' move that I have subsequently wondered why the idea had not occurred to me, given my long association with Goodwin and HOPE. Because of my wife's professional commitments in England, I was unwilling to consider a full-time appointment. But the flexibility of the American university system has made it possible for me to teach one semester a year at Duke, and spend the other six months in England – which we have done, with occasional travels elsewhere, since 1984. Apart from any contribution I may have made to the history of economic thought group in Durham, North Carolina, the most substantial and active of its kind in the world, I have also been able to continue teaching American economic history, and a more specialized course on the economics of slavery in the American South, much as I had done at Nottingham.[49] The appropriateness of the subject to the location need not be emphasized.

Oddly enough, my current position exemplifies the marginal status economic history currently occupies in too many economics departments in the United States. Despite efforts to persuade my Duke colleagues of the need for at least one full-time specialist in the field they seem content with their part-time superannuated British visitor, whose primary research interest lies outside economic and social history as conventionally defined.

Looking back over my career, I am well aware that I have had more than my fair share of good fortune. It was chance, not prescience, that led me to undertake graduate work in the United States at a time when the social sciences were seriously lagging at home; to enter the British academic labour market in the early stages of an unprecedented expansionary phase; to specialize in the history of economics some years before it burgeoned as a research field; and to treat economic methodology in historical terms just as the ahistorical positivist conception of social scientific knowledge was coming under fire from more humanistic, evolutionary and interdisciplinary approaches. Being an academic, it has always seemed to me, is a privilege. It is a vocation that offers degrees of security, freedom of action and personal autonomy far outweighing the higher material rewards of more public and stressful professions. Academic work is slow, often egocentric, and all-absorbing (as most academic spouses will attest), and only loosely constrained by deadlines (as editors and publishers know only too well!). It calls for strong motivation and self-set standards.

While I have continued to find writing disappointingly difficult (not least in the present instance), I have an almost insatiable appetite for reading, and I have never lacked enthusiasm for teaching and research. However, administration, academic politics and career promotion are, as they say, very different ball games. Some years ago, when Robert Gallman (the distinguished American economic historian) and I were on leave as visitors at Stanford University we agreed that when the external pressures were reduced, the internal pressures expanded to fill the vacuum. Longevity is characteristic of academics, and a good thing too, for there is never enough time to do all one wishes.[50] Here too, I have been fortunate: blessed with excellent health and, far more important, an exceptionally happy, durable and supportive marriage and family life. In this sensitive area, at least, there has been no appreciable dust-kicking! And, to return to the beginning of this account, with two children as permanent residents in Texas, and a third (an American citizen) resident in London, the Anglo-American connection will not readily be severed.

STRUCTURE OF THE SERIES VOLUMES

The division of subject matter between the three volumes in this series is necessarily somewhat arbitrary, given the interdependence of certain recurring themes in my work over several decades. The twenty two items in Volume I range chronologically from the late seventeenth to the late twentieth century. All but one have been published previously in one form or another – one only hitherto in Japanese – but in widely scattered locations.

All the essays in Parts I and II of this volume stem directly or indirectly from research undertaken in connection with the course on economic thought and policy, 1660–1848, which I taught intermittently at Nottingham for about twenty years, from the late 1950s. 'In Defence of Heckscher and the Idea of Mercantilism' (1958) is a response to Donald Coleman's review article published in the same journal. The exchange attracted some comment in the Swedish press. 'Mercantilism: Economic Ideas, History, Policy' (1987), orginally entitled 'Mercantilsm: Yet Again!' and written for a conference at Sassari, Sardinia, was published in Italy in 1983 and subsequently revised for presentation at the University of Newcastle, in NSW, Australia. It contains a model of the interactions between economic ideas, interests, policies and events, and comments briefly on the differences between English and continental European variants of mercantilism. 'The Relief of Poverty, Attitudes to Labour, and Economic Change in England, 1660–1782' (1976) prepared for the International Institute of Economic History 'Francesco Datini' meeting in Prato, Italy in 1974, elaborates and extends chronologically material incorporated in the two preceding items, which were published in the *Economic History Review* in 1958 and 1960. 'Adam Smith: The Modern Re-Appraisal' (1962) was delivered as a public lecture to a non-specialist audience at Nottingham, while 'Adam Smith and the Mercantile System' (1975) appeared in a volume of essays celebrating the bicentenary of *The Wealth of Nations*. 'The Classical Economists and the Labourer' was first published in a Festschrift for J.D. Chambers, and subsequently reprinted in the collection I edited, *The Classical Economists and Economic Policy* (1971). It is based on a detailed analysis of the classical economists' writings on a controversial aspect of their ideas. The topic is placed in a wider context in 'The Classical Economists, Industrialization and Poverty' (1972), a paper published in *The Long Debate on Poverty*, a volume extensively discussed in the semi-popular press. Contrary to some reports, I made no explicit references to the hotly debated question of the standard of living during the industrial revolution.

Apart from the review article on Samuel Hollander's two volume study of John Stuart Mill, which raises some general questions about the interpretation of nineteenth century British economic thought, and 'The Historist Reaction in English Political Economy, 1870–1890' (1954) – my first published article which reviews the English version of the *Methodenstreit* – all the papers in Part II are concerned with Alfred Marshall's work and his relations with his contemporaries. 'The Challenge to Free Trade: Fair Trade and Tariff Reform, 1880–1914' (1985), published here in English for the first time, provides the historical and political background to the next item, 'Political Economy and the Tariff Reform Campaign of 1903' (1968). This is a detailed analysis of a dramatic episode which thrust economists into the heart of popular controversy, exposing the deep divisions within their ranks and the severe limitations of their science as a guide to public policy. The appendix reproduces the notorious so-called 'Manifesto of the Fourteen Professors' published in *The Times* which occasioned much ridicule in the contemporary press and in parliament. The two short articles 'Alfred Marshall and Richard T. Ely' (1961), and 'Alfred Marshall and the Early Development of the London School of Economics' (1967) are both based on previously unpublished correspondence, while 'Marshall and Ethics' (1990), a hitherto neglected topic, was delivered at a University of Cambridge conference organized to mark the centenary of the publication of Marshall's *Principles*.

Part IV contains four items on American topics: a brief overview, 'Economic Thought' (1980), prepared for an *Encyclopedia of American Economic*

INTRODUCTION

History and two substantial studies of particular individuals, each of which raises issues of general significance. As its title suggests, 'Henry Carter Adams: A Case Study in the Emergence of the Social Sciences in the United States, 1850–1900' (1968), the first of these articles, based on extensive research into the Adams papers in the Michigan Historical Collections, places its subject in the broader context of the first generation of American professional academic social scientists. It is a companion piece to the article on the early history of the American Economic Association to be reprinted in Volume II of this series. 'Clarence Ayres' Place in the History of American Economics: An Interim Assessment' (1976) surveys and evaluates the work of the most prominent second generation institutionalist, a man whose contribution to economics is still the subject of considerable disagreement. The fourth item, 'Economics in the United States, 1920–1970', is an unpublished survey paper originally prepared for an interdisciplinary symposium organized by the American Academy of Arts and Sciences, in Boston. The planned volume did not materialize.

Finally, Part V contains two broad assessments of the state of economics mainly in the United States, but also in Britain. 'The Current Crisis in Economics in Historical Perspective' (1977), a lecture delivered to the Greek Economic Association in Athens, interprets the extensive 'crisis' literature of the 1960s and early 1970s as an unprecedented example of a widespread loss of professional self-confidence in the economics community resulting from a complex combination of indigenous and exogenous influences. 'The Revival of Subjectivism in Economics' (1982), originally presented to Section F of the British Association for the Advancement of Science at the University of York, examines the reasons for the resurgence of neo-Austrian economics and related ideas which formed part of a widespread reaction against the dominant positivism in economics during the 1950s and 1960s. Both these papers are designed to suggest that a historian of economics may have some advantages as a commentator on the more recent developments in the discipline.

Volume II will contain twenty or more essays on the sociology and professionalization of economics, including intellectual and institutional studies of the American Economic Association, the (American) Political Economy Club, the Royal Economic Society, and schools of economics in Chicago, Cambridge and London; the role of authority in the development of British economics; the functions and significance of scholarly journals in economics; the professionalization of economics in government; and Anglo-American differences in the culture of economics.

Volume III will contain eighteen items falling into two broad categories: (1) essays on the historiography of economics, research priorities and recent trends in economic history and the history of economics; and on the role of the history of economics in the training of economists; and (2) essays on the nature and significance of economic methodology and recent trends in the field; the methodological work of Thorstein Veblen and T.W. Hutchison; the relevance of T.S. Kuhn's and I. Lakatos' ideas for the historian of economics; value judgements; the role of explanations in economics and history; and a substantial unpublished essay on the relationships between methodology and professionalism in economics.

NOTES

1 George Berkeley, *A Treatise Concerning the Principles of Human Knowledge* (1710), Introduction, para. 3. The actual quotation is: 'Upon the whole, I am inclined to think that the far greater part, if not all, of those difficulties which have hitherto amused philosophers and blocked up the way to knowledge, are entirely owing to ourselves – that we have first raised a dust and then complain we cannot see'. I have retained the inaccurate version in the text as it is the one I have frequently quoted off-the-cuff for many years.

2 The institution, then entitled the University College of the South West, Exeter, was one of several satellites of the University of London. Thus my BSc (Econ) and MSc (Econ) degrees were external London degrees.

3 Her subsequent career as a lecturer and clinician in marital and sex therapy on both sides of the Atlantic has been rewarding for both of us.

4 Unfortunately I recall nothing whatever of the course except the textbook: Russell A. Dixon and E. Kingman Eberhart, *Economic Institutions and Cultural Change* (New York: McGraw Hill, 1941), which provided a broad, well-written, culturally focused survey of such institutions as property, the price system, free enterprise, technology, the corporation and consumption. Nevertheless, in addition to giving me my first serious taste of American institutionalism, I suspect that the novelty of the underlying approach, with its combination of generalized history and social science analysis, reinforced my disinclination to view economics in conventional neo-classical terms.

5 One explanation of the early twentieth century (i.e., largely Marshallian) British attitude to economic methodology is beautifully conveyed in one of Denis Robertson's reminiscences. Speaking of 'the topic of what sort of a study economics is and what it is about' (surely a calculatedly anti-philosophical circumlocution), he recalled: 'This is a topic which, when I started to read economics at Cambridge in 1910, it was not, I think, fashionable among us to think much about ... it seemed ... a topic more suitable for discussion by Germans than by Englishmen. There was on our reading list what I have since come to regard as a good, if dry, book about it, J.M. Keynes's *Scope and Method of Political Economy*, but to be quite honest I doubt if many of us read it. We thought we knew pretty well what sort of things we wanted to know about, and were glad enough to take the counsel given by Marshall himself near the beginning of the *Principles*, "the less we concern ourselves with scholastic enquiries as to whether a certain consideration comes within the scope of economics the better"' *idem*, 'Utility and All That', *Manchester School* vol.XIX (May, 1951), pp.111–12. There can hardly be a clearer example of the influence of an intellectual paradigm in economics.

6 Richard T. Ely, *Ground Under Our Feet: An Autobiography* (Macmillan, 1938) pp.121, 155.

7 A recent re-reading of Howard R. Bowen's analysis of the qualities required by a good graduate economics department suggests that size was by no means the only 'ideal' characteristic of the Hopkins situation. See his 'Graduate Education

in Economics', a supplement to the *American Economic Review* vol.43 (September, 1953, chapter 12.

8 It is appropriate to record here Machlup's courageous and outspoken defence of academic freedom during and after the Owen Lattimore case, which was in full spate during my Hopkins years. Also his energetic and skilful activities in the American Association of University Professors' campaign for salary increases.

9 See my essay on 'Methodology and Professionalism in Economics: A Subordinate Theme in Fritz Machlup's Writings' in Jacob S. Dreyer (ed.), *Breadth and Depth in Economics. Fritz Machlup – The Man and His Ideas* (New York: DC Heath, 1978), pp.23–35.

10 Machlup armed me with a letter of introduction to Lionel (later Lord) Robbins at the LSE thinking, I suspect, that it might lead to an offer of an appointment. The interview was memorable for one reason. When I expressed concern about my inability to read fluently the large German literature on economic methodology Robbins made it clear he considered that no cause for regret. Possibly by then he regretted some of the intellectual influences that had contributed to his famous *An Essay on the Nature and Significance of Economic Science* (London: Macmillan, 1932, 1935). For confirmation of this impression see D.P. O'Brien, *Lionel Robbins* (New York: St Martin's Press, 1988), p. 26.

11 'The Historist Reaction in English Political Economy, 1870–1890', reprinted below, pp. 220–30.

12 These lectures were subsequently incorporated into his *An Economic History of England: The Eighteenth Century* (London: Methuen, 1955), and also in *Economic Fluctuations in England, 1700–1800* (Oxford: Clarendon Press, 1959). They were responsible for my lasting interest in the economic history of the period.

13 The distinguished Hopkins economic historian, F.C. Lane, was in Europe throughout my two years in Baltimore.

14 'The Influence of Veblen's Methodology', to be reprinted in vol. III of this series.

15 Barry Gordon, *Political Economy in Parliament, 1819–1823* (New York: Harper and Row, 1976) is the kind of study I had in mind, though I wanted a greater emphasis on economic policy.

16 See, for example, 'In Defence of Heckscher and the Idea of Mercantilism', reprinted in this volume.

17 Several of these articles appear in Parts I and II of this volume.

18 An excellent example is Abraham Hirsch and Neil de Marchi, *Milton Friedman, Economics in Theory and Practice* (New York: Harvester Wheatsheaf, 1990) which admirably fulfils the promise of its title.

19 Ely, op.cit., p. 132.

20 Mary O. Furner, *Advocacy and Objectivity. A Crisis in the Professionalization of American Social Science, 1865–1905* (Lexington, KY; University of Kentucky Press, 1965). For a broader, albeit more superficial treatment of the context see Burton Bledstein, *The Culture of Professionalism* (New York: Norton, 1976).

21 See, especially, 'The Role of Authority in the Development of British Economics'; 'Sociological Aspects of British Economics c. 1880–1930'; and 'The Culture and the Economists: American–British Differences', all in vol. II of this series.

22 The lure of new ideas and interest, plus the enduring urge to try to read 'everything', also helps to account for my strong penchant for book reviewing. A comprehensive list of my reviews will appear in vol. III of this series.

23 The report was an official acknowledgement that Britain was lagging far behind her European rivals in the production of graduates – a state of affairs that still persists thirty years later! In addition to unprecedented institutional growth, there

was also a significant boost to academic career opportunities. Bliss it was in that dawn to be an upwardly mobile don.

24 Its members included James M. Buchanan, Ronald Coase, G. Warren Nutter, Gordon Tullock and James R. Schlesinger (then on sabbatical leave before embarking on his meteoric career on the national stage. He became godfather to our younger son, who was born in the university hospital). Also while at Charlottesville I attended Paul Gaston's distinguished lectures on the new South, which greatly stimulated my interest in that region. It has been a central focus of my subsequent teaching.

25 The article is reprinted in vol. II of this series. An article on 'Value Judgements in Economics' will appear in vol. III.

26 Cf. William Breit, 'Creating the Virginia School: Charlottesville as an Academic Environment in the 1960s', *Economic Inquiry* vol.35 (October, 1987), pp.645–55 for a somewhat different view of this situation.

27 Some of the matters discussed in the following paragraph are treated in my paper 'Disciplinary Self-Examination, Departments and Research Traditions in Economic History: The Anglo-American Story', to appear in vol. III of this series.

28 For further discussion see my inaugural lecture, 'Economic Growth: The Economic and Social Historian's Dilemma', (University of Nottingham, 1967). Reprinted in N.B. Harte (ed.), *The Study of Economic History* (London: Cass, 1971).

29 See 'The First Decade of HOPE (1968–1979)', in *History of Political Economy* vol. 15 (Fall, 1983) to be reprinted in vol. III of this series.

30 The prime movers were Donald Winch and R.D. Collison Black, with valuable support from Lord Robbins.

31 For a broad review of the earlier literature on this episode see 'The Current Crisis in Economics in Historical Perspective', reprinted in this volume.

32 In preparation for the first of these occasions, to be held in Leningrad in 1970, I made extensive efforts to find suitably qualified Russian participants, as those initially suggested by the organization's (non-Russian) international secretary appeared to have no record of publications in any relevant field. Eventually, having made no progress whatsoever, I approached the Soviet Academy for assistance. Some months later their reply – addressed to 'Dear Professor Nottingham' – informed me that their 'delegates' to my section (i.e., those previously dismissed as unsuitable) had already been 'selected'. So, defeated, I surrendered, gracefully.

33 This was published as R.P. Sturges (ed.), *Economists' Papers 1750–1950* (London: Macmillan, 1975).

34 The following have already appeared: *A History of Japanese Economic Thought* by Tessa Morris-Suzuki (London: Routledge, 1989); *The History of Swedish Economic Thought* edited by Bo Sandelin (London: Routledge, 1990); *A History of Australian Economic Thought* by Peter Groenewegen and Bruce McFarlane (London: Routledge, 1991); and *A History of Canadian Economic Thought* by Robin Neill (London: Routledge, 1991).

35 The following publications have already appeared from this project: (1) L. Levan Lemsele (ed.), *Les Problèmes de l'institutionalisation de l'Economie Politique en France aux XIXe siecle*, *Oeconomia* (Paris: Presses Universitaires de Grenoble, 1988); (2) M. Augello, M. Bianchini, G. Gioli and P. Roggi (eds), *The Academic Institutionalisation of Political Economy in Italy, 1750–1900* (Milan: Franco Angeli, 1988) (in Italian); (3) William J. Barber (ed.), *Breaking the Mould: Economists and Academic Higher Learning in the Nineteenth Century* (Middletown,

Conn.: Wesleyan University Press, 1991); (4) Chuhei Sugiyama and Hirosi Mizuta (eds), *Enlightenment and Beyond, Political Economy Comes to Japan* (Tokyo: University of Tokyo Press, 1988); (5) N. Waszek (ed.), *Die Institutionalisiering der Nationalökonomie an Deutschen Universitäten, Zur Erinnerung an Klaus Heinrich Hennings (1837–1896)* (St Katherinen: Scripta Mercaturae Verlag, 1988); (6) Thomas A. Boylan and Timothy P. Foley, *Political Economy and Colonial Ireland. The Propagation and Ideological Functions of Economic Discourse in the Nineteenth Century* (London: Routledge, 1992). Also forthcoming is the following: Istvan Hont and Keith Tribe (eds), *Trade, Politics and Letters. The Rise of Economics in British University Culture, 1755–1905* (London: Routledge).

36 *Supra*, p.5. The title is Methodological Controversy as an Approach to the History of American Economics, 1885–1930 (Johns Hopkins, 1953).

37 See, for example, the critical analysis in T.W. Hutchison, *Economics and Economic Policy in Britain, 1946–1966: Some Aspects of Their Interrelations* (London: Allen and Unwin, 1968); and *idem. Knowledge and Ignorance in Economics* (Oxford: Basil Blackwell, 1977) especially chapter 5; and my article referred to in note 31.

38 See the papers on these organizations in vol. II in this series.

39 *Economists in Government. An International Comparative Study* (Durham, NC: Duke University Press, 1981). See also the complete issue of *History of Political Economy*, vol. 13 (Fall, 1981).

40 *Economists in International Agencies* (New York: Praeger International, 1986).

41 Published by Princeton University Press. The contributors included economists, political scientists and specialists in international relations.

42 Published by Cambridge University Press. The contributors included economists and economic, political and intellectual historians.

43 'Is There a Structure of Scientific Revolutions in Economics?' to appear in vol. III of this series.

44 The conference yielded two widely cited volumes: Spiro Latsis (ed.), *Method and Appraisal in Economics* (Cambridge: Cambridge University Press, 1976); and Colin Howson (ed.), *Method and Appraisal in the Physical Sciences* (Cambridge: Cambridge University Press, 1976).

45 On this point see the recent paper by D. Wade Hands, 'Thirteen Theses on Progress in Economic Methodology', *Finnish Economic Papers*, vol. 3 (Spring, 1990), pp.72–6.

46 An extended review of recent developments and a concluding appraisal will appear in a hitherto unpublished essay in vol. III of this series.

47 See B. Caldwell, *Beyond Positivism: Economic Methodology in the Twentieth Century* (London: George Allen and Unwin, 1982); *idem*, 'The Case for Pluralism', in Neil de Marchi (ed.), *The Popperian Legacy in Economics* (Cambridge: Cambridge University Press, 1988); and *idem*, 'Clarifying Popper', *Journal of Economic Literature* vol. 29 (1991), pp.1–33.

48 See, for example, my 'Half a Century of Methodological Controversy in Economics: As Reflected in the Writings of T.W. Hutchison', in vol. III of this series. This is the introductory essay in A.W. Coats (ed.), *Methodological Controversy in Economics: Historical Essays in Honour of T.W. Hutchison* (Greenwich, Conn.: JAI Press, 1983).

49 The general American economic history course provides an opportunity to convey to American students the immensity of the changes in their country's international position, especially during my lifetime. The slavery course enables me to explore the problems involved in applying modern economic analysis to a socio-cultural context, markedly different from that encountered in other economics courses. My fascination with this subject is not unconnected with my love of jazz, one of the original motives for going to the United States.

50 Remember, it is said that old professors never die; they simply lose their faculties!

PART I

MERCANTILISM AND PRE-SMITHIAN ECONOMICS

2

IN DEFENCE OF HECKSCHER
AND THE IDEA
OF MERCANTILISM[1]

I

In his recent reappraisal of Heckscher's *Mercantilism*[2] Dr Coleman raised certain questions concerning Heckscher's methodological approach which transcend the immediate problem of the nature and validity of the idea of 'mercantilism' and have a bearing upon the broader issue of the relationships between economic conditions, ideas and policy. To the present writer, the danger that Heckscher's development of the idea of mercantilism will drive yet another wedge between the political and the economic historians as Dr Coleman fears,[3] is less serious than the danger that Heckscher's apparent reluctance to admit the influence of economic conditions upon economic ideas,[4] and his readiness to pass directly from generalizations about economic ideas to generalizations about economic policy, will widen the existing gap between economic historians and historians of economic doctrine, two groups of scholars whose mutual services should be considerable. To the student of economic ideas who seeks to rescue his discipline from the sterile pursuit of tracing the genealogy of particular analytic propositions, of which some of his colleagues seem inordinately fond, the matter is one of crucial importance.

The present article re-examines some of the general issues and the particular methodological problems raised by Heckscher's work, with the object of promoting a more closely integrated study of economic conditions, ideas and policy. In the final section an attempt is made to explain and demonstrate the contribution of the idea of mercantilism to this objective.

II

The general problem of the relationship between ideas and events – whether, to put the two logical extremes, ideas determine events or are determined by them – is a typical example of the kind of issue beloved of nineteenth century students of the philosophy of history[5] which nowadays seems so remote from reality. But although the contemporary distaste for these abstract questions is justified, it is not enough to ignore them entirely, or to adopt a vague eclecticism and merely assert that ideas and events act upon one another in

29

some inscrutable and incomprehensible manner. No doubt most economic historians, whether they consciously favour the economic interpretation of history or not, incline towards the position that ideas should be allotted a subordinate role in the explanation of events, whereas historians of doctrine tend to assume the contrary. This difference of emphasis is partly a product of differences of training and experience, and it helps to account for the divergent responses of the two groups of scholars to Heckscher's volumes.[6] Naturally enough, the doctrinal historians were susceptible to the argument that 'the so to speak autonomous development of the purely economic doctrines, the struggle of the mercantilists with the logical consequences of their premises, has usually been underestimated',[7] and they welcomed Heckscher's effort to identify the general characteristics of mercantilist thought. But to the economic historians his ambitious attempt (as T.H. Marshall put it) to 'establish a complete synthesis between the three elements, the situation, the ideas and the action, and demonstrate in this synthesis the presence of the unique character which he claims for his subject, Mercantilism',[8] appeared to involve dangerous oversimplification. In particular they complained that he neglected the multiplicity of factors influencing policy-making,[9] and their criticisms were buttressed by ample illustrations of the inadequacy of some of Heckscher's generalizations.

These reviewers highlighted the principal methodological weakness of Heckscher's work: his endeavour to treat all three elements in his synthesis with the same degree of generality. Whatever the causal connections between ideas and events, it is often possible to discern broad parallels between the economic ideas of any period and the economic problems posed by the contemporary situation.[10] But this parallelism does not, of itself, justify the contention that there are corresponding parallels between ideas and policy measures. At this point the theorist must descend to the study of the particular applications of general ideas. It is extremely difficult in practice to identify the causal links, if indeed they exist, between ideas and acts of policy. The requisite evidence is often lacking, and it is fatal to assume that the existence of broad similarities between the recommendations of economic writers and the details of subsequent policy measures is proof of causality.[11] Ideas often undergo radical transformation in the cut and thrust of the legislative and administrative process, or when they are subject to the influence of conflicts of personalities and interest groups, and in the study of these processes lies the key to the history of policy. It is not that it is impossible to make valid generalizations about policy, but simply that it is far more difficult to make *significant* generalizations about policy than about ideas and conditions. Abstraction is an inevitable concomitant of the decision to study economic ideas or conditions; but the attempt to isolate the economic from the non-economic aspects of policy seems to involve a far greater and perhaps unwarrantable degree of abstraction. In a real sense there is no such thing as *economic* policy, and the endeavour to trace the links between policy recommendations and policy practice[12] necessarily entails a careful investigation of the political, social, legal, constitutional and religious aspects of the situation. This explains why Heckscher's premature generalizations about 'mercantilist' thought and policy bore that air of unreality so frequently remarked upon by subsequent commentators.

Thus the comparative failure of Heckscher's attempted synthesis was not due to the vast scope of his undertaking or to his effort to force a mass of disparate factual materials into a single theoretical mould; it was inherent in the nature of the task as he had defined it. His decision to select mercantilist *policy* as the central focus of his study was doubtless inspired by Schmoller's view that the unity of any period proceeded from the characteristics of the predominant policy-making institution. Schmoller emphasized 'the dependence of the main economic institutions of any period upon the nature of the political body or bodies most important at the time', and concluded that although the evolution of the political unit 'has never accounted for all the facts of economic life, [it] has, at every period, determined and dominated it'.[13] But if, as the foregoing remarks have suggested, generalizations about policy are frequently of limited historical value, the validity of the whole idea of 'mercantilist' policy and of 'mercantilism' itself is left in doubt.

Is this a cause for concern? Would the abandonment of the idea of 'mercantilism' be a serious loss to anyone except perhaps the student of economic thought? We can agree with Professor Judges that 'the idea of a mercantile state' is misleading,[14] and sympathize with Dr Coleman's view that as a description of policy measures the idea of mercantilism is 'actively confusing',[15] while drawing attention to the importance of his concession that 'as a description of a trend of economic thought, the term may well be useful, and worth retaining'.[16]

To the present writer, the accepted usage of the term 'mercantilism' as a description of the main trend of economic thought before 1776[17] is not merely an unavoidable necessity, a further instance of the tyranny of a word that cannot be banished from the language, but an indispensable aid to historical interpretation. When carefully defined it embodies the outcome of long efforts to identify and elucidate the common characteristics of a mass of disconnected practical proposals and partisan recommendations; without it, we are left with a vast collection of seemingly unconnected writings of no conceivable relevance to any but the issues with which they are immediately concerned. The idea of 'mercantilism' is the doctrinal historian's contribution to an understanding of the nature of an important phase of economic development. It is, at least potentially, a bridge constructed by the historian of economic ideas, out of materials provided by Adam Smith and subsequent scholars, to serve as a link between the territories labelled 'economic conditions' and 'economic policy'. In Dr Coleman's account Heckscher appears as a usurper who sought, by disconnecting the bridge at the farther end, to incorporate it into his policy domain. But the shortcomings of his brilliant and ambitious scheme should not blind us to its immense constructive possibilities. The historian of doctrine may be persuaded to turn from his archeological pursuit of identifying the origins of the bricks with which the bridge is being built to the more rewarding activity of extending it in both directions and strengthening its foundations,[18] while the economic historian will benefit from the improved facilities for investigating a still largely unexplored terrain.

The nature of the doctrinal historian's contribution to this programme of collaboration is suggested by Heckscher's penetrating observation 'that economic policy is determined not so much by the economic facts as by people's conceptions of these facts'.[19] This statement not merely sheds light on the general problem of the relationships between economic history and the history of economic thought; it also provides a key to Heckscher's view of the connection between economic ideas and economic conditions.

The success or failure of an act of policy can only legitimately be assessed in terms of the objectives and the range of alternative courses of action as seen by the policy maker, and in making his assessment the present-day historian must endeavour to transcend the limitations of his own historical perspective. There are two primary limitations: the historian's knowledge of 'the facts' relevant to a given policy decision is certainly different and probably less complete than that of the policy maker; and quite apart from any deficiencies in his knowledge of the facts, his interpretation of the facts is liable to be at variance with that of the policy maker. Heckscher's training as an economist, and especially his predilection for theory, made him acutely aware of these problems.

With respect to the former limitation, it is important to understand the reason for Heckscher's distinction between 'the facts' and 'people's conceptions of the facts'. His doubts about the efficacy of mercantilist policy acts were due not so much to his 'low opinion of the economic perception of those who lived in the mercantilist era',[20] as to his general scepticism of state action. His opposition to modern public works policies, for example, was attributable not to a belief that the interventionist case was logically unsound but to his conviction that the authorities were inherently incapable of making an accurate assessment of the facts upon which their policy decisions were to be based. In the words of Erik Lundberg: 'Heckscher's opinion was that economic policy would come to be varied in accordance with current *conceptions* of business conditions and these had hitherto shown themselves to be notoriously wrong.'[21]

But the possibility that the historian might misinterpret past policies through ignorance of the prevailing view of the way in which the economy worked[22] was, to Heckscher, a more serious danger, and he was accordingly anxious to stress the historian's need to immerse himself in the ideas and attitudes of his period. Heckscher apparently believed that as a result of their predilection for empiricism, many historians tended to accept uncritically almost any attempt to explain economic ideas in terms of contemporary conditions.[23] In an effort to correct this bias he undoubtedly went too far in the opposite direction. He overemphasized the influence of economic ideas on policy, played down the influence of economic conditions upon economic ideas, and insisted so frequently upon the complexity and indirectness of the connections between conditions and ideas[24] that Dr Coleman has spoken 'of his reluctance to concede that the ideas and policies of the time might owe something to contemporary awareness of economic reality, however crude or empirical'.[25]

Nevertheless, apart from some occasional indefensible remarks,[26] there is more to be said in favour of Heckscher's treatment of the relations between ideas and reality than Dr Coleman has conceded. Heckscher regarded the *general* characteristics of mercantilist economic thought and policy as the focus of his interest, and one of his principal aims was to dispel the popular misconception that, because the mercantilist writers were usually preoccupied with the solution to pressing practical problems, their ideas consisted of little more than a miscellaneous assemblage of particular expedients designed to meet the needs of emergency situations. This explains his warning against the error of ascribing general and persistent ideas to the specific conditions of time and place.[27] It also accounts for his repeated insistence that 'the very fact that opposing practical standpoints were derived from the same principles or interpretations of economic phenomena is evidence of the fundamental uniformity of outlook'.[28] Dr Coleman's claim that Heckscher implicitly gave 'the same weight and influence' to the various constituent elements in mercantilist thought,[29] is open to misinterpretation; for although Heckscher did not always distinguish clearly between the different types of mercantilist writings, he was careful to distinguish between the general principles and the particular applications of mercantilist economics. Heckscher primarily stressed the enduring features, 'the orthodoxy which survived in spite of evolutionary changes in the component doctrines until it suffered a revolutionary overthrow at the hands of Adam Smith'.[30] When he emphasized the continuity and influence of mercantilist ideas, he was mainly concerned with the theoretical aspects of mercantilism.[31]

Heckscher's view of the relationships between economic ideas and economic conditions followed directly from this preoccupation. By their very nature and their persistence over time, the general preconceptions of mercantilist thought were not amenable to explanation in terms of particular conditions of time and place. His references to the empirical background of economic ideas amounted to more than sporadic and grudging concessions to reality,[32] as is clear from his definition of the distinctive contribution of the mercantilists. This contribution lay 'in the choice of means' by which they proposed to attain their objectives:

> Through this, mercantilism became not only a specific type of economic policy, but, even more, a characteristic body of economic ideas; for the views as to what constituted the best means were rooted in *conscious or unconscious interpretations of the tendencies of economic life.*[33]

Heckscher was not simply paying lip-service to reality; the tendencies to which he referred were not short-run contingencies, which – as his critics pointed out[34] – he deliberately neglected, but long-run trends. His sweeping vision was designed to encompass the outstanding features of the mercantilist landscape; the picture he painted was impressionistic rather than photographic, and consequently his view of the immediate foreground, with which so many specialists have been concerned, was inevitably foreshortened.

At the same time, it is undeniable that Heckscher neglected the empirical context of mercantilist ideas. Although the vast scope of his work justified his scanty attention to particular ideas and conditions, his sceptical attitude towards efforts to relate *general* economic ideas to their *general* background may have discouraged others from attempting to bridge the gap between economic historians and historians of economic thought.[35] But whatever the limitations of his own perspective, Heckscher's *Mercantilism* represented a massive contribution to the task of demonstrating 'the changes of economic theory as an historical process in which are mirrored changes in the structure of the system'[36] which should be the end product of the doctrinal historian's activity. Instead of 'inhibiting the asking of fundamental questions about the nature of economies in which certain characteristics of policy appeared'[37] these volumes marked a significant advance in our knowledge of the theoretical conceptions in terms of which these questions must be expressed, if we are to understand the contemporary approach to economic problems. The fact that Heckscher himself did not proceed to answer these questions need not prevent us from recognizing that by identifying the characteristic features of mercantilist economic thought, his work prepared the way for later scholars to investigate, in greater detail, the nature of contemporary economic conditions and policy.

III

The belief that there is a body of specifically mercantilist policy enactments is open to serious objections. But it has been suggested above[38] that there is an identifiable set of mercantilist economic doctrines, and that an understanding of the nature of these doctrines can shed considerable light on economic conditions and policy in the period before 1776. The proposal to retain the term 'mercantilism' as a description of the main characteristics of economic thought before 1776 will not, however, pass unchallenged. It has been objected that the term itself is 'ambiguous . . . undefined' and virtually undefinable;[39] and that the effort to systematize a compilation of writings that are wholly lacking in 'precise and definite principles'[40] or even 'coherent doctrine'[41] is foredoomed to failure.

An answer to these charges directly involves us in one of the most difficult problems in the interpretation of mercantilist economics: how far, and in what sense, were the mercantilist writings systematic in character? The case for the use of the term 'mercantilism' to denote a distinctive approach to economic affairs virtually stands or falls with the answer to this question.

It is immediately clear that if by 'system' in economics is meant systematic theory of the classical or Keynesian types, then there was no mercantilist system. With a few outstanding exceptions, the writings on economic affairs before 1776 were directed towards the solution of practical problems, and such progress in the analysis of economic processes as occurred was purely incidental. But mercantilism was not economic 'science', it was political economy, and in this context 'system' connotes 'an exposition of a comprehensive set of economic policies' that are advocated 'on the strength of certain unifying (normative) principles such as the principles of economic liberalism, of socialism, and so on'.[42]

It must be admitted that in the case of mercantilism the normative principles – the politico-economic ends of policy – were less clearly conceived and less consistently pursued than was the case with liberalism and socialism.[43] Moreover, it is true that 'there was never a living doctrine' of mercantilism 'that can be compared with vital philosophies of action like physiocracy or liberalism or Marxism'.[44] Yet it is not difficult to account for the absence of a specifically mercantilist philosophy of action. The mercantilists' preoccupation with practical problems extended to political as well as economic affairs, and while they made frequent references to the state, the sovereign and the system of government, they were neither interested in nor, apparently, even familiar with contemporary political theory. But, according to one modern student of this aspect of mercantilist political economy, although they 'frequently left unstated the underlying political assumptions upon which their proposals rested' the mercantilists recognized 'the interdependence of economic and political phenomena', and in this respect they measured up well to contemporary English political philosophers. 'Regarded as economic strategy', he concludes, 'aimed at the achievement of political objectives in a world of competing national states, the policies of mercantilism exhibit more logical consistency than many economists have been willing to concede to them.'[45]

The same is true of their economic ideas. Since it is well-known that there were numerous gaps and inconsistencies in their proposals, it is appropriate to describe mercantilist economics, in Schumpeter's apt phrase, as a 'quasi system'.[46] Of such 'programmes of industrial and commercial development' Schumpeter observed that:

their authors recommended or fought policies appropriate or inimical to those programmes, and reasoned in terms of individual problems. But their ideas were not unsystematic in the sense of lacking coherence. They knew how to relate one problem to another and to reduce them to unifying principles – *analytic* principles, not merely principles of policy. If these analytic principles were not always stated explicitly, they were nevertheless often worked out effectively in a way that suggests the development of English law.[47]

The existence of an interconnected body of mercantilist policy maxims is often conceded even by those who deny that mercantilist writers evinced any systematic qualities in their approach to economic problems. Thus Lipson, for example, denied that there was any 'systematic working out of a national economic system based on precise and definite principles', but elsewhere admitted that, in the discussion of the East India trade

the policy of the Company challenged many of the accepted maxims of foreign commerce and compelled a re-statement, and in some cases even an abandonment, of existing economic doctrines. In the economic, as in the constitutional, field practical problems provided a concrete basis for the formulation of new principles, and determined alike their scope and application.[48]

The late seventeenth century controversy in England over the East India trade[49] provides the clearest illustration both of the interrelationships between the various mercantilist maxims, and of the connections between these ideas and the empirical background against which they were formulated. It may be objected that this is not a typical case. As the participants in the debate centered their attention, at least initially, upon a single branch of foreign trade and the affairs of a single company, the discussion possessed a unity of focus that was often lacking in contemporary literature.[50] Moreover, the circumstances of the case required – especially from the defenders of the company's activities – a greater effort of casuistical ingenuity than was usually called for in discussions of the contribution of foreign trade to the national economy. These factors, it is true, help to account for the high level of discussion and for the theoretical advances that make this particular controversy notable. But the contributions to this debate were different in degree rather than in kind from the usual run of mercantilist polemics. Both sides regurgitated the familiar maxims of commerce, which constituted the presuppositions of contemporary economic thought, and endeavoured to interpret these general rules in a manner consistent with their respective aims and interests. The company's supporters, however, found it difficult to reconcile the needs of their case with the acknowledged criteria of a desirable trade; and this difficulty proved insurmountable when they endeavoured to defend the importation of Indian textiles. From the late

1670s the deleterious effects of these imports on production and employment in the native textile industry were becoming increasingly evident, and it was an obvious expedient for the company's opponents to claim that home goods should be given preference over foreign luxuries.

The defenders of the East India trade were therefore forced to devise novel arguments to meet this attack, although they undoubtedly endeavoured to minimize the elements of novelty in their case. Thus the two leading spokesmen, Child and Davenant, appealed for commercial freedom in only a limited sphere – the Indian trade – and were careful to note that since private gain might conflict with the national interest in other cases, they were not proposing a wholesale abolition of all regulations on foreign trade. The patent insincerity of this argument was, of course, emphasized by their opponents, who themselves employed the appeal to economic freedom in their anti-monopoly attacks on the company. On the other hand the abstract free trade reasoning of North – whose pamphlet had but a limited circulation – and the author of *Considerations on the East India Trade*, who attacked the company's monopoly while defending its imports, were too far in advance of contemporary opinion to be immediately influential.

The 'protection' versus 'free trade' issue was, however, only one of several raised in the course of this controversy.[51] And the complex questions involved cannot be comprehended in simple balance of trade terms; indeed, the balance of trade idea was subjected to severe attack, as a result of which its reliability as a test of a successful trade was permanently impaired. The question of the company's bullion exports was still prominent although it was ceasing to be the major cause for complaint by the last decades of the century. There were continued attempts to estimate the volume of specie imports and exports in relation to the country's monetary requirements, and this task was frequently coupled with a theoretical analysis of the nature and functions of money in the economy. But the question of the effects of the company's imports on the home economy and of its re-exports on the European market for our cloth industry was in the forefront of the debate. The solution of this problem also called for a combination of quantitative measurement and theoretical analysis: an account of the nature and quantity of Indian imports, an assessment of the extent of their competition with the sales of native goods at home and abroad, and an effort to trace the indirect repercussions of the trade on employment, prices, incomes and land values. Thus the debate touched upon every aspect of contemporary economic thought.

In the discussion of these matters the defenders of the company usually demonstrated greater theoretical insight than their opponents, in the sense that they showed a clearer perception of the relationships between different branches of economic life, and a more profound appreciation of the ramifications of particular acts of policy than their opponents.[52] But theoretical subtlety counted for little, at least in the short-run, against the protectionist orthodoxy. The prevailing hostility to luxury imports, and the evidence of distress and unemployment in major home industries proved overwhelming weapons against the company's interests.

The East India controversy provides a useful reminder of the importance of adopting a correct time perspective when making judgements concerning the influence of ideas and conditions upon policy. There is always a considerable lapse of time before new conditions make an impression on men's habits of thought, and an analogous, though by no means identical, delay before the new ideas make their way into the political arena. In the case of the East India trade the persistence of the accepted maxims of trade in the face of theoretical criticism and changing economic circumstances is, to the modern observer, one of the most striking lessons of the debate. It is a warning of the need to distinguish between the general premises or presuppositions of a practical argument, and the particular circumstances to which the argument is applied.

It is on the basis of this distinction that we must endeavour to strike a balance between the extremes of the ideological and the environmental determinists. While acknowledging the justice of Dr Coleman's strictures against Heckscher's underemphasis of the influence of economic conditions upon economic ideas, we must recall Heckscher's warning against the opposite error of attempting to account for persistent and general ideas on the basis of special circumstances. In attempting to account for given acts of policy it is essential to investigate the specific circumstances in which the acts were formulated; but we cannot stop at this point, unless we are prepared to forego all attempts to generalize about conditions, ideas and policy. Individual measures must be placed in their intellectual and empirical context, and seen as particular manifestations of general trends of thought and events. In the case of the East India trade the growing volume of Indian imports gave rise to an increasing concern with the level of domestic activity, and it gradually became acknowledged that the desirability of any given branch of trade depended more upon its contribution to the national aggregate of production and employment than upon its contribution to the national stock of bullion. This change of outlook was reinforced by a more profound analysis of the nature and functions of money, with a resulting shift of emphasis from the store-of-value function to the medium-of-exchange function, a shift which may be partly attributable to an increase of circulating media and a growing volume of internal trade. These connections, however, require more thorough investigation than they have so far been given.

Heckscher's *Mercantilism* was a massive contribution to this kind of activity, for it represented a pioneering effort to delineate the major themes of economic ideas and policy in Western Europe during some four or five centuries. To many historians, including the present writer, this undertaking was necessarily bound to fail; indeed, few scholars have the learning or breadth of imagination even to contemplate such an enterprise. Nevertheless, the effort was eminently worthwhile, if only for its effect in enlarging the horizons of lesser men. It would be most unfortunate if Heckscher's success in dealing with ideas were to be obscured by the shortcomings of his treatment of conditions and policy measures, for his work holds out exciting prospects for students of all aspects of economic life and thought.

NOTES

1 I am indebted to Dr Coleman for initial discussion and to Dr J.D. Chambers of the University of Nottingham and Mr J. Potter of the London School of Economics for criticism of an earlier draft. None of these persons is responsible for the opinions expressed.

2 D.C. Coleman, 'Eli Heckscher and the Idea of Mercantilism', *Scand. Econ. Hist. Rev.* vol.V, (1) (1957), pp.1–25.

3 ibid., p.11.

4 ibid., pp.12–16. See also below, pp.32–4.

5 For example, contrast Comte's dictum: 'All social mechanism rests upon opinions', *The Positive Philosophy* (London, 1853), p.14, with Marx's assertion that: 'It is not the consciousness of mankind that determines its existence, but on the contrary its social existence that determines its consciousness', *Zur Kritik der Politischen Oekonomie*, Vorwort, p.v. An intermediate view was advanced by Buckle, who held that man's (scientific) knowledge gradually enabled him to emancipate himself from the domination of the environment so that, ultimately, the progress of Europe 'is entirely due to its intellectual activity', *Introduction to the History of Civilization in England* (London, 1904), p.128. Marx, too, argued that in the classless Utopia man would be free from the domination of economic forces and 'by becoming master of his own social environment' would 'in full consciousness, make his own history'. Cf. K.R. Popper, *The Open Society* (London, 1945), II, p.98.

6 For indications of these responses see D.C. Coleman, op. cit., pp.7–10.

7 Eli Heckscher, *Mercantilism* (2nd Edition, London, 1955), vol.II, p.270.

8 T.H. Marshall, *Economic Journal*, vol.XIV (1935), p.718. It should be noted that in the next sentence Professor Marshall added: 'But the value of the two sections of his study remains unimpaired'.

9 ibid. Professor Marshall referred to Heckscher's tendency to treat policy '*in vacuo*', while Professor Heaton complained of his neglect of the statesman and the 'character of the state'. Cf. H. Heaton, 'Heckscher on Mercantilism', *The Journal of Political Economy*, vol.XIV, (3) (1937), pp.376, 386–7.

10 Cf. this volume, p.36 ff.

11 As an example of the care that must be taken in these matters see the discussion of the corn law literature in D.G. Barnes, *History of the English Corn Laws* (London, 1930), p.37.

12 There would have been much less misunderstanding of the nature and purpose of Heckscher's work if he had consistently distinguished between these two different uses of the word 'policy'. Indeed, indiscriminate references to policy have frequently acted as a barrier to understanding between historians of doctrine and economic historians. For although they are primarily concerned with different kinds of data, both groups tend to use the word policy to denote the focus of their interest. The term 'mercantilism' may well be unsuitable 'as a label for economic policy' in the sense of policy practice (Coleman, op. cit., p.24); but, as will be argued, there is a clearly identifiable set of mercantilist policy recommendations.

13 G. Schmoller, *The Mercantile System and its Historical Significance* (New York, 1896), pp.2, 3.
14 A.V. Judges, 'The Idea of a Mercantile State', *Transactions of the Royal Historical Society*, 4th Series, vol.XXI (1939), pp.41–69.
15 Coleman, op. cit., p.24.
16 ibid. This concession is in marked contrast to his earlier view that the idea of mercantilism is 'an unnecessary piece of historical baggage' which should be jettisoned. See 'Labour in the English Economy of the Seventeenth Century', *Econ. Hist. Rev.* vol.VIII, (3) (1956), pp.295, 281. In support of his later view he could have quoted Alfred Marshall, *Industry and Trade* (London, 1919), pp.719–20.
17 The precise date of the beginning and end of mercantilist economic thought is a matter for debate. Few writers would be prepared to follow Heckscher's example of embracing the whole 'time between the Middle Ages and the age of laissez-faire' (op. cit, I, p.20). In the present article the main trend of English economic ideas from 1660 to 1776 will be taken as representing the pinnacle of mercantilist thought, as a kind of 'ideal type' by which other phases of mercantilism can be understood. Cf. L. von Mises, *Human Action* (New Haven, 1949), pp.59–62.
18 Generally speaking, historians of economic thought have neglected the empirical foundations of mercantilist ideas; they appear to regard their edifice as a suspension bridge.
19 Heckscher, op. cit., vol.II, p.59.
20 Coleman, 'Eli Heckscher and the Idea of Mercantilism', op. cit., p.18.
21 E. Lundberg, *Business Cycles and Economic Policy* (London, 1957), p.115 nr. 2. Italics in original. Cf. Heckscher, op. cit., vol.II, p.181.
22 For an excellent discussion of the general problem of 'the ends and means of economic policy' see Chapter VI of Lundberg, op. cit. Among factors to be included in any assessment of past policies he mentions: (a) 'the conception of economic causality', however primitive, on which the policy was based; (b) the difficulty of distinguishing clearly between 'ends' and 'means'; (c) the possibility that the policy makers may have incorrectly diagnosed the actual or future situation with which the policies are designed to deal; and (d) the existing political conditions. (I am indebted to Mr J. Potter for this reference.)
23 Heckscher's stress on the influence of ideas stemmed partly from his objections to physical determinism, and partly from his reaction against the contemporary misuse of the teachings of Marx, Freud and the sociology of knowledge, according to which ideas could be 'explained' as rationalizations of economic interest or personal prejudice, or as a result of social conditioning. Though he did not ignore these factors, he deliberately belittled them. For example, *Mercantilism*, II, pp.30, 137, 177, 199.
   Heckscher would have approved of Maurice Dobb's remark that: 'It is a characteristic of all ideology that, while it reflects and at the same time illuminates its contemporary world, this reflection is from a particular angle, and hence largely clouds and distorts reality.' *Studies in the Development of Capitalism* (London, 1946), p.214.
24 See the discussion following the remark that: 'As the policy of provision was thus limited in time, and was later succeeded by a policy which tended in the exactly opposite direction, it is natural to search among the actual conditions of the times for factors which might explain why considerations of provision had so strong a hold on the Middle Ages. Such an explanation is not difficult, although it is certainly not to be found where one would be likely to look for it first.' *Mercantilism*, II, p.100. See also I, pp.20, 470; II, pp.54, 94, 132, 177, 222–4.
25 Coleman, op. cit., p.18.

26 For example the statement quoted by Dr Coleman from vol.II, p.347: 'There are no grounds whatsoever for supposing that the mercantilist writers constructed their system – with its frequent and marked theoretical orientation – out of any knowledge of reality however derived.'
27 ibid., II, pp.138–9, 176–7, 277.
28 ibid., II, p.183. See also I, p.27; and 'Revisions in Economic History', *Econ. Hist. Rev.*, vol.VII (1936–7), p.54.
29 Coleman, op. cit., p.20.
30 T.H. Marshall, op. cit., p.719.
31 This explains his apparent neglect of financial topics, of which his critics have complained (e.g. Coleman, op. cit., p.9; Heaton, op. cit., pp.375–8). Heckscher recognized that financial considerations determined many of the particular applications of mercantilist ideas (*Mercantilism*, II, p.96), but there was no general theory of public finance in mercantilist economics. Financial policy 'follows the line of least resistance', usually being governed by the prevailing 'general conception of what is socially useful'. ibid., II, p.97.
32 Cf. Coleman, op. cit., p.13.
33 Heckscher, 'Revisions in Economic History', p.45. Italics supplied. For some other references to his view of the relations between economic ideas and economic conditions see above, note 24.
34 Cf. Coleman, op. cit., p.23; Heaton, op. cit., p.386.
35 Heckscher did not entirely deny the validity of such activities. Cf. *Mercantilism*, II, p.354. For an excellent example of this approach see Dr Coleman's article cited above, in note 16.
36 T.H. Marshall, op. cit., p.719.
37 D.C. Coleman, *Labour in the English Economy of the Seventeenth Century*, p.281. It may be true that, owing to a misunderstanding or a neglect of the relationships between economic conditions, ideas and policy some writers have been content with vague references to 'mercantilism' as a substitute for an adequate explanation of the factors influencing given acts of policy. But this malpractice does not, in the writer's opinion, justify the conclusions that the idea of mercantilism is of no constructive value.
38 See p.31.
39 E.A.J. Johnson, *The Predecessors of Adam Smith* (New York, 1937), pp.4, 6, 8, 15. For an earlier expression of the same view see H. Higgs, *The Physiocrats* (London, 1897), p.3. Heckscher's comment on the inconsistency implicit in Johnson's reference to a pre-Smithian theory of production should be noted (*Mercantilism*, II, p.266).
40 E. Lipson, *Economic History of England* (4th Ed.) vol.III, p.1.
41 A.V. Judges, op. cit., p.41.
42 J. Schumpeter, *History of Economic Analysis* (New York, 1954), p.38.
43 Evidence of this is provided by the Heckscher–Viner dispute over the relative importance of 'power versus plenty' as the ends of mercantilist policy. For references to this see Coleman, op. cit., p.10.
44 Judges, op. cit., pp.41–2.
45 Philip H. Buck, *The Politics of Mercantilism* (New York, 1942), pp.77, 193, 179.
46 Schumpeter, op. cit., p.194.
47 ibid., italics in original. Earlier, in his *Business Cycles* (New York, 1939), vol.I, p.234, Schumpeter remarked: 'Nor does mercantilist policy embody any set of definite economic aims or principles.'
48 Lipson, op. cit., vol.III, p.1; vol.II, p.277.
49 Cf. P.J. Thomas, *Mercantilism and the East India Trade* (London, 1926), *passim*. The

following discussion relies heavily upon this valuable work. Although Thomas warned that mercantilism 'seldom possessed a unified system of policy, or even a harmonious set of doctrines', he recognized that in the late seventeenth century in the anti-East India Company case, 'protectionism . . . became a *system* with definite principles and advocating a definite policy' (op. cit., pp.3, 76. Italics in original). The latter comment is correct, but unduly restricted, for the company's opponents did not have a monopoly of systematic thought in this period.

50 Moreover there were never political or religious issues to complicate the discussion as in the case of the French trade.

51 Thomas overemphasized the importance of this aspect of the debate, while underemphasizing the influence of the discussion of the theories of money, employment and the balance of trade (op.cit., pp.24, 67–97). By classifying the protagonists as protectionists and free traders, and dealing separately with their respective arguments, he undoubtedly clarified the issues in dispute. But this treatment tended to obscure the evolution of the theoretical ideas against their historical background.

52 In the course of the debate, however, both sides were forced to re-examine and develop their own arguments. This is especially apparent in the discussion of the indirect repercussions of the company's re-exports on the European market.

3

MERCANTILISM
Economic ideas, history, policy

> Historical research must always to a certain extent begin anew each generation, regardless of whether new objective facts have been discovered. The reason for this is that every generation has by its own social experience got its eyes opened to new causes of given developments, or at least has arrived at a re-evaluation of the relative importance of different given causes.
>
> (Eli Heckscher, 1922)

A generation – or to be more precise, thirty-three years – has elapsed since the flurry of discussion generated by the publication of a revised English edition of Eli Heckscher's monumental and controversial study of *Mercantilism*, which originally appeared in Swedish (1931), German (1932) and English (1935). But the occasion would not, of itself, justify yet another reappraisal of the concept of mercantilist economic thought and policy were it not for the fact that a series of relevant articles and books on this subject has materialized within the past few years. It therefore seems an appropriate time to ask whether there have been any significant new findings, any discernible trends of scholarly opinion or any new areas of investigation opened up for students of economic thought and policy. What are the implications, if any, for parallel studies of later periods? And if the answer to any of these questions is positive, what are the implications, if any, for scholars concerned with economic thought and policy in later periods?

In the past disproportionate scholarly effort has been devoted to debates about the concept of 'mercantilism' as such, the nature and intellectual quality of 'mercantilist' ideas and the precise relationship of these ideas to the 'circumstances of the time'. In this paper I shall pass over these matters as quickly as possible since I am more concerned with the 'mercantilists' themselves, the political and administrative processes whereby their ideas became embodied in policy enactments, if ever, and the nature of the early modern or 'mercantile' state, for these are the topics on which systematic

43

research by historians of economics with appropriate historical equipment and insights promises to be most fruitful.

Although the subject of this paper may seem remote from late twentieth century professional economists' concerns there are at least two reasons why it merits attention. The first is that the terms 'mercantilism' and 'neo-mercantilism' are still to be found in scholarly and popular discussions as descriptions of contemporary economic policy goals and actions. Second, as so many economists are nowadays directly or indirectly involved in policy making – for example, as official or unofficial advisers to government, career bureaucrats, members of parliament, cabinet members or even heads of state – knowledge of policy-making processes is now becoming an integral part of the economics community's tribal lore. Given this background, studies of policy making in more distant times and places, provided they are not distorted by present-day preoccupations, can be of genuine educational interest and value.

Unfortunately in this field as elsewhere, the compartmentalization of knowledge and the accompanying specialization and division of labour have resulted in marked differences of approach and emphasis between economists, historians and historians of economics, three groups who should be working in collaboration rather than in isolation from one another. Moreover, as this paper demonstrates, the works of political and administrative historians can also be illuminating to students of economic policy making.

At the risk of some oversimplification, let me suggest that:

(a) Economists studying recent economic policy tend to treat economic ideas casually and superficially, and they frequently ignore the influence of political interests and conditions, and administrative structures and procedures. Working from some preconceived 'theory' of economic policy they generally overestimate the rationality of policy-making processes, relying on models that present policy actors as self-interested utility maximizers. Consequently their accounts are often over-schematic, understating the prevalence of chance, complexity, strong personalities and sheer confusion in policy-making contexts.

(b) By contrast economic historians, being mainly concerned with the nature and causes of economic change, focus their treatment of economic policy on conditions rather than ideas. The latter, if seriously considered at all, appear either as abstract speculations and theories with only tenuous policy linkages, or as short-term, generally partisan and self-interested reactions to events rather than as quasi-autonomous causal influences. Moreover, when they consider economic policy, economic historians seldom take full account of decision-making processes, the political and administrative context or the implementation of policy measures.

(c) Historians of economics, whose expertise can and should provide a bridge between the other two approaches, have traditionally concentrated on

44

the development of economic theory or analysis, since they consider this to be the most 'scientific' part of economics. Schumpeter, for example, even denied the possibility of progress in economic policy, as though there could be no criteria by which to assess success or failure in this field. Some excellent historical studies of economic ideas and policy have indeed appeared, but more often than not works in this genre focus unduly on policy proposals or recommendations, neglecting the processes whereby proposals are or are not adopted and enforced. Historians of economics can indeed learn much from the contemporary studies of economic advisory work.

THE CONCEPT OF 'MERCANTILISM'

Surprisingly enough, the term 'mercantilism' still arouses strong emotions. Only recently Salim Rashid suggested that it should be 'publicly burned' (i.e. banned? cf. Rashid, 1982: 863), and one of its most indefatigable opponents, D.C. Coleman, despite certain shifts of emphasis and some inconsistencies, still maintains, resignedly but evidently unrepentantly, that,

> though we may never succeed in disposing of the word we should at least understand that mercantilism is one of those non-existent entities that had to be invented in order to prevent the study of history from falling into the abyss of antiquarianism.
>
> (Coleman, 1980: 791; cf. *idem*, 1956: 281;
> 1969: 13, 117; 1977: 173)

This is not the place to engage in semantic squabbles, or to explore the epistemological implications of Coleman's reference to 'non-existent entities'. However confusing the bewildering variety of meanings ascribed to the term, 'mercantilism' is a perfectly legitimate mental construct or instrumental concept which may or may not be helpful, but certainly cannot be outlawed by mere condemnation, however authoritative and oft-repeated. As it happens, a perusal of the two volumes of the *Cambridge Economic History of Europe* devoted to the sixteenth and seventeenth centuries (Rich and Wilson, 1967, 1977) demonstrates unequivocally that a number of reputable economic historians still find the term (together with 'mercantilist' and 'mercantile state') serviceable. They evidently reject Coleman's initial contention that the concept of 'mercantilism' inhibits 'the asking of fundamental economic questions about the nature of economies in which certain characteristics of policy appeared' or that it has 'come to dictate both the questions which are asked and the answers which are found' (Coleman, 1956: 281). Nor has A.V. Judges' earlier effort to dispose of 'The idea of a Mercantile State' (cf. Coleman, 1969: 35–60) met with any success (cf. Tilly, 1975: *passim*).

Generally speaking, continental European scholars have displayed fewer inhibitions in using the term 'mercantilism' than their British counterparts, and they have undeniably added to the confusion by coining such variants as: imperial mercantilism, pseudo-mercantilism, anti-mercantilism, fiscalism and semi-fiscalism (Coleman, 1969: 3). This practice undoubtedly stems from the desire to retain the general concept while recognizing the differences between individual states at varying stages of economic, social, political and administrative development; and similar motives underlie such hyphenated descriptions as early-, middle-, late- (or high-) classical, paper money and social mercantilism – though the situation is somewhat different again in references to twentieth century new or neo-mercantilism. Moreover, British terminological reservations stem at least as much from recognition of distinctive British circumstances as from our well-known empiricist philosophical predilections.

Enough has already been said to demonstrate the improbability of any general consensus about the meaning of mercantilism, and it may therefore be necessary to settle for Charles Wilson's loose characterization of it as 'a complex of ideas and policies designed to achieve national power, and, ostensibly wealth' (1957: 16). This is, of course, to define the concept by reference to the underlying objectives, goals or 'entelechies', a term recently employed by Robert Schaeffer. This has distinct advantages as a basis for classifying scholarly and polemical interpretations of mercantilism and specifying particular entelechies, such as: the accumulation of treasure or bullion; the promotion of national wealth or economic growth; the achievement of a favourable balance of trade; the maximization of employment; protection for home industry; and the increase of state power, or unification – fiscal or more general. A further asset is that twentieth century commentators familiar with controversies about the relative importance or compatibility of specific policy objectives will, like Heckscher, be undismayed by revelations of inconsistencies or conflicts between the various entelechies. Yet, as Schaeffer notes, it is still essential, if mercantilism is to be a useful concept, to be able to 'specify where it can be said to have obtained and then explain why it is held there and not elsewhere. This has not been done.' (1981: 92). In order to rectify this omission, more detailed comparative historical analysis is required, a point to be considered later.

If the foregoing analysis is correct, there would seem to be less need for concern now, than in 1957, that the 'idea of mercantilism' will either widen the gap or diminish the collaboration between political historians, economic historians and historians of economics (cf. Coats, 1957: 173; supra, p.29). Nevertheless complacency would be premature, to judge by a recent book-length study by R.B. Ekelund Jr. and R.D. Tollison utilizing models derived from currently fashionable public choice, property rights and Chicago-style 'positive' economics, which reveals the continuing remoteness of some economic analysts from conventional historical interpretations. These authors focus attention on 'rent-seeking' – i.e., 'the activities whereby individuals seek returns from state-sanctioned monopoly rights' (1981: 13) – as the primary and central feature of mercantilism. While denying any intention of offering a monolithic or reductionist explanation of historical developments (mainly in England and France, but with some glances elsewhere in the interests of 'historical completeness', p.15), the main thrust of their argument is to emphasize that 'unvarnished rent-seeking for merchants, monarch, and ultimately the masses represented by Parliament explains most economic intervention, as well as a good deal of political–legal change' (1981: 72; cf. Appendix, *infra*, pp.59–60). This 'polinomic' version of history is, of course, an extrapolation backwards of the 'economics of politics' advocated by J.M. Buchanan, G. Tullock *et al.*, and there is a curious parallel with Coleman's latest characterization of 'mercantilist ideas and actions as utterances or moves in a bargaining process, as, so to speak, a series of games involving Crown, parliament and sets of interest groups' (Coleman, 1980: 790; for further discussion of this point see *infra*, pp.59–60). It would, however, be misleading to invoke Coleman's specialist knowledge in support of Ekelund and Tollison's version, for, curiously enough, they present their account in relation to the 'conventional paradigm' in Adam Smith (p.147) and Heckscher, who is identified with 'the historians' analysis' (pp.5, 113), and make few references to the substantial historical researches undertaken during the past three or four decades. For example, they discuss the 'high period of mercantile monarchy' in England from 1547 to the 1640s, and its subsequent decline, without a single reference to the works of Charles Wilson and his collaborators in the *Cambridge Economic History of Europe*; and their treatment of France is open to similar criticism.

No doubt contemporary economic theory can contribute something useful to our understanding of distant periods, provided that it is applied cautiously and sensitively, with due regard to available knowledge of the relevant historical circumstances. But as in the case of the 'new' economic history, one suspects that the economic aspect of political power, property rights and constitutional change appear revelatory only to those who lack formal training in history. References to 'man's eternal proclivities towards rent-seeking', and insistence that no interests are 'independent of those which drive economic man in all ages' (pp.153, 71) do not inspire confidence in the authors' grasp of the subtleties of historical change. Moreover, as they invoke 'positive' economic theory, and seek to 'refocus the methodological orientation of the study of mercantilism' (p.xi), one cannot help wondering what evidence, if any, would constitute a falsification of their theory, or what counter-examples, if any, would persuade them to abandon it?

THE NATURE OF MERCANTILIST 'IDEAS'

Schaeffer distinguishes between mercantilism – the 'theories about the history of economic thought in the seventeenth and eighteenth centuries' (1981: 82) – and the ideas of the mercantilists themselves, and this peculiar practice does at least have the virtue of recognizing the considerable and regrettable gap which has emerged between what the writers of the time said and what later generations have said about them. Of course this gap is initially due to Adam Smith and his successors, who were essentially hostile and derogatory to most pre-1776 economic writings, and a marked shift of historiographical approach occurred with Keynes and subsequent authors (though we must beware of drawing too sharp a dichotomy between the two approaches).

This is familiar stuff, not worthy of elaboration here, as is also the question of the extent to which mercantilist economics is systematic. In my view recent discussion has made no advance upon Schumpeter's description of mercantilism as a 'quasi system' consisting of 'programmes of industrial and commercial development', the authors of which

> recommended or fought policies inimical to those programmes and reasoned in terms of individual problems. But their ideas were not unsystematic in the sense of lacking coherence. They knew how to relate one problem to another and to reduce them to unifying principles – analytic principles, not merely principles of policy. If these analytic principles were not always stated explicitly, they were nevertheless often worked out effectively in a way that suggests the development of English law.
>
> (Schumpeter, 1954: 194; also *supra*, this volume pp. 35–6 for further discussion)

It is generally agreed that while mercantilist economic ideas were entirely pre-professional and largely pre-scientific, it is also acknowledged that the antecedents of modern economic theory are clearly discernible in pre-Smithian writings. They contained a highly variable admixture of 'analysis', 'theory', 'thought' and 'opinion' on a range of subjects now regarded as well outside the professional economist's special competence, and consequently it seems wise to accept a distinguished historian's verdict that 'To judge mercantilist thought by the criteria of later economic logic is wholly to misconceive its character. The concept of a separate science of wealth had not yet emerged' (Wilson, 1967: 573). Yet such a judgement has recently been offered, in at least two instances. William Letwin has applied twentieth century criteria in his attempt to identify the origins of scientific economics in the English literature of the 1690s, more especially in the works of Petty, Locke and North; but the inappropriateness of this exercise has been effectively demonstrated (cf. Blaug, 1964; Rashid, 1980), and need not be reconsidered here. More extreme and provocative were William R. Allen's two articles on mercantilist theory and modern commentators on that topic (1968, 1970), which seem to have been based on the principle of extrapolating backwards George Stigler's (to me, indefensible) dictum that 'the correct way to read Adam Smith is the correct way to read the forthcoming issues of a professional journal' (Stigler, 1969: 221, 223). The *reductio ad absurdum* of

Allen's procedure is his bland observation that Gerard de Malynes failed to formulate a correct mathematical statement of 'the general elasticity stability conditions of England's foreign exchange market' – surely a conclusion of striking originality.

Allen's approach is worth noting because it raises a fundamental historio-graphical and epistemological problem for historians of economics, namely, how far is it appropriate to apply the conceptual apparatus and standards of intellectual performance of our own day to the interpretation and evaluation of the ideas of earlier generations? However sensitive his historical imagination, the intellectual historian cannot enter fully into the minds of his subjects, especially if they lived long ago; and however hard he tries, he cannot fully emancipate himself from the ideas and beliefs of his own day, nor perhaps should he aspire to do so especially, as with Allen, when his aim is to assess the intellectual quality of the earlier writings. However, one problem here, which Rashid has noted and Allen missed, is that intellectual standards and knowledge change, especially in sciences (Rashid, 1980: 7–9). More important is the problem that

> to apply a conceptual apparatus developed under one set of conditions to those of a very different time and place involves a kind of 'trans-lation' process which, as linguistic philosophers have shown, involves compromises which necessarily affect the communication of meanings. There is no literally neutral language by which the concepts and terms of one theoretical system can be translated into those of another, and this problem arises in intellectual history as it does in contemporary science.

> (cf. Coats, 1973: 489–90).

Indeed, one of the reasons for the sharp conflicts of opinion about mercantilism among economists past and present is that they have been starting out from 'incommensurable' or even incompatible paradigms, to cite T.S. Kuhn's familiar terminology.

Allen's approach helped to pinpoint the variety of possible questions which can be asked of mercantilism, or indeed any other body of writings, and clarified the distinction between 'justifying' ideas and 'explaining' them by reference to the 'circumstances of the time'. While there was undoubtedly some coherence, consistency and evolution of mercantilist ideas, Coleman and others have done well to remind us of the variety of elements in pre-Smithian literature (Coleman, 1980; also, more generally, Hutchison, 1978: 127–35; 277–85). Given that this literature was essentially pre-professional and pre-scientific it is virtually impossible to distinguish between: logical and empirical statements; basic presuppositions, preconceptions and premises; supposedly obvious and unquestionable commonsense maxims or aphorisms; and expressions of vested interest, prejudice and ideological bias. Indeed, as Terence Hutchison and others have conclusively demonstrated, even the most supposedly sophisticated late twentieth century scientific economic writing often contains a bewildering mixture of statements of differing logical and empirical status. Is it then surprising that the precise nature and significance of mercantilist 'theory' should be the subject of controversy? For the present purpose it is surely sufficient to accept Heckscher's view that mercantilist 'theory' emerged unintentionally out of its authors' concern for practice (as reprinted in Coleman, 1969: 21), even though in doing so he over-reacted against the classical economists' denigration of mercantilist literature (cf. Herlitz, 1964: 112; Coats, 1957: 174).

Since the publication of Heckscher's first edition the classical economists' dismissal of mercantilist ideas as fundamentally fallacious and confused has been largely discredited under the combined influence of Keynes' ideas and more detailed historical research; but there has been considerable disagreement as to the precise relationship of these ideas to the circumstances of the time. With some exceptions, economic historians, lacking either interest or confidence in economic theorizing, have stressed the influence of events, especially short-term 'crises', on the pre-1750 economic literature; but while there is some justification for this interpretation it cannot explain the common features and persistent themes of writings produced at widely differing times and places. If successive crises differed from one another in certain respects, they also displayed strong family resemblances – as in more recent periods. Furthermore, the underlying economic conditions changed only gradually for several obvious reasons: poverty, under-employment and monetary stringency were endemic; technological progress was limited; and governments had to overcome considerable political, financial and administrative obstacles in their efforts to shape the course of economic and social affairs. Indeed, as indicated later, this last factor, combined with the extent of economic development of the region concerned, was usually crucial in determining both the selection of policy objectives and the types of specific policy undertaken.

Far from being simply erroneous and damaging in their effects, mercantilist ideas are now usually interpreted as relevant and applicable to the circumstances of the time, although any crude environmentalist interpretation of the connections between ideas and events must be treated with scepticism. For example, how can 'events' as such explain the co-existence of conflicting opinions unless some effort is made to demonstrate which events conditioned any particular ideas or set of attitudes? Among those who respond to events are cranks, eccentrics, partisan promoters of vested interests, office-seekers, statesmen and those rare individuals motivated chiefly by the disinterested pursuit of 'truth'. The immediate reaction to any situation may indeed be almost Pavlovian, an instinctive reliance on 'conventional wisdom' or unreflective 'commonsense'; but after a time lag the response may be very different. 'Learning by experience' is a notoriously slow, painful and uncertain process, especially on the part of politicians and government officials who may be subject to a variety of pressures, constraints and inducements. Even on the most superficial analysis, explanations of ideas in terms of events are liable to break down: for example, are we to include among 'events' the experience of conversation, reading and even spiritual inspiration? Economic ideas and events may move in opposite directions for substantial periods of time – for example, the marked extension of protectionist policies in England between 1690 and 1770, notwithstanding the concurrent growing belief in the efficacy and desirability of free trade (cf. Davis, 1966). Such anomalies can of course be explained by reference to the gap between 'theorists' and 'practical men', but this is no substitute for an examination of the evidence in order to discover which ideas are influential and which not. This may be a complex and subtle undertaking, for as Heckscher wisely remarked, 'economic policy is determined not so much by the economic facts as by people's conceptions of those facts' (Heckscher, 1955: II, 59).

Before considering the relationships between economic ideas, events and policies in the mercantilist era, it may be helpful to distinguish between three different species or levels of ideas:

(a) the ultimate ends or objectives of economic policy – e.g., the promotion of the wealth and/or power and/or security of the state or nation.

(b) The intermediate 'ends' – e.g., an adequate supply of the precious metals; a stable exchange rate; a favourable balance of trade; the provision of employment for the poor; the protection of home industry, etc. These are, in turn, 'means' to achieve the 'ends' incorporated under (a), and it is clear that very different weights were attached to them at different times and places.

(c) The more technical, low level discussion of the means to achieve these intermediate ends – e.g., bounties on exports; duties and prohibitions on imports of finished goods; prohibitions on the export of precious metals; make-work projects for the poor; subsidies for shipbuilding and fishing; the establishment of trading companies and colonies, etc.

The changing importance of these various elements is acknowledged even by those historians who are inclined to dismiss or minimize the role of mercantilist economic theories – for example, Supple's reference to the 'intellectual revolution' in England in the 1620s associated with Thomas Mun's writings (Supple, 1964: 223; cf. his inconsistent references to long and short run elements on pp.197–8; by contrast see Hinton, 1955: 284: 'The seventeenth century Commissions on trade, whose instructions embody mercantilist thought and whose enquiries encouraged it, were established in crises. This does not mean that their ideas were short term *ad hoc* and remedial to the exclusion of longer views and general concepts.'). Historians of economics recognize that without *some* conception of the way the economic system works, and the relationships between 'means' and 'ends', there can be no coherent policy making whatever; and most serious students of the period now accept that many pre-1750 economic writers perceived, if imperfectly, important interconnections between the various aspects of economic life: e.g., commerce, currency, prices, employment, manufacturing output, agriculture and the government's finances. On some topics (e.g., taxation, finance, agriculture) crude 'commonsense' arguments prevailed, especially among partisan pamphleteers. But on other topics (e.g., the supply of money, prices, the nature and effects of foreign trade, the foreign exchanges) the literature – including some official reports – was both precise and sophisticated.

MERCANTILIST ECONOMIC IDEAS AND POLICIES

As suggested at the outset, studies of the interactions between ideas and policies constitute a rich research field for students of pre-1750 economic literature. Even Adam Smith, no friend to the mercantile system he invented, acknowledged the pervasive influence of earlier economic ideas – though his polemical intention should not be overlooked (cf. Coats, 1975). But owing to the conventional division of labour and interests between doctrinal historians and specialists in political, economic, social and administrative history, we still know far too little about how, when and in what manner they were influential. The gap in our knowledge would be more excusable were it not that much valuable preliminary investigation has already been undertaken and is available for analysis and interpretation by historians of economic thought.

In this concluding section it is possible only to suggest the nature and scope of available scholarly knowledge for, like most historians of economics, the writer lacks the necessary broad and deep familiarity with the period, especially with respect to non-British conditions. The accompanying schematic presentation (see pp.53 and 54) may, however, serve as a convenient starting point for an understanding of the linkages between economic ideas and policy, which is dependent on familiarity with the relevant channels of communication, institutions and policy-making processes. Needless to say, these varied considerably over time and place, and historians of economic thought have unduly neglected the gap between policy *recommendations* and policy *actions* in the form of decrees, regulations, legislative enactments, etc. To implement policies requires enforcement, which may or may not call for a substantial body of officials equipped with appropriate information, powers and sanctions – and this calls for knowledge of public administration.

To master this knowledge over several different centuries and a bewildering mixture of states and nations would be a daunting task, and as a reaction against Heckscher's over-ambitious, but nevertheless enormously valuable pioneering effort, the writer was inclined, thirty years ago, to emphasize the particularity of policy actions and the obstacles facing those historians

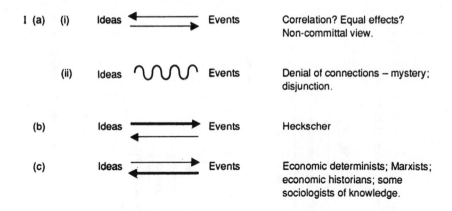

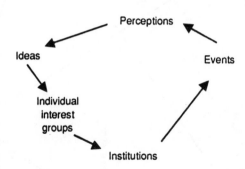

Figure 1: Economic 'ideas' and 'events': some causal connections

wishing to make *significant* generalizations about policy (cf. Coats, 1957: 175). These warnings obviously still apply today. But there is no reason in principle why generalizations about policy should not be attempted, any more than generalizations about ideas (cf. Magnusson, 1978), and in this respect substantial progress has been made in the interim. Especially notable in this connection is the work of Charles Wilson, beginning with England (which is in some respects a unique case) and extending to the Netherlands and Europe generally, both in his collected essays and in the magisterial chapter on 'Trade, Society and the State' in the *Cambridge Economic History of Europe* (Wilson, 1969; 1967). As he there remarks:

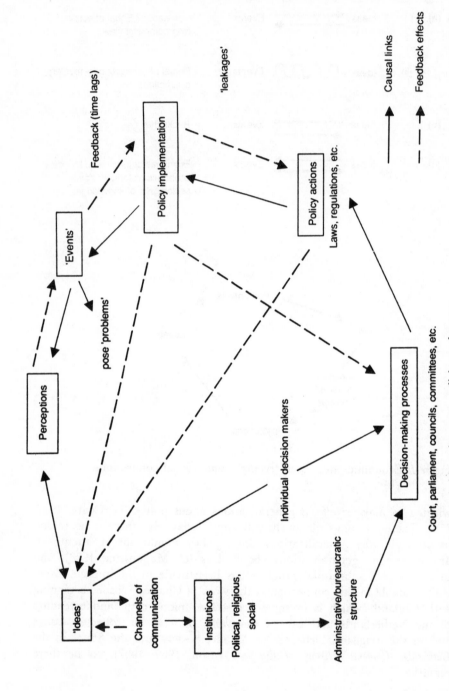

Figure 2: Interactions of economic ideas, interests, policies and events

The recurrence of similar mercantilist ideas in different countries was not accidental. Rightly or wrongly, the mercantilist prescription seemed not only appropriate but seductive to rulers, administrators and economists in search of an economic creed for local application.

(Wilson 1967: 570).

The term 'creed' is not intended to be taken literally, but it reveals Wilson's basic conviction that purely short-term crises and vested interests cannot, whether separately or in combination, dispose of the concept of mercantilist ideas.

In the case of England – which has naturally attracted the attention of doctrinal historians, because the evolution of ideas leading to modern economic 'science' is more clearly discernible there – Wilson argues that the livelier the lobbying, the more numerous the pressure groups, the more necessary the power of decision, of choosing between alternatives which resided only in the government – i.e., the Crown, privy council and ministers.

Decisions were taken on the basis of established conventions which might and often did transcend private interests, sometimes very powerful ones. Especially when the alternative choices were neatly balanced, the deciding factor might well be those economic, political, social and strategic desiderata which seemed commonplace to the governors of the time.

(Wilson, 1969: 153; cf. Hinton, quoted *supra*, p.51)

With all its imperfections, there was an element of a system of coherence and rationality in the mercantile economy which distinguished it [England] from the chaos of Spain or the Italian States and rendered it superior to that of France, or Sweden or even Holland.

(Wilson, 1969: 150)

Accordingly he concludes, of the mercantile as of the classical system of economic policy:

both economic systems derived as much from government authority and the 'encroachment of ideas' as they did from the ambiguous, often mutually destructive pressures exercised by private interests. The 'lobby' theory of economic legislation, at any rate in its simpler formulations, remains non-proven.

(Wilson, 1969: 155; *pace* Ekelund and Tollison)

This conclusion is especially important, being derived initially from a close study of seventeenth century England, because the scope for private individuals, especially merchants and interest groups, was evidently much greater there than elsewhere in Europe throughout most of the sixteenth to eighteenth centuries. Mercantilism may not have been simply a matter of state making, as Gustav Schmoller claimed, but there is much to be said for his emphasis on 'the dependence of the main economic institutions of any period upon the nature of the political body or bodies most important at the time' (cf. Schmoller, 1896: 2; quoted in Coats, 1957: 176). The relatively limited role of the state in nineteenth century England in the heyday of classical political economy tended to obscure the importance of the political context of policy making in all periods; and in pre-Smithian times the degree of 'stateness', to use a recent term, was crucial. It was in weak states that crude 'fiscalism' was likely to prevail – i.e., the attempt to raise money by any means that were to hand regardless of the social and economic consequences (cf. Betty Behrens, in Rich and Wilson, 1977: 578; also Van Klaveren, in Coleman, 1969: 140–61) – whereas in England, for example, 'where mercantilism was systematically made to serve a policy of *economic* expansion, the reinforcement of financial techniques became a powerful incentive for the development of a national economy'. In France 'mercantilism was placed too much at the service of a policy of *military* expansion during the *politique de grandeur* of Louis XIV', whereas 'in Holland, on the other hand, state mercantilism never took recognizable shape' (Herman van der Wee, in Rich and Wilson, 1977: 391–2).

The degree of 'stateness' i.e., formal autonomy, differentiation from non-governmental organizations (e.g., church, trading companies), centralization and internal coordination in the governmental apparatus (cf. Tilly, 1975: 34) was highly variable in early modern Europe, and this partly explains the many and confusing definitions of mercantilist ideas and policy proposed by scholars. It is important, moreover, not to assume (as in the Whig version of history) that there was any uniformly evolving pattern of 'political development', e.g., towards liberalism and representative democracy, and indeed pre-Smithian and Smithian conceptions of politics were so different from our own that that misinterpretation has been widespread. (For a valuable partial corrective see Winch, 1978: *passim*; also Coats, 1975.) The most recent, ambitious and stimulating effort to generalize about early modern politico-economic affairs is Immanuel Wallerstein's concept of a European world system, composed of a shifting cast of 'core', 'semi-periphery' and 'periphery' states, on the basis of which he distinguishes five determinants of power: the state's capacity to help owner–producers to compete in the world market (mercantilism); military power; public finance – i.e., mobilization of resources without eating up profits; effective bureaucracy; and extent to which 'the political rules reflect a balance of interests among owner–producers' whose 'hegemonic bloc' can support a stable polity (Wallerstein, 1980: 113). These measures, he argues, are political, not economic, because they are not measures of productive efficiency. (For another intriguing, more explicitly Marxist, attempt to relate mercantilist economic theories to the contemporary context in a variety of countries see Hajek, 1980: *passim*.)

As every schoolboy knows, the early modern period was an age of commercial expansion and shifting national rivalries, and the textbook interpretations of mercantilism in terms of bullionism, currency, balance of payments, employment, social objectives, etc., must be placed against this vivid and changing geopolitical backcloth. Some of the greater and more perceptive writers on economic affairs were themselves directly involved both in commerce, and in advising government, and the gap between theoretical and practical activity was distinctly blurred (cf. in England in such cases as Gresham, Misselden, Malynes, Mun, Cranfield, Downing, Child, Locke, etc.). For the enforcement of policies an administrative apparatus was required, but it was not always, or even usually, necessary to have such an elaborate apparatus or such an army of officials as Colbert created in France, where although the state was politically unified it was not unified economically, hence the continuing resistance to economic measures which seemed inhibiting to private individuals. To cite another example,

> The contrast between liberal Dutch and English immigration policy and Spanish or French expulsions was of the greatest economic importance. But it did not derive so much from economic expertise or economic ignorance as from the contrasting priorities accorded to material welfare or religious orthodoxy. Expert administration hardly came into the matter.
>
> (Wilson, in Rich and Wilson, 1977: 40; cf. Ekelund and Tollison; and, more specifically, Patinkin, 1981: 75–89)

Public administration is, no doubt, one of the less exciting branches of historical study, but this does not justify its neglect by historians of economic thought and policy seeking to trace the influence of ideas. Politics and administration represent the environment in which Schumpeter's mercantilist 'consultant administrators' operated, and as Terence Hutchison has recently suggested, this environment is more important even to the present-day economic scientist than most economists have been prepared to acknowledge (cf. Hutchison, 1978: 282–3, 319–20; Coats, 1981: *passim*). As a recent survey has demonstrated, there is ample scope for investigation into this aspect of the early modern context of economic policy making (cf. Wolfram Fischer and Peter Lundgreen, 'The Recruitment and Training of Administrative and Technical Personnel' in Tilly, 1975: 456–561). Particularly striking is the contrast between the situation in seventeenth century England and that in eighteenth century Germany, where a number of small states were engaged in efforts to catch up with the leading 'core' countries, England, France and, to a lesser extent, the Netherlands. It was in Germany that the concept and practice of Cameralism, so different from the English manifestation of mercantilism, was developed (cf. Wilson, in Rich and Wilson, 1977: 288, 595–6; Fischer and Lundgreen, in Tilly, 1975: 558 ff.). A comparative study of mercantilism in England, France and the states where Cameralism was practised would, I suspect, prove highly instructive.

The differing channels of communication between men of ideas and policy makers should be examined in order to provide more empirical substance to the notion of the influence of 'ideas' on policy (both in this and in later periods). For as Charles Wilson has observed, of the English case,

> The stream of petitions from clothiers, merchants, poor weavers, gilds and companies and the like did not only represent an exercise of constitutional rights; they also represented the best and often the only source of information the government could obtain on complex economic problems.

Then, as now, government officials could not operate in a vacuum, making decisions without reference to economic conditions and informed members of the community. Nowadays,

> Civil servants and even government experts have to rely on constant advice and help from private individuals on both sides of industry, from employers and industry. It is ludicrous to suppose that in an age unequipped with any kind of public economic service, government could have done anything or even known anything except with the help of those who were themselves interested parties.
>
> (Wilson, 1969: 143)

It may be an exaggeration to claim, as Christopher Hill has, that the destruction of the royal bureaucracy in the early 1640s was the most decisive reform in the whole of British history (quoted in Tilly, 1975: 295); but the changing relative power of the Crown and Parliament thereafter precluded the development of a degree of centralized control and administration of economic policy comparable to that in Colbert's France or Frederick's Prussia. To recognize these basic historical differences need not entail an abandonment of the concept of mercantilism for there were similarities as well as differences. And to retain it need not involve going to the other extreme, and committing the error referred to by George Unwin, of overestimating 'the active part which wise forethought and the deliberate pursuit of clear ideas has played in the economic history of nations' (cited by Coleman, 1980: 791). For, as Hutchison and others have argued, even among the most scientific modern economists the role of persuasion, partisanship and ideology may have been much greater and more persistent than historians of economic analysis like to think (Hutchison, 1978: chapter 10; cf. Herlitz, 1964: 119–20; Appleby, 1978; *passim*). Hence students of the more primitive ideas and policy recommendations propagated in the mercantilist era need not feel that their subject is unworthy of serious consideration.

APPENDIX

Whatever its historical shortcomings, and they are considerable, the Ekelund and Tollison study is of interest as an example of the current 'imperalist' Chicago school tendency, exemplified in the works of Gary Becker, to interpret every aspect of human experience in strictly economic terms. (For a penetrating, albeit not wholly unsympathetic, critique of this approach see Alexander Rosenberg's article, 'Can Economic Theory Explain Everything?' *Philosophy of Social Science* vol.9 (1979), pp.509–29.)

In fairness to Ekelund and Tollison it must be admitted that their claims are more modest than Becker's, for they do not set out to rewrite the entire historical record. Indeed their qualifications and reservations make it difficult to determine precisely what they are purporting to achieve. At times they make passing, and somewhat half-hearted acknowledgement of the role of non-economic factors – e.g., legal and religious objections to the exercise of royal authority (p.64), and the concept of the 'public interest' (p.65; but cf. pp.15, 91). They purport to supplement the existing (Heckscher–Viner?) explanation of mercantilism 'by viewing the manifestations of mercantilism over this period in terms of the supply of and demand for monopoly rights and of the forces that impinged on self-interested action in this process' because this provides 'a more coherent explanation of the evolution of mercantile policies and institutions' (p.xii). But while they dismiss, too summarily, Marxist explanations (p.109) presumably because of the absence of clearcut classes (cf. p.25; but contrast p.69), their reference to 'the likely existence of a self-interested economic entente between common law judges and Parliament' (p.65) is but one of many passages which must be music to Marxist ears. They cite Eileen Power in support of an interest- or pressure-group explanation of events (p.58n; but cf. p.156n), and play down the role of non-economic factors, especially ideas, in a manner congenial to Coleman and other like-minded historians (pp.14, 150–1, 154–5); but it is difficult to avoid the conclusion that they regard their interpretation as more fundamental, consistent, unified and 'simple' than the conflicting views advanced by earlier historical commentators (cf. pp.10–11, 24, 66, 71, 109, 113, etc.) – as though there were fewer disagreements among economists than among historians! On the extent of the similarities and differences between conditions in England and in France, which receives a good deal of their attention, they are equally difficult to pin down (cf. pp.74, 79, 82, 104, 108, 152). Ekelund and Tollison attach little or no weight to political aspirations – 'The unification of nation states . . . may then be interpreted as an extension of monopoly power from the local to the national level' (p.113) – while political and religious disagreements are recognized only insofar as they have by-products in rent-seeking (p.65). Administrative matters, which most commentators on mercantilism have failed to explore, are considered only because of the (admittedly crucial) problems of enforcement (cf. pp.78,

90, 108), and it is curious that the distinction between 'sanction rents' and 'enforcement rents' is mentioned only once (p.106).

In general there is a danger that unless the blanket terms 'costs' and 'benefits' are given more precise meaning the whole story will be nothing more than a rewriting of long-term economic, political, legal, constitutional and religious change in a new and unrevealing language. Rent seeking is, after all, only the profit motive in new dress, a manifestation of man's 'eternal' self interest! Unfortunately, a theory which explains 'everything' ultimately explains nothing, as Rosenberg has argued; unless its 'domain' is specified precisely, it simply applies where it applies.

NOTE

This paper was originally presented at a conference at the University of Sassari, Sardinia, in September 1983, and published in P. Roggi (ed.), *Gli Economisti e la Politica Economica* (Napoli: Edizione Scinetifiche Italiane, 1985), under the title 'Mercantilism: Yet Again!'. The present revised version was given as a joint Economics/History staff seminar at the University of Newcastle, New South Wales, on 5 June 1987. The addition of only one item (Wiles, 1987) to the original bibliography suggests that no significant new research has been published on this topic between 1983 and 1987.

BIBLIOGRAPHY

Allen, W.R., 'The Position of Mercantilism and the Early Development of International Trade', in R.V. Eagly (ed.), *Events, Ideology and Economic Theory* (Detroit, 1968), pp.65–106.
——, 'Modern Defenders of Mercantilist Theory', *History of Political Economy* 2 (1970), pp.381–97.
——, 'Rearguard Response' *History of Political Economy*, 5 (1973), pp.496–8.
Appleby, J.O., *Economic Thought and Ideology in Seventeenth Century England*, (Princeton, 1978).
Blaug, M. 'Economic Theory and Economic History in Great Britain, 1650–1776', *Past and Present* 28 (1964), pp.111–16.
Bog, I., 'Mercantilism in Germany', reprinted in Coleman (ed.), *Revisions in Mercantilism*, pp.162–89.
Coats, A.W., 'In Defence of Heckscher and the Idea of Mercantilism', *Scandinavian Economic History Review* 5 (1957), pp.173–87.
——, 'Economic Ideas and Policy in England, c. 1550–1750' in *Proceedings of Fifth International Congress of Economic History, Leningrad, 1970* vol.I (Moscow, 1974), pp.77–88.
——, 'The Interpretation of Mercantilist Economics: Some Historiographical Problems', *History of Political Economy* 5 (1973), pp.485–95. To be reprinted in vol.III of this series.
——, 'Adam Smith and the Mercantile System' in A.S. Skinner and T. Wilson (eds) *Essays on Adam Smith* (Oxford, 1975).
—— (ed.), *Economists in Government: An International Comparative Study* (Durham, NC, 1981).
Coleman, D.C., 'Labour in the English Economy of the Seventeenth Century', *Economic History Review* 2nd series, II (1956), pp.880–95.

——, 'Eli Heckscher and the Idea of Mercantilism', *Scandinavian Economic History Review* 5 (1957), pp.1–25, reprinted in Coleman (ed.), *Revisions in Mercantilism* (1969).

——, 'Editor's Introduction', in *Revisions in Mercantilism* (London, 1969) pp.1–18.

——, *The Economy of England, 1450–1750* (Oxford, 1977).

——, 'Mercantilism Revisited', *The Historical Journal* 23 (1980), pp.773–91.

Davis, R., 'The Rise of Protection in England, 1669–1786', *Economic History Review* 2nd series, 19 (1966), pp.306–17.

Ekelund, R.B. Jr. and Tollison, R.D., *Mercantilism as a Rent-Seeking Society, Economic Regulation in Historical Perspective* (College Station, Texas, 1981).

Gershenkron, A., *Europe in the Russian Mirror* (Cambridge, 1970).

Gould, J.D., 'The Trade Crisis of the Early 1620s and English Economic Thought', *Journal of Economic History* 15 (1955), pp.121–33.

Grampp, W.D., 'The Liberal Elements in English Mercantilism', *Quarterly Journal of Economics* 61 (1952), pp.465–501.

——, *Economic Liberalism, Vol.1 The Beginnings* (New York, 1965).

Hajek, J., *Comparative Research into Mercantilistic Theories in Europe of the 16th and 17th Centuries* (Prague, 1980).

Heckscher, E., *Economics and History* (1922) cited in Uhr, 'Eli Heckscher and his Treatise on Mercantilism Revisited' (1932), p.25.

——, *Mercantilism* (2nd edition, ed. E.F. Soderlund, 1955).

Herlitz, L., 'The Concept of Mercantilism', *Scandinavian Economic History Review* 2nd series, 12 (1964), pp.101–20.

Hinton, R.W.K., 'The Mercantile System at the Time of Thomas Mun', *Economic History Review* 2nd series, 7 (1955), pp.277–90.

Hume, L.J., 'Charles Davenant on Financial Administration', *History of Political Economy* 6 (1974), pp.461–77.

Hutchison, T.W., *On Revolutions and Progress in Economics* (Cambridge, 1978).

Judges, A.V., 'The Idea of a Mercantile State', reprinted in Coleman (ed.), *Revisions in Mercantilism*, pp.35–60.

Kellenbenz, H., 'Probleme der Mercantilismusforschung', in *Comite Internationale des Sciences Historiques* VI (Vienna, 1965), pp.171–90.

Letwin, W., *The Origins of Scientific Economics: English Economic Thought, 1660–1760* (London, 1963).

Magnusson, L., 'Eli Heckscher, Mercantilism, and the Favourable Balance of Trade', *Scandinavian Economic History Review* 26 (1978), pp.103–26.

Patinkin, D., 'Mercantilism and the Readmission of Jews to England' (1946) in his *Essays On and In the Chicago Tradition* (Durham, NC, 1981), pp.75–89.

Rashid, S., 'Economists, Economic Historians and Mercantilism', *Scandinavian Economic History Review* 28 (1980), pp.1–4.

——, Book Review in *History of Political Economy* 13 (1982), p.863.

Rich, E.E. and Wilson, C.H., *The Cambridge Economic History of Europe* Vol.IV, *The Economy of Expanding Europe in the Sixteenth and Seventeenth Centuries* (Cambridge, 1967).

——, *The Cambridge Economic History of Europe* Vol.V, *The Economic Organization of Early Modern Europe* (Cambridge, 1977).

Schaeffer, R.K., 'The Entelechies of Mercantilism', *Scandinavian Economic History Review* 29 (1981), pp.81–96.

Schmoller, G., *The Mercantile System and Its Historical Significance* (New York, 1896).

Schumpeter, J.A., *History of Economic Analysis* (Oxford, 1954).

Stigler, G.J., 'Does Economics Have a Useful Past?', *History of Political Economy* (1969), pp.217–30.

Thirsk, J., *Economic Policy and Projects, The Development of a Consumer Society in Early Modern England* (Oxford 1978).

Tilly, C. (ed.), *The Formation of National States in Western Europe*, (Princeton, 1975).

Uhr, C.G., 'Eli Heckscher, 1879–1932 and his Treatise on Mercantilism Revisited', *Economy and History* 23 (1980), pp.3–39.

Van Klavern, J., 'Fiscalism, Mercantilism and Corruption', reprinted in Coleman (ed.), *Revisions in Mercantilism*, pp.140–61.

Viner, J., *Studies in the Theory of International Trade* (New York, 1937).

——, 'Mercantilism', in David L. Sills (ed.), *International Encyclopedia of the Social Sciences* Vol.4 (New York, 1968).

Wallerstein, I., *The Modern World-System II, Mercantilism and the Consolidation of the European World Economy, 1600–1750* (New York, 1980).

Wiles, R.C., 'The Development of Mercantilist Economic Thought' in S. Todd Lowry (ed.), *Pre-Classical Economic Thought. From the Greeks to the Scottish Enlightenment* (Boston: Kluwer Academic Publishers, 1987), pp.147–73.

Wilson, C.H., '"Mercantilism": Some Vicissitudes of an Idea', *Economic History Review* X (1957), pp.181–8.

——, *Profit and Power* (London, 1957).

——, 'Trade Society and the State', in E.E. Rich and C.H. Wilson, *Cambridge Economic History of Europe* Vol.IV (1967), pp.487–575.

——, 'Government Policy and Private Interest in Modern Economic History', in C.H. Wilson (ed.), *Economic History and the Historian. Collected Essays* (London, 1969), pp.140–55.

Winch, D., *Adam Smith's Politics* (Cambridge, 1978).

4

CHANGING ATTITUDES TO LABOUR IN THE MID-EIGHTEENTH CENTURY

I

In recent years there have been several valuable contributions to the study of doctrinal developments in the transition from 'mercantilist' to 'classical' economics.[1] The present article is designed to suggest the need for a substantial revision of the accepted view of the attitude to labour in the literature of British economics during this transitional era.

Edgar Furniss' excellent pioneer study of eighteenth-century labour doctrines, *The Position of the Labourer in a System of Nationalism*[2] was, in certain respects, distinctly unhistorical: for instance, in the author's condemnation of 'mercantilist' theoretical fallacies, and his inadequate treatment of the socio-economic background and the temporal evolution of attitudes to labour. In chapter 7 of his volume[3] he distinguished between three distinct conceptions of the standard of living considered appropriate to the labourers, selecting his examples from a period of some eighty-odd years in which there were substantial changes in the predominant tone of economic ideas. 'A large group of writers', Furniss claimed, agreed with William Temple, the Wiltshire clothier, that wages should provide for current physical needs and no more, even for old age. The majority view, however, as represented by Sir Walter Harris, Josiah Tucker and Jacob Vanderlint, was that real wages should be slightly higher in England than abroad, while a few liberal forerunners of later thought, such as Dudley North, Bishop Berkeley and David Hume, advocated an improvement of living standards as an end in itself.

Such a classification is obviously inflexible, and Furniss seriously underestimated the importance of the last, minority viewpoint, which was receiving increasing support from the 1750s. Before the mid-century almost all British economic writers were agreed that wages must be kept low, since a rise in money wage rates would increase the cost and reduce the competitiveness of our manufactured exports. Furthermore, owing to the incorrigible idleness of most labourers, it was considered advisable to keep up the prices of provisions, so that the pressure of necessity would compel the workers to be industrious. Even in the first half of the eighteenth century, however, some writers were unwilling to give wholehearted approval to this doctrine, and their views met with increasing support from the 1750s. It was conceded that not all the workers were idle and dissolute, and that if too many of them were, it was largely the result of circumstances beyond their control. There was a greater appreciation of the hardships faced by the industrious labourer in times of high prices – a comparatively rare occurrence in the second quarter of the century[4] – and, more heretical still, it was increasingly argued that a policy of depressing wage levels in order to enforce constant and arduous toil would destroy the incentive to effort, and reduce the labouring class to despair. High wages, it was frequently asserted, would act not merely as a stimulus to effective demand, as Daniel Defoe had so insistently argued,[5] but also as a reward for skill and an inducement to further effort, so that the economy in general would benefit as well as the individual worker. Despite continued concern with the moral and economic consequences of luxury consumption, increased spending by the lower classes was not merely becoming accepted as inevitable, but was welcomed as contributing to the preservation of an equitable and stable social order, and even as an aid to the dissemination of political democracy. Adam Smith's famous proposition that 'no society can surely be flourishing or happy, of which the far greater part of the members are poor and miserable' is characteristic of the new outlook,[6] and he was not the first economist to assert that 'consumption is the sole end and purpose of all production',[7] or that 'the high price of labour . . . is the very thing in which public opulence consists'.[8] Nor is it sufficient to dismiss these anticipations of later thought as the dreams of misty-eyed idealists or the aberrant ravings of cranks. Support for these views came from some of the most profound thinkers and acute observers of their day, and was consistent with a general movement of thought affecting philosophy – the influence of the Enlightenment on the growth of sympathy for the oppressed classes, religion – particularly the decline of the Puritan conception of the shamefulness of poverty and the rise of Methodism, and literature – the emergence of romanticism and sentimentalism. It is, therefore, worth examining this neglected aspect of economic thought in some detail, in order to indicate its development and assess its precise significance.

Within the limits of a single article it is impossible to demonstrate that a more 'sympathetic' attitude to the labourer predominated in the economic writings of the period 1750–76. Instead, attention will be concentrated upon the arguments of those favouring an improvement in the standard of living, for the complexity of the issues involved has been underestimated.[9]

II

The first[10] eighteenth century writer to argue explicitly that a rise in real wages would stimulate an increase in the labourer's effort was Jacob

Vanderlint.[11] Historians of doctrine have noted his proposal to increase the money supply with the object of stimulating the demand for agricultural products, but the significance of his desire to reduce money wages by 25 per cent and the price of necessaries by 50 per cent has been generally overlooked.[12] Like the classical economists, Vanderlint regarded human wants as virtually insatiable,[13] maintaining that

> the working people can and will do a great deal more work than they do, if they were sufficiently encouraged. For I take it for a maxim, that the people of no class will ever want industry, if they don't want encouragement.

As proof of this proposition, Vanderlint cited the occasion of

> a time of general mourning for a Prince [which] necessarily requires abundance of goods to be made in a very short time, ... and we know the weavers, dyers, taylors, etc. do at such times work almost night and day, only for the encouragement of somewhat better pay and wages, which an extraordinary demand for any goods is necessarily connected with.[14]

It would be legitimate to follow the usual practice of modern writers, who either ignore Vanderlint's plea for increased real wages or dismiss it as an exception to the general rule, but for two singular circumstances: the appearance, in the year after the publication of Vanderlint's pamphlet, of the first part of Bishop Berkeley's *Querist*, which contained a somewhat analogous call for an improvement in the labourer's living standards; and the existence of Malachy Postlethwayt's plagiarism of the above-quoted passages from Vanderlint's text.

The *Querist*[15] embodied a comprehensive series of proposals for stimulating the underdeveloped economy of Ireland, including the suggestion that the Irish peasants would be more industrious if their wants were better supplied.[16] Berkeley not only referred to the degrading and discouraging effects of very low living standards, an idea which, according to Furniss, 'had already gained some support',[17] but added that if the labourer's wants were given priority over the luxuries and conveniences of the rich, the nation in general would benefit.[18] Berkeley's proposals for dealing with the problem of idleness included the enforcement of 'temporary servitude';[19] but his hostility towards the lazy and recalcitrant did not prevent him from adopting a sympathetic and understanding attitude towards the generality of labourers. Moreover, he was fully aware of the need to overcome the main contemporary obstacle to an increase in labour effort – the situation where, as Furniss says, the labourer

> is caught fast in the clutch of custom and rigid tradition. . . . Where a rigid standard of living, embracing not much more than the necessaries

of physical subsistence, obtains, any increase in wages will result in an immediate diminution in labour hours.[20]

Berkeley's solution was in accordance with that advanced by a growing number of writers in the third quarter of the century, namely, to raise the labourers' living standards and thereby create a new pattern of wants and the desire to satisfy them.

Postlethwayt, on the other hand, represents an entirely different case. It is well known that his numerous works included many passages borrowed from other writers, but his 'indebtedness' to Vanderlint seems to have passed unnoticed hitherto. This is surprising, for the above quoted extracts are reproduced in *Britain's Commercial Interest Explained and Improved*, 1757, which one authority has called 'by all odds Postlethwayt's most important contribution to economic literature'.[21] Paragraphs stolen from Vanderlint cannot, of course, be accepted unquestioningly as representing Postlethwayt's own attitude to labour, and it is easy to discover passages in his works in which he advocated low wages.[22] Nevertheless, he frequently appeared as an outspoken defender of the labourer against the familiar charges of idleness and improvidence. In a famous extract quoted by Karl Marx in *Das Kapital*[23] Postlethwayt attacked those who

> contend for the perpetual slavery of the working people of this kingdom: they forget the vulgar adage, all work and no play.

Even though the workers refused to work six days if they could maintain themselves in five, this did not mean that necessaries should be heavily taxed.

> Have not the English boasted of the ingenuity and dexterity of her working artists and manufacturers, which have hitherto given credit and reputation to British wares in general? What has this been owing to? To nothing more probably, than the relaxation of the working people in their own way . . . And if they had not unbendings, we may presume they would pine away, and become enervated as well in body as marred in understanding. And what sort of workmanship could we expect from such hard-driven animals.[24]

These arguments go beyond the earlier patriotic defence of the English worker. When taken together with his borrowings from Vanderlint, his assertion of the superiority of the native artisan over his foreign rival in respect of industriousness and ingenuity, and his recognition of the key role of mechanical devices in the development of competitive efficiency,[25] it is clear that Postlethwayt belongs with those later writers who advocated a rise in living standards as an incentive to effort.

David Hume's contribution to the emergence of a new attitude towards the labourer resembled his contribution to the general transition from 'mercantilist' to 'classical' economics,[26] for although he did not explicitly advocate an increase of real wages as a means of spurring the labourer to greater effort, his analysis indirectly lent considerable support to this viewpoint. The most direct reference to the problem in Hume's writings suggests that he favoured moderate taxes on necessaries as a means of stimulating the labourer's effort, since he argued that

in years of scarcity, if it be not extreme, . . . the poor labour more, and really live better, than in years of great plenty, when they indulge themselves in idleness and riot.[27]

This statement, however, was almost immediately followed by a warning that

exorbitant taxes, like extreme necessity, destroy industry, by producing despair; and . . . 'tis to be feared that taxes, all over *Europe*, are multiplying to such a degree, as will intirely crush all art and industry.[28]

This proviso exemplified Hume's habit of adding a particular qualification to any general proposition, a practice which makes it misleading simply to characterize him as an advocate of moderate hardship as the state of affairs most conducive to the labourer's well-being.[29] Indeed, it can be argued that the main weight of Hume's case was against any attempt to restrict the expansion of the labourer's wants and the improvement of his living standards, and this argument is reinforced by an examination of his psychological theory.

When he discussed the psychological basis of economic activity,[30] as in other parts of his writings, Hume presented both sides of the question. But while he made passing reference to the influence of 'necessity, which is the great spur to industry and invention',[31] he paid more attention to the need to provide incentives to all forms of economic activity.

It is a violent method and in most cases impracticable, to oblige the labourer to toil, in order to raise from the land more than what subsists himself and family. Furnish him with manufactures and commodities, and he will do it of himself.[32]

Professor Rotwein has recently concluded that Hume rejected the widely-held view that the best way to create a disposition towards industry was to enforce an endless repetition of toil, since he believed that human beings responded more effectively to variety and the challenge of difficulty. Whereas earlier writers

commonly viewed indulgence in the pleasures of idleness as the fulfilment of a natural craving, Hume recognises it as symptomatic of frustration – that is as an attempt to compensate through pleasure for the want of liveliness resulting from a thwarting of the design for interesting action.[33]

67

Historians of economic doctrine have long recognized that one aspect of the transition from 'mercantilism' to 'classical' economics was a growing belief in the efficacy of individual freedom in economic affairs. It could be argued that insights of the kind provided by Hume's psychological theory made a significant contribution to the willingness of upper-class writers to concede that the labourer, too, might be responsive to economic incentives.[34]

Although he did not explicitly advocate raising real wages as a means of stimulating effort, Hume's sympathetic discussion of the labourer's predicament may well have influenced other writers to adopt this view. One such writer was Nathaniel Forster, whose *Enquiry into the Causes of the Present High Price of Provisions*, 1767, bears unmistakeable traces of Hume's influence.[35] Forster castigated those who contended that 'the poor will be industrious only in the degree that they are necessitous' for propounding 'a doctrine as false, as it is inhuman'[36] and warned that the deliberate imposition of artificial burdens on the labourer would, instead of stimulating him, drive him to 'desperation and madness'.[37] Of a case in Norwich, when a rise in wages followed 'upon some particular occasion of an extraordinary demand for goods' he admitted that some persons might have worked less. But this would only

> be the consequence of a sudden rise of wages with a few idle worthless fellows ... the really industrious would never be less so from any extraordinary encouragement given to industry. And I cannot but think it as good a general maxim as ever was advanced, that the sure way of engaging a man to go through a work with vigour and spirit is, to ensure him a taste of the sweets of it.

When labourers appeared unresponsive to incentives, this was attributable to

> the fluctuating state of most manufactures and trades, and the consequent fluctuation of wages [so that] the masters and their workmen are unhappily in a perpetual state of war with each other.[38]

Perhaps the most considered and thorough-going defence of wage increases as a means of stimulating the effort of labour to be published in the period 1750–75 came from two writers whose contributions appear to have passed almost entirely unnoticed.[39] Both asserted that wages had not kept pace with rising prices and taxes, and complained that insult had been added to this injurious state of affairs, for 'those unhappy, distressed, oppressed and useful people have become the objects of abuse throughout the kingdom'.[40] Neither author was blind to the weaknesses of the labouring classes; both admitted the charge of intemperance, but they strongly attacked the government's attempt to profit from this weakness. Mortimer wanted to reduce the number and hours of opening of taverns, while his anonymous predecessor protested that the Walpole administration had encouraged

dissipation and even intemperance . . . for the sake of raising taxes . . .
making, moreover, their indulgence in vice the means of impelling them
to excessive labour.[41]

Both writers cited and enlarged upon Hume's treatment of the labour
problem, drawing the conclusions implied but not explicitly stated in Hume's
analysis. The author of the *Considerations on the Policy* accepted the view of
Petty and Sir William Temple that some degree of necessity was 'requisite to
create a spirit of industry', but after quoting Hume's warning of the dangers
of attempting to oppress the labouring classes he added that Hume

> might have looked to his own country for proof, that mere necessity
> will not always do . . . what may be effected by encouragement.

It was the opportunity for gain provided by the Union with England, not the
pressure of necessity, that had aroused Scottish manufactures and trade from
their former lethargy, making the people responsive to economic incentives.
In words strongly reminiscent of Hume's *Essays* he concluded that

> it is . . . more a turn of mind than multiplied necessities that induces
> men to become industrious, which will be better excited by encourage-
> ment than compulsion.[42]

In his *Elements of Commerce*, Thomas Mortimer carefully reviewed the
various proposals advanced by earlier writers who had considered the
labour problem, before firmly supporting those who favoured raising real
wages as the best method of encouraging industry. Mortimer denied that
the enforcement of labour would ensure an improved quality of work. When
a labourer is

> oppressed by the combined plagues of dearness of provisions, incessant
> labour and low wages, . . . indifference will take the place of emulation,
> and thus the main springs of industry will be destroyed . . . he will carry
> his industry no further, than to procure [his family] temporary and
> partial relief; and out of the little he earns by constant labour, he will
> retain a reserve, to purchase the cup of oblivion, to enable him to forget,
> for a few hours occasionally, the galling yoke of double bondage, to a
> hard hearted, mercenary master, and a numerous, distressed family.
>
> Can it be expected, that the labour or industry of a person so
> situated, will be equal to that of him, who is generously paid, in
> a degree proportioned to the advantages derived from his ingenuity,
> close application, or hard bodily labour; . . . In the one case, you must
> be satisifed with the common drudgery of an enervated slave; in the
> other, you may expect new efforts of ingenuity, extraordinary exertions
> of abilities, and every good effect of a mind at peace, and a body in the
> vigour of health.
>
> Will any man, after this, pretend to say, that manufactures can be

perfect, (the only way for them to prosper), where provisions are high, and labour low; by which all encouragement is taken away from the poor fabricator?[43]

As Mortimer's bulky volume was designed as an instruction manual for 'young gentlemen of fortune' who were to take up commerce as their profession, he proceeded to enunciate the general principles to be derived from his discussion. These were that wages should be proportioned to the price of provisions; that they should be high enough to encourage marriages, give the worker a prospect of self-improvement, and a surplus for occasional ease and plenty; that wages duly proportioned to the profits of the work would guarantee speedy and careful performance, and would discourage idleness and vice unless these were general throughout society or encouraged by the government; and that wages should never be paid in an alehouse.[44] Taken together, these principles virtually amounted to a code of 'fair labour practices' that was far removed from the prevalent tone of the writings dealing with the labourer in the first half of the century.

The writers quoted above constitute but a small sample of those who, in the period under review, defended the labouring poor against the charges of idleness and dissipation and protested against the enforced hardships caused by rising prices. By the late 1760s the literature on this subject had attained considerable proportions, and it was no longer true, as Furniss has asserted, that

> even the most compassionate was inclined toward the opinion that life had been too easy for the working-man; that discipline had been unwisely relaxed, and that [the labourer's] character had suffered from an absence of a necessity for his industry.[45]

Much of this literature lacks interest beyond the confines of the immediate problem of rising prices; some of the pamphlets published were positively puerile, and others represented partisan efforts to lay the blame on the luxury of the rich, the government's debt policy, the engrossing of farms, the middlemen or the corn bounty.[46] Partisanship, however, does not invalidate these writings as evidence of a change in the contemporary attitude towards the labourer's difficulties, and while many authors still supported the doctrine of the utility of poverty, there was some justification for Mortimer's claim that 'the advocate of the poor has one advantage on his side, he cannot be suspected of selfish views',[47] at least when he was not himself a member of the labouring class.

To say that the post-1750 writings demonstrated an increasingly sympathetic attitude towards the poor is, however, vague, for this 'sympathy' included a variety of views expressed with widely differing degrees of analytical subtlety. Some writers who expressed concern at the prevalence of 'hard times' made no reference whatsoever to wage levels, while others would clearly have opposed any scheme to raise wages for fear of damaging the export trade.[48] Not all those who recognized that low wages operated as a deterrent to effort favoured raising real or money wages as an incentive.[49] But whether they contributed systematic treatises or ephemeral pamphlets, many contemporary authors were, consciously or unconsciously, groping their way towards the concept of an optimum wage level – one which would reconcile the interests of the agricultural producers, the exporters of manufactures and the wage-earners themselves. The interests of the latter were considered not merely for humanitarian reasons, but also because it was becoming evident to all but the most prejudiced observers that the policy of allowing the wage-earner to be squeezed by rising prices had serious drawbacks, and that its continuance might lead to large-scale emigration or social disturbances.[50]

Needless to say, these attempts to define the 'optimal' level of wages met with little success, often merely amounting to a re-statement of the problem in different terms;[51] and the repeated assertion that wages should be 'proportioned to the price of provisions' was of little help until an effort was made to define the absolute level at which this proportionality was to be secured. On this matter there were clear differences of opinion,[52] partly because of the difficulty of allowing for regional and occupational variations, and partly because of the different criteria in terms of which the optimum was to be defined. The agriculturalists, for example, insisted that the prices of provisions should not be unduly depressed, and in this group Arthur Young occupied a leading role, not only because of the volume and influence of his writings, but also because of his strenuous efforts to measure the optimum level of wages.[53] Young reproduced page after page of data on family budgets, wages and prices in different areas, and while it would be foolish to expect perfect consistency from one who wrote so extensively in defence of a sectional interest his arguments may be summarized in the following propositions:

(a) Existing variations in prices and wages conclusively proved that the price of provisions did not determine the price of labour.

(b) Therefore, a guarantee of 'reasonable' prices to the farmer did not necessarily entail a high level of money wages.

(c) Owing to the labourer's inherent idleness, high prices were necessary to ensure unremitting effort.

(d) But as the cost of manufactures was determined by the quality and quantity of work performed as well as the wage rate, it was 'impossible, therefore, to assert, that our manufacturers are undersold, *because* of their high price of labour'.[54]

The second and third propositions presumably require no amplification; the underlying reasoning is obvious. The first and fourth propositions, however, are of considerable interest, both in relation to Young's own position, and to the general contemporary view of the role of labour in an expanding economy. Young was bound to reject the subsistence theory of wages (proposition a): it was incompatible with his desire for high food prices[55] and low wages, and he undoubtedly considered that his statistical evidence afforded overwhelming support for his case. Yet he did not deny that food prices and wage rates often moved together,[56] and he appeared to be advocating proportionality between prices and wages at a high absolute level. Young is usually regarded as an advocate of low wages,[57] but there are passages in his tours indicating that he recognized the advantages of rising wages under certain circumstances;[58] and although it would be misleading to suggest that he believed in the existence of a causal relationship between high wages and industriousness, it is significant that in his *Political Arithmetic*, 1774, the volume which purported to demonstrate the 'first principles' distilled from the information collected on his tours, he categorically stated that dear labour, plentiful employment, rising living standards and increasing population were the inevitable concomitants of prosperity.[59]

The argument in Young's *Political Arithmetic* does not justify his inclusion as a supporter of high wages as an incentive to effort – in view of his inconsistencies his support would in any case be of doubtful value. But when taken in conjunction with his admission that high wages did not necessarily entail high labour costs (proposition a) – a distinction drawn by several writers in the period[60] – it is clear that Young had moved some way from the early eighteenth-century view that low wages were essential to national prosperity towards the high wage doctrine of the *Wealth of Nations*.[61]

III

Apart from a few isolated advocates of a 'high wage economy',[62] most British economists before 1750 regarded low wages as an essential pre-condition of the maintenance of a high volume of exports, although the plea that the British workman should enjoy a higher standard of living than that of his continental counterpart[63] represented a tacit admission that successful competition in foreign markets did not require that home wage levels should be equal to or lower than foreign wage levels. By contrast, in the third quarter of the century there was growing support for the view that high wages and rising living standards were not merely compatible with, but were even a necessary concomitant of the prosperity of our domestic and exported manufactures. An attempt will now be made to suggest some of the reasons for this change.

From the analytical viewpoint, incomparably the most significant reason why economic writers after 1750 were less concerned than their predecessors with the high level of British wages was the growing appreciation that high money wages did not necessarily mean high labour costs. The distinction between the productivity and the money cost of labour appears to have been generally overlooked in the earlier period; but after 1750 half-a-dozen writers explicitly referred to it,[64] some of them including it as an essential part of a systematic body of reasoning, while the distinction was implicit in the works of numerous other authors. Surprisingly enough, those who advocated raising living standards as an incentive to effort did not explicitly state that this inducement would, if a significant increase in productivity occurred, lead to a reduction of effective labour costs per unit of output, although this was an obvious corollary of their general reasoning. Nevertheless, increasing attention was being paid to the skill,[65] quality and quantity of the labour performed by the English artisan, as well as to the level of money wages. It is no coincidence, though it is difficult to decide whether this was a cause or a consequence of the growing 'sympathy' towards the labourer, that favourable comparisons were being made between the British worker and his continental rivals – even the Dutch, who had so frequently been held up as a model of industry and frugality by the late seventeenth and early eighteenth-century writers.[66] If, as some were prepared to maintain, the English workman was superior to foreign workers, his higher money wages and living standards might be viewed not simply as a just recompense for his superiority, but even as a guarantee of the preservation of this differential. This is surely one reason for the widespread acknowledgement that low wages could act as a disincentive, and the increasing acceptance of the desirability of a 'high-wage economy'.

Another reason for the diminished concern over our high wage level was the growing importance attached to mechanical devices. It has recently been argued that in seventeenth century England the possibilities of increasing output by the introduction of improved techniques were very limited, a state of affairs which helps to account for the importance attached to quantitative increases in the labour supply.[67] By the 1750s however, a much wider range of mechanical appliances had become available, and the writers of this period demonstrated a correspondingly enhanced interest in the effects of labour-saving innovations. In discussing this topic they were primarily concerned with the employment effects of such devices, and some insisted that if the net effect of an innovation was a reduction of total employment it should not be adopted.[68] The majority view, however, was optimistic, and several writers attached crucial importance to labour-saving innovations as a means of reducing production costs in both agriculture and manufacturing, and thereby increasing employment and sales, both at home and abroad.[69] Of course machinery was not advocated because it would facilitate the payment of higher wages. But the growing awareness of the efficacy of mechanical aids undoubtedly reinforced the arguments of those who feared that falling real wages would have harmful effects on the labour force, while the increasing importance of capital outlays may have tended to reduce the former emphasis on wage reductions as the principal method of reducing total costs.

IV

The change in the attitude to labour in the mid-eighteenth century was not confined to such matters as wages, incentives and mechanical aids, but formed part of a generalized conception of the labourer's role in the process of economic and social development, and an attempt will now be made to place the foregoing discussion in its wider setting. An approach to this broader view may be made via a brief examination of the attitude to luxury consumption in the period 1750–75.

Mandeville's *Fable of the Bees*[70] had already enforced a shocked reappraisal of the economic consequences of luxury in the 1720s and 1730s, and the growing impact of the 'doctrine of beneficial luxury' can be traced up to Hume's 'synthesis' of the theory in the mid-century.[71] The earlier belief in the 'utility of poverty' was obviously incompatible with support for any substantial increase in the labourer's consumption, but it did not necessarily follow that the later writers who advocated raising real wages as an incentive to effort supported luxurious consumption by the labourer.[72] Moreover, it is doubtful whether there was any favourable trend in the post-1750 attitude towards luxury on the part of the public in general: indeed, there were bitter complaints of current excesses, perhaps the most famous being John Brown's *Estimate of the Manners and Principles of the Times*, 1757, which went through six editions in six months.

Like other social critics of the day, Brown blamed the upper classes for the prevalent luxury, which brought no benefit to the poor, whose money wages rose in accordance with the prices of provisions only after they had been driven by 'the last necessity and want' to commit public disturbances.[73] Many of Brown's contemporaries regarded luxury as a leading cause of present discontents and drew gloomy parallels between eighteenth-century England and the periods immediately preceeding the decay of ancient empires. There were numerous references to the dangers of a growing concentration of national wealth, and to the economic, social and political instability of a country where a great gap existed between rich and poor. Concern at this prospect inspired various egalitarian proposals, and appeals for a more equal distribution of wealth[74] or a wider diffusion of property[75] became frequent enough to constitute a characteristic feature of contemporary literature, although some authors cautiously observed that their schemes for ameliorating the condition of the lower orders would not disrupt the social hierarchy.[76] In this context the customary praise of the merchant assumed a sociological significance in addition to its familiar economic connotation. Many writers valued the contribution of 'middling people' to the preservation of 'a gradual and easy transition from rank to rank'[77] and such references assumed a kind of self-congratulatory patriotism after Montesquieu's eulogy of the English constitution.

Among the economic writers, however, a more qualified approach to luxury consumption was winning acceptance, partly through the influence of David Hume,[78] and many admitted that an increased availability of the comforts and conveniences as well as the necessities of life could operate as a powerful stimulus to industry by all ranks of society. Few persons argued that the workers should consume large quantities of the superfluities of life; but as the difficulty of defining the term luxury was acknowledged, it is reasonable to include those who favoured raising real wages as an incentive to effort among the supporters of the view that the workers should be allowed to benefit from the growing output of consumer's goods.[79] Some writers maintained that luxury consumption was an inevitable and harmless or even desirable consequence of economic progress, but the majority recognized that it might easily extend beyond the point at which it operated as a stimulus to industry. Accordingly they proposed that the government should act to prevent any excess, even though this was 'a matter of great delicacy, and requires a nice judgment'.[80]

The influence of luxury and the role of the labourer were often examined in conjunction with one another in contemporary efforts to define the conditions most conducive to a continuously high rate of economic progress. It was widely believed that Britain afforded just the right balance between the extremes of plenty and hardship and thus provided the challenge of 'difficulty' needed to stimulate the response of energy, industry and innovation (Hume's 'quick march of the spirits')[81] But although the process of development was well under way, there were many pitfalls in the path to prosperity – such as the emergence of a luxurious leisured class, a rapidly rising price level, a burdensome level of debts and taxes, and the pressure of rising living costs on the labouring classes – and appropriate policies were required to counteract these dangers.

Different writers naturally visualized the process in widely different terms, and Brown's theory of 'stages' of development was only one of the more crude attempts to develop the widespread notion that the current prosperity presaged eventual economic and social decay, an idea fostered by the popularity of classical analogies in contemporary historiography. The most sophisticated theory of economic development was that presented by Sir James Steuart, in his *Inquiry into the Principles of Political Economy*, 1767.[82] In the primitive stage, according to Steuart, luxury played an initiating role, for the growth of new wants stimulated increased effort and output, and improved consumption standards for all ranks of society constituted an essential condition of progress. But in the intermediate or 'mature' stage, rising population, food prices and wages undermined the export trade, and attempts to restrict luxury and to reduce production costs, either by utilizing mechanical devices or by stimulating the workers' effort and ingenuity, could not indefinitely postpone the day when home products were undersold by goods from less advanced countries. Consequently, in the final stage, self-sufficiency should be the object of policy, with an expanding consumption of domestic luxuries to offset the decline in export sales. Thus, despite his emphasis on rising living standards as the initial impulse to economic expansion, Steuart regarded a high wage level as the factor ultimately setting limits to this process.

In this respect Steuart agreed with Hume, who, before his conversion by Josiah Tucker, had contended that a rich country would eventually be unable to withstand the competition of a poor country, because the former would experience a rise in prices and costs resulting from a favourable balance of trade and an inflow of specie.[83] Tucker successfully controverted this view, insisting that the rich country could preserve its superiority over the poorer nation owing to its greater efficiency and its possession of 'great capital, extensive correspondence, skilful expedients of facilitating labour, dexterity, industry etc'[84]. With respect to the position of the labourer, Tucker claimed that 'the higher wages of the rich country, and the greater scope and encouragement given for the exertion of genius, industry, and ambition, will naturally determine a great many men of spirit and enterprise to forsake their own poor country, and settle in the richer',[85] so that there was no necessary reason why high wages should act as an obstacle to continuous economic expansion. Elsewhere in his writings Tucker advocated wage reductions and appeared as a bitter critic of the idleness and immorality of the English worker;[86] but in his discussion with Hume he indirectly lent powerful theoretical support to the arguments of those who viewed high wages and rising living standards for the labourer as a necessary and desirable feature of economic development. In this respect, perhaps unwittingly, his theory represented the closest approximation to that of Adam Smith, who regarded a high level of wages and a rapid growth of national wealth as inevitably associated.[87]

NOTES

1 See, for example, the works by Grampp, Hutchison, Low and Rotwein referred to in later notes.
2 New York, 1920.
3 Especially p.178 ff.
4 For a recent discussion of this period see G.E. Mingay, 'The Agricultural Depression, 1730–50', *Economic History Review* VIII, (3) (1956), pp.323–38.
5 Cf. his *Complete English Tradesman*, I (1726), pp.386–7, II (1732), pt. I, pp.138–9, 144–5, and *A Plan of the English Commerce* (1730), pp.20, 102–3.
6 *Wealth of Nations* (Everyman Ed.), I, p.70. Cf. N. Forster, *An Enquiry into the Causes of the Present High Price of Provisions* (1767), pp.62–3, and M. Postlethwayt, *Britain's Commercial Interest Explained and Improved* (1757), II, p.367.
7 Smith, op. cit., II, p.155. Cf. J. Vanderlint, *Money Answers All Things* (1734), pp.67, 120, 140.
8 Smith, op. cit., II, p.155. Cf. Forster, op. cit., pp.62–3.
9 To regard the issue merely as a dispute between the advocates of high or low wages, as is implied in Miss Gilboy's otherwise valuable discussion of luxury consumption and incentives, *Wages in Eighteenth-Century England* (Harvard, 1934), ch.9, is a serious oversimplification.

10 Although Defoe acknowledged that high wages were accompanied by increased labour effort and skill (e.g. *Plan*, op. cit., p.32 ff) he regarded high wages as a consequence of trade expansion rather than a means of raising labour productivity. Defoe was, of course, no slave to consistency. He denied the possibility of raising the living standards of the lowest paid workers (ibid., p.232), while the whole tone of this work and his *Complete English Tradesman* directly conflicted with the hostility to the labourers expressed in *Giving Alms No Charity* (1704), and *The Behaviour of Servants* (1724). His later views may conceivably reflect his experiences on his tours, e.g. the famous case of Halifax: *Tour* (Everyman Ed.), II, pp.193–5. In this respect his inconsistencies resemble those of a later traveller, Arthur Young. See this volume, pp.45–60.

11 A timber merchant of Dutch extraction, Vanderlint appears to have written only one tract, *Money Answers All Things* (London, 1734). For the few known biographical details see the *Dictionary of National Biography*, XX, p.102.

12 Vanderlint, op. cit., p.86. Although Furniss admitted that Vanderlint's advocacy of high wages represented a fundamental break with the 'doctrine of the social utility of hard times' (op. cit., p.127), he nevertheless omitted Vanderlint's name from the list of those who sought to improve the labourer's lot (ibid., p.185), apparently because Vanderlint regarded wages as normally 'settled and constituted of the price of victuals and drink' (*Money Answers All Things*, pp.6, 43, 140).

13 ibid., p.82: 'The wants of mankind are full as great, as both their abilities, and the earth too, are capable of supplying; whence it follows, that any want of employment or trade amongst the people is solely owing to this, that we have not land enough in use to employ and support them.'

14 ibid., p.122. This example was repeated by Postlethwayt (this volume, p.66). It is of incidental interest to note that an Act of 1768, raising statutory wage levels, included an allowance for abnormally high wages at a time of general mourning. See D. George, *London Life in the Eighteenth Century* (London, 1925), p.206.

15 George Berkeley's, *The Querist*, was published in Dublin and London in 1735–7, in three parts, and reprinted several times in the 1750s, cf. *The Works of George Berkeley, Bishop of Cloyne*, ed. A.A. Luce and T.E. Jessop (London, 1953), VI, pp.89–93. All subsequent references are to this edition.

There is no evidence of any connection between Berkeley and Vanderlint. The latter's tract was partly inspired by the consequences of 'the extraordinary rise of victuals a few years ago' (op. cit., p.1), probably referring to 1728–9. For a penetrating analysis of Berkeley's views see T.W. Hutchison's article 'Berkeley's *Querist* and its Place in the Economic Thought of the Eighteenth Century', *The British Journal for the Philosophy of Science* IV, (3) (1953), pp.52–77. The present writer is grateful to Professor Hutchison for many helpful comments and suggestions in connection with this study.

16 *The Querist*, Query No. 20: 'Whether the creating of wants be not the likeliest way to produce industry in a people? And whether, if our peasants were accustomed to eat beef and wear shoes, they would not be more industrious?' Cf. No. 350: 'Whether the way to make men industrious be not to let them taste the fruits of their industry?'

17 Furniss, op. cit., p.127. Cf. *Querist*, No.61: 'Whether nastiness and beggary do not, on the contrary, extinguish all such ambition, making men listless, hopeless, and slothful?'

18 ibid., No.168. Cf. No.59: 'Whether to provide plentifully for the poor be not feeding the root, the substance whereof will shoot upwards into the branches, and cause the top to flourish?'

19 ibid., Nos. 382 and 384.
20 Furniss, op. cit., pp.234–5. Characteristically, he attributes this situation to the 'rigid policies of nationalism' and the absence of any 'prospect of rising in the social scale', rather than to contemporary economic conditions. See also T.W. Hutchison's illuminating comments, op. cit., pp.55–8.
21 Professor E.A.J. Johnson, *Predecessors of Adam Smith* (New York, 1937), p.196. The above-quoted passages from Vanderlint, p.122, appear in *Britain's Commercial Interest*, I, pp.43–4. In fact Part I of Postlethwayt's 'systematically' constructed treatise is almost entirely drawn from Vanderlint, much of it consisting of word-for-word copying – an instructive commentary on Postlethwayt's method of 'integration' (Johnson, op. cit., p.205).
22 Such inconsistencies are hardly surprising in a man who, like Defoe (see note 10) and Arthur Young (see notes 53–61) wrote prolifically. In Postlethwayt's case it would be somewhat easier to reconcile these discrepancies, for he usually advocated constant or rising real wages, but reduced money wages – as he believed that a low-wage economy could always undersell a high-wage economy (cf. *Great Britain's True System*, 1757, p.158).
23 Karl Marx, *Capital* (Everyman Ed. 1930), I, p.279.
24 From the Preliminary Discourse to his *Universal Dictionary* (4th ed. written 1766, published 1774), p.xiv. For a similar argument expressed from a more hostile viewpoint see Anon., *Remarks upon the Serious Dissuasive from an Intended Subscription for Continuing the Races* (1733) quoted in A.P. Wadsworth and J. de L. Mann, *The Cotton Trade and Industrial Lancashire 1600–1780* (Manchester, 1931), p.392, fn.
25 See note 69.
26 Johnson, op. cit., p.163, remarks that Hume 'expressed ideas which *when further developed* brought about the disintegration of the whole body of ideas which . . . [he] was presenting.' (Italics in original).
27 David Hume, *Writings on Economics*, ed. Rotwein (London, 1955), p.85, fn. In the next sentence Hume cited 'the year 1740, when bread and provisions of all kinds were very dear' as an example. This supports the interpretation that Hume was mainly concerned here with the effects of *short-term* fluctuations in the harvests, whereas his general discussion of the progress of commerce and 'refinement in the arts' suggests that he favoured *long-term* improvements in the labourer's living standards. ibid., pp.21–3. For other attempts to distinguish between the long-run and the short-run see note 38.
28 ibid., p.85, fn. (Italics in original). This entire footnote last appeared, during Hume's lifetime, in the 1768 edition of his essays. Did its subsequent deletion reflect a change in Hume's views, possibly under the influence of contemporary protests against the depressing effects of rising prices on living standards?
29 Furniss, op. cit., pp.122–3.
30 On this subject I am indebted to Professor Rotwein's analysis in the introduction to his new edition of Hume's economic writings, op. cit., pp.xxxii–liii. He effectively refutes Schumpeter's dogmatic assertion, *History of Economic Analysis* (New York, 1954), p.447, fn. 4, that Hume's 'economics has nothing whatsoever to do with either his psychology or his philosophy'.
31 op. cit., pp.17–18.
32 ibid., p.12; cf. p.146: 'The most natural way, surely, of encouraging husbandry, is, first, to excite other kinds of industry, and thereby afford the labourer a ready market for his commodities, and a return of such goods as may contribute to his pleasure and enjoyment. This method is infallible and universal . . .' Also p.15.
33 ibid., p.xlix. Cf. Adam Smith, *Lectures on Justice Police Revenue and Arms, 1763*

(Cannan Ed. Oxford, 1896), p.179: 'Man is an anxious animal, and must have his care swept off by something that can exhilarate the spirits.' For a remarkable confirmation of Hume's insight see the extracts from Francis Place, *Improvement of the Working People* (1834), p.15 (quoted by D. George, op. cit., pp.208–9). Admittedly Place was referring to the late eighteenth century, but this state of affairs was doubtless also true of the mid-century.

34 Many subsequent writers quoted Hume's views on the worker's psychology or employed similar terminology, e.g. J. Massie, *A Plan for the Establishment of Charity Houses* (1758), p.50; and see p.69. This change of attitude was not, however, solely the product of a new theory; it was intimately bound up with contemporary socio-economic changes. Limitations of space preclude a discussion of this topic here.

35 Despite its title, Forster's treatise was no mere broadside fired off in haste, but an extensive and detached analysis of a wide range of economic problems. He explicitly quoted Hume on credit (p.32), taxes (p.50) and trade (pp.127–8, 197), and his whole treatment of luxury (pp.40–8) and the labour problem (pp.55–63, under the heading 'Of Taxes') was highly reminiscent of Hume, though he denied that the poor lived better in dear than in cheap years. In many respects Forster's position represented a half-way stage between Hume and Adam Smith. Like them, and other defenders of the poor, Forster quoted extensively from such writers as Mirabeau, Montesquieu and Rousseau, and it would be interesting to trace the French contribution to the discussion.

36 Forster, op. cit., p.55.

37 ibid., p.58.

38 ibid., pp.60–1. Forster's distinction between the beneficial effects of a stimulus to incentives in conditions of relative stability and the undesirable repercussions of 'sudden' increases in wages was a significant anticipation of the classical view, as embodied in J.R. McCulloch, *Essay on . . . the Condition of the Labouring Classes* (1826), pp.155, 158. McCulloch argued that although rising real wages and living standards usually led to an improvement in the worker's habits and productivity, a 'sudden and transitory' increase of wages might be followed by a growth of absenteeism, idleness and dissipation. For similar views see Sir W. Harris, *Remarks on the Affairs and Trade of England and Ireland* (1691), p.53; R. Wallace, *A Dissertation on the Numbers of Mankind* (1753), pp.151–2; and Kames, *Sketches in the History of Man* (1788 ed.), II p.393.

39 Anon., *Considerations on the Policy, Commerce, and Circumstances of the Kingdom* (1771), and Thomas Mortimer, *The Elements of Commerce, Politics and Finances* (1772).

40 Anon., *Considerations on the Policy*, p.44. Also p.196.

41 ibid., pp.57–8.

42 ibid., pp.156, 174–5, 177–8. For Hume's views see Rotwein, op. cit., p.xliii. Mortimer referred to Hume's discussion (on pp.67–8), and also cited Sir James Steuart in support of his arguments (on p.97). Steuart's position is considered later, pp.75–6.

43 Mortimer, op. cit., pp.90–1. For similar views see Francis Moore, *Considerations on the Exorbitant Price of Provisions* (1773), pp.69–70, 80–1.

44 ibid., pp.97–8. The first and third of these principles were, strictly speaking, incompatible.

45 Furniss, op. cit., p.137. See also his remarks on Arthur Young's acceptance of the doctrine of the utility of poverty on p.120: 'it is difficult to see how [his conclusions] could have been avoided by any patriotic writer of his day whose observation had convinced him of a general tendency in all branches of the

labouring population toward indolence in the face of rising wages, unless he had been endowed with a much clearer perception of the causes contributing to produce this result than may reasonably be expected of the eighteenth-century theorist.' To demonstrate that a number of writers did in fact perceive these causes is one of the aims of the present article.

46 Prominent among the partisans was William Temple, the Wiltshire clothier, whose oft-quoted attacks on the poor originated in a 1738 wage dispute (*The Case as It Now Stands Between the Clothiers, Weavers, and other Manufacturers*, 1738), and were reiterated in his later writings, *A Vindication of Commerce and the Arts* (1758), and *An Essay on Trade and Commerce* (1770). Similarly Arthur Young invariably waxed enthusiastic over the beneficial effects of high food prices on the labourer's effort when he was defending the corn bounty, e.g. *The Expediency of a Free Exportation of Corn* (1770), pp.5–23, and *The Farmer's Letters* (3rd Edition, 1771), I, pp.185–6. The author of *Considerations on the Policy* complained that Young wanted the labourer 'to toil and starve, for the benefit of landed men, farmers, and jobbers', p.112, also pp.297–8. In reply, Young called him a 'supercilious coxcomb'.

For a valuable discussion of the corn law literature see D.G. Barnes, *A History of the English Corn Laws* (London, 1930), chap.3.

47 op. cit., p.87.

48 For example, Anon., *Propositions for Improving the Manufactures, Agriculture and Commerce of Great Britain* (1763), pp.45, 53–4; Anon., *The Causes of the Dearness of Provisions Assigned* (1766), p.43; Anon., *The Occasion of the Dearness of Provisions, and the Distress of the Poor* (1767), pp.8, 27–8; [Soame Jenyns], *Thoughts on the Causes and Consequences of the Present High Price of Provisions* (1767), pp.19, 21; Anon., *An Answer to a Pamphlet entitled, Thoughts on the Causes and Consequences of the Present High Price of Provisions* (1768), pp.13, 15.

49 For example, Anon., *Considerations on the Effects which the Bounties Granted on Exported Corn, Malt and Flour, have on the Manufactures of the Kingdom* (1768), attacked as 'wicked' and 'dangerous' the policy of 'starving the useful into excessive toil in order to enable the useless to indulge themselves in all kinds of idleness and profusion', but advocated 'punishments *in terrorem*' for the idle (p.24), and made no reference to wage increases. For similar views see *Considerations on the Present High Price of Provisions and the Necessaries of Life* (1764), pp.20–1; *The Occasion of the Dearness of Provisions*, pp.8, 28, 32, and F. Moore, op. cit., pp.69–70.

50 The following is a sample of those who feared (a) large-scale emigration or (b) riots by workers who had been driven to desperation; *Considerations on the Present High Price of Provisions* (1764), pp.21, 22 (a) and (b); Postlethwayt, *Universal Dictionary, loc. cit.*, p.xxii (a); Anon., *Gentleman's Magazine* (1766), p.525 (a); *The Occasion of the Dearness of Provisions*, p.36 (a); Forster, op. cit., p.59 (b); *Considerations on the Effects which the Bounties . . . have*, p.23 (a) and (b); *Considerations on the Policy* (1771), p.46 (a) and (b); Moore, op. cit., pp.24, 78–9 (a) and (b); Anon., *Gent's Mag.* (1774), p.314 (a). The Editor of this journal observed (1766, p.525) that those who chose to emigrate would 'return with a better mind', since conditions were worse abroad. Professor W.D. Grampp's view that the mercantilist writers 'hardly ever expressed the fear of insubordination turning into sedition' is, therefore, not true of the period under review. See 'The Liberal Elements in English Mercantilism', *The Quarterly Journal of Economics*, LXVI, p.484. A general account of food riots at this time is given in Barnes, *loc.cit.*

51 One writer defined the objective as 'to make the life of the poor as comfortable and easy, as is consistent with the ends of government, and the exercise and promotion of industry': *Essays on Several Subjects* (1769), p.150; another merely stated the dilemma that if provisions were 'too dear the poor cannot live; if too

cheap, they will not work': *An Appeal to the Public* (1767), p.14; also *An Essay on the Causes of the Present High Price of Provisions* (1773), p.1.

A more careful attempt to define the problem occurred in Mildmay, *The Laws and Policy of England* (1765), pp.22–5: we should incite industry by the 'allurement of profit' which meant high wages; but this encourages idleness and reduces sales, whereas 'low wages will be a discouragement to any work at all'. Therefore he concluded that we must 'enable our poor to work . . . upon more moderate terms' by ensuring 'a general cheapness of provisions' while allowing the native worker to enjoy a higher standard of life than his continental counterpart.

52 The writer of *The Occasion of the Dearness of Provisions*, who specified actual figures, sought a wage level high enough to 'allow our manufacturers to obtain a comfortable subsistence, with a reasonable industry' (p.32) and yet low enough to enable us to compete in foreign markets. On pp.27–34 he disputed the figures and the 'unjust invectives' against the poor contained in *A Letter to an M.P. on the Present Distresses of the Poor* (1767), by J.W.

53 Perhaps the best discussion of this problem appeared in the 3rd ed. of the *Farmer's Letters* (1771), I, p.178 ff. It was based largely on information collected during his tours; e.g. *Northern Tour* (1768), IV, Letters 39 and 40. The remarks in the text are, of course, confined to Young's pre-1776 writings.

54 *Political Essays Concerning the State of the British Empire* (1772), p.206. See also his *Expediency of a Free Exportation*, p.25, where he remarked that the notion that the high price of labour ruined our manufactures was a 'vulgar error', an expression identical to that used by Josiah Tucker in his privately printed *Elements of Commerce* (1755). For a discussion of Tucker's views see this volume, p.76.

55 Young was, however, sometimes surprisingly inconsistent on this point. Although in *The Expediency of a Free Exportation*, p.42, he held that it was essential to 'keep the products of the earth at a regular price, and the higher the better', in his *Political Essays* (1772), p.220, he argued in favour of reducing the price of provisions, provided that provisions and labour were 'kept in balance'.

56 In *The Expediency of a Free Exportation*, p.27, he observed that 'although the rates of labour . . . are not decided by those of necessaries; to be in exact proportion to each other; yet in all countries, where provisions are very dear, labour must be dearer than in other countries, where provisions are very cheap.' Cf. *Political Essays*, p.205: 'Labour must rise with the necessaries of life.'

57 For example, the oft-quoted passage that 'every one but an idiot knows, that the lower classes must be kept poor or they will never be industrious', *Eastern Tour* (1771), IV, p.361.

58 For example, *Northern Tour* (1768), I, p.196: 'In a word, idle people are converted by degrees into industrious hands; youths are brought forward to work; even boys perform their share, and women at the prospect of great wages clap their hands with cheerfulness and fly to the sickle. Thus a new race of the industrious, is by degrees created.'

59 *Political Arithmetic; Containing Observations on the Present State of Great Britain; and the Principles of her Policy in the Encouragement of Agriculture* (1774), pp.ix, 61–2, 66, 68, 73–4. See also his *Expediency of a Free Exportation*, p.28, where he asserted that 'such an high price of provisions, as must be attended by an high price of labour, is absolutely requisite for the prosperity of manufactures'.

60 See note 64.

61 Op. cit., II, p.155.

62 The list is usually confined to John Cary, Dudley North and Daniel Defoe.

63 Furniss, op. cit., p.183.

64 To date I have discovered only one pre-1750 mention of this distinction: Anon.,

Considerations on the Bill for A General Naturalization (1748), p.71. Passing references to it are made in the following works: P. Murray, *Thoughts on Money, Circulation and Paper Currency* (1758), pp.29–30; Anon., *Propositions for Improving the Manufactures etc.* (1763), pp.32, 110–11. More systematic use of this distinction appears in Joseph Harris, *An Essay Upon Money and Coins* (1757), pt. I, p.17, fn; Adam Smith, *Lectures*, op. cit., p.165, and *An Early Draft of the Wealth of Nations* (1763), reproduced in W.R. Scott, *Adam Smith as Student and Professor* (Glasgow, 1937), pp.331–2; in A. Young, *Political Essays*, pp.205–6, and *Northern Tour*, IV, p.556; and also in Josiah Tucker's *Four Tracts on Political and Commercial Subjects* (2nd Edition, 1774), (written in 1748) pp.34–6, where it formed an integral part of his argument that a rich country with high wages and an efficient labour force could always undersell a poor country with low wages.

It is significant that Defoe (*Plan of the English Commerce*, pp.40–2) did not argue that the highly-paid British labourer could work cheaper than a Frenchman, but that his products would command a higher price because of their superior quality.

65 On this topic see Johnson, op. cit., chap.13.

66 For earlier references to the Dutch see Furniss, op. cit., pp.23, 101. For favourable comparisons between British and continental workers see J. Harris, *loc.cit.*; *Propositions for Improving the Manufactures*, pp.31–2, 110–11; Postlethwayt, *Universal Dictionary* (4th edition), p.xiv (but contrast this, written in 1766, with *Great Britain's True System* [1757], pp.160, 219–21); Anon., *Considerations on the Policy*, p.195; Young, *Political Essays*, pp.205–6; Mortimer, *Elements of Commerce*, p.89.

67 D.C. Coleman, 'Labour in the English Economy of the Seventeenth Century', *Economic History Review* VIII, (3) (1959), p.287. To say of this period that 'qualitative improvement' was 'virtually impossible' seems to be an overstatement of the case.

68 Arthur Young quotes several British and continental writers holding this view in his *Political Essays*, pp.209–19. To his list we may add Mortimer, op. cit., pp.104–5, and Forster, op. cit., pp.20–1, fn., who believed that most labour-saving devices would not reduce employment. Mildmay, op. cit., pp.42–3, argued that machines must be introduced even though they were likely to reduce employment, while Sir James Steuart, *An Inquiry into the Principles of Political Economy* (1767), I, Bk. I, chap.XIX, (*Works* [1805 ed.] pp.160–5) maintained that the adverse employment effects would be temporary.

69 In this group we may include Tucker, op. cit., p.30; Postlethwayt, especially *Britain's Commercial Interest*, II, pp.377–8, 420–1; Adam Smith, *An Early Draft of the Wealth of Nations*, p.332; Mildmay, *loc.cit.*; Anon., *Gents. Mag.* (1766), p.572; Steuart, op. cit., I, Bk.II, pp.390–2; Young, *loc.cit.*; F. Moore, *Considerations on the Exorbitant Price*, p.82. Postlethwayt opposed the introduction of machinery in agriculture, whereas Young was mainly concerned with this sphere. To Steuart, innovations in agriculture would release labour for industrial expansion. (See Johnson, op. cit., p.203, fn. 147).

70 Ed. F.B. Kay (Oxford 1924). For an excellent account of the economic theory of luxury and the influence of Mandeville's arguments see pp.xciv–xcviii, cxxxvi–cxxxix.

71 Johnson, op. cit., pp.293, 295–7. See also Rotwein, op. cit., pp.19–32.

72 This is attributable to the prevalent moral objections to luxury, to the fears of imported luxuries, and to the customary identification of the labourer's consumption in terms of necessaries (e.g. Vanderlint, see p.65). Even Arthur Young, whose opposition to the labourer's consumption of tea and other luxuries

is notorious, occasionally advocated substantial increases in the consumption of necessaries (e.g. *Political Essays*, p.111).

73 Brown, op. cit., pp.195–6. According to his general theory, in the first stage of economic development only necessities were produced; in the second, happy and populous stage, there were conveniences; while in the final stage wealth brought 'superfluity, avarice, effeminate refinement, and loss of principle'.

74 The following writers desired a more equal distribution of wealth or warned against the dangers of excessive inequality: Berkeley, *Querist*, No. 204; Hume op. cit., p.15; W. Hazeland, *A View of the Manner in which Trade and Civil Liberty Support each Other* (1756), pp.9–10, 20–1; Joseph Harris, op. cit., pt. I, p.70, fn., pt. II, pp.116–17; Postlethwayt, *Great Britain's True System*, pp.138–9, 157; S. Fawconer, *An Essay on Modern Luxury* (1765), p.438; Mildmay, op. cit., p.124; Forster, op. cit., pp.11, 40–1; Steuart, *Inquiry*, II, pp.155–6, advocated an 'equable' not an equal distribution; Anon., *Considerations on the Effects which the Bounties*, etc., pp.23–4; [Soame Jenyns] *Thoughts*, p.23, believed a redistribution of wealth would solve current problems, but rejected it as 'unjust and unlawful'; Anon., *An Answer to a Pamphlet entitled Thoughts*, etc. p.13; Anon., *Considerations on the Exportation of Corn, Wherein the Principal Arguments*, etc. (1770), pp.56–7; Anon., *An Inquiry into the Connection between the present Price of Provisions and the Size of Farms*, etc. (1773), pp.45–6.

75 This was usually designed to improve the agricultural situation, see Vanderlint, op. cit., pp.101, 103–4, 154; Postlethwayt, *Britain's Commercial Interest*, I, pp.35–7; Wm. Bell, *A Dissertation . . . What Causes Principally Contribute to Render a Nation Populous* (1756), p.27 (Hume, too, argued that equality of property aided population growth, op. cit., pp.128–31); Anon., *Observations on the Number and Misery of the Poor* (1765), pp.14, 31–3. In addition there were innumerable complaints of the evil consequences of the engrossing of farms.

76 For example, Anon., *An Answer to a Pamphlet*, p.12, denied that he was a 'leveller'; while Richard Woodward, *An Argument in Support of the Right of the Poor in the Kingdom of Ireland to a National Provision* (1768), pointed out, in his Advertisement to the Reader, that he had 'inculcated the reasonableness of their subordination in society, and their obligations to obedience'. Similarly F. Moore, op. cit., p.70. The desire to preserve the existing social hierarchy, though usually unstated, was implied in most of the contemporary writings on the poor.

77 J. Harris, op. cit., pt. I, p.70. fn. See also, Vanderlint, op. cit., p.101; Hume, op. cit., pp.28–9, 98–9; Forster, op. cit., p.41; Anon., *An Inquiry into the Late Mercantile Distresses in Scotland and England*, etc. (1772), pp.120, 123, 128. Many other instances could be cited.

78 op. cit., pp.19–21, 30–2. See also Johnson, op. cit., pp.168–70.

79 In discussing luxury, few writers clearly specified the social and economic classes to which their observations applied. Moreover, the distinction between luxuries, comforts and conveniences was changing over time. It is, therefore, debatable whether, apart from a few instances (e.g. Postlethwayt, *Great Britain's True System*, p.237; Forster, op. cit., p.38), a defence of the labourer's consumption of tea (e.g. *Gents. Mag.* [1773], p.60 – with the Editor's approval) and meat (e.g. Postlethwayt, *Universal Dictionary* [4th ed.] p.xxxvi; *Gents. Mag.* [1767], pp.112–13; Mortimer, op. cit., pp.97–8, where he quoted Steuart in support) should be included in this category.

80 J. Harris, op. cit., pt. I, p.29. Cf. Postlethwayt, *Britain's Commercial Interest*, I, pp.35–7; Mildmay, op. cit., pp.123–4; Forster, op. cit., pp.42, 51.

81 For Hume's views on this point see Rotwein Ed. chap.2.

82 Steuart, *Inquiry*, (*Works*, 1805 Ed.) Book II, chap.19. The position of labour in

this process is outlined in chaps. 11, 17 and 18. Steuart believed the lowest-paid workers should receive 'ample subsistence where no degree of superfluity is implied', and argued on grounds of humanity and policy against restricting this standard too vigorously (ibid., chap.21). Recognizing the dangers of a very uneven distribution of wealth (II, p.155) he did not consider modern luxury excessive (ibid., p.170) and maintained that drunkenness was decreasing (I. p.372).

83 For the materials relevant to this discussion see Rotwein, op. cit., pp.lix, lxxvii, 199–205. Also J.M. Low, 'An Eighteenth Century Controversy in the Theory of Economic Progress', *The Manchester School*, XX (1952), pp.311–30.

84 ibid., p.200. These are Hume's words, from a letter to Lord Kames, through whom the debate with Tucker was conducted. Hume's retraction apparently did not cause any change in his attitude to labour, and Kames adhered to Hume's original position. Cf. *Sketches*, I, pp.147–8. Their contemporary, John Millar, accepted Tucker's views. Cf. *Origin of the Distinction of Ranks* (1806 Ed.), p.xlviii.

85 *Four Tracts*, p.32.

86 Furniss, op. cit., p.184, fn. 3.

87 *Wealth of Nations*, pp.61–2. It is highly probable that the exchange between Hume and Tucker influenced the argument of Smith's *magnum opus*. For an intermediate stage in the development of his views see *An Early Draft of the Wealth of Nations, loc. cit.* Cf. *Lectures*, op. cit., p.165.

5

ECONOMIC THOUGHT AND POOR LAW POLICY IN THE EIGHTEENTH CENTURY[1]

I

The process of relating economic thought to policy involves the task of bridging the gap between *general* ideas and the *particular* uses to which they are put. This task can be approached either by attempting to connect the tacit or declared methods and objectives of policy with the general corpus of doctrine from which they are derived, or by endeavouring to trace the effects of the policy conclusions drawn from given theories.[2] Both approaches demand an intimate knowledge of the circumstances of the time, and most historians of doctrine have revealed pardonable shortcomings in this respect. But, beyond this, they have inexcusably neglected the gap between theory and policy,[3] and have virtually ignored the underworld of economic thought and the processes whereby theories are propagated.[4] It is, therefore, hardly surprising that their activities have usually confirmed the economic historians' suspicion that the systematic study of economic ideas contributes little to the explanation of policy.

Yet this suspicion does not justify the customary underestimate of the influence of ideas on the formation of policy. Although it is rarely possible to show that this influence is direct or conclusive, a careful study of contemporary ideas will help to clarify the objectives of policy, and may suggest that apparently, unrelated measures form part of a general programme of action. Above all, a knowledge of current ideas is essential in any effort to gauge the success of a policy, for this can only be judged in terms of the available knowledge and the range of alternative courses of action. As empiricists, most economic historians tend to be susceptible to naive 'common sense' explanations of the policymaker's intentions[5] (forgetting that the common sense of one generation often appears fallacious to the next), and their predilections encourage them to adopt an unduly sceptical attitude to any explanation that assigns a positive role to ideological forces.

Economic ideas affect policy in two distinct ways: by his definition of the problem and its solution, the economic thinker influences the selection of

85

means to attain a given end; but, beyond this, he also influences the choice of ends. For as Schumpeter and others have shown,[6] even the purest of theories is based on certain logical (philosophical) assumptions about the nature and purpose of economic activity, and these assumptions predispose the theorist towards certain types of political action. Thus despite economists' repeated and increasing claims of impartiality in the two hundred years or so since their discipline acquired the status of a recognized expertise, economic theory has been consistently permeated by the tradition of humanitarian liberalism.[7] And on the rare occasions when professional economists have refrained from entering the political arena, there have invariably been disciples or popularizers with no such inhibitions.

Nevertheless, in assessing the role of economic ideas it is essential to avoid an uncritical assumption that conformity between the recommendations of pamphleteers and the trend of policy implies a cause and effect relationship. Moreover, in considering the activities of propagandists it is easy to underrate the extent to which established doctrines are adapted or distorted to suit the needs of a particular interest group. Yet the fact that the same ideas are used by protagonists on both sides of a debate[8] makes it more, not less, necessary to undertake a careful study of their nature and effects. Although such a study may prove inconclusive, it will usually lead to a re-interpretation of the factors influencing policy, and will often reveal hitherto neglected aspects of the process of policy formation.

II

This paper is mainly concerned with the connections between the change in economic thought and the change in the predominant tone of English poor law legislation in the period from the Workhouse Test Act of 1723 to Gilbert's well-intentioned Act of 1782. Suprisingly enough, these connections have never been systematically studied,[9] although the poor law writers have often been censured for their preoccupation with the economic aspects of pauperism, and the economists repeatedly referred to the effects of the poor law system on the national economy in the course of their interminable discussions of idleness, employment, wage levels and incentives to labour. There are, moreover, significant parallels between the trend of poor law opinion and the main trend of contemporary economic thought, so that it seems reasonable to ask what light the historian of economic ideas can shed on the change of poor law policy.

It is generally accepted that Gilbert's Act was due to the emergence of a more 'sympathetic' attitude to the labouring class in general and the pauper in particular – a change in what Lecky called 'the fashions of feeling' of the upper classes[10] – but there has been no serious effort to examine the nature and sources of this new 'sympathy'. This is obviously too large a task to be undertaken here; but the following pages will provide an outline of the main features of such an investigation, followed by an examination of the circumstances leading up to Gilbert's Act and, finally, an attempt to assess the influence of economic thought on poor law policy.

Identifying the origins of such an ill-defined movement of thought as 'a wave of sympathy for the poor' is a hazardous pastime, but for present purposes we can ignore the earlier antecedents and begin with the works of the third Lord Shaftesbury, whose *Characteristics of Men, Manners, Opinions, Times* was first published in 1708–11. This is, admittedly, an arbitrary starting point, for Shaftesbury's stress on man's benevolence – the natural inclination to virtue which he termed the 'moral sense' – was a conscious repudiation of Hobbes's contention that self-interest was man's ruling passion.[11] The importance of Shaftesbury's ideas, however, lies in their influence on eighteenth century moral and social theory,[12] for although his over-optimistic view of human behaviour was superficial and unconvincing, it provoked many attempts to reconcile the seemingly conflicting aspects of man's nature – self-love and benevolence. Moreover, his influence entered directly into the mainstream of economic thought through his disciple Francis Hutcheson, the founder of the Scottish school of moral philosophy and Adam Smith's 'never-to-be-forgotten' teacher at Glasgow.

Shaftesbury's emphasis on the aristocratic virtue of benevolence gave an intellectual impetus to those periodic waves of practical philanthropy that have so often been regarded as a characteristic feature of the period. Some writers maintained that humanitarianism was a peculiarly English trait, and while modern readers may be sceptical of this claim, even the more realistic poor law reformers demonstrated a remarkable degree of confidence that voluntary charity would supply most, if not all, of the necessary funds.[13] On the other hand, there were those who feared that the current of emotional benevolence, or 'sentimentalism' as it has often been called, which reinforced this faith in private charity, might have undesirable consequences. Leslie Stephen dismissed it lightly, as merely encouraging 'fine ladies and gentlemen ... to play at sympathy with the poor and oppressed';[14] but many contemporaries feared that indiscriminate charity would do more harm than good, by undermining the pauper's habits of industry and frugality, on which his future well-being depended. The experience of the Foundling Hospital was occasionally cited as a concrete example of the harmful effects of an over-enthusiastic desire to do good.[15] This institution had apparently worked well from its inception in 1739 until 1756 when Parliament, in a fit of generosity, provided a series of financial grants on the condition that all children brought to its doors were to be admitted. During the next four years the influx of children and the rise in the death rate were so marked, that in 1760 the hospital reverted to its former, more cautious, policy and private status.[16]

The benevolent excesses of the sentimentalists were in marked contrast to the cautious and qualified tone of the Scottish philosophers who, like Bishop Butler and other eighteenth century moralists, recognized the validity of Hobbes's and Mandeville's insistence on the importance of self-interest. Although Adam Smith considered that Francis Hutcheson's theory was based on the principle of benevolence, Hutcheson himself, in his posthumously published *System of Moral Philosophy*, 1755, thought it advisable to specify the ethical limits of charity.[17] In his *Theory of Moral Sentiments*, 1759, Adam Smith went beyond this. His central principle of 'sympathy' transcended the idea of benevolence, and the subordinate role assigned to the latter is exemplified by his remark that although 'the relief and consolation of human misery depend altogether upon our compassion for' the poor and the wretched, nevertheless 'the peace and order of society is of more importance than even the relief of the miserable'.[18] This statement reflects Smith's innate conservatism, rather than any deep-seated doubt as to the compatibility of social justice with the preservation of the *status quo*, for such a doubt would have conflicted with his conception of the harmony of interests. Smith's conservatism typifies the practical, even utilitarian, attitude to the poor which was the predominant feature of contemporary social thought. Even when a writer's proposals appear to possess radical implications, closer analysis usually reveals that no such radicalism was intended.[19]

This widespread conservatism makes it difficult to distinguish between those who genuinely sought to improve the lot of the poor, and those who primarily sought to keep them in their place. Modern historians may be justified in maintaining that the latter motive had an important influence on the movements for the reformation of manners and the erection of charity schools.[20] But, as Mandeville had pointed out as early as 1723, in his *Essay on Charity and Charity Schools*, 'there is a prodigious difference between debarring the children of the poor from ever rising higher in the world, and refusing to force education upon thousands of them promiscuously, when they should be more usefully employed',[21] and this difference must be taken into account in assessing the nature and extent of contemporary 'sympathy' for the poor. Too rapid an improvement of an individual's condition and status might well have unfortunate consequences,[22] and an education appropriate to the sons of gentlemen was liable to make a labourer's children social misfits, by filling them with unattainable aspirations. The widely held belief that pauper children should be trained for 'those servile occupations which in the ordinary course of providence are most likely to fall to their share'[23] was, admittedly, strengthened by the desire to preserve the existing social and occupational hierarchy; but there was in fact little chance of success for more radical reforms. The realistic, if limited, conclusion that the most valuable contribution the upper classes could make was to ensure that the industrious workers enjoyed a 'comfortable subsistence' appropriate to their station in life, was often accompanied by approving references to the fortunate few who had successfully bettered themselves, and was tempered by the genuine, if complacent, belief that the progress of society would inevitably and automatically bring about a steady improvement for all its members.

The modest aims of most eighteenth century poor law reformers have led some historians to infer that their concern for the welfare of the lower orders was half-hearted, and this inference seems to be confirmed by the discovery that contemporary protestations on behalf of the poor were inconsistent with the harshness of the practical remedies offered. Yet in many cases the inconsistency is more apparent than real, for while there was genuine sympathy towards the *deserving* poor, the harsher remedies were to be applied to the *undeserving*. Jonas Hanway, for instance, whose charitable activities on behalf of foundling children and other distressed groups are well known, emphasized that 'coercive power and the fear of punishment, are the grand preservatives of order and the guardians of human happiness',[24] and this view had already received systematic, if extreme, expression in Henry Fielding's *Inquiry into the Late Increase of Robbers*, 1751. The honesty and integrity of Fielding's career as a London magistrate is unquestioned, and he has often been regarded as a humane and sympathetic social reformer. But although he recognized the narrowness of the dividing line between poverty and crime, Fielding nevertheless advocated rigorous enforcement of the numerous capital statutes, arguing that a magistrate who put mercy before the 'wholesome virtue' of severity was permitting his passion for benevolence to overcome his sense of duty, like the Scots clergyman who prayed to God to pardon the devil.[25] Fielding's reliance on the 'terror of the example' appears to modern eyes as a purely negative attitude;[26] yet his ambivalent approach reveals, in a somewhat exaggerated form, the dilemma facing those who were familiar with the brutal realities of contemporary life and yet wished to provide relief or employment for the deserving poor, without relaxing the stringency of the laws applicable to rogues and vagabonds. It may be unsafe to generalize, but those who were most active in promoting reform were far from being uncritical defenders of the poor. Indeed, some appreciation of the labourer's faults was an essential pre-condition of a sympathetic understanding of his predicament. Despite its obvious limitations, the discriminatory approach of the mid-century represented a distinct advance upon the tendency prevailing in the first half of the century to regard the workers as an undifferentiated mass, whose difficulties were the result not of circumstances beyond their control, but of their incurable weaknesses or the dictates of providence. It is more 'sympathetic' in the sense that there was a genuine effort to grasp the nature of these problems, and to prescribe remedies that were workable, given the existing condition of economic and social life.

Another important and unduly neglected source of sympathy for the lower orders of society was the contemporary interest in psychology, which was an especially marked feature of the Scottish theory of society.[27] According to this theory all men are fundamentally alike in their natural instincts and endowments,[28] and this similarity was held to explain the 'spirit of emulation', the desire of the lower orders to ape their betters. It followed from this interpretation that the vices and follies of the former were at least partly attributable to the bad example set by the latter, and attempts to discipline or reform the poor were futile without a reformation of manners on the part of the well-to-do. This belief found vigorous expression in such popular works of social criticism as John Brown's *Estimate of the Manners and Principles of the Times*, 1757. By placing the main responsibility for current social disorders on the shoulders of the rich, works of this kind may have contributed to a more sympathetic attitude to the poor; and some modern historians, in their firm conviction that the upper classes were chiefly concerned to keep the workers at a minimum standard of subsistence, have ignored the existence of the desire to restrict the consumption of *all* classes.

But despite widespread concern at the excessive luxury of the rich, there was a growing body of opinion that a rising standard of living for all members of society was an unmistakable indication of national well-being. David Hume was an outstanding exponent of this view, for he argued that the development of commerce was a civilizing process, which brought in its train a refinement of manners, an increase of knowledge and individual initiative, and an extension of economic, social and political freedom.[29] Moreover, Hume's psychological theory contributed to a subtle modification of the familiar notion of 'habits of industry'. It was still generally held that environmental factors played a key role in the formation of these habits; that necessity was an essential prerequisite of industriousness; and that an unwise relaxation of conditions might encourage idleness and absenteeism. But, by distinguishing between a 'passive habit' – the result of mere repetition, and an 'active habit' – which represented 'an inclination and tendency towards' the act in question, Hume undermined the belief that work is essentially irksome.[30] If the workers were to be treated as human beings, which was a corollary of the postulate that human instincts and endowments are similar, it followed that a permanent inclination towards industry was more likely to be aroused by giving them a taste of the fruits of their labours and thereby stimulating their initiative, than by attempting through the pressure of necessity, to enforce a monotonous routine of toil.

It would be fanciful to suggest that this analysis had any immediate effect upon social policy. But, as has been shown elsewhere,[31] it accorded with the existing trend of economic thought, in which an increasing reliance was being placed upon the efficacy of incentives to labour, as opposed to deterrents to idleness. This interpretation met with growing approbation as the labourer's living standards deteriorated with the rise of food prices from the late 1750s, and in this context Hume's ideas provided a theoretical foundation for some of the conclusions already reached by less sophisticated writers. For instance, he and other members of the Scottish school maintained that man possessed a natural 'impulse to action',[32] so that the poor laws, by encouraging idleness among those who had not yet developed an 'active' habit of industry and enforcing idleness upon those who had, constituted a source of individual unhappiness as well as a loss to society. And, as Joseph Massie put it, the poor suffered not only from involuntary unemployment, but also from the fact that their idleness made 'even worthy and charitably disposed persons look upon them as a nuisance' and favour 'cruel or unwarrantable treatment'.[33]

III

The foregoing account has dealt with the main intellectual elements in the emergence of a more 'sympathetic' attitude towards the poor from the mid-eighteenth century. It is, of course, by no means complete. For example, no specific reference has been made to religious impulses, partly because Quaker philanthropy and the traditional belief in the Christian virtue of charity manifested themselves in the same kind of good works that resulted from the deist Shaftesbury's advocacy of benevolence.[34] Such ideas as these helped to inspire many practical projects for assisting the sick, helpless and insane, and were indirectly responsible for a number of parliamentary enactments.[35] Yet despite the plethora of schemes for poor law reform, there were surprisingly few *general* poor law statutes in the period 1744–82, and for this reason the ensuing discussion of legislative proposals is confined to Gilbert's Act and its antecedents. The importance of this statute requires no emphasis; it has been described in one authoritative study as 'perhaps the most influential, for both good and evil, of all the scores of poor law statutes between 1601 and 1834'.[36] By reserving the workhouses in newly-formed parish unions for those unable to work, it reversed the 1723 statute (which had sought to check applications for relief from able-bodied paupers, by making entry into the house a condition of relief); and, by encouraging and regularizing outdoor relief, it directly prepared the way for the allowance system of the Napoleonic War years.

It is a commonplace of poor law history that national statutes merely promulgated or legitimized existing parochial practices, and in this sense Gilbert's Act was merely a consequence of the dissatisfaction with the workhouse system that had been apparent from the mid-century. Some reformers proposed to abandon the entire system and rely on voluntary charity; others hoped to modify it, by increasing the size of the administrative area, taking the control of workhouses out of the hands of parish officials, and building larger institutions with separate accommodation for the different categories of paupers.[37] Most of these schemes, however, entailed too drastic a change from current practice, or too much expense, to meet with general approval. This background is reflected in Gilbert's own proposals, which appeared in a series of pamphlets associated with his parliamentary activities. Some outline of his ideas and his career must be included in any attempt to assess the influence of economic and social thought upon poor law policy in this period. It will also fill a gap in the standard histories of the poor law.

Thomas Gilbert's life merits a full-scale biography, for apart from his activities as a poor law reformer and as land agent to the second Earl of

Gower, he was at times a key figure in the House of Commons, both in respect of political and financial affairs.[38] He became involved in poor law matters within a month of his entry into Parliament in November 1763, and from January to March 1764 he sat on a committee appointed to consider the case of the Gloucester workhouse, a lengthy dispute in which the merits of indoor and outdoor relief were vigorously debated.[39] There is, however, no evidence that this experience directly affected Gilbert's views; indeed, his first pamphlet, published later that year, advocated houses of industry on lines resembling the earlier schemes of Fielding, Sir Richard Lloyd and the Earl of Hillsborough.[40] Gilbert almost secured statutory implementation of this plan at the first attempt, early in 1765, but his bill was defeated in the House of Lords for reasons 'unconnected with its merits'.[41] Despite this setback he kept in touch with poor law affairs, and in a speech supporting Dowdeswell's Bill to provide contributory life annuities for the aged poor, in March 1773, he announced his intention of presenting a new plan later that session.[42] His second attempt, however, came two years later, when he attempted to introduce a modified version of his original plan. On this occasion, although a series of resolutions was accepted by the Commons, no bill was actually introduced.[43] Nevertheless, the modifications of Gilbert's first plan are of considerable interest, since they pointed the way towards the 1782 statute, in the proposal to allow temporary outdoor relief for 'the orderly and industrious poor, who, from accidental sickness, infirmities, or other unavoidable causes, shall be rendered unable to maintain themselves and their families by their labour'.[44] Further doubts about the suitability of indoor relief in all cases were apparent in his suggestion that some paupers might be permitted outside lodging and employment under carefully supervised contracts, although continuing to eat in the house; and his earlier uncritical approval of houses of correction was now qualified by a warning that these institutions had sometimes had disastrous effects, as no employment had been provided for the inmates.[45]

These provisos represent the small beginnings of Gilbert's subsequent attack on indoor relief; yet his 1775 plan was still far removed from the wholesale rejection of indoor relief for the able-bodied contemplated in his next group of pamphlets in 1781–2. Unfortunately there is only limited evidence of the reasons for the intervening change of Gilbert's ideas. According to the introduction to his plan of 1781, the change was due to the expense of erecting houses of industry and their 'precarious' success; the 'difficulties of procuring money for great works, in the present situation of public affairs'; the advice tendered by MPs in committees and meetings on his bills; and the hints and observations offered by 'other gentlemen'.[46] Some indication of the nature of these observations can be obtained from an examination of certain published letters and comments on Gilbert's plans. Several writers, including Edward Jones and Henry Zouch in 1776, and a country magistrate in 1777, complained of the hardships endured by paupers who were forced into the workhouse, and the first two quoted Blackstone's *Commentaries* in support of their claim that it was both more just and more expedient to preserve established domestic connections, and employ the poor at home whenever possible.[47] Jones claimed that since agriculture – 'the first object in every nation' – could not be taught in a poor house, such houses were only suited to large manufacturing towns which could provide appropriate occupations for the inmates.[48] Zouch employed an even more effective argument, one that is familiar to every student of nineteenth century poor law history, when he emphasized the inadequacy of workhouses at times of large-scale unemployment due to a 'stoppage in the manufactory of a country', or widespread distress resulting from a temporary dearth of corn.[49] Gilbert may have been decisively influenced by this advice. Zouch, a prominent Yorkshire magistrate, had had direct contact with manufacturing conditions; his *Remarks* had apparently met with warm approval from the 'Gentlemen of Wakefield'; and it is noteworthy that Gilbert limited the application of his 1782 plan to country districts. Zouch's views may also have strengthened Gilbert's doubts about houses of correction, for he admitted in 1782 that the defects of these institutions had discouraged him, as a magistrate, from committing offenders to them, adding that other magistrates had no doubt been similarly affected.[50] On this matter, however, Gilbert's opinion was probably influenced less by Zouch's pamphlet than by the results of a House of Commons Order of April 1775, which required the collection of information about the cost and administration of houses of correction. In the two ensuing years similar information was collected from parish overseers and charitable institutions, and the evidence of waste and inefficiency provided by these investigations undoubtedly contributed to Gilbert's loss of confidence in houses of industry.[51]

IV

It is now advisable to draw together the threads of the previous discussion, before making an attempt to identify and assess the influence of economic thought on poor law policy in the period preceding Gilbert's Act. This statute is often regarded as a triumph of the new attitude towards the poor which had emerged in the 1770s; but it is clear from the foregoing argument, and from the poor law schemes of the 1750s, that this attitude is clearly discernible at least as early as the mid-century, when William Hay expressed his pleasure at the growing prevalence of a more 'generous way of thinking' about the poor.[52] This generous thinking was compounded of various elements, of which three have been considered: the advocacy of benevolence, which stimulated private philanthropy; the increasing tendency to discriminate between the deserving and the undeserving poor; and the development of a body of moral, psychological and social theory which drew attention to the condition and duties of all ranks of society. In the third category, special emphasis has been placed upon the Scottish writings, because of their systematic character, because they reflected the typical mid-century conservative attitude to society, and because they incorporated a powerful body of liberal economic doctrine. According to this doctrine the welfare of the labouring classes was assigned an importance which contrasted sharply with the predominant mercantilist belief in the early part of the century 'that the majority must be kept in poverty [in order] that the whole might be rich'.[53] It was becoming recognized that social expediency, as well as humanity, required that the workers should be protected from excessive hardship, which would either make them listless and despondent or, alternatively, would drive them to desperation, riot or emigration.

In this way, the views of the growing number of economic writers who accepted this interpretation reinforced the opinions of those who expressed dissatisfaction with the poor law. The two groups of writers[54] were chiefly concerned with closely related classes – the deserving paupers who were unable to find work, and the industrious employed workers who were unable to make ends meet at a time of rising prices. In economic terms, the new attitude inspired demands for higher real and money wages for the British labourer, on the grounds that his former high living standard, as compared with that of his continental rivals, had been more than compensated by his superior skill and energy. Circumstances had changed, so it was argued, and it was deemed necessary to redress the balance in favour of the 'carrot' of incentives, and against the 'stick' of necessity.

As applied to the poor law, the new attitude frequently took the form of opposition to the settlement laws, or resentment at the evil conditions under which indoor relief was granted. Opposition to the settlement laws was no new phenomenon, and it would be ridiculous to claim that the economists were responsible for the prevalence of this attitude after 1750. Yet it is no coincidence that Dean Tucker and Adam Smith, two writers who made important contributions to the rise of liberal economic doctrine, reserved their strongest condemnation for this part of the poor law system. They believed that there was no overall shortage of employment opportunities, and that if these barriers to the operation of economic forces were removed, the natural progress of the economy would eventually solve the problem of involuntary unemployment. Yet the optimistic assumption that the economic system was, in the long run, always capable of generating sufficient demand to maintain full employment did not necessarily predispose its adherents to a 'sympathetic' attitude to the labourer. If employment opportunities were available, he might be idle either from choice, or because there were institutional obstacles to the operation of economic forces. It would be broadly true to say that Tucker took the former view, placing the blame largely upon the workers themselves, while Adam Smith took the latter view, regarding the labourer as the unfortunate victim of bad laws.[55]

Dissatisfaction with the workhouse system, which was another prominent theme in the writings of those concerned with the welfare of the labouring classes, has already been mentioned as an important influence on Gilbert's Act.[56] Although there were financial and administrative grounds for this dissatisfaction, the economists made a distinctive contribution by emphasizing that much poverty was of a temporary character.[57] The frequency of bad harvests from the late 1750s not only increased the numbers of those in need of relief; it may also have increased the proportion of those requiring temporary assistance, for whom the workhouse was an inappropriate remedy. In this way the economists' argument not merely strengthened the existing belief that the workhouses were too small, too expensive or too badly managed; it pointed the way to a solution, namely the return to outdoor relief. Under Gilbert's Act, however, this relief was not merely to be granted in the customary form of temporary subsidies at times of sickness, bad trade or high prices, a practice which had never ceased in many parishes, and which was already on the increase;[58] it was also to be provided as a guarantee of maintenance during an indefinite period.[59] The pendulum of policy had, indeed, swung dramatically away from the aim of enforcing labour, as embodied in the Workhouse Test Act of 1723.

This shift of policy was not, of course, simply due to the emergence of a more sympathetic attitude to the poor; circumstances also played their part. It has already been suggested that the high cost and the bad administration of the workhouses had contributed to their unpopularity, in addition to the insufficiency of the available accommodation as rising prices and expanding population helped to swell the number of applicants for relief. Moreover, political and military circumstances help to account for the delay in the passage of Gilbert's Act. On the other hand, it would be a mistake to argue that the change of policy was solely due to the change of conditions.[60] The new attitude to the poor was apparent *before* the rise of prices in the late 1750s; and a sympathetic response, on the part of the upper classes, to the workers' growing discontent, was by no means inevitable for this discontent was manifested in riots, strikes and combinations. A more hostile reaction might have been forthcoming, for, as one member of the House of Lords said, *à propos* of the food riots of 1766, 'it would ill become this place to palliate or excuse, on any account whatever, such dangerous tumults and riots, much less to incite and encourage them, by saying as I have heard it said within these walls, by one sworn to execute the laws, that the subjects . . . are made desperate'.[61] However, this unrelenting attitude did not prevail; such excuses were frequently made, not only in Parliament, but also in the press and in pamphlet literature. A more typical reaction was that of Edmund Burke who remarked, during a similar debate in the House of Commons, in 1767, that 'even legal punishments lose all appearance of justice, when too strictly inflicted on men compelled by the last extremity of distress to incur them'.[62]

Thus, the voices of those who complained of the dangerous implications of these disturbances were drowned by the voices of those who viewed the riots as proof of the need for action on behalf of the distressed,[63] and this outcome is attributable to the more sympathetic attitude towards the poor, in which the change of economic ideas had played a significant part. The change of poor law policy was, therefore, the result of a combination of ideas and events. The resort to outdoor relief may have been an obvious expedient; but Gilbert's Act went beyond this, by stressing the duty to provide employment and relief in aid of wages. In view of contemporary economic and social unrest, it may be suggested that this positive step represents the direct influence of a change in the attitude to the poor.

NOTES

1 This article is a substantially revised version of a paper given at the Economic History Conference at Swansea, March 1958.

2 In practice, particular studies of thought and policy are more likely to yield fresh insights than efforts to cover a wide period and range of ideas. Cf. my article 'In Defence of Heckscher and the Idea of Mercantilism', *Scandinavian Economic History Review* V, No.2 (1958) pp.173–87 (see this volume, pp.29–42).

3 As Jean Paul Hütter wisely remarked, 'as a general rule the economist's words have not reached the public ear until after having been simplified, exaggerated, and distorted by publicists'. Cf. A. Gray, in *Economic History* IV (1938–40), p.287.

4 Among outstanding exceptions, S.G. Checkland's unpublished M.Com. thesis, 'The Political Economists and the Politicians, From Waterloo to the Reform Bill' (Birmingham, 1947) and the study by R.D. Collison Black, 'Economic Thought and the Irish Question, 1817–70', may be cited.

5 The principal weaknesses of the empiricist's approach arise from implicit theorizing, and from the assumption that a policy can be explained merely by reference to 'vested interests' or 'the pressure of events'. On the other hand, there are obvious dangers of an undue reliance on ideological factors.

6 See J. Schumpeter, 'Science and Ideology', *American Economic Review* XXXIX (1949), pp.345–59; G. Myrdal, *The Political Element in the Development of Economic Doctrine* (1953), *passim*.

7 For some pertinent comments on this subject see G. Myrdal, *Economic Theory and Underdeveloped Regions* (1957), pp.119, 130–1. On the pre-classical period see W.D. Grampp, 'The Liberal Elements in English Mercantilism'. *The Quarterly Journal of Economics* LXVI (1952), pp.465–501.

8 An excellent example of this is afforded by the Corn Law debates of 1814–15, in which Adam Smith's arguments were skilfully employed by both parties. See W. Smart, *Economic Annals of the 19th Century* (1910), pp.410–14.

9 For example, the useful chapter on contemporary attitudes to the problem of poverty in Dorothy Marshall's *The English Poor in the 18th Century* (1926) contains no references to economic thought as such.

10 W. Lecky, *History of England in the 18th Century* (1887), VI, p.274.

11 Shaftesbury's ideas can be traced back at least as far as the seventeenth century Cambridge Platonists. See R.L. Brett, *The Third Earl of Shaftesbury* (1951), chap.1, and E.C. Mossner, *Bishop Butler and the Age of Reason* (New York, 1936), pp.59–60. His attitude to Hobbes was no doubt affected by his association with John Locke,

who had been his tutor, and an intimate friend of his grandfather. Cf. *Dictionary of National Biography* IV, pp.1054–6.

12 For accounts of Shaftesbury's influence see Brett, op. cit., chap IX; Mossner, op. cit., chap.IV; and the studies by W.E. Alderman in the *Transactions of the Wisconsin Academy* XXI (1924), pp.57–70, and XXVI (1931), pp.137–59.

13 Anon., *A Letter to Thomas Gilbert M.P. on his Plan for the Better Relief etc.* (1782), p.12; Fielding, *Inquiry into the Late Increase of Robbers* (1751), pp.46–7; Lord Kames, *Sketches of the History of Man* (1788), III, pp.97–9; and other examples are quoted in S. and B. Webb, *English Local Government: English Poor Law History*: Part 1 (1927), pp.268–9.

14 L. Stephen, *History of English Thought in the Eighteenth Century* (1902), II, p.443.

15 Joseph Massie, *A Plan for the Establishment of Charity Houses . . . Observations Relating to the Foundling Hospital etc.* (1758), p.46; Jonas Hanway, *A Candid Historical Account of the Hospital for the Reception of Young Children* (1760), pp.36–40. Among many other examples of concern about the dangers of excessive benevolence see J. Harris, *An Essay Upon Money and Coins* (1757), Part 1, p.11; R. Burn, *The History of the Poor Laws* (1764), p.206; *Gentleman's Magazine* XLIII (1773), pp.447–50.

16 D. George, *London Life in the XVIIIth Century* (1925), pp.43–5.

17 Hutcheson, op. cit., I, p.306: To make charity a legal requirement would abate the beauty of giving. Yet certain principles could be laid down: 'First, that it be not hurtful to the morals of the object . . . by encouraging them in sloth, meanness of temper, or any vicious dispositions; and again, that it be not so immoderate as to exhaust its own foundation . . . or incapacitate the donor for other offices of life toward those whom he may be more sacredly obliged to support.'

18 Smith, op. cit., (1804), II, p.77.

19 For example Hutcheson's argument that the preservation of democracy would be facilitated by 'some agrarian law or some contrivance that would prevent any dangerous degree of wealth coming into the hands of a few', op. cit., II, p.259; or Hume's more explicitly egalitarian observation, *David Hume. Writings on Economics* ed. E. Rotwein (1955), p.15, that an equalization of income 'diminishes much less from the *happiness* of the rich than it adds to that of the poor', a remark that recalls one of the more dubiously 'scientific' propositions of modern welfare economics. For other references see my article. 'Changing Attitudes to Labour in the Mid-Eighteenth Century', *Economic History Review* 2nd series XI (1958), p.49, n.2 (see this volume, p.74, n.74).

20 On the movement for the reformation of manners see S. and B. Webb, *The History of Liquor Licensing in England* (1903), chap.3 and appendix. See also M.G. Jones, *The Charity School Movement* (Cambridge, 1938), pp.4–5, who warns that 'It would be a misreading of the age of benevolence to see in the prominence enjoyed by the principle of subordination a harsh and unsympathetic attitude of the superior to the lower classes. Far from it . . . The charity schools came into being chiefly . . . to *condition* the children for their primary duty in life as hewers of wood and drawers of water.'

21 Cited by Sir F.M. Eden, *The State of the Poor* (1797), I, p.288.

22 Prof. J.J. Hecht, in his study of *The Domestic Servant Class in Eighteenth Century England* (1956), chap.8, has recently reminded us of contemporary concern about the effects of artificially high living standards on the lower orders. For a contemporary view see J. McFarlan, *Inquiries Concerning The Poor* (Edinburgh, 1782), pp.239–40.

23 Anon., *An Inquiry into the Management of the Poor* (1767), p.14. Habit was assigned a central role in contemporary psychological theory [Cf. G. Bryson, *Man and*

Society, The Scottish Inquiry of the 18th Century (Princeton, 1945), pp.141–2] and was frequently referred to in contemporary economic thought. For some comments on 'habits of industry', see n.30, this volume.

24 J. Hanway, *The Defects of Police* (1775), p.207. Similarly Joseph Massie held that most poverty was due to necessity, and complained that the poor laws drove people to despair, depravity and theft; but although he asserted that severity was ineffectual, he recommended that those unwilling to submit to the discipline of the house of correction should be forced to 'work or stand chin deep in cold water', *A Plan for the Establishment of Charity Houses . . . Considerations Relating to the Poor etc.* (1758), pp.50–9, 132.

25 Fielding, op. cit., p.118; also pp.107–8.

26 L. Radzinowicz, *A History of English Criminal Law* (1948), I, pp. 409–10.

27 Adam Smith's famous dictum that the division of labour is the outcome of man's propensity to 'truck, barter, and exchange' may be cited as an example. On the Scottish theory, to which Karl Popper's term 'psychologism' is applicable, see Bryson, op. cit., pp.25, 142. It has been argued that the Scottish writings provided the foundation for modern systematic sociology; cf. W.C. Lehmann, *Adam Ferguson and the Beginnings of Modern Sociology* (New York, 1930), *passim*.

28 For example, Hutcheson, op. cit., I, pp.119, 120–1, 299 ff. On Hume's position see Rotwein, op. cit., pp.xxviii–xxix.

29 Cf. Hume's essay 'Of Refinement in the Arts', op. cit., pp.19–32. Some contemporary writers expressed more qualified opinions, for example J. Millar, *The Origin of the Distinction of Ranks* (1806), especially pp.120–33, 289–96. The converse view can be found in Smith, *Wealth of Nations* (1910), II, p.265. For an interesting recent commentary on his position see J. Cropsey, *Economy and Polity* (The Hague, 1957), chap. III.

30 On this see Rotwein, op. cit., p.xiiii. As an illustration of a similar but less subtle version cf. Anon., *The State of the Corn Trade Considered* (1753), p.22: 'industry is more seated in the dispositions than in the outward advantages of mankind'.

31 My article reprinted in this volume, pp.63–84.

32 As Kames vividly put it, 'men by inaction degenerate into oysters', op. cit., I, p.195; cf. Hutcheson, op. cit., I, pp.21–3.

33 Massie, op. cit., p.97.

34 The Methodist revival of the mid-century is irrelevant to the present subject, for it exerted little or no direct effect upon the policy-making classes. Cf. Stephen, op. cit., II, pp.423–4.

35 For example 7 Geo. III cap. 39; 9 Geo. III cap. 31; 12 Geo. III cap. 67. For general accounts see B. Kirkman Gray, *A History of English Philanthropy* (1905), *passim*; and M.G. Jones, op. cit., *passim*.

36 Webb, *English Poor Law History*, p.171, fn.1.

37 T. Alcock, *Observations on the Defects of the Poor Laws* (1752); Anon., *Inquiry into the Management of the Poor* (1767), pp.3–4. On the other proposals see Sir F.M. Eden, op. cit., p.1, 318 ff; D. Marshall, op. cit., pp.155–9.

38 See the *DNB* VII, pp.1215–16, and Ian R. Christie, *The End of North's Ministry, 1780–2* (1958), pp.313, 333, 339.

39 *H of C Journals*, XXIX (1764), pp.737, 850, 890–1, 899, 946. Several parishes, seeking to avoid paying a share of the debt of the Gloucester workhouse (which had been closed in 1757 owing to the increase of the poor and the high cost of provisions), claimed that their paupers had been 'more easily and conveniently relieved, by pecuniary payments out of the workhouse'. There was a counterpetition from the city council. The city librarian of Gloucester has informed me that no records of this dispute have survived.

40 T. Gilbert, *A Scheme for the Better Relief and Employment of the Poor* (1764). For the earlier schemes *supra*, p.46, n.4. No doubt Gilbert was also influenced by the East Anglian experiments, cf. *V.C.H. Suffolk* 1 (1911), p.679.

41 These are Gilbert's own words, from his *Considerations on the Bills for the Better Relief and Employment of the Poor* (1787), p.4. The reasons were political, forming part of the preliminaries to the fall of Grenville's ministry six weeks later. See *Parliamentary History*, XVI, pp.77–82. There is a vivid description of the Lords' debate on the poor bill in *The Letters of Horace Walpole*, Toynbee ed. (1904), VI, pp.210–11.

42 *Parliamentary History* XVII, p.793.

43 No doubt the attention of members was diverted to the task of collecting information. Cf. *H of C Journal* XXXV, pp.392, 800–1, and this volume, n.51.

44 *Observations upon the Orders and Resolutions of the House of Commons* (1775), p.5. Gilbert commented: 'This temporary relief may often be necessary, from sickness or accidents, but should be administered with great prudence and impartiality' (35). Cf. *H of C Journal* XXXV, p.295; *Parliamentary History* XVIII, p.548.

45 T. Gilbert, *A Bill Intended to be Offered etc.* (Nov. 1775), p.50; *Observations upon the Orders*, pp.40–1. Cf. his *A Scheme for the Better Relief* (1764), p.6.

46 T. Gilbert, *Plan for the Better Relief and Employment of the Poor* (1781), pp.3–4. Unfortunately the House of Commons Committee records have been destroyed.

47 E. Jones, *Observations on the Scheme before Parliament for the Maintenance of the Poor . . . in a Letter to Thomas Gilbert* (Chester, 1776), pp.11–15; H. Zouch, *Remarks upon the Late Resolutions of the House of Commons respecting the proposed change of the Poor Laws* (Leeds, 1776), pp.6, 19–21, 34, 41–3, 45; A Country Magistrate, *Remarks Upon an Intended Bill for the Relief of the Poor, now under the consideration of Parliament* (1777), pp.3, 14. Somewhat similar views were expressed by R. Burn, a leading contemporary authority on the poor law, who had been consulted by Gilbert. See Burn's *Observations on the Bill . . . in a letter to a Member of Parliament* (London, 1776), pp.1, 22–5. Likewise, *Remarks upon the Resolutions of the House of Commons*, by a JP within the county of York (London, 1775), pp.16, 22–3; also A Kentishman, *Thoughts on the Present State of the Poor, and the Intended Bill etc.* (1776), pp.37–40. It is of some interest that Blackstone had been a member of Gilbert's committee in 1765, see *H. of C. Journal* (1765), XXX, pp.30, 38.

48 Jones, op. cit., pp.11–12.

49 Zouch, op. cit., pp.47; also 40. From 1786 Zouch was a leading figure in the campaign for the reformation of manners, cf. S. and B. Webb, *History of Liquor Licensing, loc. cit.* I am indebted to Miss M.B.C. Canney, of the Goldsmith's Library, who not only drew my attention to Zouch's pamphlet, but who has been unfailingly helpful over a long period.

50 Zouch, op. cit., p.34; Gilbert, *Observations on the Bills for amending and rendering more effectual . . . Houses of Correction* (1782), p.4. For similar views see H. Fielding, op. cit., p.64, and J. Tucker, *Six Sermons* (1772), p.74 (preached in 1745).

51 T. Gilbert, *Plan* (1781), pp.2–3.

52 W. Hay, *Remarks on the Laws Relating to the Poor* (1751), p.xii. This remark did not appear in the earlier (1735) edition. On the timing of this new attitude see the varying statements by Dorothy Marshall, op. cit., pp.14, 23, 54–6, 160. Her comment that by the mid-century 'there are to be seen the first faint signs of a more lenient attitude towards the poor' (51) underestimates the strength of this feeling.

53 E. Furniss, *The Position of the Laborer in a System of Nationalism* (New York, 1920), p.8.

54 Of course there continued to be a wide variety of attitudes to the poor and

proposals for reform. The following remarks represent an effort to generalize about the trends of thought that influenced policy, and it would be difficult to prove that they represented the majority view. Moreover the impossibility of differentiating clearly between 'economic' and 'poor law' writers, since they often discussed the same topics, further complicates the task of identifying the contribution of economic ideas to policy.

55 See *Josiah Tucker*, ed. R.L. Schuyler (New York, 1931), p.70ff. for his opposition to the settlement laws. For examples of his discriminatory attitude see *The Manifold Causes of the Increase of the Poor Distinctly Set Forth* (Gloucester, 1760), pp.23, 28, 30. Tucker believed that the competition of immigrants and the burden of taxation created problems only for the undeserving poor. For Smith's well-known opposition to the settlement laws see *Wealth of Nations*, I, p.128. He scarcely mentioned any other aspect of the poor law system. Of course many other writers could be cited. Fielding, for instance, maintained that most paupers were unwilling to work, whereas Massie held that poverty was mainly caused by the poor laws.

56 See n.37, this volume.

57 Explicit recognition of this fact can be traced back at least as far as Defoe, who distinguished between seasonal and day-to-day unemployment, and that caused by dead trade. After 1750 Massie, Hanway, Tucker, Young and many others emphasized the temporary character of distress, and proposals were made to stabilize prices, or to set aside stocks of goods or money as protection against such contingencies.

58 Cf. Marshall, op. cit., pp.128, 154–5; Webb, *English Poor Law History*, p.170.

59 See section 32 of Gilbert's Act (22 Geo. III, cap. 83) in Sir G. Nicholls's *A History of the English Poor Law* (1898), II, p.86. The author comments that 'by this provision, the Act appears to assume that there can never be a lack of employment, that is of profitable employment' (90). This optimistic assumption is characteristic of classical political economy and its liberal forerunners.

60 For a recent version of this argument see J.D. Chambers, *The Vale of Trent, 1670–1800* (Cambridge, 1957), p.58, where the author suggests that the growth of population intensified the struggle for survival, and consequently the heart of the poor law softened as its function became less compulsive.

61 *Parliamentary Debates* (1766), IV, p.387.

62 Ibid., p.506.

63 This is striking confirmation of the Webbs' generalization that the English governing classes demonstrated a growing sense of responsibility as the eighteenth century advanced. See S. and B. Webb, *English Local Government* (1906), I, p.377.

6

THE RELIEF OF POVERTY, ATTITUDES TO LABOUR, AND ECONOMIC CHANGE IN ENGLAND, 1660–1782[1]

I

During the past two or three decades economic and social historians have displayed a sustained interest in the pre-conditions of the Industrial Revolution in England, and among the many explanations of this remarkable breakthrough into modern industrialization the role of labour (including population) has been accorded a prominent place. Yet although questions about wages, labour supply, productivity, poverty and poor relief have been staple ingredients in the economic and social historian's diet ever since his discipline began to take shape in the late nineteenth century, there are still serious gaps in our knowledge of the size, composition, quality and living standards of the English labour force in the late seventeenth and eighteenth centuries. Some of these gaps may eventually be filled, at least partially, by detailed empirical studies of local and regional demographic, economic and social conditions. But even the most sanguine researcher must admit that there will continue to be deficiencies of data and unanswerable questions, so the need for interpretative, even speculative, studies will remain. The present paper falls within this latter category, for it is mainly concerned with the relationships between ideas, policies and conditions affecting the English labouring poor in the period under examination. It combines a review of the present state of knowledge of these matters with some speculative observations about causal connections and the possibilities of future research.

A cursory glance at the voluminous literature dealing with the English poor in the late seventeenth and eighteenth centuries reveals such a bewildering variety of attitudes, practices and conditions that it is legitimate to wonder whether any discernible patterns can be traced. Traditional attitudes towards poverty were disintegrating under the combined influence of the decline of religion and the spread of scientific ideas; the so-called rise of economic individualism meant, in social affairs, a decline of paternalistic central-government interference and a growth of parochial responsibility, with the inevitable result that general legislative enactments afford an even less reliable guide to local administrative realities than in the Tudor and Stuart periods; and although recent historians agree that this was a time of substantial economic advance, they also recognize that this process was very unevenly distributed, both in space and time. Consequently, although scholars have not hesitated to impose their subjective patterns on the available evidence, it is clear that any large-scale or long-term generalizations must be cautiously expressed and interpreted if they are not to do violence to the facts.

The plan of the paper is as follows. Section II outlines the general economic and social trends of the period, with special reference to prices and demographic changes. Section III describes some characteristic features of the economic literature of the time and certain broad trends in poor law ideas and practices. Section IV examines the relationship between public relief expenditures and private charity, and offers some suggestions about their combined effects, while the final section, V, reviews the argument and raises certain questions about future research prospects.

II

Recent studies of general trends in the English economy between 1660 and 1780 have stressed the multiplicity of factors at work and the extreme difficulty of disentangling them and specifying their interconnections. Yet, despite the acknowledged importance of natural advantages, political stability, social fluidity and the growth of trade, manufacturing, technology, etc., attention has lately been focused on agricultural prices and population changes – matters of direct interest to all students of labour and poverty. The period as a whole was one of substantial, if uneven, economic expansion affecting in differing degrees all sectors and regions, and despite serious shortcomings in the available evidence there is a broad consensus of opinion about the main features. In demographic terms there was a substantial growth of population from the mid-seventeenth century, probably with a marked acceleration around the 1680s and 1690s, a deceleration thereafter to about 1720 followed by stagnation until about 1745, and then a renewed upsurge which continued throughout the Industrial Revolution.[2] During the century from 1650 agricultural prices remained comparatively low, with wheat prices taking a 'decided downward plunge' until the third quarter of the eighteenth century, when 'the steep rise of population was followed by a still steeper rise of prices'. As a result there was a general upward trend in the purchasing power of the mass of the people, so that from the later 1740s 'a foundation for mass consumption was being laid by the inverse developments of population and progressive agriculture'.[3]

Owing to the lack of reliable statistical data there is, unfortunately, no parallel consensus of opinion as to the level, rate of growth and fluctuations of the national income, or its distribution among various sectors, regions or groups. There has been widespread acceptance of Professor Coleman's judgement that the initial level of living standards was low, and that contemporary observers were correct in attaching great importance to increases in the quantity and improvements in the quality of the labour force, since there was comparatively limited scope for new techniques or heavy capital investment in manufacturing processes.[4] But while many late-seventeenth and eighteenth century observers considered that the English 'poor' enjoyed higher money and real wages than their Scottish, Irish and continental European counterparts,[5] there were considerable divergences of opinion as to the desirability of this state of affairs.

In addition to these general trends there were also frequent short-term changes and significant regional variations in economic and social conditions, though they rarely fall into neat geographical or chronological patterns. Periodic crises impinged directly, and often severely, on the poorest members of the community, many of whom had no cushion of savings or alternative sources of income in times of distress. Although the progress of agriculture was tending to reduce the severity of bad harvests, which seem to have occurred less frequently between 1650 and 1750 than in earlier periods, there were many other disruptions of economic life attributable to adverse weather, epidemics (which were of diminishing severity in the eighteenth century),[6] commercial crises and wars. And as we shall see, public and private relief may have had a significant effect in reducing the impact of these misfortunes, especially for the poorest members of society.

At this point, however, we must define our terms more carefully – more carefully, that is, than contemporary commentators, most of whom failed to identify precisely or consistently the social and occupational groups to which they were referring. At the end of the period Arthur Young doubtless exaggerated in saying that 'the *labouring poor* is a term that none but the most superficial reasoners can use; it is a term that means nothing';[7] yet we must heed the late Professor T.S. Ashton's warning that

> No generalisations are more unsafe than those relating to social classes. The wide diversity of organisation in English agriculture and manufacture was matched by similar diversity in the conditions and attitudes of the workers. Many of the writers of treatises and pamphlets tended to ignore these differences; they were obsessed with the problem of the paupers; and, since in an age of economic fluctuations independent workers were liable to fall into poverty, there was a tendency to identify them with that sub-stratum of the population which was rarely, if ever, employed.[8]

For the purposes of identifying the poor, the most valuable statistical benchmarks are those provided by Gregory King in the 1680s and 1690s, who classified 23 per cent of the population as 'labouring people and out servants' and an additional 24 per cent as 'cottagers and paupers', maintaining that the annual family expenditures of both groups normally exceeded their incomes.[9] Twentieth century historians would not perhaps paint quite so bleak a picture – it has, for example, recently been suggested that about 20 per cent of the late-seventeenth century population were actually paupers in receipt of public or private charity, but that up to a further 30 per cent were at risk of becoming paupers at any given time.[10] It is virtually impossible to identify the hard core of those actually destitute for any length of time, but it is essential to distinguish between the impotent poor – such as widows, orphans, the aged, infirm, lunatics, vagrants and criminals – and the larger category of the industrious poor – mainly unskilled, low-paid labourers, weavers, manufacturers, seamen, miners, porters, etc., who were always vulnerable to any significant loss of earnings or rise in living costs. As is well known, contemporary observers usually took it for granted that the impotent poor should be supported, and that vagrants and criminals should be suitably punished, for these were straightforward Christian social duties. But they were much more concerned at the supposedly ever-growing numbers of dependent industrious poor, those able-bodied workers who were either unwilling to work or unable to find suitable or sufficient employment, whether permanent or temporary.

Any attempt to calculate the number of persons in the various categories of the poor must necessarily be treated with extreme caution owing to the lack of reliable data. Nevertheless, a rough indication of the relative magnitudes involved can be obtained by comparing two available 'guess-timates' – one, by Professor Coleman, based on a Lichfield enumeration of 1695, the other by Dr J.D. Marshall, based on official returns in the early nineteenth century.[11] In the Lichfield case it appears that 16.8 per cent of the town's population was pauperized, and of this total children under 15 comprised 47.3 per cent, and those aged 60 and over a further 17 per cent. According to Dr Marshall, children under 15 constituted approximately 50 per cent of permanent out-relief cases in the Speenhamland counties in 1802–3, while the aged, sick or infirm comprised somewhere between 9 per cent and 20 per cent of the total. The two sets of figures are, of course, strictly speaking non-comparable – for instance, Dr Marshall's figures exclude indoor relief cases, and both may be subject to considerable margins of error. Nevertheless, it seems reasonable to accept Dr Marshall estimate that able-bodied adult male labourers probably constituted less than 20 per cent of the pauper total (about 2 per cent of the entire population)[12] as broadly true of the whole period. Yet this was the category that attracted by far the greatest attention from contemporary observers. In the next section we shall consider why this was so.

III

Before reviewing contemporary attitudes to the labouring poor it is appropriate to recall some general features of late-seventeenth and eighteenth century economic literature. Although economics as a discipline was still in a pre-professional stage, for there was as yet no readily identifiable group of specialist economic writers, there was a discernible long-term development of an autonomous body of general principles of the 'science of trade', culminating in the great mid-eighteenth century systematic works by Richard Cantillon, David Hume, Sir James Steuart and Adam Smith.[13] The emergence of an autonomous body of economic ideas was accompanied by a diminished emphasis on ethical and religious considerations, which reflected the declining role of theology and the increasing influence of the natural sciences in intellectual life. These tendencies were, of course, much more apparent in the analysis of prices, monetary problems and trade than in discussions of poverty and employment, for most contemporary authors were incapable of suppressing their latent anthropocentrism and treating labour purely as a factor of production, divorced from all humanistic considerations. There was, it is true, an increasing prevalence of a 'commercial spirit' in the general literature of the time, a change which reflected the combined influence of economic progress and contemporary writers' responsiveness to the growth of a substantial new middle class readership.[14] Nevertheless, traditional Christian doctrine, unadulterated sentiment and class prejudice, continued to colour attitudes to poverty and the poor law, especially insofar as this was viewed as a matter of public or private charity. Indeed, those eighteenth century authors who were constantly discussing the relationship between reason and the passions would doubtless have understood and appreciated the current sociological distinctions between the comparative rationality of exchange relationships in the marketplace and the more emotional, affective considerations of recognition and deference entailed in gift-giving.[15] Yet there is no way of avoiding the complexities of the problem, for the question of poverty was a unifying theme linking debates about the level of economic activity, the balance of trade, prices, wages, employment, the poor law, workhouses and charity schools. The historian of economic thought and policy, as distinct from the historian of economic analysis, cannot confine himself to the embryonic treatises on systematic economics: he must go beyond the many pamphlets directly focused on poor law practice and at least sample the innumerable sermons, speeches and commentaries in the growing periodical literature of the time. Needless to say, the following summary statements will not attempt to encompass so ambitious a scope.

Despite the enormously varied and often conflicting views expressed by late-seventeenth and eighteenth century writers on economic and social questions, there was virtual unanimity on one central point – the great importance

105

attached to a large, well-ordered, healthy and industrious population. This consensus cannot be explained simply in economic terms – political, social and military considerations were also recognized. But the economic aspect was paramount. The co-existence of concern about poverty and the desire for a large population was not paradoxical, for the need to discourage idleness and prevent unemployment was generally acknowledged, and, despite all the evidence to the contrary, there remained a remarkably optimistic conviction that these difficulties could be overcome. Indeed, so great was the emphasis on the importance of employment that it came to dominate the discussion of all aspects of economic activity, including the money supply, the level of prices, the size and composition of output, and the balance of international accounts.[16] With the passage of time there was an increasing emphasis on the role of money as a medium of exchange, a positive stimulus to economic activity rather than a passive store of value; prices were considered to be too low if producers were impoverished or unemployed, and too high if our competitive power was thereby undermined; commodities produced by labour-intensive methods were preferred to those which employed few hands; and while exports were esteemed more highly than goods destined for the home market, this was not merely because they yielded foreign currency or bullion, but also because they represented an 'export of work' and therefore constituted 'foreign-paid incomes'.[17]

Although this body of ideas never acquired the systematic qualities that would justify us in describing it as economic theory, in the full present-day sense of that term, it was by no means lacking in coherence. On the contrary, the growing awareness of the interrelationships between the quantity of money, the balance of trade and the level of employment displayed by the leading economic writers of the period has persuaded some over-enthusiastic modern commentators to regard it as an embryonic form of Keynesian economics.[18] This framework of ideas formed the intellectual background to the more economically sophisticated accounts of the nature and effects of the poor law; and in certain cases the role of private charity was also taken into the reckoning.[19]

As the late seventeenth and early eighteenth centuries were the age of political arithmetic, it was inevitable that some authors would attempt to calculate the losses to the nation resulting from the failure to utilize the labour force fully and effectively, whether this was due to a shortage of money, voluntary idleness, the number of holidays or even the labourer's failure to reproduce his species.[20] But unfortunately these endeavours cannot be taken very seriously; nor can we uncritically accept the method of attaining representative opinions suggested by John Collins, who believed it possible to weigh up the views in the literature on trade so as to obtain a 'balance of doctrines'.[21] No scholar has yet been bold enough to review the voluminous and highly miscellaneous body of opinions about the problems of employment, poverty and poor law policy in an effort to identify and assess general trends of thought which could be related, with due allowance for time lags, to changes in contemporary economic and social conditions. The available secondary literature on economic ideas and policy is quite inadequate for this purpose; yet without such an undertaking there inevitably appears to be a lack of connection – other than accidental or occasional – between contemporary attitudes and practice. It is therefore necessary, while acknowledging the risks involved,[22] to offer some provisional generalizations about changes in contemporary attitudes to the poor before attempting to account for these changes in terms of the evolution of ideas and/or changes in contemporary economic and social conditions.

According to the leading poor law historians,[23] attitudes to the poor between 1660 and 1780 fall into three broad phases. From the Restoration until some time around the turn of the century, genuine concern for their welfare was coupled with an increased emphasis on the need to provide employment for the able-bodied – whether in workhouses, for those willing to work, or in houses of correction or other quasi-penal institutions, for the vagrant, recalcitrant or congenitally idle. In this phase there was genuine enthusiasm for workhouse schemes, derived largely from the over-optimistic assumption that in properly regulated conditions it would be possible to make a profit by selling the products of pauper labour. Although this expectation was waning soon after 1700, in face of accumulating evidence of past failures, workhouse schemes continued to be advocated and initiated throughout the eighteenth century by those who hoped either to defray part of the cost of maintaining the poor or to effect some reformation of their idle habits.[24]

From the beginning of the new century, however, there was a second phase, when a strident note of hostility became more widespread, and the workhouse was increasingly viewed as a device for deterring those who could find work but preferred to live off parochial relief or private charity.[25] The so-called Workhouse Test Act of 1723, which permitted parishes to form unions to construct workhouses for this purpose, was a by-product of this new approach, and, like other poor law statutes in the period, it was based directly on previous local experiments. Another feature of this second phase was the widespread support given to the practice of 'farming' either the whole poor or some special category of paupers, in the belief that this was the easiest and least expensive method of discharging a persistent and burdensome parochial responsibility. Farming involved the application of commercial methods to the poverty problem, and it usually had disastrous consequences for the poor themselves – so much so, that from the mid-century there was a growing revulsion at the foul and degrading conditions to which the indoor poor were subjected, and an outcry not only against farming, and workhouses in general, but also sometimes against the entire poor law system. It is difficult to account for this second phase in attitudes to the poor. Disappointed expectations among those who had put their faith in workhouse schemes was surely one element, and concern at rising poor rates accompanied by food riots and other public disturbances in the 1690s[26] may also have played a part. Daniel Defoe's pamphlet *Giving Alms No Charity* (1704) was probably influential; and it may have been instrumental in defeating Sir Humphrey Mackworth's workhouse bill, as the Webbs suggest;[27] but it is difficult to accept that it had a lasting impact. It seems possible that attitudes to labour became more hostile as food prices fell and real incomes rose, if the labourers responded by working less and taking more leisure time. Unfortunately this contention, too, though supported by innumerable complaints in the pamphlet literature, cannot be adequately substantiated in the present state of our knowledge. Comparisons with underdeveloped countries suggest that a negative response to the availability of higher real earnings would have been most likely in stagnant rural areas remote from expanding markets and available supplies of manufactured goods. However, further research is needed on this point, and at present we can only speculate that at a time when British exports were suffering from increased foreign competition in Europe, it appeared to many observers that opportunities for economic growth were being lost owing to an idle, unresponsive and overpaid labour force.

The third phase in attitudes towards the poor can be dated approximately from the mid-eighteenth century, and became more apparent with the rise of food prices in the late 1750s and 1760s.[28] As in earlier periods, there was no uniformity of outlook: the poor's critics could still be heard as well as their defenders.[29] But, on the whole, a more sympathetic attitude prevailed, and this was firmly based on a combination of moral philosophy and economic analysis, reinforced by growing public concern at the distress resulting from the rising prices of foodstuffs. It is surprising that public sympathy was so widespread in view of the growing evidence of social unrest, which was often serious enough to alarm the authorities responsible for law and order. But from the standpoint of the poor themselves this appears to have been largely a defensive reaction designed to preserve the higher living standards which many had enjoyed during the previous period.

Although it is a proposition virtually impossible to demonstrate conclusively, there seems little reason to doubt that the improvement in living standards enjoyed by the 'industrious poor' in the second quarter of the eighteenth century raised their conception of a decent or comfortable level of subsistence and generated rising expectations, which were frustrated when the cost of living increased in the post-1755 period.[30] At the same time a significant number of informed observers paid tribute to the skill, industry and effort of British labourers, suggesting that a more positive response to incentives may have been forthcoming after the mid-century than in earlier periods, when complaints about idleness and absenteeism were prevalent.[31] Indirect support for this general interpretation can be found in recent studies of popular disturbances, which show how frequently, and often how effectively, the lower orders ventilated their demands for a moderate subsistence in times of dearth. These outbreaks were not merely 'rebellions of the belly', unthinking Pavlovian responses to immediate pressures; they reflected positive claims and aspirations stemming from an underlying conception of natural justice, a just price or a traditional 'moral economy of provision'.[32] While the crowd's action probably depended on the existence of a hard core of leaders prepared to challenge the forces of law and order, the supporting cast was recruited from among those who were marginally indigent and threatened with pauperization by the decline in their real income.

The frequency and varied character of these outbreaks cannot be fully described here. But it is worth noting that in the earlier part of our period, when bad harvests were less frequent, the governing classes seemed comparatively untroubled by popular outbreaks, which seemed unlikely to threaten the existing social order. In the 1760s and after, however, when prices rose and bad harvests occurred more often, matters seemed very different. Rising social tensions and new social alignments, partly reflecting contemporary economic changes, were the cause of considerable concern to the government, which used the army, rather than the militia, to preserve public order. In this period the lower orders became involved in a defensive campaign to maintain the higher living standards which so many of them had enjoyed during much of the first half of the century; and their disposition to riot was certainly effective in persuading the rich to implement the machinery of parish relief and public charity.

It should be noted that the government's attitudes to these outbreaks did not necessarily accord with the responses of economic and poor law writers, many of whom were certainly more hostile to the poor in the earlier period than after the mid-century. And in terms of poor law policy the shift of opinion and intention from the Workhouse Test Act of 1723 to Gilbert's Act of 1782 was considerable.[33] The latter measure, by reserving the workhouses in newly-formed parish unions for those unable to work, reversed the earlier act, which had been designed to check applications for relief from able-bodied paupers by making entry into the house a condition of relief. It not only involved a shift from indoor to outdoor relief; it also emphasized the parish's responsibility to provide work for the unemployed, thereby preparing the way for more generous, if lax, principles and practices subsequently embodied in the Speenhamland system. And it is characteristic of Gilbert's more sympathetic attitude to the paupers – which reflected the trends of opinion in the preceding quarter century – that charitable contributions were to be enlisted to provide rewards for good behaviour.[34] Thus the line between public and private philanthropy was effectively blurred.

IV

Public and private provision for the relief of poverty in seventeenth and eighteenth century England was patently inadequate. Nevertheless there is abundant evidence of both a sense of responsibility for the less fortunate members of society and good works designed to alleviate hardship. These activities defy enumeration or neat classification. They included individual and collective efforts to inaugurate and operate institutions designed for medical, educational and social welfare; proclamations from the Lords Justices instructing parish officials to relieve distress at the time of the great recoinage; royal orders requiring the Bishop of London to organize house-to-house collections for the poor; emergency aid for the victims of natural disasters, such as fires and floods; purchases of grain and other foodstuffs in times of dearth for resale to the poor at 'normal' or customary prices below prevailing market levels; and repeated occasions when the poor were permitted or even encouraged to raid warehouses and impose their own *taxation populaire* on hated middlemen.

Historians of philanthropy have fully acknowledged the impossibility of drawing a clear-cut distinction between public and private assistance. Poor law officials often had charge of private endowments or alms houses; the well-to-do sometimes pressed them to be more generous in hard times; and charity schools were influenced as much by the desire to produce a docile, industrious labour force as to educate their pupils.[35] As Professor David Owen has noted, 'Properly administered charities can almost be thought of as instruments of mercantilist policy in so far as they tended to safeguard national power',[36] and whenever the divinely approved, 'most lasting, valuable, and exquisite pleasure'[37] of giving became careless and indiscriminate, many voices urged restraint and emphasized the need to consider the harmful consequences of such outlays for the recipients, and for society at large. It was often claimed that charity was superior to public relief, because it was prompted by a higher motive,[38] but while some maintained that the two were complementary, others regarded them as competitive.[39]

As already indicated, any overall assessment of poor relief in our period must take account of private philanthropy as well as the poor law.[40] Here, as elsewhere, generalizations are suspect; yet it seems likely that historians have tended to underestimate their combined impact. One method has been to calculate a per capita figure, either in annual or weekly terms, based on estimates of total expenditures and population at a given date.[41] Such a calculation is, of course, acknowledged to be rough and ready; but its effect is, inevitably, to make the resulting figure seem insignificant.

This procedure has two obvious shortcomings. One is that much voluntary charity was unrecorded, especially that associated with the cohesive and often paternalistic face-to-face relationships prevailing in rural communities. The second, more significant, point is that poor-relief outlays were obviously not distributed evenly over the whole population, either in space or in time, and should therefore be seen in most cases as marginal additions to income in an otherwise precarious or desperate situation.[42] In a matter of this kind timeliness is crucial. The failure to eradicate, or to effect a significant reduction in the level of poverty cannot be surprising to those familiar with its persistence in affluent industrial societies. Yet charitable and poor law payments constituted a sizeable transfer of incomes to persons with a high propensity to consume from those with a comparatively high propensity to save.[43] The impact on effective demand may have been slight, but it should not be entirely overlooked.

Far more important, however, was the effect of relief in preserving life, keeping up the labourer's morale and sense of security, and maintaining the higher levels of nutrition, energy and productivity on which many eighteenth century observers commented. Recent historians have recognized the first of these consequences, while possibly underestimating its importance at a time when rising population was probably contributing directly to economic growth.[44] But the broader social value of the poor law seems to have been lost sight of, maybe because it cannot be quantified. It may be worth recalling the views of earlier historians who considered that it encouraged social peace (a positive value transcending the interest of the governing class), helped to unite social classes, reduced the brutality of the labourer's struggle for survival and had indirect benefits even for those workers who never received public relief.[45] Its effects on the workers' psychology are even more difficult to assess, but it is at least conceivable that the situation was one whereby in growth industries in normal times labour incentives were higher than if average wages had been significantly higher or lower, and no relief had been forthcoming. When Mandeville remarked in his *Fable of the Bees* (1714) that 'the poor have nothing to stir them to labour but their wants, which it would be wisdom to relieve but folly to cure', he may have been stating an elementary truth. Jonas Hanway, a realistic philanthropist who described the poor rates as 'a stream of pure water for the support of life', added:

I question much if we should be near so rich as we are, if the common people did not live so much from hand to mouth. This is a good, though it arises seemingly from an evil; our fellow subjects enjoy an active disposition, yet generally work only in proportion to their necessities.[46]

By the third quarter of the eighteenth century it may have become increasingly clear to perceptive observers that despite the 'squalor, with spells of privation which were endured as the common lot', there were positive natural advantages in a situation where the workers could 'for the most part enjoy, when they were at work, a coarse abundance of food and drink – an abundance reflected in the published dietaries both of workhouses and large private establishments – and, above all, a jovial freedom to live irregularly, and to come and go as they please'.[47] It is, of course, impossible to assess the economic and social value of freedom, which existed despite the seemingly oppressive Settlement Laws. But present-day scholars are more likely to consider the effects of the workers' 'rude exuberance' on their energy and fertility.[48] Insofar as they prevented living standards from falling in times of distress, contemporary philanthropists may have succeeded in maintaining life, sustaining the morale and energy of the work force, and, after a long period of relatively low food prices, preserving those rising expectations on which the incentive to increased productivity so often depended. We should, after all, bear in mind that poverty is largely, if not mainly, a subjective condition.[49]

V

As indicated at the outset, the main argument of this paper is somewhat speculative. There is no reliable evidence of trends in contemporary opinion, the volume of private or public charity, or of the precise nature and effects of the poor law. Our knowledge of the labourer's living standards is depressingly meagre, not to mention his morale and productivity. But there is no doubt that poverty was the principal social problem of the period and that there is considerable scope for future research. We need to know more of contemporary attitudes and their relationship to poverty; we need detailed local studies of public and private relief payments; and more careful attempts to examine labour conditions, especially in relation to nutrition, hours of work, the number of days worked *per annum* and other influences on productivity. Whether this will lead to a revision of current conceptions of the role of labour in the economy is a matter for the future.

NOTES

1 This article was originally prepared for the sixth meeting of the International Institute of Economic History 'Francesco Datini' at Prato in April 1974.
2 Although there are significant disagreements among the experts on matters of emphasis and detail, this account is based on the work of one leading authority: J.D. Chambers, *Population, Economy, and Society in Pre-Industrial England*, ed. W.A. Armstrong (Oxford, 1972), especially pp.22–4.
3 ibid. No attempt will be made here to outline major developments in commerce, agriculture, manufacturing or technology, for such an account would take us too far afield. For reliable general textbooks see Charles Wilson, *England's Apprenticeship 1603–1763* (London, 1965) and L.A. Clarkson, *The Pre-Industrial Economy in England 1500–1750* (London, 1971).
4 D.C. Coleman, 'Labour in the English Economy of the Seventeenth century', *Economic History Review* Second Series, VIII (1955–6), especially pp.283–4. This view has been generally accepted by subsequent historians.
5 This opinion can be traced back well beyond our period. Cf. Professor F.J. Fisher's delightful quotation from a sixteenth century pamphlet: 'Oh if thou knewest thou Englishe man in what welth thou livest and in how plentifull a Countrye: Thou wouldst vii times of the day fall flat on thy face before God, and geve him thanks, that thou wart born an English man, and not a french pezant, nor an Italyan, nor Almane.' Cited in *Essays in the Economic and Social History of Tudor and Stuart England*, ed. F.J. Fisher (Cambridge, 1961), p.13.

6 This is one of the major themes of Professor Chambers's posthumous work referred to in n.2. For a general study of short-term changes see T.S. Ashton, *Economic Fluctuations in England 1700–1800* (Oxford, 1959).

7 *Northern Tour* (1768), IV, p.467.

8 *An Economic History of England: The Eighteenth Century* (London, 1955), p.201.

9 Coleman, *loc. cit.*, pp.283–4.

10 Cf. Wilson, op. cit., p.231; Clarkson, op. cit., p.233.

11 Coleman, *loc. cit.*, pp.285–6; J.D. Marshall, *The Old Poor Law 1795–1834* (London, 1968), especially pp.33–5.

12 Of course this proportion varied widely from time to time and place to place, according to local employment opportunities. As Dr Marshall suggests, careful local studies could undoubtedly provide a much more detailed and accurate picture of these variations than is currently available.

13 This is a major theme of innumerable histories of economic thought. Of special interest in the present connection is W. Letwin, *The Origins of Scientific Economics, English Economic Thought 1660–1776* (London, 1963).

14 Historians of literature seem much more aware of the significance of this point than historians of economics. See, for example, Ian Watt, *The Rise of the Novel, Studies in Defoe, Richardson and Fielding* (London, 1960); J.W. Saunders, *The Profession of English Letters* (London, 1964); and other studies of the output of seventeenth and eighteenth century novels, periodicals and newspapers. As there was then no distinct category of 'economists' or economic writers, it is necessary to view economic writings in relation to other categories of literature. This point is especially important in considering labour and poverty in view of the difficulty of distinguishing economic treatises from poor law pamphlets and the vast volume of religious tracts and ethical homilies.

15 See, for example, Neil Smelser, 'A Comparative View of Exchange Systems', *Economic Development and Cultural Change* VII (1959), pp.173–82 and Alvin Gouldner, 'The Norm of Reciprocity', *American Sociological Review* XXV (1960), pp.161–78.

16 It is noteworthy that, despite the prevalent belief that 'the majority must be kept in poverty that the whole might be rich', there was no serious discussion of the distribution of income or wealth. Cf. the classic study by Edgar S. Furniss, *The Position of the Laborer in a System of Nationalism, A Study of Labor Theories of the Later English Mercantilists* (New York, 1957; originally published in 1920). The quotation is from p.8.

17 Cf. E.A.J. Johnson, *The Predecessors of Adam Smith, The Growth of British Economic Thought* (London, 1937), ch.XV. According to Furniss, op. cit., p.41, 'In Mercantilistic thought, as in all systems of nationalism, a nationally valuable was distinguished from a nationally useless population by the test of employment, and this test comprised not only considerations of the amount but also of the kind of occupation'.

18 This view was, of course, propagated by J.M. Keynes himself, in the final chapter of his *General Theory of Employment, Interest and Money* (London, 1936). One of the principal missing links in the eighteenth century view was the failure to integrate the rate of interest and the marginal efficiency of capital into the system, largely because of a lack of understanding of the process of investment.

19 For example, by Sir James Steuart: 'provided man be made to labour, and make the earth produce abundantly, and provided that either authority, industry, or charity, can make the produce circulate for the nourishment of the free hands, the principle of a great population is brought to a full activity.' *An Inquiry into the*

Principles of Political Economy, ed. Andrew S. Skinner (Edinburgh, 1966; originally published in 1767), I, p.67. See also p.94.

20 Cf., for example, David Bindon, *A Scheme for Supplying Industrious Men with Money to Carry on their Trades* 3rd ed. (Dublin, 1750; originally published in 1729), p.62; Sir Joshua Gee, *The Trade and Navigation of Great Britain* 4th ed. (London, 1738; originally published in 1729), p.134; Lawrence Braddon, *An Abstract of the Draught of a Bill for Relieving, Reforming and Employing the Poor* (London, 1717), p.viii; and John Bellers, *An Essay toward the Improvement of Physick [. . .] with an Essay for Imploying the Able Poor* (London, 1714), p.111, who estimated the loss of every industrious labourer capable of having children as equivalent to a 'Two Hundred Pound Loss to the Kingdom'.

21 As quoted by Letwin, op. cit., pp.112–13.

22 In particular, the risks of obscuring the variety of opinions and the variations in local economic and social conditions and poor law practices.

23 Dorothy Marshall, *The English Poor in the Eighteenth Century. A Study in Social and Administrative History* (London, 1926) and Sidney and Beatrice Webb, *English Poor Law History, Part I: The Old Poor Law* [English Local Government, Vol.7] (London, 1927).

24 Just as it was widely held that the children of the poor must be 'inured to early labour', so too it was argued, for adults, 'better to burn a thousand men's labours for a time, then to let those thousand men by non-employment lose their faculty of labouring'. William Petty, *Economic Writings*, ed. C.H. Hull (Cambridge, Mass., 1899), p.60.

25 This view, of course, depended on the assumption that employment opportunities were available for the unemployed poor, a view that gained increasing support towards the mid-century. It was compatible with a growing scepticism towards interventionist 'make-work' schemes.

26 Cf. Max Beloff, *Public Order and Popular Disturbances, 1660–1714* (Oxford, 1938); R.B. Rose, 'Eighteenth Century Price Riots and Public Policy in England', *International Review of Social History* VI (1961), especially pp.279–81.

27 S. and B. Webb, op. cit., pp.113–16. They remark that Defoe threw into the discussion 'the hardest possible stone of economic disillusionment and worldly cynicism'. A comparable mood was evident in Bernard Mandeville's *Fable of the Bees* (1714) and his *Essay on Charity Schools* (1723), both of which contain a detached, cynical and calculating attitude to the problem of poverty.

28 For a more detailed account of this phase see my two articles 'Changing Attitudes to Labour in the Mid-Eighteenth Century', *Economic History Review* Second Series, XI (1958), pp.35–51 (reprinted in *Essays in Social History*, ed. M.W. Flinn and T.C. Smout (Oxford, 1974)) and 'Economic Thought and Poor Law Policy in the Eighteenth Century', *Economic History Review* XIII (1960), pp.39–51, this volume, pp.85–100.

29 In a later article Richard C. Wiles demonstrated that support for 'high wages' was less infrequent in the pre-1750 period than I had supposed. Cf. 'The Theory of Wages in Later English Mercantilism', *Economic History Review* Second Series, XXI (1968), pp.113–26. Nevertheless the main argument about the difference in attitudes between the two periods is unaffected, for this was not simply a matter of high wages. The discussion of wage levels (which was, in any case, more complex than Wiles suggested) was only part of a larger corpus of ideas and beliefs. It would, however, be inappropriate to pursue the matter further at this juncture.

30 This is in accordance with the views expressed by Professor Chambers, who emphasized the relationship between population, economic expansion and rising expectations, op. cit., pp.30, 145.

31 Any detailed examination of this possibility would, of course, call for a

careful distinction between different categories of the labouring poor, different occupations and different regions.

32 See, for example, Edward P. Thompson, 'The Moral Economy of the English Crowd in the Eighteenth Century', *Past & Present* No.50 (1971), pp.76–136; also Beloff, op. cit.; George Rudé, *The Crowd in History, A Study of Popular Disturbances in France and England 1730–1848* (London, 1964); and the recent study by Walter J. Shelton, *English Hunger and Industrial Disorders. A Study of Social Conflict During the First Decade of George III's reign* (London, 1973). This paragraph and the two following are based on these sources.

33 For further discussion of this point see my article 'Economic Thought and Poor Law Policy', this volume, pp.85–100.

34 Thomas Gilbert, *A Bill, Intended to be Offered to Parliament, for the Better Relief and Employment of the Poor, Within That Part of Great Britain Called England* (1775), p.62.

35 For example, the Bishop of Norwich: 'There must be drudges of labour (hewers of wood and drawers of water the Scriptures call them) as well as Counsellors to direct and Rulers to preside. [. . .] To which of these classes we belong, especially the more inferior ones, our birth determines. [. . .] These poor children are born to be daily labourers, for the most part to earn their bread by the sweat of their brows. It is evident then that if such children are, by charity, brought up in a manner that is only proper to qualify them for a rank to which they ought not to aspire, such children would be injurious to the Community.' Sermon preached by the Bishop of Norwich at the anniversary meeting of the charity schools in and about London and Westminster, 1 May 1755. Quoted by M.G. Jones, *The Charity School Movement, A Study of Eighteenth Century Puritanism in Action* (Cambridge, 1938), p.75.

36 David Owen, *English Philanthropy 1660–1960* (London, 1965), p.14. For example: 'British benevolence, being thus united with *native British fire*, will diffuse the *genuine* spirit of patriotism through these realms, and we may hope to see such *improvements* in maritime affairs, as posterity looking back, will view with *equal gratitude and applause.*' Jonas Hanway, *Account of the Marine Society* 6th ed. (London, 1759), p.13. Italics in original.

37 Owen, op. cit., p.14.

38 Yet not all motives were equally worthy. For example, Richard Nelson, in *An Address to Persons of Quality and Estate, Ways and Methods of Doing Good* (London, 1715), p.254, argued that charity might be immediately profitable, for 'an unexpected inheritance, the determination of a lawsuit in our favour, the success of a great adventure, an advantageous match, are sometimes the recompenses of charity in this world'.

39 For example, Henry Fielding in his *Proposal for Making an Effectual Provision for the Poor* (1753) considered that the poor unable to work could be largely or wholly supported by private charity. Other commentators maintained that the high level of poor rates discouraged private charity.

40 It is generally accepted that most poor law outlays consisted of casual doles or payments in kind. This was doubtless the easiest method by which untrained, sometimes unpaid and often overworked parochial officials could discharge their obligations. But this does not preclude the possibility that this was the most appropriate and efficacious procedure.

41 For example, Wilson, op. cit., p.235; Clarkson, op. cit., p.171–2, 231.

42 For example: 'What, too, is the condition of the great body of the poor, employed in the several branches of this manufacture [i.e. wool]? [. . .] Deplorable beyond expression. Some quite destitute of employment, and others

MERCANTILISM AND PRE-SMITHIAN ECONOMICS

half-employed, and almost all obliged to fly (where else can they fly) to the landed interest for at least partial support. [. . .] It is a fact (I speak it from knowledge) that many parishes, at this instant, pay the carriage of wool, to and from the spinning houses, at the distance of twenty, thirty, and even forty miles, for the sake of finding some employment for their poor.' Anon., *An Answer to Sir John Dalrymple's Pamphlet upon the Exportation of Wool* (1782), pp.29–30. No doubt this was a partisan statement. But the situation it described was by no means unique. For acknowledgement of the precarious situation in growing branches of manufacturing see, for example, Wilson, op. cit., p.344, and Ashton, *Economic Fluctuations*, op. cit., pp.145, 177.

43 Clarkson, op. cit., p.171. According to a much earlier pre-Keynesian writer, the poor rate was largely a wages fund, which may have helped to keep the poor from starving but probably depressed the 'industrious and competent' who were immediately above that level. B. Kirkman Gray, *A History of English Philanthropy, From the Dissolution of the Monasteries to the Taking of the First Census* (London, 1967; originally published in 1905), pp.220–1. This argument recalls the early-nineteenth century case against the Speenhamland system. It assumes a fixed wages fund or, more precisely, that sums spent on poor relief would otherwise have been spent in some other manner, so that the net employment-generating effects of poor relief would be zero or negligible. Such a contention is, of course, highly suspect.

44 The counterfactual assumption that but for private and public aid some of the poor would have starved is often implied or explicitly stated; e.g., Gray, op. cit., p.221; Wilson, op. cit., p.235: 'Often, the poor could only look for their immediate salvation to the voluntary redistribution of income through charity and poor relief'; Clarkson, op. cit., pp.237–8: for the poor, poverty 'meant receiving incomes too small to support existence without public or private charity'.

45 E.M. Leonard, *The Early History of English Poor Relief* (Cambridge, 1900), pp.302–4. Cf. S. and B. Webb, op. cit., pp.402, 404–5; Marshall, op. cit., pp.1, 250, 252–4. Recognition of the social value and, more particularly, the elevated aims of the poor law system is not, of course, incompatible with severe criticism of its actual workings.

46 Jonas Hanway, *Letters to the Guardians of the Infant Poor and to the Overseers of the Parish Poor* (1767), p.13.

47 S. and B. Webb, op. cit., p.419. For a more qualified assessment of diets in workhouses, orphanages and schools see J.C. Drummond and Anne Wilbraham, *The Englishman's Food. A History of Five Centuries of English Diet*, revised by Dorothy Hollingsworth (London, 1957), pp.223–8.

48 On the question of energy see the fascinating unpublished paper by Herman Freudenberger and Gaylord Cummins, 'Health, Work and Leisure in the Industrial Revolution' (Tulane University, March 1973). Their argument suggests that rising food consumption and improved nutrition in the first half of the eighteenth century may have significantly improved the biological quality of the English labour force and increased its energy and productivity. This supports the contention that there may have been a positive relationship between poor law expenditure and fertility. Cf. H.J. Habakkuk, *Population Growth and Economic Development Since 1750* (Leicester, 1971), p.39. A somewhat similar argument appears in Mark Blaug, 'The Myth of the Old Poor Law and the Making of the New', *Journal of Economic History* XXIII (1963), pp.151–84.

49 See, for example, Peter Townsend, 'The Meaning of Poverty', *British Journal of Sociology* XIII (1962), pp.210–27; also Peter Townsend, *The Culture of Poverty* (n.p., n.d.), p.46.

PART II

ADAM SMITH AND CLASSICAL ECONOMICS

7

ADAM SMITH
The modern re-appraisal*

I

In the literature of economic thought there are two major turning points: one marked by the publication of Adam Smith's *Inquiry into the Nature and Causes of the Wealth of Nations* in 1776, the other by the appearance of John Maynard Keynes's *General Theory of Employment, Interest and Money*, in 1936. More by design than by accident, each of these works initiated an intellectual revolution which profoundly influenced the subsequent course of human affairs and led to a dramatic reinterpretation of the past. Smith deliberately set out to discredit the doctrines and policies of his predecessors, the proponents of the so-called 'mercantile system', while Keynes vigorously attacked an intellectual tradition which, he claimed, had 'conquered England as completely as the Holy Inquisition conquered Spain'.[1]

Keynes's successful campaign against the nineteenth century tradition of economic thought, classical economics, of which Adam Smith is usually regarded as the founder, has necessarily entailed a re-appraisal of Smith's own work, as well as that of his predecessors, the mercantilists. To suggest that there is a kind of doctrinal see-saw, which brings down Smith & Co. as it raises Keynes & Co., would be an oversimplification. Yet it is a legitimate and useful one; for Smith and his nineteenth century followers had so effectively disparaged the ruling economic ideas of the seventeenth and eighteenth centuries, that Keynes's generation had been brought up to believe that mercantilist theory was 'little better than nonsense'.

In a valiant effort to rectify this injustice, Keynes appended to his *General Theory* his own, magnificently idiosyncratic version of the history of economics, in which he roundly praised or condemned earlier writers according to whether or not they had anticipated the truths of his own teachings.[2] Fortunately we can draw upon Keynes's theoretical insights without at the

119

same time committing ourselves to his wholesale revision of history, and when due allowance is made for the difference between eighteenth and twentieth century conditions there remain striking similarities between the mercantilist and the Keynesian outlook, so that our own time has sometimes been called the neo-mercantilist era of economic thought and policy.

The modern re-appraisal of Adam Smith's overall achievement has not, of course, merely been confined to his economic ideas. But as the Keynesian revolution has been followed by a radical reinterpretation of Smith's economies, this will be considered first. Before doing so, however, it will be necessary to explain the nature and significance of the Keynesian revolution, although this highly technical matter must, of necessity, be presented in rather simplified terms.

The catalyst that brought Keynes's thinking to maturity and also profoundly influenced the reception of his work was, of course, the worldwide depression of the early 1930s. Arguing that the prevailing mass unemployment was due to a deficiency in the aggregate effective demand for goods and services, he endeavoured to prove that this was caused by an excess of saving, or, in other words, an inadequate volume of private and public spending for consumption and investment purposes. This deficiency – the so-called 'deflationary gap' – could only be remedied, and the depression cured, if the government were to assume the responsibility for maintaining the level of aggregate demand by means of a carefully thought-out programme of public investment expenditure; and he developed an elaborate theoretical apparatus to buttress his argument.

Keynes's theory has been the subject of considerable controversy. But it is the conclusion, rather than the reasoning, that concerns us here. Keynes converted the younger generation of economists, many of whom became his ardent disciples; within a decade or so, the Keynesian heterodoxy had become the new orthodoxy; only a handful of conservative economists denied the necessity for a systematic full-employment policy; and Keynes's proposals received official recognition in the Government White Paper in 1944 and, soon after, in the United States and even in the United Nations.[3]

The effect of the Keynesian revolution on the history of economics has been almost as dramatic as its impact on public policy. Keynes's break with the past seemed all the more remarkable in view of his position as a leader of the Cambridge school, which had dominated British economic thought for half a century. Doctrinal cohesion and respect for tradition were among the most outstanding characteristics of this group of economists, and Keynes's outspoken attack on his predecessors for their failure to deal with the problem of general unemployment seemed at best to be rank bad form and, at worst, a kind of treachery.[4] Moreover, his crime seemed all the more heinous because his analysis led him to support state intervention.

Keynes himself was a Liberal and liberal; but his ideas had the effect of discrediting what might be called the 'Whig interpretation of the history of economics', according to which the past was viewed merely as a long and painful struggle to attain the heights of nineteenth century economic liberalism. From this viewpoint, the *Wealth of Nations* appeared as a bible, whose publication marked the end of the Dark Ages of economic ignorance and mercantile prejudice, and the dawn of a new era of economic progress, free trade and governmental *laissez-faire*. If, by contrast, we accept the Keynesian version, the *Wealth of Nations* emerges as the chief source of nineteenth century error, the beginning of a long tradition of economic thought which overemphasized the virtues of saving and ignored the vital function of spending in maintaining the level of employment.

There is, in fact, an important core of truth in the Keynesian doctrine, which has inspired a serious and fruitful re-examination of the seventeenth and eighteenth century mercantilist writings, many of which display a keen awareness of the interdependence of the quantity of money, the level of employment and the rate of economic growth.[5] The Keynesian version is far from being the whole truth; but it is an important and, until recently, an unduly neglected part. As Adam Smith was the first major writer to build a system of economic doctrine based on what became the orthodox nineteenth century view of saving, he was, in this sense too, the founder of a new tradition. Smith, however, was a practical, common sense writer, who had no intention of creating a system of economic theory. Although he was, for a time, Professor of Logic at Glasgow University, he showed little interest in that subject, giving his students only 'just so much of the ancient logic as was requisite to gratify [their] curiosity with respect to an artificial mode of reasoning'[6] and at one point in his *Theory of Moral Sentiments*, he showed his contempt for mere speculation by observing that 'the most sublime speculation of the contemplative philosopher can scarce compensate for the neglect of the smallest active duty'.[7] In these circumstances, it is hardly surprising that the greatest modern historian of economics has maintained that 'the *Wealth of Nations* does not contain a single *analytic* idea, principle, or method that was entirely new in 1776'. Yet he goes on, Smith's

> very limitations made for success. Had he been more brilliant, he would not have been taken so seriously. Had he dug more deeply, had he unearthed more recondite truth, had he used difficult and ingenious methods, he would not have been understood. But he had no such ambitions: in fact he disliked whatever went beyond plain common sense. . . . While the professional of his time found enough to command his intellectual respect, the 'educated reader' was able to assure himself that, yes, this was so, he too had always thought so . . . argument and material were enlivened by advocacy which is after all what attracts a wider public: everywhere the professor turned his chair into a seat of judgement and bestowed praise and blame. And it was Adam Smith's good fortune that he was thoroughly in sympathy with the humours of

his time. He advocated the things that were in the offing, and he made his analysis serve them.[8]

On the whole, Schumpeter's verdict was somewhat too severe, for he could not resist the temptation to deflate the celebrated and laud the lesser figures in the history of economics. Smith's great achievement was to synthesize the ideas of his predecessors and his contemporaries, express them in forceful and comprehensible prose, and apply them to vital problems that plagued his own and subsequent generations of scholars and statesmen. He was further ahead of his time than Schumpeter conceded; but he was more a man of the eighteenth century than his nineteenth century successors acknowledged. Thus the modern re-appraisal of Smith's economics centres on his view of saving and employment, rather than his advocacy of free trade and economic liberalism; and it prompts us to ask why Smith turned his attention away from the problems of unemployment at a time when pauperism was beginning to attain unprecedented proportions. What was the connection between Smith's contribution to the transition from mercantilism (with its emphasis on spending and employment) to classical economics (with its emphasis on saving and investment) and the contemporary economic and social transformation that led up to the industrial revolution?

In an attempt to answer these questions we must first examine the intellectual climate of Scottish moral philosophy, of which Smith's work forms an integral part.

II

Adam Smith was born at Kirkcaldy in Fifeshire, in 1723, the son of a successful lawyer and civil servant who had died some three months earlier.[9] Throughout the next sixty years his mother continued to be the most important woman in his life, for he never married, and this fact has given rise to speculation on the part of those who indulge in the esoteric art of posthumous psychoanalysis. Comparatively little is known about Smith's life; but it seems to have been fairly uneventful. Admittedly he was kidnapped for a few hours by gypsies at the age of three – and one otherwise reputable authority has suggested that this episode may have inspired his lifelong belief in the principle of individual freedom.[10] But apart from this incident, and a brief encounter with a highwayman, there were few adventures. Most of his life was spent in academic pursuits – as a student at Glasgow University from 1737–40, and for the next six years at Oxford under a Snell Exhibition, an award designed for those proposing to take holy orders. At Balliol he made few friends in the hostile Jacobite atmosphere of the college, but although he wrote to a relative, in the earliest surviving letter, 'it will be his own fault if any one should endanger his health at Oxford by excessive Study, our only business here being to go to prayers twice a day and to lecture twice a week',[11] he made good use of his spare time. After a brief spell of public lecturing in

Edinburgh, he became Professor at Glasgow in 1751, first of Logic, then of Moral Philosophy, retaining the latter office until he went to France in 1764. There for nearly three years, he acted as tutor to the Duke of Buccleuch – an employment that was sufficiently well paid to provide a reasonable income for the rest of his life, and this enabled him to devote almost ten more years to the completion of the *Wealth of Nations*. From 1777, until his death in 1790, he was employed as a Commissioner of Customs for Scotland, a position similar to the one his father had filled; and doubtless he relished the irony of the situation, for he had been a devastating critic of the existing customs and excise system.

As W.R. Scott has shown, Smith was an accomplished administrator. Yet he will always be regarded as a member of the genus *homo academicus*, and there are some amusing stories of his absent-mindedness. On one occasion, while engaged in an enthusiastic discussion with the Duke of Buccleuch's father, the Rt Hon. Charles Townshend, when they were standing on a plank laid across a Glasgow tanning pit, Dr Smith 'who was talking warmly on his favourite subject, the division of labour, forgetting the precarious ground on which he stood, plunged headlong into the nauseous pool. He was dragged out, stripped, and covered with blankets, and conveyed home on a sedan chair.' Another time, while similarly preoccupied, he took a piece of bread and butter, rolled it round and round and put it into the teapot, and when he had tasted it, remarked that it was the worst tea he had ever met with! One Sunday morning, Smith was walking in his garden in Kirkcaldy wearing a dressing gown, when, lost in thought, he unintentionally turned on to the turnpike road and followed it for fifteen miles until he reached Dunfermline, where his reverie was disturbed by the bells summoning the local people to church.[12] Smith evidently possessed remarkable powers of mental concentration, and an uncanny capacity for recalling conversations long past, even those during which he had appeared to be inattentive. This capacity, when coupled with his extreme dislike of the physical act of writing, helps to account for the discursive style and unsystematic arrangement of his published works, most of which were dictated to an amenuensis.

During the past fifty years or so, largely as a result of two major discoveries, scholars have increasingly recognized the essential unity of Adam Smith's life and work. These two discoveries: the one a report of Smith's lectures delivered at Glasgow University, in 1762–3, and the other, *An Early Draft of the Wealth of Nations* – a twelve thousand word manuscript that was probably written in 1763, the year before he went to France as tutor to the Duke of Buccleuch[13] – reveal that Smith's leading ideas were formulated at a much earlier stage than had been supposed, probably in the decade before the publication of his first major work, the *Theory of Moral Sentiments*, in 1759. Evidently the general influence of the Scottish tradition upon Smith's work is greater than that of the French Economistes, the Physiocrats, so that we may appropriately begin our enquiry into the nature and origins of Smith's ideas on saving and employment by considering the views of Francis Hutcheson, his predecessor as Professor of Moral Philosophy at Glasgow, and a man he revered as his 'never-to-be-forgotten' teacher, who directly influenced his economic as well as his moral ideas.[14]

Hutcheson's interest in the employment effects of different kinds of expenditure was aroused by the eighteenth century discussion of the moral and economic consequences of luxury. Was private spending on luxuries necessary in order to maintain full employment? Hutcheson admitted that such expenditures might provide some employment for the poor, but he denied that they were indispensable to the maintenance of prosperity. Like many of his contemporaries, he was shocked by Bernard de Mandeville's notorious *Fable of the Bees*, in which it was claimed that 'private vices are public benefits'; and he published a critical attack on Mandeville in 1727, when Adam Smith was four years old, in the course of which he rejected Mandeville's contention that theft and robbery benefited the public by providing employment for locksmiths:

> were there no occasion for locks, had all children and servants discretion enough never to go into chambers unseasonably, this would make no diminution of manufactures; the money saved to the housekeeper would afford either better dress, or other conveniences to a family, which would equally support artificers: even smiths themselves might have equal employment. Unless all men be already so well provided with all sorts of convenient utensils, or furniture, that nothing can be added, a necessity or constant usefulness of robbers can never be pretended, any more than the public advantage of shipwrecks and fires, which are not a little admired by the author of the fable.[15]

This passage reveals the felicitous style and aptness of illustration that Adam Smith was to inherit from his master, and it clearly foreshadows the nineteenth century orthodox view that money not spent in one way will be spent in another. In his posthumously published *System of Moral Philosophy*, based on the Glasgow lectures which Adam Smith attended, Hutcheson went even further. Frugality and abstemiousness, he insisted, would not cause unemployment, but would facilitate generosity to one's friends, charity to the poor and would encourage the diversion of commodities from home to export uses – a notion dear to present-day Chancellors of the Exchequer.

> Five families supported in sober plenty may make vastly greater consumption for every good purpose, than one living in luxury. . . . And as to sobriety, it is generally true that it makes the greatest consumption. It makes men healthy and long livers. It enables men to marry soon and support numerous families. And consider even one alone: a sober plentiful consumption for sixty or seventy years is greater than a riotous one of ten or twelve, and of fifty more in beggary.[16]

To his contemporaries Hutcheson was a liberal thinker, and in 1737, the first year of Adam Smith's attendance at Glasgow University, he was unsuccessfully prosecuted by the local presbytery for teachings that were thought to have contravened the Westminster Confession. Nevertheless he was a deist, and he found it difficult to entertain the idea that the benevolent Author of Nature had so ordered the universe that luxury and vice were necessary to economic and social welfare. By the mid-century, however, a more advanced theological outlook was in vogue in Smith's circle, and it would be unwise to assume that Smith's denial of the need for luxury and vice was merely a corollary of his religious beliefs. Like several of his close friends, he sought to explain social phenomena in naturalistic terms, rather than by reference to divine ordination. Moreover his religious beliefs are exceedingly difficult to specify. He was far from enthusiastic in the performance of his religious duties and some modern commentators have argued that the treatment of theological matters in his writings reveals a lack of moral courage, even a wilful deceptiveness.[17]

Certainly Smith was much more of a conformist than his sceptical friend, David Hume, who was barred from Scottish academic life because he was thought to be an atheist. In an important essay *Of Refinement in the Arts*, published in 1752, Hume carefully distinguished between 'innocent' luxury, which is neither morally wrong nor economically harmful, and 'vicious' luxury, which is both; and he conceded that without 'vicious' luxury there might be some unemployment, although this would be attributable to 'some other defect in human nature, such as indolence, selfishness, inattention to others, for which luxury, in some measure, provides a remedy'.[18] Hume, however, did not develop this point, and Smith did not refer to Hume's distinction, although it must have been familiar to him. In the *Theory of Moral Sentiments*, published seven years later, Smith denounced the scandalous sophistry and the pernicious implications of Mandeville's contention that private vices were public benefits. But he admitted that Mandeville's system of thought could never have exerted so much influence 'had it not in some respects bordered upon the truth'; and he acknowledged that luxury spending gave employment, for if asceticism were universally adopted 'it would be pernicious to society, by putting an end to all industry and commerce, and in a manner to the whole business of human life'.[19]

To a Keynesian this might appear as a promising start; but in his subsequent writings Smith seems to have been blissfully unaware of the possibility that luxury might be required in order to maintain full employment. Like his mercantilist predecessors, he advocated taxes on luxuries, and preferred expenditures on durable goods, such as fine houses, to expenditures on retainers and menials, because they generated more employment, augmented the nation's capital stock, and could more easily be retrenched in time of need.[20] Moreover he was firmly convinced that any retrenchment of luxury spending would be counteracted by a corresponding increase in some other kind of outlay; and here we begin to approach the crux of the argument.

Like a true Scot, Adam Smith was an outspoken advocate of the desirability of saving, or 'parsimony', and he accepted without qualification Hutcheson's doctrine that money not spent in one way would be spent in another. In characteristically forceful phrases he asserted that 'every prodigal appears to be a public enemy, and every frugal man a public benefactor' for 'capitals are increased by parsimony, and diminished by prodigality and misconduct' and 'wherever capital predominates, industry prevails'. In any society there are always spendthrifts, men dominated by the 'passion for present enjoyment'; but 'the profusion or imprudence of some, [is] always more than compensated by the frugality and good conduct of others'. What is the motive which prompts men to forgo current pleasure in order to accumulate funds for the employment of labour? In an eloquent sentence Smith replied: 'the principle which prompts to save, is the desire of bettering our condition, a desire which, though generally calm and dispassionate, comes with us from the womb, and never leaves us till we go into the grave.' So strong indeed is the operation of this principle – 'the uniform, constant, and uninterrupted effort of every man to better his condition' – that it is usually able to overcome even the extravagance and inefficiency of government. 'Like the unknown principle of animal life, it frequently restores health and vigour to the constitution, in spite, not only of the disease, but of the absurd prescriptions of the doctor.'[21]

One further argument is required, however, before we can call Smith an anti-Keynesian. Full employment is possible without luxury spending; saving is both natural and beneficial; but is there no possibility that the sums saved may lie idle in hoards? The only circumstance in which this could occur, according to Smith, was in a 'rude society', especially in times of violence and disorder, when fear of the plunderer or the arbitrary exactions of government might encourage hoarding. In all other situations, however,

> a man must be perfectly crazy who, where there is tolerable security, does not employ all the stock which he commands, whether it be his own or borrowed of other people. . . . Every individual is continually exerting himself to find out the most advantageous employment for whatever capital he can command. It is his own advantage, indeed, and not that of the society, which he has in view. But the study of his own advantage naturally, or rather necessarily, leads him to prefer that employment which is most advantageous to the society.[22]

In this passage Smith acknowledges the influence of non-economic factors, such as internal peace and the security of property, on the incentive to save. Here, too, we find one of his most penetrating contributions to the social sciences, the concept of a mechanism that coordinates the unintended consequences of individual decisions into an overall pattern of social action.

In Smith's writings this conception is indissolubly linked with the deistic idea of the 'harmony of interests'; but the fact that he occasionally used metaphorical language, referring for example to an 'invisible hand',[23] should not blind us to its importance. As Professor Viner has observed, by the time Smith published the *Wealth of Nations* he was sufficiently independent of theology to be able 'to find defects in the order of nature without casting reflections on the workmanship of its author', and although we cannot be sure about the secret mental processes by which he arrived at his conclusions, his 'argument for the existence of a natural harmony in the economic order . . . is, in form at least, built up by detailed inference from specific data and by examination of specific problems, and is not deduced from wide-sweeping generalizations concerning the universe in general'.[24]

Adam Smith was, of course, an optimist; yet he derived his optimism from a combination of broad learning and shrewd observation of contemporary society, especially the ebullient economy of Glasgow, in the midst of which he formulated his theories. If Keynes's theory was, as Schumpeter once remarked, 'depression economics',[25] Smith's theory was 'prosperity economics', for he brushed aside the possibility of unemployment, and concentrated on the problem of making the most effective use of available resources. Not that he entirely emancipated himself from the mercantilist (and Keynesian) preoccupation with the employment-generating effects of different kinds of expenditure, for he acknowledged that climatic variations, a decline in the nation's capital stock or the imposition of certain kinds of taxes, could lead to a fall in the demand for labour. But he evidently assumed that the expanding economy of his day would take up the slack, for he made no attempt to explain what happened to the displaced labourers. British capital resources were growing rapidly, Smith insisted; employment opportunities were abundant; and in one characteristic passage he mentioned the aftermath of the Seven Years' War (1756–63), when over 100,000 demobilized ex-servicemen were absorbed by the labour market, with no more than a temporary dislocation.[26]

Yet despite his optimistic view of the prospects for economic growth, Adam Smith was anxious to encourage the most efficient use of available resources, and to this end he stressed the need to divert investible funds from 'unproductive' to 'productive' employments. This distinction created considerable difficulties for his nineteenth century admirers, for whom the pecuniary logic of the business enterprise system rendered every kind of labour productive provided that it could command a price in the free market, whether it was the labour of the manufacturer, the domestic servant or the prostitute. Strangely enough, however, as a result of our current preoccupation with the problems of underdeveloped countries, the mid-twentieth century economist is able to grasp the significance of Smith's dichotomy more readily than either Keynes or the classical economists were able to.[27]

Obviously Smith had no intention of casting aspersions on the unproductive classes, for he included judges, teachers, the clergy and other worthy members of the community within this category. But the efforts of these persons merely enhanced the supply of services, whereas the productive labourers augmented the nation's stock of capital by producing durable commodities. Industry was limited by capital, and capital could be increased by savings. Savings were always spent, according to Smith; but they might be spent on the employment of either productive or unproductive workers, and the higher the proportion of productive to unproductive labourers, the higher the rate of economic growth. The present-day student of underdeveloped countries might rephrase Smith's message, without unduly distorting it, by saying that a transfer of resources from unproductive to productive employments would involve an expansion of the dynamic, industrious, high-productivity sector of the economy at the expense of the low-productivity sector, where idleness was common.

Those who endeavour to trace the connections between the ideas of economic writers and the circumstances of their times are sometimes inclined to attribute omniscience to their heroes. In the present instance, however, it is clear that Adam Smith failed to perceive some of the most important trends in the economy of his day. He was unaware of the incipient industrial revolution, and he underestimated the importance of technology – a defect that helps to explain his overemphasis on material products.[28] His concept of capital, drawn largely from the French Physiocrats, was not merely confused, it was primitive, for he regarded capital as a stockpile of food and implements accumulated *before* the process of production began and subsequently *advanced* to labourers in anticipation of the returns from the final output. On the other hand, he recognized the vital importance of capital in economic growth, and in this respect he was in accord with subsequent developments. By contrast, Smith's mercantilist predecessors had usually written as though an increase in the size and an improvement in the quality of the labour force were virtually the only means to economic expansion.

Even if Smith failed to foresee the future as plainly as some of his more uncritical admirers have supposed, his belief in the desirability of saving and productive investment was, nevertheless, based directly upon his observation of contemporary life. In the mid-eighteenth century there was no problem of mass unemployment – the involuntary idleness of full-time labourers; rather, the main employment problem arose from the under-utilization of both labour and investible funds, a situation which would nowadays be described as under-employment. There were many reasons for this state of affairs: the prevalence of casual labour, and of part-time employment in agriculture and household manufactures; seasonal disruptions caused by climatic variations and reinforced by poor transport facilities; and the large number of servants and retainers catering to the luxurious tastes of the idle rich. According to Professor T.S. Ashton, the foremost living authority on the eighteenth century economy, 'the normal condition of most domestic producers was one of under-employment. . . . Hence there existed at many points of the economy a pool of labour similar to that at the docks in our own day. More men and women were attached to each industry than could normally find full-time employment in it' and the three or four day working week was common, partly because the prevailing conditions engendered casual habits, and partly because the workers showed a strong preference for leisure over income.[29] The modern trend towards regular work and factory discipline which, as Karl Marx recognized, involved 'the conditioning of the workers', was only just beginning.

Most of Smith's predecessors had blamed the workers for this situation, which they attributed to the labourers' idle and dissolute habits, and certainly during the so-called Gin Age, in the first half of the century, when food prices were low and living conditions easy, the poor had ample opportunity to indulge their tastes for alcohol as well as leisure. By the mid-1750s, however, when Smith's leading ideas were formulated, both economic conditions and attitudes to labour were changing. Population growth, rising food prices and recurrent depressions – which may, indeed, mark the beginnings of modern cyclical unemployment – were gradually enforcing upon the workers some of that industriousness which generations of upper-class exhortation or denunciation had failed to induce.[30] Loyal son of the eighteenth century enlightenment that he was, Adam Smith considered that the main obstacles to economic progress lay not in the workers themselves, nor in the lack of investment opportunities, but in the mercantilist regulations which protected monopoly, drove an inordinate amount of capital into foreign trade and discouraged investors from switching their capital from less productive to more productive employments.

Smith was, however, essentially a pre-industrial economist, and he did not advocate the transfer of resources from agriculture to manufacturing. Indeed, he held that agriculture provided the largest amount of productive employment from a given investment of capital, and under the mercantile system as, in fact, ever since the fall of Rome, legislative interferences had unduly benefited the towns at the expense of the countryside. Yet his own argument can be turned against him, for he conceded that in agriculture there was little scope for the division of labour – the system under which a worker concentrates exclusively upon a single phase of the process of production – and he regarded the division of labour as the main cause of the growth in the skill, dexterity and inventiveness of labour, even admitting that this explained why 'the improvement of the productive powers of labour in this art [agriculture], does not always keep pace with their improvement in manufactures'.[31] Moreover, the occupational habits of the agricultural labourer who, like the country weaver, 'commonly saunters a little in turning his hand from one sort of employment to another', render him 'almost always slothful and lazy, and incapable of any vigorous application even on the most pressing occasions'. By contrast, the high wages of the artificers, even of soldiers, encourage industry 'which, like every other human quality, improves in proportion to the encouragement it receives' with the result, especially when piece rates are paid, that they endanger their health 'by excessive application to their peculiar species of work'.[32]

But although the urban artisan was far more productive than his rural counterpart, productivity was not everything, for Adam Smith anticipated some of the social and cultural dangers of industrialism. In a blistering indictment of the evils accompanying the division of labour he warned that the worker's dexterity was

> acquired at the expense of his intellectual, social, and martial virtues. ... The man whose whole life is spent in performing a few simple operations ... has no occasion to exert his understanding. ... He naturally loses, therefore, the habit of such exertion, and generally becomes as stupid and ignorant as it is possible for a human creature to become. The torpor of his mind renders him not only incapable of relishing or bearing a part in any rational conversation, but of conceiving any generous, noble, or tender sentiment, and consequently of forming any just judgement concerning many even of the ordinary duties of private life. Of the great and extensive interests of his country he is altogether incapable of judging.

With the common ploughman, however, the case is quite different. 'Though generally regarded as the pattern of stupidity and ignorance, [he] is seldom defective in this judgement and discretion.' Uncouth of speech and unaccustomed to social intercourse as he is, contact with a variety of objects widens his understanding. 'How much the lower ranks of people in the country are really superior to those of the town is well known to every man whom either business or curiosity has led to converse much with both.' Even in barbarous societies, every man 'is in some measure a statesman, and can form a tolerable judgement concerning the interest of the society and the conduct of those who govern it'.[33]

These passages reveal the author's personal prejudices, and perhaps those of his circle; but considered as a contribution to social or occupational psychology, they have a peculiarly modern ring. And they serve to remind us that Adam Smith's interests far transcended the limits of economics. He was a penetrating social commentator, whose writings foreshadowed the nineteenth century idea of class conflict, as well as the doctrine of the harmony of interest. Although the greatest intellectual achievement of the *Wealth of Nations* was to lay the foundations of modern economics by treating the economic aspect of life as an independent realm of discourse, nevertheless, political, social and moral issues were rarely far from Smith's thoughts. With his Scottish friends and colleagues, Hutcheson, Hume, Lord Kames, Adam Ferguson and John Millar, he was helping to chart the entire range of territory that is now partitioned out among the various social sciences. With the decline of Adam Smith's reputation as an economic theorist, which has accompanied the waning of classical economics of which he is the putative father, there has been a concomitant growth of interest in his sociology, especially as revealed in his first book, *The Theory of Moral Sentiments*. Accordingly, no account of the modern re-appraisal of Adam Smith's performance would be even approximately complete without some reference to the non-economic aspects of his work.

III

To call Adam Smith a sociologist may seem perverse, even uncomplimentary to one who is usually thought of as an economist! Yet this is no paradox, for while Smith made a mighty contribution to that nebulous historical movement, the rise of economic individualism, he was no mere individualist. We have already noted some of his references to contemporary labour conditions, which reveal his grasp of occupational psychology; but it is not generally recognized how persistently these psychological insights emphasized the influence of society upon individual conduct. The division of labour, for instance, was the result of man's 'propensity to truck, barter, and exchange', that is, his propensity to enter into economic relations with other members of society. Similarly, saving was prompted by man's desire to better his condition, and this reflected his need

> to be observed, to be attended to, to be taken notice of with sympathy, complacency, and approbation . . . it is the vanity, not the ease or the pleasure which interests us. . . . The rich man glories in his riches, because he feels that they naturally draw upon him the attention of the world, and that mankind are disposed to go along with him in all those agreeable emotions with which the advantages of his situation so readily inspire him . . . and he is fonder of his wealth, upon this account, than for all the other advantages it procures him. The poor man, on the contrary, is ashamed of his poverty. He feels that it either places him out of the sight of mankind, or, that if they take any notice of him, they have, however, scarce any fellow-feeling with the misery and distress which he suffers.[34]

Thus in at least two vital branches of economic activity, exchange and saving, Smith accounted for man's conduct by reference to his fellow men, rather than simply in terms of individual self-seeking; or, to use modern jargon, Smith's economic man seems to have been quite as much 'other-directed' as 'inner-directed'. Smith was not content with a purely mechanistic view of society, according to which individuals functioned as isolated, independent atoms; he was groping for a more organic approach, a truly *social* theory, and in his view of society, as Gladys Bryson has aptly remarked, 'there sometimes seem to be no individuals at all, so organic is the relation of person to person conceived to be'.[35]

In the light of these circumstances, only a blinkered specialist in the history of economic analysis would confine his attention to Smith's influence on the birth of an independent science of economics, and even he would be in serious danger of misunderstanding the subject by wrenching it from its context. Smith's conception of economic change, for example, was couched in the all-embracing form of 'stages of economic growth', a form that has recently become fashionable again, and it cannot be fully understood in isolation from this context. According to Smith's 'conjectural history' (as Dugald Stewart termed it) there were four major stages of economic and social life: hunting, pasturage, farming and commerce; and at each successive stage there were appropriate adjustments in the prevailing institutions, habits and psychological characteristics of the people, and concomitant variations in the accepted codes of behaviour and the ruling moral standards.[36] Smith regarded commercial society as the highest stage of civilization, not simply because it was the most advanced stage of economic growth, nor because he was a vulgar exponent of capitalist apologetics, but because it afforded the maximum scope for individual freedom. In a commercial society, men were brought into closer and more frequent contact with one another, and were thereby enabled to strengthen their social ties and develop a more refined sense of justice and probity; and after surveying the course of European history, Smith concluded that the progress of commerce 'gradually introduced order and good government, and with them the liberty and security of individuals'.[37]

Naturally we are not concerned with the accuracy of this interpretation, but with its bearing on Smith's conception of the social context of economic activity, and in order to elucidate this we must turn to the *Theory of Moral Sentiments*, wherein Smith disclosed his scale of values. In the vast critical literature on Smith's life and work a long-standing controversy has raged between those who have stressed its unity and those who have preferred to concentrate their admiring gaze on the *Wealth of Nations*, dismissing the *Theory of Moral Sentiments* as a kind of immature aberration. One of the by-products of the Keynesian re-interpretation of the history of economics has been a decline of interest in the theoretical aspects of Smith's economics, and a rehabilitation of his earlier volume.[38]

In the *Theory of Moral Sentiments* Smith turned his attention away from the 'supreme virtue' of benevolence, which Francis Hutcheson had made the keystone of his system, and concentrated instead upon the 'inferior virtues' of prudence, self-command and justice. Of these justice was the 'pillar' of society; it was more indispensable than benevolence, for 'society may subsist . . . without beneficence; but the prevalence of injustice must utterly destroy it'.[39] Adam Smith lived in an age when educated men laid special emphasis on moderation and good sense, and it is no surprise to find him insisting that true virtue consisted 'not in any one affection, but in the proper degree of all the affections'[40] – a desirable social equilibrium that was more likely to be achieved in a commercial society, where economic equilibrium is also attainable, than in any other. While rejecting Alexander Pope's identification of self-love with social love, Smith nevertheless acknowledged their interrelationship, believing that self-interest was not merely natural to man but also useful to society when directed into the proper channels. In a commercial society, habitual contact with his fellow men would curb the excesses of man's self-regarding instinct, for the virtue of prudence in the non-economic sphere of life had its counterpart in enlightened self-interest in the economic sphere. 'It is not from the benevolence of the butcher, the brewer, or the baker, that we expect our dinner,' he observed, in an oft-quoted passage, 'but from their regard to their own interest. We address ourselves, not to their humanity but to their self-love, and never talk to them of our own necessities but of their advantages.' And elsewhere he remarked, slyly, 'I have never known much good done by those who affected to trade for the public good. It is an affectation, indeed, not very common among merchants, and very few words need be employed in dissuading them from it.'[41]

At times Smith seems to have seriously overestimated the efficacy of 'the obvious and simple system of natural liberty' in economic affairs, from which basis he launched his devastating critique of mercantilist economic policy. Yet once we look below the surface of his polemical intent, we find that he was far from regarding commercial society as an ideal state of affairs. It is indeed ironic that his works were used as intellectual ammunition by nineteenth century merchants and manufacturers, for he singled out these groups for special condemnation. Unlike those who lived by rent and wages, whose interests coincided with the general welfare of society, those who lived by profit had 'generally an interest to deceive and even to oppress the public', and were not loath to take advantage of it. They complained bitterly about high wages, while concealing their own high profits; they combined against labour and introduced monopolies and similar conspiracies to raise prices, and Smith rarely missed an opportunity of exposing 'the sneaking arts of underling tradesmen' or 'the mean rapacity, the monopolizing spirit of merchants and manufacturers'.[42] Moreover, despite his belief in the harmonious interaction of individual interests in economic life, Smith directly, if unwittingly, laid the foundations of nineteenth century socialism by underlining the conflict between labour and capital. In a primitive society, which precedes the appropriation of land and the accumulation of capital, 'the whole produce of labour belongs to the labourer'; but in an advanced society the landlord and the capitalist demand their shares, which Smith pointedly called 'deductions' from the produce of labour. In these circumstances, he added, 'rent and profit eat up wages, and the two superior orders of people oppress the inferior one'. And as if this were not enough to fan the flames of social discontent, he stated explicitly that 'civil government, so far as it is instituted for the security of property, is in reality instituted for the defence of the rich against the poor, or of those who have some property against those who have none at all'.[43]

However, despite the serious shortcomings of commercial society, Smith considered that it was the best attainable state of affairs in an imperfect world, although he was 'constantly searching out the impact of specific institutional forms upon the human actor' in quest of 'an institutional scheme which would establish and enforce an identity of interests between the public and the private spheres' of life.[44] In economic affairs, Smith assumed (but without adducing proof), the free price mechanism would be more likely to divert individual energies into socially desirable channels than any form of government or private corporation activity; and in view of the inefficiency and corruption of eighteenth century administration his assumption seems well-founded. His virtual obsession with private saving and capital accumulation may have been one-sided and exaggerated; but it surely afforded a better solution for the contemporary problem of economic growth than any alternative programme of public policy.

Although he devoted more than half of the *Wealth of Nations* to his attack on mercantile regulations, Adam Smith was far from being a doctrinaire supporter of *laissez-faire*.[45] Nevertheless, to our sceptical modern eyes he sometimes appears to have been naive, indeed positively alarming, in his unwavering faith in the efficacy of self-interest. If the clergy, for instance, were to be more directly motivated by pecuniary gain, they would be more diligent in the performance of their duties; but in case this encouraged them to play upon the credulity and gullibility of their flocks, and thereby exert an unhealthy influence, he proposed to disestablish the church and permit such a degree of religious toleration that there would be perfect competition between two or three hundred small sects, none of which would be large enough 'to disturb the public tranquillity'.[46] Similarly in educational matters, Smith was inclined to favour competition, though he advocated compulsory education as a method of combating the debilitating social and intellectual consequences of the division of labour – and this is but one of many examples of his readiness to support government intervention when it seemed to be in the public interest. In the field of higher education, however, his faith in individual initiative was less qualified, and one wonders how the University Grants Committee (or the Robbins Committee) would react to his proposals. The contention that the dons in the 'best endowed universities . . . commonly teach very negligently and superficially', and that 'several of those learned societies have chosen to remain, for a long time, the sanctuaries in which exploded systems and obsolete prejudices found shelter and protection, after they had been hunted out of every other corner of the world' would doubtless be ascribed to provincial prejudice; and this suspicion would be confirmed by the claim that the other universities avoided these weaknesses because 'the teachers, depending upon their reputation for the greater part of their subsistence, were obliged to pay more attention to the current opinions of the world'. The committee would hardly be impressed by the familiar trade union argument (in this case attributed to Socrates) that those who teach wisdom ought themselves to be wise, and not sell their services for too paltry a sum; but the suggestion that students should select their own colleges and tutors, and that incentive payments should be introduced in order to promote rivalry and emulation among the teachers, would seem dangerously novel. And in view of recently published complaints about university lecturing, they would hardly be convinced by the assertion that students 'are generally inclined to pardon a great deal of incorrectness in the performance of [the teacher's] duty, and sometimes even to conceal from the public a good deal of gross negligence'.[47]

IV

It is a mark of the great thinker that each succeeding generation derives fresh insight from his ideas, and, as the notes to this essay reveal, Adam Smith's works still repeatedly attract the attention of scholars. He is, of course, as engaging a writer as he was a man, and while our own generation is beginning to value him more for his observations on society than for his economic theories, we must recognize that this is a comparatively recent shift of emphasis. He was the most influential economist of the stage of capitalist development that is termed the domestic system, but while he helped to lay the foundations of modern economics he was, at the same time, 'the last writer of the pre-Smithian age of economics'.[48] Admittedly the reception of his economic ideas has been unduly influenced by the rise and fall of economic liberalism; but this movement was the main medium of his influence on thought and policy, for the Declaration of Independence and the subsequent loss of the American colonies enormously strengthened the force of his plea for economic freedom. At the end of his life he was full of honours. On one occasion before a distinguished gathering, William Pitt declared, 'we will stand till you are first seated, for we are all your scholars'[49]; and in 1797 Pulteney correctly forecast that Smith 'would persuade the present generation and govern the next'.[50] Like Karl Marx, however, Adam Smith needs to be protected from his disciples, and now that the *Wealth of Nations* is no longer regarded as a bible by the existing leaders of economic thought we can remove the accumulated layers of liberal varnish and restore him to his rightful place among the intellectual masters.

NOTES

*Originally delivered as a public lecture to a non-specialist audience at the University of Nottingham in 1961.

1 Keynes, *General Theory*, p.32.
2 ibid., ch.23, especially p.335.
3 See, for example *Employment Policy* (HMSO, 1944) Cmd. 6527. Also *National and International Measures for Full Employment* (United Nations, New York, December 1949).
4 In his inaugural lecture, *The Adam Smith Tradition* (1950), H.M. Robertson recalls how 'Mr Keynes sailed into me' after a paper delivered in Cambridge in 1927, 'accusing me, indeed, of foolhardiness, if not of something almost akin to poor taste, because in Marshall's own university, I had disparaged some of Marshall's leading ideas and commended the heretic Hobson in the same breath . . . . All the same, when I consider the almost revolutionary influence of Keynes after 1936 . . . I confess I find a certain piquancy in his later *volte face* upon Marshall and Hobson' (pp.6, 8). (Alfred Marshall was the fount of Cambridge economics, and John A. Hobson a neglected, if not to say derided, outsider until Keynes rehabilitated him in the *General Theory*).
5 See, for example, D.W. Vickers, *Studies in the Theory of Money, 1690–1776* (1959) and G.L.S. Tucker, *Progress and Profits in British Economic Thought, 1650–1850,* (1960).
6 Dugald Stewart's Preface to Adam Smith's *Essays on Philosophical Subjects* (London, 1795), p.xvi.
7 Adam Smith, *The Theory of Moral Sentiments* (London, 1797), ii. pt. vi, sect.ii, ch.3, p.119. (Hereafter referred to as TMS).
8 Joseph Schumpeter, *History of Economics Analysis*, ed. E.B. Schumpeter (1954), pp.184, 185–6.
9 There are three main biographical sources: John Rae, *Life of Adam Smith*, (1895); W.R. Scott, *Adam Smith as Student and Professor* (1937); and C.R. Fay, *Adam Smith and the Scotland of his Day* (1956).
10 Scott, op. cit., p.25.
11 Adam Smith to William Smith, 24 August 1740, ibid, p.232.
12 These anecdotes are recounted by C.R. Fay, op. cit., pp.34, 79.
13 See Adam Smith's *Lectures on Justice, Police, Revenue and Arms*, ed. E. Cannan (1896); and W.R. Scott, op. cit., pp.322–56.
14 On the influence of Hutcheson's economics see the two recent articles by W.L. Taylor, 'Eighteenth Century Scottish Political Economy. The Impact on Adam Smith and his Work of his Association with Francis Hutcheson and David Hume', *South African Journal of Economics* xxiv (1956), pp.261–76; also H.M. Robertson and W.L. Taylor, 'Adam Smith's Approach to the Theory of Value', *Economic Journal* lxxii (1957), pp. 181–98.
15 Hutcheson, *Remarks Upon the Fable of the Bees* (Glasgow, 1750), p.65. Originally published in the *Dublin Journal*, February 1727.
16 Hutcheson, *A System of Moral Philosophy* (London, 1755), II. pp.320–1.
17 This question is fully discussed in Henry J. Bitterman. 'Adam Smith's Empiricism and the Law of Nature', *Journal of Political Economy* xlviii (1940), p.708 ff.
18 David Hume, *Writings on Economics*, ed. E. Rotwein (1955), p.30. Also ibid, p.19 ff. and editor's introduction p.xci ff.

19 *TMS*, ii. pt. vii, sect. ii, ch.4, pp.319, 318.
20 *The Wealth of Nations*, ed. Cannan (1904), i. pp.328–30; ii. pp.371–2, 357. (Hereafter referred to as *W. of N.*). On the definition of luxury see Schumpeter op. cit., p.324, fn.3.
21 *W. of N.*, i. pp.323, 320, 325. By contrast, the 'passion for present enjoyment', though sometimes violent and difficult to restrain is, according to Smith, 'only momentary and occasional'. Ibid., i. p.323.
22 Ibid., i. pp.267, 419.
23 Ibid., i. p.421.
24 Jacob Viner, 'Adam Smith and Laissez Faire' in *Adam Smith 1776–1926*, (1928), pp.126, 130. This has been reprinted in Viner's collected essays, *The Long View and the Short* (1958). For a similar judgement see Charles Gide and Charles Rist, *A History of Economic Doctrines* (1948), p.102.
25 By this Schumpeter meant not only that Keynes's theory was formulated in a time of depression, but also that it was less applicable to conditions of prosperity because it contained a bias in favour of inflationary policies. In fact the Keynesian *analysis* as such is equally applicable to both kinds of situation, whereas Smith's analysis is one sided in its failure to deal with the possibility of excessive saving.
26 *W. of N.*, i. pp.87–8, 74–5, 434; ii. p.350. Like the Ricardian economists in the early nineteenth century, Smith took the long-term view according to which disruptions of the economic process merely seemed transitory.
27 For useful recent studies of this aspect see V.W. Bladen, 'Adam Smith on Productive and Unproductive Labour: A Theory of Full Development', *Canadian Journal of Economics and Political Science* xxvi (1960), pp.625–30; J.J. Spengler, 'Adam Smith's Theory of Economic Growth', *The Southern Economic Journal* xxv (1959), pp.397–415 and xxvi (1959), pp.1–12; S. Moos, 'Is Adam Smith out of Date', *Oxford Economic Papers*, iii (1951), pp.187–201, who considers this question from the point of view of national income analysis.
28 Other eighteenth century writers paid more attention to these matters. See, for example E.A.J. Johnson, *Predecessors of Adam Smith, The Growth of British Economic Thought* (1937) especially ch.XIII.
29 T.S. Ashton, *An Economic History of England: The 18th Century*, (1955), ch.vii 'Labour', especially. p.203.
30 See my article, 'Changing Attitudes to Labour in the Mid-Eighteenth Century', *Economic History Review* 2nd. Series, xi (1958), pp.35–51, this volume, pp.63–84.
31 *W. of N.*, i. pp.7, 8; ii. pp.177 ff. On Smith's attitude to industrialization see R. Koebner, 'Adam Smith and the Industrial Revolution', *Economic History Review* 2nd Series., xi (1959), pp.381–91.
32 *W. of N.*, i. pp.10, 83–4.
33 *W. of N.*, ii. pp.267–8; i. pp.128–9.
34 *TMS*, i, pt. l, sect. iii, ch.2, p.122.
35 Gladys Bryson, *Man and Society, The Scottish Inquiry of the 18th Century* (1945), p.160. Cf. Albion W. Small, *Adam Smith and Modern Sociology* (1907), p.50. In this, as in many other respects, there is a marked difference between Smith and Jeremy Bentham, whose view of society was more radical and individualistic, more rational and mechanistic.
36 *Lectures on Justice, Police, Revenue and Arms*, op. cit., pp.14 ff., 107 ff., 155–6, 253 ff. Cf. *TMS*, ii, pt. v, ch.2, especially pp.30 ff.
37 *W. of N.*, i. p.383. Cf. Joseph Cropsey, *Polity and Economy, An Interpretation of the Principles of Adam Smith* (The Hague, 1957), p.x, where it is said that 'Smith advocated capitalism because it makes freedom possible – not because it *is* freedom'.

38 The following recent studies are especially valuable in this connection: Cropsey, *op. cit.*; A.L. Macfie, 'Adam Smith's *Moral Sentiments* as Foundation for his *Wealth of Nations*', *Oxford Economic Papers* xi (1959), pp.209–28; and A.L. Macfie, 'Adam Smith's Theory of Moral Sentiments', *Scottish Journal of Political Economy* viii (1960), pp.12–27.

39 *TMS*, i, pt. ii, sect. ii, ch.2., p.215.

40 ibid., ii, pt. vii, sect. ii, ch.3, p.300. 'A complete insensibility ... to vice and virtue', was for Smith, 'the vilest and most abject of all states' ibid., pt. iii, ch.2, p.298.

41 *W. of N..*, i. pp.16, 421.

42 *W. of N.*, i. pp.250, 69, 457–8.

43 ibid., p.66; ii. pp.67, 207.

44 Nathan Rosenberg, 'Some Institutional Aspects of the Wealth of Nations', *The Journal of Political Economy* lxviii (1960), pp.563, 567.

45 Viner, *loc cit.*

46 *W. of N.*, ii. p.278. Cf. pp.276–7. This proposal envisages the kind of situation that actually obtained in the American colonies where it was recognized that a 'multiplicity of sects' was a safeguard of religious rights. Cf. Daniel J. Boorstin, *The Americans; The Colonial Experience* (1958), p.180.

47 *W. of N.*, ii. p.260; i. p.134; ii. pp.250–1, 253.

48 Sir Alexander Gray, *Adam Smith* (Historical Association, London, 1948), p.20.

49 Rae, op. cit., p.405.

50 Quoted by J. Steven Watson, *The Reign of George III 1760–1815* (1960), p.329.

8

ADAM SMITH AND THE
MERCANTILE SYSTEM[1]

I

It has often been remarked that a great author has something fresh and significant to offer each succeeding generation of readers, and in Adam Smith's case this truism is especially apt. Quite apart from the multitude of ideologists and propagandists who have cited him in support of their polemical campaigns, innumerable scholars have sought to comprehend the meaning of his writings and to assess their significance for Smith's own and subsequent epochs. In recent decades there has been a considerable debate about the interrelationships between the various component elements in Smith's works, especially his conception of scientific method, his moral philosophy, his view of the process of historical change and his contributions to economic analysis.[2] The present essay is designed to place his treatment of economic policy in this broader intellectual context, by reconsidering his account of the mercantile system in relation to his theory of history and politics and his view of long-run socio-economic development.

This is, admittedly, a bold undertaking, for the range and variety of relevant issues is far too large to be treated adequately in a single essay. Nevertheless there are some compensations, for this topic does not lend itself to definitive treatment, since certain features of Smith's style and mode of presentation make it virtually impossible to determine the precise meaning and significance of his ideas. Among these is the conspicuous lack of that species of small-mindedness which makes a virtue of consistency – although Jacob Viner no doubt exaggerated when he remarked of Smith's *magnum opus* that 'traces of every conceivable sort of doctrine can be found in that most catholic book, and an economist must have peculiar theories indeed who cannot quote from *The Wealth of Nations*, to support his special purposes[3].' But in addition to the specific problems of interpreting that work, there is also the problem of relating *The Wealth of Nations* to the *Theory of Moral Sentiments*, a task which no serious student of Smith's economic ideas and policy can now avoid. Consequently there is added force in Viner's criticism that while 'the system of natural liberty' is much in evidence among Smith's interpreters, 'that natural harmony which should also result is strikingly lacking' (ibid., p.216).

II

Despite its prominence in *The Wealth of Nations*, Smith's attack on the 'Mercantile System' has too often been considered only *en passant*, possibly because his admirers have been embarrassed by its decidedly polemical tone and orientation. Yet this phase of Smith's work exemplifies the subtle combination of analysis, historical insight and policy recommendations which is to be found throughout his writings, and it also illustrates the difficulties involved in disentangling these closely interwoven strands of his thought. Although his treatment of the mercantile system has been correctly characterized as 'an emphatic piece of free trade propaganda',[4] it is also much more than this. As is well known, Smith condemned mercantilist regulations because they led to a serious mis-allocation of scarce resources and consequently inhibited economic growth; more fundamentally, such policies conflicted with 'the obvious and simple system of natural liberty', an ideal which Smith consistently advocated. This ideal was expressed in his unpublished Edinburgh lectures of the late 1740s and early 1750s[5] and was anticipated by his 'never-to-be-forgotten teacher', Frances Hutcheson, and his lifelong friend, David Hume, who published an outspoken critique of mercantilist policies more than twenty years before *The Wealth of Nations* appeared in print. Nor did Smith's central allegiance weaken in later life, despite his readiness to admit exceptions to the general principle of governmental non-interference in economic and social affairs. On the contrary, successive editions of *The Wealth of Nations* reveal Smith's determination to reinforce his anti-mercantilist position. Even in the first edition the seven chapters of Book IV devoted to the mercantile system occupied nearly a quarter of the whole work, while in the enlarged third edition he added a further chapter and several additional paragraphs. These additions contain few, if any, novel arguments; but they include much new factual material on such matters as duties, bounties and drawbacks which is probably a by-product of Smith's experience as Commissioner of Customs, a post he assumed in 1778.[6] Also noteworthy is the intensification of his attack on trading companies in the third edition, which contains a lengthy new section in Book V, chapter I, entitled 'Of the Expenses of the Sovereign or Commonwealth'. Smith described this as 'a short but, I flatter myself, a complete history of all the trading companies in Great Britain'.[7]

Smith employed the term 'mercantile system' broadly, applying it both to economic doctrines and to policy practices, though he was primarily concerned with the latter. In commenting on economic ideas he occasionally mentioned the best English writers who, he said, 'were apt to forget their own principles in the course of their reasonings and fall into confusion'; but he was far more interested in the beliefs of practical men than in intellectual achievements as such. Indeed, he maintained that self-interested merchants and manufacturers had been the 'principal architects' of the mercantile system.[8] His preoccupation with policy practice – rather than simply policy recommendations – followed directly from his definition of political economy as 'a branch of the science of a statesman or legislator'. Of 'the two different systems of political economy' which had been devised to enrich the people, namely, the mercantile system (or 'system of commerce') and the 'agricultural system', the former was the more 'modern', and it was 'best understood in our own country and our own times' (*Wealth of Nations*, IV, 2). As will be seen later, this reference to the national and temporal context is of special interest in any study of the relationship between Smith's view of economic policy and his conception of long-run socio-economic development, since it illustrates his practice of combining the analytical and historical dimensions of a given problem. He treated the mercantile system on two distinct, but interrelated levels: in terms of his atemporal ideal system of natural liberty, and by reference to the actual past and current practices of various European nations. This two-dimensional approach has been largely overlooked, or at least ignored, by many historians of economics, who have been concerned with the analytical aspects of *The Wealth of Nations*, such as the theories of value and distribution, the price mechanism and the allocation of resources. As a result they have focused their attention on the first two Books, which contain 'the central part of Smith's work as a theoretical economist',[9] while neglecting the remainder of the volume – some of which is, admittedly, tedious and long-winded. This preoccupation has encouraged the habit of viewing Smith's attack on the mercantile system simply and solely as an analysis of impediments to the smooth functioning of the competitive market economy, rather than an integral part of a larger system of moral, socio-philosophical, historical and political ideas. Yet Smith's profound impact on his own and subsequent generations was not merely due to his analytical ability. It was mainly attributable to his exceptional skill in combining analysis with empirical data, with historical examples, and with direct and incisive comments on the conditions and tendencies of his own times. In his treatment of the mercantile system the combined force of these disparate elements is well nigh irresistible; and they are so exquisitely interwoven that it is extraordinarily difficult to disentangle them for the purposes of historical reappraisal.

In recent years there has been a discernible shift of scholarly interest away from Smith's economic analysis towards his sociological and historical ideas, and it is now especially appropriate to re-examine his attack on the mercantile system in the light of his conception of the 'natural history of society'. It has long been recognized that Smith's *Lectures* embodied a theory of socio-economic development expressed in terms of four 'stages': hunting, pasturage, agriculture and commerce, each of which is based on a particular 'mode of subsistence'.[10] The discovery of a new set of *Lectures* has made it clear that this 'four-stage' theory occupied a more prominent place in Smith's mind than had formerly been supposed – so much so, that it has been claimed that the theory should now be recognized as 'the basic conceptual framework within which the major part of Smith's argument is set'.[11]

It is, of course, too early to make a considered assessment of this contention. Yet it is already apparent that the four-stage framework provides a convenient starting-point for a reappraisal of Smith's treatment of the mercantile system. For according to this theory the prevailing mode of subsistence in any society not only influences the predominant pattern of economic activity, but also the entire range of social life, including ideas and institutions of property and government, the state of manners and morals, the legal system and the division of labour. While Smith did not adopt a rigidly deterministic view of the process of change, acknowledging 'the complex interrelationships of economic, military, political, religious, moral and legal factors',[12] he seems to have regarded the economic factor as the most fundamental. However, as in Karl Marx's case, the relationship between the economic sub-structure and the cultural and institutional super-structure is by no means clear-cut.

Curiously enough, despite his unmistakable hostility to the mercantile system and his deep-seated suspicions of the activities and intentions of merchants, Smith regarded the commercial stage as the highest, most civilized form of society, and portrayed its beneficial influence on European development in glowing terms:

> commerce and manufactures gradually introduced order and good government, and with them, the liberty and security of individuals, among the inhabitants of the country, who had before lived almost in a continual state of war with their neighbours, and of servile dependency upon their superiors. This, though it has been the least observed, is by far the most important of their effects.[13]

As Joseph Cropsey has shown, Smith regarded commerce and civilization as inseparable, in the sense that:

> commerce generates freedom and civilization, and at the same time free institutions are indispensable to the preservation of commerce. If the advantages of commerce can be sufficiently impressed upon the general mind, freedom and civilization will automatically follow in its train, and mankind will perhaps be disposed to defend civilization, not necessarily out of love for freedom but out of love for commerce and gain.[14]

At first sight, these passages may suggest that Smith's attack on the mercantile system was utterly inconsistent if that system was, in fact, merely a necessary concomitant of the highest, most civilized stage of social development. Moreover, if the commercial society was also 'natural', in the sense of being inevitable, there was surely no point in fulminating against it.

There is, in fact, some justification for both these contentions. Yet it would be presumptious to suppose that a writer of Smith's stature could be dismissed so lightly. His critique of mercantilism was not merely the crude polemic it is sometimes taken to be; it was more sophisticated than this, and it is consistent with his general view of history, which is itself quite complex. For present purposes, then, the central question is: what was Smith's precise conception of the relationship between the growth of commerce and the emergence of the 'mercantile system'? Before confronting this problem directly it is necessary to consider the meaning of certain key terms in his writing and to comment on the question of his consistency and his use of historical data.

Smith obviously viewed mercantilist regulations as a perversion of the ideal of natural liberty, a state of affairs most nearly attainable in the commercial stage of development. But his account of the 'natural' progress of society through successive stages was neither clear nor detailed enough to serve as a basis for confident assertions about the inevitability or persistence of the mercantile system or the political power basis on which it rested. Despite elements of ambiguity in his semantic practice, Smith did not use the term 'natural' as equivalent to 'inevitable'. Indeed, Book III of *The Wealth of Nations*, which treats 'Of the Different Progress of Opulence in Different Nations', is specifically designed to show how, in the unfolding of European history, the 'natural' course of events has repeatedly been perverted or checked by human interference.[15] And if the mercantile system is neither inevitable nor irresistible it may succumb to a powerful polemical assault. Smith himself maintained that theories of political economy 'have had considerable influence, not only upon the opinions of men of learning, but upon the public conduct of princes and sovereign states' (*Wealth of Nations* I, lix). Although the prevailing theories and practices of government fell far short of his ideal – which he realized was unattainable in practice (see *infra*, pp.144–5) – he certainly hoped that his *magnum opus* would contribute to the reform of present discontents.

With regard to the inconsistencies in Smith's writings, Professor Macfie has reminded us that 'consistency was never the central aim or virtue of eighteenth century writers, especially of the Scottish sociological school. It certainly was not then the Ark of the Covenant that it is for our analysis-ridden age' (op. cit., p.126). Yet we need not go as far as Viner, who remarked that 'when there was a sharp conflict between his generalization and his data, [Smith] usually abandoned his generalization'.[16] Although he was sensitive to the problem of applying *general* principles to *particular* circumstances of time and place, he did not so readily discard his principles as Viner maintains.[17] In discussing the role of government, for example, he certainly recognized numerous exceptions to the general principle of *laissez-faire*, but without significantly diminishing the impact of his plea for economic freedom.

There is, unfortunately, no general rule or principle by which to explain precisely when and why Smith was prepared to admit particular exceptions to his general principles. A twentieth-century professional historian, trained to respect the evidence, may be tempted to assume that the exceptions were determined by an examination of the relevant facts; but this would be to completely misunderstand the conception of history familiar to Smith and his Scottish contemporaries. This conception is what is nowadays known as 'hypothetical' or 'conjectural' history, which is not designed as an accurate account of the historical past, but is intended to reveal the orderly unfolding of the process of change and, more often than not, also to point a moral.[18] As J.M. Clark observed many years ago, Smith's account of socio-economic development contains 'the germs of a genetic treatment', but 'they are tributary and subordinate to the system of natural liberty'.[19] His historical passages are frequently abstract and simplified in content, for they were more often designed as support for a preconceived theory than as a source of data on which to base inductive generalizations. Nevertheless Smith's use of history must be taken seriously for, unlike some of his contemporaries, he frequently cited particular facts and events, and employed this kind of material very effectively in his critique of the mercantile system. It is therefore appropriate to review this part of his work in some detail before considering its relationship to his generalized conception of the commercial stage of development.

III

As already noted, Smith recognized that a state of society 'where things were left to follow their natural course, where there was perfect liberty', was an unattainable ideal. 'The policy of Europe', he complained, 'nowhere leaves things at perfect liberty'; and even in commercial affairs, to expect 'that the freedom of trade should ever be entirely restored in Great Britain is as absurd as to expect that an Oceana or Utopia should ever be fully established in it'.[20] Civil government was a necessary evil, an imperfect remedy for the deficiencies of human wisdom and virtue, and its imperfections stemmed directly from its failure to 'sufficiently guard against the mischiefs which human wickedness gives occasion to'.[21] Like Locke and Hobbes, Smith took it for granted that government would normally be dominated by men of property and conducted in their interest. 'All for ourselves and nothing for other people', he remarked, 'seems, in every age of the world, to have been the vile maxim of the masters of mankind.'[22] Yet despite occasional outbursts of this kind he was essentially a moderate reformer. 'No government is quite perfect, but it is better to submit to some inconveniences than make attempts against it.'[23] Indeed, he specifically warned against the 'spirit of system' which leads men to embark upon far-reaching schemes of constitutional reconstruction which would entail alteration 'in some of its most essential parts that system of government under which the subjects of a great empire have enjoyed, perhaps, peace, security, and even glory, during the course of several centuries together' (*Theory of Moral Sentiments* VI, ii, 2. 15).

It is by no means clear from Smith's account which section of the propertied classes would 'naturally' have the upper hand in a commercial society, or which form of government would 'naturally' prevail. At first sight the answer seems obvious enough. In a commercial society every man 'lives by exchanging, or becomes in some measure a merchant', a state of affairs approximated in Holland, where almost every citizen is a 'man of business', or is engaged in 'some sort of trade'.[24] Such a community would, presumably, be governed by merchants or businessmen whose viewpoint should be representative of the community as a whole; and in fact Smith praised the 'orderly, vigilant and parsimonious administration' of Amsterdam which, however, he described as an aristocracy.[25] Nevertheless, despite these observations, he was utterly opposed to the notion that society should be governed by merchants. He complained bitterly of 'the mean rapacity, the monopolizing spirit of merchants and manufacturers, who neither are, nor ought to be, the rulers of mankind', and described merchants as 'an order of men whose interest is never the same with that of the public, who have generally an interest to deceive and even to oppress the public, and who accordingly have, upon many occasions, both deceived and oppressed it' (*Wealth of Nations* IV, iii, c.9; I, xi, p.10). Yet the situation would not be entirely satisfactory under a government dominated by landed proprietors, even though their interests were 'strictly and inseparably connected with the general interest of the society'. Although they 'never can mislead' the public into promoting 'the interest of their own particular order', they were too often unable to recognize that interest. Moreover, the 'indolence, which is the natural effect of the ease and security of their situation, renders them too often, not only ignorant, but incapable of that application of mind which is necessary in order to forsee and understand the consequences of any public regulation'.[26]

The only social group in which Smith displayed any confidence whatever was the so-called 'natural aristocracy', who were elsewhere described as men 'educated in the middle and inferior ranks of life, who have been carried forward by their own industry and abilities' into the highest offices 'in all governments . . . even in monarchies' (*Wealth of Nations* IV, vii, c.74; *Theory of Moral Sentiments* I, iii, 2. 5). However, this was an amorphous and somewhat ill-fated category, and for want of a better alternative Smith seemed to be more concerned, to ensure a balance of power between the various 'orders' of society – the sovereign, nobility, landed gentry, merchants and manufacturers, clergy, and labouring poor – than to advocate rule by any particular order. He recognized that statesmen, like other human beings, were necessarily imperfect, but considered that as such imperfections were unavoidable they were more tolerable than the evils wrought by merchants or any other vested interest group.[27] Generally speaking, Smith implied that historical processes had generated a balanced constitutional position in England, and that the mercantile classes represented both a source and a focus of pressure within the system, especially through the House of Commons.

Nevertheless, to the modern student of social processes and pressure group politics Smith's analysis is inadequate for it does not explain why the mercantile classes are more effective politically in some respects and contexts than in others. For example, while recognizing the primacy of national interests in all systems of political economy, and the special importance of national animosities in the growth of mercantilist regulations, he did not always clearly specify the relationship between national and sectional interests behind legislation.[28]

IV

The precise nature of Smith's attack on the mercantile system can be seen more clearly against the background of his general ideas on society and government. As Britain approximated more closely to his ideal of natural liberty than any other country, his criticisms of British economic policy were a good deal less severe than some of his more rhetorical passages might lead us to expect. Indeed they directly conflicted with Smith's own description of *The Wealth of Nations* as 'a very violent attack . . . upon the whole commercial system of Great Britain',[29] especially when his much more severe indictment of the policies of other European powers is taken into account. 'In Britain', Smith declared, 'there is a happy mixture of all the different forms of government properly restrained, and a perfect security to liberty and property . . . the nation is quite secure in the management of the public revenue, and in this manner a rational system of liberty has been introduced.'[30]

Admittedly the nation had suffered from the 'profusion of government which had retarded her natural progress'. Yet despite this, and many other setbacks, such as the fire and plague of London, the disorders of the revolution, two rebellions and a series of wars, the century or so since the restoration had been 'the happiest and most fortunate period in our history' (*Wealth of Nations* II, iii, 35). Britain's economic policy was undoubtedly bad, but its deficiencies were more than 'counter-balanced by the general liberty and security of the people', whereas at the opposite end of the scale, the civil and ecclesiastical governments of Spain and Portugal were so pernicious as to 'perpetuate their present state of poverty, even though their regulations of commerce were as wise as the greater part of them are absurd and foolish'.[31] English law, Smith maintained, was more favourable to the interests of commerce and manufactures than that of any country of Europe, 'Holland itself not excepted'.[32] Moreover even agriculture, which generally suffered under the mercantile system, was in England favoured not only indirectly, but also 'by several direct encouragements' which, though fundamentally illusory, demonstrated the legislature's 'good intention' and produced the important result that 'the yeomanry of England are rendered as secure, as independent and as respectable as law can make them'. Indeed, 'those laws and customs so favourable to the yeomanry, have perhaps contributed more to the present grandeur of England than all their boasted regulations of commerce taken together' (*Wealth of Nations* III, iv, 20; III, ii, 14). In France, by contrast, there was no legal encouragement to agriculture. The prevalence of metayage, short leases and the taille combined to produce a situation in which cultivation and improvement were markedly inferior to English standards (III, ii, 13, 18–20; III, iv, 21).

Smith fully appreciated the interdependence of commerce, manufactures and agriculture, and was especially conscious of the effects of bad taxes on output and incentives. Here, too, he was very critical of French practice. The personal taille was especially absurd and destructive since it constituted a tax on profits; the cruel, oppressive and discriminatory assessment of the corvée constituted 'one of the principal instruments of tyranny' in the hands of local administrators; and after describing the farming of taxes on salt and tobacco, which had annually resulted in several hundred people being sent to the galleys, and a considerable number to the gibbet, he concluded that these levies could be approved only by 'those who consider the blood of the people nothing in comparison with the revenue of the prince' (*Wealth of Nations* V, ii, k, 75). Here, too, the contrast between Britain and France was striking. But while the French were 'much more oppressed by taxes than the people of Great Britain', they fared better than the citizens of other countries, for they enjoyed 'the mildest and most indulgent government' of any great empire in Europe after that of Great Britain. We suffered less than most other states from the inconveniences of taxes on consumable commodities; and on the whole:

> Our present system of taxation . . . has hitherto given so little embar-
> rassment to industry that, during the course of even the most expensive
> wars, the frugality and good conduct of individuals seem to have been
> able, by saving and accumulation, to repair all the breaches which the
> waste and extravagance of government had made in the general capital
> of society.[33]

A similar emphasis is apparent in Smith's comments on Britain's colonial policy as in his discussion of domestic affairs. Although her treatment of the colonial trade had been

> dictated by the same mercantile spirit as that of other nations, it
> has, however, upon the whole, been less illiberal and oppressive
> than that of any of them . . . [indeed] the government of the English
> colonies is perhaps the only one which, since the world began,

147

could give perfect security to the inhabitants of so very distant a province.

(*Wealth of Nations* IV, vii, b, 50, 52)

There was, of course, a marked contrast 'between the genius of the British constitution which protects and governs North America, and that of the mercantile company which oppresses and domineers in the East Indies', for the latter was a prime example of that species of monopoly which 'seems to be the sole engine of the mercantile system' (*Wealth of Nations* I, viii, 26; IV, vii, c, 89). England's North American policy was better than that of any other European power, though only somewhat less illiberal and oppressive than the rest, and in his attitude to this area we encounter one of the difficulties of interpreting Smith's meaning. For despite the vigour of his polemics and his powerful analytical demonstration of the distortions of the allocation of resources resulting from our colonial policy, he made the important concession that 'the natural good effects of the colony trade, however, more than counterbalance to Great Britain the bad effects of the monopoly, so that, monopoly and all together, that trade, even as it is carried on at present, is not only advantageous, but greatly advantageous'.[34]

The grounds for this judgement were several. Despite some restraints, there was freedom to export, duty free, almost all kinds of products of domestic industry to almost any foreign country; there was also freedom of internal transport within Britain; but 'above all', there was

> that equal and impartial administration of justice which renders the rights of the meanest British subject respectable to the greatest, and which, by securing to every man the fruits of his own industry, gives the greatest and most effectual encouragement to every sort of industry.
>
> (*Wealth of Nations* IV, vii, c, 54)

After a lengthy analysis of the disadvantages of the monopoly of colonial trade, Smith concluded that owing to the heavy outlay on defence and the low level of taxation paid by the colonists, 'under the present system of management ... Great Britain derives nothing but loss from the dominion which she assumes over her colonies'. The British colonists, however, enjoyed far greater advantages than the subjects of other colonial regimes. Admittedly, their interests were sacrificed to those of British merchants, but not consistently so; and although they were prevented from 'employing their stock and industry in the way that they judge most advantageous to themselves ... [which was] a manifest violation of the most sacred rights of mankind', in practice such prohibitions had 'not hitherto been very hurtful to the colonies'. Indeed, owing to the 'plenty of good land, and liberty to manage their own affairs their own way ... there are no colonies of which the progress has been more rapid than that of the English in North America' (*Wealth of Nations* IV, vii, b, 15). By contrast, the ecclesiastical governments of France, Spain and Portugal were extremely oppressive to their colonies, especially the last two, on whose cruel, violent and arbitrary policies Smith dilated at some length, while he accused the Dutch of governing by means of an exclusive monopoly, with the inevitable restrictive consequences (*Wealth of Nations* IV, vii, b, 12).

V

This abbreviated survey of Smith's account of the mercantile system reveals his ability to combine economic principles with historical examples; it also shows that the system is far less monolithic and harmful in practice than might have been presumed on theoretical grounds alone. Yet at the same time, Smith's awareness of the national variants of the mercantile system makes it correspondingly more difficult to assess the precise relationship of the system to his broader conception of the commercial stage of development. This is largely because Smith, unlike some nineteenth century German economists and historians, did not visualize his 'stages' of development in a narrow, deterministic fashion. The mercantile system obviously represented a perversion or distortion of the ideal of natural liberty, which is most nearly attainable in a fully commercial society. But are we to infer that all the European powers whose policies Smith condemned had reached the commercial stage; or should that designation be reserved for Britain and Holland? He certainly recognized that any given nation's laws and institutions would normally lag behind its economic development,[35] hence it may be assumed that the more illiberal, authoritarian and oppressive features of the French, Spanish and Portugese régimes merely reflected their failure to cast off these inherited characteristics. But what determines how closely any given commercial society will in practice approach the ideal of natural liberty? Admittedly all fall short; but, to coin a phrase, some fall shorter than others. How far does Smith's account enable us to explain their respective positions both now and in the future?

The task of answering these questions is complicated by the fact that Smith was enough of a historian to be wary of making firm forecasts, and his writings contain a number of statements from which partially contradictory prognostications can be inferred. Whatever doubts there may be concerning the inevitability of successive stages of development, there is no reason to doubt his fundamentally optimistic belief in progress.[36] In the earlier forms of society, Smith maintained, oppressive and unjust government was almost inevitable; whereas justice and probity were, to him, such central features of the value system of a commercial society, where they were reinforced by regular face-to-face contacts in market situations, that it is tempting to suggest that these virtues will necessarily permeate government circles and eventually influence the nation's laws and economic policies. Yet Smith would probably have objected to any such simplistic extrapolation of individual behavioural characteristics from the micro- to the macro-sociological level. While at one point he spoke of the 'fated dissolution that awaits every state and constitution whatever',[37] there is no reason to suppose that this necessarily implied a prospective withering away of mercantilistic regulations. Indeed, Smith repeatedly emphasized the strength and persistence of those public prejudices which had in the past inspired so much unwise legislation, and he scorned the suggestion that any nation would ever voluntarily relinquish control of its colonies.[38] In home affairs, much would obviously depend on the shifting balance of power between the various categories of property owners, who formed the bulk of the governing classes; and while Smith was far from explicit about the forces determining this power struggle, he certainly had no faith in merchants, and he made no suggestion that society might some day be dominated by committed libertarians. Such persons would, in any case, have been examples of the 'men of system' whose influence on governments he so deeply suspected.

Smith had little faith in constitution-makers or in detailed blueprints for political and social reform; and in his review of European policies he described the pre-conditions of the good society in generalized abstract terms, such as liberty, justice and security.[39] This largely explains why his treatment of the forms and processes of government is so disappointingly sketchy and inconclusive. In *The Wealth of Nations*, the most explicitly economic of his works, the polemical driving force behind his attack on the mercantile system was his profound hostility to monopoly. The intensification of his attack in later editions may suggest that he viewed this as a growing menace, notwithstanding the comparative mildness and liberalism of the British system of government. While a trading monopoly might be justifiable for a small country, or as a temporary device for assisting the establishment of an especially remote and risky trade, he detested trading bodies like the East India Company, which had assumed functions that properly belonged to the sovereign, functions they were totally unsuited to perform (*Wealth of Nations* IV, vii, c, 103). Since monopoly was, for Smith, a simple injustice, resulting from a combination of human selfishness, unequal distribution of economic power and inadequate legal restraints, he may have assumed that no subtle or detailed social or political analysis was required. Alternatively, he may have intended to incorporate this in his projected, but unfinished 'history of law and government'.[40]

Smith traced the origins of monopoly back to the 'corporation spirit' which prevailed in medieval towns,[41] and doubtless regarded exclusive trading companies, like other state-supported monopolies, as a regrettable legacy of the past. Yet he gave no clear guidance as to the likely future trend of monopolistic activity. To a modern reader, urbanization and the growth of large-scale industry might be supposed to enhance potential monopoly powers, whereas improvements of transport and any other means of widening the market would presumably aid the forces of competition. Private monopolies gave Smith less grounds for concern than those backed by legislation, and he repeatedly warned his readers of the merchants' and manufacturers' skill in gaining government aid for their vested interests.

Nevertheless, in his treatment of the mercantile system, as elsewhere in his works, Smith was no crude advocate of *laissez-faire*. As is well known, he defended the Navigation Acts, which modern historians have generally regarded as the keystone of mercantilism, on the grounds that 'defence is of much more importance than opulence';[42] and the significance of this particular exception to the general principle of economic freedom is enhanced by his earlier acknowledgement of the fact that as societies become richer defence becomes more, not less, important, owing to the decline of the martial spirit (LJ (B) p.331; Cannan, pp.257–8).

Certainly the most remarkable, though not necessarily the most realistic, prognostication of the future of the mercantile system – or, rather, that part of it now generally known as the old colonial system – is to be found in those passages where Smith advocated a complete union of Britain and Ireland and a scheme of Imperial Federation.

As the breach between Britain and her American colonies grew wider while Smith was completing his *magnum opus* he could hardly refrain from comment on the future of our transatlantic territories; and in view of his belief that our colonial management had been a total loss to the mother country he might have been expected to recommend their complete emancipation. However, he knew that the existing empire was unlikely to be relinquished voluntarily, and suggested imperial federation (union?) as a possible alternative solution – though the language in which he presented his proposal makes it difficult to decide whether it was to be taken seriously or merely treated as *a ballon d'essai*.[43] Smith conceded that it would not be easy to develop a complete political and economic union of the colonies and the home country, but the plan was worth considering 'in a speculative work of this kind. . . . Such a speculation can at worst be regarded as a new Utopia, less amusing certainly, but not more useless and chimerical than the old.' Yet in view of his profound misgivings about the wisdom, honesty and efficiency of contemporary British government he was surprisingly untroubled by the difficulties of his proposal.[44]

As one of a group of intellectuals with a developed taste for *histoire raisonnée* Smith should perhaps be exempted from judgements of the historical validity of his attack on the mercantile system. Yet he specifically declared his interest in the system as it applied 'in our own country and in our own times' (*Wealth of Nations* IV, 2), and it would be unwise to ignore this matter completely. In fact, Smith's general assessment of the contemporary situation is borne out by the leading modern authority on the subject, who has stated that

Adam Smith's history may not have been impeccable, but there was some truth in his contention that 'the mercantile system' – that complex of rules by which the government intervened to promote a certain conception of trade – was the result of 'arguments addressed by merchants to Parliaments and the Counsels of Princes, to nobles and country gentlemen . . . Admittedly the arguments of *The Wealth of Nations* were the product of logic working upon material drawn from the observation of three relatively mature mercantile economies: those of England, France and Holland. They did not have the same appeal to those who were still concerned with the earlier stages of the transition from agrarian to mercantile economy, to whom the invisible hand seemed to manifest itself all too infrequently.[45]

Yet even in this respect Smith was probably more right than wrong, since 'with all its imperfections, there was an element of system, of coherence, and rationality in the British mercantile economy which distinguished it markedly from the chaos of Spain or the Italian States, and rendered it superior to that of France, or Sweden, or even Holland'.[46] Thus even in the most polemical parts of his writings Smith's sense of historical reality did not desert him. His insight into the nature of a commercial society was probably influenced by his association with Glasgow merchants. This did not make him an uncritical admirer of the mercantile community. But it has been suggested that his enthusiasm for liberty of commerce, though originally derived from intellectual sources, was reinforced by his knowledge of the progress of Glasgow since the Treaty of Union in 1707 (Scott, 114). His violent denunciation of trading companies may also reflect his Scottish perspective, since merchants in the 'outports' had long suspected that their metropolitan counterparts were unduly favoured by the national legislature. Yet it would be a serious mistake to reduce Adam Smith, a universal man, to the status of a mere product of specific historical circumstances. He spoke not merely for his country but for all Europe. His protest was directed against a body of restrictive regulations which had long outgrown their usefulness in Britain; and it was backed by a powerful corpus of analysis, much of which has survived to this day. His treatment of the 'mercantile system' was addressed to his contemporaries; but, like his economic theory, with which it was inextricably linked, it has retained its interest for subsequent generations.

NOTES

1 This paper has been substantially revised, following trenchant criticisms of an earlier draft by a number of readers. Although I cannot name them all, I am especially indebted to Samuel Hollander, Neil de Marchi and Andrew Skinner. They cannot, however, be held responsible for the remaining deficiencies. A first draft of this paper was completed and presented at the University of Sheffield in May 1972.

2 Andrew Skinner's editorial introduction to *The Wealth of Nations* (Penguin Books, 1970) contains a valuable survey of these issues. See also A.L. Macfie, *The Individual in Society, Papers on Adam Smith* (1967) and the works by Campbell and Meek referred to in note 11. My debt to these secondary sources will be obvious enough in the following pages. I have also benefited greatly from reading Samuel Hollander's important book, *The Economics of Adam Smith* (1972).

3 Jacob Viner, 'Adam Smith and Laissez-Faire', originally published in 1928 and reprinted in his collected essays, *The Long View and The Short* (1958), p.221.

4 Eli Heckscher, *Mercantilism*, revised ed. (1955), ii p.332. For the sake of convenience I shall treat the modern term 'mercantilism' as equivalent to Smith's usage.

5 Cf. W.R. Scott, *Adam Smith as Student and Professor* (1937), p.54, III, where he draws on the opinion of Dugald Stewart.

6 Adam Smith, *The Wealth of Nations*, ed. Cannan (1930), ii, 160, n.I. There was also a broader empirical justification for this shift of emphasis. See Ralph Davis, 'The Rise of Protection in England, 1689–1786', *Economic History Review* xix (1966), p.306–17.

7 Letter 222 addressed to his publisher, T. Cadell, dated Dec. 1782, quoted in John Rae, *Life of Adam Smith* (1895), p.362. Also in Cannan, op. cit., p.xvi.

8 *The Wealth of Nations* IV, vii, 54. (Hereafter referred to as *W. of N.*) For an elaboration of this point see J.A. La Nauze, 'The Substance of Adam Smith's Attack on Mercantilism', *The Economic Record* xiii (June 1937), pp.90–3.

9 Skinner (ed.), op. cit., p.7.

10 Adam Smith, *Lectures on Jurisprudence*, R.L. Meek, D.D. Raphael and P.G. Stein (Oxford: Clarendon Press, 1978) p.459; Cannan, p.107. Other members of the Scottish school also accepted this theory. Cf. Andrew Skinner, 'Natural History in the Age of Adam Smith', *Political Studies* xv (1967), especially pp.38–40; also his 'Economics and History: The Scottish Enlightenment', *Scottish Journal of Political Economy* xii (1965), pp.1–22.

11 Ronald L. Meek, 'Smith, Turgot, and the "Four Stages" Theory', *History of Political Economy* iii (Spring 1971), p.12; and his earlier essay, 'The Scottish Contribution to Marxist Sociology', reprinted in his *Economics and Ideology* (1967). Also T.D. Campbell, *Adam Smith's Science of Morals* (1971), pp.79–83.

12 Campbell, op. cit., p.82. It is therefore impossible to accept Leo Rogin's contention that Smith provided a 'theory of natural economic development which he imposes as a norm upon the historical career of nations since their emergence from the feudal period': *The Meaning and Validity of Economic Theory* (1956), p.76.

13 *W. of N.* III, iv, 4. Although Smith occasionally used the terms 'mercantile' and 'commercial' as equivalents, and even described 'the mercantile system' as 'the system of commerce', he used the phrase 'the mercantile system' solely as a description of those economic ideas and policies which he regarded as a perversion of the 'system of natural liberty'. The precise nature of the relationship between the mercantile system and the 'commercial' stage of societal development will be considered more fully. In this essay the term 'commercial' will be applied exclusively to that stage.

14 Joseph Cropsey, *Polity and Economy, An Interpretation of the Principles of Adam Smith* (1957), p.95.

15 As Cropsey puts it, 'man is naturally disposed to reverse the natural', ibid., p.40. In accordance with contemporary usage, Smith sometimes used the term 'natural' as equivalent to normal – i.e. spontaneous and instinctive in human behaviour, or, in social and economic affairs, what normally occurs or would occur in the

absence of some human, legal or institutional impediment. However, the term 'natural', was also used to connote 'ideal', and as Cropsey stresses, there is an important tension between the 'natural' and 'moral' elements in Smith's work. For a helpful analysis see Campbell, op. cit., pp.53–60; see also the discussion of the relationship between the 'natural' and the 'supernatural' by H.J. Bitterman, in 'Adam Smith's Empiricism and the Law of Nature', *Journal of Political Economy* xlviii (1940), pp.487–520 and 703–37 (esp.729). Another incisive treatment of this element is Jacob Viner, *The Role of Providence in the Social Order, An Essay in Intellectual History* (American Philosophical Society, 1972), esp. pp.47, 53–4, 81. According to Andrew Skinner, some members of the Scottish School, notably Kames and Millar, appeared to believe that the successive stages were, in fact, inevitable. Cf. 'Natural History in the Age of Adam Smith', pp.44–5. In his editorial introduction to *The Wealth of Nations*, p.40, he imputes this idea to Smith, but on p.34 he notes that Smith did not consider that progress beyond the second stage was inevitable. As will be shown, even if the *sequence* was in some sense inevitable, there was nevertheless scope for considerable variations *within each stage*.

16 Op. cit., p.230. Viner explained Smith's inconsistencies by referring to his polemical purpose (p.232), but this is clearly an unsatisfactory explanation. More recently Viner somewhat modified his interpretation. 'Smith worked from what he called systems and what today would be called models. He was aware that 'systems' are incomplete in the factors they take into account. Had he been able to complete his total system, he would probably have demonstrated that the apparent inconsistencies were often not real ones, but were merely the consequences of deliberate shifts from one partial model to another'; 'Adam Smith', in *International Encyclopedia of the Social Sciences* (1968), xiv, p.323.

17 Cf. Viner's classic account of this subject, 'Adam Smith and Laissez Faire'. Smith probably accepted David Hume's view that: 'General principles, if just and sound must prevail in the course of things though they fail in particular cases, and it is the chief business of philosophers to regard the general course of things.' See his *Economic Writings*, ed. E. Rotwein (1955), p.4.

18 The term 'conjectural history' derives from Dugald Stewart, to whom it was not a derogatory expression as it was for Thorstein Veblen, who described it as being 'of the nature of harmless and graceful misinformation'. Smith was a generalizing or 'philosophical' historian. 'Narrative that is not an occasion for or does not lead to, or does not in some way reinforce or illuminate a generalization or insight in sociology or economics or the like seems to have little interest for him.' Cf. Louis Schneider, *The Scottish Moralists on Human Nature and Society* (1967), p.lxii. It would take at least another article, probably a monograph, to examine Smith's merits and limitations as a historian.

19 Cf. his 'Adam Smith and the Currents of History' in J.M. Clark *et al.*, *Adam Smith, 1776–1926* (1928), p.73. Quoted in Gladys Bryson, *Man and Society: The Scottish Inquiry of the Eighteenth Century* (1968), p.86. Ch. IV of this work contains a valuable account of the Scottish approach to the past.

20 *W. of N.* I, x, a, 1; IV, ii, 43. However, it is important not to exaggerate the significance of the failure to attain the ideal. 'If a nation could not prosper without the enjoyment of perfect liberty and perfect justice, there is not in the world a nation which could ever have prospered. In the political body, however, the wisdom of nature has fortunately made ample provision for remedying many of the bad effects of the folly and injustice of man; in the same manner as it had done in the natural body, for remedying those of sloth and intemperance' (ibid., IV, ix, 28).

21 *Theory of Moral Sentiments* IV, i, 2, 2. (Hereafter referred to as *TMS.*) The most

familiar passage on the duties of the sovereign under the system of natural liberty is the following: 'first, the duty of protecting the society from the violence and invasion of other independent societies; secondly, the duty of protecting, as far as possible, every member of the society from the injustice or oppression of every other member of it, or the duty of establishing an exact administration of justice; and, thirdly, the duty of erecting and maintaining certain public works and certain public institutions which it can never be for the interest of any individual, or small number of individuals, to erect and maintain' (*W. of N.* IV, ix, 51). Although most commentators concerned with economic affairs have concentrated on the third class of governmental functions it should be noted that the second category is also ill defined and flexible. Cf. Viner, op. cit., p.237. Indeed, as will appear, it is virtually impossible to assess Smith's attitude to economic policy without taking due account of the conduct of administration and justice.

22 *W. of N.* IV, iv, 10. Elsewhere, he remarked: 'The rich, in particular, are necessarily interested to support that order of things which can alone secure them in the possession of their own advantages . . . Civil government, so far as it is instituted for the security of property, is in reality instituted for the defence of the rich against the poor, or of those who have some property against those who have none at all' (ibid., V, i, b, 12). In this respect the mercantile regulations, which tended to favour the rich at the expense of the poor, were quite characteristic.

23 *Lectures on Jurisprudence*, p.435; Cannan, p.69; Cf. *TMS* VI, ii, 2, 16: 'The man whose public spirit is prompted altogether by humanity and benevolence, will respect the established powers and privileges even of individuals, and still more of those of the great orders and societies into which the state is divided. Though he should consider some of them as in some measure abusive, he will content himself with moderating, what he cannot annihilate without great violence . . . when he cannot establish the right he will not disdain to ameliorate the wrong; but like Solon, when he cannot establish the best system of laws, he will endeavour to establish the best that the people can bear.'

24 *W. of N.* I, iv, 1; I, ix, 20. Smith did not distinguish between a government of merchants *per se* and one that is dominated or unduly influenced by merchants. But since merchants and manufacturers were treated as knowing their own interests clearly and being especially effective in getting their own way, the distinction is not of practical importance.

25 ibid., V, ii, a, 4. Elsewhere he remarked that 'The republican form of government seems to be the principal support of the present grandeur of Holland', and warned that 'The parsimony which leads to accumulation has become almost as rare in republican as in monarchical governments' (ibid., V, ii, k, 80; V, iii, 3).

26 ibid., I, xi, p, 8. Landlords, like farmers and graziers, were widely scattered and could not easily combine to promote their own interests, whereas merchants and manufacturers were already assembled in cities and could therefore put pressure on the government to give them special privileges. This helps to explain why the long-term tendency of mercantilist economic policy was in favour of towns at the expense of the countryside. In the matter of trading companies the advantages were even more concentrated than this, for in these organizations metropolitan merchants frequently gained at the expense of merchants in the 'outports'. In this connection Smith's violent attack on trading companies may reflect his long-standing association with Glasgow merchants. See p.146.

27 'The capricious ambition of kings and ministers has not, during the present and preceding century, been more fatal to the repose of Europe than the impertinent jealousy of merchants and manufacturers. The violence and injustice of the rulers

of mankind is an ancient evil, for which, I am afraid, the nature of human affairs can scarce admit of a remedy. But the mean rapacity, the monopolizing spirit of merchants and manufacturers, . . . though it cannot perhaps be corrected may easily be prevented from disturbing the tranquillity of anybody but themselves' (ibid., IV, iii, c, 9).

28 This explains some, though by no means all, of the difficulties Professor Stigler encountered in his analysis of Smith's account of the legislative process. Cf. Professor Stigler's 'Smith's Travels on the Ship of State' in *Essays on Adam Smith*, eds. A.S. Skinner and T. Wilson (Glasgow, 1975) pp.237–46 and p.150. For my comments on this see *History of Political Economy* vol.vii (1975), pp.132–6.

29 In a Letter (208) addressed to Andreas Holt, dated 26 Oct. 1780, quoted in Scott, op. cit., p.283.

30 *Lectures on Jurisprudence*, pp.421–2 (sentence order reversed); Cannon, p.45. Similar comments appear in *The Wealth of Nations*. According to Viner, 'All of the influential British eighteenth-century theologians and moral philosophers, whatever their philosophical or theological beliefs, were agreed that once the Restoration of 1660, or once the Glorious Revolution of 1688, had occurred, neither religion nor morality called for any substantial change in the political structure, or in the social structure of England, or of Scotland. With respect to matters of more direct economic interest also, there was widespread belief that no major changes in economic institutions, policies, or patterns of behaviour were urgently called for on religious or moral grounds' (*The Role of Providence*, p.58). This suggests that Smith did not regard the mercantile system as sinful or immoral. But see ibid., p.65.

31 *W. of N.* IV, v, b, 45. The overwhelming importance of 'that security which the laws in Great Britain give to every man that he shall enjoy the fruits of his own labour' was stressed a little earlier. 'This security was perfected by the revolution' of 1688, thereby encouraging individual initiative and the desire for self-improvement. 'The natural effort of every individual to better his own condition, when suffered to exert itself with freedom and security, is so powerful a principle that it is alone, and without any assistance, not only capable of carrying on the society to wealth and prosperity, but of surmounting a hundred impertinent obstructions with which the folly of human laws too often incumbers its operations' (ibid., IV, v, b, 43).

32 ibid., III, iv, 20. In contrast to agricultural systems of political economy which advocated policies contrary to the ends they proposed, the mercantile system did 'really and in the end' encourage 'that species of industry which it means to promote', though in so doing it drew resources from other, more efficient, uses (ibid., IV, ix, 49).

33 ibid., V, iii, 58. See also *Lectures on Jurispridence*, p.534 Cannan, p.245 'Upon the whole we may observe that the English are the best financiers in Europe, and their taxes are levied with more propriety than those of any country whatever.' Yet in fairness to the Dutch it should perhaps be noted that the 'load of taxes' in the singular countries of Zealand and Holland were largely due to the debt burdens incurred in fighting wars to acquire and to maintain their independence. Presumably Smith regarded these costs of freedom as legitimate. Cf. *W. of N.* V, ii, k, 80.

34 ibid, IV, vii, c, 50. Among the 'natural good effects of the colony trade' was the fact that the colonies provided a 'vent-for-surplus' of home commodities. The relationship between the conception of the influence of foreign trade on home employment and Smith's more familiar efficiency (i.e. international division of labour) argument is examined in Hollander, *Economics of Adam Smith*, ch.9. His attempt to reconcile the two theoretical approaches is ingenious, but not wholly convincing. However, a thorough discussion of the issues would not

be in accordance with the main theme of this paper. For other discussions of this matter see Charles E. Staley, 'Adam Smith's Version of the Vent for Surplus Model', *History of Political Economy* v (1973), pp.438–48, and the article by A.I. Bloomfield, 'Adam Smith and the Theory of International Trade' in *Essays on Adam Smith*, eds A.S. Skinner and T. Wilson (Glasgow, 1975), pp 455–81.

35 'Laws frequently continue in force long after the circumstances which first gave occasion to them, and which could alone render them reasonable, are no more' (*W.of.N.* III, ii, 4). It may be helpful to note that although Smith described four 'stages' of development, he considered only two 'systems' of political economy: those of 'agriculture' and 'commerce', of which the latter was 'the modern system'. The agricultural system, Smith noted, had 'never been adopted by any nation, and it at present exists only in the speculation of a few men of great learning and ingenuity in France'. However, a few pages later he acknowledged the influence of the Economistes on 'some measures of public administration in favour of agriculture'. Smith presumably considered that in the hunting and pasturage states, the institutions of government, policy ideas and practices were too underdeveloped to be compatible with any system of political economy (ibid., IV, 2; IV, ix, 2, 38).

36 This is not, of course, to deny the significance of the long-term falling trend of the rate of profit in a country which had acquired its full complement of riches. See also the essay by Robert Heilbroner, 'The Paradox of Progress: Decline and Decay on *The Wealth of Nations*' in *Essays on Adam Smith*, eds A.S. Skinner and T. Wilson (Glasgow, 1975), pp.524–39.

37 *Lectures on Jurisprudence*, p.414; Cannan, p.32. On the mortality of empires see *W.of.N.* V, ii, c, 6. For this brief comment on the early stages see the so-called 'Early Draft of the Wealth of Nations' in Scott, p.352.

38 'To propose that Great Britain should voluntarily give up all authority over her colonies, and leave them to elect their own magistrates, to enact their own laws, and to make peace and war as they might think proper, would be to propose such a measure as never was, and never will be adopted, by any nation in the world . . . The most visionary enthusiast would scarce be capable of proposing such a measure with any serious hopes at least of its ever being adopted' (*W.of.N.* IV, vii, c, 66).

39 Indeed, it has even been suggested that for Smith all the pre-conditions of economic order were reducible to one: namely, justice. Cf. Skinner, editor's introduction to *The Wealth of Nations*, p.28.

40 See Letter (248) addressed to Rochefoucauld, dated 1 Nov. 1785, quoted in Meek, *Economics and Ideology*, op. cit, p.35 n.

41 *W.of.N.* IV, ii, 21. As noted by Arthur H. Cole, Smith displayed a lower opinion of merchants in *The Wealth of Nations* than in the *Theory of Moral Sentiments*, where he remarked that they had been 'unjustly denigrated'. The earlier distaste for commercial activities, he complained, had persisted even in a refined society like England; and this 'mean and despicable idea of earlier days' had 'greatly obstructed the progress of commerce'. Cf. 'Puzzles of "The Wealth of Nations"', *Canadian Journal of Economics and Political Science* xxiv (1958), p.4.

42 *W.of.N.* I, 429; cf. IV, ii, 30. Elsewhere Smith acknowledges the wisdom of protecting certain manufactures required for purposes of defence (*ibid.* IV, v, a, 27). As Hollander notes, the principle here is that the natural liberty of individuals should be restrained where it conflicts with the security of the whole society (*Economics of Adam Smith*, p.256). Changing conceptions of the role of defence, and the interdependence of profit and power, would presumably influence government policy on this matter.

43 These problems are discussed in David Stevens's paper, 'Adam Smith and the Colonial Disturbances' in *Essays on Adam Smith* op. cit., pp.202–17.
44 Smith's views on this subject have been repeatedly discussed in recent years. See, for example, Richard Koebner, *Empire* (1961), esp. pp.220–36; Donald Winch, *Classical Political Economy and Colonies* (1965), ch. 2; and R.N. Ghosh, *Classical Macro-Economics and the Case for Colonies* (1967), ch. i. A fascinating earlier elaboration of this theme can be found in J.S. Nicholson, *A Project of Empire* (1909).
45 Charles Wilson, 'Trade, Society and the State', in *The Cambridge Economic History of Europe*, (1900), iv, ed. E.E. Rich and C.H. Wilson, pp.496, 574. This 68-page chapter is the best single survey of the historical context against which the historical validity of Smith's treatment of the mercantile system can be gauged.
46 Charles Wilson, 'Government Policy and Private Interest in Modern Economic History', in his *Economic History and the Historian, Collected Essays* (1969), p.150. This is not, of course, to suggest that Smith was necessarily correct either in matters of historical fact or in the explanations he proposed.

9

THE CLASSICAL ECONOMISTS AND THE LABOURER

In his important study, *The Making of the English Working Class* (1963), E.P. Thompson revived two familiar themes of nineteenth century romantic and socialist literature – condemnation of the social evils of the industrial revolution and bitter criticism of the classical economists; and in his treatment of the latter he went far beyond either the Hammonds or the Webbs. It was Arnold Toynbee who remarked that the protracted debate between the disciples of Ricardo and the human beings had ended with 'the conversion of the economists',[1] and as this caricature of the classical economist as the personification of man's congenital inhumanity to man has long been popular among undergraduates, it is worth re-examining the original with some care.

To sketch the main outlines of the classical economists' attitude to early nineteenth century conditions is, however, no easy task. Against the humanitarian and socialist indictment can be set an equally polemical liberal defence of classical economics, and distinguished academic authorities fully armed with apt quotations from the writings of the accused can be mustered on both sides. Any student who wishes to make up his own mind on the matter faces a formidable task, for after immersing himself in innumerable books, monographs, pamphlets, magazine articles, reports, minutes of evidence, speeches and letters, he must endeavour to condense complex discussions, reconcile inconsistencies, assess successive changes of opinion and above all thread his way through those terminological, conceptual and factual disagreements that inevitably arise whenever two or three economists are gathered together. The following pages represent a modest attempt to present an impartial summary view of the classical economists' attitude to the labourer.[2] Instead of the familiar questions about the nature and validity of the labour theory of value, the Ricardian theory of production and distribution, the wages fund, etc., which form the staple diet of historians of economic theory, we shall ask what the classical economists knew of the labourer's difficulties, his motives and his aspirations. Were they hostile,

159

sympathetic or indifferent? Were they perhaps well intentioned, but blinded by their own values and prejudices? And were their policy recommendations – especially those designed to relieve poverty and to promote economic progress – derived from abstract speculation, totally unrelated to current conditions; or were they based on genuine efforts to obtain trustworthy evidence?

Before commencing this inquiry, however, it is advisable to dispose of an elementary methodological point, one that would hardly be worth mentioning had it not been a fruitful source of serious, sometimes deliberate and wilful, misunderstanding. The classical economists were neither poets nor novelists; they were aspiring social scientists – the first 'professional economists', and therefore we should not expect to find in their writings the kind of insights into the infinite complexity, variety and subtlety of the human personality that we might legitimately seek in the works of the literary men. As the antithetical terms 'classical' and 'romantic' suggest, the Ricardians and the lakeland poets were interested in different things and asked different kinds of questions; it is, therefore, hardly surprising that they obtained very different, though not always incompatible, answers.[3] The classical economists were deeply concerned about individual freedom and happiness; but, as economists, they dealt with 'man in the aggregate – with states not with families; with general passions and propensities, not with those which occasionally influence the individual'.[4] This preoccupation does not, of course, excuse unsound generalizations, or a neglect of relevant differences – whether sex, age, family, occupational or regional – in labour conditions. But we are chiefly concerned with the nature and quality of their performance as social scientists, and we must not convict them of failure to perform a task that was no part of their intention.

I

As social scientists, the classical economists endeavoured to formulate general principles, and although they repeatedly used hypothetical 'models' – what Ricardo called 'strong cases' – to illustrate the operation of these principles, they claimed that their generalizations were based on 'fact and experiment', and did not hesitate to cite empirical data in support of their arguments. Thus the widely held notion that classical economics was a tissue of abstractions built on a priori assumptions is erroneous; but it is no easy matter to determine the exact relationship between general principles and particular facts in the classical literature.[5] Malthus's *Essay on Population*, for instance, is rightly said to have become longer and longer and duller and duller with successive editions as he incorporated the results of his extensive search for demographic evidence to buttress his central law; but while the younger authors came to the conclusion that the weight of evidence was against Malthus's theory, Malthus himself made only minor changes after his second edition.[6] Much the same is true of McCulloch, whose desire to base political economy on 'fact' rather than 'hypothesis' led him to publish several editions of his massive *Dictionary of Commerce* and his *Statistical Account of the British Empire*. He ridiculed the efforts of those 'intrepid calculators' who 'have amused themselves by framing estimates of the value of plate, furniture, clothes etc. belonging to individuals', because 'there are no data whatsoever on which to construct such estimates – which are, in fact, good for nothing unless it be to throw discredit on all statistical computations'. As far as the condition of the people was concerned, McCulloch declared that

> there is no subject about which so many contradictory assertions are made, by those pretending to be acquainted with it, as the state of the middle and lower classes in all parts of the country. We, in fact, *have no real knowledge of the matter*. There are no authentic accounts of the qualities and current prices of articles in any great market, the rent of houses and lodgings, the rate of wages in proportion to the work done, and a variety of other particulars, indispensable to be known before anyone can pretend to estimate the condition of the bulk of the people, or to compare their state at one period with their state at another. . . . Ministers are quite as much in the dark as to these matters as other people. The Secretary for the Home Department is about as well informed respecting the demand for labour, wages, diet, dress and other accommodations of the people of Canton and Manilla, as of those of Manchester and Paisley. Were he questioned on the subject, he would, of course, affirm, and perhaps truly, that the manufacturing labourers in the last-mentioned towns were highly prosperous.[7]

Nevertheless, despite his ardent desire for more extensive and reliable information, McCulloch's own appraisal of the compatibility between his theories and the facts leaves much to be desired. As is well known, he was a sincere disciple of Ricardo, and his confidence in the validity of Ricardian principles was seldom disturbed by evidence that ran counter to his presuppositions.

Before condemning this attitude, however, we must remember that the evidence was often unreliable, and could not be used to falsify *general theoretical* principles. How, for example, was Torrens to adjust his theory of wages to take account of the earnings of cotton workers employed in 'common mule spinning about No 36 weft, or 36 hanks to the lb' when his sources indicated that in computing such wages 'much depends upon the quality of cotton etc. furnished by the master; also upon the state of repair etc. in which machinery is kept, likewise upon the attention of both manager and operative'?[8] This is, of course, an extreme case, and it is no part of our purpose to offer a blanket defence of the classical economists' use of evidence. As Ricardo wisely observed, 'There are perhaps very few men who are not in some degree biased either by the love of their party or by the love of their favourite system',[9] and his fellow economists were human in this as in other respects. Since their primary objective was to construct a theoretical system, they were naturally reluctant – and often rightly so – to abandon their hard-won generalizations as a result of new and conflicting evidence which could usually be dismissed either as unsound, unrepresentative or the product of 'disturbing causes' which had been specifically excluded from the theorists' model. As the philosopher Morris Cohen has said, 'It is only as a last resort that we modify (as little as possible) the old ideas. If we did not hold on to our old ideas tenaciously, if we threw them away the moment they encountered difficulties, we could never develop any strong ideas and our science would have no continuity of development.'[10]

On the other hand, as time passed, the accumulation of evidence of contemporary economic conditions figured ever more prominently in the classical economists' writings, and their individual attitudes toward the problems of poverty, factory legislation, public health and so forth underwent significant modifications as their knowledge of the facts increased. On matters of fundamental principle they were often unduly rigid, and their conception of the labourer's predicament was undoubtedly seriously deficient. Yet, as we shall see, it was neither without empirical foundations nor wholly irrelevant to the facts of contemporary life. The classical economists were neither ignorant of nor indifferent to current evils, for their pages contain innumerable eloquent and detailed passages about the hardships encountered by such special groups as the Spitalfields silk workers, the London coal whippers, the Coventry ribbon makers, the Nottingham lace makers, the inevitable handloom weavers, and many others. Their lengthy and impassioned accounts of the degradation of the Irish peasantry and the English rural paupers were designed to warn the English working man – who, they believed, was in a significantly more favourable condition – of the dangers that accompanied reckless, idle and improvident conduct. And, with the benefit of hindsight, we can now see that their hopes for long-term improvement (and they were mainly concerned with the long run) were not wholly unjustified.

II

The classical economists' conception of the labourer's predicament and prospects was based on a theory of human nature and motivation that can broadly be termed utilitarian.[11] From Locke, Hume and Adam Smith, they inherited the notion that all men are fundamentally alike in respect of their native characteristics and potentialities, but since they also believed that environment exerted a profound influence on men's actual habits and customs, their views on specific issues comprised a changing amalgam of long-term and short-term elements which cannot easily be summarized.

On the whole, their middle-class perspective, reinforced by their genuine desire to elevate the lower orders, led the economists to underestimate the difficulties of realizing the labourer's *bourgeois* potentialities – the qualities of self-reliance, thrift, prudence, industriousness, etc., which they believed were latent in every man. According to Senior, the independent labourer was the 'normal type . . . the natural off-spring of the Saxon race', whose customary virtues would readily reassert themselves once the 'rash interference' of the State ceased, while the sanguine McCulloch maintained that:

> The poor have, upon plain and practical questions that touch their immediate interests, the same understanding, the same penetration, and the same regard to consequences as those who are rich. It is indeed a contradiction, and an absurdity to pretend, that if the labourers are capable of earning, by an ordinary degree of application, more than is sufficient to support them, they alone, of all the various classes of society, will spend the surplus in riot and debauchery. They have the same common sense, they are actuated by the same passions, feelings, and principles as other men; and when such is the case, it is clear that they cannot generally be guilty of such inconsiderate conduct.[12]

There is, accordingly, an important current of optimism in the classical literature, despite the gloomy shadow cast by the Malthusian law of population. Even Malthus, who held that the labourer's desire for self-improvement was 'perfectly feeble' by comparison with the 'passion between the sexes', allowed himself some cheerful prognostications in the later editions of his *Essay* – provided, of course, that his policy recommendations were adopted.[13] McCulloch and Senior went much further, and resembled Adam Smith in their belief that the diffusion of a spirit of emulation, a desire for respectability and the opportunity to acquire a taste for the luxuries and conveniences of life, would greatly promote the long-run economic and social improvement of the lower orders. Underlying this attitude was a residue of eighteenth century faith in progress that persisted throughout the strains and stresses of early nineteenth century industrialism.[14] When Senior observed approvingly that the gradations of wealth in England were insensible, he was echoing the eighteenth century view that a nation benefits from 'an easy gradation from rank to rank';[15] and one of the main reasons for the classical economists' stress on the need for education was their conviction that vertical social mobility was both possible and desirable.

Of course there were notable exceptions and qualifications in this as in most other matters. McCulloch, for instance, took a far more hierarchical view of the interrelationships between social classes than most of his fellow economists.

> The distinction of rich and poor, is not as some shallow sophists would seem to suppose, artificial, but real; it is as much a part of the order of Providence as the distinction of the sexes. It depends on the differences of the mental and physical powers and dispositions of

different individuals, and of the different circumstances under which they happen to be placed ... [while] riches are evidence of superior good conduct in the vast majority of cases.[16]

So influential were the standards set by the higher orders of society that the constitutional details of government were unimportant provided that its leaders were men of talent and spirit. As far as the labourer's potentialities were concerned:

> If you would develop all the native resources of a man's mind, if you would bring his every faculty and power into full activity, you must make him aware of his inferiority in relation to others, and inspire him with a determination to rise to a higher level.

But in practice, he regretfully admitted, the desire to attain wealth was much more effective a spur to ambition than the desire to excel in 'learning, benevolence, or integrity'.[17]

In educational matters also, the classical economists did not invariably overrate the possibility of indoctrinating the lower orders. On one occasion J.S. Mill threw up his hands in despair at the difficulties of the task.

> In England, it would hardly be believed to what a degree all that is morally objectionable in the lowest class of the working people is nourished, if not engendered, by the low state of their understandings. The infantine credulity to what they hear, when it is from their own class; their incapacity to observe what is before their eyes; their inability to comprehend or believe purposes in others which they have not been taught to expect, and are not conscious of in themselves – are the known characteristics of persons of low intellectual faculties in all classes. But what would not be equally credible without experience, is an amount of deficiency in the power of reasoning and calculation which makes them insensible to their own direct personal interests. Few have considered how anyone who could instil into these people the commonest worldly wisdom – who could render them capable of even selfish prudential calculations – would improve their conduct in every relation of life, and clear the soil for the growth of right feelings and worthy propensities.[18]

This outburst was not typical, either of Mill himself or of the group; but, on the other hand, it was not unique, and as time passed there was a growing realization that the process of reforming the labouring classes would be neither quick nor easy. It was recognized that the labourer's habits could not be changed overnight, whether by moral suasion, instruction or some comparatively straightforward legal or institutional change, and in these circumstances the persistence of optimism reflects the classical economists' faith in the typical English working man's natural virtues. When riots and disorders occurred they often defended the poor against the calumnies of the rich, and among the multifarious excuses they advanced for such unseemly conduct were the customs and excise laws – which tempted the people to maltreat the enforcement officers; the combination laws – which were both oppressive and ineffectual; the petty despotism of the magistrates; or 'that law for the encouragement of Murder and Robbery' (to cite McCulloch's words) which prohibited the sale of game.[19] Politically speaking, the classical economists occupied a wide spectrum, from the radicalism of James Mill to the High Toryism of De Quincey, and their attitude towards the 'mob' varied accordingly. The case of Peterloo is instructive, for it has often wrongly been regarded as a typical manifestation of early nineteenth century middle- and upper-class hostility to the poor, and it was the subject of considerable discussion in Ricardo's correspondence. Ricardo himself adopted a middle-of-the-road position, describing the affair in Manchester in 1819 as cruel, illegal and unjust, and adopting a much more temperate view of the situation than his friend Hutches Trower, who was less tolerant of the poor. Three years earlier, in 1816, Ricardo had denied that the war had degraded the morals of the people.

> The outrages of which they are at present guilty may be sufficiently accounted for from the stagnation in trade which has never failed to produce similar consequences. I am disposed to think that the people are both improved in morals and in knowledge, and therefore that they are less outrageous under these unavoidable reverses than they formerly used to be. I am in hope too that as they increase in knowledge they will more clearly perceive that the destruction of property aggravates and never relieves their difficulties.[20]

In the specific case of Peterloo, Ricardo disapproved of the magistrates' unwarranted violation of the right of assembly, and he opposed the Six Acts for similar reasons. However, mob violence presented the middle-class intellectual with a dilemma which was epitomized in Malthus's belief that although the demands of the mob 'should not be regarded', the pressure of public opinion should not be ignored.[21] James Mill and Ricardo agreed that the real test of a reformer was his willingness to allow the people to have genuinely independent representation in Parliament, and by this criterion Ricardo comes out quite well, for although he disapproved of universal suffrage, he maintained that 'it is always unwise for a Government to set itself against the declared opinion of a very large class of the people', especially in important matters! There was, however, no consensus of opinion on the question, for Malthus and McCulloch strongly opposed universal suffrage.[22]

Although the classical literature contains few instances of unqualified class hostility towards the poor, the economists viewed the development of an urban industrial society with certain misgivings. Adam Smith had

165

commented extensively on the differences in social outlook between rural and urban labourers, and his successors were fully aware that energetic and independent-minded workers would not submit to injustice or economic adversity without a struggle. McCulloch, for instance, conceded that the English populace was turbulent, inflammable and easily led astray by radical demagogues, but he regarded these characteristics as inevitable concomitants of the social conditions existing in manufacturing communities, and believed that as time passed the workers' violence would diminish as their intelligence grew.[23] On several occasions, especially in times of acute crisis, individual members of the classical school expressed grave, even hysterical anxiety at the restlessness of the people. In the summer of 1841, for instance, Senior wondered whether, if the depression of the handloom weavers became widespread, 'the Peerage, or the Church, or even the Monarchy, could resist the storm'?[24] Yet these gloomy and fearful observations were made without bitterness or hostility, and it has recently been suggested that James Mill regarded the turbulence of the people as an effective way of forcing concessions from an unwilling governing class. Ideally, he believed, the people 'should appear to be ready and impatient to break out into outrage *without* actually breaking out.'[25]

The classical economists were not, of course, invariably optimistic, even though they believed that English workers were generally more highly paid, more industrious and enjoyed better living conditions than their continental counterparts. They were aware that unfavourable environmental conditions – whether natural, institutional or psychological – could easily undermine the labourer's virtues and reduce him to that 'degraded stratum' which was 'so low intellectually as to be almost without providence, and so low morally as to be almost without self-respect'.[26] Recognition of the importance of the psychological climate is evident in Malthus's insistence that poverty ought to be held disgraceful, and in the Benthamite principle that a pauper ought to be 'less eligible' than an independent labourer. If pauperism ever became as commonplace in England as in Ireland – where a beggar was not merely regarded as an equal, but was even welcomed at a peasant's fireside – the English labourer's cherished sense of self-reliance would be crushed.[27] Socio-psychological influences could, of course, work in either direction, for even the Irish had been known to develop sound morals and industrious habits after settling in England and coming into daily contact with native workers; but it would be folly to take undue risks – hence the classical economists' almost obsessive hostility to the so-called Speenhamland system, which so dangerously blurred the crucial distinction between the pauper and the independent labourer.

At times this distinction seems to have been treated as if it defined a point of unstable equilibrium, above or below which there were prospects of continuous improvement or deterioration in the labourer's condition.[28] Certainly, in their policy recommendations the classical economists were anxious to find the right psychological balance between the stick of necessity and the carrot of incentives. In fiscal matters, for example, McCulloch accepted Hume's view that while moderate taxes would encourage effort, exorbitant taxes would engender hopelessness and despair; but only J.S. Mill among the later classical economists recognized Hume's subtle distinction between 'active' and 'passive' habits of work, for they almost exclusively emphasized the disutility of labour.[29] Similarly, Malthus repeatedly stated that although 'fear of want' (combined with the hope of bettering his condition) was necessary to keep the independent labourer industrious, 'actual want' was wholly destructive because indigence 'palsies every virtue'.[30] As McCulloch observed, in characteristically confident tones:

> It would, however, be a most detestable policy, waiving the question of practicability, to attempt to reduce the labouring classes to a scanty supply of the mere necessities of life. The experience of all ages has shown that a needy and starving populace lose a sense of their dignity and rights as men, and become depraved and enslaved. It is vain to expect industry where it does not meet with a suitable reward; men will not submit to privations and labour, but in the hope of securing corresponding comforts.[31]

This theme was repeatedly illustrated by reference to the Irish labourers, whose predicament was variously attributed to oppressive government by the English, insecurity, the prevalence of poverty in their midst and concomitant defects of character such as idleness, dissipation, improvidence, inefficiency, recklessness, cruelty, violence, vindictiveness and ignorance (a point on which there was some disagreement). Despite their belief in the influence of environment on character, the classical economists could not agree about the prospects of reforming the Irish. Some feared that Irish immigrants would contaminate the English labour force, and favoured immigration restrictions; but Senior, who had first-hand knowledge of Irish conditions, and a less favourable view of the English labourer than McCulloch, was shocked by this suggestion. As 'an inhabitant of the British Empire' he declared himself

> inexpressibly disgusted at the wish to deprive the Irish labourer of his resort to England. . . . The evidence is full of the improvement in habits, of feelings introduced into Ireland by those who have visited England.

And he endeavoured to buttress his argument by the (somewhat dubious) assertion that in counties like Lancashire, Cumberland and Westmorland, where the Irish were very numerous, wage rates were among the highest and the proportion of poor rates to population among the lowest of any part of the country.[32]

The question of the influence of insecurity on the labourers' incentives provides yet another illustration of the need for an appropriate psychological climate, and reveals the dangers of simple generalizations about the classical outlook. Fluctuations of prices and wages, like irregularities of employment, were generally believed to discourage thrift and steady industry. By comparison with the British worker, Senior observed,

> foreign labour is ill-fed, ill-clothed, ill-lodged . . . it is at least secure of employment. The only accidents to which it is subject are accidents of the seasons. Such a population necessarily acquires habits of economy and prudence.[33]

The earnings of casual workers should, therefore, not only be sufficient to support them in periods of enforced idleness; their wages 'ought also to afford them', as Adam Smith remarked, 'some compensation for those anxious and desponding moments which the thought of so precarious a situation must sometimes occasion'.[34] In dangerous trades like mining and grinding, however, recklessness was observed to be a discernible occupational trait, and this might be attributable either to the influence of occupation on character or to the fact that such occupations attracted certain types of individuals. Senior seems to have taken the latter view, for he remarked that the general dislike of 'steady, regular labour' was so strong 'that the opportunities of idleness afforded by an occupation of irregular employment are so much more than an equivalent for its anxiety as to reduce the annual wages of such occupations below the common average'.[35]

But while insecurity was harmful, security was not an unmitigated advantage. Apart from the pernicious consequences of guaranteeing a pauper his income irrespective of his efforts, even the security of property could be harmful, unless it was coupled with opportunities of self-improvement. The peasant proprietor, said McCulloch, was believed to be 'exempted from those painful anxieties that embitter the existence of day labourers, and of occupiers liable to be turned out of their holdings'; but in practice, the independence and security conferred by a patch of land is

> uniformly associated with poverty, frequently degenerating into destitution; it gives rise to the most revolting of all combinations, that of penury, pride, and laziness; and instead of expanding, contracts and benumbs every faculty . . . the happiness of peasant proprietors seems very much akin to that of the oyster – they are ignorant and satisfied.[36]

III

Industriousness and efficiency were among the English labourer's greatest merits, and in general the classical economists believed that the high average wages of labour in Britain represented a just reward for high productivity. 'To complain of our high wages', Senior caustically observed,

> is to complain that our labour is productive – to complain that our workpeople are diligent and skilful. To act on such complaints is as wise as to enact that all men should labour with only one hand, or stand idle four days in every week ... The well-directed labour of an Englishman is worth twice as much as that of any inhabitant of Europe; it is worth four or five times as much as the labour of the less advantaged European districts; and it is worth twelve or fifteen times as much as the labour of the most civilized Asiatic nations.[37]

However, Senior went far beyond his fellow economists in extolling the benefits of hard work, although he himself defined employment as 'toil, trouble, exposure, and fatigue', all of which were evils *per se*.

> The poor and half-employed Irish labourer, or the still poorer and less industrious savage is as inferior in happiness as he is in income to the hard-worked English artisan. The Englishman's industry may sometimes be excessive, his desire to better his condition may sometimes drive him to toils productive of disease ill recompensed by the increase of his wages,

but such an outcome is unusual, despite 'the apparent unhealthiness of many of their occupations [and] the atmosphere of smoke and steam in which they labour for seventy-two hours a week', as is shown by the fact that the expectation of life in England is above that of the 'lightly-toiled inhabitants of the most favoured soils and climates', and still rising. This striking inconsistency is probably due to Senior's concern at the English labourers' propensity to dissipate their surplus earnings on idleness and debauchery.

> When wages are high, they work fewer hours and inhabit better houses; and if there still remain a superfluity the women and girls waste it in dress, and the men in drink or luxurious living. When wages fall, they endeavour to increase their earnings by more assiduous labour, and to economize, first in house-rent, then in dress, then in fuel, and ultimately in food. When their earnings become insufficient for a maintenance, they throw themselves on the parish. The virtue of which they possess the least is providence.[38]

Neither Malthus nor James Mill, nor yet Ricardo, was an unqualified advocate of high wages, though in general they assumed that slowly rising wages would be accompanied by improved habits and higher productivity. McCulloch, however, unhesitatingly denounced the 'common and hackneyed complaint, which the interested views of the master manufacturers, and fanatical declamation, have contributed to make too much believed' that high wages encouraged riot and debauchery, and were therefore harmful to the workers and to the State. On the contrary, he declared, in words reminiscent of the eighteenth century economist, Malachy Postlethwayt:

> High wages are only advantageous because of the increased comforts they bring along with them; and of these, an addition to the time which may be devoted to the purposes of amusement, is certainly not one of the least. Whenever wages are high, and little subject to fluctuation, the labourers are found to be active, intelligent and industrious. But they do not prosecute their employment with the same intensity as those who are obliged, by the pressure of the severest necessity, to strain every nerve to the utmost. They are enabled to enjoy their intervals of ease and relaxation; and they would be censurable if they did not enjoy them.[39]

Malthus, too, agreed that indolence might be advantageous under certain circumstances if, by restricting labour productivity when the demand for labour was deficient, it checked an incipient tendency for wages to fall, while Ricardo on one occasion undermined the general classical attitude towards industriousness by admitting that the indolent labourer might be happier than his hard-working counterpart, provided that he had enough to eat.[40]

Whatever the effect of high wages on the effort of labour, the classical economists fully appreciated that high money wages did not necessarily mean high labour costs per unit of output. Senior contended that the Englishman's superior productivity was due to the growth of our population, the variety of wants, and our greater 'powers of production', while Torrens drew attention to our mechanical inventions, our superior manual dexterity and skill, and our more productive coalmines. In the 1840s, however, Torrens painted a gloomy picture of the decline of our comparative advantages owing to diminishing returns in agriculture, the corn laws, and the tendency of the powers of production to outgrow 'the field of employment' – presenting a kind of stagnation thesis associated with his advocacy of colonization.[41] De Quincey also feared for the English labourer who, he argued, was facing the triple threat of Irish competition, machinery and child labour. Only a determined adherence to 'the high standard of comfort inherited from his English ancestors' could protect him from experiencing 'the very basest human degradation ever witnessed amongst oriental slaves'.[42]

Before about 1830 the tendency of population to outstrip the means of subsistence seemed to be the most serious threat to the labourer's standard of living, and against this threat the economists had little better to offer than the removal of impediments to capital accumulation and the advocacy of moral restraint on the part of the labouring classes. No part of classical doctrine has aroused more hostility (either at the time or since) than the advocacy of moral restraint, and it is therefore important to recognize that Malthus, who introduced the concept, distinguished carefully between moral restraint and prudence. While both entailed the postponement of marriage until the parties concerned could afford to support a family, the former also required chastity before marriage and was an ideal – one that has aptly been said to belong more to a sermon than to political economy.[43]

As Malthus himself recognized, moral restraint was unlikely to be achieved in practice. Prudence, on the other hand, was not only attainable: at home it was the main cause of 'a degree of happiness, superior to what could be expected from the soil and climate', while in Europe it was both increasing and likely to continue to increase in the future. Habits of prudential restraint were usually due to the custom of enjoying conveniences and comforts, although liberty, security of property and the diffusion of knowledge played a contributory role.[44] Given a decent standard of living, the labourer was unlikely to propagate his species without regard to the consequences, which helps to explain the classical economists' desire to prevent real wages from falling. But here, too, apart from the level of real income, social considerations such as 'the desire to be thought respectable' played an important role. According to Senior:

> Want of actual necessaries is seldom apprehended by any except the poorest classes in any country. And in England, though it is sometimes felt, it probably is anticipated by none. When an Englishman stands hesitating between love and prudence, a family really starving is not among his terrors. Against actual want he knows that he has the fence of the poor laws. But, however humble his desires, he cannot contemplate, without anxiety, a probability that the income which supported his social rank while single, may be insufficient to maintain that when he is married; that he may be unable to give his children the advantages of education which he enjoys himself; in short, that he may lose his caste.[45]

Underlying their reliance on the prudential check was the classical economists' dedication to the principle of individual freedom, their firm belief in the labourer's capacity for self-improvement without the intervention of any external agency – whether autocratic, paternalistic or philanthropic, and their conviction that co-operation between the various social classes and ranks was both possible and desirable. The future of the labouring classes, and of society in general, depended on a kind of co-partnership between the well-to-do and the poor, in which the former provided an appropriate framework of laws and a rate of savings and capital accumulation sufficient to ensure a high demand for labour, and the latter – being the more numerous class – exercised a proper degree of restraint over the growth of numbers.[46] However unjust it might seem, postponement of marriage was less necessary among the middle and upper classes, who could afford to bear the costs of their own imprudence. But it is worth mentioning that Ricardo, Malthus and James Mill had between them a total of twenty children, and the joy with which each new arrival was recorded in Ricardo's correspondence was not unmixed with feelings of irresponsibility – even though it never produced a response like that of Francis Place, who said of a group of his utilitarian friends: 'mustering among us no less, I believe, than 36 children, rare fellows we to teach moral restraint'.[47]

Despite the grave shortcomings of Malthus's proposals, they were well intentioned, for he ardently wished to protect domestic happiness from the misery of poverty caused by overpopulation. Similarly, his stern opposition to parochial aid stemmed from his conviction that it would destroy the precious ties of parental affection and responsibility. But as he insisted that the labourer should normally support his own children, the wisdom and timing of the labourer's decision to marry became matters of great importance, and this decision was presumed to depend on the bridegroom's estimate that 'he is in a capacity to support the children that he may reasonably expect from his marriage'.[48] Even if the labourer possessed what a modern economist has called an irrational passion for dispassionate calculation, the task of estimating his probable family income and expenditure in the foreseeable future would tax the ingenuity of a trained economic forecaster, if only because of the irregularity of his prospective employment and earnings. Beyond this, however, the labourer would need to calculate his prospective progenitiveness, for Malthus ruled out contraception, and evidently assumed that the happy couple would abandon all restraint once the period of pre-marital abstinence was over.[49]

Malthus was not entirely unaware of the difficulties facing those 'who had a greater number of children than they could be expected to foresee', and in the second and subsequent editions of his *Essay* he advocated the payment of allowances for every child in excess of six, a concession that stands as a notable exception to his usual hostility to State aid for the imprudent.[50] Senior also acknowledged that it was virtually impossible in practice to demonstrate that any given marriage was improvident, because of the potential earning power of wives and children.

> A girl of 18 can attend to a power loom as well as a full-grown man; a child of 13 is more valuable as a piecer than an adult – its touch is more sensitive, and its sight is more acute. A factory lad of 18 who marries a factory girl of the same age, finds himself immediately richer; and although he may be pinched during some of the following years, yet as each child attains the age of 9 years it can earn more than its support; and the earnings of 3 children between the ages of 9 and 16 can, in prosperous times, support the whole family. It was under the influence of this enormous stimulus, with some assistance from immigration, that the population of our manufacturing districts increased during the thirty years that elapsed between 1801 and 1831 – the last period for which returns are published – at a rate equalled only in some portions of America.[51]

Thus, despite their serious lack of insight into the labourer's mind and situation, the classical economists were not wholly unconscious of the practical difficulties facing a labourer who endeavoured to decide when he was able to support a family, although they clearly underestimated them. As time passed and their fears of the effects of population growth diminished, the matter came to occupy a less prominent place in their writings, although they never abandoned their insistence on the virtues of prudence.

IV

Having considered some of the psychological determinants of the economists' view of the labourer's position and prospects, we must now examine the economic determinants, and although we are not interested in theory as such, the classical theory of wages is the most suitable starting point. This much misunderstood theory comprised two elements: a long-term equilibrium 'natural' or 'necessary' wage rate, and a series of short-term oscillations of actual or 'market' wages. The equilibrium level was believed to alter slowly from time to time and place to place according to changes in the supply and demand for labour; but for the sake of analytical simplicity it was usually treated as a minimum governed by 'the absolutely necessary subsistence, demanded by the customs of the people for the maintenance of their life and the propagation of the race'.[52] The classical economists had no illusions about the adequacy of this long-term wage rate; though significantly higher in England than in Ireland or on the continent, it was variously described as 'a miserable pittance', a sum insufficient to permit the labourer 'to economize to any extent', and an amount 'everywhere much too low for human happiness and dignity' – to select a few typical statements.[53] It is, however, essential to appreciate that this minimum was defined not in physiological terms, as a sum just sufficient for survival, but in *social* terms, as a customary or habitual minimum; and as Schumpeter observed, this 'social minimum of existence theorem' virtually amounted to accepting customary wages as an institutional datum, and abandoning the attempt at a purely *economic* explanation of the wage level.[54] Non-economic factors, such as liberty, security of property and a taste for the comforts and conveniences of life, contributed to raise this level, while despotism and ignorance lowered it; and the object of policy should be to encourage a spirit of independence, pride and a taste for cleanliness and comfort among the poor.[55] Beyond this, however, the classical economists made few constructive proposals designed to increase labour incentives or to create wants[56] – largely because they assumed that wants were virtually unlimited among non-pauperized labourers in advanced economics, and that given a minimum standard of living the labourer's desire to better his condition would more than counteract his distaste for hard work. Although the labourers as a class could not directly influence the demand for their services – which was governed mainly by the rate of profit and the quantity of capital, they could protect their accustomed living standards whenever wages fell temporarily by restricting the labour supply by postponement of marriage. This, of course, explains the importance which the classical economists attached to the prudential check. But this remedy obviously had grave limitations: its effects were delayed, it was no help at all to a married man with a large family, and self-restraint on the part of a couple contemplating marriage could make no perceptible difference to the aggregate labour supply. But the classical economists could offer no better solution, for they were desperately anxious to preserve the labourer's sense of independence and personal responsibility, and so they flatly opposed legal restraints or taxes on marriage such as existed in other European countries.

The prospects of control over the ratio between population and subsistence obviously depended on the speed with which population responded to changes in the demand for labour. If population increased rapidly when real wages rose, the numbers seeking employment would increase and money wage rates would fall as the competition for jobs became more intense. On the other hand, if the workers readily acquired a taste for additional comforts and conveniences when real wages rose, and if population changed only after a considerable timelag, then the labourers' conception of the socially acceptable minimum standard would rise and a new and higher equilibrium level of real wages would be established. Unfortunately the classical economists were neither unanimous nor individually consistent in their treatment of this possibility, and it is all too easy to judge them by casual remarks divorced from their context. On the whole Malthus, Ricardo, Torrens and the two Mills regarded population growth as a serious obstacle to any permanent rise in real wages. Yet Malthus, for instance, denied that changes in real wages were the principal determinants of population change, acknowledged that there was a considerable time-lag between a rise in marriage rates and an increase in the labour supply, and in the later editions of his *Essay* placed considerable emphasis on the effectiveness of the prudential check.[57] Senior, De Quincey and McCulloch (who periodically protested at what he called Malthus's 'mechanical theorem') also regarded the adjustment of population to changes in real wage rates as a protracted process, and considered that Malthus had exaggerated the dangers of population growth.[58] Senior 'utterly repudiated' the view that the natural rate of wages would be held down to the minimum level of subsistence, and denied that in every trade there was a stratum of workers whose ordinary wages were only equal to their necessary expenses.[59] Most of the classical economists assumed that the habits of the labouring classes changed only slowly over time, and they regarded this as both an obstacle to the reform of an impoverished and imprudent people such as the Irish and a safeguard against a deterioration of the customary standard in England when a temporary fall in real wages occurred. On the other hand, variations in the labour supply were not solely determined by changes in the number of marriages and births, for irregularity of the seasons also played a part. Despite evidence produced before the House of Commons, McCulloch insisted that money wages tended to fall in years of high prices because

> an increased number of females, and such poor children of both sexes as are fit to work, are obliged to quit their homes, or to engage in some species of employment; while those labourers who work by the piece, endeavour, by increasing the quantity of their work, to obtain the means of purchasing a greater quantity of food. It is natural, therefore, that the *immediate* effect of a rise of prices, should be to lower, not to raise the rate of wages.[60]

One important source of misunderstanding of the classical view of wages is the term 'subsistence', which was rarely defined with precision. Senior, for example, carefully distinguished between 'necessaries', 'conveniences' and 'luxuries', but admitted that the components of each category were liable to change, and added that the classification of any given commodity depended on the time, the place, the habits and the social rank of the individual consumer.[61] James Mill included 'something for enjoyment' in the category of 'necessaries', and it was invariably assumed that the English labourer's normal subsistence included some non-essentials.[62] The terms 'corn' and 'subsistence' were often used interchangeably, partly because theoretical analysis was greatly simplified by ignoring price variations between different commodities. But the distinction had important policy implications, as noted by De Quincey, who complained in 1844 that the 'corn law incendiaries' endeavoured to win converts to the anti-corn-law camp by claiming that a 10 per cent change in wheat prices was equivalent to a 10 per cent change in wages, though in other parts of their writings they denied that wages 'at all sympathize with the price of food'. Ricardo himself, whom De Quincey warmly admired, was responsible for this error.

> Yet if Ricardo were right in supposing a labourer to spend half his wages upon wheat only, then his beer, bacon, cheese, milk, butter, tea, and sugar, must proportionably cost, at the very least, all the rest of his wages; so that for clothes, lodging, fuel, to say nothing of other miscellanies, he would have no provision at all. But these are romantic estimates, and pardonable in Ricardo from his city life, which had denied him, until his latest years, all opportunities of studying the life of labourers.[63]

Although they were unable to make reliable general statistical estimates of the prices and quantities of goods consumed by the labourer and his family, the economists were well aware of the variety of components of the labourer's budget. Wheat, bread, cheese, beer, porter, sugar, tea, beef and bacon were among the foodstuffs most commonly mentioned as the English labourer's 'necessaries', while garden vegetables, fresh, butter, veal

175

and lamb were included among the 'agricultural luxuries'.[64] Inter-regional and international dietary comparisons were common, and it was persistently emphasized that any tendency to substitute inferior for superior foodstuffs, such as potatoes for bread, would be highly undesirable, because the inferior goods allowed less scope for retrenchment in time of dearth and because an inferior diet might become 'congenial from habit' and would then be accompanied by a fall in the labourer's economic and social aspirations, his capacity and his desire for work.[65] The importance of expenditure on non-foodstuffs was recognized, but was never subjected to systematic study.[66]

Among the principal short-term influences on the labourer's earnings, the classical economists listed irregularity of the seasons, the caprices of fashion, domestic commotions and policy changes at home and abroad. They recognized that time-lags occurred between price changes and movements of wages, and that in the interim some labourers and their families might either be thrown on the parish or, alternatively, might dissipate any windfall gains in idleness and luxury. The relationship between wages and 'subsistence' – i.e. the prices of those commodities that constituted the labourer's customary purchases – was held to be close, but neither direct nor exact, and Senior aptly depicted the classical view by describing the belief that wages were determined by the price of corn as a 'falsism', since it was either true or false according to the circumstances.[67] The differential effects on mortality of a *series* of bad harvests as against a particular year of dearth were fully acknowledged, and in times of extreme distress the classical economists displayed a surprising readiness to waive their usual objections to State aid for the needy. On the whole they regarded stable or slowly rising real wages as the optimum state of affairs, arguing that the equilibrium level should be high enough to provide an incentive to effort and to enable the labourer to accumulate a reserve for unforeseen contingencies.[68]

Although their theoretical reasoning was based on the assumption that factors of production were highly mobile and that wage differentials in any given place or occupation would be speedily eliminated by the process of competition, unless checked by monopolistic action or legal restraint, the classical economists frequently discussed wage differentials between occupations, places, skills and sexes. McCulloch claimed that 'the difference of a half or more, between the price of labour, etc. in the remote counties, and London and its vicinity' which had been noted by Adam Smith, had largely disappeared by 1820; but Senior regarded ignorance and inertia as significant obstacles to mobility, and asserted that between town and country, and between different regions, the differences 'in occupations, in wages, in habits, in wants, and in morals' were as great as between Paris and Berlin – a view that was fully echoed in McCulloch's writings.[69] More interesting, perhaps, was their disagreement about occupational mobility within the more advanced sectors of the economy. According to McCulloch, a person who has been trained to habits of industry and application, can easily be moved from one employment to another. The various subordinate branches of all the great departments of industry have so many things in common, that an individual who has attained to any considerable proficiency in one, has seldom much difficulty in attaining to a like proficiency in any other;

whereas Senior held that

British workmen, and more especially the most numerous classes, those employed in manufactures, resemble the component parts of the vast machine which they direct. Separately taken, they are as useless as a single wheel or a single roller. Combined with many hundreds or many thousands of others, each helpless when alone, a hundred families can produce results which could not have been obtained by the individual labour of a thousand.

Consequently, once the motive power animating this great machine ceased, the component parts lost their value – 'the engine becomes old iron, the spinners and weavers become paupers'.[70]

The workers' readiness to emigrate, given unfavourable conditions at home and a modest subsidy or other inducement to move, was the subject of extensive debate,[71] while the differential between the real incomes of single and married labourers was repeatedly referred to in discussions of the poor relief system. Ricardo, who assumed that the average current wage rate was too low to enable the married labourer to pay taxes without public assistance, denied that the single man enjoyed a surplus that encouraged him to live in an extravagant manner. According to Torrens, the unmarried labourer in an old and settled country had sufficient income 'to purchase the finer manufactured goods, and the articles of convenience and luxury, which have fallen in value as compared with the necessaries of life'; but added that a large family 'deprives the working man of the ease, the comfort, and independence which he enjoys in the single state' – and consequently the marriage rate tended to fall as a country approached the limit of its resources.[72] In general, however, the earnings of women and children were believed to encourage improvident marriages and large families. Married women were described as good earners but bad mothers, and childrens' employment was said to undercut the wages of adults, preventing them from obtaining education, and even diminishing the parents' industriousness.[73] But it was appreciated that the opportunities for family earnings were by no means uniform.

The earnings of the wife and child of many a Manchester weaver or spinner exceed, or equal, those of himself. Those of the wife and children of an agricultural labourer, or of a carpenter, or coalheaver, are generally unimportant – while the husbands, in each case, receive 15 shillings a week, the weekly income of the one family may be 40 shillings, and that of the other only 17s or 18s.[74]

As might be expected from their insistence on the need to provide incentives to effort there were occasional references to the desirability of piece-rate payments, a system which, McCulloch claimed, had been 'generally adopted' in Great Britain wherever practicable, because it

> gives the workmen an interest in being industrious; and makes them exert themselves to execute the greatest quantity of work in the least space of time. And in consequence of its prevalence, this practice materially influences even the day labourers; who, to avoid invidious comparisons, make exertions unknown in other countries.

The introduction of piece-rate payments in agriculture, he remarked a few years earlier, had emancipated the agricultural labourers from their former dependence on the farmer under the traditional hiring system.[75]

V

Both conceptually and chronologically, the classical economists represent an intermediate stage between the eighteenth century belief in the harmony of interests and the Marxian idea of class conflict, and they left it to others to draw socialistic conclusions from Ricardo's doctrine, because they broadly accepted the social system of their day, and were under the influence of inherited ideas of economic and social progress. During the early years of the century, it is true, the omnipresent fear of rising population darkened future prospects; but as time passed the once inexorable Malthusian 'law' was translated into a 'tendency' that was being counteracted by the advance of wealth, prudence and civilization. The strain of optimism was never unqualified, for it was still true at the mid-century that the Malthusian doctrine conflicted with 'those plans of easy beneficence which accord so well with the inclination of man, but so ill with the arrangements of nature'.[76] Pouring cold water on revolutionary or utopian proposals for reform was part of the classical economists' essential function as social scientists, and whenever they argued that the removal of long-established evils could not be accomplished without considerable suffering, their warnings stemmed from realism rather than from hard-heartedness. Senior may have been tragically wrong when he maintained that 'what are called severity and hardness in the administration of relief are by far the best things for the welfare of the labouring classes';[77] but, like his eighteenth century predecessors, he was anxious to discourage misplaced sentimentalism and ill-judged philanthropy which had long bedevilled the efforts of poor law reformers. As it transpired, for all their shortcomings, Senior and his ardent Benthamite collaborator

Edwin Chadwick helped to lay the foundations of an administrative revo-lution which provided an essential starting point for subsequent social services;[78] and although the classical economists undoubtedly carried their belief in uniformity and system too far, historians have generally undervalued this aspect of their influence while exaggerating the rigidity with which they adhered to their fundamental economic principles.

As the preceding pages have shown, the classical principles were capable of considerable modification and adaptation to changing circumstances – so much so, indeed, that the presentation of a brief summary of classical opinion on any important question is a hazardous undertaking. The influence of popularizers like Jane Marcet, Harriet Martineau and James Wilson of the London *Economist*,[79] who drew their authority from Ricardo and his followers, was so pervasive that it has taken a generation of scholarship to dispel the widespread view that the classical economists were dogmatic proponents of *laissez-faire*. They were, of course, generally sceptical of the value of State interference – albeit with substantial justification, considering the governmental and financial facts of contemporary life – and their influence was, in a number of specific instances, distinctly obstructive. But no serious historian will nowadays argue that either they or their ideas presented 'a solid obstacle to all plans of social reform',[80] for they were themselves essentially reformers of a piecemeal and moderate type, and were increasingly prepared to grant exceptions to the principle of non-intervention in response to the changing facts of economic and social life.

As far as the labourer was concerned, they firmly believed that his lot could and should be improved; and when Torrens claimed that political economy merited

> the peculiar attention of the benevolent and good, mainly because it explains the causes which depress and elevate wages, and thereby points out the means by which we may mitigate the distress, and improve the condition of the great majority of mankind,[81]

he was merely stating in unusually naive terms a belief that was generally accepted by members of his group.

By themselves, good intentions count for little, and the classical economists' belief in the natural operation of economic forces and their insistence on the values of individual freedom and the rights of private property undoubtedly prevented them from seriously considering some feasible proposals for reform. No twentieth century student of industrialization will argue that they possessed either an adequate knowledge of the facts or a sufficient understanding of the labourer's needs and desires. All too often their analysis was influenced by their middle-class preconceptions and prejudices, while their policy proposals as often reflected their aspirations as the practical possibilities of reform. But if their attitude to the lower orders was deficient in subtlety and sensitivity, it was neither hostile nor unsympathetic. They did not fully appreciate the richness and variety of the individuals and groups that comprised the labouring classes; but neither did they homogenize the masses into a conceptual monolith – 'the working class', as some overenthusiastic labour historians are inclined to do. They certainly failed to enter the minds of the unskilled and casual labourers, who formed a large proportion of the wage-earning population, or, at least in the short run, to win the intellectual support of a majority of workers.[82]

Nevertheless, for the most part, they endeavoured to enlist the workers as accessories to reform.[83] Taking nineteenth century British history as a whole, the classical economists were not far wrong when they assumed that the labouring classes would readily seize any opportunities to adopt middle-class attitudes, standards and patterns of behaviour.

A NOTE ON SOURCES

For the purposes of this essay, 'classical economics' means the economic writings, speeches, official evidence and correspondence of A. Smith, J. Bentham, T.R. Malthus, D. Ricardo, J. Mill, R. Torrens, E. West, T. de Quincey, J.R. McCulloch, N.W. Senior and J.S. Mill. The article deals only with the period 1800–48, because Smith's ideas are well known (see, for example, my articles in the *Economic History Review* 2nd series, XI (1958–9) (reprinted in this volume, pp.63–84) and XIII (1960–1) (reprinted in this volume, pp.85–100), and *Renaissance and Modern Studies* (Nottingham, 1962), (reprinted in this volume, pp. 119–38)) and because there are few comments on the labourer in *Bentham's Economic Writings* (ed. W. Stark, 1952–4). J.S. Mill's views changed so significantly after 1848, and in ways so intimately bound up with his opinions on non-economic issues, that they merit separate treatment. There is indeed some justice in Marx's jibe that he was 'perfectly at home in the domain of flat contradiction'.

Attention has been concentrated on published material, but this represents a large portion of the total extant, and within the selected period the coverage has been wide, though incomplete. For authorship of the numerous unsigned reviews see F.W. Fetter's articles in the *Journal of Political Economy* (1953, 1958 and 1962); and the *Scottish Journal of Political Economy* (1960). Dr Donald Winch generously lent me, in advance of publication, his edition of *James Mill, Selected Economic Writings* (1966); and I am also grateful for comments on an earlier draft by Mr M. Caplan, Dr D.P. O'Brien and Professor S. Pollard.

NOTES

1 A. Toynbee, *Lectures on the Industrial Revolution* (1884). Cf. E.P. Thompson, *The Making of the English Working Class* (1963), pp.224, 265, 313, 341, 543, 552, etc.

2 See *Note on Sources* section for an account of the sources used in this essay.

3 The same is often true, *mutatis mutandis*, of the 'optimistic' and 'pessimistic' interpreters of the industrial revolution. Cf. W. Woodruff, 'Capitalism and the Historians', *Journal of Economic History* XVI (1956), *passim*.

CLASSICAL ECONOMISTS AND THE LABOURER

4 J.R. McCulloch, *A Discourse on the Rise, Progress, Peculiar Objects and Importance of Political Economy* (1824).
5 For a recent disagreement on this point, cf. Mark Blaug, *Ricardian Economics: A Historical Study* (1958), pp.182–8, and B.A. Corry, *Money, Saving and Investment in English Economics 1800–1850* (1962), pp.10–12. (On the whole the present writer endorses Dr Corry's view.) See also W.J. Ashley's introduction to J.S. Mill's *Principles of Political Economy* (1920), pp.xviii–xx.
6 See Blaug, *Ricardian Economics*, ch.6, for a summary of the changing attitudes to the Malthusian law of population.
7 McCulloch (ed.), *A Statistical Account of the British Empire* II (1839), pp.507–8; also ibid, I, viii. McCulloch, 'State and Defects of British Statistics', *Edinburgh Review* CXXIII (1835), p.175. (Hereinafter cited as *Edin. Rev.*). Italics in original. Also McCulloch's evidence before the *Select Committee on Public Documents* (1833), pp.12–16. He advocated the establishment of a Board of Statistics in London like those in Europe, with agents in the principal manufacturing towns. For an example of a case where McCulloch claimed to have decisively changed his opinion in response to 'consideration of the historical facts with respect to the operation of the principle', see *Select Committee on the State of the Poorer Classes in Ireland* (1830), pp.590–1. In many other cases the classical economists openly admitted that there were important disagreements among qualified observers with respect both to facts and proposals for reform. For example, Senior, *Letters on the Factory Act* (2nd ed., 1844), pp.30 ff.
8 Robert Torrens, *The Budget, On Commercial and Colonial Policy* (1844), p.326. Elsewhere he distinguished between 'speaking statistically' and speaking 'hypothetically upon the principles of political economy'. *Select Committee on the Disposal of Lands in the British Colonies* (1836), p.140.
9 In a letter to James Mill, 9 Nov. 1817. Cf. P. Sraffa and M.H. Dobb (eds), *The Works and Correspondence of David Ricardo* VII (1952), p.205. (Subsequently cited as *Ricardo's Works*.)
10 Morris R. Cohen, *Reason and Nature, An Essay on the Nature of Scientific Method* (1931), p.27. For reasons why the economists were reluctant to abandon their hard-won positions, see my article 'The Role of Authority in the Development of British Economics', *Journal of Law and Economics* (Oct. (1964). Reprinted in vol. II in this series.
11 On the intellectual background see Leslie Stephen, *The English Utilitarians* (1900); and Elie Halévy, *The Growth of Philosophic Radicalism* (1928).
12 Nassau W. Senior, 'Poor Law Reform', *Edin. Rev.* CXLIX (1841), reprinted in his *Historical and Philosophical Essays* (1865), pp.97–8. Cf. McCulloch, 'Combination Laws, Restraints on Emigration', *Edin. Rev.* LXXVIII (1824), p.334.
13 William Hazlitt declared that Malthus's excessively 'amorous complexion' led him to suppose that all other men were made of 'the same combustible materials'. Cf. Stephen, op. cit., II, p.255. Cf. D.E.C. Eversley, *Social Theories of Fertility and the Malthusian Debate* (1959), pp.250–4, 294. Also Malthus, *An Essay on Population* (Everyman ed., 1914) II, pp.206, 257–61. For Malthus's attempt to defend his law of population while retaining his optimism, see Senior, *Two Lectures on Population* (1831), pp.68 ff.
14 See, for example, S.G. Checkland, 'Growth and Progress: The Nineteenth Century View in Britain', *Econ. Hist. Rev.* 2nd series, XII (1959) esp. pp.49–53.
15 Senior, 'Ireland', *Edin. Rev.* CLIX (1844), p.194. But compare his unpublished lectures of 1849–50 quoted by Leon Levy (ed.) in *Industrial Efficiency and Social Economy* (n.d.), I, p.322. For a useful background essay on this question see Asa Briggs, 'The Language of "Class" in Early Nineteenth Century England', in *Essays in Labour History*, Asa Briggs and John Saville (eds), (1960), pp.43–73.

181

16 *Ricardo's Works* VIII, pp.129, 300 (Ricardo to Malthus, 24 Nov. 1820). For Malthus's views see ibid. VIII, pp.107–8; also McCulloch, *Observations on the State of the Country, and on the Proper Policy of Administration* (1830), p.26.

17 McCulloch, *Outlines of Political Economy* (McVickar ed., 1825), p.49; *Treatise on the Succession*, pp.31, 34.

18 J.S. Mill, 'The Claims of Labour', *Edin. Rev.* CLXIV (1845), p.511. Cf. Senior, *Reviews of the Waverley Novels*, etc. (1821), p.226. For James Mill's views see 'State of the Nation', *Westminster Review* VI (1826), p.263, and Briggs, 'Language of Class', p.64.

19 See, for example, McCulloch, 'Comparative Productiveness of High and Low Taxes', *Edin. Rev.* LXXII (1822), pp.535–6; 'Impolicy of Increasing the Duties on Spirits', ibid. (1830), pp.488–9; 'Causes and Cure of Disturbances and Pauperism', ibid. CV (1831), pp.51, 60.

20 Ricardo to Trower, 15 July 1916, in Sraffa, *Ricardo's Works* VII, p.49.

21 Ibid. VIII, p.80; III, p.146; VI, p.183 (Malthus to Ricardo, 10 Mar. 1815).

22 Ibid. VIII, pp.129, 300 (Ricardo to Malthus, 24 Nov. 1820). Malthus believed that to concede universal suffrage and annual parliaments as a result of intimidation by mass meetings would be to invite a 'bloody revolution' (VIII, pp.107–8), while McCulloch, for all his generosity towards the labouring class, predicted 'nothing but insecurity, revolution and rapine' if universal suffrage were to be adopted. Cf. *Observations on the State of the Country, and on the Proper Policy of Administration* (1830), p.26.

23 McCulloch, 'Rise, Progress, Present State, and Prospects of the British Cotton Manufacture', *Edin. Rev.* XCI (1827), pp.37–8. J.S. Mill concurred; see his *Principles*, pp.756–7. For Smith's views see also Nathan Rosenberg, 'Adam Smith on The Division of Labour: Two Views or One?', *Economica* N.S. XXXII (1965), pp.127–39.

24 Senior, 'Grounds and Objects of the Budget', *Edin. Rev.* CXLVIII (1841), pp.506–11, 518. Cf. Torrens, *Address to the Farmers of the United Kingdom on the Low Rates of Profit in Agriculture and in Trade* (1831), p.13; and 'A Paper on the Means of Reducing the Poor's Rates', *The Pamphleteer* X (1817), p.524. Also McCulloch, 'Causes and Cure of Disturbances', pp.62–3.

25 Cf. Joseph Hamberger, *James Mill and the Art of Revolution* (1964), p.115. Italics in original. A severe critic of the aristocracy, Mill was nevertheless no uncritical admirer of the populace. See his 'State of the Nation', pp.263–7.

26 Senior, quoted from unpublished lectures 1849–50 by Levy, *Industrial Efficiency*, I, p.305.

27 Senior, 'The Poor Law in Ireland', *Edin. Rev.* CLVI (1843), pp.400–1. Cf. James Mill, *Elements of Political Economy* (1826), p.58; and 'State of the Nation', p.263.

28 J.S. Mill emphasized the obstacles to improvement, *Principles*, pp.348–9, and note, while Malthus identified a 'wretchedly poor' substratum incapable of reproducing themselves. *Essay* II, pp.143–4, 209, 214–15.

29 McCulloch, *An Article on Taxation*, p.5. Also 'Progress of the National Debt, Best Method of Funding', *Edin. Rev.* XCIII (1828), p.82. Cf. E. Rotwein (ed.), *David Hume, Writings on Economics* (1955), p.xiii; J.S. Mill, *Principles*, p.286.

30 Malthus, *Essay* II, pp.143, 177. For Senior's opposing view, see Levy *Industrial Efficiency* I, p.12.

31 McCulloch, *An Essay on the Question of Reducing the Interest on the National Debt* (1816), pp.132–3

32 Senior, *A Letter to Lord Howick, On a Legal Provision for the Irish Poor* (1831), pp.46–8, 50. In *An Outline of the Science of Political Economy* (1836), p.134, he hinted that in London and its environs Irish competition was pushing English labourers

up the socio-economic ladder. For contrary views see Malthus, *Select Committee on Emigration* (1827), pp.312–13; McCulloch, 'Ireland', *Edin. Rev.* LXXIII (1822), p.62, and *Statistical Account* I, p.397; Torrens, *On Wages and Combination* (1834), pp.31–2, and *The Budget*, p.117; T. de Quincey, *The Logic of Political Economy* (1844), p.145 n., 147–8 n. On immigration restrictions see James Mill, 'State of the Nation', p.246; McCulloch, *Select Committee on the State of the Poorer Classes in Ireland* (1830), pp.584–5.

33 Senior, 'Grounds and Objects of the Budget', p.504. He believed that improvidence was the British workman's greatest weakness.

34 McCulloch, *Principles of Political Economy* (1870), p.129. Similarly J.S. Mill's evidence on savings among building workers, *Select Committee on Investment for the Savings of the Middle and Working Classes* (1850), p.89.

35 Senior, *Outline of Political Economy*, p.208. Cf. McCulloch, *Treatise on Wages*, p.55.

36 McCulloch, *A Treatise on the Succession* pp.89–90. J.S. Mill took exactly the opposite view. Cf. *Principles*, Bk. II, ch.VI and VIII.

37 Senior, *Three Lectures on the Cost of Obtaining Money* (1830), p.28; *Three Lectures on the Transmission of the Precious Metals* (1830), pp.93–4. Cf. Malthus, *Essay* II, p.174.

38 Senior, *Three Lectures on the Rate of Wages* (1830), pp.52, 16–17; 'Grounds and Objects of the Budget', p.505; 'Poor Law Reform', *Edin. Rev.* CXLIX (1841), p.3; *Introductory Lecture on Political Economy* (1827), p.12. For inconsistent statements by Senior, cf. *Outline of . . . Political Economy*, p.55, and Levy, *Industrial Efficiency* II, p.298.

39 McCulloch, *Principles*, pp.93–4; *Essay on Reducing the Interest*, pp.133–4; cf. 'Effects of Machinery on Accumulation', *Edin. Rev.* LXIX (1821), pp.105–6. Also, Malthus, *Essay* II, pp.45, 215, 255; and *Ricardo's Works* VI, p.225; James Mill, *Elements*, pp.242–3, 245.

40 Malthus, 'Newenham and Others on the State of Ireland', *Edin. Rev.* XXIV (1808), p.341; Sraffa, *Ricardo's Works* VIII, p.185.

41 Torrens, *The Budget*, pp.234, 288.

42 De Quincey, *Logic of Political Economy*, pp.147–8.

43 Kenneth Smith, *The Malthusian Controversy* (1951), p.42. Cf. Malthus, 'Godwin on Malthus', *Edin. Rev.* LXX (1821), p.373.

44 Malthus, *Essay* I, pp.236, 315; II, pp.168, 175, 208, 257.

45 Senior, *Lectures on Population*, pp.26–7; *Outline of Political Economy*, p.38. Cf. Malthus, *Essay* I, pp.12–13.

46 But while population pressure was an immediate problem, capital accumulation was viewed as a slow process. See R.D. Collison Black, *Economic Thought and the Irish Question 1817–1870* (1960), p.86n.

47 Cited by James Arthur Field, *Essays on Population* (1931), pp.110–11.

48 Malthus, *Essay* II, pp.169, 243; on domestic happiness and parental responsibility, *ibid*, pp.204–6. Malthus believed that restraint increased the force of the 'passion between the sexes', but also raised its quality and hence represented a civilizing influence. *ibid*, p.156.

49 McCulloch ridiculed Sismondi's proposal that all classes should marry freely, but live in a state of continence after producing two or three children. McCulloch to Ricardo, 18 Apr. 1819; *Ricardo's Works.* VIII, p.25. On contraception see James Mill, 'Colony' in *Encyclopedia Britannica* (1818), pp.12–13; also Eversley, *Social Theories of Fertility*, pp.156–7; Field, *Essays on Population* pp.94, 125–6. Only James Mill seriously contemplated contraception as a possible solution.

50 Malthus, *Essay*, II, pp.254–5.

51 Senior, 'Grounds and Objects of the Budget', p.506.

52 Michael Theodore Wermel, *The Evolution of the Classical Wage Theory* (1939), p.162. The minimum equilibrium wage rate represented the base of a structure of wage rates that varied according to skill, length of training, unpleasantness, etc. Torrens also specified a 'moral and necessary maximum of wages'. See *On Wages and Combination*, p.8; *The Budget*, pp.107–8.

53 For passing references to factors encouraging increased productivity, which usually conflicted with the customary assumption that habits changed only slowly, see McCulloch, *Outlines of Political Economy*, p.64, and *Historical Sketch of the Bank of England* (1831), p.40; Senior, 'Report on the State of Agriculture', *Quarterly Review* XXV (1821), p.485, and *Introductory Lecture on Political Economy*, p.12.

54 Joseph A. Schumpeter, *History of Economic Analysis* (1954), pp.664–5.

55 Malthus, *Essay* II, p.215.

56 For example, McCulloch remarked that once the practice of exchange is introduced 'a spirit of industry is universally diffused, and the apathy and languor of the rude state of society disappears', *Outlines of Political Economy*, p.64. Senior maintained that an increase in the supply of corn 'will produce immediately an improvement of habits and, if permanent, an increase of numbers of the labouring part of the population', 'Report on the State of Agriculture', *Quarterly Review* XXV (1821), p.485; and elsewhere Senior claimed that 'as soon as he begins to save, a labourer becomes sober and industrious, attentive to his health and to his character ... no institution could be more beneficial to the morals of the lower orders, i.e. to at least nine-tenths of the whole body of any people, than one that should increase their power and their wish to accumulate', *Introductory Lecture on Political Economy*, p.12. Cf. McCulloch, *Historical Sketch of the Bank of England* (1831), p.40. These quotations conflict with the usual classical view that the labourer's habits changed only slowly.

57 Malthus, *Essay* II, pp.139, 257; *Principles of Political Economy* (1836), pp.257, 280. On the other hand, Malthus' discussion of emigration schemes reveals his conviction that the 'population vacuum' would rapidly be refilled. See R.N. Ghosh, 'Malthus on Emigration and Colonization', *Economica* N.S. XXX (1963), esp. pp.53–4.

58 For example, Senior, *Outline of Political Economy*, pp.43–8; and *Two Lectures on Population*, pp.68–90; but cf. his earlier opinion, 'Report on the State of Agriculture', p.484. McCulloch, *Principles*, p.182; 'Chalmers on Political Economy', *Edin. Rev.* CXI (1832), p.56; and *An Article ... On Taxation*, pp.13–14; De Quincey, *Logic of Political Economy*, p.150. Torrens, *On Wages and Combination*, p.28. It was recognized that the effects of sudden changes in real income differed from those of more gradual changes, and this is a further reason why it is risky to summarize the classical view.

59 Letter to Archbishop Whately, 20 Mar. 1845, cited by Levy, *Industrial Efficiency* II, p.26.

60 McCulloch, *Principles*, p.180.

61 Senior, *Two Lectures on Population*, pp.3–6; *Outline of Political Economy*, pp.36–7. He believed that fear of losing the 'decencies' of life was an effective check to population growth, whereas fear of losing 'necessaries' was not, at least in England. Cf. Eversley, *op. cit.*, p.93.

62 James Mill, *Elements*, p.220. Torrens and James Mill believed that the labourers could not afford to pay taxes on 'necessaries', as they had no surplus income; but McCulloch, Senior and J.S. Mill disagreed. For Ricardo's position see Carl S. Shoup, *Ricardo on Taxation* (1960), pp.65–77.

63 De Quincey, *Logic of Political Economy*, p.153.

CLASSICAL ECONOMISTS AND THE LABOURER

64 For example, Torrens, *The Budget*, pp.183–4.
65 McCulloch even suggested that the workers' taste for gin and tobacco helped to elevate their conception of an appropriate standard of living, and that without it their wages would fall (*Treatise on Wages*, pp.40–1).
66 See W.D. Grampp, 'Malthus on Money Wages and Welfare', *American Economic Review* XLVI (1956), pp.924–36; and Eversley, op. cit., p.211, for interesting comments on this matter.
67 Senior, 'The Budget of 1842', *Edin. Rev.* CLI (1842), p.197. Cf. Grampp, op. cit., *passim*.
68 Although Ricardo disapproved of the Gloucestershire practice of maintaining wage rates in periods of slack business (*Ricardo's Works* VIII, p.316), several of the classical economists supported State aid or intervention in times of acute distress to protect the labourer from a fall in his customary living standards.
69 McCulloch, *Essay on Reducing the Interest*, pp.9–10; Senior, 'Poor Law Reform', p.40; also *Three Lectures on the Rate of Wages*, p.14.
70 McCulloch, 'Effects of Machinery on Accumulation', p.115; Senior, 'Grounds and Objects of the Budget', pp.504–5.
71 Donald Winch, *Classical Political Economy and Colonies* (1965), ch.5.
72 *Ricardo's Works* VIII, pp.117–18, 124. Torrens, *On Wages and Combination*, pp.29–30. The implication of this remark for the Malthusian view need not be stressed.
73 McCulloch, *Treatises and Essays on Money, Exchange, Interest, etc.* (1859), pp.457–8; *Treatise on Wages* p.96; 'Taxation and the Corn Laws', *Edin. Rev.* LXV (1820), p.169; Malthus, 'Godwin on Malthus', p.373.
74 Senior, *Outline of Political Economy*, p.148.
75 McCulloch, *Statistical Account* I, p.619; *Observations on the State of the Country*, p.9.
76 J.S. Mill, 'The Claims of Labour', pp.501–2.
77 Senior, *House of Lords Select Committee on the Burdens Affecting Real Property* (1846), p.470. There is an almost exact parallel between the economists' desire to protect the pecuniary capital of the rich and their concern for the 'intellectual and moral capital' of the poor. In this respect they anticipate recent interest in the role of 'human capital' in economic development.
78 See, for example, S.E. Finer, *The Life and Times of Sir Edwin Chadwick* (1952), *passim*; and Marian Bowley, *Nassau Senior and Classical Economics* (1937), Part II.
79 See especially, Blaug, *Ricardian Economics*, ch.VII; and Scott Gordon, 'The London *Economist* and the High Tide of Laissez Faire', *Journal of Political Economy* LXIII (1955), pp.461–88.
80 J.L. and Barbara Hammond, *The Town Labourer, 1760–1832* (1925), p.196.
81 Torrens, *On Wages and Combination*, pp.1–2.
82 Cf. R.K. Webb, *The British Working Class Reader, 1790–1848* (1955), pp.97 ff.
83 Thompson, *The Making of the English Working Class*, p.139, with special reference to Francis Place.

10

THE CLASSICAL ECONOMISTS, INDUSTRIALIZATION AND POVERTY

I INTRODUCTION

Any brief account of the classical economists' ideas about so wide-ranging and complex a subject as industrialization and poverty must necessarily be highly selective. Even on a restricted definition, the category 'classical economics' embraces ten or a dozen individuals, most of whom were prolific authors.[1] Moreover, their collective life-span extended over a century and a half of significant economic and social transformation, from 1723 to 1875, and only the most abstract and speculative of philosophers could have been entirely unaffected by contemporary events.

Protracted controversy

There has, admittedly, been protracted controversy about the precise relationship between classical economics and the circumstances of the time.[2] But, as a group, the economists were continually seeking to understand the world around them, and they were eager to influence current and future economic and social policy. Even some of their more general theories were decisively influenced by recent events. For example, the Ricardian rent theory, which was formulated almost simultaneously in 1815 by Ricardo, Malthus and West, has with some justification been regarded as an *ex post facto* rationalization of the Napoleonic wartime experience. And both their theories and their policy proposals were repeatedly in the forefront of public discussion.

During the century that separated Smith's *The Wealth of Nations* (1776) from Cairnes's *Leading Principles of Political Economy Newly Expounded* (1874), the classical doctrines were repeatedly and bitterly attacked by a wide variety of critics, including poets, novelists, journalists, propagandists, politicians, professors, clerics, factory owners, trade unionists and other economists.

While these attacks helped to create an *esprit de corps* among the defenders of the main British doctrinal tradition, there were nevertheless important differences of opinion among them on method, theory and policy. These differences inevitably complicate the task of summarizing their views. Moreover, disagreements among the *cognoscenti* periodically attracted public attention and threatened to undermine the scientific reputation of political economy.[3] Indeed, by the mid-1870s matters had become so serious that when the Political Economy Club held a dinner in London to celebrate the centenary of *The Wealth of Nations* a writer in the *Pall Mall Gazette* commented that the economists 'had better be celebrating the obsequies of their science than its jubilee'.[4]

'Bouquets as well as brickbats'

The climate of opinion was not, of course, universally hostile: there were bouquets as well as brickbats. Yet in the five or six decades after Waterloo there was a discernible growth of individual and collective self-consciousness among the classical economists, part of a process that would nowadays be termed professionalization. When Thomas Carlyle derided 'the gloomy professors of the dismal science', he overrated the academic status and content of their work. But the trend towards academic economics was growing irresistibly, so much so that since the 1870s there have been few outstanding contributions to economic science by men and women untrained in universities. In the process of professionalization the polemical, ideological and practical ingredients in political economy were gradually repressed as attention was increasingly focused on theoretical and technical questions. This change must be borne in mind when considering the classical economists' views on such a broad theme as industrialization and poverty, for these subjects cannot be confined within the conventional boundaries of economic science. The changes in the economists' aims and self-image affected their writings in more subtle ways than changes in the economic and social environment, and failure to take both these dimensions into account has seriously misled some commentators.

'Industrialization' broadly defined

Throughout this essay the term 'industrialization' will be taken to include not only the narrowly economic and technical changes within the manufacturing sector during the industrial revolution, and the concomitant developments in industrial organization, occupational distribution, and in the level and composition of national income; it also encompasses the wider influence of these changes on the social structure and the prevailing habits, values, beliefs and attitudes.

The classical economists' writings touch upon many facets of this complex process. Since it is impossible to consider them all, attention will be concentrated on a few central themes, such as the changing balance between agriculture, manufacturing and commerce; the role of machinery and inventions; changes in the relative wealth and power of the social classes; and the predicament and prospects of the labouring population.

II STRUCTURAL CHANGES IN THE ECONOMY

When John Stuart Mill published his magisterial *Principles of Political Economy* in 1848, agriculture was still the leading occupation in Britain. But by this time agriculture's share in the national income was falling, and the focus of classical economics had shifted markedly since *The Wealth of Nations*, largely in response to the changing structure of the economy. Adam Smith attached so much importance to the role of agriculture in the economy that he has sometimes been viewed as a follower of the French Physiocrats, even though he decisively rejected their belief that the agriculturalist alone produced a 'produit net'.

Smith's nineteenth century disciple, J.R. McCulloch, regarded Smith's statement that a given capital employed in agriculture puts more productive labour into motion than an equivalent sum invested in manufacturing or commerce as 'the most objectionable passage in *The Wealth of Nations*'.[5] And a vivid, if somewhat exaggerated, impression of the differences between the two men is conveyed by the critic who protested that McCulloch

> was ready to turn the whole country into one vast manufacturing district filled with smoke and steam engines and radical weavers, and to set adrift all the gentlemen and farmers now constituting our agricultural population.[6]

Classical theory of economic growth

It is hardly surprising that manufacturing occupied an increasingly prominent role in the works of Smith's nineteenth century followers, and the theoretical reasons can be suggested by a brief account of the Malthus-Ricardo discussion of the 1815 Corn Law. This was a significant episode in the development of the classical theory of economic growth, for the theory essentially rested on the fundamental relationship between population and the food supply. For two or three decades after Malthus first published his notorious *Essay on Population* (1978) there were widespread fears that population increase was outstripping agricultural output. The inevitable consequence would be that food prices (especially corn) would continue to rise, leading to a rise in money wages and a concomitant fall in the rate of profit, not only in agriculture but throughout the economy. Since profit constituted the incentive to capital accumulation, which was the mainspring of economic growth, a fall in the rate of return would discourage investment and, if it continued, eventually bring about the 'stationary state'. Thus while economic prosperity was associated with a constant or rising output of foodstuffs *per capita*, any serious check to investment while population expansion continued would eventually depress living standards and cause general distress, especially among the poor.

This account of the classical theory is, of course, over-simplified, and individual members of the school differed in their interpretations of the growth process.[7] To Ricardo it seemed obvious that restrictions on corn imports merely made matters worse by raising food prices, whereas cheap food imports would help to counteract the pressure of population on food supplies. In Parliament in 1820, Ricardo said that.

> he conceived the duty of government to be, to give the greatest possible development to industry by removing restrictions on trade, and other obstacles of that description.[8]

Most of the later classical economists agreed, which helps to explain their support for free trade. But Malthus, who attached much more importance to agriculture than his contemporaries, argued vigorously in favour of a balanced economy, claiming that 'the principles of political economy' should be subordinated to the higher end of 'the happiness of society'. Society's gains from an indefinite extension of manufacturing might be counterbalanced by several disadvantages, he contended, including

> a greater degree of uncertainty in its supplies of corn, greater fluc-tuations in the wages of labour, greater unhealthiness and immorality owing to a larger proportion of the population being employed in manufactories, and a greater chance of long and retrograde movements occasioned by the natural progress of those countries from which corn had been imported.[9]

This passage reveals Malthus's sensitivity to the problems of industrialization which were to figure more and more prominently in the later classical writings. In defending restrictions on corn imports he recognized that he was making an exception to his general support for the free trade principle. But while ostensibly resting his case on the grounds that dependence on foreign food would lead to economic instability and would seriously weaken the nation in time of war, it is clear that he also feared the social and political consequences of a significant decline in the landed class.[10]

In this respect Malthus's disagreement with Ricardo is striking. Although Adam Smith had asserted that the interest of the landlord, unlike the merchant manufacturer, was 'strictly and inseparably connected with the general interest of society', Ricardo saw the landlord as a parasite, even as an enemy of progress.[11] Moreover, he denied that there was any necessary conflict between agriculture and manufactures:

Nations grow old as well as individuals; and in proportion as they grow old, populous, and wealthy, must they become manufacturers. If these things were allowed to take their own course, we should undoubtedly become a great manufacturing country, but we should remain a great agricultural country also. . . . There would always be a limit to our greatness, while we were growing our own supply of food; but we should always be increasing in wealth and power, whilst we obtained part of it from foreign countries, and devoted our own manufactures to the payment of it.[12]

Material wealth and social welfare

As we shall see, Ricardo and his successors were by no means unaware of the defects of an industrial society. Nevertheless, they retained their fundamental faith in the benefits of economic progress. Like their eighteenth century predecessors, David Hume and Adam Smith, who associated the expansion of commerce with the advance of civilization, they were convinced that material wealth was an essential prerequisite of social and cultural welfare. As McCulloch observed:

Where wealth has not been amassed, individuals, being constantly occupied in providing for their immediate wants, have no time left for the culture of their minds; so that their views, sentiments, and feelings, become alike contracted and illiberal. The possession of a decent competence, or the power to indulge in other pursuits than those which directly tend to satisfy our animal wants and desires, is necessary to soften the selfish passions; to improve the moral and intellectual character; and to ensure any considerable proficiency in liberal studies and pursuits. And hence, the acquisition of wealth is not desirable merely as the means of procuring immediate and direct gratifications, but is indispensably necessary to the advancement of society in civilisation and refinement.[13]

As these remarks show, the classical view of economic development was not narrowly constricted. Among later members of the school, John Stuart Mill was by far the most perceptive commentator on the relationship between wealth and welfare. Unlike his predecessors he did not view the station- ary state with 'unaffected aversion'; indeed, he regarded the competitive 'trampling, crushing, elbowing and treading on each other's heels' merely as 'disagreeable symptoms of one of the phases of industrial progress', and looked forward to the stationary state as a time when cultivation of the 'art of living' would replace the 'art of getting on'.[14] The English needed instruction not in 'the desire of wealth' but in

the use of wealth, and appreciation of the objects of desire which wealth cannot purchase. . . . Every real improvement in the character of the English, whether it consists in giving them higher aspirations, or only a juster estimate of the value of their present objects of desire, must necessarily moderate the ardour of their devotion to the pursuit of wealth.[15]

Pervasive influence of Adam Smith

One of the main analytical reasons why manufacturing figured so prominently in later classical writings was the belief that it offered scope for increasing returns, as contrasted with the prevalence of diminishing returns in agriculture.[16] This distinction had been foreshadowed in *The Wealth of Nations*, where Smith placed enormous stress on the division of labour as a source of productivity gains and new inventions; and he had acknowledged that there was little scope for the division of labour in agriculture. Smith paid comparatively little attention to mechanization, a fact that has led some commentators to suggest that he was oblivious to the industrial revolution which was gathering momentum before his very eyes;[17] and it is an inadequate excuse to say that his *magnum opus* did not appear until 1776, for scholars now agree that the 'pre-conditions' lasted several decades.

Smith's presumed insensitivity to his surroundings is all the more surprising in view of his reputation as a keen observer, for economic and social historians have long regarded his writings as a mine of valuable information about contemporary life. However, a careful recent re-reading of Smith's works has shown that he was more aware of the importance of factory production and machine technology than has usually been supposed.[18] It cannot be claimed that he foresaw the remarkable transformation of manufacturing that was to occur in the next half-century or so; but these developments were by no means incompatible with his optimistic view of economic growth, a process in which his recognition of the possibilities of manufacturing and commercial expansion occupied a central place. As a modern commentator has observed:

> Smith's long-term prognosis for capitalism is centred upon its capacity for generating technical change and thus substantially raising *per capita* income. This capacity, in turn, is made by Smith to depend overwhelmingly – indeed one may almost say exclusively – upon the division of labour and the consequences flowing from it.[19]

As we have noted, there was little scope for the division of labour in agriculture.

Smith not only emphasized the productivity-increasing effects of manufacturing, but also its adverse social consequences. In an oft-quoted passage he remarked that a worker employed on a few simple operations under the division of labour

191

has no occasion to exert his understanding or to exercise his invention
... He naturally loses, therefore, the habit of such exertion, and
generally becomes as stupid and ignorant as it is possible for a human
creature to become ... His dexterity at his own particular trade seems
... to be acquired at the expense of his intellectual, social, and martial
virtues. But in every improved and civilised society this is the state into
which the labouring poor, that is, the great body of the people, must
necessarily fall, unless government takes some pains to prevent it.[20]

Although Smith advocated state aid to education as a means of counteracting
these adverse social effects, there is no doubt that the main impact of
this passage was to draw attention to the dangers of dehumanizing the
labour force, a process that was to become a major feature of the socialist,
sentimentalist and literary indictment of nineteenth century industrialization.
Nor did Smith sugar the pill when he

recognised the existence of a hierarchy of inventions involving varying
degrees of complexity, and requiring differing amounts of technical
competence analytical sophistication and creative and synthesising
intellect.

For this implied not only continuing technical progress, but also a growing
social as well as technical division of labour, whereby those with higher skills
and attainments (and presumably superior initial opportunities) would form
the upper ranks of society, thereby becoming 'thoroughly insulated from the
ravages of the division of labour' experienced by the labouring class.[21]

Effects of mechanization on employment

On the whole Smith's followers paid comparatively little attention to
the direct effects of mechanization and the division of labour upon the
workers' outlook,[22] for they were mainly concerned to stress the productivity-
increasing results of the expansion of manufacturing.[23] There was, however,
considerable interest in the effect of machinery on the level of employment,
especially after Ricardo's dramatic *volte face* in the third (1823) edition of
his *Principles of Political Economy and Taxation*. In the first two editions
(1817 and 1819) he had assumed that machinery was beneficial to all
members of the community, and did not even consider the possibility of
technological unemployment. Indeed, Ricardo persuaded McCulloch to
abandon his earlier opinion that the introduction of machinery had an
initially depressing effect on wages. In the third edition, however, Ricardo
accepted the argument of John Barton's pamphlet *Observations on the Condition
of the Labouring Classes* (1817) that machinery might not only cause temporary
hardship to labourers by creating unemployment, but that there might also
be a permanent displacement of labour.

While most of Ricardo's classical associates conceded the temporary ill-effects,[24] they were both embarrassed by, and hostile to, his contention that there could be permanently harmful consequences – an idea enthusiastically endorsed by Karl Marx.[25] It is unnecessary to specify the details of Ricardo's analysis, which are complex and confusing;[26] but it is worth noting that although Ricardo explicitly warned against state action to discourage technical progress, which he regarded as generally beneficial, J.S. Mill insisted that if technological advances diminished the wages fund, as Ricardo suggested, 'it would be incumbent on legislators to take measures for moderating its rapidity'.[27]

The social consequences of factory employment

The classical economists displayed somewhat more uncertainty about the effects of factory production and urbanization than about other aspects of industrialization, and with the passage of time the general tone of their writings became somewhat less optimistic. As might be expected, Malthus expressed profound misgivings, arguing that the unavoidable variations of manufacturing labour constituted one of the principal causes of pauperism.

Nor did he expect to see any substantial improvement in urban manufacturing communities.

> It is undoubtedly our duty, and in every point of view highly desirable, to make towns and manufacturing employments as little injurious as possible to the duration of life; but after all our efforts, it is possible that they will always remain less healthy than country situations and country employments; and consequently, operating as positive checks, will diminish in some degree the necessity of the preventive check.[28]

In his *Essay on Population* Malthus reproduced a detailed account of the evils of child labour in cotton mills from Aikin's *Description of the Country from Thirty to Forty Miles around Manchester* (1795), and in general the classical economists were enthusiastic supporters of legislative restrictions on children's work in factories.[29] However, they were reluctant to support legislative interference with adult working conditions, and although Senior's *Letters on The Factory Act* (1837) is often cited as evidence of their uncritical attitude towards the factory system, it was by no means a typical expression of opinion.[30] Nor was Senior's notorious contention that profit was earned in the last hour of work, so that a reduction of hours would be ruinous to employers.[31] McCulloch, in particular, who wrote extensively on the subject of factory conditions over a protracted period, expressed a variety of opinions at different times. While admitting the possibility that factory work was pernicious, he bitterly attacked the 1832 House of Commons Report on Factory Conditions which, he said, 'contains more false statements and exaggerated representations than any other document of the kind ever laid before the legislature'. He conceded that great inattention to cleanliness, and some revolting abuses, have existed in some factories, particularly of the smaller class . . .; but the instances of abuse bear but a small proportion to the total numbers; and, speaking generally, factory work-people, including non-adults, are as healthy and contented as any class of the community obliged to earn their bread by the sweat of their brow.[32]

Elsewhere, however, he acknowledged that the domestic system was morally superior to the factory, because those who worked at home, especially if they owned their own goods, were free from corruption by contamination with unworthy persons in factories.[33] Moreover, they would be restrained by their parents, would benefit from the knowledge that they were working for themselves and would reap the rewards of their labours. On the other hand, properly run factories could be schools for improvement, inculcating habits of industry and of orderly and regular conduct. Furthermore, cotton factory workers were less dependent on the vagaries of the climate than domestic workers, and were therefore in a superior condition.

Some of them as are provident are in decidedly comfortable circumstances. Their money wages have somewhat declined since the peace, but they have not declined to anything like the extent that the prices of bread, beef, clothes, and almost every necessary and useful article have done; so that the manufacturing part of the population possess, at this time, a greater command over the necessaries and conveniences of life, and are in decidedly more comfortable circumstances, than at any former period.[34]

McCulloch's views have been cited at length because they reveal some of the difficulties facing the classical economist who sought to draw general conclusions about the economic and social changes during his lifetime. In the 1820s McCulloch adopted an optimistic tone, conceding that the English workers were inflammable, turbulent and liable to be misled by radical demagogues, but regarding this as merely a symptom of the growing pains of an industrializing economy.[35] During the Chartist troubles of the 1840s, however, he began to question his earlier belief that the workers' violence would diminish as their intelligence grew, and by 1859 he was taking a far more pessimistic view of the situation.

There seems, on the whole, little room for doubting that the factory system operates unfavourably on the bulk of those engaged in it . . . It is certain, too, that the demand for the services of children and other young persons, and the ease with which factory labour may in general be learned, has had a powerful influence in depressing wages, and, consequently, in preventing the wonderful inventions and discoveries of the last half century from redounding so much to the advantage of the labouring classes as might otherwise have been anticipated.[36]

Nevertheless, as his recent biographer has argued, McCulloch was less concerned about the factory system itself than its distributional consequences, which represented a threat to social order. Although he retained his fundamental optimism towards the process of economic growth, he began to share Malthus's earlier anxieties, recognizing that manufacturing was subject to fluctuations in demand, and even wondering whether the manufacturing sector of the economy should have been kept smaller than the agricultural sector.[37]

Long-term economic and social trends

Although many historians have regarded the mid-nineteenth century as the period of Britain's economic supremacy, when she was 'the workshop of the world', the later classical economists were far from complacent about either the current state of affairs or the long-term prospects. J.S. Mill and Cairnes feared that the gains from industrial progress might be counteracted by continued population growth, and despite their belief in the existence of increasing returns in manufacturing they were not convinced that technological progress in agriculture would be sufficient to offset diminishing returns from the land. Moreover, both authors considered that the rate of capital accumulation was threatened because England was one of those opulent nations where the rate of profit was 'habitually within . . . a hand's breadth of the minimum'.[38]

Partly under the influence of Edmund Gibbon Wakefield, some of the classical economists came to believe that the 'powers of production' were 'outgrowing the field of employment', and overseas colonization was advocated by Torrens, Mill and – to a lesser extent – Cairnes, as a means of providing outlets for capital investment and relieving population pressure at home.[39] Although Cairnes acknowledged that there was no tendency for the rate of wages to fall to a minimum, he argued that 'the fund available for those who live by labour tends, in the progress of society . . . to become a constantly smaller fraction of the entire national wealth'.

The recent immense industrial progress, he claimed, had made comparatively little impression on the rate of wages and profits because improvements had largely affected commodities not consumed by the labourers; and where it had, their gains had often been only temporary owing to subsequent increases in population. The distribution of wealth was already uneven, and was becoming more so, with the consequence that 'The rich will be growing richer; and the poor, at least relatively, poorer'. The decline in the rate of profit did not necessarily mean that the capitalist class suffered, for their income depended on the rate of profit multiplied by the amount of capital, which might increase indefinitely. For the working class, however, co-operation was the only means by which they could emancipate themselves from dependence on capital and share in the 'gains and honours of advancing civilisation'.[40]

Like John Stuart Mill, who also displayed a sympathetic attitude towards co-operation, Cairnes sought a means of counteracting 'the separation of industrial classes into labourers and capitalists which now prevails'.[41] His social philosophy was less complex, and less tainted with reformist sentiments, than Mill's, and in this respect he serves as a more typical example of the long-run tendencies of classical economics. All traces of Adam Smith's concept of a harmony of interests had disappeared with Ricardo's conception of the inverse relationship between wages and profits, a proposition that led Marx to hail him as the

> last of the great exponents of the classical political economy, because he consciously made the conflict of class interests, the antagonism between wages and profits and between profits and land-rents, the starting-point of his investigations, while naively conceiving these antagonisms to be a social law of nature.[42]

Present-day social historians agree that clear-cut class divisions, though not necessarily irreconcilable class conflicts, emerged in Britain during the first two or three decades of the nineteenth century.[43] But while it is clear that the later classical writings reveal more sensitivity to the social and political stresses resulting from industrialization than their predecessors', there is some danger of exaggerating the differences. Certain disharmonious remarks in *The Wealth of Nations* are sometimes cited (mistakenly) as evidence of Smith's embryonic Marxism;[44] but there is no denying the common strands of liberal political, moral and social philosophy that run throughout the classical literature.

Optimism of classical economists

Although the classical economists lived at a time of serious economic instability, acute social tensions and recurrent political disorders – circumstances which are nowdays often regarded as the inescapable accompaniments of rapid industrialization – they retained their fundamental faith in the possibilities of progress. While they were themselves members of the middle class, and can properly be charged with over-rating the merits of their social stratum, their writings were remarkably free from expressions of class hostility. Indeed, the principal exception to this generalization, James Mill, mainly directed his attacks at the aristocracy, not the labouring class, and he probably believed that reformers could only extract significant concessions from the governing classes when the workers seemed on the point of revolution.[45] Those modern commentators who have depicted the classical economists as uncritical defenders of the *status quo* have completely misinterpreted both their objectives and their historical significance. If they were, consciously or unconsciously, spokesmen for a particular class, it was the rising industrial and mercantile bourgeoisie, a social group that had not yet wrested the control of affairs from the landed interest, though it was gaining in economic and political strength throughout the first three-quarters of the nineteenth century.

It is significant that the economists were attacked from both ends of the political spectrum. Conservatives regarded them as dangerous radicals, and it is said that Ricardo, a retired stockbroker and wealthy landowner, was denied the opportunity of becoming a JP because his views were too advanced. On the other hand, working-class leaders dismissed them as exponents of capitalist apologetics, and it is true that they regarded the poverty of the masses as a threat to social peace, believing that a rise in the average standard of living would give the workers a stake in the system.

In political affairs the classical economists were moderate reformers: on the whole they did not believe in universal suffrage, and they rejected schemes for popular control of government. Indeed their political outlook was ambivalent, since it combined distrust of the people's capacity for self-government with an even deeper distrust of the influence of strong central control.[46] In general, they were less interested in political freedom than economic freedom, mainly because they considered this was the indispensable prerequisite to personal freedom in other spheres of life, not only for the upper and middle classes but for all members of society.[47]

III POPULATION, POVERTY AND WAGES

According to Adam Smith, 'no society can surely be flourishing and happy, of which the far greater part of the members are poor and miserable',[48] and this belief underlay the classical economists' pre-occupation with the problem of poverty. Throughout their writings they displayed a genuine and consistent desire to raise the lower classes in the social and economic scale by a process that might be appropriately termed 'embourgeoisement'. Despite their fears of excessive population growth and the falling trend in the rate of profit, they were anxious to raise the average level of wages as high as possible since it would encourage the labouring classes to develop a taste for the comforts and conveniences of life, a desire for respectability and a spirit of emulation.[49] By raising the labourer's economic and social aspirations they believed his desire for self-improvement would be aroused and he would be more likely to develop qualities of self-reliance, thriftiness, prudence and industriousness. The result would be not only to raise the productivity of labour, thereby providing the means to further economic gains, but also to enhance the quality of social, cultural and political life.

Belief in benefits of *laissez-faire*

These ideas underlay most of the classical economists' policy recommendations, for as Torrens remarked. 'No plan of financial or commercial improvement can be so called unless it raises the real wages of labour'.[50] Impediments to the efficient use of scarce resources tended to reduce the rate of profit and check the accumulation of capital, and it was recognized that the approach of the stationary state would be accompanied by a fall in the rate of wages as well as profits.[51] As government usually represented just such an impediment the economists were often opposed to and invariably sceptical towards state interference. From their standpoint *laissez-faire* was a progressive policy, since it entailed the reduction or removal of outmoded restrictions on economic freedom.[52] These reasons underlay their opposition to protection, excessive government expenditure, taxes on necessities, combination laws, factory legislation as applied to adults and any other measures that were likely to reduce either the rate of wages or the incentive to capital accumulation. And as Joseph Schumpeter observed, their support for the 1834 Poor Law Amendment Act

> tallied well with their views on population and wages. It tallied still better with their almost ludicrous confidence in the ability of individuals to act with energy and rationality, to look after themselves responsibly, to find work, and to save for old age and rainy days.[53]

Schumpeter's comment is somewhat exaggerated; but it highlights the classical economists' tendency, so common among social reformers, to underestimate the obstacles to the fulfilment of their hopes. Their belief in the labourers' capacity for self-improvement was partly a matter of faith; but it was also based on knowledge and reason. They were well aware that real wages were generally higher in England than on the continent or in Ireland, and they argued that this difference was mainly due to the British worker's superior industry and skill. A reduction of average wage levels would, in due course, be followed by a loss of incentive and a reduction of labour effort (whether for psychological or physiological reasons, or both); and with lower productivity and income there would be less inclination to practise moral restraint. Conversely, a rise in real wages would not be followed by an instantaneous increase in population and the labour supply;[54] and if the higher level persisted there could be a permanent upward adjustment in the wage earner's conception of a decent and proper standard of life. In the repeated discussions of the relationship between wages and 'subsistence' it was generally accepted that subsistence was determined by social (i.e. customary) rather than economic forces, since the long-term equilibrium wage level was well above the bare physical minimum necessary for survival.

Population growth and restraint

Although belief in the more rigid and mechanical version of Malthus's population theory diminished considerably from the late 1820s, the fear of excessive population growth by no means disappeared and the economists attached increasing weight to the social and psychological motives for postponing marriage or restricting the size of family. McCulloch, in particular, stressed that a taste for luxuries, comforts and enjoyments 'should be widely diffused, and, if possible, interwoven with national habits and prejudices'. Indeed he declared that it was

> the great and leading defect in the lower classes, that they submit to privations with too little reluctance. Nothing ought to be more earnestly deprecated, than any change in the sentiments of the great body of the people, which may have the effect of inducing them to lower their opinion as to what is necessary to their comfortable subsistence. Every such degradation is almost sure to be permanent; in as much as wages would always fall in a corresponding ratio; . . .[55]

No doubt this standpoint is naive, for it reveals a serious inability to comprehend the true nature of the difficulties facing the labourer. Even so, it represents a notable advance in humanity and understanding over the opinions prevalent in the early eighteenth century, when it was considered advisable to reduce wages and maintain or raise the prices of provisions so that the pressure of necessity would compel the workers to be industrious.[56] In McCulloch's complaint that the labourers too readily 'submit to privations' we find another indication of progress beyond the less sympathetic views of an earlier epoch.

In their bitter opposition to the Speenhamland system of poor law allowances the classical economists repeatedly insisted that subsidies to paupers undermined the independence of the independent labourers, and modern commentators have too readily ridiculed their overestimate of this precious quality. But in emphasizing the value of independence they were expressing their middle-class prejudices against the paternalistic emphasis on the need for dependency and deference on the part of the lower order.[57] In some quarters the eighteenth century fear that the labourers would become 'saucy' and develop ideas 'above their station' survived well into the nineteenth century; but it was increasingly on the defensive. As J.S. Mill observed, the distinguishing feature of mid-Victorian society was that 'the poor have come out of leading-strings, and cannot any longer be governed or treated like children. To their own qualities must now be commended the care of their destiny', and the prospect struck him as hopeful.[58]

Although the classical economists sometimes complained that the industrial and urban workers were riotous and disorderly, in their calmer moods they viewed this behaviour as an integral part of the progress of industrial society, and they vigorously supported educational provisions designed to narrow the gap between the middle and working classes. They viewed the lower orders not as opponents but as 'accessories to reform',[59] and it was precisely this outlook that blinded them to the difficulties of achieving their objectives.

Co-partnership the key

To historians who regard conflict as the inevitable and proper relationship between social classes their standpoint doubtless seems naive and unrealistic; but it is clear that the economists believed the future of the labouring classes, as of society in general, depended on a kind of co-partnership between the well-to-do and the poor, in which the former provided an appropriate framework of laws and a rate of saving and capital accumulation sufficient to ensure a high demand for labour, and the latter exercized a proper degree of restraint over the growth of numbers. However unjust it might appear, moral restraint was unnecessary among the upper and middle classes for if they reproduced excessively they could afford to pay the price of their imprudence. Moreover their numbers were small so that a change in their behaviour would make no significant difference to the rate of population growth. Even before Malthus formulated his notorious 'law', it was recognized that numbers made a crucial difference both to the distribution of wealth and the growth of population for, as Edmund Burke noted in 1795:

> The labouring classes are only poor, because they are numerous. Numbers in their nature imply poverty. In a fair distribution among a vast multitude, none can have very much. That class of dependent pensioners called the rich, is so extremely small that if all their throats were cut, and a distribution made of all they consume in a year, it would not give a bit of bread and cheese for one night's supper to those who labour, and who in reality feed both the pensioners and themselves.[60]

The problem of pauperism

Although the classical economists' prescriptions were really designed for the upper and middle echelons of wage-earners, they were only too well aware of the existence of extreme poverty, disease, misery and degradation at the lower end of the scale. In times of special difficulty, as for example during the Napoleonic Wars, or in bad harvest or trade depression, they recognized the widespread extent of distress,[61] and this largely explains their general conviction that the long-term equilibrium wage level was too low. They also gave eloquent descriptions of the sufferings of particular segments of the working class, especially the handloom weavers whose plight attracted national attention in the late 1830s and early 1840s.[62] The extreme poverty of the Irish peasantry was constantly held out as an awful warning of the consequences of excessive procreation and falling living standards, and despite their general suspicion of government interference in economic and social affairs they increasingly acknowledged the need for legislative controls of housing, sanitation and factory conditions.[63]

Modern commentators of all shades of opinion have criticised the classical economists, though in very differing degrees, for their failure to make constructive suggestions for relieving the hardships of the very poorest members of the community, and there is no denying that they failed to offer effective solutions for problems that have remained with us ever since. On this subject Malthus was by far the most important single voice, and unfortunately, as one recent judicious historian has observed, his work is especially difficult to interpret and evaluate.[64] As is well known, he and Ricardo advocated the *'gradual and very gradual* abolition of the poor law', not because he wished to plunge the pauper into actual want – which he recognized was so degrading that it 'palsies every virtue' – but because he believed that *fear* of want was the indispensable spur to industry, self-reliance and self-improvement.[65] Although the major poor law reform in the classical period, the famous Amendment Act of 1834, did not accord with Malthus's recommendations, his writings exerted a profound impact on the whole subject of poverty and pauperism in the first half of the nineteenth century, and had a significant indirect effect on the course of policy.

At the close of an already extended essay it is obviously impossible to discuss this topic in detail, for it is complex and still controversial. Suffice it to say that the solution adopted in 1834 was fully in harmony with the principles of political economy and its related philosophy of utilitarianism, and it is undeniable that the Act failed to alleviate the problem it was designed to solve. The principle of 'less eligibility' was based on a fallacious analysis of the nature of poverty and the psychology of the poor, and it could never have worked effectively even had it been administered efficiently. What can be said for the classical economists' solution was that it sought to ameliorate the lot of the poor by adopting a long-run solution rather than any of the numerous ill-considered and sentimental proposals then under discussion. Its exponents realised that in the short-run it would cause hardship; but they sincerely believed that without reform the long-run hardships would be much more serious. J.S. Mill's remark that Malthus's ideas conflicted with 'those plans of easy beneficence which accord so well with the inclination of man, but so ill with the arrangements of nature.'[66] could be applied to all the classical economists.

IV SUMMARY

As indicated at the beginning of this essay, it is no easy task to summarize the classical economists' ideas about industrialization and poverty. Nevertheless, the attempt must be made if the reader is not to lose sight of the main themes among the many individual differences and shifts of opinion that occurred in response to the momentous economic and social changes of the time.

Principles and beliefs

The basic principles of classical political economy were derived directly from eighteenth century liberal moral philosophy, with its emphasis on the value of individual freedom in all spheres of life, and its fundamental faith in the possibilities of progress. Admittedly this faith was severely tested under the novel and often alarming circumstances of nineteenth century industrialization in Britain. Indeed, it would be easy to compile a catalogue of statements and predictions from the classical economists' writings which, taken together and out of context, would convey an overall impression of unmitigated gloom and despondency. But that would be a false picture. While they acknowledged what are nowadays termed 'the costs of economic growth' – such as low wages, long hours, bad working conditions, child labour, technological unemployment, the dehumanizing effects of the division of labour, and the existence of over-crowded, ill-constructed and insanitary housing – they tended to underestimate these features, and they undoubtedly believed that in the long run the benefits would far outweigh the disadvantages. This was not simply because higher productivity would lead to higher standards of material welfare, but because these resources could also constitute the means to higher levels of culture and civilization.

These goals could not, of course, be attained easily. The economists recognized the dangers of ignorance, political unrest and class conflict; and from our safe distance we can see that while industrialization undoubtedly brings substantial improvements in average living standards, it neither guarantees a just distribution of wealth nor the elimination of poverty and other concomitant social evils.

Naive optimists, humane reformers

In many respects the classical economists' optimism, though rarely unqualified, was naive; and in general it reflected their bourgeois background, standards and values. In particular it led them to underestimate the hardships suffered by many wage earners and the obstacles to the improvement of their material and cultural standards. To their credit, the economists did not regard the problem of poverty as insoluble, as many earlier generations had done. But they offered few constructive proposals, and the most important single legislative enactment based on their ideas, the 1834 Poor Law Amendment Act, proved to be a lamentable failure.

It is, of course, easy to make excuses for them. Their intentions were good; the problem of poverty was unprecedented in its character and scale; they lacked adequate data; the administrative machinery was grossly inadequate, as also were the available financial resources; and at least they made a genuine effort at reform based on systematic reasoning – by contrast with many earlier emotional and utopian schemes. Despite their justifiable doubts about the efficacy of state intervention in economic and social affairs, the classical economists were neither spokesmen for dogmatic *laissez-faire* nor uncritical apologists for the *status quo*, but moderate, humane and liberal reformers. And yet when all due allowances have been made, it cannot be denied that their analysis of the problem of poverty was defective, their diagnosis inaccurate and their recommendations ineffective.

Achievements underestimated

Generally speaking, historians have underestimated the classical economists' achievements. Attention has been focused on the inadequacies of their social policy recommendations rather than on the power of their economic analysis, and of course many commentators have objected to their social and political preconceptions. At the same time, however, there has been a tendency to exaggerate their influence, and even to suggest that they directed society along the wrong 'economic and social paths'.[67] Such a criticism is meaningless unless a viable alternative solution is offered, one that is compatible with the ideas, resources and practical possibilities of the time.

From our mid-twentieth century vantage point we have become more sceptical of panaceas, and more doubtful of the efficacy of government fiscal, financial or employment policy, or in schemes designed to redistribute income or increase social welfare. And until we have demonstrated our superiority, it behoves us to be judicious and sympathetic in assessing earlier generations.

NOTES

1 The principal figures normally regarded as members of the classical 'school' are Adam Smith (1723–1790), Jeremy Bentham (1748–1832), Thomas Robert Malthus (1766–1834), David Ricardo (1772–1823), James Mill (1773–1836), Robert Torrens (1780–1864), Sir Edward West (1782–1828), John Ramsay McCulloch (1789–1864), Nassau William Senior (1790–1864), John Stuart Mill (1806–1873), John Eliot Cairnes (1823–1875). Some authorities would question the inclusion of Bentham, while others would wish to extend the list, for example, by adding Thomas de Quincey (1785–1859) and Karl Marx (1818–1883).

2 A valuable recent contribution to this discussion is Neil de Marchi, 'The Empirical Content and Longevity of Ricardian Economics', *Economica* vol.XXXII, (August 1970), pp.257–76. He argues that Ricardo's system was not incompatible with contemporary facts; that both Ricardo and J.S. Mill aimed to produce statements with refutable content; and that while Mill occasionally ignored inconvenient facts, he did not deliberately suppress historical evidence in order to protect Ricardo's economics.

3 When the Earl of Limerick complained of 'the crude opinions of the professors of political economy, no two of whom are agreed in the doctrines of their sect', James Mill questioned whether they could be called a sect if there was no agreement

among them. Cf. *Parliamentary History and Review* (1826), p.691. For a more extended account of the economists' scientific reputation see A.W. Coats, 'The Role of Authority in the Development of British Economics', *Journal of Law and Economics* vol.VII (October 1964), pp.85–106. (Also, in volume II of this series.)

4 Quoted by William Stanley Jevons, 'The Future of Political Economy', *Fortnightly Review* vol.XXVI (1876), p.190.

5 McCulloch, *Outlines of Political Economy*, ed. J. McVickar, (New York, 1825), p.94.

6 J.L. Mallet. *Political Economy Club*, Centenary Volume. Minutes of Proceedings (London, 1921), Vol.6, p.234. For McCulloch's reservations about the factory system, see pp.193–4.

7 For example, it was becoming apparent by the mid-1820s that although the British population continued to grow rapidly, food prices were low enough to cause widespread complaints from the farming community. By 1828 McCulloch had abandoned his former belief in the Malthusian 'law', probably under the influence of Senior. They were subsequently joined by Torren who, while continuing to regard population increase as a threat to the labourer's standard of living, rejected Malthus's theory as 'not conformable to experience'. Cf. D.P. O'Brien, *J.R. McCulloch. A Study in Classical Economics* (London, 1970), pp.314–19; M.E.A. Bowley, *Nassau Senior and Classical Economics*, (London, 1937), pp.117–26; and Robert Torrens, *The Principles and Practical Operation of Sir Robert Peel's Act of 1844 Explained and Defended*, 2nd edn. (London, 1857), Appendix B, p.83.

8 P. Sraffa (ed.), *Works and Correspondence of David Ricardo* (Cambridge, 1952), Vol.V, p.68.

9 Malthus, *An Essay on Population*, Everyman edn. (London, 1914), Vol.II, p.119. Malthus enlisted Adam Smith's support for this view by quoting the following passage from *The Wealth of Nations*: 'Capital which is acquired to any country by commerce and manufactures is all a very uncertain and precarious possession, till some part of it has been secured and realised in the cultivation and improvement of its lands.' (Cannan edn. (London, 1904), Vol.I, p.393: Malthus misquoted the original.)

10 Malthus also feared that a surplus of savings would develop with the growth of industrialization and argued that, as landlords had a high propensity to spend, their 'unproductive consumption' would counteract or minimize the dangers of periodic 'gluts', i.e. crises resulting from a deficiency of aggregate demand. It was this aspect of Malthus's thought that led J.M. Keynes to regard him as a precursor of his own *General Theory of Employment, Interest, and Money* (1936). (Cf. Malthus, *Principles of Political Economy* (New York, 1951), p.361 ff.)

11 Adam Smith had described rent as a 'monopoly price', stating that landlords 'love to reap where they never sowed'; but Ricardo, Senior and J.S. Mill adopted a more positively anti-landlord standpoint. According to Mill, 'They grow richer, as it were in their sleep, without working, risking, or economising. What claim have they, on the general principle of social justice, to this accession of riches?' (*Principles of Political Economy, with some of their applications to Social Philosophy* (Toronto, 1965), Vol.II, pp.819–20.)

12 Ricardo's *Works*, op. cit., Vol.V, p.180. As is so often the case, Adam Smith may be cited in support of this view also: 'England . . . is perhaps as well fitted by nature as any large country in Europe, to be the seat of foreign commerce, of manufactures for distant sale and of all the improvements which these can occasion.' (*Wealth of Nations*, I, p.391.) Whatever may be the interpretation of this passage, the contrast between Ricardo and Malthus is clearly evident from

the following extract: 'According to all general principles, it will finally answer to most landed nations, both to manufacture for themselves and to conduct their own commerce. That raw cottons should be shipped in America, carried some thousands of miles to another country, unshipped there, to be manufactured and shipped again for the American market, is a state of things which cannot be permanent.' (*Essay on Population*, Vol.II, p.90.)

13 *Principles of Political Economy* (Edinburgh, 1843), pp.8–9.

14 *Principles*, op. cit., Vol.II, pp.754, 756.

15 Ibid., Vol.I, p.105.

16 This is not the place to examine the analytical confusions in the classical treatment of the laws of returns. There is a brief account in Edmund Whitaker, *A History of Economic Ideas* (New York, 1940) pp.383–403.

17 For example, R. Koebner, 'Adam Smith and the Industrial Revolution', *Economic History Review* vol.XI (April 1959), p.382: 'There was not a line in his [Smith's] book anticipating such transformations as were to take place in mechanised production and transport.' Indeed, 'apart from having no inkling of many technical innovations which lay ahead and of the forms of organisation by which they were to be exploited – Adam Smith had been rather unfavourably disposed towards those elements of society who were to organise mechanised production and to divert it into the channels of commerce'.

18 Cf. Samuel Hollander, 'Adam Smith and the Industrial Revolution: A New View', unpublished paper delivered at the History of Economic Thought Conference, Manchester, September 1971. The substance of the argument will appear in Professor Hollander's forthcoming book, *The Economics of Adam Smith* (University of Toronto, 1972). He would probably agree with Karl Marx that 'what characterises him [Smith] as the political economist of the period of manufacture is the stress he lays on the division of labour'. (*Capital*, Everyman edn. (London, 1930), Vol.I, p.367, n.3.)

19 Nathan Rosenberg, 'Adam Smith on the Division of Labour: Two Views or One?' *Economica* vol.XXXII (May 1965), p.128.

20 *Wealth of Nations*, Vol.I, pp.7, 8; Vol.II, p.177 ff.

21 Rosenberg, op. cit., pp.131, 134, 138.

22 However, McCulloch protested at Smith's account: 'Nothing can be more marvellously incorrect than these representations. . . . The weavers and other mechanics of Glasgow, Manchester and Birmingham, possess infinitely more general and extended information than is possessed by the agricultural labourers of any country in the Empire'. (*Outlines of Political Economy*, op. cit., pp.100–1. In the 1870 edition of his *Principles of Political Economy*, p.89, he quoted Malthus in support of his view.)

23 Thus John Stuart Mill's famous outburst was untypical: 'Hitherto it is questionable if all the mechanical inventions yet made have lightened the day's toil of any human being. They have enabled a greater population to live the same life of drudgery and imprisonment, and an increased number of manufacturers and others to make fortunes. They have increased the comforts of the middle classes. But they have not yet begun to effect those great changes in human destiny, which it is in their power and in their futurity to accomplish.' (*Principles*, op. cit., Vol.II, pp.756–7.)

Generally speaking, the popularisers of political economy stressed the productivity of machinery and neglected its social effects, while the working-class press complained that the economists 'persisted in regarding human beings as soulless instruments in a great machine'. (Cf. R.K. Webb, *The British Working Class Reader 1790–1848* (London, 1955), pp.99–100.)

24 For example, while acknowledging the harmful effects of the power loom on the employment of handloom weavers, Senior ridiculed general attacks on machinery, commenting 'and when it has been made penal to give advantages to labour by any tool or instrument whatever, the last step must be to prohibit the use of the right hand'. (*Three Lectures on The Rate of Wages* (London, 1830), p.xiii.) Torrens complained of the 'fundamental and dangerous errors' in Ricardo's third edition, adding that his deviations had 'retarded the progress of the science' by exposing disagreements among its practitioners. (*An Essay on The Production of Wealth* (London, 1821), pp.xi–xii.) Elsewhere he protested vehemently about the hardships suffered by the handloom weavers, but while agreeing that the ill-effects of mechanization were usually only temporary, he granted Senior's exception in the case of machines worked by horses, which permanently diminished the subsistence (i.e. wages fund) available for labourers' consumption. He even advocated the establishment of a national fund to assist workers displaced by machinery. (*On Wages and Combination* (London, 1834), pp.34–44.)

25 'One of Ricardo's greatest services is that he realised that machinery is not only a means for producing commodities, but also a means for producing "redundant population".' Marx considered that Ricardo's renunciation of his earlier opinion on machinery reflected 'the scientific impartiality and love of truth characteristic of the man'. (*Capital*, op. cit., I, p.434, n.1; p.469, n.2; II, p.697, n.1.)

26 For example, Mark Blaug, *Ricardian Economics*, New Haven, 1958, pp.64–74; also O'Brien, op. cit., pp.302–6.

27 Blaug, op. cit., pp.69, 73.

28 *Essay on Population*, Vol.II, pp.63, 256. In this context the 'positive checks' to population growth meant the high death rate in towns; the 'preventive checks', which Malthus advocated as the most desirable method of restraining excessive population increase, referred to 'moral restraint', chiefly through the postponement of marriage.

29 With respect to restrictions on adult labour the position was more complex: cf., for example, Mark Blaug, 'The Classical Economists and the Factory Acts', *Quarterly Journal of Economics* (1958), reprinted in A.W. Coats, *The Classical Economists and Economic Policy* (London, 1971), pp.104–22.

30 Senior claimed that hours of work in cotton factories were not excessive, the work was light, working conditions were not overcrowded and the employees were healthy. 'The factory work-people in the country districts are the plumpest, best clothed, and healthiest-looking persons of the labouring class that I have ever seen. The girls, especially, are far more good-looking (and good looks are fair evidence of health and spirits) than the daughters of agricultural labourers.' However, he was shocked by the housing conditions in Manchester (as contrasted with the good houses at Hyde), which explained why the workers there were 'sallow and thinner'. (*Letters on The Factory Act*, 2nd edn., 1844.) In this edition he reproduced a long letter from Leonard Horner, the government factory inspector, contesting many of Senior's opinions and producing contradictory evidence!

In contrast to Senior, Torrens complained that the congregation of workers in factories ruined their health and destroyed their morals, and demanded a reduction of hours of work 'to save the infant labourer from the cruel oppression of excessive toil'. (Cf. *The Principles and Practical Operation of Sir Robert Peel's Act*, op. cit., p.24; and *Letters On Commercial Policy* (London, 1833), p.72).

31 *Letters on the Factory Act*, op. cit., p.4. Other members of the Political Economy Club rejected Senior's view on the ground of his faulty economic analysis.

32 *A Statistical Account of the British Empire*, 2nd edn. (1839), Vol.I, p.669. Later on the same page he declared, of Manchester, Glasgow and Leeds, 'whatever may

be the state of society in these towns, . . . *it would have been ten times worse but for the factories.*' (Italics in original.) Recent historians have generally agreed that the 1832 Factory Report was partisan and inaccurate.

33 Ibid., p.639. D.P. O'Brien, op. cit., p.283, has remarked that McCulloch 'detested the domestic system which also ran counter to the need for division of labour and was harmful to children and oppressive', but his citations are drawn from earlier sources.

34 *Statistical Account*, op. cit., p.663.

35 'Rise, Progress, Present State, and Prospects of the British Cotton Manufacture', *Edinburgh Review* vol.XCI (1827), pp.37–8.

36 *Treatises and Essays* (Edinburgh, 1859), p.455. Quoted by Blaug, *Ricardian Economics*, op. cit., p.242. The similarity between this remark and John Stuart Mill's comment on the effects of machinery (see n.23, this volume) is obvious.

37 O'Brien, op. cit., pp.284–5.

38 Mill, *Principles*, Vol.II, p.738. Cairnes expressed similar views in *Some Leading Principles of Political Economy Newly Expounded*, 1888 edn., pp.217, 230, 274.

39 On this subject Donald Winch, *Classical Political Economy and Colonies* (London 1965), *passim*; also R.N. Ghosh, *Classical Macroeconomics and the Case for Colonies* (Calcutta, 1967), *passim*. The quotation in the text is from Torrens, *The Budget. On Commercial and Colonial Policy* (London, 1844), p.288. It forms part of a very extended account of contemporary economic distress.

40 Cairnes, *Leading Principles*, op. cit., pp.281–9.

41 Ibid., p.284.

42 *Capital*, op. cit., p.867, from the author's preface to the second German edition. For Marx's distinction between 'classical' and 'vulgar' political economy, ibid., p.55n.

43 For example, Harold Perkin, *The Origins of Modern British Society, 1780–1880* (London, 1969), especially ch.VI, 'The Birth of Class'; also, from a very different standpoint, E.P. Thompson, *The Making of the English Working Class* (London, 1963), *passim*.

44 For example, in a primitive society which precedes the appropriation of land and the accumulation of capital 'the whole produce of labour belongs to the labourer'; but in an advanced society the landlord and the capitalist demand their shares, which Smith pointedly called 'deductions' from the produce of labour. In these circumstances, he added, 'rent and profit eat up wages, and the two superior orders of people oppress the inferior one'. And as if this were not enough to fan the flames of social discontent, he stated explicitly that 'civil government, so far as it is instituted for the security of property, is in reality instituted for the defence of the rich against the poor, or of those who have some property against those who have none at all'. (*Wealth of Nations*, I, p.66; II, pp.67, 207.)

45 Cf. Joseph Hamberger, *James Mill and the Art of Revolution* (1964), p.115. According to R.H. Tawney, to James Mill 'the State is not a band of brothers, but a mutual detective society: the principal advantage of popular government is that there are more detectives, and therefore, presumably, fewer thieves'. (Cf. his preface to the *Life and Struggles of William Lovett* (New York, 1920), p.xxi.) Mill was not, however, an unqualified admirer of the populace.

46 William D. Grampp, *Economic Liberalism, Vol.II: The Classical View* (New York, 1965), p.55. The whole of ch.2, 'The Political Ideas of the Classical Economists', is relevant to the present discussion.

47 This point has been especially emphasized by Joseph Cropsey, *Polity and Economy, An Interpretation of the Principles of Adam Smith* (The Hague, 1957), pp.x,

ADAM SMITH AND CLASSICAL ECONOMICS

95. Though there were significant differences of emphasis between Smith and his nineteenth century successors, their fundamental outlook was consistent.

48 *Wealth of Nations*, I, p.80.

49 Many of the matters touched on in the remainder of this essay are treated more fully in my paper 'The Classical Economists and the Labourer', originally published in E.L. Jones and G.E. Mingay (eds.), *Land, Labour and Population in the Industrial Revolution* (London, 1967), reprinted in Coats, op. cit, pp.144–79 and this volume, pp.159–85.

50 *Three Letters to the Marquis of Chandos* (1839), p.38.

51 For example, Malthus, *Essay on Population*, II, p.92.

52 The classical economists were not, of course, advocates of *laissez-faire* in any literal sense. See, for example, H. Scott Gordon, 'The Ideology of Laissez Faire', pp.180–205, and the editorial introduction in Coats, *The Classical Economists and Economic Policy*.

53 J.A. Schumpeter, *History of Economic Analysis* (New York, 1954), p.402. An admirer of classical economic analysis, Schumpeter was nevertheless highly critical of their social philosophy: 'No philosophy at all in the technical sense, unsurpassably shallow as a "philosophy of life", it [utilitarianism] fitted to perfection the streak of materialistic (anti-metaphysical) rationalism that may be associated with liberalism and the business mind.' (ibid., pp.407–8).

Not all the surviving classical economists approved of the 1834 Act: McCulloch was a determined opponent.

54 Opinions differed as to the time-lag between a rise in real income and a consequent increase of population (whether through earlier or more numerous marriages or an increase in the progeny of existing marriages). An instantaneous response was sometimes assumed for reasons of analytical convenience, whereas in later writings, e.g. Senior, De Quincey and McCulloch, it was often explicitly stated that population adjusted itself only slowly to changes in real earnings.

55 'Combination Laws – Restraints on Emigration', *Edinburgh Review* Vol.LXXVIII (January 1824); p.333; 'Ricardo's Political Economy', ibid., vol.LIX (June 1818), p.87.

In the gloomy conditions of the early 1840s, De Quincey maintained that 'the energetic spirit of the English working man' and his determination to retain his 'high domestic standard of comfort' was the sole barrier against the triple threat of machinery, child labour and Irish competition, which threatened to reduce him to 'the very basest human degradation ever witnessed amongst oriental slaves'. (*The Logic of Political Economy* (Edinburgh, 1844) pp.147–8.)

56 Cf. Edgar Furniss, *The Position of the Labourer in a System of Nationalism* (New York, 1920), *passim*; also A.W. Coats, 'Changing Attitudes to Labour in the Mid-Eighteenth Century', *Economic History Review* vol.XI (August 1958), pp.35–51 and also this volume, pp.63–84.

57 A general treatment of this theme will be found in Perkin, *Origins of Modern British Society*, op. cit., ch.2.

58 *Principles*, Vol.II, p.763.

59 Cf. E.P. Thompson, op. cit., p.139.

60 *Thoughts and Details on Scarcity, etc.*, in *Works* (1808 edn.), VII, p.376: quoted by J.R. Poynter, *Society and Pauperism* (London, 1969), p.xiv.

61 Two early examples may be given: James Mill's lengthy protest against Thomas Spence's underestimate of the poor's hardships in *Commerce Defended* (1808), pp.80–3; and the repeated expressions of concern for the sufferings caused by bad harvests in Ricardo's speeches and his correspondence with Malthus, James Mill and Hutches Trower. (Cf. Ricardo's *Works*, Vols. V and VII.)

208

62 Nassau Senior probably wrote the *Report of the Commission on the Condition of the Hand Loom Weavers*: cf. M.E.A. Bowley, *Nassau Senior and Classical Economics* (London, 1937), p.258 ff., reproduced in Coats (ed.), *The Classical Economists and Economic Policy*, op. cit., pp.57–63. Torrens and McCulloch also wrote at length on this subject, and the latter gave many detailed accounts of the hardships of particular groups in his articles in the *Edinburgh Review* and in his *Statistical Account of the British Empire*.

63 Senior became particularly concerned about bad housing, and recommended strong regulations: 'With all our reverence for the principle of non-interference, we cannot doubt that in this matter it has been pushed too far. We believe that both the ground landlord and the speculating builder ought to be compelled by law, though it should cost them a percentage on their rent and profit, to take measures which shall prevent the towns which they create from being the centre of disease.' (*Report of the Commissioners on the Condition of the Hand Loom Weavers* (P.P., 1841), p.73.) In his lectures Senior argued that the State had a right not only to prevent a man from injuring others, but also from injuring himself by living in inferior housing. (Cf. Bowley, pp.266–7.)

Readers in the 1970s may note that McCulloch not only advocated public control of ventilation, cleanliness and fencing of machinery in factories, but also suggested that smoke control might be expedient in towns or populous neighbourhoods! (Cf. *Treatises and Essays on Money, Exchange, Interest, etc.*, 2nd edn. (Edinburgh, 1859), p.462.)

64 J.R. Poynter, *Society and Pauperism, English Ideas on Poor Relief, 1795–1834* (London, 1969), p.110: 'Malthus's writings provoke prejudices; even today few can write about him without undue animus or admiration. The extreme vilification by early critics . . . was based on ignorance, or at least on misunderstanding and exaggeration. It can now be agreed that Malthus was no misanthrope, but a kind and benevolent man in his personal relationships, and quite sincere in his protestations that he deplored misery and welcomed such improvement as he thought possible. . . . [Yet] there was definite ambivalence in his writings. Malthus the sincere philanthropist was also the author of passages of harsh dogmatism and extraordinary insensitivity to human sufferings.'

65 *Essay on Population*, Vol.I, p.64; II, pp.143, 177.

66 'The Claims of Labour', *Edinburgh Review* vol.CLXIV (1845), pp.501–2. It could be said of Mill, as Schumpeter said of Ricardo, that he was 'above the unctuous phrases that cost so little and yield such ample returns'.

67 Cf. Brian Inglis, *Poverty and the Industrial Revolution* (London, 1971), p.10. This long and stimulating study, written in the humanitarian tradition of social history associated with Tawney, the Hammonds and the Webbs, has one novel feature: an almost Ruskinian belief in the power and pernicious influence of economists. According to Mr Inglis, by 1820 political economy was virtually 'a new religion, and a new God', and 'the new Government was hypnotised by Malthus, and political economy'. Yet elsewhere, he concedes that 'ministers could put it to whatever purpose they needed' because the economists disagreed among themselves and offered differing, and sometimes conflicting, policy recommendations (pp.230, 255, 402). Fortunately most present-day commentators are more sceptical of the influence of ideas and experts, and the whole question of the influence of economists and other intellectuals in the early nineteenth century is still *sub judice*. At this stage premature generalization is harmful. (Cf. Poynter, op. cit., p.324 ff.; Coats, op. cit., pp.1–32.)

PART III

LATER NINETEENTH CENTURY BRITISH ECONOMICS

11

SAMUEL HOLLANDER'S *MILL*

A review article

The reviewer of these volumes[1] faces a daunting task, not simply because of their immense size but also because they cannot adequately be considered in isolation. Together with Professor Hollander's earlier studies of *The Economics of Adam Smith* (1973: p.351) and *The Economics of David Ricardo* (1979: p.759) they constitute a sustained campaign to establish the validity of a singular unified interpretation of the central tradition of nineteenth century British economic thought. Moreover, if Hollander's main thesis is correct, it has direct implications for our understanding of orthodox (or mainstream) twentieth century economics. Under these circumstances the reviewer's responsibility is unusually onerous, and it is therefore appropriate to note that the following account reflects the standpoint of an 'outside insider' – that is, a generalist historian of economics rather than a specialist on Mill or, indeed, on classical economics. Accordingly, this review focuses less on the details than on the broader features and significance of Hollander's treatment of Mill.

Hollander's larger purpose helps to explain the ever-increasing scale of his successive studies, for this twin-barrelled instalment is swollen by repetition of themes, claims and evidence already presented *in extenso* in his controversial *Ricardo* volume.[2] Like an old-time biblical exegetist, Hollander provides innumerable lengthy quotations (many in smaller type) from Mill and other classical economists in support of his case; and he also cites a wide range of later scholars and commentators, many of whom he criticizes severely for their errors, misinterpretations, failures of judgement and unfairness. As his previous writings have demonstrated, Hollander is a formidable scholar, and he evidently believes that only a determined and persistent intellectual campaign can succeed in overthrowing the received view of the history of classical and neoclassical economics. Indeed, at one point he reveals an almost despairing sense of isolation in remarking:

> It is most regrettable that the profession cannot be shaken from the opinion that Ricardo and Mill were unable to resolve the paradox of

213

value, and that the utility contributions of the 1870s were required to break the deadlock.

(p.935; *cf.* p.929)

Hollander is, of course, referring here to the so-called marginal revolution which has long been, and still is, the subject of controversy among economists.[3] On this matter his contention that there was no 'paradigmatic transformation' or 'displacement' (pp.932–3) in the 1870s, but merely a shift in the economists' 'concentrations of attention' (Hicks's term) is less unconventional than some of his other efforts to demonstrate the essential continuities between classical and neoclassical economics, from Smith to Marshall and beyond. This is the larger purpose referred to earlier.

A prime example of Hollander's approach is method, a subject to which Mill made important contributions. It figures prominently in Hollander's opening chapter on 'The Methodological and Doctrinal Heritage', where some repetition of earlier themes is appropriate, and in the next two chapters, 'On Scope and Method' and 'The Transition to the *Principles*', which take us up to page 187. It is less prominent in chapters 5 to 7 which deal in turn with 'Allocation, Trade, and Distribution'; 'Capital, Employment and Growth'; and 'Money and Banking: Theory and Policy', which includes a discussion of business cycles; but it also underlies the most philosophical chapter 'On Utility and Liberty', and the next three chapters on policy issues, covering government, social organization and reform; and it reappears in the concluding chapter 'On Some Central Themes'. Hollander flatly rejects both Schumpeter's charge that Ricardo was guilty of the 'Ricardian Vice' and Hutchison's contention that Ricardo and James Mill were jointly responsible for a 'methodological revolution' that inaugurated the practice of using the method of extreme abstraction to determine the laws of political economy (p.4). On the contrary, Hollander claims – in opposition to most previous commentators – that Ricardo's 'balanced perspective' enabled him to appreciate the 'historical relativity of the institutional and behavioral axioms adopted in the treatment of the capitalist-exchange system' (p.5). By contrast with James Mill, Ricardo's work was characterized by

> the conscious use of strong cases as an analytical device only limited to 'scientific', in contrast to applied work; the distrust of over-simplified models for policy pronouncement; the rejection of universally valid axioms; and the view of theoretical economics as a set of investigative tools, rather than a body of descriptive truths or a set of moral exhortations.

(p.920)

To the present reviewer this sounds much more like Marshall than Ricardo;

and if the latter's appreciation of 'historical relativity' is taken seriously it implies that all the later nineteenth century historical critics of Ricardianism, both in England and elsewhere, were simply wrong. This seems a curious interpretation, to say the least, at a time when the historical dimension of the discipline is being strongly re-emphasized both by economic theorists and by methodologists.

How far does Hollander's extraordinarily charitable 'cleaned up' portrayal of Ricardo's method affect his assessment of Mill's own methodological position? No doubt he correctly highlights the major discontinuity in Mill's views *circa* 1830, when he wrote his famous (and subsequently controversial) essay on 'The Definition of Political Economy', first published in 1836. Before that, under his father's spell, he could occasionally employ 'a grotesque formal demonstration to prove a point' (p.84, *cf.* p.494); but thereafter he dissociated himself from James Mill's narrow dogmatism. Contrary to some distinguished modern scholars, such as Viner, Hollander insists that Mill did not uncritically endorse the hypothetico-deductive method in his essay, but adopted Ricardo's 'balanced position' (p.68); and despite subsequent shifts of focus in his *Logic*, his *Principles* and elsewhere, his overall position was coherent, and in general consistent. Hollander recognizes some 'anomalies' and inadequate formulations 'which must be interpreted generously'; but he refuses to acknowledge 'a ruinous internal contradiction', arguing that although Mill claimed that political economy's 'method of investigation is applicable universally', his conception of the subject nevertheless eschewed all universalistic connotation for he really believed its 'axiomatic foundation' was actually 'pertinent only to well-defined environmental conditions' (*cf.* pp.159, 166, 160). Once again, if this interpretation is correct, one wonders why so many later writers have got Mill so badly wrong.

The broader issue of Mill's consistency has troubled innumerable previous commentators, as it did some of his contemporaries, and Hollander not only fully acknowledges but also seems to revel in the difficulties of interpreting and reconciling the various shifts in Mill's ideas, beliefs and interests. It would be easy to compile a long list of his references to Mill's vacillations, vague or unclear statements and arguments, and even a few minor inconsistencies. Nevertheless, whenever a judgement is required on major matters Hollander strives his utmost to show that Mill was not seriously inconsistent, and that his ideas did not change fundamentally. Every effort is made to give Mill the benefit of the doubt, sometimes even when there is no supporting evidence. We are repeatedly warned that his words must be interpreted 'with the very greatest care' since on 'close examination' an initial impression must be revised, an apparent contradiction can be explained away or an inconsistency disappears. While Hollander scathingly dismisses some other scholars' interpretations as fit only for the 'psychiatrist's couch' (p.196; *cf.* pp.917, 928), he repeatedly refers to what 'presumably he [Mill] had in mind' (p.96; cf. pp.69, 112, 137, 164) or what Mill 'would have preferred' (p.255), and on one occasion remarks that 'it is difficult to believe that he could have believed' the implication of a certain formulation; and proceeds to supply what Mill must have meant, while admitting that his own preferred version 'is never actually spelled out by Mill' (p.359).[4]

Apart from occasional, and doubtless unintentional, passages suggesting that he has privileged access to Mill's thought processes, few of Hollander's interpretative devices are inherently reprehensible; nor can his proffered explanations, justifications and rationalizations be rejected simply because they accord so precisely with his central continuity thesis. Nevertheless, the relentless pursuit of that thesis must be emphasized both as applied to Mill himself and to the intellectual tradition to which he belongs. In the terminology of nineteenth century geology, Hollander is a strict uniformitarian rather than a catastrophist. Possibly in reaction to T.S. Kuhn, he has no patience with intellectual revolutions or breakthroughs, whether by an individual or a group. Admittedly at one point he concedes that a specific analytical development 'would have been technically impossible *given the state of the science*' (p.933; italics supplied), but this is a rare exception. On the whole he has assimilated Marshall's motto – *natura non facit saltum* – so completely that he can almost be read as saying 'it's all in Ricardo', just as Cambridge economists were once wont to declare 'it's all in Marshall'. Indeed, according to Hollander a great deal of Marshall is also in Ricardo, and the similarities between Ricardo and Smith are held to be much greater than is generally supposed.

This question of interpretation is clearly a matter of degree, not of kind. Obviously there are continuities as well as discontinuities in classical economics. No doubt Mill heavily emphasized, and probably exaggerated, his indebtedness to Ricardo; whether he repudiated his father's ideas as completely as Hollander claims, is another matter. In his *Principles*, Mill deliberately played down his differences from Ricardo, partly in order to convince the general reader of the extent of agreement among the leading classical writers (p.158). Occasionally, in later editions, he even suppressed new ideas or results that were 'not yet ripe for incorporation in a general treatise on Political Economy' (p.431n). Indeed, on reading the great Toronto edition one is struck by the limited number and extent of the changes in the economic content of successive editions, by contrast with, say, the materials on history, policy or social topics. Nevertheless, the overall effect of Hollander's emphasis on Mill's dependence on Ricardo is to diminish Mill's contribution to the development of classical economics. For example, with reference to Mill's international trade theory, which has often been regarded as a major intellectual achievement, he remarks that 'Ricardo had left the door open by his formulation so that the elaborations [by Mill] brilliant as they were, were consistent with existing doctrines' (p.932). Even where Mill's contribution was original, his analysis is said to bear 'a close family resemblance to Ricardo's discussion', whereas elsewhere Hollander maintains that the tools Mill employed 'were readily at hand throughout the full range of Ricardo's writings' (p.335).

There is a clue to Hollander's interpretative stance where he cites Hicks's view that Mill is 'the most undervalued economist of the nineteenth century' (p.ix), and Stigler's even bolder claim that he was 'one of the most original economists in the history of the science' (p.xii). In response, Hollander announces his own lack of interest in the question of Mill's 'genius', adding dismissively that 'innovation for the mere sake of innovation is no virtue' (ibid; *cf.* p.917). Presumably he fears that too much attention to Mill's originality would cast doubt on the continuity thesis. But surely innovation is crucial to the development of any science or scholarly discipline. To deny, or to denigrate it by referring to 'innovation for the mere sake of innovation' is to reduce the creative function of the intellect to the mere desire for personal fame. By placing such emphasis on doctrinal and methodological continuity Hollander tends to smooth out the filiation of ideas, homogenize the contributions of individual authors and minimize or distract attention from the anomalies, blind alleys and red herrings that obstruct the path of intellectual progress. Hollander's bland account of classical economics in retrospect obscures the manner in which conceptual and analytical advances, and solutions to problems that seem obvious *ex post* appear as serious obstacles *ex ante*. For example, contrary to earlier commentators, Hollander considers it 'inconceivable that the tools of allocation theory would have been used in one specific application [i.e., in international trade] by an economist who is ignorant of their foundation in a more general system of demand-supply analysis' (p.247) – *ergo*, this broader conception must have been present all the time, a contention compatible with his central theme.[5] Intellectual historians generally, and historians of economics and other systematic disciplines in particular, are well aware of the difficulties and time lags involved in generalizing concepts and theories initially applied to particular situations and cases; but Hollander evidently sees no difficulty here. The same kind of insensitivity to intellectual innovation is evident in his observation that the marginalist developments 'could have been absorbed by the traditional corpus of analysis' (p.931). Perhaps so; but why weren't they? The only explanation Hollander offers is a lame socio-psychological reference to the marginalists' 'impatience' to 'wipe the slate clean', a matter that deserves more careful consideration.

Hollander's initial insistence that a 'sound evaluation' of Mill's place in the history of classical economics is crucially dependent on a correct interpretation of his relation to Ricardo prepares the ground for his concluding general assessment:

in particular, their [i.e., Ricardo's and Mill's] cost-price analysis is pre-eminently an analysis of the allocation of scarce resources, proceeding in terms of general equilibrium, with allowance for final demand, and the interdependence of factor and commodity markets. There was a simultaneous (and consistent) attachment to cost theories of value to the general-equilibrium conception of economic organization as formulated by J.B. Say and much admired by Walras. The demand side, the functional relation between cost and output, the supply and demand determination of wages and profits, far from being 'radical departures' from Ricardianism, are central to that doctrine without which neither the cost theory of price nor the inverse wage-profit relation can be understood. Serious and long-lived misconceptions regarding classicism flow from a failure to recognize that its notions of wages and interest as compensations for effort and abstinence were pertinent only at the macro-economic level where the determinants of aggregate factor supplies are under investigation and not in the micro-economic context where costs refer to foregone opportunities.

(pp.931–2)

If the main theoretical claims of this passage are accepted, the prevailing view of the development of nineteenth century British economics will have to be drastically revised. Marshall's deferential comments on his classical predecessors will have to be taken seriously, rather than dismissed as more formal gestures – or what Schumpeter called an 'olive branch'. Moreover, the present day slipshod use of the term neoclassical will acquire historical legitimation, and those who regard general equilibrium as virtually coextensive with economic theory will gladly rely on this reinforcement of their pedigree.

Needless to say, Hollander's continuity thesis has already been severely attacked by some leading historians of economics, and with *Mill* these reactions are not ideological, as was so often the case with *Ricardo*. The prospect of controversy following the appearance of the projected *Malthus* and *Marx* studies is mind-boggling. One misfortune, which this review illustrates, is that the central theme necessarily distracts attention from some of the many other stimulating and provocative aspects of Hollander's study, such as: his treatment of Mill's Malthusianism (which seems over-tolerant); Mill's derogatory references to the 'old school' of political economists (which evidently included Smith and McCulloch, at least in part, as well as more vulgar authors); his complex conception of the relationship between economics and other social sciences; the role of predictions in Mill's economics; and the many shifts in his political and social views.

Hollander's *Mill* is a work of extraordinary scholarly dedication, stamina and depth. Quite aside from its length, which is enough to deter all but the most earnest and committed readers, it is in parts tedious and difficult to follow. It is therefore likely to exert its influence, whatever that may prove to be, only slowly, and initially within a limited circle of specialists. It is certainly not a study to be evaluated on the basis of one or two careful readings: the familiar cliché that even a lengthy review is inadequate for the purpose is in this instance a serious understatement. Like the massively ambitious project of which it forms an integral part, Hollander's *Mill* will leave a permanent imprint in the history of economics.

NOTES

1 Samuel Hollander, *The Economics of John Stuart Mill. Volume One: Theory and Method. Volume Two: Political Economy* (Oxford, Basil Blackwell, 1985).
2 See, for example, D.P. O'Brien. 'Ricardian Economics and the Economics of David Ricardo', *Oxford Economic Papers*, vol.33 (3) (1981), pp.352–86; Samuel Hollander, 'The Economics of David Ricardo: A Response to Professor O'Brien', *Oxford Economic Papers* vol.34 (1) (1982), pp.224–46; O'Brien. 'Ricardian Economics. A Rejoinder', ibid., pp.247–52. Unless otherwise stated, 'Mill' refers to John Stuart Mill, rather than to his father, James Mill. Page numbers refer to the volumes under review.
3 For a recent contribution to the literature re-emphasizing the revolutionary character of the 1870s episode, see Robert M. Fisher, *The Logic of Economic Discovery. Neoclassical Economics and the Marginal Revolution* (Brighton, Sussex, Wheatsheaf Books, 1986).
4 The formulation in question involves Hollander's effort to reconcile the Ricardian inverse wages/profit relationship with a neoclassical general equilibrium analysis of outputs and prices.
5 O'Brien, 'Ricardian Economics and the Economics of David Ricardo', op. cit., p.355 refers to Hollander's flights of 'negative imagination'.

12

THE HISTORIST REACTION IN ENGLISH POLITICAL ECONOMY, 1870–90[1]

During the 1870s English political economy suffered a considerable loss of public prestige. Confidence in the Ricardian 'laws' was undermined by bitter controversies between leading economists such as that which resulted from John Stuart Mill's recantation of the wages-fund theory in 1869, and the belief that the received doctrine was disintegrating found supporting evidence in Jevons' scathing attack on the Ricardian theory of value.[2] On the occasion of the dinner given by the Political Economy Club of London to mark the centenary of *The Wealth of Nations* it was suggested that the economists 'had better be celebrating the obsequies of their science than its jubilee'.[3] The nadir of this movement was reached in 1877, when it was formally proposed that Section F of the British Association, dealing with Economics and Statistics, should be dropped because its proceedings and its subject matter were unscientific.[4]

This loss of prestige was in part the consequence of a naive mis-interpretation of the nature and functions of political economy. No clear line can be drawn between the scientific and popular writings of this period, and many persons identified the teachings of the economists with policy recommendations. Accordingly, they held those teachings in high regard during the prosperous decades after the mid-century, attributing current prosperity to the success of the free trade doctrines. After 1873, however, when the tide turned, those same persons found in the state of trade ample evidence of the deficiencies of the laws of political economy. Thus the public attitude toward the science cannot be dissociated from the circumstances of the time.

Some other reasons for the decline in public esteem were suggested by economic writers. To the disturbing effects of the disagreement between its leading spokesmen must be added the undue devotion to inherited tradition. Political economy had become rigid and inflexible under the shadow of

J.S. Mill, for as Foxwell wrote, 'after the appearance of Mill's *Principles*, English economists, for a whole generation, were men of one book'.[5] Yet developments which contemporary writers considered harmful to the science sometimes appeared constructive to later commentators. Thus Foxwell, in a retrospective review of the period, grouped the progressive forces at work under three headings, 'theoretic criticism, historical method, and humanistic feelings'.[6] The wages-fund controversy and Jevons' attack on the Ricardian theory of value come under the first of these, while in the final category a wider stream of thought is encountered, embracing factory and social reform and the Christian Socialist Movement.

The present article centres attention on the second of these progressive forces – the historical method, and the debate occasioned by the attempt to make political economy an historical science. The historists led a series of critical attacks on the methods employed by the classical economists, especially Ricardo and his immediate followers, which brought forth a variety of replies from defenders of the main tradition. Both groups displayed a diversity of approaches which inhibits any brief characterization of their views, but in general the historists pressed three lines of argument: they questioned the scientific status of political economy and the purpose of the subject; they protested against the narrowness of its scope; and they complained of the excessive reliance on the abstract–deductive method of reasoning, and the dogmatic application of conclusions to policy. In the following paragraphs the principal methodological issues will be reviewed and the contribution of the discussion to subsequent advances will be appraised.

THE BACKGROUND OF ENGLISH HISTORISM

To a greater extent than is usually recognized, the historist movement in English political economy was an indigenous growth. Foxwell considered that 'perhaps the most effective of the influences which gave a new direction to economic study was that exercised by the rough but inexorable logic of events',[7] and Marshall subsequently endorsed this view.[8] The influence of Richard Jones, who had stressed the limitations of the laws of political economy when applied to different historical situations, had been revived by the publication of his collected works in 1859, and Marshall attached considerable weight to his contribution.[9] Another native source of historical thought was Sir Henry Maine, who inspired Cliffe Leslie's criticisms of political economy.

From abroad the main influence was Auguste Comte who, through John Kells Ingram, and to a lesser extent through William Cunningham, initiated many of the proposals for reorganizing economic science. J.S. Mill himself, despite a thorough Ricardian training and a destructive attack on positivist philosophy, made notable concessions to Comtist demands.[10] The rise of the German Historical School of Economics in the mid-century appears to have proceeded independently of the Comtist philosophy, although from a wider point of view the two movements had common origins. Unlike their American counterparts, who founded the American Economic Association in 1885, the English historists did not directly owe their inspiration to Germany, but rather used the German writings in support of their existing predilections.

In the following paragraphs the main arguments of the opponents of 'orthodox' political economy will be outlined, together with the principal replies made by its defenders, under the headings 'nature of the subject', 'scope' and 'method'.

NATURE OF THE SUBJECT

The crudest attack on contemporary political economy, one which probably inspired the proposal to abandon Section F, was that made by Bonamy Price, Professor of Political Economy at Oxford. The current 'wild passion for scientific treatment', Price argued, was a mistake, since political economy was not a science but a practical study. 'What are called economic laws by most writers are mere tendencies. They profess no absolute and uniform character.' Political economy 'is the application of common sense to familiar processes. It explains their nature and manner of working.'[11]

This denial of scientific status to political economy was welcomed by some popular writers but was rejected by most academicians, including Leslie and Ingram. Price's hostility to the term 'tendency' is reminiscent of Whewell's introduction to Richard Jones' works,[12] and his rigid view of science was shared by Robert Lowe, one of the most outspoken supporters of Ricardianism. Defining science as 'knowledge in its clearest and most absolute form', of which the 'one crucial test' was prediction, Lowe exhibited strong positivist leanings;[13] but in this, as in other matters, he was out of touch with the prevailing trend in economic literature. The leading writers accepted Mill's view that 'all laws of causation, in consequence of their liability to be counteracted, require to be stated in words affirmative of tendencies only, and not of actual results',[14] an interpretation which reflects the more precise and qualified tone of their writings.

There was greater support for the notion that practical precepts constituted the end product of political economy, and it was to counter this view that J.E. Cairnes published his famous essay, 'Political Economy and Laissez-Faire'.[15] Cairnes denied that economists were committed to a laissez-faire programme and affirmed the validity of the concept as a theoretical first approximation, from which reasoning could proceed to more complex cases. In modern terminology, laissez-faire was a simple 'model', not a practical policy.

Walter Bagehot, editor of the *Economist*, also rejected the contention that economists should concentrate on policy recommendations, although he wished to strengthen the link between theory and practice. 'Political economy', he complained, 'is an abstract science which labours under a special hardship. Those who are conversant with its abstractions are usually without a true contact with its facts; those who are in contact with its facts have usually little sympathy with and little cognisance of its abstractions;'[16] but he did not deny the discipline scientific status.

SCOPE

An attack on the narrowness of the current view of the proper scope of political economy was the main feature of Ingram's presidential address to Section F of the British Association in 1878, an address which met with an enthusiastic response in America and in Germany. Ingram, who was profoundly influenced by Comte, emphasized the need for a unified science of society. While accepting the argument in favour of doing 'one thing at a time', he warned that the social sciences were still branches of one subject, 'and the relations of the branches may be precisely the most important thing to be kept in view respecting them'.[17] The parallel between sociology and biology was relevant here, and the organic analogy loomed large in his exposition. Mill had conceded that in practical questions the different aspects of society were interconnected, and Ingram insisted that this was also true for theoretical purposes. In separating related matters, he said, economists had neglected moral issues, and for this they had been justly criticized by Carlyle, Ruskin and their followers.[18]

Cliffe Leslie, though not a disciple of Comte, shared Ingram's views on the scope of economics. Economic, moral and intellectual forces were identical, Leslie maintained, and 'political economy is thus a department of the science of society which selects a special class of social phenomena for special investigation, but for this purpose must investigate all the forces and laws by which they are governed. The deductive economist misconceives altogether the method of isolation permissible in philosophy.'[19]

However, the fallacy underlying this view had already been exposed by Henry Fawcett. 'Political economy', Fawcett said, 'does not investigate all the laws which concern the production of wealth; for if it did investigate those laws, chemistry, physiology, mathematics, and various other branches of knowledge would form a part of the science of political economy. It will be necessary therefore to place some limit upon our investigation.'[20] Henry Sidgwick likewise contended that while political economy was not an independent study, it was best pursued separately, if properly qualified.[21] Only by this method could economic problems be clearly distinguished from political or ethical issues, and it was essential to recognize the limits of the economist's province. With other writers, he held that it was useless to rely on Ingram's 'laws of social evolution', for the Comtist sociology was still in embryo. It was generally agreed that different problems required different admixtures of economic and non-economic considerations and Sidgwick, like Cairnes, was anxious to avoid dogmatism on the matter.

Thus the representatives of the dominant tradition claimed scientific independence for the theoretical branch of the subject while admitting the relevance of non-economic factors in the application of economic principles to practical questions. But a change of emphasis in the interpretation of the scope of economics occurred during the period as a reliance on an economic 'approach' to social phenomena tended to supplant references to a specifically 'economic' range of subject-matter.[22] William Cunningham, a historist sympathiser, regarded this modification as highly significant, adding that 'the historians isolate a group of facts and try to account for them; the normalists isolate certain motives and measure them, and formulate laws according to which these motives act. Professor Marshall describes economics as the science of measurable motives.'[23] It is likely that this change indicated an increased unwillingness to differentiate rigidly between economic and non-economic facts, and was a response to the historist criticisms.

METHOD

The dispute over method, *per se*, centred around two main issues. Firstly, should political economy be based on more specific or more general propositions? Secondly, to what extent is a general theory applicable to different concrete situations? Much of the controversy sprang from a failure to recognize that a theoretical proposition is valid only under given conditions, although this had been vigorously stated in earlier methodological writings. The historists appealed for more induction, more attention to the facts of economic and social life, both as a source of fruitful hypotheses and as a means of testing conclusions.

On the issue of the generality of the assumptions of political economy Ingram and Leslie were in close agreement. The Ricardian premises were termed 'viciously abstract' in that they represented such broad categories that the essential realities were hidden. Assumptions such as 'self-interest' and the 'desire of wealth' had been treated as 'simple, universal, and invariable principles', whereas more specific assumptions should have been made, based on careful observations. The 'desire of wealth', Leslie said, occupied a central place in political economy comparable to that of natural selection in Darwinian theory, but 'Mr Darwin's hypothesis was based on many previous inductions, and followed by minute and elaborate verification, for which the sole substitute in political economy has been an ignoratio elenchi'.[24]

The argument was then directed against the practice of isolating certain motives as sufficient for the explanation of economic phenomena. Earlier economists had admitted the existence of non-economic motives, but Leslie suggested 'with respect to the deductive economists' practice of setting aside a number of forces as 'friction', that the best corrective would be a demonstration that this so-called friction is capable of scientific analysis and measurement'.[25] Supporters of the traditional method must either argue that no other motives were relevant, or claim an intuitive knowledge of such motives.

In their reply to the charge that the premises of political economy were too broad to serve as the basis for theoretical reasoning the defenders of the classical system presented a united front. They maintained that these premises were founded on experience and were, for practical purposes, universally true. Nevertheless, Sidgwick emphasized the need for qualifications, adding that the writers of the 'opposite school' had performed a valuable service in drawing attention to them. However, the basic methodological question, he claimed, was 'not whether the play of the ordinary motives of self-interest ought to be limited or supplemented by the operation of other motives; but whether these other motives actually do, or can be reasonably expected to operate in such a way as to destroy the applicability of the method of economic analysis which assumes that each party to any free exchange will prefer his own interest to that of the other party'.[26] This he categorically denied.

The demand for an historical method arose partly as a protest against the dogmatic application of economic reasoning to practical affairs. The 'deductive economists' were charged with a neglect of the changing structure of society, and the catchwords 'perpetualism' and 'cosmopolitanism' – derived from the German Historical School – were applied to the practice of attributing validity to basic principles at all times and in all places. As an alternative the historists proposed to compare societies at different stages of development and to formulate 'laws of social evolution'. For Ingram, the historical method aimed at 'describing objectively existing economic relations, not as immutable necessities, but as products of a gradual historical past, and susceptible of gradual modification in the future', while the laws of the 'economic constitution and movement of society' were to be obtained by observation.[27] Leslie, who used the terms 'inductive' and 'historical' as equivalents, also referred to 'laws of social evolution' as the 'ultimate causes' of economic phenomena. Deduction was not irrelevant, but he considered that 'political economy has not reached the stage of a deductive science; that the fundamental laws of the economic world are still imperfectly known; and that they can be fully known only by patient induction'.[28]

Walter Bagehot stood somewhat apart from the academic tradition, though his work was warmly approved by Marshall. Admitting that English economists had shown an excessive desire for universality, Bagehot proceeded to examine the extent to which the basic postulates were relevant to different historical and geographical situations. In this respect he showed a leaning toward the historist position. J.S. Mill had claimed universality for the laws of production, but Bagehot held that all the doctrines of political economy applied to modern commercial nations alone. To limit the claims of the subject would sustain its authority, for 'by marking the frontier of our property, we shall learn its use, and we shall have a positive and reliable basis for estimating its value'.[29]

The orthodox economists shared the historist desire to avoid excessive rigidity in the laws of political economy and in the application of doctrines to different historical situations. In general they agreed with Mill that Comte had not demonstrated the futility of social generalizations, but had merely shown 'that these generalisations must necessarily be relative to a given form of civilisation and a given stage of social advancement. This, we apprehend, is what no political economist would deny.'[30] Orthodox writers accepted this judgement as relevant to the applications of economic theory while insisting on the universality of the basic principles, when suitably qualified. In the 'seventies and 'eighties historical pronouncements became very fashionable, though it is difficult to judge how far the central body of economic analysis was affected by the change. Assumptions were more carefully stated, conclusions were more cautiously applied, and parallel comments can be cited from Ingram and Sidgwick to illustrate that the two groups were not far apart in this respect.[31] To Marshall, the change represented an enhanced appreciation of scientific method, amounting to 'the abandonment of general propositions and dogmas in favour of processes of analysis and reasoning, carefully worked out and held ready for application to the special circumstances of particular problems relating to different countries and different ages, to different races and different classes of industry'.[32]

In answer to frequent charges that the Ricardians had placed undue reliance on deduction, Sidgwick replied that 'the opposition between the Inductive and Deductive methods appears to have been urged by writers on both sides in needlessly sharp and uncompromising terms'.[33] Both methods were needed, but in different proportions in different parts of the subject. J.S. Mill, for instance, had relied on the inductive method in his theory of production, whereas in the theory of distribution, which had been a central part of economic analysis since Ricardo's day, the questions posed demanded a predominantly deductive treatment. The deductive method was indispensable because of the need to begin with simple cases and to interpret the motives of human agents. Successful deduction was largely dependent upon the ability of the reasoner to recognize the divergence between simplifying assumptions and the actual facts, and to judge the effects of modifying causes neglected in the premises. 'It is obvious', Sidgwick concluded, 'that answers so obtained do not by themselves enable us accurately to interpret or to predict economic phenomena; but it is commonly held that when modified by a rough conjectural allowance for the difference between our hypothetical premises and the actual facts in any case, they do materially assist us in attaining approximate correctness in our interpretations and predictions'. Useful criticisms had been made by opposing writers, he added, 'but I cannot accept the conclusion which some of them have proceeded to draw, that the traditional method of English political economy is essentially faulty and misleading'.[34]

CONCLUSION

Treatises on the history of economic thought frequently proclaim the years 1870–1 as the beginning of a new era of theoretical advance, centring around the subjective theory of value. The years 1890–1 can be regarded as another turning point, closing off a phase of continuous methodological controversy and ushering in a period conspicuous for the development of a widely accepted body of theory. In various quarters there were indications of a new harmony and moderation – Adolf Wagner in Germany, Charles Dunbar and the American Economic Association in the United States, Alfred Marshall and John Neville Keynes in England, all produced important attempts to survey the condition of economic thought, and to establish the areas of agreement between different schools.[35]

While the methodological debates continued in Germany and Austria, this was not the case in the Anglo-Saxon countries. In England the new atmosphere must be credited largely to the Cambridge school, which had been gathering strength in the two preceding decades. This group had acquired its prestige through the outstanding abilities of its leaders, Marshall, Sidgwick, J.N. Keynes and Foxwell, and, it must be acknowledged, through the absence of any serious rivals, a state of affairs partly to be accounted for by the recent premature decease of several eminent contemporaries.[36] Marshall's work, for instance, showed a notable emphasis on the continuity of doctrine, and an attempt at the reconciliation of diverging views with the object of eliminating unnecessary controversy, for he denied an interest in compromise as such. Although the historists failed to gain the ascendancy, significant, if subtle modifications in the received doctrine had taken place.

In considering these modifications it must be recalled that some of the early historist enthusiasm subsequently found expression in the new field of economic history, while some of those who desired a unified social science turned their attentions to sociology. In political economy itself, apart from major developments in systematic theory, there was an increased understanding of scientific method. A specialized terminology was fashioned; a clarification of basic concepts occurred, from which a new set of definitions emerged; new theoretical tools were forged; assumptions were explicitly stated and more carefully qualified; and, above all, a more cautious set of policy recommendations was outlined, with a more modest statement of the contributions of pure theory. There was a better understanding of the relationship between theory and policy, and a wider recognition of the complementary nature of induction and deduction.

On the latter question there was a marked continuity in the orthodox methodology, although the leading classical writers had at times unduly relied on deductions from general premises. Popularisers had transformed this overemphasis into a rigid system of laws which they dogmatically applied to a variety of current problems. The historist criticisms had a salutary effect in discrediting this practice for, as Marshall said, 'general economic principles had to justify their existence before a court which no longer had any bias in their favour. . . . Consequently they became less dictatorial, and more willing to admit their own limitations. Never again will a Mrs Trimmer, a Mrs Marcet or a Miss Martineau earn a goodly reputation by throwing them into the form of a catechism or of simple tales, by aid of which any intelligent governess might make clear to the children nestling around her where lies economic truth.'[37]

The positive contributions of the historists, however, were more modest. Political economy could not and did not become an historical science. Most of the critics greatly undervalued deductive analysis, and their proposals were innocent of any systematic theory. They largely failed to distinguish the generality of economic principles from the relativity of economic applications, and since the Comtist vision of sociology inspired a misguided belief that 'laws of social evolution' were readily attainable or even in existence, their methodological programme was lacking in content.

Historist criticism was not, of course, the sole stimulus to the advance of economic science. This was, as Edgeworth remarked, an 'age of luxuriant speculation, when novel theories teem in so many new Economic Journals'.[38] Even J.N. Keynes may be accused of having somewhat overrated the influence of the historists and the contribution of history to certain areas of economic theory.[39] Yet the influence of historism was undoubtedly significant. As Professor Nicholson said, in 1893, the traditional method had been modified and supplemented, rather than being revolutionized and supplanted; 'the dogmatic slumber induced by popular approval has been rudely shattered, and although some of the more timid followers of the orthodox camp thought they had been killed when they were only frightened and awakened, the central positions are more secure than before'.[40] This, we may conclude, is explained by the fact that the defenders of classical political economy recognized many of its weaknesses, made appropriate adjustments in their teachings to allow for them, and thus preserved the tradition by cutting away the ground from under their critics' feet.

NOTES

1 The term 'historism' is here used as in Professor Hayek's 'Scientism and the Study of Society – Part II', *Economica* vol.X (1943), pp.50–1, as the view that history was the source from which the theoretical science of society would spring. The term was introduced by Karl Menger in *Die Irrthümer des Historismus* (1884). In preparing this paper I have received many helpful suggestions from Professors Evans and Machlup and fellow members of the Political Economy Seminar at

the Johns Hopkins University, and also from Mr T.W. Hutchison of the London School of Economics.

2 Jevons, *Theory of Political Economy* (London, 1871), Preface. *A propos* of the bad effects of controversies on political economy, John Ramsay McCulloch said that 'the differences which have subsisted among the most eminent of its professors have proved exceedingly unfavourable to its progress, and have generated a disposition to distrust its best established conclusions'. Quoted by Henry Sidgwick, *Principles of Political Economy* (London, 1901), p.5.

3 Quoted by Jevons in 'The Future of Political Economy', *Fortnightly Review* vol. XXVI (1876), p.190.

4 See the *Journal of the Royal Statistical Society* (1877), pp.468–75. The state of English political economy in the early 1870s is more fully discussed in T.W. Hutchison's book, *A Review of Economic Doctrines 1870–1929* (Oxford, 1953), pp.1–31.

5 Herbert Somerton Foxwell, Introduction to Anton Menger's *The Right to the Whole Produce of Labour* (London, 1899), p.lxxviii. It has been pertinently suggested that this was not the only time that English economists were 'men of one book'.

6 Foxwell, 'The Economic Movement in England', *Quarterly Journal of Economics* vol.II (1888), p.87.

7 ibid., pp.85–6.

8 Alfred Marshall, 'The Old Generation of Economists and the New', *Quarterly Journal of Economics* vol.XI (1897), p.116.

9 ibid., p.117, where Marshall wrote that Jones 'said just what was wanted at the time; and his influence, though little heard of in the outer world, largely dominated the minds of those Englishmen who came to the serious study of economics after his works had been published by Dr Whewell in 1859'. Though referring to his own generation Marshall's judgement appears to grant too much to Jones's influence.

10 Mill's comment that 'we know not of any thinker who, before M. Comte had penetrated to the philosophy of the matter, and placed the necessity of historical studies as the foundation of sociological speculation on the true footing', was of the kind calculated to appeal to the advocates of historism. See J.S. Mill, *Auguste Comte and Positivism* (London, 1865), p.86.

11 Price, *Chapters on Practical Political Economy* (London, 1878), pp.16, 15.

12 Whewell, *Literary Remains of the late Richard Jones* (London, 1859), pp.xiv–xv.

13 Lowe, 'Recent Attacks on Political Economy', *The Nineteenth Century* (November, 1878), p.860.

14 J.S. Mill, *System of Logic* (New York, 1846), Bk. 3, ch.X, sec.5, p.258.

15 Cairnes, 'Political Economy and Laissez-Faire', *Essays in Political Economy: Theoretical and Applied* (London, 1873), pp.232–64.

16 Bagehot, *Economic Studies* (London, 1888), p.7.

17 Ingram, *Proceedings of the British Association for the Advancement of Science* (1878), p.646.

18 The link between moralism, historism and humanitarianism is exemplified by the work of Arnold Toynbee, a writer who had a significant impact on Oxford opinion in the 1870s. On methodological issues Toynbee was close to Bagehot's position. See Toynbee, *Lectures on the Industrial Revolution in England* (London, 1884); also Hutchison, op. cit., pp.11, 19.

19 Leslie, *Essays in Moral and Political Philosophy* (London, 1879), p.212.

20 Fawcett, *Manual of Political Economy* (London, 1863), pp.44–5.

21 Sidgwick, *Principles of Political Economy* (London, 1883), p.24.

22 Compare Cairnes, *The Character and Logical Method of Political Economy* (New

York, 1875), Lecture, I, with John Neville Keynes, *The Scope and Method of Political Economy* (London, 1891), p.132.

23 Cunningham, 'A Plea for Pure Theory', *The Economic Review* vol.II (1892), p.34. See also his article, 'Why had Roscher so little Influence in England?', *Annals of the American Academy* vol.V (1894–5), pp.317–34, which further indicates his divergence from Marshall's position.

24 Leslie, op. cit., p.186.

25 ibid, p.194. This suggestion, he said, was made by Sir Henry Maine.

26 Sidgwick, *Proceedings of the British Association* (1885), p.1148. In the following paragraphs Sidgwick rather than Marshall has been cited as the principal spokesman for the orthodox position since his views are less familiar to modern readers.

27 Ingram, *loc. cit.*, p.654. To this Marshall replied: 'Observation discovers nothing of the action of causes, but only of sequences in time': *Memorials of Alfred Marshall*, ed. A.C. Pigou, (1925), p.166.

28 Leslie, op. cit., p.24.

29 Bagehot, op. cit., p.21.

30 Mill, *Auguste Comte and Positivism*, p.81.

31 See Ingram, *Proceedings of the British Association* (1878), p.653; Sidgwick, *Proceedings* (1885), p.1150.

32 Marshall, *Proceedings of the British Association* (1890), p.899.

33 Sidgwick, op. cit., p.7.

34 ibid., p.44.

35 Wagner, Review of Marshall's 'Principles', *Quarterly Journal of Economics* vol.V (1891), pp.319–38; Dunbar, 'The Reaction in Political Economy', *Quarterly Journal of Economics* vol.I (1887), pp.1–27; (Dunbar's appointment as President of the American Economic Association in 1892 marked a widening of the organization's membership, and signified the increased respect for divergent approaches to the subject.) Marshall, *Principles of Economics* (London, 1890); J.N. Keynes, *Scope and Method of Political Economy* (London, 1891).

36 J.S. Mill died in 1873; Cairnes in 1875; Bagehot in 1877; Jevons in 1882; Leslie in 1882; and Fawcett in 1884.

37 Marshall, 'The Old Generation of Economists and the New', *Quarterly Journal of Economics* vol.XI (1897), p.117.

38 F.Y. Edgeworth, *Proceedings of the British Association* (1889), p.676.

39 See his references to the relativity of economic doctrines, op. cit., p.262, and to historical laws of economic development, ibid., pp.135, 267.

40 J.S. Nicholson, *Proceedings of the British Association* (1893), reprinted in the *Journal of Political Economy* vol.II (1893), p.119.

13

MARSHALL AND ETHICS

I PREAMBLE

In all economic questions, considerations of the higher ethics will always assert themselves, however much we try to limit our inquiry for an immediate practical purpose.

(Alfred Marshall, 1887: xxvi)

The key note ... of the whole of Marshall's life as an economist, was that double nature – scientist and pastor, thinker and moralizer – that Keynes perceived as the clue to Marshall's mingled strength and weakness; to his conflicting purposes and wasted strength.

(Whitaker, 1972: 37–8)

The interrelationship between economics and ethics is a fundamental and pervasive theme in Marshall's career and writings. An adequate treatment of this theme is obviously impossible within the space available here since it would call for a detailed analysis of the condition and development of the two disciplines during Marshall's lifetime against the broader background of mid- and late-Victorian British intellectual, social and economic history, with special reference to the growing specialization and professionalization of the social (or moral) sciences. Consequently, what follows is highly selective.

II ECONOMICS AMONG THE MORAL SCIENCES

Given my special interests, and John Maloney's recent perceptive account of Marshall's role in the development – perhaps one should say the emergence – of the economics profession in Britain (Maloney, 1985), it is convenient to begin with the last of the above-mentioned subjects. As is well known, Marshall did not practise what Beatrice Webb termed 'a Self-Contained, Separate, Abstract Political Economy' (Webb, 1926: 422); and Maynard Keynes was seriously misleading in describing him as:

the first great economist ... who devoted his life to building up the subject as a *separate* science, standing on its own foundations with

231

as high standards of scientific activity as the physical or biological sciences.

(Keynes, 1925: 56–7; emphasis added)

To discuss 'standards of scientific activity' or 'the professional scientific attitude' (another phrase in the same passage) would take us too far into methodology and sociology. The more immediately relevant issue here is the concept of a 'separate' science, a term Marshall himself occasionally applied to his economics, which pointed towards the growing division of labour in an expanding academic universe. No doubt Keynes was right in claiming that after Marshall 'Economics could never again be [merely?] one of a number of subjects which a Moral Philosopher would take in his stride, one Moral Science out of several, as Mill, Jevons and Sidgwick took it' (ibid.: 57).

Developments in economics during Marshall's lifetime were part of a much broader process – though, admittedly, the eventual success of Marshall's protracted campaign to establish an independent Economics Tripos (Groenewegen, 1988) had significant repercussions, both within Cambridge and beyond. He would surely have deplored the narrowing, fragmentation, excessive abstraction and mathematization that has occurred in economics since his death, although he would have welcomed the growth of quantification, within limits.

Nevertheless, given the pedagogical and professional circumstances of his time, he favoured greater specialization, since the ambitious Comtean plan for a unified social science 'showed no signs of coming into existence'. The progress of knowledge, Marshall argued, required a 'common sense' breakdown of social problems into their component parts, and a corresponding division of academic labour, with each discipline utilizing its 'specialised scientific organon, if there be one ready'.[1] Needless to say, economics was fully prepared for the new dispensation, even if the other social sciences were not.

Five years later, when the *Principles* first appeared, Marshall professed indifference to academic demarcation disputes, declaring that 'the less we trouble ourselves with the scholastic inquiries as to whether a certain consideration comes within the scope of economics, the better' (Marshall, 1961: vol.1, 9). In his hands this constituted a licence for a comprehensive approach that some critics have dubbed 'imperialistic' (Boulding, 1969: 8; Collini *et al.*, 1984: 312). Marshall's own procedure was characteristically ambivalent. As recently noted, he sought

> to retain a hold on all possibilities simultaneously – to claim that there was a well-delimited area for economic science, one that could be expanded indefinitely by the cumulative efforts of dedicated students, while at the same time maintaining immediate contact with all ethical questions of the present and future, without claiming to solve them by its own methods, or losing its qualities as a science in the process.

(Collini *et al.*, 1984: 318)

This was, indeed, a curious species of separateness. Like many of his generation, Marshall initially studied and taught what would nowadays be regarded as several distinct disciplines before deciding to dedicate his life to economics. But unlike his close colleague and contemporary, Henry Sidgwick, who wrote major treatises on *Ethics* (1874), *Political Economy* (1883) and *Politics* (1891), he subsequently more or less stuck to his last, thereby directly contributing to the irresistible march of scholarly compartmentalization that has subsequently dominated twentieth century academic knowledge.

Ethics was one of the subjects, together with mathematics, philosophy, politics and psychology, that absorbed Marshall's energies during his early years, and his characterizations of its relationship to economics provide a rare opportunity to derive some amusement from this solemn occasion. Ethics was both the 'sister' of economics (Marshall, 1874: 430) and 'the good Abigail', the 'mistress' of economics (Marshall, 1893: 390, 389); and as has been wittily observed of the latter designation: 'Although . . . separate establishments were, as usual with such relationships, the wisest arrangement, Marshall continued to speak as though economics enjoyed privileged access to that establishment' (Collini *et al.*, 1984: 318). For those familiar with Margaret Attwood's chilling novel, *The Handmaid's Tale* (parts of which were filmed at Duke University), the scope for Freudian interpretations is further enhanced by A.C. Pigou's guileless suggestion that Marshall saw ethics as 'a handmaid of economics and a servant of practice' rather than 'an intellectual gymnastic [or] even as a means of winning truth for its own sake' (Pigou, 1925: 84).

Although the ethics–economics connection was being actively discussed throughout much of his career (Maloney, 1985: ch.9), Marshall did not actively participate in the debate.[2] He steadfastly refrained from engaging in philosophical controversy or committing himself to any formal ethical doctrine, preferring instead to rely on 'our ethical instincts and common sense, when they as *ultimate* arbiters come to apply to practical issues the knowledge obtained by economics and other sciences' (Marshall, 1961: vol.1, 28; emphasis in original).

Marshall's reservations about utilitarianism – or, for that matter, any other formal philosophical system – are well known,[3] hence his insistence that while

> some of the greatest economists have been utilitarians . . . that was an accident. Their analysis was wholly independent of utilitarian doctrine; it was, when rightly understood, *common property to all ethical creeds*.
>
> (Marshall, 1893: 388; emphasis in original)

Given his reluctance to explicate his ethical beliefs, it is hardly surprising that so many commentators have concluded that Marshall simply took for granted the conventional moral ideas and standards of his social and intellectual group. There is substantial warrant for this general interpretation; but it is possible to be more specific. For example, in *Industry and Trade*, as earlier in his sermon to the younger generation of economists, he acknowledged the difficulty of defining the true nature of the 'social good', but added that there was a fundamental 'substratum' of agreement that consisted 'mainly in that healthful exercise and development of faculties which yields happiness without pall, because it sustains self-respect and is sustained by hope' (Marshall, 1923: 664; cf. Marshall, 1897: 310). The key term here is not 'happiness', but 'self-respect'. As Marshall informed the evolution sociologist, Benjamin Kidd, his 'religion of self-respect' required no 'supernatural sanctions' of the kind needed 'in an earlier stage of development'; for

> the sanctions of religion are moral, and that morality may be a product of instinct, but in the ultimate appeal must rely mainly on reason. My reason . . . tells me that an unmoral life is not likely to be a happy one at all, and cannot be a very happy one; because – according to my personal experience, and according to that of all those whom I know, who have tried both methods of living – the times I have least respect for myself have been my unhappiest, physical conditions count for little in comparison.[4]

In a rare concession to contemporary ethical debate, in two revealing footnotes, Marshall endeavoured to dispel the misconception that the desire to do one's duty is no different from any other 'pleasure', by proposing the broad, neutral term 'satisfaction' to refer to 'the aims of all desires, whether appertaining to man's higher or lower nature'. For the Benthamites, however, an additional 'independent major premise was required' to 'serve as a bridge by which to pass from individualistic Hedonism to a complete ethical creed'. For some, the Kantian 'Categorical Imperative' would serve the purpose; but for others, obviously including Marshall himself, whatever 'the origin of our moral instincts', it would be sufficient to rely on 'self-respect', which 'is to be had only on the condition of endeavouring so to live as to promote the progress of the human race'.[5]

The ethical significance of Marshall's concern with 'the progress of the human race' appears more clearly in his 1875 unpublished talk on 'Some Features of American Industry', which ends with the statement that he was working his way 'towards that ethical creed which is according to the Doctrine of Evolution'. There were two key factors in the human evolutionary process: firstly, 'the peaceful moulding of character into harmony with the conditions by which it is surrounded, so that a man . . . will without conscious moral effort be impelled in that course which is in union with the actions, the sympathies, and the interests of the society amid which he spends his life', and secondly, 'the education of a firm will through the overcoming of difficulties . . . [a will that] submits every particular action to the judgement of reason' (reproduced in Whitaker, 1975a: vol.2, 375, 377). As John Whitaker has observed, Marshall's approach combined a powerful internalized individual commitment to duty with the external pressure to conform to community ethical standards. But

> only if there are agreed ethical axioms can the internal and external pressures be regarded as always working together. . . . This kind of ethical absolutism – the belief that there exist universal values which merely need to be discovered – was a quite common unconscious presumption of nineteenth century thinkers.[6]

III 'PURE' ECONOMIC SCIENCE AND APPLIED ECONOMIC ETHICS?

There are at least four reasons why Marshall could not contemplate a complete severance of economics from ethics.

1. On a personal level he was, as Keynes said, 'too anxious' to do good, and this led him to undervalue the more theoretical as against the practical aspects of economics. In his later years he seemed to lose interest in pure theory, apart from continuing efforts to reinterpret and defend his own work in response to criticism; and he became increasingly preoccupied with ethical ideals, historical development, and problems of economic and social policy.

2. To Marshall, the economist's mission was itself an ethical undertaking. Its purpose was not merely to relieve poverty and suffering, but to help raise the 'quality of human life'; and the scientific economist's work could, at least sometimes, 'suggest a moral or practical precept' which, through human effort, could 'modify the action of laws of nature' (Marshall, 1961: vol.1, 36). And, as the economist (ideally?) had 'no class or personal interests to make him afraid of any conclusions which the figures (or the analysis?) when carefully interpreted may indicate', he was 'fortified by the consciousness of his own rectitude' (ibid.: vol.2, 757; Marshall, 1897: 305). Like others of his intellectual circle, Marshall had abandoned his youthful religion and could salve his conscience by viewing his career as a species of secular priesthood. Indeed, on his deathbed he told Keynes 'how he first came to study economics and how such a study was a sort of religious work for the sake of the human race'.[7]

3. In 'positive' scientific terms, the economist was obliged to take ethical forces 'into account' (Marshall, 1961: vol.1, vi), because they directly and significantly influenced individual and social behaviour and, therefore, the operation of economic laws and tendencies. For example, in the *Economics of Industry* (1879: ch.2), 'moral character' was listed as one of the principal 'agents of production', and this agent played a central role in Marshall's conception of evolutionary socio-economic change. (See *infra*, section IV).

4. Together with his rejection of the concept of 'economic man', Marshall incorporated ethical factors into his economics also because he wished to align himself, in general terms, with the 'new economic movement' (Foxwell,

1887) associated with the reformist ideas of Thomas Carlyle, John Ruskin, Arnold Toynbee (Marshall's predecessor at Balliol College, Oxford) and the more moderate Christian Socialists. Like Marshall, these writers held that political economy should be a study of human welfare rather than merely material wealth.[8]

In Marshall's sociological system the relationship between economics, ethics and psychology was crucial. It explains both his rejection of the concept of an economic man 'who is under no ethical influences and who pursues pecuniary gain warily and energetically, but mechanically and selfishly' (Marshall, 1961: vol.1, vi), and his claim that one of the 'chief features' of his *Principles* was the inclusion of all motives relevant to human action. More important still, it underlies the claim of economics to be a 'separate' science, because economic motives are measurable, albeit indirectly. Admittedly, not all motives are measurable; and the available indirect monetary measure is imperfect and inexact, so that economics cannot hope to achieve the precision and generality of physics. Nevertheless, 'it is this definite and exact measurement of the steadiest motives in business life, which has enabled economics to far outrun every other branch of the study of man' (ibid.: vol.1, 14). Ethics, of course, lacks this advantage:

> The pure science of Ethics halts for lack of a system of measurement of efforts, sacrifices, desires, etc., fit for her wide purpose. But the pure science of Political Economy has found a system that will serve her narrower aims. This discovery, rather than any particular proposition, is the great fact of the pure science.
>
> (Marshall, 1876: 126)

However, as noted above, Marshall was unwilling to confine himself within the boundaries of 'the pure science of Political Economy'. He was eager to embrace all motives, both higher and lower, whether measurable or non-measurable; and as one of his more penetrating critics, Walter Weisskopf, has argued, he provided no solution to the problem of handling the qualitative ethical differences entailed in taking account of the higher motives of life:

> Although the restriction of economics to the money motive seems to be completely vindicated on purely intellectual grounds, . . . [because] conduct motivated by money gains is supposedly measurable, verifiable, predictable, and subject to laws, regularities and uniformities . . . its combination with deliberate rationality contains an ethical element, because deliberateness is considered by Marshall to be a moral virtue. At the end of his discussion Marshall acknowledges the importance of the ethical: the money measurement is used for the sake of greater exactness; but for practical issues we must 'take some sort of account of our ethical instincts and common sense'.[9]

Marshall's determination to take account of ethical factors explains his rejection of Sidgwick's conventional distinction between the 'science' and the 'art' of political economy (Sidgwick, 1883: xix, 12, 21ff, 403) and John Neville Keynes' tripartite division between: (a) the 'positive' scientific study of economic laws, (b) 'applied' political economy, focusing on the practical precepts for attaining given ends; and (c) the ethical norms and criteria required for policy recommendations (Keynes, 1890: 31–6). Unlike Sidgwick, who devoted nine chapters of his *Principles* to the art of political economy, including such topics as 'The Principles of Distributive Justice' and 'Political Economy and Private Morality', Marshall had no patience with elaborate classifications. He simply drew the line between the relatively 'pure' and the relatively 'applied' parts of the science, arguing that

> it seems better to regard the science as pursuing its inquiries with more or less direct reference to certain practical issues, and as pointing the way towards solutions of them, than to make pretension to the authority of an Art, complete and self-contained, and responsible for the entire direction of conduct in certain matters.
>
> (Marshall, 1961: vol.2, 154)

However, in his quest for realism and his impatience with mere abstraction, he severely limited the sphere of the 'pure' science, even claiming that 'in a sense the whole of economics is an applied science' (ibid.: vol.2, 153). In this respect his approach resembled that of his predecessor, Henry Fawcett (cf. Deane, 1989: 97–8).

Marshall clearly believed it was both possible and desirable to avoid the confusions between the imperative and the indicative mood which had bedevilled the writings of earlier economists, including Adam Smith (Marshall, 1961: vol.1, 756–8; vi), and he periodically issued strong injunctions against this malpractice. An unusually specific example occurs in his *Bee-Hive* article, where he distinguished between the consequences of a certain course of action and the question whether actions having such consequences were justifiable. In many cases, he said, the issues 'are so clear that our moral judgement is given without hesitation, almost instinctively, and we are scarcely aware that any other judgement than that of political economy can be given'. However other cases 'which political economy presents to our judgement' are not so clear, and here:

> It is absolutely necessary to keep entirely distinct two questions, that which must be decided according to the laws of political economy, viz. what consequences will follow from a postponed [sic][10] course of action, and that which will be decided by our moral judgement, viz. whether an action which produces these consequences is right.
>
> (Marshall, 1874: 425)

The economist's 'special science' gives him no special competence to answer the second question, for political economy:

lacks the power of giving direct and complete answers on points involving questions of right and wrong . . . and if the rigidly scientific character of political economy be forgotten, those questions even, which belong strictly to her domain, will not be discussed with scientific calm and thoroughness.

(ibid.: 425–6)

In later years Marshall seems to have been somewhat more flexible towards 'the rigidly scientific character of political economy'; and in differentiating between conclusions based securely on scientific method and judgements on matters lying outside the economist's professional competence and authority he employed what later became the familiar (and notorious) Robbinsian distinction between the economist *qua* scientist and *qua* citizen – one that has provoked perennial controversy and mixed responses from twentieth century economic writers, many of them angry, sceptical or merely cynical. Marshall's own practice was, to say the least, permissive;[11] and he overlooked, or perhaps simply chose to ignore the problem of individual judgement involved in deciding where the boundary should be drawn between scientific and non-scientific matters.[12] In the absence of an explicit definition of the discipline's scope – which he was certainly unwilling to provide – the decision must necessarily be based either on personal, extra-scientific value premises or, alternatively, on an inter-subjective professional consensus which necessarily has normative and/or ideological implications. As Maloney has persuasively argued, the establishment of such a consensus under Marshall's leadership, and on his terms, became one of his long-term career objectives (Maloney, 1985: especially chs 2, 10 and 11).

IV ETHICS, PSYCHOLOGY AND THE EVOLUTIONARY PROCESS

Although Marshall said he had 'come to economics out of ethics, intending to stay there only a short while' (Marshall, 1961: vol.2, 36), his study of psychology left a lasting imprint on his mind for, late in life he remarked: 'If I had to live my life over again I should have devoted it to psychology. Economics has too little to do with ideals. If I said much about them I should not be read by businessmen' (Keynes, 1925: 37); and the business community was a major segment of the audience he wished to address.

Psychological – or, more strictly speaking, characterological – factors were central in Marshall's account of economic, social and moral development, and in this he was probably influenced by John Stuart Mill's conception of a science of 'ethology' – i.e., the study of character formation, which Mill thought might possibly constitute the foundation of a general science of society. In his *System of Logic* (1843), Mill referred to 'progressive changes both in the character of the human race' and in 'their outward circumstances

238

as far as moulded by themselves' (cited in Hollander: (1985) vol.1, 194), whereas Marshall spoke in similar terms of 'the ever changing and subtle forces of human nature' and the social scientist's need to recognize that there would be 'no sudden improvement in man's conditions of life, because he forms them as much as they form him, and he himself cannot change fast' (Marshall, 1897: 311). At first sight Marshall's statements about the speed of change of human nature seem inconsistent. He frequently referred to 'human nature being what it is', as though it were a fixed datum, whereas at other times he gave a quite different impression of human pliability and adaptability (for example, Marshall, 1885: 173–4; cited in Reisman, 1987: 370). The differences could, however, be reconciled by distinguishing between the 'tactics' and the 'strategy' of man's conflict with nature; for

> though there is a kernel of man's nature that has scarcely changed, yet many elements of his character, that are most effective for economic uses, are of modern growth. . . . To carry over from one age to another both strategical and tactical lessons, is to incline somewhat towards a mechanical view of economics; to carry over strategical lessons is characteristic of a biological view.[13]

Unlike his price theory, where the analytical distinction between the immediate, short and long periods was clearly specified, in discussing changes in character, morals and social conditions he suggested no time periods, although he was probably thinking in terms of secular, or very long-term developments.[14] The 'progress of industry', for example, was attributable to a combination of influences including: 'the religious, the moral, the intellectual and the artistic faculties . . . [and the] organization of a well-ordered state. . . . [It is] the product of an infinite variety of motives, many of which have no direct connection with the pursuit of wealth.'[15] This was no simple deterministic scheme, although

> man's character has been moulded by his everyday work, and the material resources which he thereby procures; more than by any other influence unless it be that of his religious ideals; and the two great forming agencies of the world's history have been the religious and the economic.
>
> (Marshall, 1961: vol.1, 1; see also 'Some Features of American Industry' in Whitaker, 1975 a: vol.2, 359)

Religious motives were more intense than economic motives; but the latter were more pervasive, and Marshall attached extraordinary weight to the influence of occupation on character and behaviour. 'Work, in its best sense, the healthy and energetic exercise of faculties, is the aim of life, is life itself' (Marshall, 1873: 115) and ideally no man (or woman?) 'should have any occupation which tends to make him less than a gentleman' (ibid.: 110). In his youthful enthusiasm, Marshall believed that the progress of society would eventually obliterate the distinction between the working man and the gentleman; and once this was achieved 'everyone who is not a gentleman will have only himself to blame for it' (ibid.: 111). Under such circumstances, 'no one is to do in the day so much manual work as will leave him little time or little aptitude for intelligent and artistic enjoyment in the evening' (ibid.: 110).

These passages may seem naive to modern readers, but they illustrate the importance Marshall attached to activities as against mere wants. Human beings were not simply Benthamite pleasure machines, consuming for the sake of consumption – although that might unfortunately be the case with some of the lowest income groups; and, contrary to William Stanley Jevons' idea that 'the Theory of Consumption is the scientific basis of economics', Marshall believed that

> much that is of chief interest in the science of wants is borrowed from the science of efforts and activities. These two supplement each other; each is incomplete without the other. But if either, more than the other, may claim to be the interpreter of the history of man, whether on the economic side or any other, it is the science of activities and not that of want.
>
> (Marshall, 1961: vol.1, 90)

Thus, although the causal relationship between them was sometimes expressed in neutral terms, and a cumulative process of deterioration presumably could not be entirely ruled out, the general thrust of Marshall's account was undeniably optimistic, with activities as the more powerful element; for 'Although it is man's wants in the early stages of development that give rise to activities, yet afterwards each new step *upwards* is to be regarded as the development of new activities giving rise to new wants' (ibid.: 38; emphasis in original).

The ethical significance of the distinction between wants and activities underlies Marshall's concept of the standard of life, which is much broader than the standard of comfort, that is, mere conventional necessities (ibid.: vol.1, 504). Thus,

> a rise in the standard of life implies an increase in intelligence and energy and self-respect; leading to more care and judgement in expenditure, and to an avoidance of food and drink that gratify the appetite but afford no strength, and of ways of living that are unwholesome physically and morally.
>
> (ibid.: vol.1, 689; cf. 504)

Given Marshall's 'religion of self-respect', the long-run interdependence and compatibility of economic, social, characterological and ethical changes seemed assured; and this constituted the basis of Marshall's belief in the superiority of late nineteenth century British society by comparison with both its past, and the contemporary state of less developed nations. To some critics this complacent attitude has seemed outrageous. For example, following his pathbreaking analysis of the wants/activities' interrelationship in Marshall's system, Talcott Parsons offered some scathing comments on Marshall's sociology in general, and his concept of character in particular:

> Englishmen have often ridiculed Hegel for supposing that the evolution of the *Weltgeist* had taken place solely for the purpose of producing the Prussian State of the early nineteenth century. And yet Marshall, good Englishman that he was, supposes that the whole process leads to the production of the English businessman and artisan of the latter part of the same century. With all due respect for these worthy gentlemen, does anyone really suppose that they alone will inherit the earth? I am not here concerned with disputing the validity or propriety of Marshall's ethical conviction of the supreme value of one type of character. What is important is whether such subjective ethical convictions should be allowed to colour the whole perspective of the past and present tendencies of social development as it undoubtedly does in the case of Marshall. The complete disregard of most other things which it entails is a narrowness hardly compatible with the ideal of scientific objectivity.[16]

V MARSHALL'S ETHICS AND THE NEW MOVEMENT IN ENGLISH ECONOMICS

In his important survey published in the second volume of the new *Quarterly Journal of Economics*, Marshall's former pupil and colleague, Herbert Somerton Foxwell, who was by no means an uncritical admirer, characterized the new movement in English economic thought as comprising three main elements: 'theoretic criticism, historical method, and humanistic feeling' (Foxwell, 1887: 87). Marshall's contribution to the last of these is of special interest in the present context for it has been unduly neglected by historians of economics – though not by social and more general intellectual historians.

According to Foxwell, the strengths of the authors who emphasized 'the moral and humanistic criticism of our economic life and institutions' lay in 'their opposition to materialism, and their healthy estimate of the real objects of existence'; whereas their weakness was the tendency to 'sometimes allow reason to be overbalanced by emotion'. However, economists like General Walker in the United states, and Jevons and Marshall in England, were contributing to the current convergence of the three lines of inquiry – those of the theorist, the historian and the moralist – so as to form a 'new school', whose members reject

> the old notion that a positive science of economics can be constructed, which even in the industrial sphere can be independent of morality

241

and justice, purely rigid and mechanical in its principles. ... It is the mechanical unmoral economics, even more than the policy of laissez faire, which the new school has banished to Saturn. ... It is their decided conviction that, if competition is to remain the basis of economic relations, society must see that it is so held in check that it shall not violate the older and deeper principles of justice and humanity

(ibid.: 90–1, 100–1)

Whether Marshall saw and/or approved of this passage is not clear; but, setting aside some of the more recent methodological connotations of the phrase 'positive science of economics', it represents a reasonable interpretation of his overall position. And it provides a suitable entrée to a brief account of the contemporary significance of the humanistic side of his work.

In the oft-quoted peroration that concluded his inaugural lecture Marshall disclosed his

most cherished ambition ... to increase the number of those, whom Cambridge, the great mother of strong men, sends out into the world with cool heads but warm hearts, willing to give some at least of their best powers to grappling with the social suffering around them; resolved not to rest content till they have done what in them lies to discover how far it is possible to open up to all the material means of a refined and noble life

(Marshall, 1885: 174).

In this characteristically evangelical Victorian manifesto, with its combination of moral earnestness, duty, manliness, professional commitment and social responsibility, the juxtaposition of 'cool heads' and 'warm hearts' is especially pertinent given Marshall's double nature'.[17] For most of his career he felt obliged to rein in his natural moral enthusiasm; so there was an unmistakable sense of relief in his confidential admission of his intention, in the final part of his forthcoming book 'to give a little freedom to my *sentiment*, as distinguished from my reason, and to speak as a citizen rather than especially as an economist'. And yet immediately he reimposed the restraint, adding that 'sentiment is like a butterfly; no amount of discipline will make him go by a rational bee-line'.[18] As sometimes suggested, Marshall may have absorbed some of the Toynbee aura while at Balliol. But the influence of T.H. Green's concept of citizenship was probably more powerful, for Marshall certainly believed that Toynbee had been altogether too emotional.[19] Nevertheless, there is a curiously Toynbeean implication in the above-quoted letter to the effect that the economist as such was entirely lacking in sentiment – a view fully compatible with Toynbee's well known contrast between the economists and the human beings.[20]

MARSHALL AND ETHICS

During the years when Marshall was writing the first edition of the *Principles*, England was in a ferment of social reform; and it is in this sense that the book was 'a kind of counter-Reformation . . . directed against doubts from within and without the fold' (Shove, 1942: 310). As a recent social historian has observed:

> Alfred Marshall was a liberator of the more cautious. Christians worried by the relation of economics to social justice found in him a thinker more systematic than Toynbee (whom he succeeded at Balliol) and more respectable than George (with whom he debated publicly at Oxford). . . . Whether or not they read Marshall in detail, Christians with a desire for social justice but a respect for the body of professional opinion could assure themselves and others that here was an orthodox economist who blessed efforts to remove social misery, whose notion of economic theory was quite friendly to what Scott Holland called the 'unfaltering assertion of moral as supreme over mechanical laws'.
>
> (Inglis, 1963: 257–8)

The question of the relationship between moral and mechanical (or economic) laws was the subject of a fundamental debate between the economists and certain sections of the clergy in England, as in the United States, during the 1880s and 1890s; and this constitutes an essential part of the context of Marshall's treatment of the economics–ethics issue. The aforementioned Canon Henry Scott Holland was chairman of the Christian Social Union (CSU), an organization formed in 1889 by a group of scholarly Oxford clergy who had been deeply influenced by the Toynbee–Green reformist movement; and their action in launching a new periodical, the *Economic Review*, in 1890, shortly before the appearance of the inaugural issue of the *Economic Journal*, was deeply disturbing to Marshall, for it was an open public challenge to the hegemony of Cambridge economics, of which he was undeniably the leading exponent and custodian (Kadish, 1982: ch.6).

By proposing to concentrate on 'the moral and social bearing of economic problems', the *Review*'s editors were evidently trying to divide the territory between the two camps. But the establishment of the CSU and its new organ reveal the continuing sensitivity to the respective spheres of the more narrowly scientific and the broader ethical–social approaches to the subject; and this helps to explain Marshall's desire to encompass both in his *Principles*. The issues were complex, for they included religious, philosophical, methodological, doctrinal, policy and professional elements, which have been carefully explored by Alon Kadish and John Maloney (Kadish, 1982; Maloney, 1985). Theologian–economists like Wilfred Richmond, who lacked professional credentials (whatever they were at the time) nevertheless reached a considerable audience;[21] and by flatly asserting the superiority of moral over economic principles they tended to undermine the economists' intellectual authority and thereby limit their sphere of influence. Marshall did not challenge this claim directly; and he characteristically occupied an ambivalent middling position on the spectrum of economists' views on the ethics–economics issue,[22] although he was clearly unwilling to abandon all claims to the ethical implications of economic and social problems.

It seems doubtful that Marshall made any significant adjustments to the *Principles* in response to the Oxford clerical–reformist movement, although he was already in general sympathy with its broader aims and objectives, which formed part of the general current of Christian Socialism.[23] This is clear from his conception of the economist's 'mission', and his statement of the qualities the economist requires for the effective performance of his task. These include the qualities of 'a shrewd mother-wit, of a sound sense of proportion, and of a large experience of life'. Beyond this, the economist must possess not only

> the three great intellectual faculties, perception, imagination and reason; and most of all he needs imagination . . . . [but also] the faculty of sympathy, and especially that rare sympathy which enables people to put themselves in the place, not only of their comrades, but also of other classes.
>
> (Marshall, 1961: vol.1 43 and 45)

One may only speculate how far modern professional training helps to develop these capacities.

VI CONCLUSION

Marshall invariably emphasized – many historians of economics nowadays would say overemphasized – the essential unities and continuities in the long-run development of economic ideas; and it is therefore fitting, in this centenary year, that he should appear to us as a great transitional and synthesizing figure spanning the classical and modern ages of our discipline. Moreover, notwithstanding his characteristic British complacency and insularity, we now more fully appreciate that he incorporated a considerable variety of non-British components into his capacious architectonic edifice.

Of course, late twentieth century economics is very different from anything Marshall himself could have foreseen or would have wished to see, and not merely in respect of its sheer scale, fragmentation and technical complexity. Surely he would disapprove of the massive investment of intellectual and material resources into the 'pure' science, and especially into highly abstract mathematization. On the other hand, he would no doubt welcome the immense expansion of the 'applied' side – data collection and analysis and economic/historical research; and he might feel gratified, albeit with some reservations, by the manifest success of his professionalization campaign, which paved the way for the employment of thousands of economists in a remarkable variety of useful and important non-academic positions.

Whether the profession still has the requisite commitment to the relief of poverty and other good causes so dear to Marshall's heart is quite another matter.

But while much of the core of Marshall's theoretical analysis still survives, and has been absorbed so effectively into twentieth century mainstream economics that it takes a conscious effort of historical reconstruction to identify it, what can be said of the ethical components of his writings? Is it the case, as even some of the more sympathetic commentators have asserted, that his 'pious asides and prim moralisings have "dated" badly; that the line of attack against which they were in part a defence has faded out' (Shove, 1942: 316); and that consequently the reader of the *Principles* should 'pass over, without too much feeling of annoyance, those passages which are a reflection, in Schumpeter's phrase, of Marshall's "mid-Victorian morality seasoned by Benthamism", much of which the present generation finds almost intolerably tiresome' (Guillebaud, 1952: 113, 114). A more recent, somewhat less sympathetic, commentator has questioned the wisdom of this advice, not only because 'Marshall's constant sermonizing page after page was integral and substantive to his work, that indeed in a strange and fundamental way this *was* his work' (Levitt, 1976: 44; emphasis in original), but because (as Keynes remarked), its 'concealed crevices' contain 'buried treasure' of value to our own and subsequent generations (quoted by Levitt, ibid.).

Of course, most of professional economics in the 1990s is far more formal, precise and rigorous than its Marshallian counterpart, and correspondingly narrower in vision, scope and content, notwithstanding determined efforts in some quarters to extend its domain by applying a simplified utility-maximizing model to every conceivable subject under the sun. Ironically, Marshall, who was so wary of the dangers of utilitarianism and simple theories, would undoubtedly have deplored this species of social science imperialism.

While much Marshallian ground has undoubtedly been lost (admittedly with some compensatory gains) in the process of whoring after false positivist scientific gods, there has recently been increasing evidence of a counteracting tendency that promises to bear fruit in the foreseeable future. This involves, in particular, a considerable number of varied and thoughtful efforts to incorporate into the main body of economic analysis elements that Marshall deemed integral to his broad concept of economic science (pure and applied). A central theme here is the revival of serious interest in economics as a 'moral' science that takes ethics more fully 'into account'.

This revival goes much deeper than the vague, amorphous, and too often untheoretical expanding field of 'social' or 'humanistic' economics (e.g., Lutz and Lux, 1979; cf., *infra*, p.246, n.1). It includes such varied works as: Boulding, 1969, 1973; Etzioni, 1988; Hardin, 1988; Hirschman, 1981; McPherson, 1984; Matthews, 1981; and Sen, 1987. Titles such as

Economics for a Civilized Society (Davidson and Davidson, 1988) suggest that Marshall's concept of economic 'chivalry', which seems so quaint to some modern readers, still has purchase. Studies of 'non-selfish' economics such as: Baumol, 1986; Collard, 1978; and Phelps, 1975; co-operation: Axelrod, 1984; status and the passions: Frank, 1985; 1988 (*pace* David Hume, of blessed memory), indicate that some current economists wish, as did Marshall, to go beyond the confines of a disembodied 'agent' or 'economic man' to a human being of flesh and blood. And the fruitful revival of interdisciplinary work, both in economics and psychology (cf. Earl, 1988; Hogarth and Reder, 1987) and more generally, might also earn Marshall's approval – though he became suspicious of academic psychology.

Needless to say, this brief catalogue gives no adequate impression of the richness and variety of the recent range of literature on what might be termed 'some neglected Marshallian themes'. No attempt has been made to include, for example, the huge body of writing on the subjects of evolutionary institutional change, or on the traditional value-laden topic of efficiency versus equity (or the ethics of the market), which appears so often in the public policy literature.

Of course, in most instances where comparisons can be found between recent contributions and Marshall's broader interests, the similarities are superficial, given the great differences in method and approach. And although there has been a marked recovery of interest in ethical or normative economics, the positivist, 'objective' natural-science conception of economics is still dominant. The promise of Marshall's organismic–biological approach has yet to be realized.

NOTES AND REFERENCES

1 Marshall (1885a: 164); from his inaugural address. Most historians of economics do not realize that, for a time, 'that noble science of politics' was conceived in Cambridge as the umbrella under which economics and other moral sciences should be classified. This helps to explain why Marshall was eager to drop the term 'Political' from the title of his discipline, although in 1889, probably for tactical reasons, he proposed that Political Economy should be included in a new Political Sciences Tripos. (Note the plural.) For a revealing account of this situation see Collini *et al.* (1984: ch.11). In the third and fourth editions of the *Principles*, Marshall implied that Social Economics would be as acceptable a title for his subject as Economics *simpliciter* (Marshall, 1961: vol.1, 159).

2 There are, of course, occasional brief comments on the economics–ethics relationship in Marshall's writings. The most explicit and/or detailed are in the *Bee-Hive* articles (which few of his fellow economists probably read), and in his response to Lord Goschen's *Presidential Address* to the British Economic Association (Marshall, 1874; 1893).

3 R.D. Collison Black has recently questioned the conventional view that 'Jevons was a thoroughgoing Benthamite, whereas Marshall was hardly a Utilitarian at all', arguing that both men 'blended the new evolutionism with the old Utilitarianism' in their efforts to reconstruct economic studies, but in different

proportions (Black, 1990: 7, 14). The implications for Marshall's work are considered on pp.234, 240 in this volume.

4 Marshall to Benjamin Kidd, 6 June 1894, Cambridge University Library, Add 8069 M251. Rita McWilliams Tullberg kindly provided a copy of this letter. Marshall was often evasive on matters of ethical principle, as indeed on other matters too. In the course of a public discussion on Henry George's views, for example, he said he did not know what was meant by a 'just distribution of proceeds between capital and labour' (Marshall, 1883: 198). However, this did not prevent him from making frequent observations on the desirability of redistribution on both economic and ethical grounds. For an unusually outspoken example, in a letter to Bishop Wescott, with respect to schemes 'to take from the rich and give to those who are less rich', he said: 'I would promote all such by every means in my power that were legitimate; and I would not be especially scrupulous in interpreting that word' (24 January 1900; cited in Pigou, 1925: 386). Presumably this was Marshall the citizen speaking!

5 See Marshall (1961: vol.1, 17; vol.2, 137). For a valuable discussion of these matters, see Henderson (1989 and 1990); also Whitaker (1977). I greatly appreciate the opportunity to examine Professor Henderson's paper of 1990 in advance of publication.

6 Whitaker (1977: 172). Marshall may have derived his 'common sense' view of ethical principles from Kant, via Sidgwick, whose work he presumably read, although there is no reference to Sidgwick's *Ethics* in Marshall's writings. According-ing to the Kant–Sidgwick approach, the object of ethics (moral philosophy) is not to discover new truths but to systematize available knowledge so as to demonstrate the ultimate rationale of the moral knowledge and practices man already has. 'There should be no wholesale rejection of practical moral claims, but an attempt should be made to unify and show the objective justification of most of those claims' (Nielsen, 1967: 117). Sidgwick tried to provide a logical bridge between inclination and obligation, 'is' and 'ought', by 'combining the Kantian theory of rational duty with the utilitarian theory of value, maintaining that we are intuitively aware of the duty to obey moral principles at the expense of self-interest but that moral principles, in turn, are justified by their utility in promoting the common good' (Abelson and Nielsen, 1967: 97). This seems to capture the essence of Marshall's approach. See also Schneewind (1977).

7 Hill and Keynes (1989: 195); I owe this reference to Rita McWilliams Tullberg. Religious language and imagery occurs so frequently in Marshall's writings it would repay separate study. It was by no means uncommon at the time. For a thoughtful discussion of the context see Skidelsky (1983: ch.2 'Cambridge Civilization: Sidgwick and Marshall').

8 See p.241 of this volume for further discussion.

9 Weisskopf (1955: 70); citing vol.1, 28. Weisskopf complains of Marshall's 'moral–economic casuistry' because so often in his account ethical problems are implied in the logical ones. Marshall's strong emphasis on the value of rational, deliberative conduct involves 'a moral–economic calculus of a compulsively obsessional and neurotic character' (ibid: 184, 183).

10 [A number of corrections have been made, probably in Marshall's hand, to the press-cuttings from the *Bee-Hive* of Marshall's two articles, kept in the Marshall Archive. The word 'postponed' is crossed through and 'proposed' written above – Ed (i.e. Rita McWilliams Tullberg).]

11 Recent scholars have derived some harmless amusement from this permis-siveness which, in the past, has often been the focus of severe criticism. For example, John Maloney refers to the 'unhealthy give-and-take between Marshall

the economist and Marshall the private citizen'. To Marshall, the economist as private citizen had much to do. And Marshall the private citizen was everywhere. He attended Professor Marshall's lectures doggedly; his constant interruptions must have been very frustrating to the latter, who had not come along to tell students that one of the best ways to use their wealth was to buy pictures, exhibit them and leave them to the nation, or to tell them that keeping up with fashion was a 'crime'. . . . In the end, Marshall the moralist dressed up as Marshall the economic biologist, egged on Marshall the ordinary citizen to speak out in public by telling him he was speaking more or less professionally after all' (Maloney, 1985: 198, 200; cf. Levitt, 1976: 435: 'Even when speaking strictly *qua* economist, Marshall unhesitatingly intruded normative and moral prescripts into his discussion, and these his readers learned to ignore almost totally; and if not ignore, treat as either solecistic quaintness or irrelevant mush. Yet they show that Marshall each time he faced an impasse in the use of economics to solve problems of general social well-being, was forced, and had no hesitation in returning, to strictly personal judgements of moral rightness and social oughtness.') Levitt provides a comprehensive catalogue of these pronouncements. See also Reisman (1987: chs.1 and 2).

12 In this respect the parallel with Mill is striking. Mill informed a correspondent that his *Principles* was 'essentially, a book of applications exhibiting the principles of the science in the concrete . . . I was the more prompted to do this inasmuch as it would enable me to bring in, or rather to bring out, a great number of opinions on incidental matters, moral and social, for which one has not often so good an opportunity, and I have used this privilege as freely as Adam Smith did, and I fully expect to offend and scandalise ten times as many people as I shall please' (quoted by Whitaker, 1975b: 1047). On the issue of principle involved, see Hutchison (1964: 142). He considers that Marshall violated sound methodological practice much less frequently than Pigou and some of his Cambridge colleagues (cf. Hutchison, 1981: especially 65, 99, 110).

13 Marshall (1898: 44). Elsewhere Marshall stated that 'partly through the suggestions of biological study, the influence of circumstances in fashioning character is generally recognized as the dominant fact in social science' (Marshall, 1961: vol.1, 48).

14 As Weisskopf has noted, changes of character completely undermine the concept of diminishing marginal utility, which presupposes fixed preferences and tastes. Marshall ignored this problem. 'By making constancy of character a prerequisite for the stationary state and, with this, for the establishment of an equilibrium price, Marshall has unified his system and assured its ethical justification with one stroke' (Weisskopf, 1955: 217; cf. 177. For a more sophisticated analysis of this problem, see Whitaker, 1977: 183–5).

15 Chasse (1984: 392). Cf. Whitaker (1977: especially 182–3).

16 Parsons (1932: 335). For a somewhat less negative interpretation, see Chasse (1984).

17 See the second epigraph to this paper, p.231 in this volume. Also Keynes' beautifully expressed reference to Marshall's 'evangelical moraliser of an imp somewhere inside him, that was so ill advised as to disapprove' of any preoccupation with the purely abstract (in Pigou, 1925: 37).

18 To A.W. Flux, 19 March 1904; in Pigou (1925: 408); emphasis in original. Oddly enough, when *Industry and Trade* appeared, a reviewer in the *Athanaeum* complained that its moral tone was out of place in a scientific work (cf. Flubacher, 1950: 390).

19 For valuable comments on this relationship, see Kadish (1986: 234–6).

Foxwell seems to have been somewhat more sympathetic to Toynbee. On the Toynbee–Green relationship, Richter (1964), is indispensable.

20 'At last it is apparent to all the world, that the long and bitter controversy between the economists and human beings has ended in the conversion of the economists. The economists now dares to say that the end of his practical science is not wealth but man; and further, he owns that his intellectual theories have undergone a vast change. He has learnt to recognise that the laws which he supposed were universal are only partial and provisional' (quoted from p.1 of his posthumously published *Lectures on the Industrial Revolution*, 1884, with valuable supplementary comments in Kitson Clark, 1973: 289–90).

21 Richmond (1881 and 1890). The latter work contains a remarkably revealing preface by Scott Holland. Richmond is one of the ethicists discussed in Henderson (1990).

22 Maloney (1985: ch.9) reviews a representative, but incomplete, selection of contemporary economists' views on this subject.

23 For a comprehensive review, see Jones (1968); also Norman (1976).

BIBLIOGRAPHY

Abelson, R. and Nielsen, K. (1967) 'Ethics, History of', in P. Edwards (ed.) *The Encyclopedia of Philosophy* (New York: Macmillan and Free Press) vol.3, pp.81–116.

Axelrod, R. (1984) *The Evolution of Cooperation* (New York: Basic Books).

Baumol, W. (1986) *Superfairness: Applications and Theory* (Cambridge, Mass: MIT Press).

Black, R.D.C. (1990) 'Jevons, Marshall and the Utilitarian Tradition', *Scottish Journal of Political Economy*, vol.37, pp.5–17.

Boulding, K. (1969) 'Economics as a Moral Science', *American Economic Review*, vol.59, pp.1–12.

Boulding, K. (1973) *The Economy of Love and Fear: A Preface to Grant Economics* (Belmont, Ca.: Wadsworth).

Chasse, J.D. (1984) 'Marshall, the Human Agent and Economic Growth: Wants and Activities Revisited', *History of Political Economy*, vol.16, pp.381–404.

Collard, D. (1978) *Altruism and Economy: A Study in Non-Selfish Economics* (Oxford: Martin Robertson).

Collini, S., Burrow, J. and Winch, D. (1984) *That Noble Science of Politics* (Cambridge: Cambridge University Press).

Davidson, G. and Davidson, P. (1988) *Economics for a Civilized Society* (New York: Norton).

Deane, P. (1989) 'Henry Fawcett: The Plain Man's Economist', in L. Goldman (ed.) *The Blind Victorian: Henry Fawcett and British Liberalism* (Cambridge: Cambridge University Press) ch.4.

Earl, P. (ed.) (1988) *Psychological Economics: Development, Tensions, Prospects*, (Boston, Dordrecht: Kluwer).

Etzioni, A. (1988) *The Moral Dimension: Toward a New Economics* (New York: Free Press).

Flubacher, J. (1950) *The Concept of Ethics in the History of Economics* (New York: Vantage Press).

Foxwell, H.S. (1887) 'The Economic Movement in England', *Quarterly Journal of Economics*, vol.2, pp.84–103.

Frank, R.H. (1985) *Choosing the Right Pond: Human Behavior and the Quest for Status* (Oxford: Oxford University Press).

Frank, R.H. (1988) *Passions Within Reason: The Strategic Role of the Emotions* (New York: Norton).

Groenewegen, P.D. (1988) 'Alfred Marshall and the Establishment of the Cambridge Economic Tripos', *History of Political Economy*, vol.20, pp.627–67.

Groenewegen, P.D. (1990) 'Teaching Economics at Cambridge at the Turn of the Century: Alfred Marshall as Lecturer in Political Economy', *Scottish Journal of Political Economy*, vol.37, pp.40–60.

Haan, N., Bellah, R., Rabinow, P. and Sullivan, W.N. (1983) *Social Science as Moral Inquiry* (New York: Columbia University Press).

Hardin, R. (1988) *Morality within the Limits of Reason.* (Chicago: University of Chicago Press).

Henderson, J.P. (1989) 'The relation of Ethics to Economics: J.S. Mackenzie's Challenge to Neoclassical Economics', *Review of Social Economy*, vol.47, pp.240–65.

Henderson, J.P. (1990) 'The Ethicists' View of Marshall's *Principles*', unpublished paper, 41 pp.

Hill, P. and Keynes, R. (1989) *Lydia and Maynard* (London: Andre Deutsch).

Hirschman, A.O. (1981) 'Morality and the Social Sciences: A durable Tension', in his *Essays in Trespassing: Economics to Politics and Beyond* (Cambridge: Cambridge University Press), pp.294–306; also in Haan, N. et al. (1983), pp.21–32.

Hogarth, R.M. and Reder, M.W. (1987) *Rational Choice: The Contrast Between Economics and Psychology* (Chicago: Chicago University Press).

Hollander, S. (1985) *The Economics of John Stuart Mill*, vol.1, *Theory and Method* (Oxford: Basil Blackwell).

Hutchison, T.W. (1964) *'Positive' Economics and Policy Objectives* (London: George Allen and Unwin).

Hutchison, T.W. (1981) *The Politics and Philosophy of Economics: Marxists, Keynesians and Austrians* (New York: New York University Press).

Inglis, K.S. (1963) *Churches and the Working Classes in Victorian England* (London: Routledge and Kegan Paul).

Jones, P.D.A. (1968) *The Christian Socialist Revival: Religion, Class and Social Conscience in Victorian England* (Princeton: Princeton University Press).

Kadish, A. (1982) *The Oxford Economists in the Late Nineteenth Century* (Clarendon Press: Oxford).

Kadish, A. (1986) *Apostle Arnold: The Life and Death of Arnold Toynbee 1852–1883* (Durham, N.C.: Duke University Press).

Keynes, J.M. (1925) 'Alfred Marshall, 1842–1924', in Pigou (1925), pp.1–65.

Keynes, J.N. (1904) [1890] *The Scope and Method of Political Economy* (London: Macmillan, third edition).

Kitson Clark, G. (1973) *Churchmen and the Condition of England, 1832–1885: A Study in the Development of Social Ideas and Practice from the Old Regime to the Modern State* (London: Methuen).

Levitt, T. (1976) 'Alfred Marshall: Victorian Relevance for Modern Economics', *Quarterly Journal of Economics*, vol.90, pp.425–43. Reprinted in Wood (1982), vol.1, no.23.

Lutz, M.A. and Lux, K. (1979) *The Challenge of Humanistic Economics* (Menlo Park, California: Benjamin/Cummings).

Maloney, J. (1985) *Marshall, Orthodoxy and the Professionalisation of Economics* (Cambridge: Cambridge University Press).

Marshall, A. (1873) 'The Future of the Working Classes', in Pigou (1925), pp.101–18.

Marshall, A. (1874) 'The Laws of Political Economy' and 'The Province of Political Economy', in R. Harrison, 1963, 'Two Early Articles by Alfred Marshall', *Economic*

Journal, vol.73, pp.422–30, originally published in *The Bee-Hive*. Reprinted in Wood (1982), vol.4, no.106.

Marshall, A. (1876) 'Mr Mill's Theory of Value', in Pigou (1925), pp.119–33.

Marshall, A. (1883) 'Three Lectures on Progress and Poverty', in G.J. Stigler, 'Alfred Marshall's Lectures on Progress and Poverty', *Journal of Law and Economics*, 1969, vol.12, April, pp.184–226. Reprinted in Wood (1982), vol.4, no.106.

Marshall, A. (1885a) 'The Present Position of Economics', in Pigou (1925), pp.152–74.

Marshall, A. (1885b) 'How Far Do Remediable Causes Influence Prejudicially (a) the Continuity of Employment, (b) the Rate of Wages? With Four Appendices', in C.W. Dilke (ed.) *Report of Proceedings and Papers on the Industrial Remuneration Conference* (London: Cassel).

Marshall, A. (1887) Preface to L.L.F.R. Price, *Industrial Peace: Its Advantages, Methods and Difficulties. A Report on an Inquiry Made for the Toynbee Trustees* (London: Macmillan).

Marshall, A. (1889) 'Cooperation', in Pigou (1925), pp.227–55.

Marshall, A. (1893) Response to the President's Address, *Economic Journal*, vol.3, pp.387–90.

Marshall, A. (1897) 'The Old Generation of Economists and the New', in Pigou (1925), pp.295–311.

Marshall, A. (1898) 'Mechanical and Biological Analogies in Economics', in Pigou (1925), pp.312–18.

Marshall, A. (1900) [1892] *Elements of Economics of Industry: Being the First Volume of Elements of Economics* (London: Macmillan, third edition).

Marshall, A. (1907) 'Social Possibilities of Economic Chivalry'. Reprinted in Pigou (1925), pp.323–46.

Marshall, A. (1923) [1919] *Industry and Trade: A Study of Industrial Technique and Business Organization; and of Their Influences on the Conditions of Various Classes and Nations* (London: Macmillan, fifth edition).

Marshall, A. (1961) [1890] *Principles of Economics*, C.W. Guillebaud (ed.,) (London: Macmillan for the Royal Economic Society) ninth (variorum) edition in two volumes, vol.1 – text; vol.2 – notes.

Marshall, A. and Marshall, M.P. (1879) *Economics of Industry* (London: Macmillan, first edition).

Matthews, R.C.O. (1981) 'Morality, Competition and Efficiency', *The Manchester School*, vol.49, pp.289–309.

McPherson, M.S. (1983) 'Want Formation, Morality, and Some Interpretative Aspects of Economic Inquiry', in Haan *et al.* (1983), pp.96–124.

Nielsen, K. (1967) 'Ethics, Problems of', in P. Edwards (ed.,) *The Encyclopedia of Philosophy* (New York: Macmillan and Free Press) vol.3, pp.117–34.

Norman, E.R. (1976) *Church and Society in England 1770–1970: A Historical Study* (Oxford, Clarendon Press).

Parsons, T. (1931/32) 'Economics and Sociology; Marshall in Relation to the Thought of His Time', *Quarterly Journal of Economics*, vol.46, pp.310–45.

Parsons, T. (1931/32) 'Wants and Activities in Marshall', *Quarterly Journal of Economics*, vol.46, pp.101–40.

Paul, E.F., Miller, F.D. and Paul, J. (eds) (1985) *Ethics and Economics* (Oxford: Basil Blackwell).

Phelps, E.S. (ed) (1975) *Altruism, Morality and Economic Theory* (New York: Russell Sage Foundation).

Pigou, A.C. (ed.) (1925) *Memorials of Alfred Marshall* (London: Macmillan).

Reisman, D. (1987) *Alfred Marshall: Progress and Politics* (London: Macmillan).

Richmond, W. (1888) *Christian Economics* (London: Rivingon's).

Richmond, W. (1890) *Four Lectures on Economic Morals* (London: W.H. Allen).

Richter, M. (1964) *The Politics of Conscience: T.H. Green and His Age* (London, Weidenfeld and Nicholson).

Schneewind, J.B. (1977) *Sidgwick's Ethics and Victorian Moral Philosophy* (Oxford: Clarendon Press).

Sen, A. (1987) *On Ethics and Economics* (Oxford: Basil Blackwell).

Shove, G.F. (1942) 'The Place of Marshall's *Principles* in the Development of Economic Theory', *Economic Journal*, vol.52, pp.294–329. Reprinted in Wood (1982), vol.2, no.38.

Sidgwick, H. (1901) [1883] *The Principles of Political Economy* (London: Macmillan, third edition).

Skidelsky, R. (1983) *John Maynard Keynes, Vol.1: Hopes Betrayed, 1883–1920* (London: Macmillan, and New York: Viking Penguin Inc., 1986).

Webb, B. (1926) *My Apprenticeship* (London and New York: Longman Green).

Weisskopf, W.A. (1955) *The Psychology of Economics* (London: Routledge and Kegan Paul).

Whitaker, J.K. (1972) 'Alfred Marshall: The Years 1877–1885', *History of Political Economy*, vol.4, pp.1–61. Reprinted in Wood (1982), vol.1, no.8.

Whitaker, J.K. (ed.) (1975a) *The Early Economics Writings of Alfred Marshall 1867–1890* (London: Macmillan for the Royal Economic Society, and New York: Free Press) 2 volumes.

Whitaker, J.K. (1975b) 'John Stuart Mill's Methodology', *Journal of Political Economy*, vol.83, pp.1033–49.

Whitaker, J.K. (1977) 'Some Neglected Aspects of Alfred Marshall's Economic and Social Thought', *History of Political Economy*, vol.9, pp.161–97. Reprinted in Wood (1982), vol.1, no.25.

Wood, J.C. (ed.) (1982) *Alfred Marshall: Critical Assessments* (London: Croom Helm) four volumes.

14

ALFRED MARSHALL AND
RICHARD T. ELY
Some unpublished letters

The following correspondence between Alfred Marshall and Richard T. Ely was recently discovered in the course of an examination of the Ely Papers in the Wisconsin State Historical Society.[1] As so few of Marshall's letters have been published, almost any addition to the available supply is likely to be welcomed.

By way of background, it should be mentioned that John A. Hobson's *The Economics of Distribution* (1900) was published in Ely's series, The Citizen's Library of Economics, Politics and Sociology. Ely was at this time President of the American Economic Association, and Director of the School of Economics and Political Science at the University of Wisconsin.

Marshall to Ely: 11 July 1901

Perhaps Dr Hobson has communicated to you the fact that the particular passages on wh. he bases what I regard as misinterpretations of my views, in his 'Distribution' in your series, were mostly expunged from my book; because I had found them to be capable of being taken – with an adequate disregard of the context – in senses in wh. I had not designed them. I sent him my last edition; and he wrote me a friendly and straightforward answer as to this matter, and similar comments of mine on his *Social Problem*. He is so very busy with other things that he may probably not have thought it necessary to write to you about this. There is an immense deal that is most fascinating about him; and he is certainly very able. But he is in a hurry: and so he disappoints me whenever the only good work is slow work.

But perhaps like some other oldish men, I have an 'epidemic' of supposing that younger men polish off difficulties too hastily.

Ely to Marshall: 11 October 1901

I am much interested in what you write about Mr Hobson . . . I am confident that at the time when he wrote his book he was as far as possible from a desire to do you an injustice. I am sure you will also believe that I should regret being instrumental, in any way, in presenting your views, incorrectly to the public . . . Mr Hobson's manuscript was submitted by me to another economist, who is very careful in his statements of theory, and he did not discover any mistake in the presentation of your views. I am glad to learn that you have made the changes to which you refer.

I think there is a feeling in this country that the English economists have not done justice to Hobson. I speak, of course, only in a general way, and without reference to any specific utterances. I must confess that I, myself, have had a feeling of this kind, although I have never given so strong an expression to it as I have seen in one of our leading periodicals. At the same time, although I would not like to make the statement publicly, I must say to you, personally, that I fear your judgement concerning Hobson is correct. . . . There is enough in his 'Economics of Distribution' for a very large volume, if the thought should be elaborated properly. I am disappointed, as you are, because he seems to lack continuity. . . .

I could wish that there were a closer connection between American economists and English economists, but I am not sure how strong the desire for this closer connection may be on the part of your people. The few references to American writers would, to be perfectly frank, indicate that the English economists do not esteem their work very highly. I suppose the connection, today, between the German economists and the Americans is closer than that between the American and the English writers. I am speaking about the personal connection as much as about the connection of thought.

I must say that, so far as I am individually concerned, I do not feel that I have always been treated fairly by English writers. A recent reviewer, in speaking about my 'Outlines of Economics' alluded to the 'self advertising' of the author. His assertion was based upon the number of references to books and articles of my own, given in the bibliography at the close of the work. As a matter of fact I had nothing to do with the preparation of the bibliography, which is in fine print, and no essential part of the book. . . . Of course, every friend of mine must have felt indignant at such a calumny, and so entirely unwarranted.

As you put a certain, personal element in your letter, I trust you will not take it amiss that I have, in a measure, unburdened myself to you. I do not wish to complain unduly, and least of all, would I bring an accusation against a whole class on account of the sins of one or two.

I may add one thing more, and that is this: my 'Principles of Scientific Work' is still in manuscript. . . . I am doing far less popular work than in earlier days, both because owing to changed conditions it is less needed, and also because I feel that I must put my strength upon more serious scientific work. I trust that when it appears you will not feel that I am one of those younger men alluded to by you who 'polish off difficulties too hastily'.

Marshall to Ely: 28 October 1901

As to English and American economists not being in touch – I think there is some fear of that. But the causes seem to me largely transitional.

There is relatively little academic study of economics in England: the type of student who fill German and American economic lecture rooms scarcely is to be found here. So, though American books are much read by the few students who, rather against their pecuniary interest, take up economics here, those books are chiefly terse slowly written books, addressed to the few and not the many. E.g. on banking Dunbar's book is much more read than any other here except Bagehot's *Lombard Street*. I myself read at least as much of American as of English economic literature: such as the Reports of the Industrial Commission, articles in the Journals describing business from the inside etc. I am too old to read many academic articles or books, in whatever country they may appear. I read hardly any English academic books.

Next as to English etiquette. I think few Americans know how far that reaches in the Chinese direction. A Chinaman may be bursting with conceit that he has the most beautiful wife and the most splendid house within a hundred miles. But he will say to a stranger, of lower rank than himself and one on whom he looks down, 'will you deign to honour with your magnificent presence my small and contemptible hovel, where I may have the high honour of introducing that ugly old hag my wife to you'. But he would be amused if this stranger took him literally, and expressed pity for his misfortunes in having such a house and wife. We don't go as far as that. But our etiquette does not allow anyone to praise his own work, or even to claim originality, on penalty of being judged an offender against our rather artificial canons of reticence. So Englishmen are rather amused if Americans (whose etiquette, at all events in the West, seems to have no Chinese element, and to allow people to say whatever they think is true and useful to the reader) assume that when they do not claim originality, it is because they do not believe they have anything new to say.

I have, for the present at all events, entirely gone out of all but so called 'advanced' teaching. So your address on 'Competition' has more interest to me than your 'Outlines'; though I think that may have a use in England if Economics should ever come into fashion at our Universities and Colleges for general study. I think your address on Competition is highly suggestive. I hope you will develop it.

Marshall's second letter reveals his tact and gentle humour, and sheds some light on the differences between British and American economics in the early years of this century. It also suggests a reason, other than that afforded by the customary references to Marshall's temperament, why there are 'no labels of salesmanship' in the *Principles*, and why his 'references to the question of priority are extremely reserved'.[2] Marshall's respect for English 'etiquette' undoubtedly reflects his personal outlook, as exemplified by his confession to Edwin Cannan that 'I did not dare to set myself in opposition to the English tradition',[3] for it is clear, as Edgworth pointed out, that Marshall 'deferred to the prejudices of those whom he wished to persuade', especially if they were, like Jowett, 'representative of cultivated opinion'.[4] Yet Marshall's distaste for aggressive dissent from economic orthodoxy was shared by his colleague Henry Sidgwick, who had earlier complained that Jevons' attitude in the *Theory of Political Economy* was 'almost similar to that which each new metaphysical system has hitherto adopted towards its predecessors'.[5] By contrast the 'distinctively American' attitude was described by J. Laurence Laughlin in 1906, when he remarked that among his countrymen 'no authoritative writer, no sacrosanct doctrine, no prestige of years, protects any part of economic results from criticism or attack; indeed, radical reconstruction is the order of the day'.[6] Is it unreasonable to contend that 'etiquette' or ancestor-worship (to develop Marshall's analogy) helps to explain why English economists have so often been 'men of one book'?[7] Moreover, is it not apparent that we must examine the sociological context of academic economics in Britain if we are to comprehend the force of classical and subsequently neoclassical economics? Such an investigation would provide valuable insights into the relationships between economic doctrine and economic policy, thereby drawing attention to a grossly neglected phase of the history of economic thought.

NOTES

1 The Ely collection consists of 51 volumes and over 100,000 letters, and the correspondents include leading politicians (including two future Commonwealth Prime Ministers), prominent business, social and religious figures, and academicians of many lands.

2 Cf. J.M. Keynes in A.C. Pigou (ed.), *Memorials of Alfred Marshall* (1925), pp.48, 22.

3 Ibid., p.405, with reference to the definition of capital.

4 Ibid., pp.66–7.

5 Cited by T.W. Hutchison, *Review of Economic Doctrines, 1870–1929* (1953), p.15. Fear of the ruling orthodoxy, mingled with strong distate for it, is evident in W.S. Jevons's correspondence, and in the concerns of such other 'outsiders' as William Smart and J.A. Hobson.

6 J.L. Laughlin, *Industrial America* (1906), pp.228–9. Laughlin was the first chairman of the Department of Economics at the University of Chicago.

7 This was H.S. Foxwell's description of the generation following the appearance of Mill's *Principles*. See his introduction to Anton Menger, *The Right to the Whole Produce of Labour*, (1899), p.lxxviii.

15

ALFRED MARSHALL AND THE EARLY DEVELOPMENT OF THE LONDON SCHOOL OF ECONOMICS

Some unpublished letters

The founding and early history of the London School of Economics has repeatedly attracted the attention of historians, but its place in the development of British economics has hitherto been unduly neglected. As is well known, the Webbs and their co-founders were not seeking to establish a new centre of socialist propaganda, for, as Fabians, they believed that 'it only needed patient explanation of facts to persuade others of the truths of Socialism and the desirability of socialistic reforms'.[1] Nevertheless, they undoubtedly intended to encourage the ideas of schools of thought other than 'the theoretical and individualist economics of Ricardo and Mill',[2] and to this end they chose as the first Director a young Oxford scholar, W.A.S. Hewins. Hewins' undergraduate studies had reinforced his initial prejudices against orthodox economics, and he became an active member of an important group of young Oxford dissidents whose number included the economic historian W.J. Ashley; the clergyman-editor of the *Economic Review*, John Carter; the economist and journalist, J.A. Hobson; the geographer (and subsequently, second Director of the LSE), Halford J. Mackinder; and the educationist, Michael E. Sadler. Despite friendly warnings from the Oxford economic historian, J.E. Thorold Rogers, that he would jeopardize his career if he adopted too radical an approach, Hewins went ahead with his plans to reorganize the teaching of economics, and these proposals formed the basis of the scheme for the new institution which he submitted to Sidney Webb in 1894.[3]

In view of the precarious financial position of the LSE and the inevitable suspicions aroused by its links with the Fabian society, Hewins launched a vigorous publicity campaign designed to emphasize the novelty and the importance of this new educational venture. Naturally enough, he drew heavily upon the report of an authoritative sub-committee of the British Association for the Advancement of Science, published in 1894, which had stressed the urgent need to improve the facilities for teaching and examining economics in British universities and colleges,[4] and in so doing he offended Alfred Marshall, who was not only the leading contemporary British economist, but also one of the principal defenders of the received tradition of British economic thought.

In his autobiography Hewins mentioned W.J. Ashley's report that Marshall

> was very angry with me on account of an official report published by the Education Department on the London School of Economics. Ashley said to him, 'Why, what is there wrong in it?' and Marshall replied, 'There is nothing wrong in it, it is the devilish subtlety of it'.[5]

This disclosure is, to say the least, enigmatic. However, the substance of Marshall's objection can now be revealed, for some of his letters to Hewins have recently come to light.[6] They are of interest for three distinct reasons: they disclose Marshall's conception of economics as a science and as a practical study; they explain his objections to Hewins' report on the LSE; and they contain significant remarks on the state of economics teaching and study at Cambridge shortly before Marshall began his campaign for an Economics Tripos – a campaign that was crowned with success in 1903. Marshall evidently considered that Hewins' account of the LSE, which appeared in a government publication in 1898,[7] did less than justice to the situation at Cambridge; and he probably felt that Hewins had painted far too gloomy a picture of the state of British economics prior to 1895. At that time, according to Hewins, scarcely any branch of English higher education was so ill provided for as economics. Scientific work had usually been subordinated to the study of practical questions, and economics had been neglected by existing educational institutions and starved of both state and private funds. The leading British economic writers had rarely derived their inspiration or their preparatory training from elementary economics; the number of academic economists was small; professorships were few and poorly paid; and consequently talented men turned to other matters, refusing to embark upon a scholarly and scientific career 'in which bare subsistence is uncertain'. It was, admittedly, 'just possible to earn enough to live with extreme economy by combining together several different economic sources of income. But this requires unusual ability, perfect health, and unremitting toil'; and the associated activities might well prove detrimental to scientific work.

In commenting on conditions outside London, Hewins spoke more severely of Oxford than of Cambridge, where 'economic studies have been organized up to a certain point with energy and success ... and the teaching at Cambridge is more systematic and continuous'. Even so, Marshall may have regarded this concession as patronizing, for although Hewins had acknowledged the LSE's debt to its precursors, he had proudly claimed that the School's performance already showed 'that the problem of organizing higher economic teaching in England is not insoluble' – a matter that had presumably remained in doubt up to 1895.

Unfortunately Hewins' letters to Marshall have not survived. Earlier correspondence in the Hewins papers indicates that the two men were on friendly though not intimate terms, but the first reference to the LSE occurs in the following.

Balliol Croft, 12.10.99

My dear Hewins,

It seems strange to me to be asked my views as to the study of pure economic theory; as tho' that were a subject on wh I were fit to speak. For indeed I was never a partisan of it; and for more than a quarter of a century I have set my face away from it. As early as 1873 (I think that was the year) Walras pressed me to publish something about it; and I declined with emphasis.[8]

The fact is I am the dull mean man, who holds Economics to be an organic whole, and has as little respect for pure theory (otherwise than as a branch of mathematics or the science of numbers), as for that crude collection and interpretation of facts without the aid of high analysis which sometimes claims to be a part of economic history.

In the next two paragraphs, Marshall made some unfavourable remarks on Wilhelm Launhardt's *Die Betriebskosten der Eisenbahnen* (1877), arguing that the author had gone to work by a 'wrong route':

My route would be parallel to his – or what I believe to be his, but turned round through 180°. I would not let students look at Launhardt, till they had attained enough of railway instinct to know beforehand whether passenger rates would be high or low relating to goods rates in America, and in what parts of the world the quickest trains speed would bear the lowest ratio to (I mean be the least in excess of) the average passenger train speed and so on. Then I would give them several concrete books such as Hadley's,[9] and tell them to put into mathematical phrase (if they happened to like mathematics) but anyhow into precise quantitative phrases, such parts of their reasoning as were capable of it; *not* throwing away the rest, but keeping it formulated by side of the mathematics. Next they should try to find the general mathematical proposition of wh that proposition was a special case: next they should try to interpret that general proposition into English, and not lightly take a denial: that should be their main effort to wh they should give most weeks and months of work; and when they had done it they might throw away their mathematics; unless indeed they cared to keep a few specimens of such work in an old curiosity shop.

When they had got that proposition they might turn round again thro' 180°; and starting from it take the various special problems as

259

illustrations. Having discovered the One in the Many, they might set forth afresh the Many in the One. I repeat I regard the use of mathematics on the way as a gain when convenient, but not as of the essence of the work. In my view the *Many* is the ground of study; the *One* is the Holy Grail to be sought by the pious and laborious pilgrim; and the One where so found is to help as a guide through life over the broken ground of the Many. Launhardt's plan *seems* to me (I have not read him) that of standing where he happens to be, and jumping in the air and jumping again, in hopes that the Holy Grail will come floating past and stick in his fingers as he jumps.

This prolix exposition of what I conceive to be *the* method of economics would be of absurd length, if it were really an answer to your question. But really it is evoked by your remark as to the Church Congress.

The plain fact is that I have felt rather sore since I read your account of 'the position of Economics in England' in Sadlers Educational Blue Book. Some newspaper reports of public speeches by you had fretted me a little before: but when I read that I felt that I must make a protest, in public or private, sooner or later.

I think it is certain there are virtues in the London School wh I do not know of, and you do; and I think it is probable that you know more about its shortcomings than I do. Nor do I blame you in the least for setting forth its merits, and leaving others to find out the deficiencies; some of wh are perhaps inseparable from those merits, while others will be removed as the School grows stronger with time.

But while impelled to lay stress on one side of the case as to London, it seems rather hard that you should have laid stress on the other side as regards Cambridge. I gather that you really do not know what is being done here, nor how it is being done. Taking the least important point of all, the number of lectures given, I think you would be astonished if you counted up the number that are given in the year here on subjects of the same order as those treated in the London School: I believe you would find that our number is not less than yours; though of course the proportion of them that are elementary is large; because the average age of our students is low.[10]

But the main point is that Cambridge has an idea of its own which asserts itself in spite of the partially non-Cambridge idiosyncracies of one or two members of the staff. The incidental work wh we do not advertise, but should be compelled to advertise if we were starting a new place like the London School (or to quote my own experience Bristol University College in 1879, where my duties as advertiser in chief were specially onerous) – this incidental work is very great. I regard it as the more important half of my own work; and it is governed vy much by a central idea, Cambridge born.

You will say – why then not write a separate and peculiar panegyric of Cambridge? I have sometimes thought that that is what I ought to have done when Sadlers blue book appeared. But my personal disinclination for such work, my loathing for it is beyond conception. What I had to do of it at Bristol nearly killed me. And it would have been difficult to keep quite clear of controversy, by implication if not explicitly. For one thing I could hardly have fully admitted that Cambridge has the faults that attach to its virtues (as well as others), without implying that in my opinion London also has those faults which attach to *its* virtues.

So I have tried to indicate what I mean by the guiding principle of those Cambridge men who are – in my view most truly Cambridge men – the Search of the One in the Many and the Many in the One.

For I hope that in the address, wh I am delighted that you are to give at the Church Congress,[11] your text will be 'Economics should be studied, and it can be studied in London', and that you will *stop there*; that you will *not* add as you did, I think in the blue book: – 'and it cannot be studied anywhere else in England! So down with the cash please, for without the London School there would be no true economic study at least on this side of salt water.'

Yours very heartily   Alfred Marshall.

Returning to Launhardt. I have been looking at him again. I see he is not quite so wooden as I thought. But he still seems to talk of Betriebs-Kosten as tho experts had not agreed to deny the existence of such a thing. As perhaps you know, I think experts overstate the case. But to ignore the difficulty, is the work of a 'pure' theorist in the dyslogistic sense of the term.

You know that I have begged of Berry's[12] Goodness – he is not paid save by microscopic fees – to lecture on 'The Diagrammatic treatment of Pure Economic Theory' (mathematics being added for mathematicians): but these are really lectures on method and language: aimed at strengthening grasp, not inculcating doctrine.

I think lectures on Cournot for the same purpose would be useful to some persons.

A few days later Marshall added a further explanation.

Balliol Croft, 17.10.99

My dear Hewins,

Many thanks for your friendly letter, and for your particularly kind remarks about myself. But of course it is for Cambridge that I am jealous. I did not see why the scope of your paper required you to make implicit comparisons between London and other centres of instruction. Had you stuck to your subject: which, I understand, was the London School of Economics, no one could have blamed you: for it is obviously

261

a good subject and one on all fours with those of many other articles in the Report. But you took your subject to be the London School in its relation to other schools; and, you must forgive me for saying, that, whatever your intention, the effect of your words was to give people a wrong impression of that relation, both as regards the methods and the volume of teaching, and of initiating original work.

I say this the more freely, because I know from experience how difficult it is to give to others a correct impression of one's own feelings in matters of proportion. I often find that one half of my remarks, especially on controversial and personal matters, gets home, and the other half does not: so that 'the taste left in the mouth' is different from what I had designed, and from what I believed it had been, till informed to the contrary. In speaking thus frankly, I am but doing as I would be done by in all such cases. I know well that newspaper reports are misleading as regards the general tendency of speeches as well as their details.

Again thanking you. I am Yours sincerely, Alfred Marshall. I thought your paper at the Church Congress was excellent in every way.

This postscript suggests that Hewins may have accepted Marshall's advice about his address to the Church Congress, but Marshall's interest in the LSE did not end here, for seven months later (by which time the School had been incorporated into the University of London) he raised a semantic issue that obviously seemed to him of some importance.

Balliol Croft 29.5.00

My dear Hewins,

I have just looked at the London University Calendar. I find that the subject wh you had described as economic *science* is officially called 'pure theory'. I knew that that had been assigned some place: but I am rather indifferent about it. Much of 'pure theory' seems to me to be elegant toying: I habitually describe my own pure theory of international trade as a 'toy'. I understand economic science to be the application of powerful analytical methods to unravelling the actions of economic and social causes, to assigning each its part, to tracing mutual interactions and modifications; and above all to laying bare the hidden *causas causantes*.

The M.A. Scheme in the hands of good examiners may conceivably promote the scientific study of past facts to a very limited extent. But it seems to me to have no room for the scientific study of those facts which are of the most importance and most fully alive [?].

In the hands of second-rate examiners it will I think foster sciolism as regard facts, and frivolity as regards reasoning.

Marshall's interest in matters of terminology and curriculae probably stemmed from his involvement in Cambridge academic politics, for sometime during the ensuing year he was appointed to a committee of the Historical Board whose task was to report on methods of extending the study of modern economics and politics in the university,[13] and his next letter to Hewins directly reflects this activity.

6.6.01

My dear Hewins,

I hear little of what is going on; especially just now. But an accident brought to my ears a rumour that rapid progress is being made with the scheme for the new London University course in Economics, and that it pays a scant honour to the Scientific as distinguished from the technical aspects of economics: while it finds room for Ancient history – an important subject in itself, but one to wh English youth already give a disproportionate amount of time, and one wh already has far more than its proper share of endowment direct and indirect.

The whole rumour may be based on a mistake: for, in the form in wh it reached me, it represented this policy as having been carried to a grotesque extreme. And if there is *no* truth in it, just drop me a card to put me out of my anxiety; and trouble no more about it.

In any case you will perhaps be so good as to excuse me from a discussion of details. I know you are extremely busy. I am never fit for correspondence; and I am specially unfit just now.

But this reminds me that I cannot recollect whether I have ever sent you of the scheme, now inclosed,[14] wh I drew up a few weeks ago for a Tripos here. It may interest you possibly: though it is laid on the shelf for the present. It is based on long discussions wh were held here some years back: but the titles of the papers on politics are new; and Dickinson is responsible for them. He may perhaps have shown you the paper.

The only distinct trend of opinion as to it – outside of vague polite phrases – is characteristic. It is a restive suspicion that Commercial Law is not a good subject for undergraduate study.

I never thought it was by itself: and I am not at all sure that it is even as subsidiary to economic analysis. Perhaps it will disappear from the next draft.

Forgive my bluntness and abruptness

From yr sincerely

Alfred Marshall

P.T.O. I inclose also a short list of books supplementary to the Tripos lists, wh I am giving to people who are carrying the study of economics even that vy little way for wh alone present Cambridge arrangements makes provision.

I think a Faculty of Economic and Political Science is unworthy of its name unless it makes it to the examination-interest of students to give time enough for reading those books (in addition to the Tripos books); or other books of equivalent substance.

Rumours about London University affairs seem to have been rife in Cambridge about this time, as shown by the following communication, written four months earlier than the one quoted immediately above, which raised a matter that subsequently became the subject of public controversy.[15]

19.2.1901

My dear Hewins,

I did not answer your letter, because I thought I might meet you at the Political Economy Club, to which, by rare exception I went last Friday week. Failing that, I again delayed till I should have seen Acworth.[16] He came here yesterday, delighted the young men's Club beyond measure by his talk about railways, and has just left. I had heard rumours that led me to think there was some danger that the economic department of the London University might be 'captured' by people acting more or less in alliance with the Fabians. I am more in accord with some Fabian opinions and aims than are many academic economists: but I could not contemplate such a danger without grave anxiety. I have spoken without reserve on this subject to Miss Brooke and to Bowley: and I think you may have heard something of my views on it. So I write at once to say that Acworth has convinced me that my fears were based on a misapprehension.

You and I are busy, and it is difficult to arrange for a talk about anything. Also, both because I am ignorant of the resources and difficulties of London education, and for other reasons, I think it most unlikely that I could contribute anything useful to the solution of those difficult problems of organization in which you are immersed. But those problems are of vital importance for the economic wellbeing of England: London and Cambridge have in many respects a closer kinship with one another than with any other economic schools on this side of the Atlantic; and, if at any time you would like to arrange a talk, I would gladly try to hit it off with you.

Yours sincerely,

Alfred Marshall.

These letters require no detailed commentary. They reveal something of the uncertainties and conflicts of loyalty resulting from the founding of a new centre of economics teaching and research, and, appropriately enough, the two correspondents exemplified the outspokenness and impetuosity of youth and the cautious conservatism of age (Hewins was 34, Marshall 57). As the acknowledged leader of British academic economics, Marshall felt obliged to apply some paternal restraint to the new foundling, though his motives were not wholly disinterested given his ambitions for Cambridge economics. The correspondence suggests that his well-known distaste for controversy dates back to his period as Principal and Professor of Political Economy at the new University College, Bristol, from 1877 to 1883 – though it evidently did not deter him from engaging in a famous public debate with Henry George, in 1883.[17]

Marshall's references to 'pure' economic theory and the distinction between the 'scientific' and 'technical' aspects of economics are explicable when viewed against the background of his campaign to promote economics at Cambridge. Here it was academic prejudices and vested interests that chiefly concerned him; whereas his earlier objections to the phrase 'empirical study' in the above-mentioned report of the British Association for the Advancement of Science[18] must be seen in the context of the public debate about the respective merits of the historical and deductive methods, which had plagued British academic economists during the 1870s and 1880s. By the turn of the century the subject was on the point of achieving full academic recognition, and Marshall was naturally anxious that its twentieth-century development should be based on solid foundations. While discouraging the study of pure theory for its own sake, he believed that the discipline should be based on systematic economic analysis which would constitute a 'centre of intense intellectual activity',[19] and the student would then need to acquire skill in the application of principles to actual problems. All these matters were the subject of intense interest to the leading professional economists of the day, and although there were deeper undercurrents of personal, methodological and policy disagreements, the discussion seems on the whole to have been conducted in a commendably calm and rational manner.

NOTES

1 Margaret Cole, *The Story of Fabian Socialism* (1961), p.32, and ch.VIII. See also Janet Beveridge, *An Epic of Clare Market, Birth and Early Days of the London School of Economics* (1960); Sir Sidney Caine, *The History of the Founding of The London School of Economics and Political Science* (1963).
2 F.A. H[ayek], 'The London School of Economics, 1895–1945', *Economica* vol.XIII (1946), p.5.
3 W.A.S. Hewins, *The Apologia of an Imperialist* (1929), vol.1, pp.15, 19, 20.
4 'The Methods of Economic Training Adopted in This and Other Countries', *Report of the British Association for the Advancement of Science* (1894), pp.365–91. The Committee consisted of W. Cunningham, E.C.K. Gonner, F.Y. Edgeworth, J.N. Keynes and H. Higgs.
5 Hewins, op. cit., pp.26–7.
6 They form part of a substantial collection of Hewins' papers, which are now in the possession of his grandson, Mr Richard Hewins. I am most grateful for Mr Hewins' permission to publish them.
7 W.A.S. Hewins, 'The London School of Economics and Political Science', *Special Reports on Educational Subjects* (ed. Michael E. Sadler), C.8943 (1898), pp.76–98. The following quotations are on pp.80, 80–1, 77.

Hewins' accounts of the obstacles to a scientific career in economics were at least partly based on personal experiences, for his father had gone bankrupt shortly before he went to Oxford, and he subsequently lived modestly and worked assiduously, giving University Extension lectures and writing numerous articles for the *Dictionary of National Biography*, Palgrave's *Dictionary of Political Economy*, and so on.

8 There is no record of this. The first known contact between Marshall and Walras was in March 1883. See W. Jaffe (ed.), *The Correspondence of Leon Walras and Related Papers*, 3 vols, (1965).

   For some revealing evidence of Marshall's reluctance to discuss theoretical questions, see his correspondence with Wicksell, reproduced in T. Gardlund, *The Life of Knut Wicksell* (1958), pp.339–45.

9 Presumably A.T. Hadley's *Railroad Transportation* (1885), a leading American work on the subject.

10 Hewins' account of the LSE included details of lectures and attendances, which reveal that audiences were much larger in 'practical' subjects like Railway Economics and Law of Accident Insurance than in more conventional topics like economic theory, economic history and statistics. However, substantial numbers attended a lecture on the Measurement of Economic Quantities and two lectures on the Theory of Bimetallism, the latter being then a subject of popular controversy.

11 'The Relations of Economic Knowledge to Christian Charity', *Report of the Church Congress* (1899). The paper contained no explicit references to economics at London or Cambridge.

12 Arthur Berry, of King's College, Cambridge.

13 The other members of the Committee were Goldsworthy Lowes Dickinson of King's College, Cambridge, who also taught politics at LSE, and A.W. Ward, the Master of Peterhouse. See Marshall to H.S. Foxwell, 8 May, 1901, in Marshall Library, Cambridge: 'At the meeting before last, I urged that if our studies were made to give no room for what business men want, we must expect their money to go to new Universities; and we should continue money-starved. I find that some thought that I was going for a "commercial school".'

   About this time new universities were being started or planned in Birmingham, Sheffield, Leeds, and elsewhere, and the LSE had obtained some financial support from the London Chamber of Commerce. Two days later Marshall informed Foxwell of an abortive attempt to obtain money from the American steel magnate, Andrew Carnegie, who had recently made a substantial gift to the University of Glasgow.

14 Unfortunately Marshall's 'scheme' is not attached to his letter. Various proposals were under discussion among the Cambridge economists during the 1890s, and after 1900 the controversy about the future of economics became vigorous and sometimes heated. A useful collection of fly sheets can be seen in a Guard Book on Economics and Associated Branches of Political Sciences, in the Cambridge University Archives.

15 On this occasion the leading economist-critics were Clara Collett and Henry Higgs, who were members of the London Economic Club (based at University College, London) and close associates of the Cambridge economist, H.S. Foxwell. In addition to the normal complexities of London University politics, there was also the question of housing Foxwell's great economic library which had recently been purchased by the Goldsmiths' Company. See, for example, Beveridge, op. cit., p.51, and Hewins to S. Webb, 14 and 26 Jan., 1903, in Passfield Papers, British Library of Political and Economic Science.

16 W. Acworth, who lectured in Railway Economics at the LSE. The other persons referred to in this letter are A.L. Bowley, the statistician, and Miss Brooke, who is still unidentified. (Emma Brooke, the Fabian and Suffragist, and Gertrude Mary Brooke, B.A., London, 1892, are possible candidates.)

17 See, for example, E.P. Lawrence, *Henry George in the British Isles* (1957), p.70; C.A. Barker, *Henry George* (1955), pp.403–4.

18 Marshall to J.N. Keynes, 10 June, 1894, in Marshall Library, Cambridge: 'I think Edgeworth has spoken to you about the objectionable phrase "empirical study" in the last report of the Committee of the British Association of which you are a member. In these cases there is always a danger that one or two men of ardent, polemical zeal will arrange between them a report, so worded as to commit more moderate men to phrases which they would not themselves have chosen; and thus do a great deal of harm by publishing in a report, having high authority, opinions which would have been harmless if published only in the names of those who have been most active in formulating them . . . those very few students of economics whom we get at our English universities are taught to use the inductive method in a scientific way. I believe that scarcely any of the great German Economists of the historical School could endorse the suggestion that the "empirical method" should be encouraged; . . . Given the number of our students I think we make the most of them; because we encourage specialized inductive study only after and not before the B.A. degree . . . And should we make any arrangements of a more formal kind for post-graduate study, we shall, I have no doubt, include aid and guidance in the investigation by trained students of special points in economic history.'

19 The quotation is from Marshall's brochure, *The New Cambridge Curriculum in Economics* (1903), which, with its citation of the opinions of leading businessmen and public officials and its references to the importance of the 'professional study' of economics and the 'national interest in the supply of trained economists', has a curiously up-to-date ring.

16

THE CHALLENGE TO FREE TRADE
Fair trade and tariff reform
1880–1914[1]

> It will no doubt be one of the great puzzles for future historians
> to explain the strange tenacity with which intelligent and civilized
> nations have clung to this doctrine [of protection]. It has been refuted
> in the United States, for example, as completely as here . . . And yet
> protection was never much stronger in America than it is now. It is a
> terrible rebuke to the labors of economists, to the Cobden Club, and
> similar agencies of enlightenment, that they have not visibly weakened
> that great economical heresy.
>
> (*The Times* 24 March 1881)

This quotation dating from the early days of the so-called 'fair trade'
movement, provides a suitable introductory text for our subject. No doubt
most of the readers of *The Times* who thought about the matter at all did
indeed regard protection as an economical heresy and free trade doctrine as
tantamount to holy writ. Moreover, although there had been certain economic
difficulties which some later historians have treated as the beginnings of a
'great depression', few observers in 1881 questioned that free trade was the
best policy for Britain, and many found it difficult to understand why other
countries were so reluctant to follow her along the primrose path leading to
the Cobdenite liberation of commerce and thence to international peace. The
later twentieth century reader, however, with the benefit of hindsight, is likely
to react quite differently. Unlike *The Times*, he is more liable to be puzzled by
the question: Why did Britain continue to adhere to her free trade policy right
up to World War I, throughout a period when her principal industrial rivals
and many of her imperial partners were either clinging or adding to existing
trade barriers?

In seeking an answer to this question today neither scholars nor laymen
will be satisfied with superficial references to the 'labors of economists' or

other 'agencies of enlightenment', despite frequent references to J.M. Keynes's familiar dictum that practical men (presumably including politicians and policy makers) 'are usually the slaves of some defunct economist'. Ours is a less gullible age than either Keynes or *The Times* supposed. We have encountered too many situations in which leading economists can be quoted on all sides of complex issues; and we more readily appreciate the subtlety of the interrelationships between economic ideas, institutional conditions and vested interests in the formulation and implemention of economic policy. From this standpoint the late nineteenth and early twentieth century challenge to free trade in Britain is still a fascinating case study. Admittedly the main outlines of the story are familiar from innumerable textbooks, scholarly monographs, articles and biographies, and we know that the outcome was a resounding defeat for the challengers. Nevertheless, there is still ample scope for differences of interpretation and controversy over the relative importance of the various causal influences at work. Nor is this solely due to the inherent complexities of the story, which is full of striking *dramatis personae* and unexpected twists and turns of events. It is also attributable to the regrettable over-specialization and compartmentalization of modern scholarship which leads each group of specialists to focus attention on those aspects that fall within its disciplinary domain. Thus while historians of economic thought concentrate on, and thereby usually over-emphasize, the role of ideas, economic historians tend to veer in the opposite direction, treating economic policy as though it were simply the direct product of events, while at the same time dissociating themselves from any form of economic determinism. Both these groups tend to underestimate the importance of political attitudes, beliefs and processes, whereas the political historians – many of whom have been fascinated by the later phases of our subject – are too often preoccupied with political party alignments and manoeuvers and the role of leading personalities.

Of course all these factors are relevant. As with the debate over Britain's entry into the European Economic Community, the challenge to free trade posed fundamental economic, fiscal, political, social and strategic questions, both domestic and international. No wonder, then, that interpretations of the story vary so markedly.

Let us return to our citation from *The Times*. During the 1860s and 1870s Britain's external trade policy more closely approximated the doctrinaire free traders' ideal than ever before or since, and many contemporary observers attributed this state of affairs to the classical economists' influence on the sequence of legislative enactments from Peel's budgetary reforms of the early 1840s, through the repeal of the Corn Laws in 1846 and the Navigation Acts in 1849, Gladstone's budgets of 1853 and 1860, to the signing of the Anglo-French Treaty of Commerce in 1860, which is rightly regarded as the Cobdenite movement's highest achievement. There is, however, a different version of the story, one in which economic ideas play a much less active part. For as Friedrich List and many of his contemporaries appreciated, these policy innovations suited Britain, the first industrial nation and workshop of the world, for she had nothing to fear from foreign competition and plenty to gain from reduced trade barriers, in the form of expanding markets for her exports and cheaper imports of foodstuffs and raw materials. Moreover, in accordance with the economic interpretation of politics, free trade was wholly compatible with the rising political influence of the urban electorate and the manufacturing interests whose power could not be checked by a declining landed class which had suffered a defeat of profound symbolic, and considerable practical, significance in 1846.

So far, then, the story seems straightforward and unproblematic; and the same highly generalized explanatory model can be applied to the 1880–1914 period. Despite significant changes in economic, social and political conditions favourable to their cause, neither the fair traders in the 1880s and early 1890s nor the tariff reformers after the turn of the century were able to defeat the combination of free trade dogma and the political and economic vested interests that were threatened by prospective innovations in external economic policy. Yet the outcome was by no means inevitable. Without venturing into counter-factual hypothesizing, we need not accept the banal supposition that what in fact happened had to happen and could not have happened in any other way. Although the fair traders gained only limited public support their campaign prepared the ground for later developments, and the tariff reformers made a decisive impact on politics after 1900, especially among the Conservatives and Unionists, at times coming close to capturing the government. In the decade before World War I commercial policy and fiscal reform dominated the political stage for lengthy periods, becoming central policy issues over which major economic, social and political groups struggled for mastery. Both then, and during the fair trade period, economic ideas were crucial to the definition of those issues, and in the innumerable efforts to specify the advantages and disadvantages of the various contending policy options. While repudiating *The Times's* simplistic assumption that the persistence of protectionism abroad was in some sense evidence of the Cobdenites' failure, we must not go to the opposite extreme and underestimate the role of economic ideas in parliamentary debates, on party platforms, in political speeches, in the civil service and the inner councils of state, in the press, and in the literally millions of books, articles and propaganda pamphlets and leaflets that were circulated throughout the land. More often than not the intellectual content was low, from which some historians of economics have drawn the erroneous conclusion that such material is unworthy of their attention. Yet most of the leading economists and economic historians of the time participated in the public controversy, some very openly, others behind the scenes, and economic ideas were integral to the processes of policy formation and public persuasion. Indeed, they formed an important element in popular culture. Thus unless we assume that there was a massive collective delusion, it follows that many serious-minded late Victorians and Edwardians evidently thought that economic ideas were both relevant and serviceable to their cause, whether in crude party political or self-interested terms, or as a contribution to the general enlightenment. Not all men and women are persuaded by reasoned argument, but some are; and the persistence and intensity of the debate, and the repeated efforts to employ logic and to expose fallacious reasoning, continued throughout the period.

The strategic role of economic ideas is obvious once we appreciate that the central policy issue could not be reduced to a straightforward choice between 'free trade' and 'protection', although political propagandists often presented it in those terms. With the passage of time the leading political actors, the general public and to some extent even the economists themselves, became aware of the variety of options under consideration once the ideal of universal free trade was discredited. In the midst of the dramatic Cabinet crisis in 1903, Arthur Balfour, the philosophically-minded Prime Minister, issued a supposedly non-controversial pamphlet entitled *Economic Notes on Insular Free Trade*. This formulation was by no means novel. The crucial distinction between 'universal' and 'insular' (i.e., 'one-sided' or 'isolated') free trade had been recognized at least half a century earlier – for example when Benjamin Disraeli remarked in the House of Commons: 'I look on one-sided free trade as an obsolete opinion'[2] – and that concept became increasingly significant as barriers to international trade rose from the late 1870s, raising doubts whether the Cobdenite ideal was either intellectually defensible or desirable on practical grounds. As a free trade country in an increasingly protectionist world from the 1880s Britain had nothing to offer but exhortations as a means of securing concessions from her trading partners or in return for concessions offered to her. Under the reciprocity treaties which Britain and a number of other European countries had negotiated with some enthusiasm in the 1860s,[3] the inclusion of most favoured nation clauses severely limited the scope for piecemeal concessions. Indeed, some doctrinaire free traders objected to all such treaties on principle, despite their contribution to the reduction of commercial barriers, on the grounds that they involved an unwarrantable governmental interference with commercial affairs. When the treaties came up for renewal they were often allowed to lapse because Britain's treaty partners had renounced Cobdenite practices; and it is no coincidence that the failure to renew the Anglo-French Treaty of 1860 was soon followed by the formation of the Fair Trade League in 1881.

Such qualifying terms as 'insular' or 'one-sided' constitute semantic testimony to the power of free trade orthodoxy, for during much of our period the term 'protection' was anathema to all but a minority of industrialists and agriculturalists. The widespread coining of euphemisms or other substitute expressions, such as free imports, free food, fair trade, reciprocal or mutual free trade, imperial preference, customs union, reciprocity, retaliation, tariff reform, or fiscal reform, inevitably created confusion in the minds of political leaders and the general public. While extreme free traders viewed any change of policy as the thin end of a protectionist wedge, many of their opponents (including Balfour and Joseph Chamberlain) strenuously denied that they were protectionists. In fact not all the above terminological variants are synonymous with protection; yet there were genuine grounds for disagreement as to the short or long-run, domestic or international effects of any deviation from established practices since all significant policy innovations involve some degree of uncertainty. While the divisions of opinion among the would-be innovators necessarily weakened their combined persuasive power, the free traders, who were more united, had no difficulty in finding objections to any new departures. Little wonder, then, that the debate was so bewildering to many contemporaries.

The existence of a variety of policy proposals between the extremes of free trade and protection is crucial to the politics as well as the economics of our subject. In an age lacking reliable opinion polls it was virtually impossible to gauge the extent of support for any given policy innovation either among MPs or the electorate at large.[4] Yet such information was essential, especially after 1886, when established party allegiances had been shattered by the conflict over Home Rule, and political survival depended on the maintenance of alliances between various political factions. Broadly speaking, the Liberals were much more firmly committed to free trade and, indeed, to ideas generally, than their opponents. In the Gladstonian era the 'ideal of economical and therefore virtuous government . . . became a religion of financial orthodoxy whose Trinity was Free Trade, Balanced Budgets and the Gold Standard, whose Original Sin was the National Debt'.[5] Free trade – the words were usually capitalized – was much more than simply a commercial policy: it was an ideology reflecting a certain conception of society. As the *Edinburgh Review* had observed in 1843: 'Be assured that freedom of trade, freedom of thought, freedom of speech, and freedom of action, are but modifications of one fundamental truth, and that all must be maintained or all risked; they stand or fall together'.[6] The abandonment of free trade, it was held, would lead to the corruption of political life by vested interests seeking to control fiscal policy for their own venial ends. Under such a regime there would be no restraints on the growth of centralized political power, a prospect that alarmed all genuine Liberals. The Conservatives, by contrast, were much more flexible, and both Balfour and Lord Salisbury (his uncle and immediate predecessor as Prime Minister) intermittently revealed their sympathy for deviations from strict adherence to free trade. Yet neither man adopted a strong and consistent line, putting party unity before principle; and although the Conservatives were in power throughout most of the period between 1886 and 1906, they lacked sufficient strength to impose their will without concessions to specific groups within their own or the opposition's ranks, especially the Liberal Unionists. The fact that over the period as a whole many prominent politicians equivocated, changed sides in the debate, or exposed their ignorance and uncertainties either in private discussion and correspondence or even in public, merely added to the general atmosphere of confusion among the critics of free trade, and encouraged periodic calls for guidance from economists and/or other recognized or professed experts.[7] Despite the long-standing custom of poking fun at the 'gloomy professors of the dismal science', to cite Carlyle's immortal jibe, the economists had a golden opportunity to demonstrate their knowledge, their grasp of complex current issues and their capacity to shape public opinion and policy measures.

This point is sufficiently important to students of economic thought and policy to warrant separate consideration later in the following essay.[8] At this juncture, however, it is appropriate to emphasize the obvious fact that economic policy can rarely be treated in isolation from political and social issues without serious distortion. This is especially true of our subject, for the challenge to free trade was so intimately bound up with questions of imperial relations, national defence, domestic politics and social reform, that shifts of interest and opinion on these and other contemporary problems[9] necessarily had a direct and vital impact on the discussion of trade and fiscal matters.

When Joseph Chamberlain launched his dramatic tariff reform campaign in 1903, his proposals differed little in substance from those advanced by the fair traders twenty years earlier, except for the addition of imperial preference.[10] Moreover, the essential continuity between the two main phases in the challenge to free trade must be emphasized, for it has been well said that in 1903 'Chamberlain had merely to put himself at the head of a sizeable following which had long been seeking a leader of his stature and had in fact singled him out as a likely candidate'.[11] Nevertheless, the historical context changed markedly between the 1880s and the 1900s. While it is true that the fair traders were protectionists first and imperialists second, their movement became caught up in the enthusiasm for empire.[12] At the first Colonial Conference, in 1887, Jan Hofmeyr of South Africa put imperial preference squarely on the political agenda by suggesting that Britain and the self-governing colonies should introduce a 2 per cent tariff to raise funds for imperial defence. Although Chamberlain displayed some interest in imperial preference, he became an enthusiast for empire only after his appointment as Colonial Secretary in 1895, a post he preferred to one of the more prominent Cabinet positions.[13] At that time he was more interested in the prospects of trade expansion than protection, believing that our imperial possessions could make a valuable contribution to domestic prosperity. The connection between imperialism and social reform, which was becoming increasingly important at that time, is illustrated by Chamberlain's surprising readiness to support a tax on wheat imports if this was the only way to raise revenue for old age pensions,

273

one of his current enthusiasms.[14] By the 1900s the need to raise additional government revenue was becoming acute, not only in order to pay for social reforms but also to meet the costs of the South African war and other claims on public expenditure; and as Britain appeared to be suffering increasingly severe competition from foreign manufactures, the link between fiscal reform and some modification of our traditional free trade policy became increasingly obvious.

When the change of policy occurred it came from an unexpected quarter, for the Chancellor of the Exchequer, Sir Michael Hicks Beach, a free trader, decided to reintroduce a corn registration duty in his 1902 Budget.[15] Although designed simply as a temporary revenue raising measure, it was widely seen as a potential weapon for use against foreign competitors or in favour of friendly trading countries. At the Colonial Conference shortly thereafter the protectionist Prime Minister of Canada, Sir Wilfred Laurier, seized the opportunity to use the only new duty as a basis for renewed proposals for imperial preference. However, unlike Chamberlain and some earlier preferentialists, Laurier did not envisage free trade within the empire. Instead, as Peter Fraser has pointed out,

> The colonies were dependent for their revenues upon tariffs raised on important manufactures, which came almost exclusively from Britain, and the preferences which they wanted to give consisted not in the remission of heavy duties on British goods, but in laying even heavier duties on foreign goods. Thus they did not offer Britain a customs union with no internal tariffs, but invited the mother country to become a party to an extension of protection.[16]

Although the government decided to remit the corn duty in favour of Canada after the Colonial Conference of 1902, Laurier's scheme was unlikely to win support in Britain since it would involve food taxes, which were anathema to many, perhaps most, members of the public. And the political situation became much more delicate during the following spring when, during Chamberlain's absence in South Africa, the new Chancellor, C.T. Ritchie, forced the Cabinet to agree to the abolition of the corn duty under the threat of his resignation. This action deeply divided the government, preparing the way for Chamberlain's decision to support tariff reform publicly in the month following Ritchie's budget. The political consequences of this decision and the role of the economists in the ensuing public debate are examined in some detail in the next item in this collection (*infra*, pp. 284–337).

It is neither necessary nor appropriate to describe in detail the subsequent course of events, which has fascinated historians and biographers ever since.[17] For the present purpose it is sufficient to emphasize that Chamberlain's tariff reform campaign was a major landmark both in politics and in the development of economic thought and policy. Its political significance, which will be considered here first, does not simply consist of its relationship to

274

the remarkable crisis in Balfour's Cabinet and the ensuing tortuous politics; it was also an unprecedented effort by a single political leader to change the course of public opinion and official policy. With Balfour's blessing, Chamberlain resigned from the cabinet in order to preserve his freedom of action and to maximize his effectiveness in winning supporters for his cause, while Balfour saw this move both as a way of at least temporarily neutralizing a difficult colleague and as a means of discovering the extent of public sympathy for reform of the nation's commercial policy.[18] In the meantime it became known that Balfour had 'no settled convictions' on the subject.

The striking differences in personality and background between Chamberlain and Balfour help to underline the historical importance of the tariff reform campaign, for they personified two sharply contrasting political styles and traditions. Like Salisbury, Balfour represented the patrician political elite, whereas Chamberlain was a comparative upstart, a new breed of democratic politician. An able, eloquent and wealthy middle-class non-conformist manufacturer who had initially established his reputation as a successful radical mayor of Birmingham, a great industrial centre that continued to serve as his political base after he entered the national arena, Chamberlain combined ambition and opportunism with a readiness to make personal sacrifices for the sake of great causes, such as union with Ireland and imperial relations. Whereas Balfour was a distinguished philosopher, intellectually subtle, politically devious and unwilling to make firm commitments, Chamberlain was not a consistent thinker but a political pragmatist who was widely distrusted by his critics. Despite his active promotion of municipal socialism in Birmingham he has been regarded as a believer in individualism and *laissez-faire*.[19] Initially a supporter of J.S. Mill and Cobden, a member of the Cobden Club and occasional speaker at its dinners until his resignation in 1886, he became aware of the case for the reform of commercial policy when he was required to speak on behalf of free trade in the House of Commons, in 1881.[20] Like many Liberals he 'hated bureaucracy and central direction', preferring instead to strengthen political responsibility in more limited communities against the power of the aristocracy and the established church. After he quit the Liberals over Home Rule he became effectively a captive of the Unionists, and old style Conservatives were shocked by his eagerness to make vulgar appeals to the masses. Whereas Balfour was lazy, concerned primarily to hold his divided party together rather than to lead it, Chamberlain possessed the energy and ability to arouse enormous enthusiasm among his followers, and 'he did more than any other man of his times to create organized politics'.[21] So effective were his efforts from 1903 that the whole country began to take sides 'over an abstract, not to say highly technical economic theory'.[22] While the traditional Tory leaders feared that the Tariff Reform League created by Chamberlain and his supporters would alienate those party members who did not endorse its platform – as was evident in the formation of the Unionist Free Food

League – after the Liberal landslide in 1906 this was the party's only credible issue. Even Balfour came off the fence he had occupied for so long describing fiscal reform as the party's 'first constructive work'.[23]

In the end, of course, the campaign was a failure. The Conservatives and Unionists lost the next three elections after 1903 and Chamberlain died a broken man after suffering a severe stroke. Fiscal reform, without any change in commercial policy, was taken over by the Liberals and generated a major political crisis over Lloyd George's 1909 budget. The challenge to free trade did not come even close to success in parliamentary or legislative terms. One curious manifestation of this was in Balfour's so-called 'two election' proposal, according to which the case for imperial preference would be put to the public in an election and, if the outcome was favourable to tariff reform, specific recommendations would be worked out and put into practice at a second election after a 'free' colonial conference.[24] Whether this delaying tactic was ever feasible does not concern us here, for as already noted, the electoral test never produced the requisite body of support.

One further political aspect must be mentioned before turning to more strictly economic and intellectual matters. Both during the 1880s and 1900s the efforts to enlist trade unionists and other working-class electors into the movement against free trade were conspicuously unsuccessful.[25] This may seem strange to present-day observers given the late nineteenth century extension of the franchise, the growth of organized labour and the development of working-class political consciousness, for example with the emergence of the Labour party. The failure to undermine the workers' allegiance to free trade and the cheap loaf is more readily understandable in the 1880s when there were some poorly organized and disreputable attempts to create an impression of trade unionist enthusiasm for fair trade. But by the turn of the century the growth of foreign competition, the increased public awareness of the problems of poverty and unemployment,[26] and the strong link between imperialism and social reform, combined to create conditions much more favourable to Chamberlain's cause. Yet despite the Tariff Reform League's massive effort to enlist the workers in its cause, utilizing all the available apparatus of mass political propaganda, neither the principal labour organizations, including the Trade Union Congress, nor the bulk of unaffected workers (many of whom either did not register as voters or did not exercise their franchise) responded to Chamberlain's powerful appeals for support, although they attended his meetings in huge numbers. In an atmosphere of increasing industrial conflict they rejected the tariff reformers' claim that their programme was in the mutual interests of employers and employees. And they were not moved by Chamberlain's argument that it would generate enough economic activity and employment opportunities to offset the sacrifices involved in the imposition of 'stomach taxes', as they became widely known.[27]

Most present-day economic historians would undoubtedly endorse this judgement, although it is impossible to demonstrate precisely what would have been the effects of the implementation of Chamberlain's proposals on the volume and direction of foreign trade, the level of employment and the cost of living. It seems clear that the empire could not provide either a sufficiently expansive market for our exports nor the requisite supplies of cheap foodstuffs and raw materials to justify the risks involved in imposing a significant level of tariffs on products from non-empire sources.[28] Moreover by the early 1900s, as noted earlier, the ideal of empire free trade was unattainable given the self-governing colonies' power to raise tariffs, their need for revenue from such duties and in some cases (e.g., Canada) their strongly protectionist sentiments. Nevertheless despite these objections, there is no denying that Chamberlain's programme was both idealistic enough to inspire passionate enthusiasm among many of his supporters and realistic enough to merit serious consideration by uncommitted observers and contemporary experts. And this is where the economists come into our story.

As the relevant context is familiar to historians of economics, it can be summarized briefly here. By the early 1890s, when the fair trade movement was in decline, there were numerous encouraging signs that economics was entering a new phase in Britain. The publication of Alfred Marshall's influential *Principles* in 1890, following his election to the Cambridge chair five years earlier, signalled the emergence of the most important academic school of the next forty years. Likewise, the founding of the British Economic Association (later the Royal Economic Society), and the launching of its *Economic Journal* shortly after the new *Economic Review* produced at Oxford, provide further testimony to the discipline's intellectual and academic recovery from the low public esteem and the methodological controversies of the two preceding decades.[29] Although the professionalization of economics in the universities was still in its early stages, given the lack of systematic training at least until the early 1900s when full degree courses were inaugurated at the London School of Economics and at Cambridge,[30] there was a small and growing band of university teachers able to bring their specialist knowledge to bear on the issues raised by the advocates of new commercial policies. The academics were still greatly outnumbered by the conventional nineteenth century 'practical' businessman, city financier or civil servant type of economist, but the tariff reform episode is unprecedented in the extent to which every species of economic expertise was either openly or privately brought into the formulation and discussion of policy recommendations, and the provision of critical analysis and advice.[31] Both within and beyond the academic community there were deep divisions of opinion as to the desirability and consequences of any significant departure from free trade; but political leaders and the public were so eager for assistance that almost anyone with pretensions to expertise was guaranteed a hearing. Nor were the academics unwilling to participate, although some had reservations about the advisability of becoming involved in public policy, especially on an issue

277

where economic considerations were so tightly entwined in a complex network of non-economic affairs.[32]

Generally speaking, the economics played a much more significant and prominent role in the latter than in the earlier phase of the challenge, for free trade doctrine was much stronger and less qualified in the 1880s than twenty years later, by which time there was a small but vigorous and vocal band of historically-minded scholars who questioned whether a policy which had apparently been so successful in the mid-Victorian period was still appropriate to the changed domestic and international conditions of the twentieth century.[33] Some of the more orthodox economists sympathized with the political arguments for closer economic ties with the empire, while nevertheless recognizing that certain economic costs would have to be borne in order to achieve the imperialists' broader objectives.[34] Also, in the development of economic theory there was a growing recognition of the limitations and exceptions to pure free trade doctrine which can be traced at least as far back as John Stuart Mill's famous 'infant industry' argument.[35] Curiously enough, as Donald Winch has observed, 'the most telling arguments in favour of tariffs have been advanced by economists who have favoured free trade as a general rule',[36] partly because some of the proposals advanced by critics of free trade posed issues calling for a degree of analytical sophistication, ability to handle empirical data, and historical insight well beyond the average layman's grasp.[37]

Especially in its post-1900 tariff reform phase, the challenge to free trade was undoubtedly a major landmark in British economic thought and policy. Not since the Corn Law debates of the 1840s had the public and the politicians been so preoccupied with or so divided over an economic question; and there was no comparable degree of intensity of controversy in economic affairs thereafter until the depression of the 1930s. It is, moreover, appropriate to emphasize the global significance of Britain's choice between free trade and protection or imperial preference, for she was a leading centre of economic ideas and the world's greatest international trader, shipper, banker and investor, in addition to her extensive imperial interests, responsibilities and influence. Indeed, the sheer range and complexity of the issues involved helps to explain the challengers' failure to overthrow free trade, for despite the widespread anxiety about the country's domestic and international economic performance and prospects, and the manifest loss of faith in the traditional commercial policy, it proved impossible to get a sufficient consensus on any of the numerous alternative policy options. There were too many conflicting interpretations of past economic experience and its extrapolation into the future; and too much uncertainty about the prospects for imperial development and the reactions of our rivals and competitors to the imposition of protectionist or preferential barriers or the introduction of retaliatory measures. While the critics of free trade were numerous, vigorous and often persuasive, their efforts too often seemed to cancel each other out, both intellectually and politically. Even the Tariff Reform League – by far the most lavishly endowed, energetic and organizationally effective agency working against the established economic policy – was much less successful than the Anti-Corn Law League had been in focusing the public's attention on clear and feasible proposals for legislative change.

In the preceding account more attention has been devoted to political conditions and alignments than is customary in discussions of economic thought and policy. Nevertheless, it is important to emphasize the limitations of this undertaking. Any serious attempt to assess the importance of commercial policy in relation to other major contentious political questions of the age – such as the Irish problem, the Boer War, national defence, the need for increased government revenue, the constitutional role of the House of Lords, social welfare policy, and even such lesser but still divisive issues as education and licencing laws – would require a substantial monograph.[38] All these issues must be taken into consideration in any comprehensive effort to account for the failure of the challenge to free trade prior to World War I.

This obvious point highlights the unavoidable difficulties encountered by those who seek to evaluate the role of economic, or indeed any other ideas, in history, for ideas are usually so firmly embedded in the total historical context that they cannot readily be isolated for separate study without distortion, as with the Heisenberg principle. As already noted, economic ideas were utilized prominently and extensively by all parties in the controversy, and at several different levels. To the historian of economics the episode is especially significant because it broadly coincided with the beginnings of the academic professionalization of the subject in Britain, and because the active participation of a number of leading economists raised sensitive questions of professional ethics when they made pronouncements on matters beyond the boundaries of their intellectual expertise.[39] Fortunately for them, unlike the situation in the USA at that time, the open conflict between scientific objectivity and public advocacy did not also entail a serious threat to academic freedom and security.[40] But there is little doubt that the economists' collective reputation was damaged, and this experience may have had a lasting impact on the prevailing conception of acceptable professional conduct. The division of opinion on theoretical and policy questions within the 'community of the competent' was too marked to enable them to present a united front to the public. But in this respect, at least, the challenge to free trade was by no means unique.

NOTES

1 This is the first part of an essay which drew on and supplemented material already published in the next item in this collection, pp.284–337 of this volume.
2 Quoted by William Cunningham, *The Rise and Decline of the Free Trade Movement* (Cambridge: Cambridge University Press, 1912), p.106. (From *Hansard*, 1852, vol.CXXIII, p.858.)

3 See, for example, Carl Johannes Fuchs, *The Trade Policy of Great Britain and Her Colonies Since 1860* (London: Macmillan, 1905), chapters 1 and 2. Also Charles P. Kindleberger, 'The Rise of Free Trade in Western Europe 1820–1875', *Journal of Economic History* vol.35 (March 1975), pp.20–55.

4 For example in April 1905 Chamberlain's supporters gave Balfour the following analysis of Unionist parliamentary strength:

(1) Preferentialists who have publicly expressed their support of the whole policy: 172

(2) Preferentialists who would support the whole policy if it were recognized as being the policy of the government: 73

(3) Retaliationists, many of whom would support preference also, if adopted by the government, but some of whom would in any case refuse to go further: 98

(4) Members totally opposed to any change in our fiscal system – most of whom are retiring at the next election: 27

(5) [others]:   4

                                                                                           TOTAL 374

Cf. Peter Fraser, *Joseph Chamberlain, Radicalism and Empire, 1868–1914* (London: Cassell, 1966), p.262; See also pp.259–60.

5 Henry Roseveare, *The Treasury. The Evolution of a British Institution* (London: Allen Lane, 1969), p.118. See also, for example, Kindleberger, op.cit., and H.C.G. Matthew, *The Liberal Imperialists. The Ideas and Politics of a Post-Gladstonian Elite* (Oxford: Oxford University Press, 1973).

6 Quoted by Jacob Viner, 'The Intellectual History of Laissez-Faire', *Journal of Law and Economics* vol.3 (October 1960), p.55.

7 For example 'Puzzled' asked *The Times*: 'Is there no one amongst our experts of sufficiently unprejudiced mind to put the *pros* and *cons* before us in a dispassionate manner?' 5 December 1983.

8 See p.284ff. in this volume.

9 This is especially true of Home Rule and the South African war. It is also clear that the opposition to free trade waxed and waned roughly in inverse ratio to the state of the economy, possibly with a time lag of about a year.

10 'With the exception of imperial preference, however, the details of his programme were taken almost word for word from the fair traders of the 1880s: a duty of two shillings a quarter would be imposed on foreign corn (with the exception of maize); a duty of the same amount on flour; a duty of five per cent on meat and dairy produce (with the exception of bacon); and an average duty of ten per cent on articles of foreign manufacture. By way of compensation for so many duties on foodstuffs there was to be a reduction of three quarters in the duty on tea, of a half in the duty on sugar and corresponding reductions of the duties on coffee and cocoa. In all cases colonial produce would be exempt.' Richard A Rempel, *Unionists Divided. Arthur Balfour. Joseph Chamberlain and the Unionist Free Traders* (Newton Abbott, Devon: David and Charles, 1972), p.64.

11 Benjamin H. Brown, *The Tariff Reform Movement in Great Britain 1881–1895* (New York: Columbia University Press, 1943), p.1. This valuable study of the fair trade movement was reprinted in 1966. In chapter 1, Brown provides a useful

account of the early protests against free trade. See also Denis Judd, *Radical Joe. A Life of Joseph Chamberlain* (London: Hamish Hamilton, 1977), p.109: 'the tariff reform campaign of Chamberlain's last years did not, therefore, materialize fully fashioned out of the thin air of Edwardian politics as a blatant response to current economic and political needs. The ideas were germinating twenty years before.'

12 Cf. Brown, op. cit., chapter IV 'Tariff Reform and Imperialism'. Also Sidney H. Zebel, 'Fair Trade: An English Reaction to the Breakdown of the Cobden Treaty System', *Journal of Modern History* vol.12 (June 1960), pp.161–85; *Idem*, 'Joseph Chamberlain and the Genesis of Tariff Reform', *Journal of British Studies* vol.7 (November, 1967), pp.131–57; and the biographical studies by Fraser and Judd, previously referred to in this volume.

13 On all these matters there is much detailed information in the massive official *Life of Joseph Chamberlain* published by Macmillan, London. The first three volumes were written by J.L. Garvin, between 1932 and 1934, the last three by Julian Amery, between 1951 and 1969.

14 Cf. Fraser, op. cit., p.277 and Rempel, op. cit., p.19. However, from the later 1890s Chamberlain's interest in old age pensions was subordinated to his preoccupations with imperialism and tariff reform. For background see Bernard Semmel, *Imperialism and Social Reform* (London: Allen & Unwin, 1960). In May 1908, shortly after becoming Prime Minister, H.H. Asquith told St Loe Strachey that he has 'realized from the first that if it could not be proved that social reform (not Socialism) can be financed on Free Trade lines a return to Protection is a moral certainty. This has been one of the mainsprings of my policy at the Exchequer.' Quoted by Jose Harris, *Unemployment and Politics. A Study in English Social Policy 1886–1914* (Oxford: Clarendon Press, 1972), p.270.

15 A similar duty had been allowed to lapse in 1869. There were, incidentally some other government interventions in commercial policy despite the predominance of free trade. For example, the Merchandise Marks Act 1887; the 1895 duties for Indian cotton; the Contagious Diseases (Animals) Act; the 1901 coal export duty; and the subsidies to the Cunard Shipping Line and the West Indian Cane Sugar producers, both in 1902. The decision to remit part of the Corn Registration Duty on Canadian grain was yet another deviation from pure free trade.

16 Fraser, op. cit., p.229.

17 See, for example, the studies by Amery, Fraser, Judd and Rempel, already cited. Also Alfred Gollin, *Balfour's Burden. Arthur Balfour and Imperial Defence* (London: Anthony Blond, 1965); and Kenneth Young, *Arthur James Balfour* (London: Bell, 1963), p.213.

18 On the subsequent divisions within the Unionist party see the appendices in Rempel, op. cit., pp.225–30.

19 Fraser, op. cit., pp.21–2. However Amery describes him as an interventionist, adding that he began as a radical critic of the aristocracy and ended as a defender of the House of Lords. Amery, op. cit., vol.6 pp.993–4.

20 Curiously enough, on that occasion he was opposed by Ritchie, who subsequently became a committed free trader. Cf. Rempel, op. cit., p.14, p.132; Zebel, 'Joseph Chamberlain and the Genesis of Tariff Reform', op. cit., p.132.

21 Judd, op. cit., pp.xv–xvi; Fraser, op. cit., pp.xxii–xxv. This paragraph draws heavily on these two studies. For hostile Liberal reactions to his political style see, for example, Matthew, op. cit., p.129. Winston Churchill complained that Chamberlain was responsible for the Americanization of politics. Cf. Fraser, op. cit., p.211; Gollin, op. cit., p.58.

22 Young, op. cit., p.213.

23 Gollin, op. cit., p.278.
24 Cf. ibid., pp.228, 234. Fraser, op. cit., p.255.
25 See, for example, Brown, op. cit., chapter II 'Tariff Reform', Labour, and the Anti-Bounty Movement, 1881–1895', also Kenneth Brown, 'The Trade Union Tariff Reform Association 1904–1913', *Journal of British Studies* vol.IX (May, 1970), pp.141–53. He refers to 'the almost unanimous hostility [to protection] officially expressed by labour organizations' on p.142. There is a valuable account of 'Chamberlain's Crusade' in Gollin, op. cit., chapter 12, also in Amery, op. cit., vol.6, especially Books 24 and 25.
26 Cf. Harris, op. cit., *passim*, for an authoritative treatment of this theme.
27 According to Amery, imperialism and tariff reform were more than a policy to Chamberlain: they represented a faith in the possibilities of economic expansion, full employment and social progress. Amery, op. cit., vol.6, pp.996, 999. However the rise of socialism and organized labour politics reflected an entirely different ideology.
28 This was widely recognized by supporters of free trade. For discussion of this subject by recent economic historians see, for example, F. Crouzet, 'Trade and Empire: The British Experience from the Establishment of Free Trade Until the First World War', in B.M. Radcliffe (ed.), *Great Britain and her World 1750–1914: Essays in Honour of W.O. Henderson* (Manchester: University of Manchester Press, 1975), pp.209–35; idem, *The Victorian Economy* (London: Methuen, 1982), pp.209–35; C.K. Harley and D.N. McCloskey, 'Foreign Trade: Competition and the Expanding International Economy', especially pp.88–97, in R. Floud and D. McCloskey, *The Economic History of Britain Since 1700, vol.2, 1860 to the 1970s* (Cambridge: Cambridge University Press, 1981); P.J. Cain, 'Political Economy in Edwardian England', in A. O'Day (ed.), *The Edwardian Age, Conflict and Stability 1900–1914* (London: Macmillan, 1979), pp.35–59; Forest Capie, 'Tariff Protection and Economic Performance in the Nineteenth Century', in John Black and L. Alan Winters, *Policy and Performance in International Trade. Papers of the 6th Annual Conference of the International Study Group* (London: Macmillan, 1983), pp.1–24.
29 Among many other sources see, for example, A.W. Coats, 'The Historist Reaction in English Political Economy, 1870–1890', reprinted in this volume, pp.220–30; idem, 'The Origins and Early Development of the Royal Economic Society', *Economic Journal* vol.78 (June 1968), pp.349–71; idem, 'Sociological Aspects of British Economic Thought, c1880–1930', *Journal of Political Economy* vol.75 (October 1967), pp.706–29; both to be reprinted in vol. II of the series, and T.W. Hutchison, *A Review of Economic Doctrines 1870–1929* (Oxford: Clarendon Press, 1953), chapters 1–7.
30 For example, John Maloney, 'Marshall, Cunningham and the Emerging Economics Profession', *Economic History Review* 2nd Ser., vol. 29 (August 1976), pp.440–51; and idem, *Marshall, Orthodoxy and the Professionalization of Economics* (Cambridge: Cambridge University Press, 1985).
31 See especially, A.W. Coats, 'Political Economy and the Tariff Reform Debate of 1903' reprinted in this volume, pp.284–337; also idem, 'The Role of Authority in the Development of British Economics', *Journal of Law and Economics* vol.7 (October 1964), especially pp.99–103. To be reprinted in vol.II of this series. For a valuable recent study bearing on this subject see John Cunningham Wood, *British Economists and the Empire* (London: Croom Helm, 1983).
32 The remainder of this essay draws heavily on Coats 'Political Economy and the Tariff Reform Debate', reprinted in this volume, pp.284–337.
33 See, for example, Gerard Koot, 'English Historical Economics and the Emergence of Economic History', *History of Political Economy* vol.12 (Summer 1980), pp.174–205; also Sections Two and Three in Wood, op. cit. W.S. Jevons, for instance, who is not usually regarded as a doctrinaire economist, wrote: 'We

may welcome *bona fide* investigation into the state of trade, and the causes of the present depression, but we can no more expect to have our opinions on free trade altered by such an investigation, than the Mathematical Society would expect to have axioms of Euclid disproved during the investigation of a complex problem.' *Methods of Social Reform* (London: Macmillan, 1883), pp.181–2. Quoted by Wood, p.105.

34 For example, Sir Robert Giffen. Some other economists, e.g., W.J. Ashley in 1888 and J.S. Nicholson in 1909, were either undecided or agnostic. Cf. Wood, op. cit., pp.169–72, 185, 155–60.

35 The best brief account of this development after 1890 is in Narmadeshwar Jha, *The Age of Marshall* (Patra, India: Novelty & Co, 1963), chapter 4, which also contains a useful survey of the discussion of commercial policy and statistical and historical studies in the *Economic Journal*. During the public controversy lay critics of free trade took great delight in citing passages deemed favourable to their cause from the great economists of the past, both British and foreign.

36 Quoted by Wood, op. cit., p.143 from Winch's *Economics and Policy. A Historical Study* (London: Hodder and Stoughton, 1969), p.60.

37 The role of political economy in the post-1900 discussion of tariff reform is examined in the next essay in this collection.

38 For a useful brief discussion of these issues see Walter L. Arnstein, 'Edwardian Politics: Turbulent Spring or Indian Summer?', in O'Day, op. cit., pp.60–78; also Cain, op. cit., in the same volume.

39 See p.310ff. in this volume.

40 On the US situation see, for example, Mary O. Furner, *Advocacy and Objectivity: A Crisis in the Professionalization of American Social Science, 1865–1905* (Lexington KY: University of Kentucky Press, 1975).

17

POLITICAL ECONOMY AND THE TARIFF REFORM CAMPAIGN OF 1903

I

Joseph Chamberlain's spectacular attempt to convert the country to tariff reform dominated the British political stage from 1903 until the general election of 1905, and has been a subject of continuing interest to economic, social and political historians ever since. It has, however, been surprisingly neglected by students of economic thought and policy despite the fact that during these years the entire country was called upon to take sides 'over an abstract not to say highly technical economic theory.'[1] There are striking parallels between this episode in British history and the sensational presidential campaign of 1896 in the United States, in which public controversy centred on the respective merits of gold and silver as the basis of the nation's currency.[2] In both instances the economists had an unusually favourable opportunity to apply their expertise to a problem of outstanding public importance, and for this reason alone the tariff reform debate deserves more serious study than it has hitherto received from historians of economics.

A thoroughgoing assessment of the role of economic ideas in the tariff reform campaign would far transcend the scope of an article; it was far too vigorous, too protracted and too deeply embedded in a complex political situation. In the following pages attention will therefore be concentrated on the first hectic phase of debate from May to December 1903, for this was the period when the 'professional' economists had their greatest opportunity to influence the course of events.

Joseph Chamberlain's Birmingham speech on 15 May 1903, is usually regarded as the effective beginning of the tariff reform debate,[3] but its significance cannot be appreciated without reference to the April Budget, in which the new Chancellor of the Exchequer, C.T. Ritchie, had repealed the nominal duty on corn imports imposed a year earlier by his predecessor, Sir Michael Hicks-Beach. Ritchie took this step because he was determined to prevent the duty being used as the thin end of a protectionist wedge, not because he objected to the duty as such, and although his decision took his cabinet colleagues by surprise,[4] he was adamant, even threatening to resign if he did not get his way. The repeal was correctly interpreted by all parties as a direct, orthodox free trader's challenge to the tariff reformers, and thereafter the breach within the Cabinet ranks widened and became the subject of intense public interest, especially when Chamberlain, the Secretary of the Colonies, declared his faith in imperial preference and refused to be

> bound by any purely technical definition of free trade ... [or by] an entirely artificial and wrong interpretation which has been placed upon the doctrines of free trade by a small remnant of Little Englanders of the Manchester School who now profess to be the sole repositories of the doctrines of Mr Cobden and Mr Bright.[5]

During the ensuing summer the Prime Minister, A.J. Balfour, employed all his immense dialectial and political talents in an effort to devise a compromise solution that would preserve the unity of his Cabinet and the Conservative party in face of the growing hostility between the free traders and the advocates of imperial preference and tariff reform, and the fascinating events of this period have been discussed in innumerable historical and biographical studies.[6] Matters came to a head in the Cabinet on 13 August, when Balfour presented two documents on fiscal reform – one a compromise memorandum, which was approved for publication and appeared under Balfour's name as *Economic Notes on Insular Free Trade* on 16 September, 1903, and the other, a confidential 'blue paper', which revealed the Prime Minister's provisional support for preferential tariffs and the taxation of food imports. The 'blue paper' – which has never seen the light of day – irreparably widened the existing breach in the Cabinet ranks, for it was regarded as evidence that Balfour had capitulated to Chamberlain; but it was agreed that the final decision would be postponed until the next Cabinet meeting, a month later. Balfour realized that some of the free trade ministers might resign in the interim, but the full gravity of the situation became clear when he learned on 15 September that the Duke of Devonshire – a distinguished elder statesman and moderate free trader, who might conceivably become the leader of a dissident Tory faction – also proposed to resign.

This is not the place to show how Balfour, with consummate skill, and with some disregard for the proprieties of the situation managed to persuade the Duke to withdraw his resignation while at the same time securing the resignations of Ritchie, three other free traders and Chamberlain, who had decided to take the tariff reform question to the country.[7] The public was astonished by the news. With one fell swoop, it seemed that Balfour had saved his Cabinet, his administration and his party, and had ridden himself of the extremists in both camps, while retaining the loyalty and the services of the Duke of Devonshire. The methods by which he had performed this master stroke were avidly discussed, both in private and in public, for many months; but behind the scenes there was an intricate network of politics and personalities in which economic ideas played a prominent and significant role.

II

Throughout the tariff reform debate the interdependence of the economic, political and strategic aspects of the problem was generally acknowledged; but as far as possible the following pages will concentrate on the economic aspect, which aroused sharp disagreements among the leading protagonists. To the propagandists the central issue was simple – it involved a choice between free trade and protection – and despite the government's protest that this involved a gross misrepresentation of their case, the opposition repeatedly emphasized this theme, evidently appreciating the truth of Balfour's remark that 'popular disputation insists on labels and likes its labels old'.[8] Unprejudiced observers were well aware that neither Balfour's nor Chamberlain's position could be adequately expressed in these simplistic terms. As Chamberlain's critics noted, he had been an outspoken supporter of free trade during the 'fair-trade' controversy of the mid-1880s (when Ritchie, curiously enough, was in the opposite camp), and despite his growing preoccupation with the economic elements in his 1903 programme he consistently maintained that commercial considerations were subordinate to considerations of imperial union and domestic social welfare. Balfour, on the other hand, was mainly concerned to preserve his government by avoiding an outright commitment either to free trade or protection, and after the Cabinet crisis had been resolved he offered a qualified programme of fiscal reform while professing to hold the interests of free trade at heart. His success in isolating the Duke of Devonshire from the doctrinaire free traders in the Cabinet rested in part on the Duke's inability to understand the precise differences between Balfour's position and Chamberlain's.[9] In this, the Duke was in distinguished company, which included many other leading politicians, members of the public and even the Monarch himself, and as time passed the confusion increased as the conflicting mass of economic theory, statistics and crude propaganda continued to swell. For as long as he could, Balfour took advantage of the demand for an expert and impartial inquiry into the economic issues at stake, while 'drawing a mantle of indecision' over the differences within the Cabinet, although he fully realized that eager partisans in both camps would prejudge the outcome of any such inquiry, and that once the results were published there would be ample opportunity to question the reliability of the evidence and to dispute any interpretation placed upon it.

In this situation there was an urgent need for expert 'scientific' advice on economic affairs; but how far were the 'economists' willing and able to respond to the opportunity? This question does not, unfortunately, admit of a simple answer. There was as yet no substantial body of 'professional' economists, if only because systematic university training in economics was still in its infancy. Cambridge, the leading university centre of theoretical economics, launched its first Economics Tripos a few weeks after the Cabinet crisis, but this was only after considerable internal apathy and prejudice had been overcome. Oxford never has had a specialist undergraduate economics degree, and although the first degree course in economics had been inaugurated at the London School of Economics in 1901, that diminutive institution had been in existence less than a decade and had been seriously hampered by academic and political prejudice, as well as by lack of funds. A few students studied political economy in the provincial, Scottish and Irish universities, usually in conjunction with moral philosophy or history, and there were about a dozen professors who could act as spokesmen for the subject. However, the deficiencies of university preparation meant that the conventional nineteenth century 'practical' businessman or city financier type of economist still predominated, and the views of such ex-Chancellors of the Exchequer as Viscount Goschen and Hicks-Beach, leading statisticians like Robert Giffen and Charles Booth, and, behind the scenes, permanent officials of the Treasury and the Board of Trade, usually carried more weight than academic opinion. Where the professors and the practical men were in agreement, as was the case in many matters, there was no problem; but on the question of tariff reform there were deep divisions both within and outside the academic walls, and the customary reluctance to consult academic opinion was enhanced by the fact that in the tariff reform debate many people considered that the non-economic aspects were paramount.

Nevertheless, despite all these obstacles, the academic economists' advice was eagerly sought; indeed, so pressing was the desire for expert theoretical and statistical information that almost anyone with pretensions to specialized knowledge of economic phenomena was guaranteed a hearing. Letters, articles, pamphlets, speeches, books and memoranda poured from the presses, and the voice of the professor was heard both in the public forum and in the inner-most councils of state. The most widely publicized incident involving the academic economists was the appearance of a letter to *The Times* on 15 August, near the climax of the Cabinet crisis, a document which soon became generally known as the 'manifesto' of the 'fourteen professors'. This document provoked a series of lively replies and rejoinders which have been discussed elsewhere;[10] and it is of permanent interest, since it represented a concerted effort to bring the weight of academic authority to bear against the economic aspects of Chamberlain's programme, and it initiated a general discussion of the role of economics in public affairs.

Behind the scenes various experts, some of whom were currently holding academic posts, played a direct and vital part in the formulation of government policy. Unfortunately the surviving evidence is insufficient to justify a detailed account of the economic advice offered to the leading politicians, but the positions of Ritchie, Chamberlain and Balfour merit consideration. The opponents of fiscal reform had the easier task because the weight of tradition and experience was on their side, and the constructive work of devising acceptable new policies is usually more difficult than the negative function of defending the *status quo* and finding fault with proposals for reform. Ritchie, the leading free trader in the Cabinet, was strongly supported by a number of pro-free-trade Treasury officials, headed by Sir Francis Mowat, the Permanent Secretary. In the background, though by no means entirely in agreement with him, were his predecessors, Hicks-Beach and Goschen, both of whom were regarded as weighty authorities in financial affairs, and it is no coincidence that when he resigned Ritchie's example was followed by the recently appointed Financial Secretary, Arthur Elliott. The Chancellor of the Exchequer appears to have been a sacrificial victim rather than an independent intellectual force, for according to Winston Churchill, who was bitterly opposed to Chamberlain's proposals,

> Mr Ritchie, the blameless Chancellor of the Exchequer, was held up by Mowat, his chief adviser, right in the forefront of the battle, and went down with his free trade colours flying. Mowat, going far beyond the ordinary limits of a Civil Servant, making no secret of his views, courting dismissal, challenging the administration in admirable State papers, carried on the struggle himself. He armed me with facts and arguments of a general character and equipped me with a knowledge of ecocomics, very necessary to a young man who, at twenty-eight, is called upon to take a prominent part in a national controversy.[11]

Balfour considered that Ritchie's vital Budget speech, in which

> he used arguments absolutely inconsistent with those used by Beach, myself, and others, when the duty was originally imposed . . . was so gratuitous that it can only be explained by the fact that he was already completely under the control of Mowat and E. Hamilton and that he was resolved to make it as difficult as possible for anyone else ever to resort to a tax on corn again.[12]

After Ritchie's retirement, Mowat's hostility to the policies of the new Chancellor, Austen Chamberlain, became the subject of outspoken public as well as private criticism. J.L. Garvin, in the *National Review*, suggested that pending the preparation of the 'big revolver' of retaliatory duties against foreign powers, the Prime Minister

> might usefully employ a small revolver upon the large and disorderly mob of permanent Civil Servants, who have got completely out of hand

during the last few months. We can make considerable allowance for hide-bound officials brought up in narrowly Gladstonian traditions and imbued with the spirit of Little Englandism from their earliest youth when they see their favourite fetish challenged. But there is a limit to the licence which is permissible to the permanent servants of the State. The Treasury has notoriously been the centre of the cabal against Tariff Reform, and the manner in which its clerks have forsaken their departmental duties in order to lobby and intrigue, and prime the enemies of the Government with materials to be used against Ministers, is a matter of common knowledge and universal condemnation. Other departments have followed suit. We do not make the complaint because they are on the opposite camp to ourselves. We should equally object to seeing Protectionist opposition. The Civil Service has seriously injured its reputation since the opening of the tariff controversy, and it is high time that discipline were restored.[13]

The proponents of tariff reform not only had to agree upon their proposals – which eventually proved impossible – they also had to justify them by reference to their probable effects, a task which was greatly exacerbated by the political and strategic complications of the situation. Chamberlain, whose limited knowledge and occasional wilful disregard of political economy soon became notorious, was for a time the somewhat impulsive and recalcitrant pupil of W.A.S. Hewins, who was Professor of Economics and Director of the London School of Economics before he became Secretary to the Tariff Commission established by Chamberlain's supporters in November 1903.

Hewins' first contact with Chamberlain occurred in 1900, but there was no further communication until June 1903, and there are no grounds for the opinion that Hewins was responsible for Chamberlain's decision to undertake the tariff reform campaign.[14] An account of their dealings during the six months prior to the decision to form the Tariff Commission, in November 1903, is given in Hewins' autobiography, *The Apologia of an Imperialist*, but unfortunately there is almost no direct evidence of the economic advice he gave. On their first meeting, in June, the two men carefully discussed the plans for Hewins' series of polemical articles in *The Times*, which appeared under the pseudonym 'An Economist', and Chamberlain's dependence is suggested by his confession: 'I do not pretend to be an economic expert. I once read Mill and tried to read Marshall. You must supply the economic arguments,'[15] which Hewins eagerly proceeded to do. In a hitherto unpublished passage in his diary he recorded that Chamberlain

referred several things to me in July, and part of one of my memoranda seems to have found its way into Balfour's *Economic Notes*, how I do not know. When Chamberlain's autumn campaign began I regularly during his earlier speeches sent him a weekly resume of the arguments used against him and the replies thereto. I wrote for the Birmingham

289

[Tariff Reform] League a tract on the Food Taxes. He also knew that I was the leader writer of the *Morning Post* [wherein Hewins wrote 'all the fiscal leaders . . . and some special articles and reviews' after Balfour's Sheffield speech of 1 October]. I always complied with any request he made me whether direct or indirect. My argument on the food taxes was very generally adopted and Garvin worked out a good many of my suggestions both in his *Daily Telegraph* articles and his contributions to the *National Review*. Both directly and indirectly it is probable that I influenced Mr Chamberlain but I had no means of access to him in any way exceptional.[16]

In dealing with Hewins, as later with W.J. Ashley, Chamberlain emphasized that working men and audiences at public meetings would not be impressed by many figures or by abstract economics, and added, on 12 October:

> What, however, I do ask from you is that, wherever possible, you should take up these and other criticisms and deal with them from an expert point of view. At present I am somewhat in the position of Athanasius contra mundum, and of course I cannot deal separately with all my opponents, but their mis-statements and mistakes ought not to go uncorrected but should be answered as fast as they are made, by responsible authorities.
>
> Anonymous letters in small type are of little value, but an article or letter from a recognized authority which the Editor will place in the front and comment upon is of the utmost advantage in such a controversy.[17]

Chamberlain required help in dealing with his Cabinet colleagues, as well as with the general public, and there is a tantalizingly incomplete glimpse of Hewins' advice in connection with the following inquiry about the balance of payments from 'a correspondent' – who, on examination of the Chamberlain papers, proves to be none other than the Duke of Devonshire himself.

> You seem to think that for some reason it must always be necessary for us to export something, whether such exports are required to pay for our imports or not. It seems to me that if, to take the extreme case, our Imports were balanced by our shipping receipts and by the interest on our foreign investments, the country would be just as much better off than it is now, as a man who lives on invested capital is better off than a man who has to work with his hands. And if the country is better off, I cannot see that any class should be worse off.
>
> I cannot follow exactly what would happen in such a case, but I imagine that the work which is now done to pay for our Imports would be employed in providing for the enhanced wants and requirements of a richer people . . .

I wish we could give Parliament something to show that we are really enquiring. If it is only the statistics on which you only are proving the reduction or stagnation of some of our industries it would be something. I think it is for you to open your case first, and the counter statistics or statements, if there are any, would follow.[18]

This inquiry was doubly important, for it came from one of the key figures in the political debate, one whose mind was apparently not yet made up, and it cast doubt on Chamberlain's fundamental argument that a policy of preference would raise the general level of employment. There is no trace of Hewins' reply, but it undoubtedly influenced Chamberlain's answer to the Duke, a week later:

All economic arguments are speculative and in my opinion, as apparently in yours, they are inconclusive.

I prefer a little common sense and business experience. Both of us see that there is ample room for the investment of untold millions in this country and if it gives manufacturers here some security there would be an enormous development of Home Industries both by British and Foreign capital.

There will also be a sufficiency of labour although its cost per man will increase. Not necessarily its cost in the goods made as new inventions constantly take the place of manual labour.

There are always millions unemployed in this country or with only partial employment and besides this there is a large continuous emigration. . . .

In any case, we have 4 facts to go upon – viz.:

(1) British exports have been stagnant for 10 years.

(2) They would have shown an immense decline but for the increase of Colonial trade and the larger export of coal.

(3) British Industries will be in the most serious danger when Germany and America have a large over-production.

(4) Tariffs and Preference, which might remedy the above evils, are consistent with a growth and progress of protected nations enormously greater than our own.[19]

This letter does not suggest that Chamberlain paid much attention to economic reasoning in endeavouring to allay Devonshire's doubts, despite his limited knowledge of the subject. Nor, indeed, was he any more careful in his use of evidence, for as Hewins recalled:

I begged him to allow me to have his figures worked out by competent statisticians, but he would not adopt this suggestion. He preferred his own methods and said that was his way of getting up the subject. It was rather difficult to help him though I always complied with any request he made to me whether direct or indirect.[20]

One of Chamberlain's contemporaries remarked that his career was 'strewn with the debris of abandoned hypotheses' and in this respect, as in many others, he was the antithesis of Balfour. Cautious and indolent, where Chamberlain was impetuous and zealous, Balfour was much better prepared for a debate of this kind, and although Sir William Harcourt complained, with some justification, that the country was 'awaiting the education of the Prime Minister',[21] Balfour was already possessed of some knowledge and a genuine interest in political economy. He had been a student of Henry Sidgwick at Cambridge, and while disputing Sidgwick's philosophy he endorsed his economic ideas, and indeed Sidgwick's personal influence may help to explain Balfour's philosophical subtlety and his skill in finding a *via media* between rival economic ideas.[22] A Vice President of the Royal Economic Society, Balfour drew upon the advice of Percy Ashley, of the London School of Economics and, to a lesser extent, of Herbert Somerton Foxwell of Cambridge, as well as various officials at the Custom House and the Treasury. Unfortunately, Foxwell's comments on a draft version of Balfour's *Economic Notes* have not survived,[23] but the Balfour papers contain a volume of more than two hundred pages of memoranda and replies to questions contributed by his other advisers. Between early June and the beginning of August, Percy Ashley submitted lengthy reviews of British and foreign – especially German – economists' opinions concerning tariffs, British trade statistics and the comparative fluctuations of corn prices and pauperism, together with analyses of dumping and foreign competition in British markets, and, as befitted an academic expert, his tone throughout was moderate and detached. At one point he expressed his 'strong Imperialist' sympathy towards Imperial Union, but went on to voice his fear that the economic legislation necessary to achieve that goal would involve a price 'a great deal too heavy'. He was not disturbed by Britain's tendency to become 'relatively more a banking and financial country and relatively less an industrial one', and he saw no insuperable objections to Chamberlain's proposal to raise the corn duty, for his study of corn prices and pauperism led to the cautious conclusion 'that a moderate rise in the price of corn does not mean of necessity an increase in pauperism, i.e., it does not (as we have often been told) *force a number of people who are on the line over the line to pauperism*' – a view that was subsequently endorsed by no less an authority than Charles Booth, the leading contemporary student of poverty.[24] From his Civil Servants, however, the Prime Minister obtained much more conflicting recommendations. The most favourable response to Chamberlain's scheme came in a memorandum from three officials at the Custom House entitled 'Can our Import Duties be so Modified as to Become a Means of Promoting our Export Trade, and Lightening the Present Charge on the Food of the People?', in which they offered a qualified affirmative reply, proposing moderate duties on non-British foodstuffs, preferential rates on food from British possessions offering reciprocal terms, a reduction of existing duties on tea, coffee, sugar and fruit, and a higher scale of charges on imports of finished manufactures. The net effect, they concluded, would be slight – little more than a token of imperial goodwill; but although there were dangers in complicating the established procedure they considered it possible to maintain the existing import volume and level of customs revenue 'and at the same time to obtain machinery for smiting back against those who smite us, favouring those who deserve it, and reducing certain heavy charges on food'.[25]

However, very different advice was received from the Treasury. In a substantial memorandum 'Notes on some points connected with Preferential Treatment', Chamberlain's proposals were denounced as 'a leap in the dark', and the consequent changes in the fiscal system were attacked in unambiguous terms.

> Of all things in taxation we ought to beware, it is change, for I believe that there is much truth in those who hold that there is nothing so unjust in taxation as change. Moreover, the very object of the change is to do what taxation ought not to do, that is, to interfere with trade, which it is very easy to dislocate and most difficult to organise.[26]

The Treasury view of the effect of food taxes was exactly opposite to Ashley's.

> Just think what a tax on food means! The nation as a whole may be lightly taxed; but we must remember that there is unfortunately always a by no means negligible quantity of the population who are in straits to keep body and soul together, and that anything which tends to enhance the cost of living – and it must do that – aggravates and extends those straits.[27]

What, if any, were the effects of this expert advice on the three principal recipients? Ritchie, as we have seen, was a captive of the Treasury view, whereas Chamberlain was so independent-minded, and his pronouncements on economic matters were so numerous and so erratic, that Hewins' influence upon him cannot be reliably assessed without far more detailed evidence than we now have. However, Balfour's case is different; his ideas are well-documented, and although he was chiefly concerned with the political aspects of the situation, the precise formulation of his economic position was a matter of vital importance both to his Cabinet and his party. Balfour's opponents repeatedly protested at his delaying tactics and complained, with some justification, that his speeches and his *Economic Notes* were deliberately vague and obscure. But the Prime Minister was far too astute a politician to commit himself to detailed and specific policy statements in a situation where there were so many unknown and unpredictable factors – especially the state of public opinion at home and the reactions of colonial governments. On questions of principle his position was obscure only to those who saw the problem exclusively in terms of free trade versus protection. Undoubtedly the *Economic Notes* was, as some critics maintained, a somewhat 'academic treatise' – indeed Balfour himself confided to Austen Chamberlain that the whole debate was a fit subject for 'schoolmen';[28] but as he explained when despatching the first instalment to the Duke of Devonshire:

> the only practical point to which it is immediately directed is that we should openly and avowedly announce that this country no longer considers itself debarred by economic theories from making the best commercial bargain it can with other countries. I have long held this view, and publicly expressed it twenty years ago.

Among the underlying principles he listed the following:

> 1. No retaliatory duty should be threatened, or fiscal preference offered, *with a view to protecting any industry in this country against legitimate competition.*
> 2. No such duty and no such preference should introduce any change into our fiscal system which would increase the average cost of living to the working man.
> 3. I do not think that, as at present advised, we ought to attempt to carry out a retaliatory policy by the continental method of *starting with heavy protective duties against the world*, and relaxing them in favour of those countries which give us privileges.[29]

Balfour's concept of 'insular' free trade was prompted by the question *'whether a fiscal system suited to a free trade nation in a world of free traders, remains suited in every detail to a free trade nation in a world of protectionists'*; and his main plea, in the *Economic Notes* and in his crucial speech at Sheffield on 1 October, was summed up in the slogan 'freedom to negotiate that freedom of exchange may be increased'.[30] Balfour considered that the country was not yet ready to accept taxes on food for the sake of Imperial unity; but he did not dissociate himself from Chamberlain's campaign to win support for this position, and the close association in Balfour's mind between 'retaliation' and preference is clear from his correspondence with Windsor. After explaining the need to strengthen the government's bargaining power in defence of our legitimate commercial interests he added:

> There are, however, two quite different shapes in which this 'freedom to negotiate' may be employed – one against Foreign governments, the other in favour of our own Colonies. In dealing with foreign governments we may threaten – and if need be employ – 'retaliation'. In dealing with our own Colonies we can only offer 'preference'. The second is perhaps the most important; *if*, that is, a really good bargain could be struck between the Mother Country and her children. But it is also by far the most difficult. It is difficult because a bargain is always

294

difficult:it is especially difficult because it is hard to see how any bargain could be contrived which the Colonies would accept, *and which would not involve some taxation on food in this country*. In Mr Balfour's opinion there are ways in which such taxation *might* be imposed, which would in no degree add to the cost of living of the working classes. But he is also of opinion that in the present state of public feeling, no such plan would get a fair hearing; to make it part of the Government programme would be to break up the Party and to endanger the *other* half of the Policy – that which authorises retaliation – for which the country is better prepared. Mr Balfour therefore, as at present advised, intends to say that, though Colonial preference is eminently desirable, in the interests both of Brit. Commercial and Imperial Unity, it has not yet come within the sphere of practical politics.[31]

This letter demonstrates that political considerations outweighed the economic advice of those who argued that taxes on food could be imposed without raising the cost of living. But, as is so often the case with efforts at compromise, Balfour's position was attacked from both sides. Despite his clear cut declaration of support for fiscal reform, Chamberlain's supporters were disappointed, for 'retaliation' fell far short of a systematic programme of imperial preference or protection. On the other hand, as the Duke of Devonshire had correctly forecast, Balfour's statements were widely interpreted as 'a victory for Chamberlain and the extremists', mainly because

> your declaration must involve some attack on the principle of Free Imports which will give great hope and encouragement to every Protectionist, and will, in the first instance at least, alienate from you every Free Trader, until you have been able to persuade them, if you can persuade them, that you are working in the interests of real Free Trade.[32]

Torn as he was between loyalty to Balfour and the party and adherence to his principles, the Duke's response was vital to the administration. He correctly described himself as a 'convinced, but not bigoted free trader', and, as Lord President of the Council, he was the government's spokesman in the House of Lords, a position that was exceedingly uncomfortable for him.

> My knowledge of political economy is very small, and I should find it difficult to argue with either an expert Free Trader or Protectionist, and I am too old to begin a new study. But I feel like Balfour of B[urleigh] that this policy, if it is to be adopted, must be supported by those who believe in it with a whole heart, and of this I am quite incapable. After giving away so much as we are asked to do of Free Trade principles, I do not know whether I should have most difficulty in answering the Protectionists who want more, or the Free Traders who would concede

nothing. I am more and more convinced that this is and must be a fight between Free Trade and Protection, and that no such compromise is possible between them.[33]

As it transpired, he probably got the worst of both worlds, for his decision not to resign on 18 September with Hamilton, Ritchie and Balfour of Burleigh, exposed him to the charge of breaking his promise and betraying his friends, while his subsequent resignation, immediately following Balfour's Sheffield speech of 1 October, angered the Prime Minister and some who remained in the Cabinet. Nor did his resignation bring an end to his troubles for he became President of the Unionist Free Food League, an organization which before the close of the year was threatening to split the party by advising Unionist voters to withold their support from candidates who supported Chamberlain; and in the New Year he had to face the ordeal of justifying his action before the House of Lords. To his staunch free trade friend, the Liberal, Leonard Courtney, he confided:

> Our Free Traders are extraordinarily weak, and I think by that time I may be left almost alone and representing nobody but myself. Strongly as I feel on the subject I find a great difficulty in speaking about it. It is too big and my political economy is not strong. What do you think is the best line for a man who does not profess to be a political economist? I am sure that more and more ought to be made than has been made of the Colonial and Imperial side of the Question,: but then I do not know much about Colonies either.[34]

Thus it can be seen that economic ideas played a crucial part in the political events of 1903 within the government, especially in relation to the Duke of Devonshire's conduct. It is now time to review the public response to Chamberlain's proposals and the role of the economists in the ensuing controversy.

III

If the King's ministers found it difficult to grasp their leader's position, it is hardly surprising that many rank and file party members found their allegiances painfully divided. The unfortunate layman who sought to inform himself of the issues at stake was immediately confronted with a bewildering variety of policy recommendations, for although the schemes could be grouped under four headings – free trade; imperial preference; retaliation; and protection – many subtle variations on these themes were heard, and there was considerable terminological confusion.[35] In addition, several leading public men had either recently changed their minds about the tariff question, or were in process of doing so, and when such reputable financial spokesmen as Goschen and Hicks-Beach appeared to adopt shifting and inconsistent positions one can sympathize with the writer who cried: 'Will not one of the omniscient Fourteen Professors write a monograph to explain Sir Michael Hicks-Beach to plain people?'[36] In an attempt to educate their countrymen, that is, to lead them away from their blind, unthinking adherence to free trade into the clear light of fiscal reform – Chamberlain's supporters printed literally millions of pamphlets and other publications; and gave innumerable lectures and speeches in their endeavour to promote their cause. Somewhat similar tactics were adopted on a more modest scale by the free traders, and the nation's leaders emphasized the public's duty to inform themselves of the arguments on both sides. But the prospect was hardly encouraging when a brilliant opposition spokesman like Lord Rosebery, after advising his audience to read recent speeches rather than 'dry' economics textbooks, confessed that some of the arguments were beyond him and even conceded that protection might be beneficial under certain circumstances.[37]

At a time when the country was suffering from what Asquith termed 'fiscalitis', economic reasoning inevitably tended to be swamped by propaganda, for most commentators acknowledged the interdependence of the political and economic issues in debate. In an effort to patch over the differences with his Cabinet Balfour claimed that the utmost variety of opinion on abstract questions was permissible provided that a consensus could be achieved on policy matters, and Akers Douglas, the Home Secretary, tartly informed the House of Commons that economic questions had never been made the test of party loyalty.[38] But Balfour admitted that political economy was being used as a propaganda weapon,[39] and as the controversy became more heated even the academic economists were accused of political prejudice, especially when the 'manifesto' of the fourteen professors was criticized as a misguided and illegitimate attempt to bring academic influence to bear upon an essentially political issue.[40] Nor was this opinion confined to the laity: Foxwell informed Balfour that the original draft had been toned down, partly as a result of his own objections to 'some passages of a markedly political character, especially the last which ended with a sneer at Mr Chamberlain'. After it was printed, however, he regretted the changes, 'for if the document had appeared in its original form, its political and personal bias would have been obvious'.[41]

To some dejected observers, events seemed to be confirming Goschen's prediction that mass democracy and scientific political economy were incompatible, for despite the weight of authoritative economic opinion against him, it was said that Chamberlain

> knew upon what a stolid mass of ignorance, passion, prejudice and cupidity he could rely if he supported the Protectionist banner ... [he] knew he could count upon the pot-house and the music-hall to drown in drink and discord any glimmering of reason and sound sense in the fuddled brain of his boozy contingent.[42]

Even some of his supporters admitted that Chamberlain was appealing to passion and prejudice rather than to reason,[43] but he evidently failed to shake the average working man's faith in free trade. Although some free traders linked protection and socialism, condemning both, moderate trade union spokesmen like John Burns attacked Chamberlain's proposals as a threat to the cheap loaf, and the Cobden Club's massive collection of 940 signatures of Trade Unionists and Cooperative leaders seemed to bear him out.[44] To the doctrinaire socialist, the entire debate was merely 'a quarrel between two sections of the capitalist classes as to the best method of securing the fruits of the exploitation of labour';[45] but there were those who retained their confidence in the wisdom of the masses.

> The English labouring man, whether artisan or clod-hopper, has always shown better judgement and been more teachable in the fundamental parts of economy, than chambers of commerce, brokers, manufacturers on a large scale. The superior education of the latter does not carry them far enough to see much beyond their own interest. But as to their education in political economy, it is rarely superior to that of the masses. The right and duty of private judgement in politics belongs to every man; many, however, have not the time and opportunity to get hold of the learning regarding Free Trade. These must follow authority, and they had better follow the 14 professors than those who prove by their talk that they have never read a line of Ricardo and John Stuart Mill and who are evolving their political economy out of the profundity of their own consciousness. Everything is to be expected of the English masses when they are called on to decide the proposals of Protection and Retaliation.[46]

Soon after Chamberlain's Birmingham speech of 15 May Balfour announced that the government intended to conduct an 'inquiry' into the condition of British trade before deciding the future course of fiscal policy, and this seemingly innocent proposal provides an excellent example of the complex interaction of political and economic influences on the debate. Under normal circumstances such an inquiry would have been undertaken by a Select Committee or a Royal Commission, and Balfour's statement that it would be 'an inquiry by the Cabinet for the Cabinet'[47] disappointed those who favoured a more open and systematic investigation and exposed the administration to ridicule by its opponents. Liberal spokesmen like Rosebery and James Bryce denounced the manoeuvre as a 'hollow sham', and there were many who believed that

> To avoid the responsibility of committing the Cabinet and perhaps of precipitating resignations, Mr Balfour allowed the Corn Duty to be withdrawn, and then invented the quaint theory of Inquiry; or, in other words, authorised his colleagues to quarrel among themselves

and to leave it to the public, in some indeterminate fashion, to decide the dispute.[48]

The opposition's suspicions were, indeed, justified, for at the height of the Cabinet crisis the Duke of Devonshire reminded Balfour that an earlier crisis had only been 'averted by the invention of the formula of the Enquiry',[49] and at the time the Prime Minister's move only served to heighten the general confusion. Torn between their loyalty to traditional Tory free trade policy and the appeals of Chamberlain and his allies, Balfour's supporters could not return the opposition's fire until an official 'party line' had been announced, and the problem was exacerbated when Devonshire, under pressure from Goschen, confessed his inability to specify the precise points on which enlightenment was being sought. The object, he explained, was 'not so much to obtain information, because all the necessary information, I believe, exists, but to arrange it in a manner which they [that is, the Cabinet] will be able to consider themselves';[50] but this admission merely gave comfort to the opposition, for it re-emphasized the government's indecision and suggested that there was no startling new evidence to warrant any radical departure from established policy. Some advocates of tariff reform consoled themselves with the thought that the mere existence of an inquiry was 'fatal to the prestige of the hitherto accepted creed because it necessarily destroys its divine attributes',[51] but there were few on either side who accepted at face value Lord Lansdowne's assurance that the object of the exercise was to reach the truth, rather than to confirm a preconceived theory.[52]

Before considering the results of the inquiry it is worth asking why Balfour consistently refused to appoint a Royal Commission on the fiscal question, despite persistent pressure from a variety of quarters, including Windsor. As Dr Gollin has noted, the King 'was intensely interested in the Ministerial crisis . . . [for] this was the first major political clash of his reign, and he was anxious to assert his constitutional right to be consulted, to encourage and to warn'.[53] In a letter written to Balfour from Marienbad three days after the economists' 'manifesto' appeared in *The Times*, Edward VII expressed his satisfaction that

the Cabinet had postponed till its mid-September meeting any final decision regarding the important matter of fiscal reform which is occupying the attention of the whole country. The King sees the great difficulties which beset Mr Balfour on this all-important subject, and much regrets the dissension of opinion in the Cabinet which may entail certain changes amongst the Ministers which would weaken the government. Would it not be possible to refer the whole matter to a Royal Commission which has been suggested by Mr Price of Oxford? The matter is mostly of too serious a character for any Cabinet to arrive at a just conclusion in one or two meetings, but if the Royal Commission were appointed without loss of time, consisting of the ablest men in the country and thoroughly conversant with so difficult a problem, it would relieve Mr Balfour and the Cabinet of a great responsibility.[54]

There are several reasons why Balfour rejected the King's apparently wise and helpful advice. Undoubtedly, as Dr Gollin has argued, he regarded the issue as a political one, and considered that the country would be unwilling to listen to Professors of Economics or other experts; he may also have taken account of the King's known free trade sympathies, feeling that His Majesty's proposal was motivated by the suggestion that a Royal Commission would reveal the weight of expert opinion against Chamberlain's scheme. According to a well authenticated story (which must have been known to Balfour) a few days before his departure for Marienbad the King had expressed his approval of taxes on the rich, and when Ritchie had inquired 'Your Majesty does not approve of taxing the food of the poor?' the monarch replied 'No, and I do not care who knows it!' Whereupon Devonshire turned to Lord Balfour of Burleigh saying, 'We really must get this man on the stump'.[55] This anecdote became so well known that in October the proprietor of the *Devon Herald* wrote to Windsor seeking official confirmation of the report, only to be rebuked with the lofty reply that 'The King never expresses any opinion on political matters except on the advice of his responsible ministers';[56] and a month later, a doubtless overconfident Joseph Chamberlain left Windsor believing, 'as he boasted on his way up to London, that he had converted the whole Royal family, and that the Queen was an ardent Protectionist'.[57] But whatever the King's opinion, he renewed his suggestion in December, when Chamberlain announced 'the formation of a non-political commission of experts which would undertake the drafting of a scientific tariff'. According to his official biographer, Edward VII was 'somewhat perturbed' by Chamberlain's 'independent action',[58] and Balfour had to reassure his Majesty and reaffirm his objections to a Royal Commission.

Unlike some of Chamberlain's critics who regarded the appropriation of the term 'Commission' as a shocking act of *lèse majesté*, Balfour characteristically contemplated the new body 'with serenity'. 'This soi-disant Commission', he maintained, was an offspring of the Tariff Reform League, a body similar in nature and function to the Anti-Corn Law League; it involved no usurpation of authority; it lacked the King's approval, and was financed entirely from private sources.

> If the Government *had* proposed to appoint a Commission one thing is certain. Any invitation addressed to the Opposition to take part would have been rejected with scorn. The argument would have been that, if the Government proposed to tamper with our present fiscal policy, upon them must rest the responsibility; and they – the Opposition – would have nothing of it. Then when the Government had framed the Commission under these circumstances, the Party cry against them

would have been – as it is against *this* Commission – that it was a packed Commission of protectionists.[59]

Balfour had already revealed to a correspondent that his objections to a Royal Commission rested on grounds of expediency rather than principle:

> I have always had grave doubts about the value of a Commission to examine what I may call 'fundamentals', whether in economics or anythings [sic] else. An enquiry of this kind drags on for months, and sometimes years, and it is extremely difficult to get really competent persons to give their time to it, and when the inquiry is finished, it probably produces a series of widely divergent Reports upon all the really important issues. The Labour Commission, for example, dealt with, on the whole, far simpler problems. How many people are there who have read the report – to say nothing of the Evidence? And what degree of agreement has followed from its protracted labours?[60]

Even the formation of the Tariff Commission did not terminate the demands for a bona fide Royal Commission. When Parliament reassembled in February 1904 the Earl of Wemyss pressed the Government to act, and the matter was carefully debated in the Lords on 9 March. Once again the King seemed surprised and perhaps disappointed by Balfour's attitude, for the Prime Minister once again felt it necessary to justify his refusal. 'Lord Lansdowne's first instinct was to grant Lord Wemyss' request – at least in part', Balfour reported, but on mature consideration, he added, the Cabinet decided against such a course, for a variety of reasons.

> Lord Goschen is the only person of authority who seems to approve Lord Wemyss' motion; and *he* only approved that part of it which dealt with an investigation into *facts*, feeling that the suggestion of *remedies* could not be left to a Commission . . .

> The fact is, any such enquiry is not likely to end in a unanimous Report. And if it ends in several Reports, signed by Members of the various Schools of economic thought, the general public will be more puzzled than ever. Moreover, it will be quite impossible to find materials for a Commission which the public would regard as impartial. Almost every man – I might go further, and say every man – in public life has committed himself more or less one way or the other. John Morley has, I think, publicly expressed his disapproval of any enquiry; and no member of the Opposition in the House of Commons has given it the slightest encouragement. For the present, therefore, it would probably be wise to allow the matter to rest. But a time may come when, on particular subjects, or aspects of the case, an enquiry into facts may be desirable; and it must by no means be supposed that the decision of the Cabinet necessarily excludes such investigations.[61]

And there the matter rested. No Royal Commission was appointed and in retrospect, Balfour's attitude seems wise in view of the overheated state of public opinion. As might have been expected, the Tariff Commission was heavily attacked by Chamberlain's opponents, who rightly regarded it as a handpicked body of protectionist sympathizers[62] – apart from Charles Booth, the noted social statistician, who appeared as a misguided pawn in the propagandists' game.[63] Winston Churchill and others pointed out that the body included no bankers, and no representatives of the cotton industry or the learned professions,[64] and so confused was the current state of opinion that Arthur Pearson, the proprietor of the Daily Express and head of the Tariff Reform League, was said to have been 'continually annoyed by the difficulty of finding out whether this man or that was a Protectionist or a Free Trader. He himself always knew what he believed and what he did not believe, and he never had any faith with the Laodicean.'[65]

But although there was no Royal Commission, the results of Balfour's Cabinet inquiry were published, at least in part, in a Board of Trade 'Blue Book'[66] which became the subject of widespread comment. Even before it appeared, on 22 September, there was dissatisfaction because some of Chamberlain's fellow ministers felt he had broken the tacit agreement to postpone public discussion until the results of the inquiry were available, and it was claimed that Balfour had made up his own mind before the inquiry was concluded. As the Duke of Devonshire complained:

> I have done my best to persuade myself and to persuade others that a real enquiry was being carried on, that Free Trade was on its trial, and that by the results of the enquiry it would be judged. But I cannot admit that the collection of a mass of statistics without any attempt to enlighten the country as to what they prove, or an abstract essay such as you intend to publish, constitute the kind of Enquiry which I at least have been promising.[67]

Needless to say, the available statistical data were subject to varied and conflicting interpretations, which further added to the public's confusion. Free traders gleefully claimed that the Blue Book demonstrated the thriving state of the nation's trade, but while one writer spoke of the 'unimpeachable figures of the Board of Trade' another called the Blue Book 'a booby trap for every dabbler in fiscal statistics'.[68] On the whole, the weight of expert opinion favoured circumspection. One of Balfour's economic advisers cautioned

> that no undue inference should be drawn from figures published in the Trade Returns, which, to those not acquainted with the methods of compilation and collateral circumstances, may seem to bear an exaggerated significance quite at variance with their true and natural meaning.[69]

This warning was underlined a year later by a distinguished panel of experts working under the auspices of the Royal Statistical Society.[70] These problems of statistical interpretation soon became known to the general public when, for example, a revealing exchange of letters between Chamberlain and Giffen, the eminent statistician, was printed in *The Times*. Chamberlain had cited the increase of manufacturing imports between 1872 and 1902 as evidence of our growing industrial weakness in a world of protective tariffs and 'dumping' by international cartels, and when he indicated, in response to Giffen's inquiry, the official source from which he had derived his figures, Giffen provided a dramatic lesson in the fallibility of such statistics. In a long, and carefully argued letter, he explained that owing to certain peculiarities in the method of presentation, Chamberlain's figure was subject to an error of approximately 70 per cent; and it did not soften the blow when Giffen added, *a propos* of the technical adjustments necessary to the official returns:

> Both parties to this great fiscal controversy will be offended, I fear, at so much being required of them, but we all have an interest in having good statistics, and a good logical use of them, whatever our opinions on policy may be.[71]

However, this was too much for some laymen to bear. One correspondent protested, in reply to Giffen's letter, that his distinctions were 'too fine for explanation to a popular audience', adding that leading economists treated statistics as expressive of tendencies rather than exact magnitudes. Mr Chamberlain had cited authoritative sources, and if these were ambiguous he could not be blamed. The misunderstanding was attributable to 'the connotative terms used by those who are responsible for the statistical statements'; and in any case his arguments had not been invalidated for they rested on premises which required no formal specification since 'as everybody knows . . . they are identical to those upon which economic science rests'.[72] In what one observer described as the 'fearful fog of figures which overhangs this controversy', such a retreat to self-evident, self-validating premises was doubtless irresistible; and many contemporaries probably sympathized with *The Times* editorial comment that

> The manipulation of figures is so easy, and the art of deriving direct conclusions from them is so profoundly difficult, that there is perhaps but small prospect of materially influencing the judgement of the people of this country, in one direction or the other, by a mere parade of millions, the fluctuations in which may possibly be dependent on none of the causes to which ardent controversialists ascribe them.[73]

Consolation for those dissatisfied with statistics was offered in a variety of forms: the economist, A.C. Pigou, emphasized that statistics proved nothing about causes; Booth asserted that the outcome of the controversy would be decided by general principles rather than figures; Mr Punch employed ridicule in noting the deficiency of the official returns resulting from neglect of the glass eye industry; but the *reductio ad absurdum* was provided by the Chamberlainite who concluded that the leader's appeal to 'human nature' would ultimately prevail, whatever the statistics showed.[74]

IV

Faced with a torrent of conflicting evidence and opinions, many members of the public became impatient with the slogans offered by partisan writers and sought unbiased advice and instruction. 'Is there no one amongst our experts of sufficiently unprejudiced mind to put the *pros* and *cons* before us in a dispassionate manner?',[75] wrote 'Puzzled' to *The Times*, while another correspondent, Oswald Crawfurd, maintained that the size of the body of 'neutral observers' was attributable to the prevalence of partisanship,

> for it is impossible for an impartial inquirer to fail to observe that the *data* on which arguments on either side of the debate are grounded are almost invariably and immediately controverted and disputed, and often proved to be incorrect by the other.[76]

One reader of the *Spectator* begged the editor to treat the controversy seriously and to

> engage some trained political economist who shall defend the present fiscal system ... [and explain] how it is that other countries with a smaller Customs revenue but a higher tariff are able to show a much larger proportionate increase in foreign trade, in growth of income, in shipping, of savings bank deposits, and a much larger decrease in pauperism.

But the invitation was declined:

> We cannot say that we are encouraged by the results achieved by another newspaper, *The Times*, in adopting that course. We are content with the knowledge that two and two make four, that though you may make a few individuals rich by Acts of Parliament which prevent people buying freely what others desire to sell freely, you cannot perform that feat for a whole nation, and that it is an eternal law that he who will not buy neither shall he sell. These things can be learnt without a trained economist. For the rest, and here we think we shall have the support of our ablest trained economists, we venture to assert that the policy of Free Trade is no mystery which the mere layman must not dare to defend.[77]

In thus referring to *The Times*, the editor of the *Spectator* was, of course, recalling the sixteen articles written by Hewins under the pseudonym. 'An Economist', a series that continued for a longer period than originally planned partly because it proved impossible to persuade any anti-Chamberlain academic economist to reply in that journal.[78] Hence when the so-called 'manifesto' was printed on 15 August its impact on readers of *The Times* had already been undermined, for Hewins had revealed that there were at least two academic sides to the question, and within the next few weeks there appeared numerous letters of dissent, including several from academic economists and others citing appropriate references from the works of notable British and foreign economists whose views were in conflict with the 'manifesto'.

Thus the division of opinion among the academic economists soon became public knowledge, and its significance was interpreted in a variety of ways – most of them unflattering. There were innumerable references to 'musty theorists', 'evangelists of a fossilized orthodoxy', and 'slaves to economic pedantry', while the appeal to immutable economic principles or laws was dismissed with the caustic observation that 'when a professor of political economy tries to teach us an eternal truth we may be certain that he is talking ancient nonsense'.[79] The most fashionable idiom of abuse was anti-clerical – and anti-Papist as contrasted with the anti-rabbinical references of the 'fair trade' controversy. The 'manifesto' was repeatedly described as an 'encyclical'; the economists were called 'priests' and their doctrines 'sacred dogma,' 'the Ten Commandments' or 'Sermon-on-the-Mount principles'.[80] Even so sober a critic as L.L. Price, the Oxford economist and historian, enriched this literature by his reference to free trade economists who propounded 'an *odium theologicum* which could discern no via media between economic salvation and damnation', and this view was unintentionally confirmed by the Bishop of Hereford who, after condemning the 'Birmingham Gospel' of tariff reform as sacrificing the needs of the poor to the vested interests of the rich, concluded that 'every Minister of Christ is bound to do his part in banishing and driving it away'.[81]

Probably more telling than these generalized anti-intellectual lunges were the more specific references to rival schools of economic thought. Chamberlain's opponents were frequently termed the 'old' or 'cosmopolitan' school, which was presumably meant to include the Ricardian economists and mid-nineteenth century supporters of Cobden and Bright – whereas the advocates of tariff reform were variously termed the 'new', 'modern', 'historical', 'imperial', 'nationalist' or 'young' school. The implication was, of course, that the free traders were outmoded, inflexible and dogmatic. However, a more significant division was that between British and foreign economists, for the public was reminded that

> there are economists abroad just as authoritative as any we have at home. . . . One of the saddest things about political economy is that what it declares absolute truth under one set of political ideas may be totally rejected by its professors living under a different political system. . . . It is a little odd that political economy, claiming to be a science, changes its complexion entirely when cultivated across the channel.[82]

Another obvious and popular line of attack was the contention that professors

305

were unrealistic and incompetent to judge practical policy questions. According to one Member of Parliament

> The rival schools of economists who represent the extreme abstract theories of free trade and protection could not be reconciled. They started on absolutely opposed premises and denoted differing first principles. Business men did not accept these extreme abstract theories on either side.[83]

and the Duke of Bedford, in a similar vein, doubtless expressed a widely held prejudice when he voiced his suspicions of

> the business capacity of the academic mind, which strains at the gnat of a shilling registration duty on corn and swallows the camel of State socialism. I prefer the ripe experience of men who are engaged in commercial life, or who have travelled and worked abroad, to the hard-and-fast rules of professors of political economy.[84]

Chamberlain himself, of course, did not hesitate to play on the prejudices of his audiences. Knowing that a majority of accredited teachers of economics were aligned against him he retorted that 'the working classes of this country, the business men of this country, they know where the shoe pinches much better than the political economists and the lawyers who profess to instruct them',[85] and as one of his supporters shrewdly observed,

> he will have to leave to other hands the task of defending his proposals from the economic point of view. But this will not trouble a man of his brilliant audacity and resourcefulness. It is not to political economy, or even to the facts of our past history, that Mr Chamberlain really wishes to appeal. He knows full well that the weight of the experts, the authorities in economics, is against him. So he turns his back upon a dreary science and a dead past, and looks for argument in the life, the prejudices, the passions of today.[86]

Faced with this challenge to their professional expertise, what reply could the academic economists offer? Pigou, though an inexperienced young don, provided the most explicit defence, insisting that

> economic science is not a subject in which persons, however eminent, can expect, without special training to negotiate an argument successfully. It is unpleasant, and may appear impertinent, to call attention to confusions of thought into which distinguished men have fallen. But if the public can be brought to see that even Dr Crozier and Sir Vincent Caillard find themselves 'in wandering mazes lost' when they set out on predatory excursions into the domain of economics, the conclusions of 'the man in the street' may perhaps assume a less wild and confident tone.

However, he went beyond this calm appraisal to poke fun at the numerous confident articles written by

> persons whose claim to distinction rests upon work done in fields other than that of economic science. In fact, it seems that a few distinguished men in various professions, perceiving that our financial specialists and Professors of Political Economy are either prejudiced or incompetent, have kindly consented to step down from their own loftier avocations and, with the swift insight of genius, to reveal the truth.[87]

Even so, Pigou was much more restrained than Edwin Cannan, who abandoned his academic detachment and expostulated

> to think that the principal member of the Government which has made capital less abundant . . . [by excessive spending] should be going about the country whining that the wicked foreigner has reduced our exports, makes my blood boil. I decline to take it lying down.[88]

Of course the economists faced a dilemma: if they held their peace, they could be accused of indifference, lack of courage, failure to grasp a golden opportunity to demonstrate the importance of their special knowledge, or neglecting their professional responsibility to society; whereas if they intervened they could be held guilty of transcending their pedagogical and scientific functions. It was difficult to decide when, and even more important, how to intervene in such a way as to influence the debate while preserving their academic dignity. Marshall subsequently regretted having signed the 'manifesto' and, despite his customary reserve and self-restraint, he was accused of addressing the layman in condescending terms;[89] W.J. Ashley, on the contrary, though praised as Chamberlain's most (even his sole) authoritative scholarly supporter, was accused of treating 'the average citizen as a philosopher, perceiving infallibly the true interest of the community, and going straight for that'.[90] In their efforts to impress the public some of the economic experts undoubtedly went to undignified lengths. A.L. Bowley, after stressing the need for skill and experience in the interpretation of statistics, boasted ten year's work on the trend of wage rates; Pigou tried to exploit the advantage of access to a privileged circle by saying 'nearly all economists would subscribe to a remark which one of the most distinguished of them once made in the presence of the writer, that any one who advocates Protection for England now does not know how Protection works'; while Goschen rejected academic economics for the sake of 'facts', declaring 'I have worked out these problems for myself. I have been a patient observer of commercial banking and trade affairs, and it is from that point of view I speak to you as a business man.'[91] But the palm should perhaps be accorded to William Smart, who held the Adam Smith Chair at Glasgow, for in the preface of his *Return to Protection* he sought the best of both worlds. Economic theory, he maintained, merited serious attention because it was 'the soul of facts', and after proudly declaring he had co-signed the 'manifesto' of the fourteen professors he also proceeded to claim special knowledge and experience of business, for 'I was a Free trade manufacturer in this country and a Protectionist manufacturer in the United States long before I became a teacher'.[92]

During the course of the debate every conceivable source of authoritative knowledge was drawn upon, with the inevitable consequence that all became suspect and no man's reputation stood unquestioned. The views of well known economic writers were cited *ad nauseam*: as in earlier public controversies *The Wealth of Nations* rendered conspicuous service to both sides, and Haldane communicated the growing boredom resulting from the endless parade of 'authorities' by remarking that 'in these days when everybody has studied everything it is of no avail to quote the economists from Adam Smith to Professor Marshall'.[93] Nor was the citation of sources free from hazards, for Chamberlain perpetrated a well publicized *faux pas* in quoting Joseph Shield Nicholson in support of his programme, only to have that outspoken professor flatly reject Chamberlain's interpretation of his writings and pronounce his disapproval of imperial preference.[94]

As we have seen, official statistics were soon shown to be an unreliable basis on which to judge the contending claims of free traders and fiscal reformers, and before long it became clear that rival versions of economic theory also had to be taken into account, especially with regard to the mobility of labour and the incidence of taxation. After citing Walter Bagehot's views that 'the transferability of labour' was one of the two fundamental postulates of ortho-dox political economy, a moderate academic tariff reformer like W.J. Ashley could conclude that 'the older writers minimised unduly the difficulty with which labour transfers itself from one industry to another, even a closely allied one',[95] but in Chamberlain's hands this qualified type of criticism became an effective political weapon against the free trade doctrine. In an oft-quoted passage from a speech at Greenock concerned with the harmful consequences of foreign trusts he reminded his audience that a House of Commons speaker had recently conceded that our primary industries might be doomed, but had claimed that we could find compensation in our subsidiary trades. Thus, Chamberlain went on,

> We are to lose the great industries for which this country has been celebrated, which have made it prosperous in the past. We are to deal with inferior and subsidiary industries. Sugar has gone. Let us not weep for it, jam and pickles remain! Now, of all these workmen, these intelligent artisans, who were engaged tending and making the machinery for sugar refining in this country, I would like to know how many have found a resting-place, have found equivalent wages and comfort, in stirring up jam-pots and bottling pickles.
>
> This doctrine, this favourite doctrine, of the 'transfer of labour' is a doctrine of pedants who know nothing of business, nothing of labour.

It is not true. . . . You cannot teach men who have attained to skill and efficiency in one trade, you cannot teach them on a moment's notice, skill and efficiency in another.[96]

This attempt to enlist the bogey of unemployment into the cause of tariff reform seems not to have been politically effective to judge by organized labour's reluctance to support the Chamberlain cause. However, it probably added another smear to the tarnished image of political economy, for the 'fourteen professors' had explicitly denied that a rise in imports brought a corresponding decline in home employment. *The Times* echoed Chamberlain's criticism of the 'foolish and pedantic arguments of the textbooks that, when an industry is destroyed, capital and labour can turn without loss to another', and the writings of Edgeworth, Price and Nicholson were cited in support of the view that workers displaced by foreign competition might remain unemployed.[97] Nevertheless, although Chamberlain reawakened a familiar old prejudice, the theoretical issue involved attracted far less attention than that of the incidence of taxation.

One of the main points of difference between Chamberlain and Balfour arose from the Prime Minister's unwillingness to support taxes on food – the so-called 'stomach taxes' – because he realized the extent of public hostility to such impositions. Chamberlain had accepted the Hicks-Beach corn duty as a basis for imperial preference and had claimed, after its repeal by Ritchie, that food taxes could be levied in such a way as to grant a worthwhile measure of preference to colonial produce without raising the home cost of living – indeed, actually lowering it, while the labourer would benefit from increased employment and higher wages. This claim met with a generally sceptical or hostile response. Goschen, with uncharacteristic bluntness denounced it as 'a gamble with the food of the people',[98] but it provoked a vigorous and protracted discussion of the theoretical and practical issues involved. As we have seen, Balfour's inner circle of advisers were deeply divided on the subject, and the public was baffled by what Hicks-Beach called the 'terrible conflict between the economists as to whether the duty is paid by the consumer or the producer'.[99] There were still some laymen who expected enlightenment from that quarter: in response to Nicholson's repudiation of Chamberlain's scheme J.M. Craggs wrote to *The Times* asking if 'eminent and skilled political economists would inform us what would most likely be the incidence of a wheat duty in the event of such a preferential scheme as Mr Chamberlain has suggested';[100] but if Pigou's reply to 'Tariff Reformer' (that is, L.S. Amery of *The Times*) is anything to go by, the average layman was unlikely to be any the wiser in consequence.[101] Pigou was, of course, quite right in drawing attention to the repercussions of a preferential duty on colonial and foreign output, as well as on home prices and living costs; but while acknowledging the impossibility of assessing the long run cost of implementing Chamberlain's proposals, because of the lack of information about the supply and demand conditions of most of the commodities involved, he nevertheless condemned the scheme on the grounds of its harmful effects on the redistribution of wealth.[102]

Such sophisticated attempts to explain the economic effects of Chamberlain's proposals were hardly likely to interest or convince the public, and various attempts were made to provide rule-of-thumb guides to the incidence of taxation. Sidgwick was quoted as saying that the foreigner pays a small tax whereas the home consumer pays a large one, while Chamberlain estimated, on the basis of several leading economic writers and 'one of the highest authorities of this country, one of the highest of the official experts whom the government consult', that if the foreigner supplied three quarters of the consumption he would pay three quarters of the tax.[103] One writer made a promising and surprisingly mid-twentieth century sounding distinction between the static 'revenue taxes' favoured by free traders and the dynamic 'development taxes' advocated by the tariff reformers,[104] but did not attempt to elaborate the analytical possibilities inherent in it; indeed, on the whole the level of sophistication in the non-specialist publications was extremely low, and the tariff reformers' attitude was neatly epitomized in the remark that 'England expects that every foreigner will pay his duty'.[105] In a sense, the establishment of the Tariff Commission was a confession of failure to solve the problem of tax incidence, for one of its primary functions was to devise a 'scientific tariff' which would not

> add one farthing to the burden of any taxpayer, but which by the transference of taxation from one shoulder to another, and from the shoulders to the back, may not only produce the same amount of revenue which will always be necessary for our home exports, but may incidentally do something to develop and extend our trade.

As the editor of the *National Review* remarked, by way of a footnote to his endorsement of this ideal, 'Mr Chamberlain refused to accept the pessimistic view that our scientific economists and our manufacturers were unable to do what every other country and British Colony had been able to do'.[106]

V

What conclusions can be drawn from this extensive, but by no means exhaustive survey of the economic issues in the tariff reform controversy of 1903? What was the contribution of the economic experts, whether academic or otherwise, and what influence, if any, did they exert? And what was the effect of the economists' involvement in this public controversy on the economics profession itself?

There was certainly no lack of interest in economic questions: and the economists had innumerable opportunities to be heard on public platforms, in Parliament, in the press, in a wide variety of general and specialist periodicals, and in pamphlets and books; and despite the volume of scorn and abuse levelled at political economy it is clear that at least some members of the public were willing and eager to listen. Thus in many ways the circumstances were propitious. How successfully did the economists seize their opportunity?

Unfortunately there are no simple criteria by which to assess the role of economic ideas in the making of public policy. Economic policy is never purely economic, and in this case, even more than most, political, diplomatic and strategic factors were preponderant.[107] Admittedly the Prime Minister saw fit to consult economic experts before committing himself to a declaration of policy; but both he and his opponents were acutely conscious of the political implications of his position; and although at first sight the differences between the main protagonists appeared to turn upon the finer points of economic theory, it should be remembered that the lines of battle between the free traders and their critics had been firmly drawn during the 'fair trade' discussions of the two preceding decades. Chamberlain's campaign undoubtedly aroused great public excitement; and it was more than a nine day wonder, for it helped to shape the course of domestic politics throughout the dramatic decade of constitutional and international crises that preceded World War I. Nevertheless, there is no reason to question the accepted view that despite Chamberlain's outstanding gifts of oratory and political leadership, he was unable to shake the British public's deep-rooted faith in the free trade policy to which it had clung ever since the Repeal of the Corn Laws in 1846.[108]

But while this re-examination of the role of economic ideas in the tariff reform debate may not have necessitated any drastic re-interpretation of the period, it nevertheless sheds considerable light on the history of British economic thought and on the relations between economic ideas and policy. Despite the undeniable importance of the economic and statistical issues at stake, it is clear that the public, as always, wanted simple solutions to complex problems – solutions of a kind which the economists were unable or unwilling to give. For at least a decade the main trend of British economics had been away from the dogmatic simple-minded doctrines of the mid-Victorian era towards a more cautious and qualified statement of principles and their applications.[109] Moreover, the leading economists were anxious to minimize the divisions within the academic ranks, whether on questions of method, theory or policy; and yet the events of 1903 swept them along in a whirl of controversy which, on the whole, seemed likely to diminish rather than to enhance the prestige of their discipline.

In this respect, the so-called 'manifesto' to *The Times* was a key incident, which deserves more attention from historians of economics than it has hitherto received. One need not accept Leo Amery's opinion that this 'over-whelming barrage of the heaviest artillery' had a 'shattering effect on the morale of Chamberlain's supporters and, still more, on the great majority who were still undecided', for this might entail acceptance of his exaggerated judgement of the effectiveness of his own 'counterblast', written under the pseudonym 'Tariff Reformer', which, he contended, so successfully ridiculed the manifesto that 'in subsequent controversy a reference to the fourteen professors only evoked hilarity'.[110] Hilarity and ridicule there certainly was; and both Balfour and Chamberlain made effective platform use of jibes against academic pedantry and the 'orthodox' economists' dogmatic resistance to change; but it would be pointless to try to weigh this type of popular denigration against the many deferential obeisances to professorial opinion in the writings of those who defended the status quo.

But while the public's response to the 'manifesto' was mixed, there is less reason to doubt the effect of the incident on the economists themselves. Indeed, for some it was apparently a traumatic experience. Admittedly there were those who boldly reiterated their support for it with a defiant touch of professional loyalty;[111] but the leading representative of the signatories, Alfred Marshall – who, despite his unwavering advocacy of free trade, had never been enthusiastic about the manifesto – openly declared a year later his objections 'to all manifestos by economists on political questions', although he added that 'the only fault he had to find with it was that there were one or two sentences which seemed to be constructive, and there was no room for construction in so short a document'.[112] According to Foxwell who was among those who had repudiated the 'manifesto', James Bonar had 'induced Marshall, against M.'s better judgement, and after M. had twice refused, to sign the Professors' Manifesto. It was just because he felt that his signature was a blunder that he was so angry with me for attacking it'; and Foxwell considered that

the Manifesto has had the effect which so many of us foresaw at the time of putting economists out of court altogether. We are now hopelessly discredited: in fact political economy seems to me to have fallen back in public opinion to the position it held about the 70s. I hoped that the more realistic and liberal tone of the work of the last generation would have gained for English economists something of the respect which German economists enjoy in the world of affairs. However the mischief is done and silence is now the most fitting attitude for a 'professor'.[113]

No doubt Foxwell somewhat overstated the case; but Marshall's own reaction was similar, for he confided to the German economist, Lujo Brentano, that in view of the public reaction to the manifesto the best thing for the signatories to do was 'to lie low, and bend our backs to the smiters';[114] and this chastening mood was reinforced the following year by no less a person than the Prime Minister who, in his capacity as Vice President of the Royal Economic Society, warned the assembled company that

If a man of science once lets the public think that he is speaking not in the interests of his science, but in the interests of his party, if he once allows the view to get abroad that his expression of opinion may have its origin in his scientific views, but has a double parentage, and that the scientific views are in some sense moulded in conformity with our political differences, his whole authority from that moment will absolutely vanish; he will sink to the level of the unfortunate person who now addresses you. Let him at all costs avoid that danger. (Laughter.)[115]

Whatever Balfour's motives in making these remarks, his conclusions were shared by several of the leading academic economists, especially the older men.[116] Marshall, for instance, had refused to reply to Hewins' articles in *The Times* partly because of the mixture of economics and politics involved, explaining:

> For that work the better class of newspapers and members of Parliament are better fitted than economists of the chair, who make it a duty to bring out arguments which tell against their ultimate conclusion, as faithfully as those which tell for it. . . . I feel that Chamberlain needs to be combated by rough and – to speak frankly – more crude and unscientific arguments and methods than I have either the taste or the faculty for.[117]

Those economists who were less cautious than Marshall, and decided to take an active part in the controversy, were nevertheless fully aware of the possible implications for their academic reputations, as is shown by Sidney Chapman's excellent letter to *The Times*, to cite but one instance.[118] Chamberlain's supporters were equally sensitive to this problem. W.J. Ashley, for example, who became known as Chamberlain's chief professorial defender, took comparatively little part in the popular debate, though he wrote *The Tariff Problem* at Chamberlain's suggestion,[119] a book that became widely regarded as the best statement of the anti-free trade case. Yet he felt uneasy at being described by a fellow Liberal, John Morley, as 'this excellent writer, who lives very near to the centre of authority, very near to Mecca',[120] and he felt impelled to defend himself both in public and in private. He wrote to assure Morley

> less formally that there has been no sort of conference between Mr Chamberlain and myself. He can't be held responsible for anything I may have said; and I am not responsible for anything he may have said – except in the sense that he may have read my book with others. Until very recently I have had no conversation at all with him on Economic matters. My book was written entirely of my own motion, and without the slightest inspiration direct or indirect.
>
> I want to make this clear because I realized at once, when the issue

was raised, that for a Professor in the University of Birmingham to write on the subject was to expose himself to grave misrepresentation. I am thankful that the leading Liberal organs have not doubted my scientific independence; but some of them have attributed an influence which I have no reason at all to suppose I have ever exercised. It was a mere accident which brought me, on my return to England, to Birmingham. I might just as well have gone to Manchester; and there the Manifesto of the Fourteen Economists would have forced my little book out of me just the same.

Mr Chamberlain has realized the dangers of my position; and careful as he has always been not to interfere with academic independence here, he has been most delicately careful not to influence in any way my opinions or actions as an Economist.

The situation is so difficult; there is so much need for criticism and thought all round; and the movement of affairs is the result of the co-operation of so many forces, that you will believe me sincere when I sign myself with great respect and regard,

Truly yours.[121]

There is no evidence that Ashley experienced any restriction of his academic freedom as a result of his association with Chamberlain; but if his position was delicate, it was much less so than that of Hewins at the London School of Economics, an institution whose Fabian origins had already made it the object of both public and private criticism. The Fabians were seriously split on the tariff reform question, and although there were certain obvious advantages in having a Tory imperialist as Director of a supposedly socialist institution, Sidney Webb, who was much less sympathetic to Chamberlain's policies than his wife Beatrice, feared that Hewins' active involvement might embarrass the School. At the end of May he expressed the hope that Hewins would not become an active partisan, and this helps to explain why Hewins' articles in *The Times* were signed 'An Economist', despite the endeavours of some Chamberlainites to persuade him to lend the weight of his academic authority to the cause. In his diary, Hewins expressed his 'contempt' for Fabianism, and referred disparagingly to Sidney Webb as 'a born little Englander', explaining that he had first become seriously interested in lecturing on the history of commercial policy as part of his effort 'to bring into prominence the commercial and practical side of the School work . . . with the view of winning the support of the business world . . . with the outbreak of the South African war I went openly on to his [that is, Chamberlain's] side and not only advocated wherever I could an Imperialist policy but identified it with Mr Chamberlain'. Even so, Hewins did not welcome the tariff reform campaign, preferring that the 'commercial revolution' resulting from the adoption of an Imperial policy 'should be carried as far as possible by purely administrative methods and that any violent breach with Free Trade should if possible be avoided, and the beneficial results of that policy as distinguished from those of a mischievous character safeguarded'. But this, he acknowledged, was 'an academic view' and, like Ashley, though more willingly, he became caught in the tide of events.[122] Despite his cloak of anonymity, his position became more and more difficult and a few months later he recalled that 'even before I left the School of Economics it was becoming practically impossible for me to give any lectures for the simple reason that the most ordinary common place observations which I had been accustomed to make for ten years had suddenly assumed a controversial importance'.[123] When the Tariff Commission was first proposed in November, Chamberlain hoped that Hewins would be able to combine his secretaryship with his existing post, but Hewins was able to persuade him that the two were incompatible, and accordingly he severed his academic connections.[124]

Not only is it likely that the tariff reform controversy damaged the public reputation of political economy; it also seems clear that the dispute reopened earlier divisions within the economists' ranks which had been patched over since the methodological armistice of the early 1890s.[125] As was generally recognized at the time, the economic historians and the advocates of historical method (especially Ashley, Cunningham, Foxwell, Hewins, Mavor[126] and Price) were, in varying degrees, sympathetic to Chamberlain and opposed to the 'manifesto', whereas those who either signed or publicly endorsed it were, by and large, exponents or defenders of 'orthodox' abstract economic theory.[127] The reasons for this were various, including differences of temperament, doctrine and method; but on the whole the 'historicists' were more pro-German, and therefore sympathetic to German tariff and social reform policy, as well as to the historical school of economics;[128] they were less inhibited by theoretical objections to a retreat from free trade; and they were more sensitive to the process of historical change, and accordingly susceptible to the idea that new circumstances demanded the modification or abandonment of traditional policy.[129]

Divisive and acrimonious tones crept into the economists' debate, even in the pages of the two leading professional periodicals, the *Economic Journal* and *Economic Review*,[130] and there is no reason to suppose that the effects were transitory, if only because tariff reform remained the subject of active public interest for a decade. Indeed, there is reason to believe that the events of 1903 may have directly influenced the choice of Pigou as successor to Marshall at Cambridge in 1908, a decision that ensured the pre-eminence of economic theory at the leading academic centre of British economics. The evidence is, inevitably, only circumstantial and indirect; but Foxwell, the chief Cambridge contender and the most bitterly disappointed candidate, always believed that his rejection of the free trade doctrine had counted decisively against him.[131] Marshall was said to have actively canvassed on Pigou's behalf, and there is abundant evidence that he strongly disagreed with the views of those

315

economists who actively supported Chamberlain, as the following hitherto unpublished letter to Hewins demonstrates.

> I must not let you remain under the impression that there is 'not any substantial difference of opinion between us on the economic question'. I have no time for controversy, and least of all controversy by post. So I indicated, or tried to indicate, my differences as mildly as possible. But misconceptions in such a case are to be avoided. And so I trust you will forgive me if I state bluntly and categorically that I dissent from your economic arguments, and even from your statements as to fact, to an extent which I had not anticipated in the very least.
>
> If I really thought that there was any danger that the scheme which you advocate would be put into practice, I should feel bound to break through my rule against taking active part in the discussions of the market place . . . [A preferential duty on wheat, by itself, would do no harm; but] whatever your original intentions, you seem to me to have been entangled in the meshes of a very articulate body of Protectionists. Your position – in the same way though not to the same extent as those of Chamberlain himself – seem to me incapable of being maintained – permanently, and worked out to their logical consequences, without resulting in Protection of the most malignant kind, to which I understand that you, if not he, are truly opposed.

Marshall admitted that German protectionists approved of Chamberlain's scheme. 'But most of the intelligent Germans whom I meet agree that free trade is the only policy which really suits England. And the same is true of Americans and others.' Moreover, Chamberlain's scheme would lead to friction with the Colonies and would estrange the US.[132]

L.L. Price vividly described Marshall's reaction to his criticism of the 'manifesto' and pointedly referred to Pigou's determined partisanship on behalf of free trade, and to his almost 'filial respect' for Marshall's utterances,[133] while Edgeworth, a free trader who was certainly an influential elector, praised Pigou's theoretical contributions to the debate in eulogistic terms.[134]

Direct evidence that echoes of 1903 were still being heard five years later, and that Pigou and his rivals were still being judged by those actively involved in the tariff reform controversy, is afforded by an exchange of letters between Hewins and Balfour, one of the Cambridge electors. Shortly before the election Balfour wrote:

> I am on the Cambridge Board which elects Marshall's successor. I was appointed to it years ago – long before the fiscal question was thought of. I wrote to the Vice-Chancellor, and said that, in existing circumstances, I was too much mixed up with the economic controversy in its party aspect to make it altogether fitting that I should take part in the Election

on Saturday. The Vice-Chancellor has replied by asking me privately
for my opinion upon the three Candidates. I have dictated the enclosed
letter, which really is the best I can do. If you have any comments to
make upon it, I shall be delighted to hear them. The letter must go off
by today's post.

Of course this is *very confidential*.[135]

Hewins' reply, in which he evaluated the respective claims of Pigou, Ashley
and Foxwell, is in the Balfour papers:

I have the highest opinion of all three candidates; I do not think that
any of them will do much for Cambridge economics; but of the three
I shd appoint Foxwell.

Pigou may become a great economist. I understand that he is a man
of unusual ability. He has not so impressed me. He has not read widely
enough, or handled enough materials or had sufficient experience, to
give the proper finish to his work, which always strikes me as being
clever but crude and ill prepared. He wd. gain by waiting for a few
years before he occupies a position in wh. he wd. constantly be called
upon for his opinion (and be bound to express it) on subjects he knows
nothing about.

Ashley is by far the ablest and best equipped of the three and has
done most original work. Since he went to Birmingham he has been
much taken up with the organisation of the Commercial faculty there.
At the time when his scheme was drafted I did not think it good
educationally or fitted for the Birmingham University. I have not seen
any recent evidence of its success or failure, I doubt whether Ashley
wd. work well with the Cambridge History Tutors, or the Historical
Tripos; and the Economic Scheme is scarcely on his lines. But my
experience is not recent. I shd. feel that Ashley's case required very
careful consideration before I appointed him.

Foxwell wd. be a very safe appointment and in the circumstances
wd. probably meet with widespread approval.[136]

As it transpired, Pigou was elected two days later, and Foxwell apparently
considered that Balfour had let him down by failing to attend, for he had
supported his application for the Chair of Commerce at Birmingham, in
1901.[137] Is it, then, too much to suggest that but for the tariff reform debate
of 1903 the election of 1908 might have gone differently, and that it would
not have ensued that, for the next twenty years, under Pigou's leadership
'theoretical economics in England consisted very largely of the discussion
and interpretation, often textual, of Marshall's *Principles*?'[138]

Obviously no general conclusions about the influence of economic ideas
on policy can be drawn from a single example, however interesting and
important it may be. But the tariff reform controversy of 1903 illustrates

317

the difficulties encountered by economists when they participate in public controversy, even in cases where the public is appealing for help, and where some of the principal issues at stake clearly fall within their sphere of competence. In a sense there is no such thing as economic policy *per se*: all policies involve non-economic issues and possess implications that transcend the economist's special province, though this does not mean that he should hold himself aloof, for he has responsibilities both as an expert and a citizen. In the case we have examined, it seems doubtful whether the economists' intervention raised the quality of the debate, and it certainly appears to have diminished their prestige in the eyes of the public. Moreover, it deepened existing divisions among the economists both within and outside the academic community, and the animosities aroused or strengthened by their conspicuous disagreements undoubtedly weakened their professional *esprit de corps*. Indeed, one of the general lessons to be drawn from this example is that such quasi-political activities pose a threat to the economics profession; but one suspects that few economists would conclude that this is too high a price to be paid for the opportunity of shaping policy.

NOTES

1   Kenneth Young, *Arthur James Balfour* (London: G. Bell, 1963), p.213.
2   Joseph Dorfman, *The Economic Mind in American Civilization* (New York: Viking Press, 1949), vol.3, p.228.
3   The ground had, however, been so well prepared 'that in the end Joseph Chamberlain had merely to put himself at the head of a sizeable following which had long been seeking a leader of his stature and had in fact singled him out as the likely candidate'. Benjamin H. Brown, *The Tariff Reform Movement in Great Britain 1881–1895* (New York: Columbia University Press, 1943), p.1.
4   Chamberlain and Balfour were under the impression that the Cabinet had provisionally agreed in November 1902 to support the corn tax but with a preferential remission in favour of the British Empire. Blanche Dugdale, 1 *Arthur James Balfour* (London: Hutchinson, 1936), vol.1 p.340. Cf. Julian Amery, 4 *The Life of Joseph Chamberlain* (London: Macmillan, 1951), vol.4, p.527; idem., Joseph Chamberlain and the Tariff Reform Campaign. *The Life of Joseph Chamberlain*, vol.5 1901–1903 (London: Macmillan, 1969) pp.154–6, 158–9. I am most grateful to Mr Amery for allowing me to see the proofs of this volume, in advance of publication, and the Chamberlain papers in his possession.
5   See *The Times*, 16 May 1903, p.8, col.4.
6   Alfred Gollin's recent book *Balfour's Burden* (London: Anthony Bland, 1965), contains an excellent account of the political background to the tariff reform debate. See also Peter Fraser, *Joseph Chamberlain* (London: Cassell, 1966), chs. 10–11 and Sydney H. Zebel, 'Joseph Chamberlain and the Genesis of Tariff Reform', *J. British Studies* 7 (Nov. 1967), pp.131–57.
7   In addition to Ritchie and Chamberlain, Sir George Hamilton, Secretary of State for India, Lord Balfour of Burleigh, Secretary of State for Scotland and Sir Arthur Elliott, Financial Secretary to the Treasury, also resigned. Some witty observers suggested that Balfour and Chamberlain had arranged a 'collusive

divorce', and when Austen Chamberlain, Joseph's son, was appointed as Ritchie's successor at the Treasury, Lord Rosebery asked whether he was 'a hostage or a scout'.

8 Cited by Burrell, 'Mr Balfour, The Fiscal Problem and England's Fate', 161 *Westminster Rev.* (1904), pp.161, 162, from Arthur James Balfour's *Economic Notes on Insular Free Trade* (1903) 1. Balfour informed Lord Knollys, the King's Private Secretary, that Asquith had said 'in private conversation that, whether we like it or not, they – the opposition – meant to dub us Protectionists as a Government, and to fight under the banner Free Trade versus Protection'. *Royal Archives* (R.A.) R. 24, 51, 31 Dec. 1903. See also Gerald Balfour, 129 *Parl. Debate* (1904) (4th ser.) pp.656–7.

9 Twenty years later, speaking of his *Economic Notes on Insular Free Trade*, Balfour recalled: 'The Duke never read it, you know. I remember hearing he had confessed to somebody that he tried, but couldn't understand it. Dear Devonshire! Of course he hadn't. He told me once that he had been content to leave his financial conscience in the hands of Mr Gladstone. But it was all a muddle. He got himself into such a position that he had to behave badly to somebody – and there it was! But it never made the slightest difference to my love for him.' 1 Blanche Dugdale, op.cit, vol.1 pp.360–1.

10 Coats, 'The Role of Authority in the Development of British Economics', *J. Law and Econ.* 7 (1964), pp.85, 99–103. To be reprinted in vol.II of this series.

11 Winston Churchill, *Thoughts and Adventures* (London: Thornton Butterworth, 1932), p.55. Mowat 'represented the complete triumphant Victorian view of economics and finance; strict parsimony; exact accounting; free imports whatever the rest of the world might do; suave, steady government; no wars; no flag waving; just paying off debt and reducing taxation and keeping out of scrapes; and for the rest – for trade, industry, agriculture, social life – *laissez-faire* and *laissez-aller* . . .

'Tall, spare, with a noble brow, a bright eye and strong jaws, this faithful servant of the Crown, self-effacing, but self-respecting, resolute, convinced, sure of himself, sure of his theme, dwelt modestly and frugally for nearly fifty years at or near the centre of the British governing machine. Governments, Liberal or Tory, came and went. He served them all with equal fidelity, cherishing his Gladstonian sentiment as a purely private affair.' ibid., p.54. But evidently he broke the habits of a lifetime after Ritchie's resignation, and resigned himself on 30 September 1903. W.A.S. Hewins described Ritchie as 'an instrument of other people more important than himself. He was called upon by circumstances to take part in a controversy, the significance of which he did not understand'. 1 W.A.S. Hewins, *The Apologia of an Imperialist, Forty Years of Empire Policy* (London: Constable, 1929), p.63, n.1. It appears that Marshall's *Memorandum on Fiscal Policy of International Trade* (reprinted in *Official Papers by Alfred Marshall*, 365, J.M. Keynes Ed., London: Macmillan, 1926) was originally drafted in July 1903 at Ritchie's request. Cf. McCready, 'Alfred Marshall and Tariff Reform', *J. Pol. Econ.* 63, (1955), pp.259, 263, 267 n.21.

12 1 Blanche Dugdale, op.cit. at p.346. See also the revealing letter from Mowat to Ritchie quoted by Alfred Gollin, op.cit. note 6 at pp.49–50.

13 J.L. Garvin, 'The Economics of the Empire', *Nat'l Rev. Spec. Supp.* 42 (Oct. 1903) p.156. There is, however, no truth in the report that Chamberlain was unable to obtain help from the Civil Service. Like Balfour, he was in touch with such Customs Board Officers as Sir George Ryder (who later, for a short time, joined the Tariff Commission) and Sir Thomas Pittar, and he received important memoranda from the Board of Trade. For evidence of his use of

this assistance see letter from Gerald Balfour to Joseph Chamberlain, 7 May 1903; letter from Duke of Devonshire to Joseph Chamberlain, 23 Aug. 1903 and Joseph Chamberlain's detailed reply of 25 Aug. 1903. Quoted by Amery, op.cit., in vol.5 pp.372–4. Unfortunately there is no collection of these memoranda in the Chamberlain papers, as in the Balfour papers.

14 See Bertrand Russell, *Portraits from Memory and Other Essays* (London: Allen & Unwin, 1956), p.76. Chamberlain himself, perhaps over-generously, acknowledged the influence of Sir Vincent Caillard's articles published in 1902 in the *National Review*. Cf. Amery, op.cit. vol.5. p.218.

15 W.A.S. Hewins, op.cit., vol.1 p.68. Mowat was reported as being 'very much struck by the extraordinary ignorance certain ministers have displayed upon the very basis of economic theory. It was a revelation to Chamberlain that goods exported were not paid for in cash, and another seemed equally surprised to be told, when he drew the line at the taxation of raw materials, that the food of the people was raw material at its rawest and most absolute form, being the very substance out of which the brain and sinew of the worker have to be evolved.' Almeric Fitzroy, *Memoirs* (London: Hutchinson, no date), vol.1 p.144.

16 In W.A.S. Hewins papers, now at the University of Sheffield Library. J.L. Garvin and Leo Maxse formed part of what Mr Amery terms Chamberlain's 'Brains trust'. Though both were primarily journalists rather than economists, there are some long and abstruse letters on economic and statistical matters from Garvin in the Chamberlain papers.

17 Letter from Joseph Chamberlain to W.A.S. Hewins, 12 Oct. 1903, in Hewins papers. Cf. letter from Joseph Chamberlain to W.J. Ashley, 26 Oct. 1905, in Chamberlain papers.

18 Letter from Duke of Devonshire to Joseph Chamberlain, 13 July 1903, in Chamberlain papers. The first two paragraphs were included in a letter from Joseph Chamberlain to W.A.S. Hewins, 14 July 1903, in Hewins papers, which began with the following appeal for help:

Is it more advantageous for a country that its imports should be paid for by corresponding exports of the goods which it is able to produce, or that they should be paid for by the interest on its investments in the countries with which it is dealing?

and secondly, what is the effect of payment for imports by interest on securities? Is it not the effect that such payment does not promote employment of labour, and that, therefore, although the *wealth* of the country so paid may not be less in the aggregate, the national health will be worse in the sense that it will tend to cease being a manufacturing and producing nation and will become instead a nation of consumers, chiefly rich men and their dependents.

After the quotation from Devonshire he concluded:

Surely this is false reasoning, but I cannot be quite certain what political economy has to say in such a case, and should be very much obliged if you would help me.

For evidence that he had still not resolved this problem eighteen months later see letter from Joseph Chamberlain to W.J. Ashley, 6 Dec. 1904, in Chamberlain papers.

19 Letter from Joseph Chamberlain to Duke of Devonshire, 25 July 1903, in Devonshire papers, Chatsworth, Derbyshire. Quoted by Julian Amery, op.cit., vol.5, p.364.

20 W.A.S. Hewins, op.cit., vol.1 at p.73. On Chamberlain's use of statistics see his exchanges with Giffen, see note 71 below.

21 *The Times*, 13 July 1903, at p.8, col.1. There was only figurative truth in the report from the House of Commons Lobby that Balfour's 'frequent absences from the front bench during the debates ... were due to the fact that he was engaged in his room, behind the Speaker's chair, in reading up a pile of elementary books on Political Economy, with the object of equipping himself for a discussion and a decision in the Cabinet on the momentous questions raised so unexpectedly by his colleague, Mr Chamberlain'. Lefevre, 'Mr Balfour and Retaliation', *Fortnightly Rev.*74 (1903), p.941.

22 Arthur James Balfour was the brother-in-law of Henry Sidgwick, of whom Leslie Stephen once complained, 'A man has no right to be so fair to his opponents'. Cf. Noel Annan, *Leslie Stephen, His Thought and Character in Relation to his Time* (London: McGibbon & Kee, 1951), p.206.

23 The Balfour papers contain two letters from Foxwell, one conveying a full account of his reactions to the economists' manifesto of 15 August, the other some hasty and incomplete preliminary reactions to the draft. In the latter, which is undated, Foxwell observed:

As far as I can see, there will be no room for criticism, but some additional points may suggest themselves. . . .
   I find myself in absolute agreement with your concluding paragraph and have been so for twenty years past. . . .
   My difficulty in this matter is not with principles, but with their application to the particular circumstances of time and place. . . .
   Thus in 1840, when a strong tide of first class emigration was leaving Europe, a well arranged policy of Colonial preference might have altered the political centre of gravity of North America. Today, when that stream has nearly run dry, it is doubtful whether the game would be worth the candle. . . .
   As I read economic history, we abandoned Colonial preference just when it would have been worth while to have sacrificed anything for it. . . .
   The other principle of reserving the right to defend our trade interests by whatever policy promises at the time to be most effective, seems to me true of all times and places, and as nearly universal in its validity as any economic principle can be.
   Letter from Herbert Somerton Foxwell to Arthur Balfour, undated, B.M. (British Museum) Add. Mss. 49855.

Among other Cambridge 'economists' preparing statistical data for the Board of Trade were C.P. Sanger and W.T. Layton. Cf. Lord Layton, *Dorothy*, (London: Collins, 1961), pp.29–30.

24 B.M. Add. Mss. 49870 (Balfour Papers). The quotations are from Ashley's submissions of 4 July 1903 and 5 Aug. 1903. Italics in original. For Charles Booth's views, which were received with enthusiasm by Chamberlain's supporters and shocked disapproval by his opponents, see his article, 'Fiscal Reform', *Nat'l Rev.*42 (1904) p.686. Booth considered that a small rise in the cost of living would be more than compensated by the increase in employment consequent upon fiscal reform. Booth subsequently became a member of Chamberlain's Tariff Commission and was regarded by its opponents as the only reputable figure on it.

25 B.M. Add. Mss. 49870 (Balfour Papers), dated 13 July 1903, and signed by G.L.R., J.A.K., T.J.P. (that is, Sir George L. Ryder, John Arrow Kempe and Sir Thomas J. Pittar). This was a supplement to a memorandum of 4 July 1903 entitled 'Mr Chamberlain's Scheme of Preferential and Protective Duties' in which the aim was to raise revenue. Slightly different levels of duty

were proposed in the two cases. The earlier memorandum was designed to 'carefully avoid any material increase of the prices of the necessities of life in this country, and any artificial development of industries which would inevitably be extinguished as soon as a change of policy is adopted, and any system of continual bargaining and contention between the Mother Country, her Colonies and the Foreigner, with its consequent unending disturbance of our Tariff, which would be absolutely intolerable to Traders'. Their proposals would entail an 'intrinsically slight, but relatively considerable differentiation between duties which are very light in either case' and would 'stimulate competition, not check importation, and will not give offence to foreign countries, all of whom favour their own colonies if they have any'.

26 B.M. Add. Mss. 49870 (Balfour Papers) 6 June 1903 signed by Entt (?). I have been unable to identify the signatory.

27 B.M. Add. Mss. 49870 (Balfour Papers). The immediately preceding sentence reads: 'It comes, then, to this – the foreign articles we must tax, in order to give the Colonies a "pull", are articles of food, and it must be an appreciable tax in order to raise a sum worth raising and in order to give the Colonies a preference worth having.'

An earlier memorandum signed by Entt, on 'The Corn Duty', dated 14 May 1903 gave arguments justifying Ritchie's abandonment of the duty in his April Budget.

28 Austen Chamberlain, *Politics From Inside* (London, 1936), p.31.

29 B.M. Add. Mss. 49770 (Balfour Papers). Letter from Arthur James Balfour to Duke of Devonshire, 30 July 1903. Italics in original.

30 Arthur James Balfour, *Economic Notes on Insular Free Trade* (London: Longmans, 1903), pp.9, 24. Italics in original.

31 R.A. 23 84. Letter from Arthur James Balfour to the King, 15 Sept. 1903. This was written at the height of the Cabinet crisis. A more complete, but slightly different version appears in 1 Blanche Dugdale, op.cit., vol.1, pp.353–5.

32 B.M. Add. Mss. 49770 (Balfour Papers). Letter from Duke of Devonshire to Arthur James Balfour, 15 Sept. 1903. Ritchie complained that Balfour was asking for a 'blank cheque' while Asquith, for the opposition demanded to know how the government would use its 'fiscal liberty', and Haldane privately warned that 'it is easy to put modified protection into a nutshell, but much more difficult to keep it there', Cf. B.M. Add. Mss. 49724 (Balfour Papers). Letter from Richard Burton Haldane to Arthur James Balfour, 20 Sept. 1903.

33 B.M. Add. Mss. 49770. Letter from Duke of Devonshire to Arthur James Balfour, 9 Sept. 1903. On the same day, he wrote a very similar letter to Ritchie, adding 'I cannot see myself defending either in the House of Lords or elsewhere the kind of compromise to which we are asked to consent, and I am afraid therefore that there is no alternative to the disruption of the Government'. Letter from Duke of Devonshire to Charles T. Ritchie, 9 Sept. 1903. See the Ritchie papers, in the National Register of Archives. For confirmation of the Duke's prediction about the trend of the debate, see Nicholson, 'Book Review', *Econ. Journal* 14 (1904), p.61.

34 Letter from Duke of Devonshire to Leonard Courtney, 3 Jan. 1904. Reprinted in George Peabody Gooch, *Life of Lord Courtney* (London: Macmillan, 1920), p.485.

35 For example, both Balfour and Chamberlain claimed to be free traders, but 'free trade' was subdivided and qualified by various spokesmen into: 'insular' or 'one-sided' versus 'cosmopolitan' or 'ideal' free trade; 'free imports'; 'free food'

etc. One enquirer asked whether the Unionist Free Food League proposed to give food away free of charge, and their position was in principle compatible with preferential or protectionist treatment of non-food imports. See the report of the Tariff Reform League's Executive Committee, in *The Times*, 30 July 1903, at p.9, Col.6.

36 Editorial [L.J. Maxse], 'Episodes of the Month', *Nat'l Rev*.42 (1903), p.514. Beach, it will be recalled, had imposed the corn duty in his 1902 budget; he subsequently supported its repeal in 1903, criticized Balfour's and Chamberlain's schemes, and then appeared at a banquet with Balfour in his constituency and pledged support for the Prime Minister. Lord George Hamilton, who resigned with Ritchie, subsequently became a scathing critic of the Manchester School and doctrinaire free trade. See Lord George Francis Hamilton, *Parliamentary Reminiscences and Reflections* (London: John Murray), vol.1, pp.327–31; *idem.*, vol.2 pp.318–25, 329 (1917).

37 Lord Rosebery at Sheffield, reported in *The Times*, 14 Oct. 1903, at p.5, col.6. See also Cadogan's advice to his tenants, *The Times*, 19 Oct., 1903, at p.7, col.1.

38 131 Parl. Deb. (4th ser.) (1904) p.689; 129 Parl. Deb. (4th ser.) (1904) p.1442.

39 'Mr Speaker, I always regret the manner in which political economy is treated in this House and on public platforms. It is not treated as a science, or as a subject which people ought to approach impartially with a view to discovering what the truth is, either from theory or experience. Not at all. They find some formula in a book of authority and throw it at their opponents' heads. They bandy the old watchwords backwards and forwards, they rouse old bitternesses, wholly alien, as far as I can see, to any modern question, and our controversies are apt to alternate between outworn formulae imperfectly remembered, and modern doctrines imperfectly understood. That is not a fortunate state of things, and I should hope that one result of my honourable friends' speech and of the debate today will be that the country will devote itself, not in a partisan spirit, to the consideration of the real economic position in which we stand, and the real difficulties we have to face now and in the immediate future, and the best way of meeting these difficulties. . . . It is a question of our future fiscal policy, which requires a most careful study on its strictly scientific and economic side, and a most careful study on what I might call its Imperial and social side.' 123 Parl. Deb. (4th ser.) (1903) p.163.

40 See the ensuing discussion in the correspondence columns of *The Times*; and also my article, 'The Role of Authority in the Development of British Economics', *J. Law & Econ.* (1964), p.85. To be reprinted in vol.II of this series.

41 B.M. Add. Mss. 49855 (Balfour Papers). Letter from Herbert S. Foxwell to Arthur James Balfour, 17 Aug. 1903. Foxwell's remarks tend to confirm Alfred Emmott's contention that 'Political economy . . . is not an exact science, it is sometimes as opportunist as theology or even politics.' *The Times*, 15 June 1903, at p.12, col.5. See also Balfour's warning against political bias in his address to the Royal Economic Society, see note 115 below.

Chamberlain probably learned from Hewins of the proposed counter-manifesto which, in fact, never materialized. Cf. letter from Joseph Chamberlain to W.J. Ashley, 19 Aug. 1903, cited in Amery, op.cit., vol.5, pp.292–3.

'The fourteen Economists who produced, as the Times correspondent says, "seven platitudes and a preamble" will, I think, regret their boldness. I suspect they were brought into the field by [Leonard] Courtney and [Viscount] Goschen.

I was aware of the counter pronouncement and suggested your name as one of the signatories.

I hope you will be able to produce a complete answer to what I think is one of the weakest productions ever sent out by clever men.'

42 Lord Monkswell,'A Broad View of the Fiscal Controversy', *Independent Rev*.4 (1904), p.441. Cf. Goschen's speech in the House of Commons on 29 June 1877, opposing the extension of the franchise: 'It might be an unpopular thing to say it, but Political Economy had been dethroned in the House and Philanthropy had been allowed to take its place. Political Economy was the bugbear of the working classes, and philanthropy, he was sorry to say, was their idol. In all legislative assemblies wherever numbers and numbers alone had prevailed, the doctrines of political economy had never taken root. . . . It was the teaching of history that the reign of numbers endangered not the Throne, not the Constitution, not Property – these were all bugbears – but Political Economy and the teaching that made Englishmen self-reliant.' George Peabody Gooch, op.cit. p.163.

43 Weymss Reid, 'Last Month', *Nineteenth Century* 54 (1903), p.345.

44 John Burns, 'Labour and Free Trade', *Independent Rev*.9. (1903) p.209; 'Expansion and Expenditure', *Edinburgh Rev*. (1903) p.364; 'Labour Leaders and Preferential Trading', *The Free Trader*, 11 Sept. 1903, at p.55. Both in 1903 and 1904 the Trades Union Congress overwhelmingly endorsed anti-protectionist resolutions.

45 Quoted from a speech by Will Thomas, Socialist and Trade Unionist candidate for West Ham, *The Times* at p.5, col. c, 12 Nov. 1903. On the Fabian attitudes see A.M. McBriar, *Fabian Socialism and English Politics 1884–1918* (Cambridge: Cambridge University Press, 1962), pp.131–4.

46 Charles Baron Clarke, *On Free Trade* (1903), p.19.

47 Arthur James Balfour, 124 Parl. Deb. (4th ser.) (1903) p.1159.

48 Sigma, 'The Wreck of the Unionist Administration', *Fortnightly Rev*.74 (1903), p.378. Cf. James Bryce, in *The Times* 6 July 1903, at p.8, col.3. Lord Rosebery declared that this 'hole and corner' approach really involved an enquiry into the constituencies' response to fiscal reform, while Sir Edward Grey dryly remarked that 'if the length of life of the Government was to be measured by the length of time during which Mr Balfour may continue to have no settled convictions it might have a long life'. Lord Rosebery, 124 Parl. Deb. (4th ser.) (1903) p.744; Grey, *The Times*, 1 July 1903 at p.13, col.4.

49 B.M. Add. Mss. 49770. Letter from Duke of Devonshire to Arthur James Balfour, 15 Sept. 1903. See also Lord George Hamilton, *Parliamentary Reminiscences and Reflections*, vol.1 p.320.

50 Duke of Devonshire, 124 Parl. Deb. (4th ser.) (1903) pp.755–9. In response to this admission Asquith predicted the publication of a 'new and revised edition of the Statistical Abstract of the United Kingdom, with a preface by Mr Chamberlain, a commentary and annotations by Mr Ritchie, and *apparatus criticus* by the Prime Minister, and, he supposed, a dedication to the British public by the united Cabinet. (Cheers and laughter). He was sure it would be the success of the publishing season (laughter).' *The Times*, 2 July 1903 at p.4, col.1.

It is worth noting that Asquith, one of the most effective opposition spokesmen, was less ignorant of political economy than most of his fellow politicians. He had studied Mill at school, and given University Extension lectures on the subject. Cf. 1 John Alfred Spender and Cyril Asquith, *Life of Herbert Henry Asquith, Lord Oxford and Asquith* (London: 1932), p.153.

51 [L.J. Maxse], 'Episodes of the Month', *Nat'l. Rev.*41 (1903) p.702. It was said that 'a Free Trader who inquires is in the perilous position of a lady who hesitates'. 'Episodes of the Month', ibid., 42 (1904), p.674.

52 Lord Lansdowne, 123 Parl. Deb. (4th ser.) (1903) p.868.

53 Alfred Gollin, op.cit. note 6 at pp.82, 179.

54 Sidney Lee, *King Edward VII* (London: Macmillan, 1927), vol.II, pp.173–4. Cf. L.L. Price's letter to *The Times*, 15 Aug. 1903, at p.4, cols.2–3, expressing his dissent from the 'manifesto' of the 'fourteen professors'.

55 1 Almeric Fitzroy, *supra*, vol. I, p.146. A slightly different version of this story appears in George Ranken Askwith, *Lord James of Hereford* (London: Ernest Benn, 1930), pp.277–8, also vol.II *Journals and Letters of Reginald Viscount Esher*, Maurice Vyner Brett (ed.) (London: Nicholson & Watson, 1934), vol.II, pp.1–2. Lord Esher was a confidant of the King, whose free trade sympathies are confirmed by Sidney Lee, op.cit., vol.1, p.173.

56 The reply, from Buckingham Palace, dated 19 Oct. 1903, in *The Times*, 21 Oct. 1903, at p.12, col.2.

57 Almeric Fitzroy, op.cit., vol.1 p.470.

58 Sidney Lee, op.cit., vol 1, p.128.

59 R.A. 24 49. Letter from J.S. Sanders to Lord Knollys, 27 Dec. 1903. Italics in original.

60 B.M. Add. Mss. 49856 (Balfour Papers). Letter from Arthur James Balfour to Edward Chapman, 2 Nov. 1903.

61 R.A. 24 71. Letter from Arthur James Balfour to Lord Knollys, 12 Mar. 1904. Italics in original. In fact, despite Balfour's confident assertion, Lord Rosebery had stated in the House of Commons that a Royal Commission would be preferable to the Government's 'hole and corner' inquiry. 124 Parl. Deb. (4th ser.) (1903) p.744.

62 In his draft scheme for the Commission Hewins stated that all its members should be 'favourable to Mr Chamberlain's views' because:

(i)   It is not desirable to waste time in general discussions;
(ii)   criticism must be constructive;
(iii) unanimity as to the desirability of adopting an Imperial policy will make the inquiry more manageable and economize time and material.

If however on general political grounds it may be thought desirable to broaden the base of the committee it should be clearly understood that its objects are entirely practical.

It may make it easier to obtain information in some quarters if Free Traders are included. This is a point for discussion.

His concluding remarks revealed both his sense of urgency and his prescience: '*It is absolutely necessary that Mr Chamberlain's policy should be adopted before the next great periodic improvement in trade. If it is postponed beyond that point the scheme will subside.*' [And this, of course, is exactly what happened.]

Although the Commission was 'packed', Hewins repeatedly insisted that its investigations were scientific and impartial. In a lecture to the Women's Branch of the Tariff Reform League at St Peter's Institute, London, on 22 Feb. 1904, he declared: 'If anybody can suggest a more thorough and comprehensive method of inquiry into the condition of our industry than has been set on foot by the Tariff Commission I can only say I will resign my post.'

The draft scheme, and the lecture, are in the Hewins papers. Italics in original. For the background see W.A.S. Hewins, op.cit., vol.I, ch. 3, n.11.

63 In his diary Hewins, who persuaded Booth to join the Commission, quotes him as saying he 'did not believe the food taxes would do a ha'p'orth of mischief to anyone'. In W.A.S. Hewins papers.
64 Winston Churchill, speech to the Halifax & District Anti-Protection Society, reported in *The Times*, 22 Dec. 1903, at p.8, col.1. In an editorial *The Times* commented that bankers were 'constitutionally timid about new departures', 18 Dec. 1903, at p.9, col.3.
65 Sidney Dark, *The Life of Sir Arthur Pearson* (London: Hodder & Stoughton, 1922), p.108.
66 British and Foreign Trade and Industry: Memoranda, Statistical Tables and Charts Prepared in the Board of Trade, with Reference to Various Matters Bearing on British and Foreign Trade and Industrial Conditions', Cmd. No. 1761 (1903). Edwin Cannan commented: 'It will probably not affect the judgment of ten persons in the whole country. . . . It was a desperate undertaking to attempt to settle a question of this kind by reprinting a few statistics when what was wanted was a good deal of common sense and a little skill in economic reasoning.' *Econ. Rev.* vol.13 (1903), p.470. Chamberlain was reported as having dismissed it, somewhat tactlessly, as the 'library of the Free Importers'– thereby suggesting that it reinforced his opponents' case. Cf. *The Free Trader*, 22 Jan. 1904.
67 B.M. Add. Mss. 49770 (Balfour Papers). Letter from Duke of Devonshire to Arthur James Balfour, 15 Sep. 1903. The 'abstract essay' referred to was, of course, Balfour's *Economic Notes on Insular Free Trade* (1903).
68 John Burns, 'Labour and Free Trade', *Independent Rev.* I (1903), p.123. 'Episodes of the Month', *Nat'l Rev.*42 (1903), p.860.
69 B.M. Add. Mss. 49780 (Balfour Papers). Letter from Sir Thomas Pittar to Davies, 11 May 1903 (probably a paper sent to C.T. Ritchie's secretary).
70 The Committee were 'much impressed by the difficulty of handling statistics of International Trade, even when dealing with the reports of the United Kingdom, whose genesis and meaning are well known to them. They recommend extreme caution in using any such statistics, for even when regard is paid to all the defects, limitations, and sources of error analysed above, it is not at all easy to know within what limits of error the statistics may be trusted.' Extracts from the 'Report of the Committee of the British Association for the Advancement of Science Appointed to Inquire into the Accuracy and Comparability of British and Foreign Statistics of International Trade', *J. Roy. Stat. Soc'y* 57 (1904) p.445. See also the account of the preparation of the Blue Book by Sir Alfred Bateman, ibid., 56 (1903), p.684.
71 Giffen to *The Times*, 29 Oct. 1903, at p.6, col.2. The earlier letters appeared on 24 Oct. at p.13, col.1, and 27 Oct. 1903, at p.9, col.5. There are several more letters between the two in the Chamberlain papers, together with Garvin's efforts to advise Chamberlain on statistical matters. On 26 Oct. 1903, Giffen asked Chamberlain to give the sources of any new figures he might quote in the future, to avoid confusion, and explained that the official practice of 'grouping' countries in the blue book made it impossible, without further investigation, to ascertain the underlying causes of changes in the currents of trade. Moreover, he disagreed with Chamberlain's efforts to dismiss coal exports as a special case, for 'if coal is not among our "manufactures", neither should we put stones and slates among imports of "manufactures" from the continent, or unwrought copper and crude zinc among imports of "manufactures" from the United States.'
He then proceeded to give his reasons for opposing Chamberlain. 'You force

myself, and many others like me, to choose between adherence to free trade and Imperial federation, because you affirm that a complete reversal of free trade policy is necessary to bind the empire together. Your appeal is to protectionists and in consequence you array free traders against you. If you had been careful to explain that we might concede *something* to protectionist prejudices in the Colonies for the sake of union, and that you should deprecate any substantial reversal of free trade policy, I believe you would have gained your object, or had a chance of doing so; but as matters stand I doubt. At any rate a policy of free trade is so essential to the prosperity of the United Kingdom that if its reversal is proposed I must vote for free trade and let the imperial question wait, and many others whom you might have had for supporters will do the same. Only a free trade country, or rather a free import country, can be the centre of the world's international commerce, as we are, which brings us an enormous business and gain, whatever special disadvantages it *may* have in the shape of "dumping" and so on. I fear you are rather overlooking this aspect of the question.' Italics in original.

72 William V. Craig, *The Times*, 9 Nov. 1903, at p.4, col.2.
73 *The Times*, 12 Oct. 1903, at p.7, col.2.
74 Pigou,'Free Trade and its Critics', *Fortnightly Rev.*73 (1903) p.544; Charles Booth, 'Fiscal Reform', *Nat'l Rev.* (1904) p.696; 'Fiscal Letters', Punch 126 (1904), p.59 also; ibid., 125 (1903), p.149; Francis R. Jones, *The Times* (London), 19 Aug. 1903, at p.8, col.3.
75 *The Times*, 5 Dec. 1903, at p.12, col.5. Italics in original.
76 *The Times*, 30 Nov. 1903, at p.14, col.4. Italics in original. Cf. the similar letter by 'Inquirer' who, writing on behalf of those whose minds were not yet made up, posed fourteen questions requiring to be answered. *The Times*, 3 Aug. 1903, at p.9, cols.5–6.
77 'Open Mind' and editorial reply, *The Spectator* 9 (1903), p.14. Earlier the Principal of McGill University, W. Peterson, had suggested that a 'commission' of 'modern and up to date University Professors of Economics' should be appointed to answer questions posed by 'convinced' free traders and to issue an impartial report. If they failed to give clear answers and to forecast the effect of the new proposals on the Empire they 'would fall back into the ranks of "academic economists", instead of posing as professors of a "useful science"'. If they succeeded the voter will have every reason to bless them.' *The Times*, 24 June 1903, at p.4, col.5. A somewhat similar proposal emanated from W.J. Ashley who proposed that if retaliation were adopted, the government would have to adjust duties by executive decree, in which case a Ministry of Trade and Commerce should be established, and assisted by local correspondents or delegates advised by provincial university professors of commerce. William James Ashley, *The Tariff Problem* (London: P.S. King, 1903), pp.133–6. This was heavily attacked on both constitutional grounds and because professors were not equipped to give such advice. Cf. 129 Parl. Deb. (4th ser.) (1904) p.640; 130 Parl. Deb. (4th ser.) (1904) pp.406–7; Autonomous, 'Pinchbeck Protectionism', *Fortnightly Rev.*74 (1903), pp.719, 729–31.
78 1 W.A.S. Hewins, op.cit., vol.I p.67.
79 Goschen, 17 Oct. 1903, at p.8, col.2; Asquith, 15 Oct. 1903, at p.5, cols.2–3; editorial 26 Nov. 1903, at p.9, col.3, all in *The Times*; Mr Griffith Boscawen, 129 Parl. Deb. (4th ser.) (1904) p.818; Garvin, *Economics of Empire*, op. cit., p.99. It would be folly, said another author, to adhere to the shibboleths of the past, for 'in political economy above all, where every factor is changing

yearly, the very meaning of the shibboleths become distorted by age'. 'Open Mind,' *The Spectator* 90 (1903), p.933.

80 Esme Wingfield-Stratford, *The Victorian Aftermath* (London: Routledge & Kegan Paul, 1933) p.88; 'Last Month', *Nineteenth Century* 54 (1903) p. 1044; James Lowther, 123 Parl. Deb. (4th ser.) (1903) p.462.

81 Price, 'The Economic Prejudice Against Tariff Reform', *Fortnightly Rev.*74 (1903), p.747. Italics in original. For the Bishop of Hereford's view see William Scovell Adams, *Edwardian Heritage, A Study in British History 1901–6* (London: Frederick Muller, 1949), p.197. Also the discussion in the *Spectator* vol.91, pp.858–9, 907–8, 1020, 1077–8 (1903). This provides a curious parallel with the participation of the clergy in early nineteenth century social and economic reform movements.

82 Editorial, *The Times*, 29 Oct. 1903, at p.7, col.2.

83 Mr Cripps, addressing his constituents. *The Times*, 14 Nov. 1903, at p. 8, col.3.

84 The Duke of Bedford, 'Some Reflections on the Fiscal Question', *Nat'l Rev.*43 (1904) pp.50, 54–5. This provides an interesting account of the change of views, under Chamberlain's influence, of a great landowner who had studied political economy under Benjamin Jowett at Balliol. Even 'after a lapse of a quarter of a century', he observed, 'I cannot think, without a shudder, of the reception with which an essay advocating Protection would have met at the then head of my College'. One can only speculate how many of his contemporaries having undergone similar educational experiences, had learned 'to mistrust political economy', and had come to the conclusion that free trade 'has no claim to be regarded as a scientific system of commercial policy, and that some of its fundamental principles are shattered by sentiment, riddled by contradictions, and honeycombed with inconsistencies'. ibid., p.58.

85 Chamberlain in a speech at Birmingham, reported in *The Times*, 5 Nov. 1903, at p.9, col 1.

86 Reid, 'Last Month', *Nineteenth Century* 54 (1903), p.345.

87 Pigou, op.cit., note 74 at pp.545, 542. John Beattie Crozier was a kind of latter day Spencerian philosopher-cum-economist. See his *The Wheel of Wealth: Being A Reconstruction of the Science and Art of Political Economy on the Lines of Modern Evolution* (London: Longmans Green, 1906). Sir Vincent Caillard, a director of Vickers, Sons & Maxim Ltd., another 'amateur' economist, became a member of the Executive Committee of Chamberlain's Tariff Commission. Both men had recently written pro-tariff reform articles.

88 Letter to *The Times*, 28 Nov. 1903, at p.14, col.2. See the reply by Benedict W. Ginsburg, Secretary to the Royal Statistical Society, ibid., 1 Dec. 1903, at p.12, col.1. Cannan's letter was quoted, with approval, in the *The Free Trader*, 4 Dec. 1903.

89 F. Carne Rasch (MP) to *The Times*, 26 Nov. 1903, at p.5, col.3.

90 Lightbody, 'Taxing the Foreigner', *Westminster Rev.* 160 (1903), pp.606, 611. The author of this article emphasized how easy it was to compile statements from 'the much abused "doctrinaire" economists which seemed to support change, provided that the accompanying qualifications were neglected'. ibid., p.609.

91 Bowley, *The Times*, 27 Oct. 1903, at p.10, cols.1–2, and 3 Nov. 1903, at p.10, col.4; Pigou, op.cit., note 74, p.547; Goschen, *The Times*, 7 Nov. 1903, at p.14, col.1, reporting a speech at Liverpool. Goschen explicitly refused to 'theorize' and protested: 'Are we to be dealt with by authorities or are we to be dealt with by the facts of the case? We have been warned off the field of political economy, which we are told is obfuscating and

nebulous (Laughter), So I take my refuge in facts; but when we go to facts they come out and fire at our heads the pistol of authority.' ibid., col.3.

92 William Smart, *The Return to Protection* (London: Macmillan, 1904), Preface; quoted in Mr Chamberlain's 'Proposals', *Edinburgh Rev.*200 (1904), pp.258–9. See also Smart's letter in the *Spectator* 91 (1903), p.128.

93 In a letter, the *Spectator* 91 (1903), p.601.

94 J.S. Nicholson, *The Times*, 31 Oct. 1903 at p.9, col.5. Nicholson emphasized the theoretical possibility but practical improbability of a situation in which part of a tax on imports was paid by the foreigner. For Sir William Harcourt's gleeful response to Nicholson's reproof, ibid., 2 Nov. 1903, at p.11, col.3. Chamberlain, he said, was unfortunate 'in the people who cram him. They give him inaccurate figures, and they give him professors who are really against him'.

95 Ashley, op.cit., pp.34–5.

96 See S.H. Jeyes, *Mr Chamberlain, His Life and Public Career* (London, Edinburgh: Sands & Co., 1904), p.330 (Greenock, 7 Oct.).

97 *The Times*, 16 Oct. 1903, at p.7, col.3. For quotations from various economic writers see Vincent Caillard, 'Free Trade and its Defenders', *Nat'l Rev.*41 (1903), p.420. See also the exchange of letters between Sir Arthur Conan Doyle and William Smart in the *Spectator* 91 (1903), pp.12–13, 55, 90–1, 128.

98 123 Parl. Deb. (4th ser.) (1903) p.846.

99 *The Times*, 6 Nov. 1903, at p.9, col.2, reporting a speech at Manchester.

100 *The Times*, 11 Nov. 1903 at p.5, col.4. Craggs himself thought that part of the tax would always be paid by the foreigner. 'Inquirer' had already appealed for advice on various matters, including the effect of food taxes on the cost of living, and of import duties on foreign manufactures. ibid., 3 Aug. 1903, at p.9, cols.5–6.

101 After stressing the crucial relationship between 'the elasticities of production in the taxed and untaxed sources respectively', Pigou explained that 'upon the basis of the statistics of wheat production given in Broomhall's Corn Trade Year Book it can be proved mathematically that, if these elasticities are equal, and if our tax is small enough to justify neglect of consequent changes in elasticity, then the price in England will be raised above the level at which it would otherwise have stood by more than four fifths of the duty. It is probably true that the hypothesis of equal elasticities exaggerates the expansibility of colonial production. In order, however, to justify Tariff Reformer's assertion that the "major part" of the tax will be borne by the consumer, it is necessary to assume that the elasticity in the United Kingdom and the Colonies together is not merely equal to, but is nearly six times as great as, the elasticity in the foreign countries – an assumption which it is impossible to defend.' *The Times*, 3 Dec. 1903, at p.5, col.3.

102 A.C. Pigou, 'The Known and the Unknown in Mr Chamberlain's Policy', *Fortnightly Rev.*75 (1904), p.36.

103 Sidgwick, as quoted in *The Times*, 19 Oct, 1903, at p.9, col.3; Chamberlain's estimate was given in his Glasgow speech of 6 Oct. Cf. the version printed in *Nat'l Rev.*42 (1903), pp.351, 367.

104 J.L. Garvin, 'The Economics of Empire – II, Preference and the Food Supply', *Nat'l Rev.* Spec. Supp., 42 (Dec., 1903), p.34.

105 [L.J. Maxse] 'Episodes of the Month', p.34. *Nat'l Rev.*42 (1904), p.682. The phrase was apparently originated by a writer in the Daily Telegraph.

106 *Nat'l Rev.*42 (1904), p.682, citing Chamberlain's speech at Leeds on 16 Dec. 1903.

107 Apart from the relative importance of the economic and non-economic issues, the principal questions were: What was the correct or 'orthodox' free trade theory, and how far was it applicable to the changed circumstances of the time? What, if any, alternative theory was applicable to the situation? What, indeed, were the 'facts' of Britain's trade position both in relation to her past experience and by comparison with the experience of other nations, especially Germany and the USA? How far did these comparative experiences shed light on the efficacy of free trade policy as against protection or some alternative? How far could past experience, whatever that was, be a guide to future developments – for example, the reaction of Colonial governments to an offer of preferential terms; the response of protectionist nations to British tariffs or retaliatory measures? What would be the effects on domestic conditions of various types and levels of import taxes? (A problem complicated by the uncertainty of Balfour's intentions and the contending forces within the ranks of the tariff reformers.)

   In some ways the situation resembled the range and complexity of issues raised during the debate about Britain's entry into the Common Market, especially as it was widely asserted that tariff reform entailed protection, the growth of monopolies, parliamentary lobbying and the corruption of political life, as was suggested in the economists' 'manifesto' of 15 Aug. 1903.

108 For striking evidence of the public's lack of response to Chamberlain's pleas, despite all the superficial enthusiasm, see the results of the Daily Mail polls referred to in Alfred Gollin, op.cit., pp.199–201.

109 Thus while Pigou denied that Balfour's proposals were in conflict with established economic principles, Hewins asserted that Chamberlain's policy was compatible with scientific political economy. Cf. Pigou, 'The Economics of Mr Balfour's Manifesto', *The Times* 18 Sept. 1903, at p.4, col.3; Hewins, Lecture at St Peter's Institute, 22 Feb. 1904. Copy in Hewins' papers.

   Ever since J.S. Mill's recognition of the 'infant industry' argument for protection, the number of admitted exceptions and qualifications to the pure theory of free trade had been growing steadily. This, indeed, was the source of much of the 'authoritative' ammunition collected by tariff reformers. For a useful survey of the current state of international trade theory see Narmadeshwar Jha, *Age of Marshall* (Patna, India: Novelty & Co., 1963), ch.4. The current state of theory undoubtedly discouraged some of the leading economists from participating actively in the debate. Cf. Edgeworth's comment, citing Giffen, Goschen and Sidgwick in support, that the complexity of the issues involved was 'calculated to stablish [sic] in their faith those Free Traders whose conviction is founded not so much on knowledge that Free Trade is the best course, as on ignorance of what course is better'. Review of J.W. Root, The Trade Relations of the British Empire', Econ. Journal 13 (1903), pp.375, 381. As Goschen said, 'there are a great many agnostics in economics', 123 Parl. Deb. (4th ser.) (1903) p.838.

110 1 L.S. Amery, *My Political Life* (London: Hutchinson 1953), pp.244–6. Winston Churchill, in the House of Commons, put Amery's contributions in their true perspective by his reference to 'that able young gentleman who spent his afternoons in writing letters over the signature "Tariff Reformer" and his evenings in writing leading articles saying how excellent and conclusive those letters were'. 129 Parl. Deb. (4th ser.) (1904) p.916. On the other hand, Andrew Bonar Law wrote to W.J. Ashley, 'There is one point, however, which, if you agree with me as to its importance, I wish you would bring to the notice of Mr Chamberlain. There is nothing, I think, which so tells more against us

than the idea that *scientific* authority is against us'. Italics in original. Cf. Anne Ashley, *William James Ashley: A Life* (London: P.S. King, 1932). p.135. Unfortunately this letter is undated.

111 For example Bowley, Cannan, Pigou and Smart. S.J. Chapman and J.H. Clapham, who gave a belated endorsement to the manifesto, might also be included in this group.

112 At the August 1904 meeting of the British Association for the Advancement of Science, in reply to the criticisms of L.L. Price. Cf. *Econ. Journal* 14 (1904), pp.483–4. Marshall was abroad when the manifesto appeared and after refusing to draft it subsequently suggested that it should be drafted in England. His first reaction was 'on the whole we can be proud of it'; but a week later he acknowledged certain 'blemishes in the drafting', adding that 'On the whole my first feeling that a Manifesto is more vulnerable than a letter by an individual remains. The Manifesto must be short, and yet must cover a large ground. And as no one feels its wording is exactly what he would have chosen himself, no one is very eager or even well qualified to defend it.' Marshall to Lujo Brentano, 18 Aug. and 26 Aug. 1903. Cited by H.W. McCready, 'Alfred Marshall and Tariff Reform, 1903, Some Unpublished Letters', *Journal Pol. Econ.* 63 (1955), pp.259, 266.

113 Letter from Herbert S. Foxwell to W.R. Scott, 18 Feb. 1903; letter from Herbert S. Foxwell to James Bonar, 22 Nov. 1903. Both in Kress Library, Harvard University.

114 Cf. McCready, op.cit., p.266.

115 At the Annual Dinner meeting in July 1904. Cf. *Econ. Journal* 14 (1904), p.353.

116 In the popular debate (that is, pamphlets and contributions to newspapers rather than respectable periodicals and books), the most active participants among the academic economists, were Bowley, Cannan, Chapman, Hewins and Pigou.

117 McCready, op. cit., pp.261, 267. The two parts of the quotation come from Marshall's letters to Brentano of 17 July 1903 and 29 Sept. 1903, respectively. Other leading economists gave similar explanations of their reluctance to participate.

118 *The Times*, 17 Sept. 1903 at p.5, col.1. Quoted in part in my article, 'The Role of Authority in the Development of British Economics', *Journal Law & Econ*, (1964), pp.85, 102–3. To be reprinted in vol.II of this series.

119 See letter from Joseph Chamberlain to W.J. Ashley, 13 May 1903. Typescript copy in Chamberlain papers. Chamberlain's list of eleven questions needing investigation prompted Ashley to spend the summer writing his book. Cf. Amery, op.cit., note 4 in vol.5.

120 See 129 Parl Deb. (4th ser.) (1904) p.640.

121 Letter from W.J. Ashley to John Morley, 9 Feb. 1904; and Morley's reply, 11 Feb. 1904, both in Joseph Chamberlain papers. See also, *The Times*, 9 Feb. 1904, at p.7, col.a, and 11 Feb. 1904, at p.5, col.c.

122 See letter from Sidney Webb to W.A.S. Hewins, 30 May 1903, and Hewins' Diary, in Hewins' papers. For the early history of the London School of Economics see Hewins op.cit., vol.I, and Janet Beveridge, *An Epic of Clare Market: Birth and Early Days of the London School of Economics* (London School of Economics and Political Science, 1960).

123 Letter from Joseph Chamberlain to W.A.S. Hewins, 9 and 16 Nov. 1903, in Chamberlain papers.

124 From W.A.S. Hewins' lecture at St Peter's Institute. In Hewins' papers. This

lecture contains some outspoken comments on the behaviour of 'my old friends and colleagues in the Economic World'.

125 For the background see Coats, 'The Historist Reaction in English Political Economy, 1870–90', *Economica* (N.S.) 21 (1954), p.143, reprinted in this volume, pp.220–30.

126 James Mavor, the former Glasgow Professor (then at Toronto), though he disagreed with Chamberlain, wrote to Foxwell 'deploring the manifesto . . . as leading the world to believe that the only contribution we could offer upon a question of the utmost difficulty was to flourish a few abstract principles of elementary simplicity at the heads of our leading statesmen'. Foxwell to Bonar, 22 Nov. 1903 (unpublished letter in Kress Library, Harvard University). The dividing line between economists and economic historians was not, however, rigid. Apart from Marshall's *Industry and Trade* (London: Macmillan, 1919), S.J. Chapman wrote economic history, as did H.O. Meredith, another supporter of the manifesto. Cf. Audrey Cunningham, *William Cunningham* (London: SPCK, 1950), p.100.

127 The extent and the persistence of this division is suggested by T.S. Ashton's reminiscence of his undergraduate days at Manchester in 1908–10. 'Under Chapman we had been brought up as strong Free Traders, and had even been encouraged to lecture for the Free Trade Union. It was a shock when in 1932 Chapman became the chief architect of the new British tariff system.' Quoted, by permission, from a private letter of 10 Sept. 1966.

128 For a revealing account of Ashley's and Cunningham's views, see B. Semmel, *Imperialism and Social Reform*, (London: Allen & Unwin, 1960), chs.10 and 11.

129 Whereas Free Traders constantly emphasized the theoretical and practical risks, advocates of tariff reform favoured action, fearing the consequences of a policy of drift. Cf. the views of Edgeworth, *Econ. Journal* 13 (1903), pp.381–2 and Cunningham, 'The Failure of Free Traders', *Econ. Rev.*14, (1904), esp. at pp.51–2. Also Ashley's revealing article 'The Tariff Problem', ibid., 14 pp.255–78. As another writer remarked, with reference to the growth of England's wealth under free trade, '*The real question surely is not whether England is becoming more wealthy, but whether she is becoming as much more wealthy as she might become if the markets of the world were not being closed against her*', R.E. Macnaughten, 'Is Free Trade a Fallacy', ibid., p.35. Italics in original.

130 See, for example, Ashley, *The Tariff Problem*, op.cit., *passim*, and the writings of L.L. Price, especially his scathing review of Pigou's *The Riddle of the Tariff*, *Econ. Rev.*14 (1904), p.232, and Smart's 'The Return to Protection', ibid., p.366. Though chiefly an economic historian Price had reviewed many theoretical works in the *Economic Journal*, including Marshall's *Principles*, which he had warmly praised. See his articles 'The Economic Possibilities of an Imperial Fiscal Policy', *Econ. Journal* 13 (1903), p.486; 'Economic Theory and Fiscal Policy', *Econ. Journal* 14 (1904), p.372 (which provoked Marshall's response, ibid., pp.483–4); and 'The Economic Prejudice Against Tariff Reform', *Fortnightly Rev.*14 (1903), p.747

For other examples of acrimonious comment see Edwin Cannan, 'Professor Ashley on the Tariff Problem', *Free Trader*, 25 Sept. 1903, pp.71–2: 'It has always been plain that, like several other economic historians of his particular generation, he has been disinclined to admit the validity of ordinary methods of economic reasoning.' In the other direction, see, William Cunningham, *Richard Cobden and Adam Smith* (London: Tariff Reform League, 1904), pp.33–4, and *The Wisdom of the Wise: Three Lectures on Free Trade and Imperialism* (Cambridge: Cambridge University Press, 1906), pp.6–7. For a review of Cunningham's activities see Audrey Cunningham, *William Cunningham*, op.cit., pp.102–4.

131 Cf. Audrey Foxwell, *Herbert Somerton Foxwell: A Portrait*, in Harvard Graduate School of Business Administration, Kress Library of Business and Economics, Publication No.1, The Kress Library of Business and Economics (1939) p.9. Also letter from Foxwell to W.R. Scott, 18 Feb. 1903, in Kress Library. Cf. C.W. Guillebaud's obituary in *The Eagle* (St John's College, Cambridge) 69 (1937), p.275 and Keynes' obituary article, 'Herbert Somerton Foxwell', *Econ. Journal* 46 (1936), p.589 especially pp.590–4. Foxwell's opinion was endorsed by L.L. Price, who had been Chairman of the Oxford University Tariff Reform League. See his unpublished memoir, 'Retrospect of an Oxford Economist', pt.4, ch.3, pp.29–30, in Oriel College, Oxford. This is another part of the manuscript referred to in note 133 below. They are not identical.
132 Letter from Alfred Marshall to W.A.S. Hewins, 14 July 1903, in Hewins papers.
133 In his unpublished autobiography, L.L. Price wrote '. . . at the Cambridge meeting of the British Association in 1904 . . . Marshall chid me like an irate dominie flogging a naughty schoolboy, for my support of Tariff Reform. I imagine that he had not liked the ridicule in *The Times* of the damning pontifical manifesto of the Free Trade professors against Chamberlain and had nursed his wrath'. Of Pigou's election, Price recalled that 'on good assurance I learnt that by every means open Marshall had urged Pigou's success. However brought about, and Foxwell gave me subsequently an account of what he had heard of the proceedings at the election, with the division of the votes, the event finally disrupted the long friendship there had been between him and Marshall . . . Ashley . . . told me later that he had been in some sense stimulated by Marshall to become a candidate, or understood that he was not dissuaded from this step. As he gathered, such action, so he put it, was likely to "spoil" or harm the field for Foxwell.' *Memories and Notes on British Economists, 1881–1947*, (1946), ch.2, pp.14–16. (Typescript in the Brotherton Library, University of Leeds.)

Price complained of Pigou's 'intellectual arrogance', his 'inability to abstain from dogmatic declarations on political questions', and his failure, together with his cosignatories, to recognize the paramount importance of the political issues involved or recognize the large modifications necessary before the pure theory of international trade could be applied to the circumstances of the case. *Econ. Rev.*14 (1904), pp.233, 238–9.
134 Edgeworth, reviewing the same work, praised 'the power with which he yields the organon of economic theory' as 'of the highest promise' and compared Pigou to Clerk Maxwell, of whom it had been said 'it is impossible for that man to go wrong in physics', Edgeworth, Book Review, *Econ. Journal* 14 (1904), pp.65, 67.
135 Letter from Arthur James Balfour to W.A.S. Hewins, 28 May 1908, in Hewins' papers.
136 B.M. Add. Mss. 49779 (Balfour Papers). Letter from W.A.S. Hewins to Arthur James Balfour, 28 May, 1908.
137 Cf. C.R. Fay's letter to Harry Johnson, 27 Aug., 1959, in the possession of Mr John Saltmarsh, of King's College, Cambridge. On the Birmingham election, where Ashley was the successful candidate, see Keynes' obituary of Foxwell, op.cit., note 131, p.598.

W.T. Layton, who was a Cambridge University Lecturer in economics at the time of the election subsequently claimed that Balfour's support for Pigou was 'decisive'. See Layton, op.cit., note 23, p.32. However, the surviving evidence provides no support for this interpretation. I am most grateful to Professor E.A.G. Robinson and G.A. Dick of Nuffield College, for their help in this matter.

Sidney Webb's reaction is worth quoting: 'What a jump for Pigou is the Cambridge appointment! I don't at all approve, for more reasons than one. But Marshall seems to have moved Heaven and earth to exclude you and Foxwell. I happen to have quite accidentally learned, a couple of years ago, that Marshall intended and expected Pigou to succeed him, but scarcely believed it possible with much more experienced and distinguished persons in the field. University affairs seem to me to be governed with as little wisdom as those of the unlearned world, and with quite as much simple prejudice – not to say envy, malice and uncharitableness.' Letter from Sidney Webb to W.J. Ashley, in Ashley papers, University of Birmingham Library.

138 T.W. Hutchison, *A Review of Economic Doctrines, 1870–1929*, (Oxford: Clarendon Press, 1953), p.62. Cf. the following comment on Pigou's economics by a warm admirer: 'Pigou was a man of the Temple of Truth, fixed in Cambridge. His system never greatly changed. He gave the impression of using *one* machine, most beautiful and powerful in its construction, to solve a series of problems, the solutions all tending, after he had settled down into middle age, to have a certain family likeness. [By contrast] Keynes was always inventing new machines and new ways of using old machines. The solutions he offered were much more varied.' Hugh Dalton, *Memoirs – Call Back Yesterday, 1887–1931*, (London: Frederick Muller, 1953), p.60.

ADDITIONAL NOTE

For discussion of the relationship between the tariff reform debate and the succession to Marshall's chair see the following articles: 1. A.W. Coats, 'The Role of Authority in the Development of British Economics', *Journal of Law and Economics* (October, 1964) vol.VII pp.85–106. (To be published in Volume II of this series.); 2. Ronald H. Coase, 'The Appointment of Pigou as Marshall's Successor', *Journal of Law and Economics* (October, 1972) vol.15, pp.473–85; 3. A.W. Coats, 'The Appointment of Pigou as Marshall's Successor: Comment', *Journal of Law and Economics* (October, 1972) vol.15, pp.487–95; 4. Trevor W. Jones, 'The Appointment of Pigou as Marshall's Successor: The Other Side of the Coin', *Journal of Law and Economics* (April, 1978) vol.21, pp.235–43; and 5. John C. Wood, 'Alfred Marshall and the Tariff Reform Debate', *Journal of Law and Economics* (October, 1980) vol.23, pp.481–95.

APPENDIX:
PROFESSORS OF ECONOMICS AND THE TARIFF QUESTION
TO THE EDITOR OF *THE TIMES*,
15 AUGUST 1903

Sir:

We, the undersigned, beg leave to express our opinions on certain matters of a more or less technical character connected with the fiscal proposals which now occupy the attention of the country.

One of the main objects aimed at in these proposals – the cultivation of friendly feelings between the United Kingdom and other parts of the Empire – is ardently desired by us; and we should not regard it as a fatal objection to a fiscal scheme adapted to this purpose that it was attended with a considerable sacrifice of material wealth. But the suggested means for obtaining this desirable end do not seem to us advisable, first, because there would probably be incurred an immense and permanent sacrifice, not only of material, but also of higher goods; and, secondly, because the means suggested would be likely, in our judgment, to defeat rather than attain the end in view.

First, having regard to the prevalence of certain erroneous opinions, to which we advert below, we think that any system of preferential tariffs would most probably lead to the reintroduction of protection into the fiscal system of the United Kingdom. But a return to protection would, we hold, be detrimental to the material prosperity of this country, partly for reasons of the same kind as those which, as now universally admitted, justified the adoption of free trade – reasons which are now stronger than formerly, in consequence of the greater proportion of food and raw materials imported from foreign countries, and the greater extent and complexity of our foreign trade. The evil would probably be a lasting one since experience shows that protection, when it has once taken root, is likely to extend beyond the limits at first assigned to it and is very difficult to extirpate. There are also to be apprehended those evils other than material which protection brings in its train, the loss of purity in politics, the unfair advantage given to those who wield the powers of jobbery and corruption, unjust distribution of wealth, and the growth of 'sinister interests'.

Secondly, we apprehend that the suggested arrangements, far from promoting amity, may engender irritating controversies between the different members of the Empire. The growing sense of solidarity would be strained by an opposition of interests such as was experienced in our country under protection, and has been noticeable in the history of the United States and of other countries. Such an opposition of interests would be all the more disruptive in the case of the British Empire, as it is not held together by a central government.

Our convictions on this subject are opposed to certain popular opinions, with respect to which we offer the following observations:

1. It is not true that an increase of imports involves the diminished employment of workmen in the importing country. The statement is universally rejected by those who have thought about the subject, and is completely refuted by experience.

2. It is very improbable that a tax on food imported into the United Kingdom would result in an equivalent – or more than equivalent – rise in wages. The result which may be anticipated as a direct consequence of the tax is a lowering of the real remuneration of labour.

3. The injury which the British consumer would receive from an import tax on wheat might be slightly reduced in the possible, but under existing conditions very improbable, event of a small portion of the burden being thrown permanently on the foreign producer.

4. To the statement that a tax on food will raise the price of food, it is not a valid reply that this result may possibly in fact not follow. When we say that an import duty raises price, we mean, of course, unless its effect is overborne by other causes operating at the same time in the other direction. Or, in other words, we mean that in consequence of the import duty the price is generally higher by the amount of the duty than it would have been if other things had remained the same.

5. It seems to us impossible to devise any tariff regulation which shall at once expand the wheat-growing areas in the Colonies, encourage agriculture in the United Kingdom, and at the same time not injure the British consumer.

6. The suggestion that the public, though directly damnified by an impost, may yet obtain a full equivalent from its yield is incorrect, because it leaves out of account the interference with the free circulation of goods, the detriment incidental to diverting industry from the course which it would otherwise have taken, and the circumstance that, in the case of a tax on foreign wheat – English and Colonial wheat being free – while the consumer would have to pay the whole or nearly the whole tax on all the wheat, the government would get the tax only on foreign wheat.

7. In general, those who lightly undertake to reorganize the supply of food and otherwise divert the course of industry do not adequately realize what a burden of proof rests on the politician who, leaving the plain rule of taxation for the sake of revenue only, seeks to attain ulterior objects by manipulating tariffs.

C.F. Bastable (Professor of Political Economy at the University of Dublin); A.L. Bowley (appointed Teacher of Statistics in the University of London at the London School of Economics); Edwin Cannan (appointed Teacher of Economic Theory in the University of London at the London School of Economics); Leonard Courtney (formerly Professor of Political Economy at University College, London); F.Y. Edgeworth (Professor of Political Economy at the University of Oxford); E.C.K. Gonner (Professor of Economic Science at the University of Liverpool); Alfred Marshall (Professor of Political Economy at the University of Cambridge); J.S. Nicholson (Professor of Political Economy at the University of Edinburgh); L.R. Phelps (Editor of the *Economic Review*); A. Pigou (Jevons Memorial Lecturer at

University College, London); C.P. Sanger (Lecturer in Political Economy at University College); W.R. Scott (Lecturer in Political Economy at the University of St Andrews); W. Smart (Professor of Political Economy at the University of Glasgow); Armitage Smith (Lecturer in Political Economy at the Birkbeck College, Recognized Teacher of the University of London in Economics).

PART IV
AMERICAN ECONOMICS

18

ECONOMIC THOUGHT

In a brief panoramic survey of American economic ideas, compromise is unavoidable. Limitations of space preclude the adoption of an encyclopedic cultural approach (like Joseph Dorfman's *The Economic Mind in American Civilization*), yet to go to the opposite extreme and focus narrowly on the development of economic science would involve concentrating mainly on the twentieth century, thereby obscuring both the continuity and the essentially pragmatic character of much of the national economic literature. Two interrelated major themes will therefore be highlighted: the repeated efforts to adapt the inherited corpus of European ideas to perceived domestic needs and conditions, and the gradual emergence and professionalization of economics as a social science discipline. This procedure is designed to avoid dichotomizing theory and practice, since adaptation includes modifications and extensions of theory as well as its application to current and prospective problems; and economic writers can function in both fields as specialists or generalists, amateurs or professionals.

The two themes converge in the post-Civil War decades, when academics increasingly took the lead in the advancement, refinement and dissemination of economic ideas. The end of the first century of independence forms a convenient watershed. Charles Dunbar's oft-quoted judgement that 'the United States have, thus far, done nothing toward developing the theory of political economy, notwithstanding their vast and immediate interest in its practical applications' ('Economic Science in America 1776–1876', p.122) reflected his orthodox classical standpoint. But subsequent historians, after making due allowance for the cases of Henry C. Carey and John Rae, have generally endorsed his opinion and accepted his explanation that Americans were too preoccupied with the urgent practical needs of a new society to devote themselves to original thought.

Despite its superficial attractiveness, this interpretation is too simplistic. Admittedly, economic thought has generally followed rather than anticipated

341

economic development. The early leadership of Great Britain in the field was not uninfluenced by the economic and social changes associated with the industrial revolution; and since comparable changes occurred much later in the United States, some time lag in American economic thought is only to be expected. Yet, as Frank A. Fetter argued, the effect of a new environment is to stimulate novel ideas appropriate to the circumstances; and American economic writers were by no means lacking in originality, flexibility and ingenuity, particularly on policy issues but also quite frequently in theoretical matters. Indeed, in a sense they were too inventive, too ready to scrap or modify existing ideas in response to some new intellectual impulse or the pressure of current concerns, and unwilling to undertake sustained analysis. Hence, their thoughts on economic subjects were rarely expressed in a mature, consistent and systematic form.

These deficiencies cannot be explained without reference to the wider intellectual and social context. The American distaste for abstract and speculative inquiry, whether in philosophy, politics or natural science, is a historiographical commonplace; and this bias persisted long after the late nineteenth century expansion of the academic profession. Indeed, caustic critics claim that when a sophisticated indigenous intellectual system – pragmatism – eventually emerged, it was little more than an elaborate rationalization of deep-rooted and widely held beliefs and values. Doubtless this contention is exaggerated; but the mainstream of American religious, political, social and economic ideas has demonstrated remarkable continuity and conservatism, with comparatively little support for the more extreme forms of European radicalism. British empiricist philosophy was preferred to French rationalism, and the powerful influence of Scottish 'common sense' doctrines helps to explain the persistence of dogmatism in antebellum college teaching of moral philosophy and political economy.

Given the widespread distaste for pure theory, it is hardly surprising that the conspicuous early American intellectual achievements were in empirical studies directly dependent on keen observation and assiduous data gathering. In producing works of travel or natural history, or in undertaking investigations in geology rather than, say physics, American authors were less constrained by the European heritage, which was a source of strength in elementary work but inhibiting to advanced thinking or research in more theoretical fields. Fetter claims that the American lag in political economy was due to the 'false authority of English orthodoxy', which had 'rested like a dead hand' on efforts to account for essentially different and abnormal conditions, and that the prevalence of 'personal prejudices and pecuniary or class interests' had obstructed disinterested scientific effort. There is some justification for both these contentions, especially the former; but the latter condition was by no means unique. As Joseph Schumpeter noted, mere partisanship did not prevent English economic writers from producing major analytic contributions. In America the exceptional opportunities for business enterprise had absorbed a disproportionate share of the available creative talent, so consequently the 'circles that did cultivate intellect and scholarship were quantitatively unimportant and sterile in scientific initiative'.

There are, unfortunately, no reliable measures of the social and geographical distribution of creative ability. The American intellectual community was certainly small and weak, especially during the colonial era, and the climate of opinion was hostile to the growth of a specialist class of 'knowers'. The absence of professional economists in Britain at the time did not prevent the development of systematic economic analysis; but in the colonies clerical influence was dominant, and the emancipation of political economy from the constraints of theology and moral philosophy was delayed for almost a century after its liberation in England. Somewhat similar ideas of natural law and economic 'laws of motion' were recognized in both countries. But the influence of deism, which churchmen on both sides of the Atlantic considered shocking – even blasphemous – was much weaker in America; and the fundamental conception of a Newtonian-type mechanism operating independently of divine intervention, which underlay systematic economic thinking in England and France, was not fully grasped in America until well into the nineteenth century. Even then it appeared only in a crude and unimaginative form.

Clerical influence delayed the development of an independent tradition of academic economics both in Britain and America, especially in the latter. Until the late nineteenth century many American college professors were selected more for their piety and moral leadership than for their learning. Colleges were endowed to train ministers and propagate approved ideas. All studies were subservient to theology, and independent research was viewed with suspicion. Emoluments were poor; teaching was elementary and often conducted by rote; security of tenure was lacking. Hence, the academic profession offered few attractions for men of vigour, originality and independence.

Admittedly a few significant economic writers temporarily became professors before the Civil War, usually after failure in business, journalism or public service, or as a springboard to better things. Special chairs were occasionally endowed for such men, who were expected to express 'sound' views on current issues such as commercial policy or the currency. Although they sometimes disappointed the donor's expectations, it is hardly surprising that the public generally regarded professors of political economy as paid hirelings or partisans, rather than as disinterested truth seekers. Indeed, as late as the 1880s, Cornell University took the logical step of simultaneously appointing one lecturer to expound protectionism and another to present free trade views, and the University of Pennsylvania still insisted that its economists should not support free trade.

By that time a revolution in American higher education was already under way in response to rapid population growth, industrialization, urbanization and the consequent expansion of demand for specialized occupational knowl-edge and skills. The extension of settlement generated demands for regional colleges and universities designed to emulate or surpass older seaboard institutions. Intense public interest in economic and social questions was stimulated by popular writers such as Henry George, and economics led in the growth of academic posts in the emerging social sciences. In 1879, three years after his discouraging report cited earlier, Dunbar became head of the first American university economics department independent of philosophy, at Harvard; and in 1886 he and his colleagues launched the first English-language scholarly periodical in economics, *Quarterly Journal of Economics*, which was soon followed by several competitors. A decade earlier the opening of the Johns Hopkins University in Baltimore had furthered graduate training; but the most important single impulse to the subject was the founding of the American Economic Association (AEA) in 1885, by a group of young scholars recently returned from studies in Germany.

Despite its early troubles, the AEA soon became the organizational focus for serious discussion and research in economics – and not only for profes-sional academics. Admittedly, until well into the twentieth century, resistance to English orthodoxy was usually more conspicuous than intellectual con-solidation or scientific advance, for both intellectual and sociological reasons. In terms of ideas, the influence of German historical economics doubtless impeded scientific progress because it discouraged systematic theorizing and emphasized the historical relativity of economic doctrines and the value of detailed factual and statistical studies. The Germans' contention that English classical economists assumed static social conditions and overemphasized the limitations of natural resources appealed to young Americans impressed by the past record of the nation and its prospects of economic development. In their eagerness to promulgate doctrines relevant to American needs and conditions, they endeavoured, sometimes indiscriminately, to combine elements from English, German and Austrian economic literature. But the resulting syntheses were invariably unsatisfactory. A certain restlessness of spirit and exaggerated enthusiasm for innovation generated variations of received doctrines that were distinguished more by semantic ingenuity than by analytic merit.

Sociological as well as intellectual factors help to account for the delayed emergence of doctrinal coherence and more uniform professional standards and training. The shortage of personnel competent to satisfy the rapidly expanding demand for social science instruction, the obstacles to scholarly communication across a continent, the number and heterogeneity of educa-tional institutions, and the variety of professional beliefs and values all help to account for the diversity that so sharply differentiated American economics from its European counterparts.

Nevertheless, by the early twentieth century the professionalization of American economics was well advanced. There were few outstanding theorists, but the volume and quality of contributions to scholarship were already attracting widespread and favourable international attention. Despite some well-publicized academic freedom cases involving the dismissal of or severe pressure on prominent economists, the academic status, conditions and emoluments of the profession were generally rising – although still lagging behind aspirations derived from comparisons with the position of the German professoriat. Around the turn of the century, American economists played a leading role in defending their peers against persecutors, and they were prominent among founder-members of the American Association of University Professors in 1915. In endeavouring to have an impact on a society that undervalued purely intellectual achievements, they were torn between the ideals of scientific objectivity and non-partisanship, and the desire to shape policy, solve contemporary problems and promote the cause of social reform.

The United States long remained a net debtor in the international exchange of economic knowledge. It did not become a net creditor until the 1940s, and then only with the aid of a number of remarkable European émigrés. Since World War II it has unquestionably taken the lead, and it is noteworthy that seven of the first fifteen Nobel laureates in economics have been born in America or work there.

In this article it is impossible to cover more than a small fraction of the significant ideas and techniques developed in recent times. And before attempting this task, it is necessary to look more closely at some of the outstanding features and figures of earlier periods.

THE COLONIAL PERIOD

Colonial society and culture were not merely European in origin and character: they were predominantly English. Consequently, English mercantilist ideas naturally provided the background for American economic writers. The broad compatibility among commerce, religion and the maintenance of a hierarchical social structure was a continuing theme. The Puritan conscience readily reconciled piety and the accumulation of riches as evidence of successful endeavour, if not of divine grace. As in England, trade was valued as an agent of economic growth, regarded as an expansive and liberating force rather than as a threat to the socioeconomic order; and praise of the merchant's achievements represented both a rationalization of and a contribution to colonial expansion.

The major themes of English mercantilist economics were echoed, even literally copied, by colonial writers, but with significant modifications and differences of emphasis. While the positive role of the state in economic affairs was acknowledged in English, and strongly emphasized in continental economic literature, the colonists, being on the receiving end of much British legislation, frequently questioned the desirability and efficacy of government restrictions. Even in England, of course, there were innumerable complaints from specific producer, occupational or regional interests; but colonial opposition to taxation, currency, trade and commodity regulations were endemic and growing in strength. There were frequent appeals for commercial freedom; but, as in England, these appeals were usually partisan and practical rather than abstract and general, as in the works of Adam Smith and his supporters.

Recognition of the mutuality of interests among trading nations, which reflected the expansion of overseas commerce and the emergence of more systematic economic analysis in later English mercantilist writings, had no counterpart in the colonies. On the contrary, nationalist sentiment grew, especially during and after the turbulent phase of Anglo-American relations, 1763–1783. Yet even in the revolutionary period some authors acknowledged the substantial economic benefits derived from the British connection, and ingenious efforts were made to demonstrate the compatibility of British and colonial interests. After independence, similar arguments were deployed in appeals for the relaxation of British restrictions on the lucrative West Indies trade.

Echoing later English mercantilists, colonial writers acknowledged the importance of a favourable balance of trade as the means of ensuring an adequate bullion supply in a country lacking gold and silver mines, and laid even greater stress on the dynamic functions of money as a stimulus to economic activity, rather than as merely a passive store of value. Indeed, the money supply became an obsession, for periodic desperate shortages of currency were exacerbated by British opposition to colonial legal tender issues and insistence on payment of debts in specie. Consequently there were numerous proposals to found public or private land or credit banks, and heated debates about the benefits and dangers of paper money.

The colonists' preoccupation with monetary affairs meant that there was no tendency, as in later English mercantilism, to emphasize the role of employment as a key element in economic growth. The importance of population increase and labour supply was acknowledged, but underemployment and poverty attracted comparatively little attention, for these problems were much less acute than in England; and there was no disposition to calculate the employment content of imports and exports or to substitute a 'balance of labour' for the conventional balance-of-trade concept. Idleness was attacked on moral and religious grounds, but there were few advocates of low wages as a means of ensuring labour effort. The English poor law system was frequently criticized; and imitations of English price- and wage-fixing practices, and settlement and apprenticeship laws, were neither effective nor long-lasting.

The outstanding colonial economic writer, Benjamin Franklin, was in many respects a representative figure of his age. Printer, journalist, newspaper proprietor, scientist, land promoter and distinguished public servant, he personified the characteristic American blend of thought and action, and facilitated the transition of the country from colonial dependence to nationhood. A personal link between leading European intellectuals and American readers, his voluminous writings usually reflected domestic concerns. Franklin's economic ideas embraced mercantilist, physiocratic and liberal elements. He opposed English trade restrictions, denied that the colonies drained the mother country of population, followed French economists in stressing the primacy of agriculture over manufactures, deplored the shortage of currency, favoured the use of paper money – albeit subsequently with reservations – and advocated the establishment of a colonial bank, to be managed from England. While powerfully preaching Puritan virtues, he was an enlightened and cosmopolitan thinker, and not unduly inhibited by religion. Franklin's most notable publication was *Observations Concerning the Increase of Mankind* (1751), which anticipated – some would claim surpassed – Thomas Malthus' theory of population.

THE FIRST CENTURY OF INDEPENDENCE

Political independence did not mean economic or intellectual independence: the same basic problems persisted – some in excacerbated form – and economic issues continued to be treated mainly in a piecemeal fashion. There was, admittedly, a growing awareness of the systematic ideas emerging in Europe; and works by David Hume, Adam Smith, Dugald Stewart, the Physiocrats, and (later) John Ramsay McCulloch, Thomas Malthus, David Ricardo and Jean-Baptiste Say were quoted increasingly. But the use of these sources was both varied and conflicting, and the attitudes toward them were often ambivalent and confusing. While their authority was repeatedly cited by leading men of affairs and contending parties in policy debates, there was no hesitation to modify or dismiss European economic ideas whenever they seemed irrelevant or inappropriate to American interests, needs and conditions. On at least one occasion it was suggested that political economy should receive government aid because it could contribute to the solution of the national economic problems.

But while political economy was becoming part of everyday public discourse, there were concomitant drawbacks. It was repeatedly attacked as a useless, erroneous, even pernicious body of alien doctrines; economists were dismissed as mere partisans or members of warring sects; and any claims to scientific status were ridiculed. Daniel Webster's declaration in 1830 that the subject consisted solely of 'mere truisms' or 'doubtful propositions' was hardly untypical. Of course, political economy encountered similar vociferous opposition in England; but anti-intellectualism may indeed be a more powerful phenomenon in America, according to Richard Hofstadter. As Fetter has noted, the full flowering of American economics had to await the emergence of a judicious and scholarly spirit in the social sciences, a congenial climate of public opinion and the establishment of social institutions capable of safeguarding intellectual independence.

There was a marked expansion in the teaching of political economy in American colleges about 1820, but it usually comprised a dogmatically simplified version of classical doctrines, frequently as modified by J.B. Say, presented as part of a moral philosophy course taught by a clergyman–academic who possessed neither the requisite competence nor interest. It was generally treated as a vehicle for moral improvement; and even after the Civil War Arthur Latham Perry, author of the text most widely used for several decades, frankly acknowledged that the instructor using his volume need have no prior knowledge of the subject. Earlier textbook authors viewed political economy as a systematic arrangement of God's laws 'in unison with the voice of morality', and divine support was invoked on behalf of sound policy as well as righteous conduct. As John McVickar, author of the first American political economy textbook, *Outlines of Political Economy* (1825), based largely on McCulloch's *Encyclopaedia Britannica* article, declared, 'I cannot but reverence the claims of commerce as something holy', and Perry, thirty years later, described free trade as 'in accordance with the natural dictates of Providence', it is hardly surprising that some readers questioned their scientific detachment.

Since the tariff was the most important single economic policy issue during the century after independence, and protection has often been regarded as a distinctively American doctrine, it is easy to understand why so many Americans regarded economists as committed spokesmen for free trade who were under the spell of alien physiocratic or classical doctrines. Classical economics and *laissez-faire* seemed irrelevant to American conditions, so the rise of a rival indigenous 'nationalist' school was doubtless inevitable.

Patriotic sentiment and competing visions of economic development underlay the conflict between the Hamiltonian and Jeffersonian ideals that profoundly influenced political and social attitudes in this period. The conflict is usually depicted in oversimplified terms; but it is broadly true that while Alexander Hamilton and his intellectual collaborator, Tench Coxe, advocated a 'balanced' economy in which commerce and manufactures would be prominent, Thomas Jefferson and his supporters, partly following physiocratic ideas, were more favourably disposed toward agriculture. In general, while the Jeffersonians usually won the early skirmishes, the Hamiltonians were ultimately victorious, their doctrines being enshrined in the 'American system' so effectively propagated by Henry Clay. Strictly speaking, this was not a logically coherent system but a miscellaneous set of practical policies designed to promote the effective utilization of the national resources. All its components – strong federal government, a national bank, the tariff, internal improvements and the national debt – were controversial, and several became central issues in the growing antebellum sectional hostility. Among supporters of the 'American system', the Pennsylvania protectionists constituted an extreme and monolithic pressure group from whose ranks emerged the first internationally known American economist, Henry C. Carey.

Carey's ideas were a characteristically American blend of European doctrines and domestic interests and prejudices. His father, Mathew Carey, who owned a leading publishing firm, was a prolific author, prominent protectionist campaigner and associate of Georg Friedrich List, who absorbed American political economy before returning to Germany to write his protectionist classic, *The National System of Political Economy* (1841). Henry Carey was no slavish disciple, for in the 1830s he advocated completely free trade. But from 1847, after some years of hesitation, he joined the protectionists and wrote prolifically on a variety of topics. Like Frédéric Bastiat in France, he believed in the harmony of interests, and his optimism largely explains his famous attack on Ricardo's rent doctrine and Malthus' gloomy population theory, both of which he considered irrelevant to America, with its abundant land and scarce labour. In his notable *Essay on the Rate of Wages* (1835), *Principles of Political Economy* (1837–1840) and *The Past, the Present and the Future* (1848), Carey reversed the customary sequence, arguing that cultivation proceeded from inferior to superior soils, with concomitantly increasing returns. In the long run, he contended, capital grew more rapidly than population, and wages rose both absolutely and relatively. An almost uncritical admirer of the Bank of the United States, he defended the moneyed interests and was himself a wealthy man closely associated with the Philadelphia social elite. In general his writings reinforced the growing conviction that America required doctrines appropriate to its institutions and environment, and his relativistic concept of the role of representative government harmonized with the ideas of later American disciples of the German historical school.

Only two of the many other able and indigenous economic writers of the period can be mentioned here: John Rae and Francis Amasa Walker. A Scotsman who lived mainly in North America, Rae had a checkered and ill-starred career. Like the Careys he was a protectionist, but he is nowadays admired for the strikingly original theory of capital in his *Statement of Some New Principles on the Subject of Political Economy* (1834), which, according to Schumpeter, was 'conceived in unprecedented depth and breadth'. Rae's book anticipated a major part of Eugen Böhm-Bawerk's later theory; but while John Stuart Mill, the most widely known economist of the age, generously acknowledged Rae's achievement, his work was virtually ignored until the turn of the century.

Walker, by contrast, achieved international recognition during his lifetime both for his economic ideas and for his many official activities. An outstanding leader and able administrator, he had a brilliant career as a Civil War general, superintendent of the census and president of the Massachusetts Institute of Technology. His election as the first president of the AEA symbolized his transitional position between the 'old' and 'new' schools of political economy. A severe critic of doctrinaire *laissez-faire* and the classical wages-fund theory, Walker also attacked contemporary socialists and popular radicals, describing Henry George's proposals as 'steeped in infamy'. His father, Amasa, had published a widely used textbook, *The Science of Wealth*, in 1866. Walker's own principal works were *The Wages Question* (1876), in which he advanced a 'residual claimant' theory, *Political Economy* (1883) and *International Bimetallism* (1896), dealing with a movement of which he was a prominent international leader.

THE SECOND CENTURY OF INDEPENDENCE

Since the centennial, American economics has been utterly transformed. The number of currently practising professionals far exceeds that in any other country for which data are available, and most qualified observers acknowledge that American standards of academic training and publication are, on the average, significantly higher than elsewhere. The professionalization process gathered momentum in the 1880s and 1890s under the leadership of a young generation of scholars trained in Germany, who took advantage of the expansion of academic employment opportunities and the sustained public interest in such current policy questions as the currency, the labour movement, railroads and the trusts. In the twentieth century the pace has accelerated rapidly, especially since 1945. It has truly been an 'age of opportunity' for economists, in terms of remunerative employment in universities, business, and government, research funds, publication outlets and influence on the public. Yet while academic economics has become ever more esoteric and technical, there has nevertheless been a substantial growth in awareness of economic issues among the public.

The disastrous depression of the 1930s constituted a watershed in both professional and lay economics. Despite the persistence of popular fallacies, there has been a marked rise in the general level of economic literacy. Millions of Americans have taken elementary college courses in the subject and, especially in recent years, outstanding professional academics have publicly expounded and debated economic affairs alongside financial journalists, business analysts and numerous public or private educational and propaganda agencies. Most important has been the dramatic growth of government participation in and responsibility for economic and social conditions through the New Deal, the so-called Keynesian revolution, and the post-1945 acceptance of economic interventionism by both major political parties. No present-day government can contemplate an economic downturn with equanimity. Economic affairs have become highly politicized, with concomitant risks to the economists' professional integrity. Economic 'indicators' now constitute part of everyday conversation and reports in the mass media, making it difficult for even the purest of pure theorists to forget that his or her discipline is widely considered to be highly relevant to the current mixed-capitalist society.

In the early post Civil War decades the tremendous enthusiasm for business enterprise was such that the courts seemed, according to Sidney Fine, to view unrestricted economic freedom as one of the inalienable rights enshrined in the Constitution. The conservative *laissez-faire* ideology was vigorously propagated in both academic and popular circles, especially by the prolific Yale economist and sociologist William Graham Sumner, who adapted Herbert Spencer's social Darwinist ideas to the domestic situation. Near the end of the century the climate of opinion shifted toward a more activist concept of a 'general welfare state' with the growing desire to check the abuses of business power and to remedy the social and economic evils of uncontrolled industrialization and urbanization.

The young economist founder-members of the AEA, especially Henry Carter Adams, John Bates Clark, Richard Theodore Ely, Edmund Janes James, Simon Nelson Patten and Edwin Robert Anderson Seligman, contributed directly to this movement. Their studies in Germany had sensitized them to the dangers of *laissez-faire* individualism, and the initial AEA 'declaration of principles' included the statement that 'We regard the State as an agency whose positive assistance is one of the indispensable conditions of human progress'. Given the existing economic and social unrest and the prevailing pro-business ideology, this deliberately toned-down pronouncement was still radical enough to deter some economists and conservative laymen, including Sumner, from joining. The declaration provoked embarrassing charges of socialism, and some of the prime movers of the organization feared that Ely's aggressive Christian socialist proselytizing would jeopardize its scholarly and scientific reputation.

After a brief phase of uncertainty and the waning of methodological controversy between the 'old' and 'new' schools of economics, the 'declaration of principles' was dropped and compromise over policy was reached in 1892 with Ely's resignation as secretary and Dunbar's election as president, in succession to Walker. These changes are not merely of parochial interest. They symbolize the determination to abandon the open partisanship of earlier generations and to adopt the new ideal of detached and objective professionalism that has increasingly dominated American economic thought ever since. The adoption of a more conservative and scientific tone was designed, according to Daniel Horowitz, 'to protect a shaky academic freedom and to avoid arousing suspicion about the nature of their policy pretensions'. Of course, practice has not always been in conformity with that ideal. But the subsequent deliberate abstention by the AEA, as a body, from direct commitments to specific policy positions has undoubtedly enhanced its scientific reputation.

The men who laid the foundations of twentieth century American economics were extraordinarily energetic, versatile and long-lived. While their first duty was to teach the expanding student population and publish scholarly works, they also founded and managed learned periodicals and societies, and administered academic departments, schools, research institutes and even universities. And although American economists made few outstanding contributions to the central corpus of formal theory until the 1930s, they actively shaped public opinion through their popular lectures, speeches, miscellaneous writings on current issues and participation in a wide variety of official investigatory commissions and statutory bodies.

The growth of conservatism in the profession did not entail a retreat into academic ivory towers. On the contrary, the flow of systematic descriptive and statistical studies that commanded international scholarly respect from the 1880s on contributed directly to understanding by the educated public of current and prospective economic and social developments. The heated political controversy over the monetary standard, a central issue before and during the 1896 presidential campaign, not only revealed sharp theoretical and policy disagreements among the academics, but also demonstrated that their work was relevant to major policy issues. Not all were German-trained, or hostile to classical economics and *laissez-faire*. But the main thrust of the profession was toward moderate reform, and scholarly research reinforced the 'progressive' tide of educated opinion after the turn of the century.

Richard T. Ely was an outstanding example of the new academic breed. After studying in the United States and Germany, he became the first full-time economics teacher at the influential Johns Hopkins University in 1881 and was soon notorious as an outspoken and emotional critic of 'old school' economics and an advocate of seemingly socialistic reforms. His insistence on the intimate relationship between Christian ethics and economics makes him, like several of his contemporaries, a transitional figure between the theologically coloured, collegiate tradition of political economy and the new secular professionalism. After resigning his AEA secretaryship in 1892, Ely moved to Wisconsin, where he was director of the School of Economics, Political Science and History, the staff and students of which made major contributions both to academic research and to state (and subsequently federal) economic and social legislation. Having been accused of socialism in the 1880s and 1890s, he later substantially moderated his views and was in fact attacked as a spokesman for conservative propertied interests in the 1920s.

Although distinctly limited as an economic theorist, Ely was a stimulating teacher and a major academic entrepreneur who, by his energy and enthusiasm, shaped the careers of many students and colleagues. In the most important single case, that of John R. Commons, he acted as a direct link between nineteenth century German historicism and American institutionalism. He wrote incessantly, producing and editing numerous treatises, textbooks, scholarly and popular articles, and pioneering studies: *French and German Socialism in Modern Times* (1883); *The Labor Movement in America* (1886); *Property and Contract in Their Relations to the Distribution of Wealth* (1914); *Elements of Land Economics* (1924, with Edward W. Morehouse); and

Land Economics (1940, with George S. Wehrwein). His *Introduction to Political Economy* (1889) became, in its later collaborative version, entitled *Outlines of Economics* (1893), the most widely used economics textbook in the 1920s. His 'new school' polemic, *The Past and the Present of Political Economy* (1884), and his autobiography, *Ground Under Our Feet* (1938), are valuable as historical sources.

John Bates Clark was unquestionably the leading economic theorist of his generation. An independent discoverer of the marginal utility principle in the 1870s, he revealed in his innovative *The Philosophy of Wealth* (1886) the strong ethical interest and moderate reformism that he shared with several of his contemporaries. Yet his crowning achievement, *The Distribution of Wealth* (1899), which contained a powerful and elegant formulation of marginal productivity theory, appeared to justify the current socioeconomic order by contending that it gave 'to each what he creates' in economic terms. This doctrine was developed partly as a rebuttal of the leading American popular economic radical, Henry George, whose astonishingly successful *Progress and Poverty* (1879) inspired the 'single tax' movement on both sides of the Atlantic. George's analysis of land values rested on Ricardo's rent doctrine and was presented with evangelical fervour. Even Walker, who described George's ideas as 'steeped in infamy', acknowledged his effectiveness in arousing public interest in economic affairs. Although George dismissed the professoriat as allies of the ruling class, the combined impact of his ideas on both academic and lay readers reveals that American economics was not yet insulated from popular radicalism.

From the late nineteenth century, American economists increasingly became assimilated into the international scientific community through the interchange of ideas, publications and personnel. They were receptive not only to German teachings; they also readily adopted Austrian marginalism and English neo-classical economics, especially following the publication of Alfred Marshall's magisterial *Principles of Economics* (1890). Americans welcomed his undogmatic eclecticism as disseminated through the remarkably effective teaching and writings of Frank William Taussig, at Harvard, until the late 1930s. A moderate traditionalist and long-time editor of the *Quarterly Journal of Economics* in succession to Dunbar, Taussig was no great theorist. But he produced the classic *Tariff History of the United States* (1888) and served on a variety of government bodies, including a term as chairman of the Tariff Commission, established in 1916. He also published important works on international trade and business leadership.

Another young conservative, Arthur Twining Hadley, a colleague of Sumner's who became president of Yale, produced a textbook and the constructive theoretical and practical study *Railroad Transportation* (1885), and served as commissioner of the Connecticut Bureau of Labor Statistics. Despite methodological and doctrinal disagreements with Henry Carter Adams, a member of the 'new' school, he welcomed the latter's appointment as chief statistician to the Interstate Commerce Commission in 1888. Economists of various shades of opinion were enjoying increasing opportunities to enter the public policy arena.

James Laurence Laughlin was a third, more dogmatic young traditionalist. A staunch conservative who held aloof from the AEA until 1904, he taught at Harvard, Cornell and Chicago, where he became head of the political economy department and founded the *Journal of Political Economy* (1892). An ardent gold monometallist, Laughlin actively participated in public controversy and was ridiculed by the leading contemporary pro-silver pamphleteer, William 'Coin' Harvey. Yet, despite his partisanship, Laughlin tolerated heterodoxy among his colleagues, who included such brilliant and original thinkers as Thorstein Bunde Veblen, Herbert Joseph Davenport, Wesley Clair Mitchell, Robert Hoxie and John Maurice Clark. He probably constituted the stereotype of the rigid 'orthodox' economist featured so prominently in heterodox writings.

During the twentieth century the growth of professionalism has gradually obliterated some of the more distinctive indigenous features and themes in American economic thought. By comparison with Europe, the spread of professionally acceptable ideas, standards and values has been slow, with certain established eastern seaboard institutions and a handful of midwestern and far western universities leading the way. The sheer size and diversity of the country have made it virtually impossible for any one individual, department or doctrinal school to gain complete ascendancy – although some observers would claim that this situation was approached in the post-1945 Keynesian movement. But intellectual and sociological, as well as geographical factors have encouraged diversity: for example, the premium on innovation; the prevalence of competitive assertiveness; the comparative lack of inhibition and reticence; and the heterogeneity of academic conditions, training and objectives. Even among 'orthodox' writers there was a remarkable proliferation of rival theoretical systems and approaches, many of which revealed a taste for intellectual product differentiation rather than creative scientific ability. And there was, in addition, a strong current of heterodox or dissenting economics, usually known as institutionalism, of which Veblen was the undoubted initiator and guiding spirit.

The most brilliant, penetrating and destructive critic of economic orthodoxy who ever lived, Thorstein Veblen was, above all, a marginal man. During his student days at Carleton College, Johns Hopkins and Yale, where he wrote a dissertation on Kant's philosophy in 1884; in the seven-year jobless rural exile that followed; and in a succession of unsatisfactory academic positions at Cornell, Chicago, Stanford, Missouri and the New School for Social Research, he made life difficult for himself and his colleagues. A dreadful teacher, he was openly subversive of academic routine, discouraging students and, as Mitchell recalled, practising 'vivisection' on his colleagues without benefit of anaesthetic. His style was calculated, circuitous and at times opaque, and he attacked the 'preconceptions' of the received doctrine rather than the doctrines *per se*. His most explicitly economic book, *The Theory of Business Enterprise* (1904), contained a powerful and topical critique of the destructive effects on the machine industry of finance capitalism, with its built-in tendency to depressions caused by overproduction and/or speculative manipulation.

Owing something to Karl Marx, for whom he had a certain regard, Veblen was no respecter of German historicism, to which he also owed something. But his most persistent and effective attacks were directed against classical orthodoxy, with its Newtonian preoccupation with static equilibrium, its ridiculous 'animism' and hedonistic psychology, its 'normalization' of data, and its theological view of economic change. In its place Veblen proposed to substitute a Darwinian approach, incorporating the neutral concept of cumulative causation, an 'instinct' theory of human behaviour and a demonstration of the eventual dominance of the engineer and the machine process over the captain of industry and 'imbecile' pecuniary institutions. No brief summary can convey his effective deployment of a wide variety of esoteric sources and illustrative examples. His principal methodological essays were reprinted in *The Place of Science in Modern Civilization* (1919) and *Essays in Our Changing Order* (1934). *The Higher Learning in America, A Memorandum on the Conduct of Universities by Businessmen* (1918) contains a devastating exposé of contemporary academic life, while *Imperial Germany and the Industrial Revolution* (1915), *The Vested Interests and the State of the Industrial Arts* (1919), *The Engineers and the Price System* (1921) and *Absentee Ownership and Business Enterprise in Recent Times* (1923) embody his main critiques of the existing socioeconomic order.

Although Veblen left no direct disciples and formed no doctrinal school, his ideas exerted a powerful influence on subsequent generations of American economists and social scientists, for example, through the writings of Clarence Edwin Ayres and John Kenneth Galbraith. A philosopher by training and follower of John Dewey, Ayres became the leader of a regional school of institutionalists in Texas, where he taught for more than thirty years. His most significant work, *The Theory of Economic Progress* (1944), constitutes a direct link between Veblen's generation and the post-1945 dissidents sometimes known as neo-institutionalists. Galbraith is less clearly Veblenian, although he shares some of the familiar institutionalist concerns. By training an agricultural economist, and subsequently a government employee, editor of *Fortune* magazine, professor at Harvard and ambassador to India, he has been the principal post-war link between the economics profession and the lay public through his extraordinarily successful books: *American Capitalism: The Concept of Countervailing Power* (1952), *The Affluent Society* (1958), *The New Industrial State* (1967) *Economics and the Public Purpose* (1973) and many others. Although most of the main themes of these works have long been familiar to professionals, taken together they provide the most incisive analysis of American capitalism since Veblen's. And the fact that Galbraith was elected president of the AEA in 1972 indicates that public and professional value judgements are not always incompatible.

Wesley Clair Mitchell, the second outstanding member of the institutionalist triumvirate, studied at Chicago during the 1890s. Laughlin proposed the dissertation topic that led to Mitchell's first two substantial publications, *A History of the Greenbacks* (1903) and *Gold, Prices, and Wages Under the Greenback Standard* (1908), both skilfully combining theory and history with detailed statistical analysis. But it was Veblen who reinforced Mitchell's distaste for abstract theory and shaped his vision of the business cycle as 'the economic process in motion' and his urge to reconstruct the psychological foundations of economics. These views were expounded in a series of journal articles, in the famous lecture course 'Types of Economic Theory', which he delivered at Columbia for several decades, and at the beginning of his classic, *Business Cycles* (1913). Mitchell's subsequent research on this subject was unique in its breadth of scope and continuity, especially after he became co-founder and first director of the National Bureau of Economic Research (1920). The numerous publications of the bureau have constituted the main empirical component of twentieth century American economics and economic history. Through the work of Mitchell's colleagues and students, especially Simon Kuznets, its national income studies and economic indicators now form an essential basis for government economic policy making in many countries.

Although Mitchell's work has been attacked as 'measurement without theory' by Tjalling Koopmans, more sympathetic interpreters, such as Milton Friedman, have discerned an underlying conceptual framework of considerable subtlety. Mitchell was greatly respected both by orthodox and heterodox economists and by leading public figures, and participated in many important investigations of contemporary economic and social problems. His belief in the intellectual's contribution to 'social engineering' reflected the influence of the instrumentalist philosopher John Dewey, his Chicago teacher and Columbia colleague. But after the Great Depression he tended to concentrate more on the completion of his lifetime research.

Like Veblen and Mitchell, John R. Commons, the third great institutionalist, was born and raised in the Middle West. Like Veblen, he had a checkered student and early professional career, failing to complete his doctorate at Johns Hopkins and being dismissed from or deprived of several university posts. After five years of non-academic research, he joined his former teacher, Ely, at Wisconsin in 1904, remaining there until his retirement. In a sense Commons had three distinct but related careers: as a labour historian, for which he is best remembered today; as a remarkably successful policy maker; and as a theoretical social scientist. With his Wisconsin collaborators, Commons produced *A Documentary History of Industrial Society* (1910–1911) and *History of Labor in the United States* (1918–1935). His seminal article 'American Shoemakers, 1648–1895: A Sketch of Industrial Evolution' stressed the historical importance of product markets; while his concept of job rights, derived partly from H.C. Adams, formed the basis of the influential *A Theory of the Labor Movement* (1928), by his student Selig Perlman.

While engaged in labour history, Commons also conducted investigations of civil service reform, public utility regulation, workmen's compensation, unemployment insurance and small loans; and although he remained neutral, he took full account of the vested interests involved. The fruits of this work were later embodied in state legislation, making Wisconsin a laboratory in economic and social affairs, the experiments of which were widely copied on both state and federal levels. Some of Commons' former students made notable contributions to such legislation during the New Deal.

Much of Commons' theorizing was derived from his varied experiences. His first significant theoretical work, the idiosyncratic *The Distribution of Wealth* (1893), was an unsuccessful blend of Austrian marginalism and historical analysis. His impressive historicist *Legal Foundations of Capitalism* (1924) and the massive attempted synthesis *Institutional Economics: Its Place in Political Economy* (1934) represented mature efforts to supplement orthodox economics, which Commons regarded as narrowly Newtonian and individualistic. Instead, he emphasized the role of group behaviour, or 'collective action in control of individual actions', especially as manifested in organizations or 'going concerns'. His central concept of 'transactions' embraced but also transcended mere exchange relationships, and his seminal articles entitled 'A Sociological View of Sovereignty' anticipated later ideas of 'counterpoise' or 'countervailing' power in a mixed economy.

Unfortunately, Commons' theoretical ideas, in contrast with his more practical studies, were often expressed in maddeningly obscure and tortuous prose. But he was an exceptionally stimulating teacher and policy maker, and his central ideas anticipated much recent work in such modern social science disciplines as organization theory, managerial and administrative decision making, and conflict resolution. Above all, his life epitomizes the combination of scholarship and practical action that has so long been a feature of American economics.

Viewed as a whole, the institutionalist legacy has been decidedly mixed. Against Veblen's failure to provide an 'evolutionary' alternative to traditional doctrines one must set Mitchell's and Commons' substantial contributions to the scope, method and empirical content of applied economics. Historians of economic analysis frequently dismiss the 1920s, especially in America, as a period marked more by intellectual vigour and variety than by conceptual progress or logical synthesis. Admittedly the persistence of heterodox assaults on conventional assumptions and doctrines contributed to the decline of interest in value and distribution theory; and the sheer growth and subdivision of subject matter gave prominence to quasi-independent subdisciplines, such as agricultural, labour, and transportation economics, money and banking, and business cycles, as against general theory, which remained largely confined to the textbooks. The prevailing range of interests partly reflected the shift of educational resources into business schools, where scientific management and other vocational areas were studied, subjects often crossing borderlines between economics and other social science disciplines.

In this era of business hegemony the impulse to progressive reform died away, and few economists offered radical criticisms of the socioeconomic system. The sharp depression of the early 1920s stimulated one major issue of interest to both businessmen and academics, price stabilization. Leading economists such as Commons, Irving Fisher and J.M. Keynes combined with practical men in support of the Stable Money League (later the National Monetary Association); and the economics profession faced a direct challenge from two 'outsiders', William Trufant Foster and Waddill Catchings, whose Pollak Foundation for Economic Research published popular studies: *Money* (1923), *Profits* (1925), *Business Without a Buyer* (1927) and *The Road to Plenty* (1928). Offering a prize to successful critics of their underconsumptionist explanation of depressions, whose replies were published in *Pollak Prize Essays* (1927), they generated widespread interest in questions that occupied centre stage a few years later.

Irving Fisher was undoubtedly the outstanding American economic theorist of this period. Introduced to mathematical economics at Yale by Sumner, he produced a brilliant dissertation, *Mathematical Investigations in the Theory of Value and Prices* (1892), that drew on the penetrating *Principles of Political Economy* (1885) of the astronomer and amateur economist Simon Newcomb, Ely's critic at Johns Hopkins, who had introduced the concept of 'societary circulation' and utilized the distinction between stocks and flows. Fisher subsequently published a stream of fundamental theoretical studies, including *The Nature of Capital and Income* (1906), *The Purchasing Power of Money* (1911), *The Making of Index Numbers* (1922), which was sponsored by the Pollak Foundation, and *The Theory of Interest* (1930). His formulation of the quantity theory of money has become an integral part of basic economics; his ideas of time discounting and impatience linked Austrian capital theory to Keynes' analysis; and his adoption of the logic of choice in place of hedonistic psychology paved the way for subsequent developments in demand theory.

Gifted with great creative energy, Fisher was an effective expositor through textbooks and many popular writings, and his enthusiastic campaigning on behalf of monetary reform, the League of Nations, eugenics, prohibition and healthy living possessed crankish features that, for a time, detracted from his scientific reputation. To many he was known for his losses in the stock market after his failure to predict the Great Depression.

Needless to say, the depression stunned both the economics profession and the general public. Despite renewed doubts about the economists' expertise, their help was sought from all quarters, including the administration of Herbert Hoover; and many and varied were the moderate, piecemeal proposals that they offered. There was widespread professional recognition of the need for reforms of monetary and credit policy, guarantees of bank deposits, regulation of the stock exchange, the readjustment of private debts, the expansion of public works and the maintenance of deficit financing. Contrary to later impressions fostered by Keynes' disciples, economists of various doctrinal and ideological views opposed wage cuts and other supposedly 'orthodox' remedies. There was, indeed, a marked proclivity for combining in support of various petitions and memorials, the most famous being that opposing the 1930 Smoot-Hawley Tariff, signed by more than one thousand economists. What was sorely needed at the professional level was comprehensive theoretical reconstruction rather than displays of solidarity. This was lacking until 1936, when J.M. Keynes' pathbreaking *General Theory of Employment, Interest, and Money* met with an enthusiastic reception.

Keynes' principal American propagator was the Harvard economist Alvin Hansen. Like many of his predecessors, Hansen had taught school for several years before obtaining his Ph.D. at Wisconsin, in 1918; he then taught at Brown and Minnesota. An acknowledged specialist on economic fluctuations, he revealed in *Business Cycle Theory* (1927) and *Economic Stabilization in an Unbalanced World* (1932) that he was a mild deflationist and supporter of Say's law, and his initial response to the *General Theory* was only mildly favourable. But at Harvard (from 1937) Hansen's renowned fiscal policy seminars and his books – *Full Recovery or Stagnation?* (1938), *Fiscal Policy and Business Cycles* (1941), *Economic Policy and Full Employment* (1947) and *Monetary Theory and Fiscal Policy* (1949) – were largely responsible for making Keynesianism (as distinct from Keynes' own ideas) into the post-war professional economic orthodoxy. Hansen's own controversial belief that the United States was suffering from secular stagnation, hints of which had appeared in his earlier writings, helped to create a climate of opinion favourable to post-war government macroeconomic management.

Some of Hansen's supporters regarded the dramatic World War II expansion as confirmatory evidence of his stagnationist thesis, which underlay their startlingly inaccurate predictions of massive post-war unemployment; others regarded the recession of the late 1950s as evidence of the continuing deficiency of private investment opportunities. More generally, Keynesian ideas not merely encouraged advocates of economic interventionism, but also stimulated the demand for economists in government, which had begun to grow under the New Deal. A major watershed was the mildly Keynesian, but hotly debated, Employment Act of 1946, which created the Council of Economic Advisers, thus indicating that the 'new' economics had put professional economists in the saddle as far as policy making was concerned. Unfortunately, the period since about 1970 reveals that they were riding for a fall after the peak of their public success with the 'Kennedy' tax cut of 1964. The subsequent combination of slow economic growth and inflation ('stagflation') has not responded to Keynesian medicines, with the result that there has been a crisis of professional self-confidence and a resurgence of rival doctrines.

Although Keynesianism has undoubtedly been the dominant stream of economic thought and policy in America since the late 1930s, even a brief survey must pay due attention to other elements that have sustained diversity, a term that embraces conflict as well as mere variety. Like other disciplines, economics has been directly affected by the explosive growth in the production and distribution of knowledge, the increasing global interdependence of the scholarly community and the seemingly irresistible tendency toward mathematization and quantification in the social sciences. Mathematics is of course a language that facilitates international communication – as, for example, in the case of the Econometric Society since 1930. American international links have increased not only because of the vast material and educational resources of the nation, but also through its continuing capacity to attract and retain outstanding talent from abroad.

Even a brief sampling will reveal the richness of the roster of illustrious immigrant economists since the disintegration of the Austro-Hungarian Empire and the rise of Nazism in the 1930s. Those born or trained abroad include Joseph A. Schumpeter, Friedrich A. von Hayek, Fritz Machlup and Gottfried Haberler (Austria); Oskar Morgenstern (Germany); John von Neumann (Hungary); Abraham Wald and Nicholas Georgescu-Roegen (Rumania); Tjalling Koopmans (the Netherlands); Henry Schultz (Poland); Wassily Leontief and Paul Baran (the Soviet Union); Kenneth Boulding (England); and John Kenneth Galbraith (Canada). Several of these scholars have developed theories or techniques that have opened up new sub-disciplines, while others have reinforced existing trends or taken up themes already present. In at least one instance a foreign-born economist, Henry Schultz, built upon the work of statistical estimation of economic variables by an American, Henry Ludwell Moore, who had no native-born disciples. In other cases – for example, Galbraith and Boulding – immigrants have made significant contributions to that supposedly distinctive American movement, institutionalism. An even more striking convergence, perhaps, has been that between the Austrian libertarian economists and the main current of American economics rivalling the post-war Keynesians, the 'Chicago school'.

Nowadays identified, often too exclusively, with its brilliant 'monetarist' leader Milton Friedman, this methodological, doctrinal and ideological tradition can be traced to the 1920s in the work of Jacob Viner and, more especially, Frank Hyneman Knight. A student at Cornell under Herbert Davenport, who was himself a severe and independent-minded critic of Marshallian economics, Knight produced a distinguished dissertation that was subsequently published as *Risk, Uncertainty and Profit* (1921). Designed primarily to clarify existing economic theory, this study advanced the theory of entrepreneurial profit by concentrating on the uncertainty-bearing, rather than merely the risk-bearing, function. In a stream of later essays and reviews, Knight revealed exceptionally penetrating critical powers stemming partly from his early training in philosophy. Dismissing important parts of classical and Austrian economics as erroneous and confused, he attacked the scientific pretensions of conventional economic methodology and proposed a bifurcation between an a priori concept of price theory devoid of historical or normative implications, and economic behaviour, which was conditioned by custom, institutions and the legal framework. Conceding late in his life that this gave him some affiliation with institutionalism, he was nevertheless sceptical toward most institutionalist ideas and hostile to New Deal-type social reform proposals.

This, like his constant emphasis on the value of freedom, links Knight with Friedman, especially through the ideas of his colleague and Friedman's teacher, Henry Calvert Simons. A powerful thinker who wrote comparatively little, Simons was an undogmatic libertarian whose posthumously collected essays, *Economic Policy for a Free Society* (1948), indicated that he valued equality only a little less highly than freedom. An outspoken opponent of labour union power, Simons favoured monetary expansion as an anti-depression policy but was opposed to discretionary economic intervention and was concerned by the trend toward monopoly. His brief *Personal Income Tax* (1938) and *Federal Tax Reform* (1950, written in 1943) exerted an important influence on later Chicago economists.

Friedman, one of the most eloquent and persuasive of living economists, is known throughout the world as an outspoken defender of capitalism and critic of simplistic Keynesian orthodoxy. Few economists can display the unity of methodology, theory, policy recommendations and ideology to be found, for example, in his *Essays in Positive Economics* (1953), *Capitalism and Freedom* (1962, with Rose D. Friedman), *A Monetary History of the United States, 1867–1960* (1963, with Anna Jacobson Schwartz) and *The Optimum Quantity of Money and Other Essays* (1969). His study of the consumption function and emphasis on the principle that income is the yield on capital, and capital the present value of income, are significant theoretical contributions; and even the most ardent Keynesians would concede that Friedman's vigorous polemics have brought about a considerable re-emphasis on monetary factors in contemporary theoretical and policy discussions. With his Chicago colleagues, who have in recent years been ingeniously – if not ingenuously – applying competitive price analysis to a range of hitherto untouched problems, Friedman has ensured that American economics did not become monolithic during the 'age of Keynes'.

Three further major American contributions must be mentioned, however briefly, before closing the account. The first is the *Theory of Monopolistic Competition: A Re-orientation of the Theory of Value* (1933), by the Harvard economist Edward H. Chamberlin, which represented a major breakthrough in microeconomic theory. By identifying a spectrum of market positions extending from monopoly to perfect competition, this work stimulated numerous studies of such matters as product differentiation, selling costs and interactions between firms, that had far-reaching implications for the allocation of resources, welfare economics, taxation and public policy with regard to monopoly power.

Even more fundamental and far-reaching was the publication of the *Foundations of Economic Analysis* (1947) by Paul A. Samuelson, which was designed to reveal the underlying unity of micro and macro theory in terms of general hypotheses concerning the conditions and stability of equilibrium. A fertile and prolific mathematical theorist who aims to develop 'operationally meaningful theorems', author of the most successful economics textbook ever produced, a spare-time historian of economics, and a witty and influential contributor to public policy discussion, Samuelson has demonstrated a remarkable range of abilities of the highest order. He has led the way both in the application of mathematical analysis to a wide variety of theoretical problems and in establishing the post-Keynesian synthesis, which has recently been under widespread attack.

The third and last contribution to be recorded here, the lifework of John Maurice Clark, is of a very different character. The son of the great turn-of-the-century economic theorist John Bates Clark, and eventually his successor at Columbia, John Maurice Clark's writings not merely linked the generations but also, in large measure, bridged the gap between orthodoxy and heterodoxy in American economics. His most important book, *Studies in the Economics of Overhead Costs* (1923), explored the distinction between social and private costs, and the differences between economists' and accountants' conceptions. An independent discoverer of the 'acceleration principle' in 1927, Clark later developed a seminal concept of 'workable competition' that was a fruitful tool for studies of industrial organization and market power. A fertile thinker who made almost no use of mathematical formulations, he continued to make thoughtful contributions to a wide variety of conceptual and policy issues; for example, in his books *Alternative to Serfdom* (1948), *The Ethical Basis of Economic Freedom* (1955) and *Competition as a Dynamic Process* (1961). Respected and admired by economists of very divergent views, Clark's work can be regarded as an authentic representation of the mainstream of American economic thought.

CONCLUSION

Since colonial times American economic thought has developed remarkably in range, analytical power, technical sophistication and capacity to influence public opinion and policy making. Indeed, arguably it has been too successful – some professional economists have been too eager to profit from naive public expectations and the exaggerated ambitions of overly sanguine politicians and legislators. Despite George J. Stigler's claim that, since the 1870s, 'the dominant influence upon the working range of economic theorists is the set of internal values and pressures of the discipline' (G.J. Stigler, *Essays in the History of Economics* [Chicago, 1965] p.22), a number of significant exogenous factors have profoundly affected the questions asked, the methods employed and the answers obtained. These factors include the politicization of economic issues, the availability of non-academic employment opportunities, the growth of research funds, the data explosion and far-reaching technological innovations affecting the economists' capacity to construct theoretical models and to process information. Deep divisions of opinion remain within the profession, with respect to both means and ends. Yet despite widespread comment on the so-called crisis in the discipline earlier in the 1970s, and hitherto disappointed hopes of a new post-Keynesian synthesis, American economic thought is as rich, diversified and as full of promise as ever.

BIBLIOGRAPHY

Robert L. Church, 'Economists as Experts: The Rise of an Academic Profession in the United States, 1870–1920', in Lawrence Stone (ed.), *The University in Society* (Princeton, 1974), vol.II, is a stimulating survey of changing attitudes toward the application of economic theory to practice and the social role of the professional economist. A.W. Coats, 'The First Two Decades of the American Economic Association', *American Economic Review*, 50 (Sept. 1960), is an account of the beginnings and early difficulties of the leading organization of American economists; and 'The American Economic Association, 1904–1929', *American Economic Review*, 54 (June 1964), is an account of further development of the leading organization of American economists. Joseph Dorfman, *The Economic Mind in American Civilization*, 5 vols (New York, 1947–1959), is an extraordinarily comprehensive and balanced survey of economic opinion by the leading authority on the subject. Charles F. Dunbar, 'Economic Science in America 1776–1876', *North American Review*, 122 (Jan. 1876), is the earliest general review of the state of American economics by an important economist. Frank A. Fetter, 'The Early History of Political Economy in the United States', *Proceedings of the American Philosophical Society*, 87 (July 1943), is a thoughtful and balanced general survey by a leading economist. Sidney Fine, *Laissez-Faire and the General-Welfare State* (Ann Arbor, Mich., 1964), is a balanced and detailed survey of economic and social ideas.

Milton Friedman, 'The Economic Theorist', in *Wesley Clair Mitchell. The Economic Scientist*, Arthur F. Burns, (ed.) (New York, 1952), is a perceptive analysis of Mitchell's theoretical ideas. Mary O. Furner, *Advocacy and Objectivity: A Crisis in the Professionalization of American Social Science, 1865-1905* (Lexington, Ky., 1975), is an authoritative study of the developing social science community. Allan G. Gruchy, *Modern Economic Thought: The American Contribution* (New York, 1947), is a sympathetic review of the main institutionalist writers; and his *Contemporary Economic Thought: The Contribution of Neo-Institutional Economics* (Englewood Cliffs, N.J., 1972), reviews writings of earlier institutionalist writers and Clarence Ayres. Richard Hofstadter, *Anti-Intellectualism in American Life* (New York, 1962), offers a stimulating review of an important but neglected theme. Daniel Horowitz, 'Textbook Models of American Economic Growth, 1837–1911', *History of Political Economy*, 7 (Summer 1975), reveals the conceptions of economic development held by American economists. Harry G. Johnson, 'The American Tradition in Economics', *Nebraska Journal of Economics and Business*, 16 (Summer 1977), is a perceptive review of some distinctive features of American economics by an outstanding economist.

Tjalling C. Koopmans, 'Measurement Without Theory', *Review of Economics and Statistics*, 29 (Aug. 1947), is a penetrating critique of Mitchell's ideas. Walter P. Metzger, *Academic Freedom in the Age of the University* (New York, 1961), is a perceptive account of the late nineteenth century and early twentieth century academic environment. Michael J.L. O'Connor, *The Origins of Academic Economics in the United States* (New York, 1944), is an authoritative review of pre- and post-Civil War teaching of economics. Paul A. Samuelson, 'Economic Thought and the New Industrialism', in *Paths of American Thought*, Arthur M. Schlesinger, Jr. and Morton White (eds.) (London, 1964), is a stimulating survey of economic science in America by an outstanding economist. Joseph A. Schumpeter, *History of Economic Analysis* (New York, 1954), is a magisterial survey of economic ideas by an outstanding economist. Joseph J. Spengler, 'Economics: Its Direct and Indirect Impact in America, 1776–1976', *Social Science Quarterly*, 57 (June 1976), is a densely packed bicentenial survey of economic ideas by a leading historian of economics.

19

HENRY CARTER ADAMS
A case study in the emergence of the social sciences in the United States, 1850–1900

I

Few scholars would nowadays question the importance of the United States in the world of learning; but the process whereby that nation attained its present eminence still remains obscure. Among the *cognoscenti*, it is generally acknowledged that American scholarship had come of age by the early 1900s, whereas fifty years earlier there had been only a handful of American scholars and scientists of international repute, and the country's higher education lagged far behind its European counterparts. Yet despite the recent popularity of intellectual history and research in higher education, which has produced a veritable flood of publications touching on various aspects of this theme, the heart of the process – the emergence of the academic profession – is still inadequately documented and imperfectly understood.[1]

Given the limitations of our knowledge, an accumulation of case studies may help to reveal the underlying pattern of ideas and events; and the present article is designed to contribute to this end, by examining the career of Henry Carter Adams, a leading member of the first generation of American academic economists.

Adams had no intention of becoming a social scientist when he first entered college in 1870; indeed at that time there was no such academic species, for, as is well known, college professors were often responsible for such a wide variety of subjects that they were said to occupy settees rather than chairs. Adams was carried into the academic profession by a combination of hereditary, environmental and accidental circumstances, and his career affords some general insights into the development of American scholarship because political economy was the leading discipline among the social sciences – a group of subjects virtually created out of nothing in the post-Civil War period. Admittedly political economy had been taught in a few American colleges before that time; but it had rarely been regarded as an independent academic discipline, and had usually been treated in the eighteenth century Scottish fashion as a subordinate part of a general course in moral philosophy taught by clergymen, most of whom possessed neither special interest nor qualifications in the field.[2] After the Civil War, American institutions of higher education rapidly adapted themselves to the demands of an expanding industrial society, and academic economics – together with history, sociology, political science and a variety of other social and natural science disciplines – developed in response to both intellectual and vocational needs. There was a rapid growth in the number of college and university appointments in these new subjects and consequently men like Henry Carter Adams enjoyed career opportunities which were virtually unknown when they began their student days.

Adams' career is of special interest not only because of its representative character, but also because it is so fully documented.[3] From the time he first left home to attend school in the late 1860s, until after he became established as Professor of Political Economy at the University of Michigan in 1887, he corresponded regularly with members of his family, especially his mother, with whom he shared his private thoughts and aspirations. As he did not marry until 1890, shortly before his thirty-ninth birthday, this correspondence spans the formative stages of his career, and it constituted a channel of communication that helped to sustain the powerful religious influences of his home background. Yet despite these strong ties of love and loyalty, he gradually grew away from his early beliefs and standards, and his letters reveal his efforts to justify his later ideas and activities and to preserve his personal, intellectual and spiritual links with his family. He was an honest, clear-headed, self-aware and independent-minded man, who continued to gauge his ideas and achievements by reference to the standards acquired in his childhood and early youth, and the effort to reconcile the two often made him despondent and self-critical. Hence the Adams correspondence provides revealing glimpses of some of the personal strains experienced by new recruits to the academic profession.

II

In many respects, Henry Carter Adams' career was typical of the younger generation of late nineteenth century American academics, and in the following pages attention will be concentrated on its more representative features. He was born in Davenport, Iowa, on 31 December 1851, and grew up in a series of small rural Iowa towns during a hectic phase of pioneer settlement. Henry's father, Ephraim Adams, was a founder-member of the Iowa Band – a group of young Congregationalist missionaries from Andover

Theological Seminary who had dedicated themselves to the task of bringing spiritual succour to the trans-Mississippi West; and he soon became one of the leading ministers in the state.[4] Ephraim Adams was not an intellectual; but he came from a highly respectable New Hampshire family in which education was regarded as the handmaiden of the church, and this outlook also dominated the Adams household. Henry received little formal schooling owing to his ill health, but no doubt family instruction amply compensated for this deficiency, since his parents were conscientious and their educational attainments were well above the average for that region.[5] In 1870, when he was ready to commence his higher education, he continued in the family tradition by enrolling at Grinnell, a conventional small denominational liberal arts college, of which his father was co-founder and (for sixty-one years) a trustee.[6]

The theological atmosphere at Grinnell was somewhat less constricting than in many such institutions, for the Congregationalists possessed a comparatively weak sense of denominational loyalty and did not insist on strict doctrinal conformity. Nevertheless it was during this period that Adams experienced his first serious spiritual doubts and began to question the desirability of following in his father's footsteps. He evidently enjoyed student life, representing Grinnell in an inter-state collegiate debating contest, and doing especially well in 'political economy and all those studies bearing on political science' (11 June 1876). But although he participated conscientiously in the many regular religious exercises and took an active part in occasional local revivals, he became deeply dissatisfied with his progress as a Christian. At one stage, in a fit of depression, he even contemplated removing his name from the Church roll, an action that would have meant virtually severing his precious family ties; and his letters and personal diaries reveal his recurrent spiritual doubts and anxieties. On one occasion he appealed to his father: '. . . if I could only *know* the ministry would be my first and only choice. You have faith in God's providence . . . [but] perhaps God does not want me to be a minister, and knowing that I would be one if I could have sufficient faith in Him and His Son, He does not give it to me' (22 April 1873).

Unfortunately Ephraim Adams' faith was too simple and unsophisticated to provide answers to his son's questions, and on one occasion he confided to his wife:

Dear Boy: why don't he remember that a steady honest purpose to do right, to call Jesus Master and do His work as a true follower as far as he knows how, is all that is asked of him and not worry about feelings. I think I never feel when I am trying to, but responses will come to one who trusts. [A hand-written note on Henry's letter to his mother, 16 February 1873.]

To Henry, 'feeling' was of the essence, for after participating in a local revival he remarked: 'It is easy enough to live Christianity outwardly and to do work with apparent success; but to *feel* the effects of the Spirit as described by others is a different thing' (6 May 1873). Henry realized his growing intellectual powers were undermining his childhood faith, but when he asked his father: 'Is belief an act of the will or intellect?', the reply was cautious and qualified. Ultimately, Ephraim Adams maintained, belief was derived from 'evidence, facts, testimony, etc., presented to and handled by the intellect' (to his son, 27 April 1873), and this statement unintentionally prepared the ground for Henry's subsequent examination of the historical evidences for Christian faith, as presented by his Andover professors.

Adams obtained his B.A. from Grinnell in 1874, and in the ensuing year he worked as a country schoolmaster, a job he had already undertaken during his student days as a means of helping to pay his way through college. He was obviously unwilling to make a firm decision about his future career, for he was torn between his spiritual doubts and his desire to please his parents, who hoped he would enter the ministry; and although he agreed to enter Andover Theological Seminary at Andover, Massachusetts, in 1875, he undoubtedly regarded it as a trial rather than an irrevocable commitment.[7] At Andover he acquired his first real taste for learning, reporting that whenever he entered the library: 'I always begrudge the hours of sleep and wish that I might invent a shorthand memory' (3 October 1875), and his intellect chafed increasingly at the restraints imposed by the strait-jacket of theological orthodoxy. He began a serious 'investigation of the credibility of the new Testament', explaining to his mother:

To me this question is of great importance for by it Christianity stands or falls as a true system. It is true – as one of my classmates said to me – that 'whether it originated in the first or second century it is a mighty good thing'. Yet unless it can on historic grounds be proven credible it seems to lose much of its power and I would not preach it. You think me foolish for wanting to go over the ground myself but such is my nature and it would be against my intellect to refuse to do it. [10 October 1875.]

Doubtless he was guilty of intellectual pride; but the inquiry left him mentally exhausted, for 'every question is a personal question. It has been a continual appealing to self, and I have not been allowed to be a spectator or an impartial judge – I have sought earnestly for *truth* – and that is of more importance than anything else in this world' (28 May 1876).

Nor did the outcome fulfil his father's optimistic assurance that his faith would be confirmed. A year after he left Andover he commented retrospectively in his diary:

I studied as far as inspiration. Then I broke down. Philosophic abstraction I do not care anything about – I only want common sense, and not be forced to believe about *our* things what we won't allow others to believe about theirs. It is the legendary argument that gets me. And so I have drifted away from my educated belief. [Diary, 2 August 1877.]

This passage is of crucial importance for it explains Adams' resistance to doctrinaire theology, an attitude that paralleled his response to orthodox political economy. It also explains why he was subsequently attracted by Felix Adler's non-theological religion of ethical culture, and why he sympathized with the heterodoxy of the German historical school of economics. Even before he went to Andover he had virtually decided not to enter the ministry, and doubtless his decision was wise, for while he could have become an earnest, devout and hardworking minister, any success he had in this vocation would have been hollow. He was too introspective and self-critical to suppress his doubts about the foundations of his belief, and his frank outspokenness would undoubtedly have brought him into conflict with his co-religionists.

In the year after he left Grinnell Adams drafted his first scheme for a political magazine, and when he eventually announced his intention to become a journalist his father somewhat reluctantly gave his blessing, provided that his motives were right and the work was noble and useful.[8] Mrs Adams, however, found it difficult to conceal her disappointment, for she hated to see her son

> going into the hard and uncertain employment of journalism, planning to begin by hunting up all the mean and dirty things happening, as a city reporter . . .
>
> After all, it does seem to me that a good minister has a better field of labour than an editor or a journalist. He comes nearer to the people, touches them more closely with a stronger influence though his sphere is much narrower and the good news is *so* good, so ever new . . . Well both callings are necessary, and to all will the 'well done' be given, if they have served Him in their day and generation. [9 April and 7 May 1876.]

As it transpired, Henry was providentially rescued from a sordid career as a city reporter by the unexpected success of his application for a graduate fellowship at Johns Hopkins, an application he had submitted not on impulse but as a step towards the fulfilment of his plan to establish a political quarterly. This scheme had been taking shape in his mind for nearly two years, and it came to a head following a discussion in April 1876 with the outstanding political journalist of the day, E.L. Godkin of *The Nation*. Godkin 'advised very strongly against going into the reporter's school if I desired to become a political writer' because 'very few came through it not mentally broken. They practice writing in a sensational manner – and do not practice clearness of style and clearness of thought.' Instead, Godkin recommended that he should pursue some course of study which would make him 'an accurate and strong thinker', adding that:

> A knowledge of constitutional law is necessary, also of the constitution in its history. He depreciated the idea of studying theology a year longer. There is a distinction, said he, between Religion and Theology. In the former people are becoming more and more interested and demand that their papers be so too, with the latter their sympathy is decreasing. [Diary, 19 April 1876, and undated letter written to his mother shortly thereafter.]

Adams did not report to his mother Godkin's unfavourable comments on theology. But while eagerly seizing the opportunity to study 'political science' in Baltimore, he still felt impelled to seek his parents' approval, and even promised: 'If I find myself wanting for the work to which I think myself called I shall return gladly and cheerfully to the seminary and preach the *truth in Christ*' (12 June 1876).

Under these circumstances Adams'parents could hardly deny his request. His father conceded that 'God of course don't want all men to be Ministers', and though he added that 'the studies will not hurt you if in the end you should be a Minister' (15 June 1876), he probably realized that this was a remote possibility.

<h1 style="text-align:center">III</h1>

Adams' move to Baltimore in 1876 was a turning-point in his life, for it symbolized both his rejection of the ministry and his entry into the mainstream of American higher education. The new Johns Hopkins University was about to assume the leadership of the American academic profession and two years later Adams' pioneer status was authenticated when an alphabetical accident made him the first of the university's distinguished line of Ph.Ds.[9] Acceptance of a fellowship did not entail any commitment to an academic career: his course was still set towards political journalism rather than the professoriat. But during the Baltimore years he made the crucial decisions that shaped his future, although their ultimate significance was not immediately apparent

The Johns Hopkins climate of opinion was congenial, for despite its vital role in the development of American scholarship the university was not solely orientated towards academic affairs. President Gilman's inaugural emphasized the need for men 'prepared by intellectual and moral discipline to advance the public interests irrespective of party and indifferent to the attainment of official stations'; and while he described learned works as 'the noblest fruits of academic culture', he also stressed the value of less exalted publications such as textbooks, lyceum lectures, magazine articles and letters to the daily press, and expressed the hope that scholarly research would result in 'less misery among the poor, less ignorance in schools, less bigotry in the temple, less suffering in the hospitals, less fraud in business, less folly in politics'.[10] Yet it was the intellectual aspect of Hopkins that most decisively influenced Adams' career. Even before his classes began he was reading widely on matters 'in no way connected with the curriculum', presumably along the lines suggested by Godkin; and for some time thereafter he was examining the history and current state of journalism, with the aim of elevating its standards. However, in three months or so he was preparing some lectures to be delivered to a group of local businessmen because: 'There seems to be such a free independent spirit here that it does not seem presumptuous in the least to say so. Everyone is trying to do something that no one ever did before, and that (as father thinks) is what is my greatest fault – and perhaps it is' (7 January 1877).

This early venture into political economy was apparently a spontaneous response to the Hopkins practice of *Lernfreiheit*, which was in direct contrast to the rigidity of the Andover system; and his active interest in political economy antedates the first university lectures in the subject, which were given by the leading contemporary American economist, General Francis A. Walker, in April 1877. But whatever the source of the initial impetus, Walker undoubtedly influenced and encouraged Adams' economic studies, advising him towards the end of the first academic year to concentrate on taxation, as the subject 'affording the best field of all at the present time for thought and research', and to abandon his plan to write a doctoral thesis on 'English History in its relations to political economy', for this ambitious scheme would require 'a veteran scholar' in both fields (30 August 1877). Among the specific topics proposed by Walker were government revenue and public debts – on which Adams later became the leading American authority; but he took up this subject with an uneasy conscience, recalling the promises he had made to his parents, and endeavouring to justify his decision by saying:

> There is no subject which comes into daily life – affecting the conditions and happiness of men – as much [as] Political Economy. If all men were honest and unselfish and yet the institutions in which they find their existence not based on economic principles, society would by no means have reached its true ideal conditions. The fact that our legislators for ninety years have known nothing of it, and the fact that Editors write articles contradictory of the first principles of Economy does not argue that there should not be some recognized qualifications for Editorship. [22 October 1877.]

Adams still conceived his mission in quasi-religious terms, as a crusade against the sin of ignorance, and he had no intention of becoming a specialist on taxation. 'Although my studies now seem far from the course I had marked out, and distant from the influences which directly affect the morality of men', he wrote near the beginning of his second year at Hopkins, he insisted that

371

his specialist knowledge would enhance his capacity to influence the course of economic and social life.

It takes no prophet to discern that we are on the eve of a great religious upheaval. Not by enthusiasts is it to be wrought but by those who study religion comparatively. The world will depend on Economy for its motive to right action – upon religion for the feeling of adoration and praise.

This is not separating the two, but it is uniting them in their true relations. [Diary, 2 August 1877.]

He now possessed a sense of purpose that had been lacking at Andover, and when President Gilman hinted that he might eventually be considered a suitable candidate for the headship of the university's department of political economy he eagerly seized the opportunity of going to Germany for a further period of study. Nevertheless, once again, he sought his parents' approval, commenting:

If I succeed I shall be useful. If I do not I shall be conscious of a patient endeavour, and also as I firmly believe – the consciousness of no selfishness in my motives. I know that Economy cannot reach everything – for evils are too deep – but there are so many sins of humanity which are sins of ignorance, not wilful, that the desire to teach still admits of an honest enthusiasm. Can you and father tell me heartily to go? [18 April 1878.]

IV

Armed with his parents' blessing, and encouraged by Gilman's advice and financial support, Adams embarked on a year's study in Europe in the summer of 1878. Naturally enough, he went in an optimistic frame of mind; but in fact neither his personal nor his professional troubles were yet over. During his year in Germany he experienced recurrent doubts about his chosen calling, doubts of a kind that must have disturbed many of his fellow academic pilgrims. In addition to arousing misgivings about the wisdom of his decision to defer the joys of a home and marriage for the sake of his studies,[11] his European experiences widened his intellectual horizons, and led him to question the value of political economy as a field of specialization. Before attending his first lecture on Politik at Berlin University, he observed:

I have a dream, if I go back to the University in Baltimore – of turning over from Political Economy to Political Philosophy in about ten years. For the first I feel to be a little cramping as it seems at present necessary to teach it. One cannot take into consideration the entire range of social experience in the first and in the second he can. If the truth were told

I expect it would be that there is not enough chance to preach in the first. [29 October 1878.]

On one level his changing attitude towards political economy reflects his intellectual development, for his contact with eminent historical economists like Adolph Wagner and Ernest Engel and his observation of an entirely different socio-political system combined to heighten his appreciation of the interdependence of history, jurisprudence, government and economic affairs.[12] But on a deeper, more personal level, there were times when he questioned his ability to fulfil his promises to his parents and to himself:

> I am so burdened with this state of uncertainty and doubt. There is no ambition, no desire, *no love* which I would not abandon for the certainty of knowing what is truth and following it . . . I have drifted into the condition where it seems to me that I am properly following Christ by rejecting Him, that is, the truths of his teaching. . . . After leaving the Seminary I was for a time enthusiastic concerning Economy and [the] labor of love for men which a study of it would bring. But after three years of study [of political economy] from the rankest laissez-faireism to the ethnological duty of the state, it only remains to be said that nothing radical can be done here – a readjustment of the evils is all that is possible. [Diary, 2 March [1879].]

The only real hope for social amelioration, he concluded, was universal love, a matter that far transcended the economist's mundane realm; but he was far too realistic to entertain any utopian dreams of radical reform via a transformation of human nature. Continual doubts about his professional future added to his uneasiness, for his negotiations with Gilman dragged on for months until he eventually felt bound to resign his Hopkins fellowship, 'because I did not in the least wish to make his [Gilman's] favours to me a trouble for him. All that I do not like is his reticence and his letting me run on without answers' (3 August 1879). However, professional insecurity did not deter him from publishing an essay on 'The Position of Socialism in the Historical Development of Political Economy', even though he realized it might damage his prospects.[13] As he confided to his mother: 'There are one or two things slightly socialistic in it and the thought came, dare I put them in? Will it not endanger my position at Balt? That was but for a moment. Endanger it or not I will write what I believe' [18 January 1879]. This determination to speak his mind, even on delicate or controversial questions, was consistently maintained in his subsequent time of trial at Cornell in 1886.[14]

While he awaited the outcome of his negotiations with Gilman, Adams contemplated various alternative employment opportunities. Like other scholarly pilgrims he found it difficult to obtain a satisfactory permanent academic post in the United States, for the secular boom in higher education was only just beginning in the late 1870s and early 1880s. Adams' personal problem was temporarily resolved by sheer accident when he was offered a part-time appointment at Cornell University as the result of an interview with Andrew D. White, who initially confused him with the Johns Hopkins historian Herbert Baxter Adams.[15] Shortly thereafter Gilman, who may have been glad to be relieved of his embarrassment, offered him a short course of lectures at Johns Hopkins, and although his reception at Cornell by the Acting President, William C. Russell, was less than enthusiastic, Henry put up a brave front, declaring that 'a wandering lectureship is something which I should have chosen had I dared to do so, and now it is forced upon me' (14 September 1879). A few months later, by another curious coincidence, James Burrell Angell, President of the University of Michigan, invited Adams to act as a substitute during his forthcoming tour of duty as American Minister to China, thereby establishing an institutional connection that lasted until Adams' death forty years later.

Adams' peripatetic status in the years 1881–7 indicates that some of the leading American universities still regarded a full-time economist as a luxury beyond their limited means; but his travels enabled him to obtain invaluable insight into the differences between the three institutions at which he was employed. He realized that Michigan and Cornell were academically inferior to Johns Hopkins, and for a time he still hoped to secure a permanent post in Baltimore, where another budding leader of American economics, Richard T. Ely, enjoyed a humble and somewhat impermanent footing. However, there were compensations at Ann Arbor, for 'they treat a man decently here and not as though he were an everlasting experiment, as they do at Baltimore' (17 April 1881); and he soon came to prefer Michigan to Cornell, maintaining that 'the poverty of Ann Arbor . . . gives it for me a certain quality of charm, for I feel that the institution is living fully up to its capacity', whereas the wealthier Cornell struck him as 'a brilliant prison rather than a charming home'.[16]

An economist faced certain definite professional disadvantages at Cornell where, by an arrangement which *The Nation* scathingly referred to as 'the Duplex Professorship', two different sets of lectures were provided on the free trade versus protection issue, a practice that accurately reflected the contemporary belief that an economist must necessarily be an advocate of one or other of these policies. Like other economists, Adams expected public criticism – which, as we shall see, he also encountered in Michigan; but Cornell was unduly influenced by the autocratic Chairman of the Board of Trustees, Henry Sage, a lumber millionaire, with an 'undisguised contempt' for unpractical college professors.[17] Despite Adams' outspokenness, an open clash with Sage was delayed until 1886, a year of bitter controversy over the Haymarket incident in Chicago, and the circumstances reveal Adams' growing preoccupation with 'the social question'. He had first witnessed the evils of a modern industrial society during his Hopkins days, when he began to formulate a more coherent and systematic conception of society, and by the early 1880s he conceived his pedagogical task as that of making the students 'alive to the necessity of thinking on these [social and economic] topics that are now coming to make up my life, indeed to take the place of religion'.[18] While at Ann Arbor he was attacked in the local and national press when he questioned the sanctity of property; but the opposition subsided after he had explained his position in a newspaper interview, and the university authorities took no action, even though there had been earlier complaints about his free trade views.[19]

However, Mr Sage was not so readily appeased when Adams expressed sympathy towards the Knights of Labor in an impromptu speech at Cornell in April 1886, for when he read a report of it in the *New York Times* he marched into the President's office and declared: 'This man must go, he is sapping the foundations of our society.'[20] The incident was significant, not only because it jeopardized Adams' academic career, but also because it occurred at a time when his social and political ideas were beginning to crystallize. A month earlier he had presented the first version of his essay on the 'Relation of the State to Industrial Action' at the New York Constitution Club, and at Cornell he was elaborating one of his key ideas about the role of labour unions in American society.[21] He neither approved of the recent violence, nor did he advocate socialism or anarchy – as Sage and other critics imagined. On the contrary, he offered a peaceful alternative, the essence of which involved an extension of the concept of property rights so as to give organized labour a share in the government of industry. Admittedly he was somewhat naïve, as he subsequently acknowledged, in supposing that the leaders of the Knights of Labor shared his high ideals; and he unnecessarily gave hostages to fortune by claiming that his scheme would initiate a social revolution comparable to the abandonment of the divine right of kings – including eventually 'the overthrow of the wages system and the establishment of what may be termed "Industrial Federation".'[22] But his most serious mistake was his failure to appreciate that the public was in no mood to contemplate such far-reaching long-term reforms.

There was apparently no question of an instant dismissal, for his temporary appointment had only a year to run, and his correspondence even suggests that it might have been renewed, at a reduced salary, through the good offices of his former Ann Arbor colleague Charles Kendall Adams, the new President of Cornell. But Adams refused to negotiate on these terms, believing himself entitled to a full professorship,[23] and so his professional hopes now rested on his friend, President Angell of Michigan.

The possibility of a full professorship at Ann Arbor had been under consideration for several years, but Angell genuinely questioned whether the university could afford a full-time economist. Adams' scholarly reputation had been growing steadily, even though his first major book, *Public Debts*, did not appear until 1887,[24] but Angell evidently did not feel confident that his academic contributions would be distinguished enough to outweigh the embarrassments which might result from his views on current affairs. While he liked and respected Adams, he felt uneasy about the precise nature and long-run tendencies of Adams' thought and feared that a premature attempt to promote him might be turned down by the Board of Regent's.[25]

Shortly before the Cornell affair, in response to Adams' inquiry about his prospects, Angell had asked certain questions about his views on private property, inheritance and state socialism; and Adams' full and frank replies deserve attention, for they fairly accurately depict the drift of opinion among the younger, reform-minded social scientists. Adams denied that he was a socialist, and maintained that 'the only tenable defence of property is its necessity'. The problem of appropriate limits of control of productive agents was 'wholly a question of expediency, that can be answered only by experience and the common sense of men'. The right of inheritance, he considered, was 'the weakest of all the claims that spring from the theory of personal property', and the economic question was simply 'to what extent must we allow men to control their property after death in order to get the best work out of them while they live?' Inheritance should be restricted by progressive taxation, and limits should also be placed on the ownership of agricultural lands. City ground rents should not be subject to private ownership, and there should be no private monopoly of natural resources. While opposing anything resembling 'paternal government', such as 'the old English poor law', he advocated federal control of the post office and telegraph, state ownership of mines, state control of forestry and public education (including the university), and municipal control of gas works, water works and street railways.[26] He concluded by expressing surprise at Angell's questions, since the President had the power to drop him without explanation (although such an action would, of course, be unfair), and in a subsequent letter, written in response to a further series of questions, Adams expressed his frank opinion of the issue of principle involved:

> in my opinion, your point of view in this matter is not the right one. If you make a man's opinions the basis of his election to a professorship you do, whether you intend it or not, place bonds upon the free movement of his intellect. It seems to me that a Board has two things to hold in view. First, is a man a scholar? Can he teach in a scholarly manner? Is he fair to all parties in the controverted questions which come before him? Second, is he intellectually honest? If these two questions are answered in the affirmative, his influence on young men cannot be detrimental.[27]

In his reply, Angell explained his conception of the limitations on academic freedom to which he was subject.

> Your theory as to the grounds of appointing a Professor cannot, I

think, be accepted in an American college or university. It would permit the appointment of a Buddhist to the chair of Philosophy. While as you know I favor large liberty in respect to the views of a Professor, the German idea of Lehrfreiheit cannot be fully accepted in this country, when colleges depend on friendly public sentiment for their support.[28]

Nevertheless he appreciated the essence of Adams' problem, that is, the difficulty of giving a precise account of ideas which were not yet fully formulated, and the impossibility of giving an assurance that their subsequent development would not embarrass the university authorities. As Angell acknowledged:

Your letter of the 15th inst. was intensely, almost painfully interesting to me. It showed me that my guesses as to the processes you had been going through were substantially correct, though I did not guess all the details. It showed that my impression was correct that you had made the mistake of speaking prematurely, before your mind had really settled on its leanings and that you see and regret the mistake, as I have done for you for some time. But it shows – what I did not need the letter to convince me of – the frankness, sincerity, and openness of your mind.[29]

These personal remarks can be taken at their face value, for they are consistent with other evidence of Angell's opinions about Adams, who had been a frequent and welcome visitor to the Angell household. Like Presidents Gilman, White and C.K. Adams, Angell was impressed by his frankness and honesty,[30] and although it is dangerous to generalize about academic freedom cases, the President's support could often be decisive in tipping the balance in favour of a professor whose position was in jeopardy.[31] Angell must have realized that nothing could be gained by prolonging his investigation of Adams' ideas and scholarly purposes, and he was soon able to give him the welcome news that he would be appointed to a full professorship.

V

While the details of the events leading up to Adams' appointment in Michigan were obviously untypical, his trials at Cornell and Ann Arbor are of general interest since they foreshadowed the growing conflict between the new university governing elite and the rising generation of social scientists – a conflict that was to produce some sensational incidents in the next two decades.[32] As a spokesman for reform, Adams was invariably moderate, but persistent and unflinching despite the risks to his professional career; and his experiences not only revealed the limits of academic freedom, but also gave him the satisfaction of knowing that his professorial utterances could shake the complacency of the rich. His appointment as Professor in the University of Michigan set the seal upon his academic career, and this was further enhanced a year later when he became Chief Statistician to the Interstate Commerce Commission. This post represented an ideal combination of academic expertise and public service, and his work in establishing a uniform basis for railway accountancy laid the foundations for the subsequent development of an effective federal system of rate regulation.

Although he gradually became assimilated into the Eastern educational establishment, Henry Carter Adams did not forswear his Midwestern Congregationalist origins, but always maintained a certain sceptical detachment towards the Eastern middle and upper classes, especially the wealthier, more hedonistic and conservative members of that society. He consciously strove, with considerable success, to dissociate his views as a social scientist from his personal feelings, and he accordingly became an acute observer of contemporary values and practices. He continued to live modestly – at least up to the time of his marriage – but permitted himself some relaxation of the stern prohibitions against tobacco, alcohol and dancing which he had learnt at home.

In addition to his normal university work, Adams took an active interest in the development of higher education in Michigan, especially education for business, and given his background it is hardly surprising that he became a staunch supporter of state, as against private, universities. Yet apart from his personal experiences, this preference was entirely consistent with his fundamental faith in democracy. 'Education supported by the gifts of the wealthy must inevitably respect and support the interest of the wealthy classes', he wrote to one correspondent, and while the people might occasionally make fools of themselves, their interests were 'more nearly in harmony with the national interest, than that of any particular class'. Like other progressives, Adams had great faith in publicity, maintaining that, in contrast to private universities, 'whatever is done in a public institution must be done openly and . . . [therefore] must receive the criticism of the press'. Moreover, 'an error committed in a state institution will not probably perpetuate itself, whereas the prejudices of rich men who found private institutions can . . . although they are in a small minority and represent interests that should be temporary because they are class interests'.[33]

In his economic and social thought, as in his political philosophy, Adams was neither an abstract nor a highly systematic thinker. Yet he was a consistent and effective advocate of 'industrial liberty', which he viewed as a logical corollary of the religious and political liberty embodied in the Anglo-American constitutional tradition. Starting as a 'pronounced individualist', he subsequently accepted the socialist critique of contemporary society; but he rejected the socialist solution as 'contrary to the fundamental principle of English political philosophy'. As an alternative, he emphasized 'the principle of personal responsibility in the administration of all social power, no matter in what shape that power may exist', for the realization of this principle would 'cure the ills of which socialists complain without curbing or crushing that which is highest in the individual'.[34] The evolution of Adams' attitude to socialism is too complex a matter to be discussed adequately here,[35] but it is important both because his pronouncements on this subject influenced his professional position, and because socialism formed a link between his original plan for a political quarterly and his later preoccupation with the role of the state in modern society. By temperament and training Adams was incapable of adopting either a purely theoretical or a narrowly economic view of society, and the political, social, economic, legal and ethical aspects of his thought were virtually inseparable. His view of the business corporation, for example, as a factor in the growth of monopoly, was derived from his knowledge of history and jurisprudence, to which he added a powerful element of economic analysis when he explained the significance of such industries as transportation, the telegraph and public utilities – the so-called 'natural monopolies' – which were subject to increasing returns to scale.[36] His Interstate Commerce Commission appointment placed him at the heart of the American effort to reconcile the customary rights of private enterprise with the public interest and, characteristically, he regarded his railway accounting work not merely as a rate-regulation device but also as a means of extending the principle of public control to other economic activities.[37] As Joseph Dorfman, the leading authority on American economic thought, has justly observed, 'Adams was in a very real sense the philosophical parent of much of the political–economic legislation of the next fifty years'; and he has aptly designated Adams as 'the harmonizer of liberty and reform'.[38] In conjunction with other contemporary social scientists, he helped to elaborate the American conception of the 'general welfare state'.[39] Adams' European pilgrimage had both strengthened his patriotic sentiments and enhanced his awareness of his country's shortcomings, and like others of his generation he sought specifically American solutions to American problems – solutions that drew upon the European legacy of ideas and experience and adapted them to American needs.

As his academic career progressed during the 1880s, Adams gradually became more confident that he was performing a useful social function, and he accordingly became less concerned to justify his life in strictly religious terms. Religion continued to be extremely important to him even though he abandoned the effort to define his faith, and he increasingly came to regard it as a matter of the heart rather than the intellect. He did not abandon his faith; but faith fought a losing battle against intellect, and the spiritual doubts which had convinced him of his unsuitability for the ministry eventually led him to adopt what he termed a 'theoretically agnostic, yet practically theistic view of things' (Diary, 14 May 1882). During the final decade of his bachelorhood his most intimate friends were Hamilton Bartlett and William

McIntyre Salter, dedicated men who, like himself, were engaged in the quest for spiritual truth and a vocation worthy of their high social ideals. Bartlett, a fellow student at Grinnell and Andover, evidently appealed to the emotional side of Adams' nature, for they exchanged confidences about their relations with the fair sex and Bartlett's difficulties in his Presbyterian, and subsequent Episcopalian ministries. Salter, on the other hand, was an intellectual, the son of the most scholarly member of the Iowa Band, who, after studying at Knox College, Andover, the Yale and Harvard Divinity schools, and Göttingen, served a brief term as a Unitarian minister before joining Felix Adler's Ethical Culture movement.[40]

Salter's career, up to the point where he renounced his inherited faith, indicates the pattern that Henry Carter Adams' life might have assumed had he actually decided to enter the ministry, a suggestion reinforced by his warm response to Adler when Salter first brought them together in New York in 1882.[41] Like Salter, Adler had abandoned his (Jewish) orthodoxy under the influence of the German critical and historical approach to theology, and his Ethical Culture Society, with its slogan 'deed not creed', was conceived as a school of 'moral idealism' that would be 'practical as well as spiritual, and unhampered by sectarian dogmas'. These aims were congenial to Adams, and though he regarded Adler's view of human nature as too idealistic, both men believed that reform of social institutions was dependent on a parallel reformation of personal character. They shared a common general approach to such familiar contemporary reform issues as socialism, co-operation, the ideas of Henry George, the conflict between capital and labour, and the urgent need to remedy the evils of an urban industrial society,[42] but while Adams expressed certain reservations about Adler's programme and his methods, his unwillingness to become a disciple was really due to his independent-mindedness and firm attachment to the Protestant tradition. Nevertheless he co-operated with Adler as far as his academic career and public service permitted, serving as a co-director of Adler's Plymouth School of Ethics in the 1890s, giving addresses to local ethical culture groups, and becoming a founder-member of the editorial board of the *International Journal of Ethics*.

VII

Towards the close of the nineteenth century the interdependence of religion, scholarship and social reform was still manifest on both sides of the Atlantic, but as the influence of religion declined and the growth of professionalism continued, the gap widened between the clergy, the academic social scientist and the reformer. Henry Carter Adams' career is of general interest because his departure from his inherited beliefs, his rejection of the ministry as a vocation and his decision to become an academic economist reflected a lasting, if still incipient, occupational trend. His correspondence reveals, in an especially vivid manner, both the aspirations that motivated him and the strains and stresses he experienced.

NOTES

1 The most important single study of this process is Richard Hofstadter and Walter P. Metzger, *The Development of Academic Freedom in the United States* (New York, 1955). More recently a number of studies of particular individuals, disciplines and institutions have appeared, suggesting that there is a growing awareness of the general problem.

2 The most authoritative source on these matters is the first three volumes of Joseph Dorfman's *The Economic Mind in American Civilization* (New York, 1947–9), *passim*; see also M.J.L. O'Connor, *Origins of Academic Economics in the United States* (New York, 1944).

3 The Henry Carter Adams papers are in the Michigan Historical Collections, Ann Arbor, Michigan. Unless otherwise stated, all subsequent quotations are taken from Adams' letters to his mother. Individual letters will be identified in the text. The best account of Adams' life and thought is Joseph Dorfman's introductory essay to his edition of Adams' essays: *Relation of the State to Industrial Action, and Economics and Jurisprudence* (New York, 1954), pp.1–55 (in subsequent notes this will be cited as 'Dorfman (ed.), *Essays*'). I am most grateful for the assistance I have received from the Adams family and the Department of Economics at the University of Michigan.

4 Ephraim Adams eventually became Superintendent of Home Missions in Iowa, and one obituarist claimed that 'he was the real leader of our Congregational hosts in Iowa'. He was an effective administrator, spending two periods as financial agent of Grinnell College, and an active historian of the missionary movement. His book, *The Iowa Band* (Boston, n.d. [1st ed. 1870, 2nd ed. 1902]) is a minor classic of nineteenth century American protestantism. For background studies of the missionary movement see Colin Brummit Goodykoontz, *Home Missions on the American Frontier* (Caldwell, Idaho, 1939); Trueman O. Douglass, *Pilgrims of Iowa* (Boston, 1911); Julius A. Reed, *Reminiscences of Early Congregationalism in Iowa* (Grinnell, 1885); George F. Magoun, *Asa Turner, A Home Missionary Patriarch and His Times* (Boston, 1889).

5 His mother, Elizabeth Douglass Adams, had been raised 'in the literary atmosphere of Dartmouth' and had probably met Ephraim Adams during his student days at Dartmouth College.

6 The founding of a college had been one of the original purposes of the Iowa Band. Cf. John Scholte Nollen. *Grinnell College* (Iowa City, 1953).

7 Although Adams' decision to enter Andover was obviously the result of an agreement with his parents, there is no correspondence bearing directly upon it. It was probably the outcome of family discussions at home.

8 Ephraim Adams expressed his fear that his son's decision stemmed from 'an unwillingness to surrender some darling project or object that in your mind must be surrendered if you become a minister . . . If for self will we avoid doing God's will it will prove bitter in the end – This I say not to drive you to the Ministry for I don't know that it is God's will that you should be one . . . I want you to say to God I am there to follow what so far as you can see He would have you' (8 June 1876).

9 Cf. Hugh Hawkins, *Pioneer: A History of the Johns Hopkins University, 1874–1889* (Ithaca, 1960). For a recent general history see Laurence R. Veysey, *The Emergence of the American University* (Chicago, 1965).

10 Quoted by Hawkins, op. cit, p.68. See also D.C. Gilman, *University Problems* (New York, 1898), pp.7–30.

11 On 17 March 1879, he confided to his Berlin diary: 'The difficulty is one cannot always be satisfied with his work. I am beginning to lose faith in myself and my studies. . . . The news of the engagement of Mollie and Clara has had something of an unsettling effect on me – probably because I am not [a] dead hand at anything this week. It is not that I cared for either of them though they are both splendid girls, but the thought brings me to my age and the fact that the world is moving. Am I being left behind it? All such questions are signs of weakness, but to myself they may be confessed. I look up at my books in their black binding, Nationalökom, Finanzwissenschaft, Völkerrecht, Socialism, German and French grammars and dictionaries. I look into my drawer, there are my lectures, plans for articles, notes, half-finished definitions and an immense amount of other rubbish. I look away across the ocean, there are my friends settling down to contented happy useful private lives, with the love of the world in their hearts because of the love for one above all others. . . . Love and ambition are always at war, and I am not strong enough to say damn ambition or to cut the love.' In contrast to Adams' frustration, other American expatriates experienced a profound sense of emotional release during their German student days. For example, see G. Stanley Hall, *Life and Confessions of a Psychologist* (New York, 1923), pp.219, 223.

12 As he wrote to D.C. Gilman on 15 December 1878, 'I have learned so much actually new economy from the simple study of old subjects under new relations that I am quite anxious to repeat the experiment in France' (Gilman Papers, Johns Hopkins University Library, Baltimore).

13 It appeared in the *Penn Monthly*, April 1879, pp.285–94, and was his first published article.

14 See later, pp.374–5.

15 White was then on leave from Cornell as United States Ambassador to Germany, and needed a substitute to teach his history course at Cornell. Their correspondence suggests that White was tactful enough to conceal his mistake.

16 To Herbert Baxter Adams, 13 and 23 April 1883. (In Johns Hopkins University Library.)

17 Anna Shafer Goodstein, *Biography of a Businessman: Henry W. Sage, 1814–1897* (Ithaca, 1962), esp. pp.223–4, 230, 233–5

18 To Herbert Baxter Adams, 13 and 23 April 1883, *loc. cit.*

19 After quoting from a report of Adams' lectures, the editor of the *Kansas City Journal* (January, 1884) added: 'We think it about time the professor should be bounced from his position. The man who preaches such doctrines is an enemy to society, and unworthy of being countenanced by any honest man.' The cutting, with others, is in a scrapbook in the Adams Collection. Two years earlier Henry had informed his mother: 'One disadvantage of a State institution cropped out the other day. The President spoke to the Regents about a permanent appointment for me here. It came out that every one of the Regents had received [a] complaint that I was a free trader. They happened to be all protectionists. Dr Angell said that this was the first time that a question had ever come to their meeting of a political character. I still feel a boy. These little incidents come up now and then to show me that I am doing the work and exerting the influence of a man' (14 January 1882). Two weeks later he added: 'I do not think there was anything serious in the inquiry of the Regents about my principles upon Free Trade. At least I do not think it was sufficient to endanger my position. If so, I should gladly go, for I don't want to be anywhere with a rag over my mouth. There are plenty of things I could do. I could go to New York City and in a year have a good position on some paper. . . . So don't fret about that.' (30 January 1883.)

20 Quoted by Adams in his scrapbook, which contains a copy of his address, and

the comment: 'The effect of this essay upon myself was: to learn that what I said might possibly be of some importance.'

21 Like John R. Commons, Adams 'interpreted the labor movement as a historical institution striving to give proprietary significance to job rights'. It was an integral part of the evolution of industrial democracy, and in this Adams anticipated the recent idea of 'countervailing power'. Cf. Mark Perlman, *Labor Union Theories in America, Background and Development* (Evanston, 1958), esp. pp.162–3, 168, 208–10.

22 This is quoted from an Ithaca newspaper report dated 26 April 1886, in Adams' scrapbook. The Adams Collection also includes an unidentifiable newspaper article 'What Do These Strikes Mean?', dated 25 March 1886. His Cornell address was eventually published in the *Scientific American Supplement*, 22 (21 August 1886), pp.8861–3. Sage replied in the same magazine on 28 August 1886, p.8877. See also Adams' article, 'Shall We Muzzle the Anarchists?', *The Forum I* (July 1886), pp.445–54, which contains some interesting reminiscences of the 'detestable system' of 'police surveillance' in Germany.

23 In 1890 Cornell offered Adams a full professorship, but he rejected it – a decision that doubtless gave him some satisfaction.

24 At the time of his negotiations with Angell, Adams had published about twenty articles, comments, etc., in a variety of periodicals and newspapers, in addition to his doctoral thesis, *Taxation in the United States, 1789–1816* (Baltimore, 1884) and his *Outlines of Lectures upon Political Economy* (Ann Arbor, 1881, 1886). His important monograph, *Relation of the State to Industrial Action*, first appeared in 1886 as a pamphlet issued by the New York Constitution Club, and subsequently in the *Publications of the American Economic Association, I*, no.6 (January 1887). Adams had been elected first vice-president of the Association in 1885; Francis Walker was its president. It is worth noting that some of Adams' early writings represented journalistic work of a type then common among aspiring young social scientists. However, there were few purely scholarly journals, and a man could usefully supplement his income, pay off his debts and enhance his academic reputation, while contributing to the solution of current economic and social problems.

25 On 10 June 1885, shortly before White resigned as President of Cornell, Angell had written asking what had been decided about Adams. 'Is he like the baby before Solomon to be [in a] divided state, or dropped? He has such merits and such limitations that I confess I hardly know whether we want him permanently or not.' A year earlier he had written that the university was 'too impecunious' to employ Henry for more than six months (17 July 1884) (in J.B. Angell papers, Michigan Historical Collections, Ann Arbor).

26 Adams to Angell, 25 March 1886, in Angell papers. This was a reply to Angell's letter of 19 March 1886, in Adams papers.

27 Adams to Angell, 15 March 1887, in Angell papers. This long letter is reproduced in full in Dorfman (ed.), *Essays*, pp.37–42. It is a reply to Angell's letter of 12 March 1887, in Adams papers.

28 Angell to Adams, 26 March 1887, in Adams papers.

29 Ibid.

30 Adams did not stand in awe of University Presidents, possibly because once, during his Grinnell days, he was brought into intimate contact with President Magoun of Grinnell. After visiting 'Uncle Lane', a member of the Iowa Band, he confided to his diary: 'Miserable old Prex. Magoun was there and I wished myself anywhere but there. To clap the climax I had to sleep with the old coon. The only consolation I found was that the bed was wide.' However, the next day his opinion rose, for Magoun gave a splendid sermon and 'even walked to church with me

– after dark – and talked with me about *England and his tour abroad* (15 January 1871, italics in original). Magoun had succeed Ephraim Adams as minister of the First Congregational Church in Davenport, Iowa, Henry's birthplace.

31 Angell's attitude was not, of course, Adams' sole asset. Apart from his own academic reputation, the University of Michigan was widely regarded as the leading State University and it enjoyed an unusually strong position *vis-à-vis* the state, and a tradition of non-interference with faculty affairs. For a more general view of the influences on academic freedom cases, see Hofstadter and Metzger, op. cit., p.176.

32 ibid., chap.IX.

33 Adams to C.O. Pauley (of Cornell College, Iowa), 28 February 1899 (in Adams collection). Henry took an active interest in subsequent academic freedom cases involving economists, and his own free trade views were again vigorously attacked in the local and national press early in 1889. Yet his conviction that freedom of teaching and expression was greater in state than in private institutions remained unshaken. It is not, however, supported by later writers. Cf. Hofstadter and Metzger, op. cit.

34 Adams to Angell, 15 March 1887 (in Angell papers).

35 The following quotations are suggestive: 'The United States taken as a whole . . . has nothing to do with the question of socialism at present, but if the men at the helm are wise, they will take care that conditions are not produced that will give rise to such an agitation as Germany is having and has been having this century' (October 29 1878). 'I am a socialist – to tell the truth – with the very characteristic exception of questioning their plan of reconstruction – and the study of the question has given me again a foothold on Political Economy' (Diary, 7 December 1878). 'He who properly understands the position of socialism in economic history holds the key to the great economic problem of the present day'. We must repudiate both 'the centralizing tendency of German Economy' and the 'unrestrained activity of private enterprise. . . . From this dilemma must arise an American Political Economy – an economy which is to be legal rather than industrial in its character' ('The Position of Socialism', *Penn Monthly*. [April 1879] pp.286, 294). 'As an economic idea, [socialism] is simply the opposite of individualism; as an economic system, it is a revolt against the doctrines of the Manchester school; judged from the standpoint of the organization of industries, it may be said to embrace all those plans for organization based upon the exercise by the state of the coercive power with which every state is clothed. A study of socialism must be historical, analytical, and critical' (*Outlines of . . . Political Economy* [Ann Arbor, 1881] p.73). 'Do you want to know what I am? I am a Socialist of the general Philosophy of Karl Marx . . . [I do not] think he has the true method of work and agitation but his criticisms upon our present society are just and true' (to his mother, 7 November 1883). 'The control of railways by Commissions is the truly conservative method of control. If it succeeds, we may look for a solution to all the vexed industrial problems in harmony with the fundamental principles of English liberty. If it fails, there is nothing for the future of our civilization but the tyranny of socialism' ('The Interstate Commerce Act: Discussion', *Publications of the Michigan Political Science Association*, [May 1893], p.143).

36 His 'Relation of the State to Industrial Action' (in Dorfman (ed.), *Essays*) provides the best introduction to these matters.

37 The Adams family seem to have been adept at figures. Ephraim Adams spent two periods as financial agent of Grinnell College, and as Superintendent of Home Missions in Iowa it was his duty to collect 'facts and statistics' about the

movement. In a letter written when Henry was at school, he gave him detailed instructions about keeping his accounts, thereby initiating a habit which his son eventually put to professional use in the ICC.

38 Dorfman, *The Economic Mind*, vol, III, p.174; also Dorfman (ed.), *Essays* (introduction).

39 On this general movement see Sidney Fine, *Laissez-Faire and The General Welfare State, A Study of Conflict in American Economic Thought 1865–1901* (Ann Arbor, 1956, 1967).

40 In a large, but unsatisfactory literature, see Felix Adler, *An Ethical Philosophy of Life* (London, 1918), which contains an autobiographical introduction; William McIntyre Salter, *Ethical Religion* (London, 1905); *The Fiftieth Anniversary of the Ethical Movement, 1876–1916* (New York, 1926, no editor or author); also the excellent critical bibliography in James Ward Smith and A. Leland Jamison (eds.), *Religion in American Life*, vol.IV (Princeton, 1961), pp.264 ff.

41 Adams' reactions appear in his New York diary, as well as in his correspondence.

42 One of Adler's followers expressed views exactly in conformity with Adams' beliefs and experiences: 'The plan of the undertaking is, that a number of thorougly educated men, who have studied at home and foreign universities on the subjects of political science and economics, sociology and ethics, comparative religion and the history of philosophy, should take up the great practical issues of the day and treat them from a broad, free, ethical standpoint. Thus far in our country no such platforms have existed. It is seldom, even in our universities, that our teachers are free, and doubtless it would cost many of them their official heads if they were to speak exactly what they think. But for want of such utterances society is in jeopardy. The public is coming to see that there is more danger from a restriction of free speech than from free utterance, where the utterance comes from educated minds. There will be no crude radicalism where there has been thorough education' (W.L. Sheldon, *Sketch of the History of the Ethical Culture Movement* [St Louis, 1890] pp.21–2).

20

CLARENCE AYRES' PLACE IN THE HISTORY OF AMERICAN ECONOMICS
An interim assessment

I

A comprehensive scholarly assessment of Clarence Ayres' place in the development of American economics is long overdue, and it is to be hoped that it will soon be forthcoming. Yet it is a task that should not be undertaken lightly, for, in addition to Ayres' voluminous and scattered writings, the author will have to familiarize himself with several major streams of twentieth century American intellectual activity, not only in the social sciences but also in philosophy and politics. And he will find it difficult to avoid partisanship.

Given these circumstances and the proverbial folly of those who rush in, the tentative character of this essay must be stressed. It stems from the belief that a comparatively detached, sympathetic but neutral, transatlantic viewpoint may be of some value in appraising the work of so distinctively American a writer.

Generalizations about national character are often more confusing than helpful. Nevertheless the 'Americanness' of Ayres' economics is undeniable, whether one considers his intellectual antecedents and associations, his principal themes and preoccupations, his professional style, or even his academic location and influence. He was, of course, an institutionalist, and institutionalism has generally been regarded as a distinctly, even uniquely American contribution to modern economic thought.[1] Ayres repeatedly and generously acknowledged his personal indebtedness to those characteristically American thinkers, Thorstein Veblen and John Dewey; and it is worth noting that all three were decisively shaped, albeit in different ways, by the late nineteenth and early twentieth century Middle West, a region which also nurtured the other two leading co-founders of institutional economics, Wesley C. Mitchell and John R. Commons. By 1917, when Ayres completed his graduate studies at the University of Chicago, Mitchell, Veblen and Dewey had already left the faculty. But the influence of the last two on Ayres' economics and philosophy teachers was still strong, and the Chicago tradition was still thriving a decade or more later when he published his first book and a shorter statement of his philosophical beliefs.[2]

Ayres has recently been depicted as a member of the post-1945 generation of so-called neo-institutionalists.[3] If there is indeed such a movement, he may legitimately be regarded as its father figure. Yet Ayres himself was manifestly of an intermediate generation, a personification of the intellectual links between the original, *fin de siècle* institutionalist triumvirate and the more dedicated younger adherents of the Association for Evolutionary Economics. To the latter generation Ayres represents a voice from the past, for even a casual perusal of his writings reveals the essential continuity and repetitiveness of his basic themes and concerns. Like Veblen, Ayres took his doctorate in philosophy, and throughout his subsequent career he maintained an essentially philosophical approach to his subject matter. Admittedly neither he nor Veblen was really interested in those pedantic and narrowly technical questions which preoccupy many academic specialists in philosophy and economics. On the contrary, they were concerned with broader issues, such as the preconceptions of established doctrines, especially orthodox economics, and the general nature and processes of economic and cultural change. Both men displayed a sustained interest in matters far beyond the conventional boundaries of the social sciences; and, seeking a broad interdisciplinary synthesis, they aimed to present their findings to intelligent laymen as well as to their academic peers. On policy matters they were usually vague and general, rather than detailed and specific. Yet they undoubtedly sought to influence the course of events as well as the main currents of educated opinion. Like many late nineteenth and early twentieth century American progressives, they were moral and social reformers, preachers as well as teachers, fundamentally optimistic in their conception of American society, its problems and prospects.[4] And, like other reformist intellectuals, they were far less radical in practice than some of their contemporary critics supposed.

In several respects both Veblen and Ayres now seem somewhat old-fashioned – though their admirers will undoubtedly add: so much the worse for current styles! Comparatively unconcerned with conventional academic success in the disciplines they nominally professed, they earned respect and acquired followers largely because they were intellectual mavericks, surviving (sometimes not without difficulty) as generalists in a university environment increasingly dominated by specialists. It has often been noted that Veblen's nearest British counterpart, J.A. Hobson, never obtained an academic appointment and was almost certainly refused permission to undertake university extension lectures in economics on the grounds of his presumed professional incompetence. Difficult and subversive as he was, Veblen nevertheless managed to hold, albeit precariously, a series of academic appointments in leading universities, and his experience may consequently be cited as evidence of the tolerance and heterogeneity of the American academic community.

Somewhat the same is true, *mutatis mutandis*, of Ayres' career.[5] It is surely impossible to find a parallel case among European professors of economics – that is to say, a leading figure in an important university possessing a similar journalistic and disciplinary background, an equally limited technical expertise and interest in his nominal field, a comparable list of non-specialist publications, and an equivalent combination of pedagogic charisma and personal influence. Admittedly this assessment is somewhat speculative, for the relevant data have not yet been assembled. Nevertheless, Professor John S. Gambs' lighthearted reference to the 'Cactus League of Dissenting Economists' should be taken seriously,[6] for a study of regional 'schools' of American economics should not be confined to Chicago, Wisconsin and Harvard. Now that Thomas S. Kuhn and others have sensitized us to the interrelations between the epistemological, social and institutional dimensions of the scientific process, we must be prepared to examine these matters in detail. And if institutional economics survives as a distinct intellectual movement in America – a matter on which even some of its faithful adherents have expressed reservations – then Ayres' career is of much more than merely biographical interest.

II

In order to understand Ayres' version of institutionalism, some account of his philosophical presuppositions is unavoidable, even though this will take us into an obscure terrain far beyond the conventional boundaries of economics. Most economists prefer to take their metaphysics and values for granted, but Ayres, unlike Veblen, made no attempt to conceal his feelings in satire or convoluted prose. Veblen's basic dichotomies – between science and ceremonialism, technology and institutions, industry and business, workmanship and waste – recur throughout Ayres' writings, though he was constantly reformulating, elaborating and synthesizing these elements. His conception of socioeconomic development bore marked resemblances to Veblen's, and in later years his acknowledgments to Veblen became more frequent and explicit.[7] Yet he was no mere disciple, largely because his ideas were securely grounded in Dewey's pragmatist/instrumentalist epistemology, a doctrine which Veblen had treated with considerable scepticism around the turn of the century. Moreover, Ayres' commitment to specific values was much more explicit than Veblen's, and his intellectual system was consequently much more coherent and purposeful.

Ayres' critics accused him of preaching technological determinism,[8] and indeed he so strongly emphasized the technological circumstances that 'shape and modify and attenuate the institutional heritage' of modern society that the charge is not unreasonable (1951, 'The Co-ordinates of Institutionalism', p.51). While denying that the technological process was the whole of culture, that technology was an external force, or that machines invent themselves, Ayres nevertheless described technology as the 'life process' and 'hope' of mankind and declared that machines are 'the ultimate reality of modern civilization' (1951, 'The Co-ordinates of Institutionalism', p.51; 1953, 'The Role of Technology in Economic Theory', p.287; 1943, 'Capitalism in Retrospect', p.301).

Yet his concept of technology extended far beyond mere machines: it was essentially epistemological, hence his willingness to view his system as an offspring of Dewey's instrumentalism. As he explained 'I have done my best to state explicitly and repeatedly that I am using the word [technology] in the broadest possible sense to refer to that whole aspect of human experience and activity which some logicians call "operational", and to the entire complement of artifacts with which mankind operates. So defined, technology includes mathematical journals and symphonic scores no less than skyscrapers and assembly lines, since all these are equally the product of human hands as well as brains.'[9]

Given his later insistence on the value and importance of science and technology, Ayres' treatment of science in some of his earlier writings comes as a considerable surprise. In his first book, *Science: The False Messiah* (1927), he attacked the current worship of pure science as an end in itself, warning that scientists were becoming the high priests of modern society. Strongly contesting the view that popular thought was wholly confused or that science was superior to the 'homely ideas' on which civilization turns, Ayres asserted that 'from the human point of view science is utterly unsatisfactory . . . science never solves the mysteries of the Forces which rule our lives. In the field of mystery – and human life is all mystery – religion remains supreme' (1927, SFM., p.154).

Two years later, in a philosophical essay, he reiterated his opinion that science was incapable of dealing with the entire range of human concerns – especially the most important ones. Accepting the Kantian distinction between the *ding an sich*, the philosophical realm and things as they seem, which he identified with science, he declared that such certainty as science could muster merely stemmed from its 'instruments of precision' and its consequent capacity to extend the powers of sensory observation (1927, SFM, pp.47, 156–8). 'No subject matter', he remarked, 'can be understood except as derived from a certain type of mental discipline' (1929, 'A Critique of Pure Science', p.178), and, as he offered no criterion by which to compare the validity of one mental discipline with another, his assertion that the study of science and the study of society 'have nothing whatever in common except the fact that both are pursued by men' is perplexing (1929, 'A Critique of Pure Science', p.178). The limitations of science, he continued, 'arise from the fact that not all matters of interest and importance to mankind are perceptible to eye and ear. . . . Social behavior is just as real as any behavior, and concepts which arise in social behavior are therefore just as real and sound as concepts which arise in the tinkering of hand and eye.'[10]

These passages are of the greatest interest in the light of Ayres' subsequent tendency to adopt a monistic ontology parallel with the monistic epistemology he derived from Dewey. As a loyal instrumentalist, he consistently opposed dualistic disjunctions between body and mind, facts and values, means and ends, knowing and doing. Technology was the only *source* of knowledge and genuine values, for 'operational' values derived from tools were uniform and consistent moral values, by contrast with the variability of 'false' cultural values.[11] It was the positivistic disassociation of truth and value which defined the moral crisis of the twentieth century, for the crucial issue was not to separate knowledge from values but to distinguish between true and false, both in knowledge and values (1961, TRS, pp.49–50). As an instrumentalist, Ayres claimed that value judgements could be objectively verified, and he repeatedly referred to technological criteria of value judgements and human welfare (1961, TRS, p.61; 1967, 'The Theory of Institutional Adjustment', p.14).

By contrast with his earlier acknowledgement of the disjunction between science and 'the human point of view', Ayres subsequently stressed their fundamental compatibility, for both modern science and 'the values of man's achieving' reflected the underlying uniformities of nature (1961, TRS, p.51). This may explain why at one point he described machines as the 'ultimate reality' of modern civilization, while elsewhere he defined reality as 'the unique coherence of . . . the non-material culture' (1943, 'Capitalism in Retrospect', p.301; 1967, 'The Theory of Institutional Adjustment', p.7). In emphasizing the fundamental unity and uniformity of the 'mutually intensifying system of concerted values' (1959, 'The Industrial Way of Life', p.9), which he sometimes vaguely referred to as the 'life process' (a term to be found in Veblen, Hobson and Ruskin), he became increasingly critical of the pestilential 'moral agnosticism' of those who believed in the relativity of cultural standards (1957, 'The Pestilence of Moral Agnosticism', pp.116–25). If, as he claimed, culture was an 'aspect of nature' like science and technology, presumably the two aspects could not be indefinitely out of phase or at odds with one another, even though he repeatedly referred to the conflict between institutions and technology and declared that institutional and instrumentalist standards were 'absolutely opposed' (1935, 'The Gospel of Technology', p.40; 1967, 'The Theory of Institutional Adjustment', p.5).

There was, of course, as Veblen had demonstrated, an institutional lag as society adjusted itself, sometimes slowly and painfully, to the ongoing process of technological advance. But toward the end of his life Ayres appeared to be looking beyond Veblen to a time when the lag would be significantly reduced, if not entirely eliminated. Despite institutional impediments, technology proceeded at an accelerating pace, and twenty years earlier Ayres had acknowledged the 'logical and ethical and therefore economic significance of the continuity which is actually present in the technological process and in it alone' (1945, 'Addendum to *The Theory of Economic Progress* p.939). Hence, notwithstanding his Veblenian distaste for teleological statements and his reluctance to indulge in prophecies, Ayres' later writings convey an ineradicable impression of the ultimate supremacy of technology. A 'de-institutionalization' process was under way, directly parallel to the 'de-mythologization of modern culture' which results from the inexorable growth of science and technology (1967, 'The Theory of Institutional Adjustment', pp.8, 16). But since, in his earliest writings, Ayres maintained that even science was ultimately based on folklore, one wonders what credence can be given to this *Weltanschauung*.

In his first book, Ayres had sneered at the Hegelian dialectic as 'a sort of patent Absolute detector' (1927, SFM, p.165); but subsequently, despite occasional denials, he was preaching his own species of absolutism. This was entailed in his attack on cultural relativism, in which he distinguished between 'the fancied values to which each different culture conditions its community . . . [and] the genuine values which are common to all' (1959, 'The Industrial Way of Life', p.14). In culture, as in technology, non-operational norms and practices were false and irrational, and, although 'supernatural fancies' could be culturally transmitted as readily as 'clear and certain knowledge' (1959, 'The Industrial Way of Life', p.15; 1961, TRS, p.289), in due course the predominant influence of technology would presumably obliterate most, if not all, the spurious variations.[12] Ayres' warm endorsement of Dewey's famous critique of *The Quest for Certainty* seems curiously at odds with his own confidence in 'the progressive certainty of science' and his conviction that true knowledge and values can be distinguished from false (1946, DRC, p.185). As early as 1935 he conceded that 'sooner or later any theory of historical process faces the problem of absolute value', adding that technology must constitute its ultimate foundation since it 'does indeed afford a basis of judgment which is absolute in the sense that it is in no wise dependent upon any sort of moral inwardness nor upon any moral tradition whatever . . . I am therefore, in this sense, a complete materialist' (1934–35, 'Confusion Thrice Confounded', p.358). In his last book, *Toward a Reasonable Society* [1961], he explicated his set of interacting, mutually compatible values: freedom, equality, security, abundance and excellence. Taken together, these constituted the essence of the 'life process' which it was the economist's duty to promote.

If, as seems likely, the foregoing account of Ayres' philosophy is somewhat obscure and bewildering, it is at least partly due to his unwillingness to employ precise philosophical terms and concepts. This limitation particularly inhibits the effort to understand his conception of the nature of and relationships between institutions, technology and values. For example, he never precisely specified the meaning and extension of the term *technology*, although he repeatedly and unambiguously stressed that the development of technology was continuous, increasingly influential and compatible with human values. In later writings he tried to specify the principal values embodied in that compendious expression 'the life process', but he never cleared up certain earlier difficulties arising from his shifting emphasis on the nature, sources, foundation and criteria of values. In the preface to the new edition of his first two books he made a final attempt to explain his meaning. Whereas the continuity of the technological process 'means that it is *a* locus of value . . . Human life itself is *the* "locus" of value – not in the animistic sense of totem and taboo, but in the continuously progressive sense of the "instinct" [or process] of workmanship.' Two pages later he went further, almost repudiating his Deweyite insistence on the means–ends continuum, concluding that 'human life and well being *depends upon* the furtherance' of the technological process, thereby implying that technology is merely a means to an end rather than an end in itself, since 'the values we seek are those of human life and well-being' (1927, SFM, first two quotations from p.x, third quotation from p.xii; italics supplied). Yet if this is the core of his message is it more than a statement of the obvious?

III

Although Ayres was sometimes regarded as a dangerous radical, he was never in fact an extremist, either in political or economic affairs. Consistently hostile to fascism, Marxism and doctrinaire socialism, he stood squarely in the mainstream of moderate American social and economic reformers alongside the progressives and new dealers. To a transatlantic reader it is noticeable how frequently he cited such British liberal reformers as Hobson, R.H. Tawney and J.M. Keynes, with whom he was associated in the 1920s during his *New Republic* days; and, when William Beveridge published his *Full Employment in a Free Society* in 1944, Ayres welcomed his social security programme as a means of bypassing the traditional controversy between socialism and capitalism.[13] A staunch opponent of *laissez-faire*, Ayres naturally favoured a form of interventionist policy which, he hoped, would produce what he called 'limited capitalism'. Unlike the first generation of American institutionalists, Ayres developed his economic ideas against the background of the Great Depression of the early thirties and Roosevelt's recovery programmes, and contemporary preoccupations influenced his ideas more directly and profoundly than has been generally appreciated. Despite his severe criticisms of business, he wished to extend business principles,[14] and during the New Deal he was advocating regulation of machine industry and some form of social control or guidance of the productive mechanism which would deal with the central problem of idle resources (1933, 'The Basis of Economic Statesmanship', p.215; 1939, 'The Principles of Economic Strategy', pp.460–70). In the mid–1940s Ayres welcomed the new Keynesian macroeconomics, and despite his profound reservations about all forms of economic orthodoxy, he declared, in 1948, that institutionalism, underconsumptionist ideas (which he associated with Hobson and Keynes), and economic planning were mutually reinforcing (1948, 'The New Economics', pp.226–32).

His conception of planning was no more extreme than his other policy ideas. He considered that a general economic strategy was required, not a detailed blueprint, and he opposed planning against competition and sweeping nationalization or expropriation of industrial property (1939, 'The Principles of Economic Strategy'; 1943, 'The Significance of Economic Planning'; 1946, DRC, p.164; 1948, 'The New Economics'). Indeed, considering his advocacy of piecemeal economic and social reform and his rejection of fears that increased government activity represented the road to serfdom, it would not be farfetched to describe him as a typical Fabian.

Another central characteristic Ayres possessed in common with other American progressives and instrumentalists was his underlying confidence in the future of American society – and, indeed, of industrial capitalism in general. He was not, of course, a blind optimist. He repeatedly stated that progress was not inevitable, warning against the dangers of complacency. He often referred to current 'crises', and sometimes suggested that capitalism or 'society' was in danger of collapsing (1943, 'The Twilight of the Price System', p.180; 1943, 'The Significance of Economic Planning', p.470; 1946, DRC, p.80; 1961, TRS, pp.207–8). Nevertheless, even in periods of the greatest difficulty he never seemed to doubt that some remedy was available, and his pessimistic statements are far outweighed by his fundamentally optimistic views. He vigorously rejected the predictions of the 'prophets of scientific doom' (1943, 'The Significance of Economic Planning', p.479), arguing that 'human experience does manifest a developmental pattern of some sort' (1945, 'Addendum to the *Theory of Economic Progress*', p.938) and entitling 'his magnum opus *The Theory of Economic Progress*.

Underlying this optimism was his belief in the 'inner law of progress in technology' (1943, 'Technology and Progress', p.11), and he had no fear that the growth of science would lead to cultural decay or a loss of freedom. On the contrary, he anticipated the progressive replacement of superstition by knowledge, of prejudice by reason (1961, TRS, p.138). He claimed that there was an increasing awareness of the importance of machines among the general public, and even among the economists, after the Great Depression (1944, TEP, p.306), and that there was no incompatibility between economic progress and other values (1952, IE, p.403). In more specifically economic affairs he saw no serious obstacle to sound policies – for example, the need to set farm prices so as to obtain the desired volume of production (1948, 'The New Economics', p.232). Nor was there any economic barrier to the attainment of social security, though there might be political obstacles (1946, DRC, p.104). Technological progress might be checked for a time by institutional impediments, but this would only be a temporary setback (1952, IE, p.402). And his comparative lack of concern with the human and environmental damage caused by industrial technology, a theme which has recently become almost obsessive, is yet another indication of his membership in an earlier generation of social commentators.[15] There was no ultimate conflict of values: without being Utopian, Ayres evidently believed that freedom, equality, security, abundance and excellence were all within man's eager grasp.

Like many intellectuals, Ayres possessed a fundamentally optimistic faith in the 'power of ideas' (1944, TEP, chap.13), confidently asserting that 'intellectual progress is never destructive' (1948, 'The New Economics', p.230). Yet, although he claimed that the power of propaganda was greatly exaggerated (1944, TEP, p.295), his optimism was by no means unqualified. In the late 1940s, when the anti-communist phobia was gaining momentum, he warned that society would collapse if intellectual freedom was suppressed (1947, 'Are Professors Dangerous?'), and in economic and social affairs he was deeply concerned at the persistence of outworn dogmas and pernicious fallacies. He not only attacked the orthodox tradition of economics as providing ideological support for *laissez-faire* capitalism, but he also suggested that, if the ideas of the founding fathers were not repudiated, disaster would ensue (1956, 'The Classical Tradition Versus Economic Growth', p.350). Like other economic dissenters he thought that the economics profession had great influence over the general public, arguing that 'the consummate fault of the whole classical theory' was that it prevented the community from recognizing the dangers of 'bigness' and its implications for economic power (1952, IE, p.390). And in his later writings he accused the economics profession of moral irresponsibility on the grounds of its persistent failure to warn the public of the pernicious influence of business power.

Given his background, training, literary skills and wide-ranging intellectual interests, it is perhaps surprising that Ayres ever became, let alone remained, a professor of economics. But once he was situated within the academic community it was surely inevitable that he would become a dissenter. When he joined the University of Texas faculty in 1930 the obsequies of institutionalism were already being celebrated in some quarters, and the movement's younger adherents lacked leadership. Of the three co-founders, Veblen was dead; Mitchell had turned from his more heterodox ideas to the statistical study of business cycles; and Commons, though still active in the field, had become increasingly isolated and incomprehensible even to his closest admirers. Although Ayres was obviously a critic of economic orthodoxy, his precise intellectual allegiances remained obscure during the 1930s, probably because he was still feeling his way. During that decade he published much less than in his journalist days of the 1920s, or in the 1940s and 1950s, when he was expounding and elaborating his intellectual system. However, he was neither ignored nor rejected by the professional economic establishment in the 1930s, for he published occasional articles in the *American Economic Review* and became an active and effective member of its editorial board for three years, from 1935 to 1938. This was the closest he ever came to the professional centre of American economics. In the mid-1940s his intellectual position became much clearer with the publication of *The Theory of Economic Progress* (1944) and *The Divine Right of Capital* (1946), and it is significant that chapters of these works first appeared in general periodicals, such as *The Antioch Review* and the *Southwestern Social Science Quarterly*, rather than in the professional economic journals. He continued this practice in the next two decades, thereby revealing his detachment from the mainstream of American economics and his desire to reach a less specialized readership.

Dissenters and outsiders are often effective and perspicacious critics of established doctrines and opinion leaders, and Ayres was no exception. A brief résumé of his objections to classical and neo-classical economics contains few surprises for those familiar with earlier heterodox effusions.[16] Economic theory, he complained, was comprised of a melange of absurdities, truisms, meaningless tautologies and circular reasoning. Its philosophical and psychological premises were unsound; its propositions were not merely unrealistic, but false; and as an intellectual system it was devoid of human, moral or social merit. Despite its positivistic pose, classical economics had never been purely descriptive, and Adam Smith's desire to overthrow the mercantilist economic order merely exemplified the economists' perennial and unavoidable concern with social problems (1918, 'The Function and Problems of Economic Theory', pp.74–8). Unlike some heterodox writers, Ayres did not regard orthodox economics as static, nor did he entirely reject the concept of equilibrium (1939, 'The Principles of Economic Strategy', p.463). On the contrary, he insisted that classical political economy was 'fundamentally a theory of economic dynamics' and the founding fathers' conception of the equilibrium of institutions and technology was their greatest achievement (1934, 'Values: Ethical and Economic', p.453; 1951, 'The Co-ordinates of Institutionalism', p.50; 1943, 'The Twilight of the Price System', p.163; 1944, TEP, pp.20–1).

Much of his hostility – which, he subsequently admitted, was exaggerated – was directed at the price system. Its importance had been overrated both by its defenders and by the institutionalist opposition. Price theory was the 'Freemasonry' of the professional economists (1966, 'Nature and Significance of Institutionalism', p.73), who, for technical reasons, had elaborated it to the point where it became an arcane mystery inaccessible to the layman, and therefore a basis for professional status and recognition (1951, 'The

Co-ordinates of Institutionalism', p.49; 1952, IE, pp.18–19). Ayres considered that this analytical apparatus had no meaning or significance once it was detached from its original conception of the harmonious, atomistic, self-regulating socioeconomic order; and he criticized the institutionalists for their failure to provide an alternative theory or to proceed successfully from analysis to policy (1934–35, 'Moral Confusion in Economics', pp.172–4; 1943, 'The Twilight of the Price System', p.179; 1944, TEP, pp.11–12). But although the economists were not merely vulgar apologists of the capitalist system (1938, PEO, p.34), as the socialists claimed, price theory had in fact afforded intellectual support for capitalism. Moreover, classical economics had provided a moral justification for the prevailing uneven distribution of wealth (1934, 'Values: Ethical and Economic', p.454; 1944, TEP, p.52), and at times Ayres even accused the economists of perpetrating a confidence trick on the public in claiming that savings and abstinence, rather than technological progress, constituted the main source of capital accumulation (1938, PEO, pp.73–4; 1944, TEP, p.54; 1961, TRS, p.238).

Ayres occasionally adopted a carping and satirical tone when referring to his colleagues in the economics profession,[17] complaining that they had failed to keep pace with the development of Western civilization or to comprehend the existing economic order. Nevertheless, he credited them with sincerity, honesty and modesty – indeed, they greatly underestimated their influence on the general public (1944, TEP, p.284; 1952, IE, p.297; 1966, 'Nature and Significance of Institutionalism', p.78). Ayres naturally sympathized with outsiders like Hobson, who had been 'professionally ostracized' because he had challenged the moral basis of capitalism (1946, DRC, p.195); and at one point he even referred to the 'atmosphere of intimidation' in which economic instruction 'commonly proceeds' (1944, TEP, p.54). He stoutly defended the dissenters against false accusations, denying that 'institutionalism is the work of men who are failures and who have therefore in anger and bitterness turned against the economic order they blame for their own failure'. Nor was it true, he insisted, that the movement had its origin in 'emotional disaffection' or that it led to 'social revolution' (1952, IE, pp.3, 14).

Throughout the greater part of the 1930s, Ayres remained a detached commentator on institutionalism, as in his first published article, which appeared in 1918. Institutionalism was 'bad economics', he declared in 1935: its exponents dismissed orthodox theory too lightly, and they offered no alternative theory – merely 'a few stray uncoordinated hints' (1934–35, 'Moral Confusion in Economics', pp.172, 182, 197–8; 1934–35, 'Confusion Thrice Confounded', p.357). Indeed, in 1944 he complained that many of Veblen's followers had displayed 'a contempt for theory as such which has led them to eschew "abstract" thinking and to concentrate their efforts upon empirical studies of actual economic situations . . . with results which are not clearly distinguishable from' the work of students who have never strayed from the classical fold, as the latter never tire of pointing out' (1944, TEP, pp.11–12).

In his magnum opus Ayres aimed to set out 'a new way of thinking about economic problems', while acknowledging that there was as yet no viable alternative to the orthodox model. 'Whatever the defects of the classical design, it still remains the only over-all design we have, and will remain until another conception of the meaning of the economy has taken form' (1944, TEP, p.21). To provide this alternative design was Ayres' principal aim, for he considered that the primary task of economics was 'to elicit the meaning' of the economy, and its proper focus was 'the theory of economic order' rather than the narrower range of theoretical, technical and statistical topics which engaged the attention of most professional economists (1944, TEP, p.85; 1934–35, 'Moral Confusion in Economics', p.171; 1938, PEO).

By 1952, when he published his textbook *The Industrial Economy: Its Technological Basis and Institutional Destiny*, he had abandoned his detachment and adopted institutionalism (or instrumentalism) as the required 'new way of thinking'. In so doing he took up a 'frankly partisan' standpoint, declaring: 'I confess I have no patience with the notion that the business of teachers (and, I presume, writers) is to "present both sides" of any matter that is in dispute, leaving it to their students (or readers) to "decide for themselves" where the truth resides . . . the eventual effect of such a practice is likely to be that the teachers and writers gradually acquire indecisiveness as a sort of occupational disease' (1952, IE, p.ix). Ayres considered it the teacher's or writer's duty, 'seeking all the knowledge and all the wisdom he can manage, to present his understanding of the matter in hand as clearly as he can, together with the clearest possible account of the procedures by which he has arrived at his conclusions, leaving it to others to present similarly sympathetic accounts of alternative interpretations of the matter. There is no reason why anyone who reads this book should not read others that declare otherwise, and every reason why he should' (1952, IE, pp.ix–x).

Ayres' reasons for declaring his allegiance to institutionalism (or instrumentalism, or technologism, as he would have preferred to call it) were expressed in his earlier writings. Classical economics was a foreign importation which failed to take account of the post-industrial revolution, development of technology and post-Darwinian scientific ideas. By contrast, institutionalism was an indigenous American ideology, and its central tenet was the instrumental or technological conception of value, 'which takes the place of the "moral sense" of Adam Smith and the moral nihilism of his present-day successors' (1952, IE, p.27). Following Dewey, Ayres claimed that valuations in terms of instruments and techniques are not irrational, like tribal beliefs and sentiments, for 'whereas the institutional values are culture-limited, the instrumental (or technological) values are the same for all cultures' (1952, IE, p.26). This new body of ideas, with its modern conception of human nature as a 'social or cultural phenomenon' entirely replaced the erroneous 'atomistic Newtonian–Lockean conception of human nature . . . and the whole Hobbesian–Smithian conception of the economy as a natural

397

outgrowth of the natural activities of naturally reasonable beings' (1952, IE, pp.12–13).

As the foregoing passages reveal, Ayres' primary aim was to reconstruct the philosophical foundations of economics in accordance with his conception of the economic and cultural development of Western civilization. He admitted in 1935, in response to F.H. Knight, that 'any value theory, economic or other, must have a basis which is somehow absolute' and that 'technological process does indeed afford a basis of judgment which is absolute in the sense that it is in no way dependent upon any sort of moral inwardness nor upon any moral tradition whatever' (1934–35, 'Confusion Thrice Confounded', p.358).

To put the matter differently, he subsequently agreed with Galbraith that mankind 'cannot live without an economic theology' (1956, 'The Classical Tradition Versus Economic Growth', p.347), and instrumentalism (or technology) was the central article of his faith. As we shall see, Ayres did not entirely ignore the conventional preoccupations of economists; nor did he endorse Veblen's wholesale and destructive attacks on economic orthodoxy. He was chiefly concerned with other, deeper and more general issues, and it was on this broad philosophical level – where most economists feel uncomfortable – that he functioned most persuasively. He must be answered, if at all, on an equally high level of generality, a plane of discourse on which mere economics may have comparatively little to contribute.

This is especially true of his *Theory of Economic Progress*, where, despite the opening salvos against conventional economic doctrines, Ayres' main purpose was to develop a comprehensive philosophy of cultural development. With his optimism, his moderation and his belief in reason, he can be viewed as a latter day exponent of the eighteenth century enlightenment, with its refined taste for *histoire raisonnée*. Like other leading institutionalists, especially Veblen and Commons, he used history selectively to buttress arguments derived from his philosophical preconceptions, not as a source of evidence to be critically examined and tested. Though he frequently spoke of economic history, he did so in terms almost unrecognizable – or at least unacceptable – to most specialist practitioners in the field; and, it seems, few of them have heeded his message. Admittedly there are now some small indications of a revival of interest in large-scale historical growth models,[18] but these owe nothing to Ayres, being largely a reaction against the limitations imposed by mathematical growth models in economics and the new 'cliometric' economic history. No doubt, Ayres' conception of economic development has stimulated young dissenting economists – not only in the ranks of the Association for Evolutionary Economics. But although his message is much clearer than Veblen's, it is almost as difficult to follow his lead, for, as Benjamin Higgins has remarked, Ayres tells us virtually nothing about specific programmes and policies.[19]

Despite his attachment to Veblen, Ayres took comparatively little notice of the methodological controversies in which his predecessor figured so prominently – with the sole exception of the question of the psychological foundations of economics, a matter he took very seriously. However, this, too, is an issue which now attracts much less attention than it did in the earlier decades of the century – at least if Allan Gruchy's account of neo-institutionalism is accurate.[20]

IV

Orthodox critics claim that when institutionalists turn from polemical attacks on classical and neo-classical economics to constructive work they inevitably draw upon the conventional corpus of economic analysis for the simple reason that they have not yet developed their own alternative theories. It is appropriate to consider how far this observation applies to Ayres, for an examination of his writings suggests that he drew more heavily on orthodox economics than many of his followers have appreciated.

As we have seen, Ayres was a philosopher rather than an economist, and his earlier economic writings mainly represent commentaries on past and present economic doctrines, rather than substantive exercises in economic theory or policy. Indeed, throughout his life he confined himself to the most elementary kinds of economic reasoning, eschewing complex theories, whether mathematical or verbal, and making only the most sparing use of statistical data. He was always more interested in policy problems than in economic analysis. But toward the end of the 1930s his economic ideas began to assume a more definite shape.

A central tenet of Ayres' economics, one that was directly linked to his technological interpretation of history, was his repudiation of the orthodox concept of capital. Classical economics, he maintained, had emerged under conditions where a rapid expansion of the national dividend was accompanied by gross inequality in the distribution of wealth, and this had fostered the misconception that inequality was an essential precondition of economic progress. Orthodox capital theory, he declared in 1938, was responsible for 'the greatest confusion in economics'. The idea of saving as the source of capital accumulation was a 'hoax', perpetrated by those seeking to defend the status quo; and he cited J.M. Keynes in support of his contention.[21] The accumulation of capital was due to the growth of industrial tools, not the expansion of investible funds.[22] Indeed, the growth of financial assets by large business organizations during the 1920s had restricted the expansion of consumers' demand, thereby creating the fundamental economic problem of the 1930s, which the New Deal administrators had tried to solve by expanding the volume of purchasing power. From this point Ayres proceeded in the 1940s to draw upon Keynes' *General Theory*, with its attack on Say's Law (i.e., the idea that supply creates its own demand), its use of the multiplier concept and its general endorsement of the underconsumptionist tradition in economic thought. Even in 1935 Ayres had acknowledged the falsity of the supposed conflict between neo-classical economics and institutionalism, and later in life he periodically stressed their compatibility, speaking of the convergence of orthodox and heterodox ideas on the lines of institutionalism, underconsumption and economic planning.[23] Hence in this respect he was closer to Commons than to Veblen, who had presented his evolutionary economics as being fundamentally incompatible with orthodox economics.[24]

During the 1940s and earlier 1950s Ayres came closer to orthodox economics than at any other time in his career. In his *Divine Right of Capital* (1946) – a book which, he said, bore 'a general and pervasive relationship' to *The Theory of Economic Progress* (1944) – and in *The Industrial Economy* (1952) he expounded an elementary form of Keynesianism compatible with his belief that the 'full employment' criterion was virtually equivalent to the technological criterion of 'full production'. Full employment, he maintained, was a good bargain, for the accompanying benefits of increased output could be achieved with little or no additional cost. 'What we require, and all we require, to make the industrial economy work is a flow of mass-consumption purchasing power sufficient to absorb the entire product of industry at whatever level of production we may be able to achieve' (1946, DRC, p.95).

He devoted considerable space to a discussion of income flows and what he called the 'income diversion' required to achieve this end, giving assurances that this did not entail either confiscation of property or a deliberate campaign to soak the rich. In both volumes he paid some attention to the problems involved in achieving economic stability, such as increased government expenditure, deficit financing, various types of taxation, public works and the debt burden, and in the 1952 text he even included eleven diagrams and a statistical table – for Ayres, an unprecedented concession to conventional economic pedagogy.[25] It must be admitted that by the standards of orthodox economic theory Ayres' analysis was superficial and lacking in originality. Matters of this kind were simply not his forte; nor was he really interested in them. Moreover, it would be utterly misleading to suggest that Ayres was merely a marginal Keynesian with an idiosyncratic view of economic development and a predilection for encyclopaedic sociology. His writings reveal some confusion about the functional relationships between consumption, production and distribution, for sometimes he stressed their interdependence whereas on other occasions he emphasized the primacy of one over the others.

But his most distinctive theme was his emphasis on physical production, as contrasted with the orthodox concern with exchange values, and in this respect his work is directly reminiscent of Veblen's. During the 1930s he referred to certain essentially quantitative criteria of the success of any society (1935, 'The Gospel of Technology', p.28), and by the end of the decade he advanced the notion that 'the first principle of all economic strategy is physical stability' in place of the traditional concept of price stability (1939, 'The Principles of Economic Strategy', p.464). The key to classical economic strategy was 'the idea of natural harmony', and classical price theory was meaningless when detached from that idea. But since the idea of natural harmony was no longer acceptable it must be replaced by the concept of 'physical stability', which is 'the stability without which civilization is impossible, the reality behind all enlightened social theories' (1939, 'The Principles of Economic Strategy', p.464).

> economic stability can certainly be understood in such physical terms as the relation of food supply to population, the regularity of the working habits of the people, continuity of operation of machines, and so forth. There is nothing esoteric about it, or even complicated. For it must be understood at once that the adoption of the principle of physical stability does not by any means require a set of blue prints showing the place of every man and every tool at every hour of the day to an indefinite future, any more than our past reliance on the principle of price equilibrium presupposed a similarly detailed knowledge of the movements of all prices whatsoever and of all the things of which they were the prices. A principle of strategy undertakes to state in general terms what it is that we are trying to do, and no more.
>
> (1939, 'The Principles of Economic Strategy', p.464)

In opposition to the generally accepted view, Ayres maintained that the classical economists had underestimated the importance of production. In considering the general principle of economic strategy, the question 'Production of what?' was irrelevant. Here, as elsewhere, he was concerned with society as a whole, not with individual tastes and motivations. 'There is no point in saying before you can begin to produce you must know what people want. No society begins to produce. Society is a going concern largely by virtue of the fact that we produce what we can. The effective modification of our habits of consumption does not come about as a result of spiritual revelation made manifest in wants, or by the imposition of some people's ideals on other people. The actual changes come through the adjustment of consumption to the exigencies of production' (1939, 'The Principles of Economic Strategy', p.466).

In his later writings Ayres repeatedly referred to the idea of 'full production', which he preferred to the widely accepted notion of 'full employment'. It was not a new idea in economics, he insisted, but earlier generations had failed to grasp its true significance – which hardly seems surprising when one considers Ayres' comprehensive definition of the concept: 'Full production means the sum of human achievement . . . We need have no hesitation in committing ourselves to the ideal of full production, conceived as the life process of mankind. No conception on the whole range of human thought is richer in meaning, of surer logical validity or scientific soundness' (1946, DRC, p.187).

401

Given such a generalized, even metaphysical interpretation, it is hardly surprising that mere economists failed to accept – or even comprehend – Ayres' doctrine, especially when he claimed that it was already unconsciously accepted by more empirically minded economists. Indeed, there was no modesty in his pretensions. 'Without being fully aware of its implications (since, after all, most people are not social philosophers), the whole world has come to accept physical production as the criterion of a sound economy. Institutionalism is nothing more, and nothing less, than the intellectual implications of that axiom' (1951, 'The Co-ordinates of Institutionalism', p.55).

As a historian of economics, rather than a metaphysician or social philosopher, the writer is understandably reluctant to accept Ayres' challenge and explore these implications fully. However, it may be appropriate to ask why the notion of 'full production' seems bizarre by contrast with the long familiar notion of 'full employment'. 'Keeping the machines running', as Ayres put it, seems intrinsically less interesting and desirable than the objective of keeping men in employment, whether in digging holes in the ground or building pyramids. Idleness of physical plant and idleness of manpower both involve waste; machines, like men, deteriorate if they are not cared for. But the essential difference is surely that the various factors of production are not equally worthy of human concern: as social scientists we necessarily take an anthropocentric view of society, caring more for the sufferings of idle men than for idle machines. It is certainly true, as Ayres repeatedly insisted, that orthodox economics is postulated on the idea of scarcity, while modern technology has revealed possibilities of abundance (subject to the limits of global natural resources) undreamt of by earlier generations. But his preoccupation with technology led Ayres to put machines into a more prominent position in the hierarchy of values than any other economist; and, despite his continual warnings, it is difficult to abandon the traditional notion of consumption as 'the sole end and purpose' of production. In Ayres' case, unlike Veblen's, an obsession with full production is understandable, for during the 1930s, when crops and livestock were destroyed in an effort to keep up prices, the spectacle of 'poverty in the midst of plenty' was profoundly shocking. In this very real sense, Ayres' technological version of institutionalism, with its key emphasis on physical output, may be regarded as a response to the depression, just as much as was Keynes' *General Theory*. One important difference, however, was that Ayres explicated the underlying epistemological and moral judgements involved and deliberately erected his version of institutionalism upon these foundations.

V

Ayres' relationship to the mainstream of American economics was always that of an outsider, a marginal man, a philosophical critic rather than a practising economist. His writings contain little or nothing of interest to the historian of economic theory, and at this distance in time his criticisms of orthodox economics seem stale, exaggerated and often misconceived. For the historian of institutional economics, however, and for all students of the intellectual history of twentieth century America, Ayres has an undeniable fascination. As mentioned earlier, he is a key figure linking the founding fathers of institutionalism to the recent post-war generation of their descendants, for whom he has been an important source of stimulus and encouragement. But is he more than that? Notwithstanding Professor Gruchy's attempt to stake a claim on behalf of a contemporary neo-institutionalist movement, it is still too early to say. Despite widespread and highly miscellaneous dissatisfaction with economic orthodoxy, there is as yet very little evidence of interest in the core of Ayres' system – the instrumental (or technological) theory of value. Nor do many young dissenters seem willing to adopt a 'holistic' philosophy or a cultural interpretation of economics. Much lip service is paid to the ideal of interdisciplinary study, and some genuine progress has undoubtedly been made. The preoccupation with economic development, both among advanced and backward societies, has flourished mightily, and this movement, while owing nothing to Ayres' system as such, has certainly provided an audience for his views.

Thus, as a system builder, it appears that Ayres' has earned few literal disciples, and his general theory has not as yet been fruitful in the sense that others have tried to follow his example and elaborate his central ideas. His work has, therefore, passed into the mainstream of American economic dissent, and it will take a careful and impartial scholar to trace and evaluate its influence.

NOTES

1 In the 1957 preface to the Japanese edition of *The Theory of Economic Progress* (subsequently referred to as TEP), Ayres tried to define the 'Americanness' of institutionalism, describing it as 'a manifestation of the American spirit of impatience with tradition and dissent from commonly accepted dogma' (not paginated – only typescript version available). In stressing the importance of the state of the industrial arts the institutionalists were not concerned with a uniquely American phenomenon. Nevertheless, he said, owing to 'a medley of historical circumstances', machines had played 'a greater part in the lives of Americans than is true of other peoples'. This is not the place to discuss the parallels and links between American institutionalists and the European authors who have sometimes been classified with them. As in the case of Veblen, there have been no avowed European disciples of Ayres. However, his work has occasionally been warmly praised by leading European economists, for example Joan Robinson, *Economic Philosophy* (Chicago: Aldine Publishing Co., 1962), pp.110–13; also, Eric Roll, *A History of Economic Thought* (London: Faber & Faber, 1973), p.586, n.4. Ayres is usually either completely ignored or merely cited *en passant* in general histories of economic thought. There is a brief account of his ideas in Joseph Dorfman, *The Economic Mind in American Civilization* (New York: Viking Press, 1959), 4, pp.126–9.

2 *Science: The False Messiah* (Indianapolis: Bobbs-Merrill, 1927) (subsequently referred to as SFM). The legacy of the University of Chicago and the Middle West region was acknowledged in the editorial introduction to *Essays in Philosophy by Seventeen Doctors of Philosophy in the University of Chicago*, Thomas Vernor Smith and William Kelley Wright (eds), (Chicago: Open Court Publishing Co., 1929), p.xi. The volume contained Ayres' essay 'A Critique of Pure Science'. See also his own acknowledgement in *The Divine Right of Capital* (Boston: Houghton Mifflin Co., 1946), pp.188–9 (subsequently referred to as DRC).

3 See Allan G. Gruchy, *Contemporary Economic Thought: The Contribution of Neo-Institutional Economics* (Clifton, NJ: Augustus M. Kelley Publishers, 1972). For a critique of this claim see my review in the *Journal of Economic Issues* 8 (September 1974) pp.597–605.

4 This unduly neglected aspect of Veblen's thought is examined in, for example, David W. Noble, *The Paradox of Progressive Thought* (Minneapolis: University of Minnesota Press, 1958), chap.9. On the presuppositions of the pragmatists and instrumentalists see also Louis Hartz, *The Liberal Tradition in America* (New York: Harcourt, Brace and Co., 1955), especially pp.10, 59. For Ayres' views see below.

5 See, for example, Gruchy, *Contemporary Economic Thought*, chap.3 and p.341; also, William Breit, 'The Development of Clarence Ayres's Theoretical Institutional-ism', *Social Science Quarterly* 53 (September 1973), pp.244–57. Ayres' personality and lifestyle were, of course, entirely different from Veblen's. However, his views were bitterly attacked in the Texas legislature and his professorship was sometimes at risk. For one of his public reactions see 'Are Professors Dangerous?', *Southwest Review* 32 (Winter 1947), pp.8–15.

6 John S. Gambs, 'What Next for the Association for Evolutionary Economics?', *Journal of Economic Issues* 3 (March 1968), p.76.

7 See, for example, his articles 'Veblen's Theory of Instincts Reconsidered', in *Thorstein Veblen: A Critical Reappraisal*, Douglas F. Dowd (ed.) (Ithaca: Cornell University Press, 1958) and 'The Legacy of Thorstein Veblen', in *Institutional Economics: Veblen, Commons and Mitchell Reconsidered*, by Joseph Dorfman *et al.* (Berkeley and Los Angeles: University of California Press, 1963). In the former essay he claimed that Veblen's theory of instincts was 'by far his most important scientific contribution', even though 'the very notion of instincts is now scientifically obsolete', and Veblen's account was conspicuous for its 'vagueness' (pp.25, 28). Acknowledgements to Veblen appear very prominently in Ayres' last published item, 'Prolegomenon to Institutionalism', Preface to the new edition of *Science: The False Messiah and Holier Than Thou: The Way of the Righteous* (New York: Augustus M. Kelley, 1973), pp.iii–xii. (The two volumes are bound together with pagination identical to the originals.)

8 For example, Frank H. Knight, 'Intellectual Confusion in Morals and Eco-nomics', *International Journal of Ethics* 45 (1935), pp.208–9. See Ayres' reply, ibid., pp.356–8.

9 C.E. Ayres, 'The Industrial Way of Life', *Texas Quarterly* 2 (Summer 1959), p.5. Ayres' definition of technology presents very considerable difficulties, for it is almost indefinitely extensible. Consequently, the relationship between science and technology, on the one hand, and institutions or ceremonialism, on the other, becomes very blurred – possibly because Ayres wished to emphasize the increasing predominance of the former over the latter. As science and technology are indissociable, being respectively the 'thinking' and 'doing' aspects of technology, it would be helpful to know the precise epistemological boundary between scientific and non-scientific thinking and doing. Unfortunately, Ayres never demarcates these realms.

10 C.E. Ayres, 'A Critique of Pure Science', pp.184, 189. I am indebted to a philosopher colleague, R.K. Black, for drawing attention to a point in this passage which had worried me. The claim that the concepts which arise in social behaviour are 'just as real and sound' as instrumental concepts seems basically incompatible with Ayres' subsequent distinction between true and false knowledge and values. However, it seems advisable to regard this remark as an isolated aberration.

11 C.E. Ayres, *Toward a Reasonable Society* (Austin: University of Texas Press, 1961), p.9 (subsequently cited as TRS).

12 There is some residue of ambiguity or inconsistency in Ayres' position, for he made few specific predictions. Thus, although he spoke with conviction of the 'progressive abandonment of what might be called the life of fancy and a progressive commitment to the realities of a life of doing and making', he warned against complacency and denied that progress was inevitable (see TRS, concluding chapter). Nevertheless, despite these caveats, Ayres exemplifies Max Weber's observation that the claim to a single universal future is an important characteristic of Westerm civilization. I owe this point to Paul Streeten; see his 'Some Problems in the Use and Transfer of an Intellectual Technology', in *The Social Sciences and Development* (Washington, DC: International Bank for Reconstruction and Development, 1974), p.21.

13 DRC, p.176. In Ayres' last five books Adam Smith was by far the most frequently quoted author, followed at some distance by Veblen, Keynes, Marx, Beveridge and Hobson. Ayres also regarded Edwin Cannan as an ally on the basis of a single article. A somewhat curious bedfellow, indeed!

14 C.E. Ayres, *The Industrial Economy: Its Technological Basis and Institutional Destiny* (Boston: Houghton Mifflin Co., 1952), p.397 (subsequently referred to as IE).

15 Apart from a passing reference to the dangers of the automobile and the possibility of pollution (TRS, p.160), Ayres was remarkably insensitive to the damage caused both to human beings and the environment by twentieth century urbanization and machine technology. One of his former students, Dorothy Reinders, has suggested to me that his long residence in Texas, amid abundance and close to the 'frontier', may have helped to preserve his optimistic view of contemporary reality.

16 C.E. Ayres, *The Problem of Economic Order*, passim (subsequently referred to as PEO). Also, TEP (Chapel Hill: University of North Carolina Press, 1944), chaps. 1 and 2.

17 The economists, he once observed, were a highly skilled profession. 'By long practice and by use of a multitude of adroit literary devices, they have been able to bring the art of double-vision and double-talk to a high degree of perfection ... it might be said that if two things are utterly and completely distinct, but if you nevertheless think of them as being identical, then you have an economic mind' (DRC, p.4). This is an uncharacteristically mocking statement from one of his avowedly popular books. Its journalistic tone resembles that of his earlier books *Science: The False Messiah* and *Holier Than Thou: The Way of the Righteous*.

18 For example, Sir John Hicks, *A Theory of Economic History* (Oxford: Clarendon Press, 1969) and D.C. North and R.P. Thomas *The Rise of the Western World: A New Economic History* (Cambridge: Cambridge University Press, 1973).

19 Benjamin Higgins, 'Some Introductory Remarks on Institutionalism and Economic Development', *Southwestern Social Science Quarterly* 41 (1960–61), p.17.

20 Gruchy, *Contemporary Economic Thought*, passim. For a general background see my Ph.D. thesis, 'Methodological Controversy as an Approach to the History of American Economics, 1885–1930', Johns Hopkins University, 1953, chap.5.

21 PEO, pp.73–5. It is noteworthy that Ayres did not cite the *General Theory* but Keynes' earlier writings – in this instance, *The Economic Consequences of the Peace* (1920) and *Unemployment as a World Problem* (1931). This supports the general impression that Ayres had not yet grasped the underconsumptionist implications of the 'new' economics.

22 Ayres argued that the accumulation of funds and the enlargement of industrial tools and equipment were two distinct processes, either of which could occur independently. In a capitalist system the link was the power which the accumulation of funds confers on its possessors ('The Significance of Economic Planning', in *The Development of Collective Enterprise*, Seba Eldridge (ed.) [Lawrence: University of Kansas Press, 1943], p.473). Ayres' severe critique of Joseph A. Schumpeter's conception of capitalism is of especial interest in this connection ('Capitalism in Retrospect', *Southern Economic Journal* 9 [April 1943], p.299).

23 The instrumentalist concept of value, he maintained, was just what was needed to make the combination fully effective ('The New Economics', *Southwest Review* 33 [Summer 1948], p.231). His subsequent work was largely devoted to the elaboration of this contention. In his later writings Ayres' conception of the relationship between institutionalism and economic orthodoxy became very blurred. While the institutionalists of the late 1930s had 'in part at least ... become Keynesians', he claimed that by the mid-1960s 'most practising economists have become institutionalists' and the 'instrumental, process-oriented conception of value' is present 'at least by implication in the thinking of virtually all institutionalists' ('Nature and Significance of Institutionalism', *Antioch Review* 26 [Spring 1966], pp.72,88–9).

24 For Ayres' brief, early, but penetrating attempt to compare his own ideas to Commons' *Institutional Economics*, see 'Moral Confusion in Economics', *International Journal of Ethics* 45 (1934–35), pp.198–9.

25 It is significant that Ayres' account of demand and supply is relegated to chaps. 13 and 14 (IE, pp.320–73). His later essay 'Guaranteed Income: An Institutionalist View' represents a development of matters referred to in DRC and IE ('Guaranteed Income: An Institutionalist View', in *The Guaranteed Income: Next Step in Economic Evolution?*, Robert Theobald (ed.) [Garden City, NY: Doubleday and Co., 1966]).

21

ECONOMICS IN THE UNITED STATES, 1920-70*

I PREAMBLE

It may never be easy to provide a brief and balanced assessment of the development of economics in the United States from 1920 to 1970. At the present juncture the task is especially difficult for several reasons. The intervening lapse of time is insufficient for the requisite detached historical perspective and 'the fullness of available data for adequate description',[1] and the terminal date for this essay coincides with an unprecedented intellectual and professional crisis in the discipline.[2] Admittedly other disciplines, especially social sciences, were also undergoing an agonizing reappraisal at that time. But the trauma seems to have been especially acute in economics, a subject in the forefront of public affairs which has often been described as the 'hardest' of the 'soft' sciences. The public dimension of American economics will be examined in some detail later in this essay. The more fundamental issue of economics' scientific character and status cannot, however, be deferred since it necessarily affects the interpretative standpoint adopted in a synoptic review of this kind. The crisis around 1970 left a legacy of doubts and a deep division of opinion about the past record, present condition and future prospects of economics; and the usual problems of historical judgement are exacerbated by the currently confused state of debate in the philosophy, history and sociology of science, which has a direct bearing on my subject. It therefore seems advisable to begin with some brief explanatory remarks on the approach adopted here in the hope that they may offset the inescapably subjective and selective features of the following account.

II PROBLEMS OF INTERPRETATION

Until recently, economists usually viewed the development of their subject from an 'internalist' standpoint, focusing on the progress of theory or analysis,

407

the ostensibly 'scientific' core of the discipline, almost as though this were an autonomous, self-contained process that could fruitfully be studied without reference to the majority of personnel by whom it was developed, the historical and institutional context in which it evolved and the uses to which the analysis was put. This standpoint is compatible with the discipline's predominantly liberal–individualist tradition in methodology, as well as in policy matters, and with the economists' deep-seated urge to emulate physics, the supposedly paradigmatic exemplar of an exact, objective, predictive and positive science. But there has also been a long-standing dissenting 'externalist' conception, rejecting a purely naturalistic treatment of economic and social phenomena, and emphasizing the changing interdependencies between economic ideas, the circumstances from which they emerged, and their practical impact on society. This latter, more relativistic, approach is especially appropriate in the present instance for several reasons.

First, I am more concerned here with general intellectual and cultural history than with theory or analysis as such. Indeed, a strictly internalist account might conceivably exclude the major proportion of American economists' work prior to World War II, for they made few significant contributions to the central corpus of economic theory during that period. Nevertheless, it will be argued later that some of their most valuable contributions to modern economic science, interpreted broadly, were made during the 1920s and 1930s. Second, an internalist interpretation would omit entirely, or seriously underrate the importance of the institutionalist movement, often regarded as the most distinctively 'American' stream of economic thought, for many of its proponents had a more or less anti-theoretical bias. The presumed decline of this influential dissenting tradition in the 1930s, and its renaissance after 1945, is one of the essential subordinate themes in our story.[3] The third reason for adopting a sociological, though not necessarily exclusively externalist approach, is its suitability as a method of handling more recent developments in economics, a point that requires some amplification.

The conventional orthodox history of economics in terms of great thinkers, ideas and systems, may not have been seriously misleading as applied to periods when the number of economists was small, and individual contributions to the subject were comparatively easy to identify and evaluate. But it is increasingly inappropriate to the mid and late twentieth century, as the economics profession expanded enormously, as the subject became highly specialized and compartmentalized, and as joint authorship, team research projects and possibly multiple discoveries became more frequent. Instead of the traditional history emphasizing great imaginative achievements, major breakthroughs, watersheds or turning points, the growth of a modern academic discipline is pre-eminently a collective professionalized phenomenon, a relatively continuous or evolutionary process shaped by many hands, even in phases when some of the actors believe themselves participants in a dramatic intellectual revolution. And this collective evolutionary process was clearly apparent in economics at an earlier time in the United States than elsewhere.

The adoption of a sociological standpoint need not entail any under-valuation of purely theoretical developments within the discipline, which have indeed been dramatic in the post-1945 period. On the contrary, the expansion of higher education, the growth of non-academic employment opportunities and the economists' enhanced public reputation have, arguably, so strengthened their status in the community that there is nowadays much greater scope for the autonomous development of the science than in earlier times. This has brought its problems, however, for many powerful professional and lay critics have maintained that the pursuit of abstract theorizing and sophisticated technique have become ends in themselves, resulting in a serious misallocation of intellectual resources. This contention will be considered later.

Against this background, the crisis in economics at the end of our period illustrates the difficulty of providing a methodologically balanced account of the development of American economics, for it resulted from a peculiar conjuncture of internal and external influences. During the first two post-World War II decades economists in the USA, as in some other countries, enjoyed an unprecedented wave of success. Only the most hardened sceptics and ideologues refused to grant them some credit for the remarkable contrast between the depression of the 1930s and the sustained post-war prosperity and high employment, and this vote of confidence was reflected in the rapidly expanding demand for their services in academia, business and government. Of course, significant disagreements about theoretical, technical and policy issues persisted within the economics community, but they could be viewed as evidence of intellectual vigour. More unusual to any historian of economics, however, was the exceptional measure of doctrinal harmony, now sometimes described as the 'Keynesian consensus'. The mood of the time was aptly conveyed in 1959 by Paul Samuelson, subsequently the first American Nobel prizewinner in economics, when he observed that economists presented 'a united front that reflects *too little* basic disagreement on fundamentals'. Furthermore, referring to the absence of post-war depressions, he added, somewhat complacently,

> Many economists feel technologically unemployed: having helped banish the worst economic diseases of capitalism, they feel like the ear surgeons whose functions modern antibiotics has reduced to a low level of priority.[4]

Samuelson need not have worried. Within a decade the American economy was faltering under the combined evils of inflation and slackening economic growth – a conjuncture which many of the early post-war Keynesians would have regarded as highly improbable, if not impossible. Naturally enough, this state of affairs undermined both the public's confidence in the economists, and their confidence in themselves. It also gave heart to various dissident groups of neo-Austrians, Marxists, radicals and institutionalists, whose protests had been either silent or muted during the Keynesian hegemony.

Part of the revival of heterodoxy from the late 1960s is undoubtedly traceable to peculiarly American economic, social and political conditions – especially the Vietnam War, urban unrest and racial problems – for the sense of crisis was undoubtedly stronger in the USA than in Europe, parts of which were suffering (or were to suffer) from similar economic difficulties. But its strength was also attributable to conditions within the profession, for the professionalization process had advanced much further in the USA than elsewhere, as had also the development of specialization, mathematization and quantification, the most distinctive features of the modernization movement in the post-war social sciences. To some critics the so-called 'positivist' movement had been carried to excess in the case of American economics, a discipline in which it was easy to cherish the illusion that progress was bringing convergence towards precision and predictability of the kind associated with the natural sciences. As with the Great Depression of the early 1930s, the preceding 'collective hubris' – a term that seems peculiarly suited to describe the state of American economics in the early 1960s – was followed by a correspondingly sharp reaction. In the 1970s it was no longer fashionable to speak of the economists' ability to 'fine tune' the economy; and it now seems surprising to find that another (subsequent) Nobel prizewinner, George Stigler, could have declared, in 1965, that as a result of the post-war 'quantitative revolution', economics

> is finally at the threshold of its Golden Age – nay, we already have one foot through the door. . . . Our expanding theoretical and empirical studies will inevitably and irresistibly enter into the subject of public policy, and we shall develop a body of knowledge essential to policy making. And then, quite frankly, I hope we become the ornaments of democratic society whose opinions on economic policy shall prevail.[5]

Stigler is a distinguished historian of economics, noted as a pungent critic of woolly thinking, and his claim is all the more remarkable given that his conception of appropriate economic policies differed substantially from Samuelson's. In 1953, Stigler's Chicago colleague, Milton Friedman, another (subsequent) Nobel laureate, had argued that the progress of 'positive' economics would eliminate most policy disagreements, since they stemmed from different predictions of the effects of policy measures, rather than from normative considerations. But when the crisis came, the public reaction was seriously disquieting, and Friedman was inclined to blame his professional colleagues:

> we economists have done great harm – to society at large and to our profession in particular – by claiming more than we can deliver. We

have therefore encouraged politicians to make extravagant promises, inculcate unrealistic expectations in the public at large, and promote discontent with reasonably satisfactory results because they fall short of the economists' promised land.[6]

It would, of course, be easy to provide a selective parade of quotations designed to reveal the variety of opinion within the economics profession at the end of our period, especially if the range was broadened to include dissenters as well as established leaders. There is now a veritable babel of tongues, a variety of groups, schools and splinter movements, and almost as many standpoints from which to assess the current state of the art. The crisis of the early 1970s may, indeed, eventually prove to be transitory – a collective psychological neurosis rather than a degenerating phase in the orthodox research programme. Nor are matters any clearer if we turn to methodology for guidance, for the 'positivism' which was virtually the official doctrine approved by most mainstream economists during the post-war so-called mathematical–quantitative revolution, is now wholly discredited by philosophers of science. And whether this means that we need a new methodology, a vigorous reassertion of the old or the abandonment of methodology in any form, is now the subject of lively controversy.[7]

In short, this is hardly the ideal time for a comprehensive survey of the development of economics in America during our period; and this prolegomenon is designed to alert the reader to some of the limitations in the following account.

III SCALE, SCOPE AND CONTENT

Like other academic disciplines, economics expanded very rapidly in the USA during our period. Indeed, for much of the time it was one of the most popular subjects taught in colleges and universities, earning considerable fortunes for the most successful textbook writers. But unfortunately, there are no reliable statistics of the number of 'economists', quite apart from the problem of differentiating between 'professionals' and others.

For data on this matter it is natural to turn to the records of the leading scholarly organization, the American Economic Association (AEA), founded in 1885. These show an increase of membership from 2,301 in 1920 to 4,154 in 1945 and 18,908 by 1970 – that is, just over 82 per cent, less than the concurrent rate of US population growth (92 per cent) and the estimated fourteenfold increase in the academic staff in higher education during the same period.[8] However, these statistics may be more confusing than helpful. The AEA was an open organization with no entry conditions other than payment of the modest subscription for the *American Economic Review* (AER), and during the early part of our period vigorous membership campaigns were conducted to enlist businessmen and other interested laymen.[9] Thus by no means all AEA members were qualified economists; the above figures also include foreign members, and many academically trained economists did not join. As the discipline expanded some economists have joined other, potentially competing, scholarly organizations catering for particular regions and/or groups of specialists in economics, while business and government economists have formed what might loosely be termed 'craft unions'. Even more disconcerting was the disclosure, in a careful study conducted in the 1960s, of huge discrepancies between the AEA's figures and those for economists listed in the Census and the National Roster for Scientific Personnel, both of which are much larger.[10] Nor is this surprising. The number of academically trained economists employed outside higher education has grown remarkably, especially since the 1930s, and as the subject has become more technical and esoteric many have been reluctant to join the AEA, or to remain as members if they joined as graduate students. Beyond this, it must be acknowledged that the title 'economist' has no specific 'professional' significance. As anyone can use it, the economists' ranks may be swollen by amateurs, quacks and charlatans, and this is a problem that has periodically worried leaders of the profession.[11]

But although the AEA's membership figures are unrepresentative, they are not insignificant. The demand for fully trained economists has been high and sustained since World War II, notwithstanding some vicissitudes in the profession's public standing. Almost three quarters of the growth of AEA membership has occurred since 1945, and broadly similar results would probably emerge from a full count of Ph.D.s granted by American colleges and universities. Between 1920 and 1970, 32,109 US doctorates were awarded in the social sciences, of which 12,293 were in economics, 330 in econometrics and 419 in statistics. The accelerating pace of expansion is suggested by the fact that 40 per cent of all doctorates in economics and 54 per cent of those in econometrics were awarded in the 1960–70 period.[12]

There are no reliable statistics on the distribution of economists within the labour force,[13] but data on first intentions of doctorates provide some indication of the initial linkages between academic training and subsequent careers. A comparison of first employment intentions of 1960–74 economics and econometric doctorates with those of behavioural science doctorates as a whole (in brackets) yields the following results: college and university appointments 68.1 per cent (67.1); business and industry 5.6 per cent (3.8); federal government 7.5 per cent (4.8); state and local government 1.3 per cent (6.5); non-profit organizations 4.1 per cent (6.3); other and unclassified employment 13.4 per cent (11.5).[14] These differences are less marked than might have been expected considering the direct relevance of economics to business, and the economists' growing public prominence in the higher echelons of government – including the Cabinet and the Council of Economic Advisers – the press and elsewhere. The percentage of economics Ph.D.s in the 1960–74 cohorts who took academic posts was significantly higher than that for psychologists, many of whom work in hospitals, other public health agencies and in private practice; and only slightly higher than for behavioural scientists generally (the respective figures are 68.5 per cent, 53.5 per cent and 67.1 per cent). This is surprising, given the economists' alternative employment opportunities.[15] However, in interpreting these figures it is necessary to note that as academic training has become more advanced there has been some tendency to regard the Ph.D. as too specialized, and some non-academic employers may prefer ABD's – that is, candidates with the requisite qualifications 'all but dissertation'.

Turning to more strictly academic matters, in economics, as in other disciplines, Ph.D. production was highly concentrated in a limited number of centres throughout the period, despite the rapid growth in the number of institutions offering Ph.D. programmes after World War II. Between 1920 and 1974 the leading producers of Ph.D.s in economics and econometrics were: Harvard, 1,235; Wisconsin 947; Columbia 832; California (Berkeley) 757; Illinois (Champaign-Urbana) 592; Pennsylvania 582; Chicago 544; Cornell 512; Minnesota 436; Iowa State 391; MIT 377; and Ohio State 369.[16] The first ten of these accounted for more than 55 per cent of the total, and ten of the dozen listed here were also among the top dozen producers of doctorates in the behavioural sciences as a whole, although not in the same rank order.

Given the competitiveness of American higher education there have naturally been various efforts to assess the quality of graduate faculty and graduate programmes, especially since the 1950s, and despite the acknowledged deficiencies of the data the results have been widely quoted. Some commentators argue that these publications, like political polls, tend to have a self-confirming character:

> They tend, first, to make the rich richer and the poor poorer; second, the example of the highly ranked clearly imposes constraints on those lower down the scale,

with the effect of reducing diversity, rewarding conformity or respectability, penalizing genuine experiment and risk, and promoting the prevalence of disciplinary dogma and orthodoxy.[17] Moreover, it is clear that the polls tend to measure (if anything) prestige rather than quality, and from this standpoint perhaps the most significant feature is the persistence of certain leading institutions in economics and, to a lesser extent, in the social sciences as a whole, throughout the half century. This is so even when we include the first survey (in 1925) which was much more limited in scope than the two 1960s surveys, which were basically comparable in approach.[18]

In 1925 the rank order in economics was: Harvard, Chicago, Columbia, Wisconsin, Yale, Johns Hopkins, Michigan, Pennsylvania, Illinois and Cornell. By the first post-1945 survey, in 1957, Johns Hopkins, Illinois and Cornell had disappeared from the first ten, and did not reappear thereafter, whereas Berkeley and Stanford had risen to fifth and sixth places in the 1960s, while Columbia and Pennsylvania had sunk to eleventh and twelfth by that time. The most spectacular post-war rise was that of MIT, which did not appear in the first ten in 1957, but tied for first place with Harvard in 1964 and 1969.[19] Two further points deserve notice: the lack of any close correlation between prestige (quality?) and size of Ph.D. output, and the fact that most of the leading institutions in economics were also regarded as leaders in the social sciences as a whole, even though some of them acquired departments such as Anthropology or Geography only late in the game, if at all.[20] The implications of these findings will be considered briefly later.[21]

There is no brief and painless way of describing the main changes in the scope and content of American economics between 1920 and 1970. According to the invaluable AEA *Index of Economic Journals* the number of periodicals published in 1920 was fifteen; in 1963 it was 112; and by 1970 it had risen to 197. This was a rate of growth broadly similar to that of all scientific journals taken together. The *Index* has been used as the basis for a number of revealing studies of the structure and functioning of the economics profession (which will be considered later) as well as changing trends, fads and fashions in the discipline. Articles are usually regarded as a more sensitive index of the state of a discipline than books, especially in the natural sciences, where there is keen competition to publish results quickly in order to establish priority claims in research.[22] The situation is somewhat different in economics, a discipline in which there are marked divergencies between the changing content of articles, as against books and dissertations. Even after allowing for problems of definition and classification, the striking increase in the percentage of articles on economic theory (including monetary theory) between 1920 and 1970[23] is not matched by a comparable expansion in the percentage of books and dissertations in these subjects. Thus in the 1920 AER listing of books the sixty-nine general works, theory and history came tenth in size behind economic history and geography (210); labour, social problems and reforms; accounting and business methods; agriculture and related activities, and other applied or empirical categories. A broadly similar ranking appeared in 1939, even in respect of foreign language books, and the composition of book output seems not to have changed dramatically after World War II, notwithstanding the greatly enhanced importance of mathematics and technical sophistication in the discipline.

Admittedly the earlier book classifications differ from those adopted after 1945, when theory and related studies sometimes appeared under the same heading. Yet economic theory and general economics ranked only seventh among new books in 1950, and twelfth in 1968. The largest categories were international economics and economic history, economic development and national economics – subjects that reflected the economists' new post-war preoccupations. Yet such pre-war standbys as land economics, agricultural economics and economic geography, labour economics and various aspects of business studies still figured prominently. Curiously enough, economic theory led among foreign language books in 1950 and was fifth in 1968. How far editorial policy affected these outcomes is impossible to say, but it probably accounts for the strange fluctuations in the composition of book reviews, which do not correspond with the numbers of books listed. In 1920 book reviews of general works, theory and history came only tenth, but first in 1939. In 1950 reviews on economic theory, general economics ranked first but only equal eleventh in 1968 (together with public finance and fiscal policy, population, and welfare and consumer economics).

No doubt it would be unwise to draw firm conclusions from this unsatisfactory data; but it does shed some light on the relative importance of economic theory, which is a kind of umbilical cord linking all members of the profession. J.M. Clark probably underestimated its role in 1927 when he suggested that only 2 per cent of economists could be classified as 'theorists'.[24] Yet theory was, and still is the central focus of most controversy and the principal basis on which many distinguished careers are built – another point to be considered later.[25]

In addition to publications, dissertations also provide some indication of the changing content of a discipline, for they reflect the current research of the youngest generation of scholars (and their advisers' recommendations), and they usually have a period of gestation shorter than books but longer than articles. Unfortunately, the AEA's annual dissertation lists are sometimes confined to degrees granted, but in other cases include theses in progress, some of which may never be completed. This helps to account for the erratic fluctuations of the totals: 1920 – 245; 1930 – 544; 1950 – 215; 1968 – 694. Yet if we concentrate on the 1955, 1960, 1965 and 1970 lists, which were compiled on a uniform basis, economic theory still comes well down the ranking after such topics as labour, land and agricultural economics, business administration and industrial economics. This ordering undoubtedly conceals the extent to which theory and advanced techniques have been utilized in dealing with traditional 'applied' problems, for this has been one of the most noteworthy features of post-1945 economics. Whether this has narrowed the 'gap' between 'theory' and 'policy' (or the so-called 'real world') is quite another issue.

Yet another standpoint from which to view the shape of the discipline is the distribution of economists between given 'fields of special competence', as revealed in self-descriptions compiled by the AEA. The following table also includes the percentages of journal articles in various major subdivisions of the discipline, and can therefore serve as a check on the above quoted statistics on books and dissertations (although, of course, it applies only to a single year).[26] One intriguing feature of this table is that economists specializing in general theory, monetary and fiscal theory and institutions, international economics, and industrial organization, appear to have produced a disproportionately greater share of articles, whereas those specializing in economic development, planning, business administration and finance produced relatively less.

Table 1 Distribution of economists and journal articles by fields of special competence (1964 percentage distribution)

Field of special competence	Registered economists	Journal articles
General economic theory	10.2	19.1
Economic history, history of thought	2.2	5.3
Economic development and planning	7.1	6.9
Economic statistics	4.0	4.6
Monetary and fiscal theory and institutions	8.0	20.2
International economics	4.4	9.7
Business finance and administration	39.0	5.7
Industrial organization	6.6	11.0
Land economics	10.3	10.4
Population, welfare	1.4	3.0
Other	1.3	5.9

Given the lack of precise information about the output of publications in economics it is impossible to know whether these results reflect differences in the market or in levels of productivity between fields.

The above list of fields gives only a very rough indication of the subject matter of economics. At the end of our period the *Index of Economic Journals* was organized into twenty-three categories and some seven hundred sub-categories, while the important Behavioural and Social Sciences Survey of Economics conducted in the late 1960s employed a classification different from both the *Index* and the table reproduced above.[27] More revealing about the state of the discipline is the Survey's panel of experts' concern at the 'communications crisis in the discipline' as the result of the post-World War II process of expansion and decentralization. It was estimated that the abstracts in the recently founded AEA *Journal of Economic Literature* covered only about 25 per cent of the current literature; the *Index* only 50 per cent of the articles published in English (and none in foreign languages); and the AEA *Handbook* only about half the profession (and that half preponderantly American). Owing to the increased number of societies, it was said, there was 'both inadequate coverage and excessive duplication' of information on publications and research activities; the annual meetings of the AEA and the related group of Allied Social Science Associations were seriously overcrowded; and despite the proliferation of national and international conferences with widely differing composition and subject matter, these gatherings had not increased in number 'commensurately with the growth in the profession'. The communications gap was much too great to be filled by individual university departments, research organizations or libraries. The only hope for a solution rested with the professional societies which should co-operate in providing comprehensive bibliographies, abstracts and directories 'for the discipline as a whole'.[28] There has, in fact, been some progress in this direction since the survey was published, but there is still a long way to go.

IV GENERAL FEATURES AND TRENDS: THE INTER-WAR PERIOD

Historians of economics who equate economic science with economic theory generally refer disparagingly to the work of American economists in the 1920s, and certainly there were few major theoretical advances during that decade. Yet this was also a comparatively lean period for economic theory in other countries, and as it is generally acknowledged that the USA attained world leadership in the discipline during the 1940s it is natural to inquire when the foundations of that achievement were laid. Some would maintain that the importance of economists grew during World War II, while others might focus attention on the 1930s when a handful of brilliant future Nobel prizewinners published their first articles and a number of 'illustrous immigrants' from Europe set new standards in teaching and research.[29] Even so, a scientific community does not appear overnight: young seedlings must be sown in fertile ground, and in this sense it may appear that the 1920s warrant a more favourable appraisal than they have generally been accorded hitherto.

After World War I, American economists undoubtedly enjoyed clear advantages over their European counterparts. The higher education sector was much larger, grew more rapidly and was far more affluent in the United States than in Europe. New institutions, schools and departments were being formed, and academic curricula were proliferating in directions favourable to the social sciences generally, and to economic and business studies in particular. Thus there were ample employment opportunities in undergraduate teaching, and in the training of graduates who would attain professional maturity in the next decade or so. Despite the size of the country, intellectual communications were good – internationally as well as domestically – and there were numerous and expanding scientific and scholarly publication outlets, and a sustained public interest in economic affairs. Moreover the numbers were sufficient to provide the critical mass necessary to support new research projects, the formation of academic societies, the launching of new journals and the maintenance of contacts with other scholars in the various subdisciplines which were proliferating as a result of the growing specialization and division of scholarly labour.

No doubt academic standards were more heterogeneous and frequently less stringent than in Europe, as is hardly surprising in an era of rapid growth and experiment. Consequently, the spread of professionally acceptable ideas, standards and values was slow, with certain established eastern seaboard institutions and a handful of mid- and far-western universities leading the way.[30] The more superficial manifestations of intellectual and professional competition were both unseemly, and doubtless wasteful of resources. Even before World War I orthodox economists had developed a remarkable variety of rival theoretical versions of received doctrines and approaches, some of which reflected the desire for product differentiation rather than dedication to creative scientific progress. Nevertheless, in the long run the premium on innovation, the prevalence of personal assertiveness, the comparative lack of inhibition and reticence, and the heterogeneity of academic conditions, training and objectives proved advantageous. Already by 1920 much had been learned from Europe, as might be expected of a latecomer; and a corollary of decentralization and diversity was the absence of any narrow or authoritarian scholarly or scientific elite with the power to inhibit intellectual exploration and inventiveness. As Merle Curti remarked in a comprehensive survey of American scholarship:

> Judged even by European standards American scholarship in the first decades of the twentieth century was substantial in quantity and competent in quality. . . . In the field of the social sciences, Americans were truly creating a vigorous, original, and significant body of knowledge. But American and European scholars alike were often misled by the tendency of American scholars to be self-critical, to belittle the emphasis on fact-finding and the frequent failure to relate new discoveries to traditional knowledge and to larger perspectives.[31]

Of course, self-criticism can be carried to the point where it becomes merely destructive, and some balanced commentators on American economics perceived this danger in the later 1920s.[32] Many of the younger generation of economists were scornful or dismissive of the inherited corpus of orthodox neo-classical theory, regarding it as unduly abstract, static and incapable of fruitful application to the contemporary problems that preoccupied them. Yet there was no available substitute for the existing paradigm, which provided a common professional language and conceptual apparatus, if only as a focus for dissent; and conventional economic theory could be either utilized if so desired, or slighted, apparently without serious professional risks, for there were no groups or institutions to enforce conformity. By the 1920s the subject had spawned a bewildering array of doctrines, formulations, viewpoints and subdisciplines, and there was a pressing need for consolidation, especially in theory and methodology. Indeed, towards the end of the decade Wesley Mitchell, the most important American economist between the World Wars, who was by no means deficient in historical perspective, even suggested that the subject might be disintegrating.[33] However he was not unduly alarmed, for the was confident of the prospects for 'realistic' economics, and he had limited faith in comprehensive intellectual frameworks, preferring instead to entitle his famous Columbia doctrinal history course 'Lectures on *Types* of Economic Theory'. In a number of the new specialisms, economists were forging links with scholars in cognate disciplines, a practice Mitchell heartily welcomed, and many of his professional colleagues seemed to be finding it increasingly difficult to conceive of the subject in its entirety. The absence of grand theoretical syntheses has often been noted, and Dorfman has drawn attention to the growing number of large or two-volume textbooks produced by two or more authors, as a response to the ever-expanding subject matter.[34] By the mid-1940s, when the American Economic Association decided to sponsor a survey of contemporary economics, it proved necessary to organize a pair of collaborative volumes, with a considerable team of authors and commentators.[35] However, the trend towards specialism and empiricism in the 1920s reflected not merely scale, but also the contemporary climate of intellectual life; what Morton White has termed 'the revolt against formalism', a pragmatist/instrumentalist attitude evident throughout the social sciences.[36] The links between this attitude and public policy issues will become clear shortly.

Generally speaking, the tone of American economics after World War I was eager, optimistic, experimental and workmanlike without being overconfident. There were few if any traces of the post-1945 'collective hubris' which prompted J.K. Galbraith to declare: 'Whatever its failings, economics as a discipline cannot be faulted for inadequately fostering scholarly ego.'[37] Whether World War I represented a clear watershed, or merely a temporary hiatus in the modernization of America, is a question much debated by political, social and intellectual historians. To the historian of economic ideas and conditions it is the continuities that stand out, if only because some of the leading pre-war personalities (e.g., J.B. Clark, J.R. Commons, R.T. Ely, F.W. Fetter, I. Fisher, F.W. Taussig, E.R.A. Seligman) were still active and influential in the 1920s. If the war did in fact mark 'the end of American innocence', to cite Henry F. May's vivid title,[38] perhaps economists had already been initiated into the ways of the world well before that revelation. Even if the war had blighted the more moralistic strains in progressive reformism, the leading economists had already anticipated that trend when they dissociated themselves from Richard T. Ely and his Christian Socialist allies during the early days of the American Economic Association (AEA).[39] The economists had played a leading role among the humanists and social scientists in the academic transformation which had enhanced the status of research relative to teaching, promoted advanced graduate training, and fostered the emergence of a new professional ethic designed to reconcile the conflicting attractions of 'advocacy and objectivity'.[40] In the process they had also been in the front line during the pre-war assaults on academic freedom, for their subject matter had inevitably thrust them into confrontation with a variety of powerful vested interests.[41]

The economists' reactions to World War I were mixed. Some, like Arthur

T. Hadley and Henry W. Farnam, were ambivalent, but unequivocally declared their support for the allies despite their personal ties and indebtedness to their German training. Others, like Ely and Commons, embraced the crusade with enthusiasm, demonstrating a crude emotional patriotism and anti-German sentiment entirely at odds with the spirit of scholarship.[42] Many, of course, became directly or indirectly involved in the war effort as professionals, and predictably enough Irving Fisher, an inveterate enthusiast, considered that his academic colleagues had failed to respond adequately to the call to fulfil their public responsibilities. In his December 1918 Presidential Address to the AEA he appealed to them to venture beyond their ivory towers and make themselves available to government on a permanent basis.[43] Nevertheless, any who hoped that the wartime emergency, so favourable to economic and social planning and the utilization of economic expertise, would leave a lasting peacetime legacy were due for disappointment. As Dorfman has observed, since there was no

> permanent provision for a high level of economic service, it was not surprising that the government called the economists into the war effort belatedly, used them sparingly and inefficiently, and was disposed to drop them without regret. Their utility in the war certainly enhanced the prestige and authority of economics. . . . But the habits developed over a century were not easily broken. The relevance of their theories to economic practice in peacetime was still questioned; the motives behind their thinking still seemed suspect; and the value of their authority remained equivocal.[44]

The public's ambivalence towards the economics profession has proved durable, and not only in America. Nevertheless, there has been a long run growth in the employment of professional economists outside academe, the beginnings of which in the United States are usually associated with the New Deal. Yet Dorfman reveals that in the 1918–29 period more than sixty economists were employed by leading politicians, congress, government agencies and a variety of other bodies as specialist advisers or technical experts. No doubt systematic inquiries would reveal many more examples.[45]

For the present purpose, however, the career of Wesley Mitchell will serve to illustrate certain general tendencies in the period. Mitchell had established his reputation before World War I with the publication of his masterly *Business Cycles* (1913), probably his most successful book. In wartime Washington his main task was 'to reduce the confusion through organizing statistical materials so that quick and relatively reliable answers might be given to the many pressing practical questions raised by war emergencies'.[46] He became Chief of the Price Section of the War Industries Board and worked closely with E.F. Gay, the Harvard economic historian, who headed the Division of Planning and Statistics at the Shipping Board. Together with Gay, he succeeded in forming a Central Bureau of Planning and Statistics as a clearing house of statistical data for the War Industries Board, the War Trade Board and the Shipping Board. After the armistice he stayed on to prepare a *History of Prices During the War*, published in 1920, as 'he felt very strongly that there should be some permanent carry-over within the government of the machinery that had been set up for gathering statistics and making them available to research workers and businessmen'.[47] In his 1919 Presidential Address to the American Statistical Association, on 'Statistics and Government', he expounded what became one of his most insistently reiterated themes: the need for 'intelligent experimenting and detailed planning rather than for agitation or class struggle. What is lacking to achieve that end, indeed, is not so much good will as it is knowledge – above all, knowledge of human behavior.' While believing that the development of social science offered 'more hope for solving our social problems than any other line of endeavour', he conceded that the constituent disciplines were 'immature, speculative, filled with controversies'. Nevertheless, 'social statistics, which is concerned with measurement of social phenomena, has many of the progressive features of the physical sciences . . . [and] even in its present state is directly applicable over a wide range to the management of practical affairs'. In building up 'quantitative knowledge of social facts' and making it available to 'responsible officials, we are contributing a crucially important part' of 'the task of developing a method by which we may make cumulative progress in social organization'.[48]

These stirring sentiments were to have powerful resonances throughout the inter-war years and beyond, not simply in Mitchell's own work and in American economics as a whole, but also in the social sciences generally. They embody the instrumentalist conception of knowledge propagated so effectively by Mitchell's Columbia (and formerly Chicago) colleague, John Dewey, and proclaim a cautious but optimistic faith in the results to be achieved by applying trained intelligence to contemporary social problems. Mitchell shared Dewey's impatience with philosophical speculation and theoretical abstractions, and though his personal interpretation of 'method' was frequently criticized by his professional colleagues for overemphasizing the accumulation of 'quantitative knowledge of social facts', it became a major component in the growth of knowledge in American economics during the next half century. Beyond this, his work with the National Bureau of Economic Research (NBER) helped to lay more secure empirical foundations for the economists' contributions to public policy throughout the post-1945 world.

Another element in Mitchell's credo reinforced by wartime experience was his stress on the need for 'scientific planning for social change'. He anticipated that the future would see an increased use of intelligence 'for guiding the social forces, relying more and more on trained people to plan changes for us, to follow them up, to suggest alterations', and he may well have been correct in thinking that 'most [economic] writers approve a policy of conscious social control through government agencies', thus revealing that 'the preconceptions of economic theory are changing'.[49] Peacetime certainly brought him greatly enhanced opportunities to study and pronounce upon economic and social problems in his capacity as a leading academic economist, a director of the increasingly prestigious NBER and a prominent member of and contributor to various public bodies and official reports. In all these contexts the challenge to what Mitchell called (following Veblen) the 'preconceptions of economic theory' deriving from the 'progressive' utilization of 'scientific planning for social change', has proved to be a continuing theme in American economics.

To the more impatient and idealistic American progressives the 'Republican ascendancy' of the 1920s was doubtless deeply discouraging. Yet the shift from the strongly moralistic, quasi-evangelical tone so characteristic of the turn-of-the-century reformist propaganda to a more restrained, secular and scientific approach to economic and social affairs was entirely congenial to most social scientists, particularly the economists. Despite abundant evidence of dissatisfaction with the state of their discipline, and a readiness to challenge the ruling orthodoxy, the prevailing mood was by no means radical in a political sense. One manifestation of acceptance of the status quo was the decline in the number of academic freedom cases involving economists. Another was the growing concern about questions of professional ethics as some of their colleagues became more 'useful' to government, business and private interest groups. Once again Mitchell can serve as an exemplar when he informed the New York Bureau of Personnel Administration, in 1929, that

A cautious scientific inquirer is sometimes gravely disturbed by the confidence with which a businessman will ask his opinion upon some delicate problem and still more disturbed by the practical man's disregard of the limitations and conditions with which he feels it necessary to hedge his answers about. The time was when such folk as economists complained about the neglect of their findings by men of affairs. Now they are frequently called upon to advise about matters of which their knowledge is slight. They do not always decline the over-flattering invitations with the firmness which befits a scientific conscience.[50]

The increasing numbers of economists engaged in advisory positions and other non-academic activities during the 1920s was an obvious byproduct of the modernization of American society, with its familiar concomitants of industrialization, urbanization, bureaucratization, professionalization, specialization and the division of intellectual and technical labour. For the economists, the expanding role of the state was especially pertinent, for as often noted, a strictly *laissez-faire* government would have few if any policies calling for economic expertise. By the turn of the century the evolving idea of a 'general-welfare state' had created the situation envisaged by the young professionals who had endorsed the AEA's initial, but short-lived, commitment to more positive government;[51] and although the wave of World War I interventionism proved transitory it was succeeded by a marked but insufficiently appreciated trend towards large scale organization in the private sector. To Mitchell and other less cautious advocates of a new 'institutional' economics as a substitute for or complement to economic orthodoxy, this movement was welcome on doctrinal and methodological, as well as practical, policy grounds. To the enthusiasts, the changes in American economic and social life supported their contention that the neo-classical theoretical framework, with its static individualistic assumptions and mechanistic 'pre-Darwinian' conception of economic processes,[52] was an inadequate basis for the study of contemporary problems. Even for those with less activist intellectual inclinations, the expanding scope of economic studies and the quest for social control were combining to blur the disciplinary boundaries which orthodox economists had been defending since the late nineteenth century. Economic and social problems obviously could not be neatly confined within existing subject compartments. The fluidity and rapidly changing character of the American academic situation meant that despite the growth of specialization, disciplinary boundaries were constantly being challenged, whether because of theoretical or policy disputes, or academic power struggles.

Here too, Mitchell's career and writings exemplify contemporary trends both in economics and in society at large, for he directly influenced the growth in the scale, organization and utilization of economic knowledge. In this regard his friendship and collaboration with Herbert Hoover is of both practical and symbolic significance, since both men were engaged in what Robert Wiebe has termed 'the search for order', a distinctively American movement towards a form of 'social control' or 'social engineering'.[53] The typical New Deal caricature of Hoover as a spokesman for *laissez-faire* is both inaccurate and unjust. No doubt his conception of the role of government in American life was limited by present-day standards, but it was positive, and it stemmed directly from his personal experience as a successful engineer, businessman and advocate of efficiency in public administration. In some respects Hoover personified Veblen's conception of the technocrat, for he once attacked the economists for adhering to a supply and demand theory of wages instead of recognizing that 'in these days of international flow of labor, commodities, and capital the real controlling factor in wages is efficiency'.[54]

Mitchell undertook various commissions for Hoover both as an individual and, as he preferred, in his capacity as director of the NBER – for example in producing a report on *Business Cycles and Unemployment* (1922) – and he refused numerous invitations to undertake government work. He played a leading role in two major multi-author studies initiated by Hoover: *Recent Economic Changes in the United States* (1929) and *Recent Social Trends in the United States*

(1933). In the following year the two men had a friendly disagreement in correspondence over the concept of national 'planning', a weasel word that had acquired sinister connotations for Hoover by the New Deal period.[55] There was, of course, a marked change of mood, emphasis and objectives as a result of the depression, especially from Hoover's standpoint, and the impact of that experience on the economics profession in general will be considered later. At this point, however, it is appropriate to emphasize the underlying continuities between the 1920s and the 1930s, in the long run trend towards rationalization, centralization, bureaucratic order and control. The 1920s are no longer seen as a bleak hiatus in the history of progressivism. On the contrary, the growth of what Louis Galambos has termed 'primary' organizations was greater than in earlier periods, and leading businessmen (as well as social scientists) were caught up in and contributed to this collectivist trend.[56]

Needless to say, the depression reinforced this movement, for the federal government was the only institution powerful enough to do anything substantial at the national level to remedy the economic crisis. A decade earlier Hoover had advocated national planning on a voluntary, co-operative basis under 'central direction',[57] but he opposed most of the more innovative proposals for federal anti-depression intervention. He supported public works and welcomed the 1931 Employment Stabilization Act designed to make the timing of federal construction projects compatible with national economic needs. In the present context the various early 1930s proposals to create some kind of National Economic Council or National Planning Board are of particular interest, for they involved professional economists either directly as members or indirectly as suppliers of economic expertise and statistical data. A number of prominent economists gave evidence in the lengthy hearings on Senator LaFollette's bill to establish a National Economic Council, and there was even support for a 'conservative' version of the idea from the US Chamber of Commerce Committee on the Continuity of Business and Employment, which favoured a 'planning board'.[58] No doubt, as a recent historian has observed, 'the planning idea was plastic and flexible, and fuzzy at the edges always, but it was put forward in a decidedly flexible American way, as a cooperative, open, democratic way of collectively responding to the obvious imbalance between productivity and purchasing power'.[59]

To the historian of economics, the lengthy report on 'Long Range Planning for the Regularization of Industry', written by J.M. Clark for the National Progressive Conference, is of special significance.[60] If Mitchell was the most influential American professional economist of the inter-war period, his Columbia colleague Clark was probably the most representative, for he combined a profound understanding of orthodox economics with broad institutionalist sympathies. His concepts of 'overhead costs' and 'workable competition' provided a bridge between the discipline's two main intellectual traditions prior to the early 1950s, when a contributor to an AEA *Survey of*

Contemporary Economics could remark that institutionalism had 'permeated the whole of economic analysis and has become more or less integrated with the other approaches'.[61] This was, of course, the institutionalism of Mitchell and Commons, which its authors viewed as complementary to economic orthodoxy, not that of T.B. Veblen and C.E. Ayres, who were seeking a substitute.

The planning discussions of the early 1930s bore tangible fruit in the New Deal period, and can be viewed from a longer perspective as a half-way house to the 1946 Employment Act, which established the Council of Economic Advisers. The intermediate steps from Roosevelt's National Emergency Council and National Planning Board of 1933 to the National Resources Planning Board, which was abolished by Congress in 1943 because it was too ambitious (i.e., Keynesian?), are too numerous and complicated to be retraced here, but the links with the development of the economics profession do deserve attention.[62] The National Planning Board was in part a byproduct of the Hoover Committee's report on *Social Trends*, chaired by Mitchell, who served for two and a half years as one of the three original Board members. Nor is it coincidental that the whole experiment now appears more as an 'impressive' intellectual achievement than as an effective influence on policy,[63] for Mitchell's ideas on national planning were always rather vague[64] – and therefore innocuous – and none of his professional contemporaries seems to have fully anticipated the strength of the political and administrative obstacles such advisory bodies inevitably encounter. Originally conceived, perhaps appropriately, as an agency of the Public Works Administration, the board initially reported directly to the President, not to its nominal superior, the Secretary of the Interior.[65] But this privileged access did not last, and the 370 reports eventually produced by the Board and its successors had little or no direct impact on the course of events.

Some attempts have been made, not without justification, to identify the Board and the planning experiment generally with the institutionalist tradition, rather than with mainstream economic orthodoxy.[66] It should therefore be noted that the list of economists who wrote for or were otherwise employed by the agency included several leaders of the post-war generation who do not belong under even the most capacious institutionalist umbrella.[67] Yet there is no denying that the planning idea gathered considerable momentum in the New Deal era, and the shaping of new institutional forms proved of great intellectual and practical significance in later years.[68]

Whether John Maynard Keynes' *General Theory of Employment, Interest and Money* (1936) was responsible for a basic paradigm change or intellectual revolution in economics is still in dispute. But there is no denying his profound impact on American economic ideas and policy. Keynes' name was already widely known in the United States before the depression through his sensational polemic *The Economic Consequences of the Peace* (1920), and his periodical articles in the reformist *New Republic*, in addition to his professional economic writings and his editorship of the *Economic Journal*. In 1924, together with some other European economists, he gave evidence to the Senate Gold and Silver Inquiry Commission, and he actively supported various organizations advocating monetary stabilization, in collaboration with Fisher, Commons, the popularizer Stuart Chase and other economists.[69] His participation in the Harris Foundation meetings at the University of Chicago in 1931 is of special interest in relation to the *General Theory* for, together with a number of other prominent economists – many of whom have usually been regarded as orthodox conservatives, he firmly endorsed proposals for interventionist federal anti-depression policies.[70] Although the claim that the *General Theory* contained 'really very little new', and what 'was new was largely in error', is misleadingly oversimplified,[71] it is now clear that the supposed chasm between the so-called 'old' and 'new' economists was much narrower than Keynes' more enthusiastic disciples believed.

The long run intellectual and professional importance of Keynes' *magnum opus* lay in its provision of a new theoretical framework, rather than any novel policy recommendations, and the book came as a revelation to some of the younger American economists. The *wunderkind* of that epoch, Paul Samuelson, who subsequently produced a dazzling sequence of theoretical contributions, wrote the most influential post-war textbook in the subject, and became the first American Nobel laureate in economics, evocatively conveyed the Harvard economists' response to the *General Theory* by reiterating Wordsworth's initial, overenthusiastic response to the French revolution: 'Bliss was it in that dawn to be alive, but to be young was very heaven!'.[72] This was not, however, the unanimous response. For the next decade or so the profession was deeply divided over Keynes' contribution, on theoretical, policy and ideological grounds, and broadly on generation lines, for the *General Theory* was wilfully provocative, deeply disrespectful of tradition and unnecessarily difficult to comprehend.[73] As Samuelson's contemporary, Galbraith, has recalled, the book 'inspired bitter-end conservatives to panegyrics of unexampled banality. ... For a long while, to be known as an active Keynesian was to invite the wrath of those who equate social advance with subversion.'[74] Indeed, the powerful opposition to Keynes' ideas – or even to his name, especially by those who had not read his writings! – from conservative businessmen and politicians seriously impaired the effort to secure full employment legislation after World War II.[75]

Since the late 1930s successive swings of the pendulum of professional opinion have inspired innumerable additions to the large inventory of summaries, dissections and evaluations of the Keynesian 'revolution'. This literature cannot be reviewed here, though it must be profoundly dispiriting to anyone who believes that the growth of knowledge in economics is either linear or continuous. However, some things have become clear as the result of scholarly investigation. For example, despite Keynes' personal attentions, President Roosevelt was never a disciple, and the initial infiltration of

Keynes' ideas into the corridors of federal power owed more to a Utah banker, Marriner Eccles, than to any professional economist.[76] Curiously enough, when the crucial decisions were made Keynes himself 'was not an important part and the *General Theory* was as yet an insignificant part' of the administration's thinking. Roosevelt's reluctant acceptance of the need for spending to promote recovery came only in 1938, but it paved the way for the employment of increasing numbers of professional economists imbued with Keynesian ideas in the federal government – a trickle that became a flood as the European war gathered momentum. The appointment of Laughlin Currie – an ex-Harvard economist, 'probably the intellectual leader' of the 'spenders' – as administrative assistant to the President was an important step on the road to the creation of the Council of Economic Advisers in 1946. Like the Harvard economist Alvin Hansen, the main academic proponent of Keynesian economics, Currie's initial reaction to the *General Theory* had been negative, and despite his access to the President, his 'role in domestic financial affairs was actually quite limited'. Nevertheless, in 1939 he proposed Richard V. Gilbert, another Harvard man and a committed Keynesian, as director of the newly created Division of Industrial Economics in the Department of Commerce, and the 'new economics' bandwagon was soon rolling strongly in Washington.[77]

As already indicated, there is still considerable controversy about the precise nature and significance of Keynes' impact on the development of American economic thought and policy partly owing to disagreements about the differences between Keynes' own ideas, which were difficult to interpret unambiguously, and the distorted and vulgarized version of his doctrine propagated by some of his followers, the Keynesians.[78] Nevertheless, the *General Theory* unquestionably provided the main conceptual impetus to the marked shift towards macroeconomics which dominated the economics profession in the three decades following its publication, and provided the rationale for more active and effective management of the economy. Admittedly, the acceptance and implementation of these ideas was slower and less complete in the United States than in Keynes' own territory, and it is likely that the long run trend towards increased federal government intervention in economic and social affairs would have continued even if Keynes had never lived. But as James Tobin (a Nobel prizewinner) has noted, 'One of Keynes' objectives, and eventual triumphs, was to liberate economists and statesmen from misplaced inhibitions on pragmatic measures to relieve unemployment, inhibitions supported by orthodox modes of economic analysis'.[79]

In the public policy domain the crucial turning point for Keynes' ideas in America was the passing of the Employment Act of 1946, which incorporated the federal government's acknowledgement of its ultimate responsibility for the maintenance of a high and stable level of economic activity. To Keynes' more enthusiastic disciples the measure seemed half-hearted, since it had to be toned down in response to strong anti-interventionist lobbying and

Congressional opinion, a move symbolized by the rejection of the expression 'full employment' in the Act.[80] Nevertheless, it was a more institutionally innovative development than its British counterpart for it established two new bodies – the Council of Economic Advisers in the Executive Office of the President and the Joint Economic Committee of Congress.[81] While these two organs were potentially in adversary roles, they combined to ensure the professional economists a prominent and influential place in subsequent economic policy debates. This was also true in the international sphere. During World War II it was generally recognized that depression in one country necessarily had adverse effects on others, especially if the first impulse came from a leading power such as the United States. But while international institutions to promote full employment were not contemplated, the United States and Britain led a powerful movement to create international financial, investment and trading organizations that would help to create conditions conductive to international economic growth and stability. Within these organizations – such as the IMF, World Bank, GATT (the remnant of an abortive ITO) and the United Nations Secretariat – influential groups of professional economists, at first mainly American and British, have exerted an important, and sometimes even dominant, influence on the organizations' policies.[82] This international post-war diffusion of non-academic economists is exactly analogous to the spread of their national counterparts in federal agencies, corporations, banks, private research institutions, and state and local governments.

Limitations of space preclude a thorough examination of the American economists' vastly expanded World War II and post-war role in public policy making,[83] although some reference will be made later to the impact of this development on conditions within, and public attitudes towards, the economics profession. At the present juncture it is sufficient to mention that the economists' capacity to understand, chart and influence the movements of the economy would have been seriously constrained but for major developments in economic theory and quantitative data and techniques, to which we must now turn.

V INNOVATIONS, AND THE EMERGENCE OF AMERICAN GLOBAL LEADERSHIP

The Keynesian revolution was but one of three major intellectual break-throughs in the 1930s which transformed twentieth century economics, and it was the one that exerted by far the greatest impact on public policy. The other two – the theory of monopolistic or imperfect competition, published in 1933 by E.H. Chamberlin of Harvard and Joan Robinson of Cambridge,[84] and the mathematization of economic analysis, among American economists associated especially with Paul Samuelson of MIT, among many others – were less obviously dramatic because they worked through the professional networks, rather than via more public channels.

The relationships between firms and industries were already a matter of great interest before Chamberlin's book[85] appeared hard on the heels of a major institutionalist study, Adolph Berle and Gardner C. Means's *The Modern Corporation and Private Property* (1932).[86] Together they stimulated a vast literature in the next two decades on the theory of the firm, the functioning of markets, economic concentration and antitrust policy. Having been allowed to lapse in the early 1930s, this policy was revived in the later stages of the New Deal, and it inspired a massive Congressional inquiry by the Temporary National Economic Committee (1938–41).

Mathematization is, of course, a much more general process which has had parallel, though far less striking, manifestations in the other social sciences. Its American roots can be traced back long before our period, for example in the pre-World War I works of Simon Newcomb, Irving Fisher and Henry Ludwell Moore.[87] But on the whole Americans were slow to take advantage of European developments in mathematical economics, partly because of their strong empirical and pragmatic bias and their distaste for formalism. Paul Samuelson has given a vivid personal impression of the state of economics when he began his remarkable career:

> to a person of analytic ability, perceptive enough to realize that mathematical equipment was a powerful sword in economics, the world of economics was his or her oyster in 1935. The terrain was strewn with beautiful theorems waiting to be picked up and arranged in unified order. . . . [As a result] the people with analytical equipment came to dominate in every dimension of the vector the practitioners of literary economics.[88]

After producing a number of precociously brilliant articles in the late 1930s Samuelson eventually performed this unifying task, after a wartime delay, in his *Foundations of Economic Analysis* (1947). This pathbreaking study exerted a profound impact on the next generation of economic theorists. However the dissemination of mathematics in economics was slow, and Samuelson has always acknowledged the contributions of his predecessors and contemporaries, whose combined efforts have enormously extended the theoretical range and increased the precision of the central corpus of orthodox theory.

Mathematical economics is not a 'subject' as such but a technique, a language, which can be utilized in many different parts of the discipline. Its greatest significance has been in advancing the basic theory of the subject – increasing the rigour of argument, enhancing the theorists' capacity to analyse complex problems involving several variables, and significantly raising the level of theoretical abstraction. The mathematical and econometric movement has had considerable sociological, as well as intellectual significance for the professionalization of economics. It has acquired a strong hold on graduate training, becoming a kind of pedagogical *pons asinorum* for students, an entry barrier to the upper echelons of the profession, and a factor widening the gap between the professionals and the general public.

No summary can do justice to the technical advances in American economics during the past half century. For the present purpose it must suffice to cite the sole or joint American contributions to the economic entries in Karl Deutsch's well-known list of sixty-two basic innovations in the social sciences between 1900 and 1965:[89]

Role of innovations in socioeconomic change (J.A. Schumpeter 1908–14; 1946–50; A.P. Usher 1924; J. Schmookler 1966)

Theories of economic development (R. Nurkse, A.O. Hirschman, E. Domar, H. Chenery, all 1943–58)

Economics of monopolistic competition (E.H. Chamberlin 1930–33)

National Income Accounting (S. Kuznets 1933–40)

Input–Output analysis (W. Leontief 1936–53)

Linear programming (G. Dantzig 1948; R. Dorfman 1958)

Econometrics (P. Samuelson 1947)

Computer simulations of economic systems (L. Klein, G. Orcutt 1947–60)

Social welfare function in politics and economics (K. Arrow 1951).

Any such list is obviously open to challenge. For example, Samuelson should probably be regarded primarily as a theorist rather than an econometrician, and some economists would object to the omission of O. Morgenstern (1944–58), the economist co-developer of game theory with John Von Neumann, which Deutsch classifies as mathematics. Also, if linear programming is economics, why not statistical decision theory (credited to A. Wald 1939–50, also defined as mathematics)? Cost-benefit analysis, attributed to C. Hitch (1956–63) is classified as politics, although it has given employment to hundreds, perhaps even thousands of economists; and even more anomalous, at first sight, is the fact that Herbert Simon, a Nobel prizewinner in economics, is credited with two innovations: hierarchical computerized decision models (1950–65), defined as mathematics, and – jointly with others – computer simulations of social and political systems (1955–66), defined as politics. Admittedly Simon's Nobel award came as a surprise to many economists, who should perhaps have known better; but his example, like the others cited here, illustrates the technical and conceptual links that have developed among the social science disciplines, especially mathematical modelling and other quantitative techniques. The fact that another American economist, K. Boulding, appears as a contributor to general systems analysis (1956, listed under philosophy, logic, history of science) reinforces this point.

Although Deutsch's data may be influenced by the compiler's national background, it is worth noting that the sixteen Americans mentioned (twenty-one if we add those cited in the preceding paragraph) constitute a high proportion of the thirty-five economists listed by him. More striking still is the distribution of economics innovations in time and space. Whereas only about one-third of the American contributions date from the pre-1945 period, the proportions are almost exactly opposite for foreigners; and the differences would be much greater if economic development – manifestly a subject of international scope – were to be excluded. The shift of innovative leadership to the USA, mainly from Europe, becomes even more apparent when we note that several of the pre-war American contributions were made by immigrants from Europe, a pattern similar to that found in some other disciplines.

The influx of distinguished foreign economists appears in a different form in the list of Presidents of the AEA, the leading national scholarly organization. Prior to 1948 only one President (J.A. Schumpeter) had been both born and completely trained abroad, whereas there were five additional incumbents with these characteristics in the 1963–70 period.[90] In other words, it took some time for foreign born and trained economists who settled in the United States during the 1930s to reach the peak of the profession. Prior to 1944, only two AEA Presidents had been born abroad and completed their education in the USA (though eleven born at home had been partly trained abroad); but by 1959 the number in this category had risen to nine, and to seventeen by 1978 – ten of whom had obtained at least one higher degree in the country. In fact, the influx of 'illustrious immigrants' in the 1930s fertilized a profession largely dominated by economists born and trained in the United States.[91]

The profession's greatly increased post-war public influence is only partly attributable to the major scientific advances referred to in this section, most of which were known to and understood by only a limited audience. The rapid growth in the non-academic demand for the economists' services is also attributable to the sustained expansion in the role of the state in economic and social affairs, the acceptance of political responsibility for the level of economic activity, the availability of an intellectual framework for handling the central macroeconomic problems and – a factor so far neglected – the vast accumulation of statistical data pertinent to the functioning of a complex modern economy. In this connection there has been a growing effort since the 1920s to escape from the limitations of traditional 'literary' and qualitative economics, and to test theoretical hypotheses against the available empirical (usually statistical) evidence. As the Behavioral and Social Sciences Survey showed in the late 1960s, much remained to be achieved before hypothesis testing and economic forecasting could be said to meet the highest scientific standards. But great advances had been made since the late 1930s, and nowhere was this more clearly the case than in national income analysis and accounting, which provided the basic empirical substructure for Keynesian theory and policy making.

The unchallenged American leader in this field has been Simon Kuznets, whose career exemplifies three central strands in this essay: the continuities between pre- and post-World War II economics; the fundamental importance of the empirical work begun in the 1920s to the subsequent progress of economics as a science and a profession; and the rise of the United States from a laggard to the leading position in world economics.

The development of national income analysis and statistics was one of the National Bureau's initial purposes and, like his colleague Wesley Mitchell, Kuznets was somewhat suspicious of large, overarching theories, preferring instead to work on limited aspects of business cycle processes and the basic concepts and measurements required for a system of national accounts.[92] But although he was initially sceptical of the pioneer national income research undertaken in Europe, he was more willing than Mitchell to propose and examine imaginative hypotheses about 'strategic factors' in economic growth processes – a subject in which he was an innovator long before it became fashionable after World War II. Although he was reluctant to engage in public policy debates or economic forecasting, his work has been fundamental to both these post-war activities, internationally as well as domestically. Most advanced, and many less developed countries now have comprehensive or partial systems of national accounts based on the procedures developed by Kuznets and his collaborators, and there have also been major advances in other categories of aggregate statistics, both in government agencies like the Departments of Commerce, Agriculture and Labor, in the Federal Reserve System, and in innumerable private and public organizations.[93] This data has transformed knowledge and research in business cycles, economic growth, international economics, economic history and other fields; but the demand for more statistical data is insatiable, partly because the mountainous volume of material has largely emerged as a by-product of business and governmental activities, rather than having been generated by the economists' scientific demands. At the end of our period there was still strong pressure for a national database for social and economic research, a series of large scale social science research centres and the provision of networks of computer facilities, with linkages to ensure easy access for researchers at various locations.[94]

VI GENERAL FEATURES AND TRENDS: WORLD WAR II AND AFTER

During the half century traversed in this essay there has been substantial progress towards Mitchell's goal: the application of trained intelligence to the solution of economic and social problems. Yet as indicated at the outset,[95] serious difficulties remained for professional economists, both in their relations with the general public and in their domestic affairs. Underlying the vigorous intellectual, scientific and ideological disagreements within their ranks at the end of the period were deeper structural issues, such as the degree of concentration of leadership and control in the profession and the widespread dissatisfaction with the allocation of intellectual and financial resources in the discipline. Unfortunately there appears to be no basis from which to achieve a consensus on these matters, given the variety of interests and values involved; certainly none will be offered here. Nevertheless these contentious issues should not be ignored for they provide insights into the development of the subject since the 1920s.

Judged by international standards, American higher education and research have been highly decentralized, and this has often been deemed a source of strength. But as in many other private and public spheres, there has been a marked growth in the number and scale of the organizations involved – including the universities, some of which have attained elephantine proportions by nineteenth century standards, with matching administrative bureaucracies. Scale and quality have not been closely correlated, but the reputational evidence,[96] for all its defects, reveals the persistence of certain centres of presumed excellence throughout the period. What have been the causes and consequences of this state of affairs?

Among efforts to answer this question there has been a high ratio of strong prejudice to reliable evidence, but most commentators agree that government and the large foundations have exerted a profound influence on the scale and direction of research, and consequently the status of certain institutions. In the case of economics the story can be traced back at least to World War I, with the genesis of the NBER and (what later became, in 1928) the Brookings Institution, the two most prestigious and venerable research bodies.[97] Another early landmark was the foundation of the Social Science Research Council, in 1923, the product of a group of 'knowledge intermediaries' – men like Mitchell, Charles Merriam, W.F. Ogburn and Beardsley Ruml.[98] In due course, however, their place was taken by a class of professional research administrators, partly for reasons of organizational convenience, but also because the growth of specialization meant that fewer full-time scholars and scientists were competent to make reliable judgements outside their own discipline or field of expertise.

Before World War II the larger private foundations (e.g., Rockefeller, Laura Spellman Rockefeller, Carnegie, Russell Sage) constituted the principal suppliers of social science research funding, for the federal government demonstrated little or no interest at the time. As these foundations tended to invest their resources in already well-established private institutions, they helped to promote the prosperity of the fittest; and some conservative critics have considered this a healthy state of affairs.[99] However, as early as 1953, a like-minded commentator expressed concern at the emergence of an elaborate organizational structure for furthering and financing economic research, viewing it as yet another manifestation of the general trend towards centralized control and planning in American life.[100]

Since the 1940s the federal government has played an increasingly important role in financing economic research, both within and outside government agencies, and there has also been a vast expansion of support from innumerable private sources – with the Ford Foundation being outstanding. Yet even at the end of the period it seems that less than 2 per cent of outside research support from public and private sources has gone to the social sciences, with economics well ahead of its sister disciplines (psychology being defined as a natural science).[101] Federal support has been more generally diffused than private funding, for obvious reasons, and some critics argue that there have been adverse consequences in the quality of research. Another oft-repeated charge has been the politicization of research, with government agencies promoting their own activities while discouraging serious criticism of their own work, and supposedly detached and impartial scholars overeagerly accommodating themselves to the presumed wishes of potential grantors.[102] Consequently scholarly independence has been compromised, and genuinely original and creative work discouraged, for both grantors and grantees have tended to follow fashion or defer to the contemporary leaders of professional opinion. Part of the problem, it is said, is attributable to the university departments' inability to compete with specialized research institutions both because they lack the requisite funds, and because they are poorly organized, especially for team research (although this does not seem to have been a serious impediment in the case of the natural sciences). Another defect is the lack of close supervision and criticism of Ph.D. students by academics who are too preoccupied with their own research or other interests.[103]

Of course these contentions often derive from personal and/or professional self-interest, and it is consequently difficult to assess their validity and significance. Doubtless similar views could be culled from many other disciplines, but they have a peculiar pertinence to economics, a subject in which the analysis of market forces has traditionally played a central and generally approved role. In responding to the demand for their services the economists have been subjected to the inescapable tensions between the public and private spheres; and this helps to explain the variety of forms and sources of dissatisfaction, which cannot be ascribed solely to differences between orthodox and heterodox conceptions of the subject, or to ideological convictions, significant though they have been. In responding to the demands of various publics the economists may indeed have contributed to 'the institutionalization of bias in economics', as one critic has argued.[104] Yet many who deplore the existing allocation of intellectual and financial resources in the discipline also blame it on the economists' demand for their own services – with the literature 'feeding on itself', and the economists' tendency to 'take in each other's esoteric verbal wash'.[105]

Towards the end of our period serious divisions appeared within the professional economists' ranks, and they became much deeper and disturbingly public in the early 1970s. Of course there had always been disagreements, even among orthodox economists during the halcyon days of the Keynesian 'hegemony' (i.e., roughly speaking, 1945–65), despite the obvious achievements of the mathematical/quantitative revolution which, its proponents contended, were bringing the discipline much closer to physics, the positivists' 'icon of scientificity'.[106] Whether the profession could claim credit, and if so how much, for the absence of the expected post-war depression and the sustained economic growth into the 1960s was, and still is, a highly debatable question; and there were many who had serious reservations about the efforts to treat economics as a natural science.[107] Nevertheless these misgivings seemed of secondary significance, given the high and sustained demand for the economists' services, both in universities and elsewhere, which demonstrated the public's confidence in the profession, and reinforced the economists' confidence in themselves. In view of the American economists' unprecedented national and international prestige up to the mid-1960s, the shock of the subsequent crisis seemed correspondingly greater, a curious parallel to the traumatic impact of the post-1929 depression in America following the prosperity of the 1920s.

The nature and causes of the crisis in economics have been endlessly debated, and obviously cannot be fully explored here.[108] Competing interpretations of this episode turn largely on the weights assigned to 'external' as against 'internal' factors, and on the importance attached to the various components such as: methodology, theory, technique, policy recommendations, and professional goals, values and standards. As noted earlier,[109] both external and internal conditions must be taken into account, and economics was by no means the only discipline, let alone social science, to undergo an agonizing reappraisal at the time. For the present purpose two partially contradictory features stand out: the fact that all the main intellectual issues in the crisis were familiar to historians of economics, especially students of American economic thought; and, on the other hand, the unprecedented extent to which concern about the condition and prospects of the subject was expressed by outstanding leaders of the subject.[110] Dissatisfaction, or more than this, was by no means confined to dissident, maverick or heterodox economists, although it gave special aid and comfort to institutionalists, radicals, Marxists and subjectivists.

Among the non-orthodox streams of thought institutionalism is by far the most relevant here, for although it virtually defies definition, except negatively, it is generally acknowledged to be a distinctively American movement.[111] Despite a number of premature obituaries, especially in the late 1920s and early 1930s, the ideas of the original triumvirate – Thorstein Veblen, John R. Commons and Mitchell – have never lacked admirers and disciples. But while avowed institutionalists made important contributions to the conception and implementation of the New Deal, institutionalism as a doctrine failed to provide an intellectually satisfactory analysis of the nature and causes of the depression,[112] by contrast with Keynesianism, which effectively destroyed the remnants of Veblen's claim that a Darwinian evolutionary economics would emerge as an alternative to the orthodox theory. During the post-war expansion of the profession there were abundant employment opportunities for institutionalists both in higher education and, perhaps particularly so, in non-academic employment; and there was some compatibility between their outlook and the Keynesians' policy-oriented interventionism. Another favourable condition was the strong revival of professional interest in long-run economic growth and development, which was compatible with the institutionalists' historical orientation. The failure of numerous ingenious post-war efforts to formulate general mathematical growth theories came as no surprise to them, any more than the professions' belated appreciation of the importance of the political, sociological and cultural dimensions of economic change, especially in Third World countries. These dimensions had generally been excluded from orthodox economic theory, and the contention that such theory was culture-bound, emphasized by such prominent figures as Gunnar Myrdal, was entirely consistent with Veblen's analysis. Against this background, the emergence of a neo-institutionalist movement with its own organization and journal was a natural evolutionary process,[113] and it acquired more adherents as economic orthodoxy appeared to be in increasing difficulties. In due course there was a split between the followers of Veblen and C.E. Ayres,[114] who viewed institutionalism as a substitute for economic orthodoxy, and those who, like Commons and Mitchell, regarded the two as complementary, and hoped that a synthesis was possible. So far, this hope has not been fulfilled.

In their politics, as in their policy recommendations, the institutionalists have generally been closer to the progressive tradition in American thought than to the socialists, with whom they have often been identified by their opponents. However in the late 1960s a more genuinely socialist movement gained strength in the economics profession with the revival of Marxist doctrine, which had long been weak in America, and the formation of the Union for Radical Political Economics.[115] The relationship between these two elements has been complex and confusing, both intellectually and in personal terms. Marxism, of course, has had long antecedents and strong European links, and has been of theoretical and practical interest to many economists, including some who have rejected its main tenets. Radical economics, on the other hand, appealed especially to the younger generation protesting against such contemporary evils as the Vietnam war, the urban crisis, environmental pollution, and discrimination against women and minority groups. Whereas Marxian economics tended to be more rigorous, posing intellectual puzzles in the theory of value, economic crises and cycles, and long-run structural changes in the economy, and was often studied by mathematical theorists, radical economics was primarily issue-oriented, especially in its initial mani-festations. Its 'spokespersons' aimed to persuade professional economists to recognize the need to restructure society, by changing its basic institutions, instead of concentrating on marginal changes and piecemeal reforms. There was a considerable overlap of interest between the radicals and the Marxists, and to some extent they shared the institutionalists' desire to broaden the scope of economics in order to make it more directly applicable to current issues.

The growing heterogeneity of American economics in the third post-war decade has not simply been due to the rise of dissident and heterodox viewpoints. Even more significant, as far as the stability and reputation of the profession is concerned, have been the divisions within the orthodox ranks following the disintegration of the Keynesian consensus, for such divisions cannot so easily be dismissed as the product of ignorance, incompetence and soft-headedness, charges often levelled at heterodox economics by mainstream professionals. Some of these splinter movements have long and respectable intellectual pedigrees, such as subjectivist economics, which is directly traceable to late nineteenth century marginalist theories of value and distribution, especially the Austrian variant, which exerted a considerable if diffused impact on American economic theory prior to World War I. The post-1945 revival of subjectivism has been largely due to a number of distinguished third and fourth generation Austrian immigrants to the US, especially Friedrich von Hayek (a Nobel prizewinner), Fritz Machlup and Ludwig von Mises, an intellectually powerful but idiosyncratic figure whose disciples at New York University acquired a growing audience in the 1970s.[116] Despite sharp disagreements among the neo-Austrians, the most important subgroup of subjectivists, they constitute a significant reaction against the positivist, behaviourist and mathematical/quantitative movement. They emphasize methodological individualism, the fundamental differences between the social and the natural sciences, economic processes rather than equilibrium, and are generally critical of government intervention in economic and social affairs.

The growing challenge to Keynesian economics both within and from outside the economic profession was, of course, partly attributable to its failure to provide a satisfactory explanation and remedy for the problems of inflation and unemployment, which became increasingly obvious during the later 1960s and early 1970s. Yet well before this time there had been a growing but unspectacular resistance to the dominance of Keynesian macroeconomics in teaching and research.[117] and this brought to the fore two further streams of thought – Neo- or Post-Keynesianism, from withing the Keynesian tradition, and Monetarism, its principal opponent.

Post-Keynesianism has taken a variety of forms which cannot be adequately summarized here; [118] but in its emphasis on historical time (rather than the logical distinction between statics and dynamics, which has been familiar to

American economists since the late nineteenth century work of J.B. Clark), the role of uncertainty and expectations, and the influence of economic and political institutions on economic outcomes, it can be viewed as a bridge between orthodox economics and the institutionalist and radical dissenting approaches. Whether it constitutes a new paradium, as some of its exponents claim, is still unclear. However, it is intellectually more rigorous and more mathematical than other quasi-historical currents of economic thought, and this enhances its attractions to economists who are unwilling to abandon orthodox analystical methods.

Like the Neo-Austrian movement, Monetarism is an intellectually and ideologically more conservative reaction to Keynesian ideas than institutionalism, radicalism, Marxism or post-Keynesian economics. It is of special interest in the present context for two reasons: like subjectivism, its roots stretch back far beyond Keynes' *General Theory* to the quantity theory, which has late medieval origins; and it is directly identified, in part wrongly, with the most significant institutionally-based doctrinal tradition in American academic economics, the Chicago School. Although the leading exponent of Monetarism, Milton Friedman, was at the University of Chicago for many years, where he exerted a strong personal influence on many graduate students, few of his departmental colleagues wholeheartedly endorsed his views on monetary theory and policy. Yet Friedman's personal prominence was crucial in establishing Chicago's reputation in the eyes of the public and the profession.

The term 'Monetarism' was coined in 1968[119] to highlight the crucial role of the money stock in accounting for variations in three key macro-economic variables: output, employment and prices. It was a direct reaction against the earlier vulgarized Keynesian slogan that 'money does not matter'. Friedman's writings provoked a vast literature on the theory and measurement of monetary components in the economy; and in addition to the monetarists' impact on the protracted post-war controversy over the respective merits and efficacy of fiscal versus monetary policy in macro-economic management, they also provided strong intellectual support for conservative opponents of intervention by the monetary authorities – in accordance with Friedman's advocacy of 'rules versus authorities'. For a time it appeared that Monetarism constituted an effective 'counter-revolution' against the ruling Keynesian orthodoxy,[120] and many commentators argue that it has exerted a powerful influence in the recent policies adopted in the USA, Britain, Chile and elsewhere. During the crisis, however, it constituted one further, significant, manifestation of the breakdown of consensus.

Perhaps more than the other movements considered in this section Monetarism operated on a variety of different levels, since it embraced methodology, theory, measurement, policy, ideology and professional commitment. In the final section attention will be focused on the interaction of these elements in American economics at the end of our period.

VII CONCLUDING REFLECTIONS

At earlier points in this essay attention was drawn to the consistently high ratings of certain American universities in economics and other social sciences in the eyes of the academic profession, and the influence of private foundations in reinforcing this pattern of leadership.[121] Curiously enough, although Chicago has never led the formal ratings in economics it has been unique in the possession of the most readily identifiable professional image of any economics department throughout much of our period, notwithstanding major changes of personnel and developments in the theory, technique and focus of its work. Chicago has not been monolithic; yet it has consistently had a more clearly defined character than its principal rivals, for example, Harvard, Yale, Berkeley or MIT.

The precise nature of Chicago economics has been the subject of endless professional gossip and a number of scholarly commentaries and analyses, especially during the past twenty years. By far the most revealing of these has been an article by Melvin Reder,[122] which admirably combines the insider and outsider perspective, and focuses on the interaction of ideas, personalities and institutional conditions. Despite some of its members' strenuous denials, Reder demonstrates that Chicago has indeed developed a distinctive approach to 'scientific' economics, especially since 1946, which has transcended the succession of key individuals and reflected the department's exceptionally strong emphasis on research and postgraduate training. To most American economists the Chicago School has represented an amalgam of elements: Milton Friedman's methodology of 'positive' economics (to which not all of his colleagues have subscribed); a consistent defence of economic theory against those seeking to dilute it or to incorporate non-economic assumptions; a determination to 'test' economic analysis by reference to empirical data; and an unwavering belief in the efficacy of markets and scepticism towards all government interference in economic affairs. The more technical focus on what Reder terms 'Tight Prior Equilibrium', as the correct basis for scientific economics, as contrasted with the 'Diffuse Prior Equilibrium' employed by non-Chicago economists, may oversimplify the differences between the various species of economic orthodoxy. Nevertheless, he fully acknowledges the more diffuse influence on Chicago economics exerted by earlier outstanding members of the department, such as Frank H. Knight, Jacob Viner, Henry C. Simons and Aaron Director, none of whom practised, and some of whom would not have approved of, the latest Chicago methods. Of potentially greater interest beyond our period has been the 'economistic' challenge by a younger generation of Chicagoans who view economics as the only truly scientific discipline in the social sciences, and are ingeniously and imperialistically applying their approach to such varied topics as government bureaucracy, law, crime, marriage and the family.[123]

Most of the Chicago economists have either refused to acknowledge the existence of a crisis in the subject, or have not taken it seriously. They have constituted an island of confidence and continuity amid troubled waters, and would doubtless subscribe to Schumpeter's view that

> there is no room for schools in our discipline. As a matter of fact we do find a great convergence of the really leading and capable brain workers in our discipline. . . . There is no use in fighting something which life will sooner or later eliminate anyway. . . . All we can say is that if in science something wins through it will have proved its right to exist, and if the thing is not worth anything, it will surely wither.[124]

During the past decade or so the intensity of controversy has decreased somewhat because of dimishing intellectual returns and the exhaustion of the leading protagonists, rather than the emergence of a new paradigm or consensus. One of the lasting legacies has been the heightening of professional self-consciousness and the fostering of a more sociological, though not necessarily more detached, view of the scientific status and prospects of the subject. Paradoxically, despite the wide range of current views on theoretical and policy issues, and the growth of sub-disciplines and minority groups, each with its own scholarly association and publications, there have been growing complaints about the professional 'establishment'.[125] This body is said to dominate the American Economic Association, choose speakers at the main sessions of its annual conference, control the selection of articles in the leading professional journals, and, through its influence over the content and standards of graduate training, shape the outlook and careers of new recruits to the profession. This impression has been strengthened by a substantial number of statistical studies[126] which suggest that the discipline has become more centralized and homogeneous in its activities and membership. Whether this is peculiar to economics, or characteristic of all mature social sciences, is not yet clear, given the absence of systematic comparative investigations. But research on these matters has been both a byproduct and an influence on the growing awareness of the structure and functioning of the scientific community in economics.

Despite its strong and remarkably durable analytical core, and its vast body of empirical data by comparison with other social sciences, the discipline's public prominence and deep involvement in public policy issues has made it impossible to develop the degree of autonomy and insulation from current affairs some authorities claim is essential for continuous and uninterrupted scientific progress. Moreover, it is clear that this old-fashioned ideal is no longer feasible, given the new insights into the history, sociology and philosophy of science of the past two decades. The decline of positivism has reduced the barriers to those who advocate the role of subjective, normative and ideological influences in economics.[127] While there can be no denying economics' growth, technical advance and continued prosperity, its critics still maintain that the profession is 'embarrassed', in 'disarray', even 'at bay'! The debate continues.

NOTES

* This previously unpublished paper was originally prepared for an inter-disciplinary symposium sponsored by the American Academy of Arts and Sciences. No attempt has been made to update the citation of secondary sources. I wish to thank Mary S. Morgan for correcting some errors in an earlier version.

1 Joseph Dorfman's *The Economic Mind in American Civilization, 1918–1933* (New York, 1959), p.x. Every student of American economic thought is heavily indebted to Dorfman's encyclopaedic work.

2 For a general review see my 'The Current "Crisis" in Economics in Historical Perspective', *Nebraska Journal of Economics and Business*, reprinted in this volume (see pp.459–71), and the references cited therein. Also Daniel Bell and Irving Kristol (eds), *The Crisis in Economic Theory* (New York, 1981).

3 The two most important, if over-enthusiastic studies of this tradition are by Allan G. Gruchy, *Modern Economic Thought, The American Contribution*, (New York, 1947); and *Contemporary Economic Thought, The Contribution of Neo-Institutional Economics* (Clifton, New Jersey, 1972). For my highly critical review of the latter volume see *The Journal of Economic Issues* vol. 8 (Sept 1974), pp.597–605.

4 'What Economists Know', reprinted in *The Collected Scientific Papers of Paul A. Samuelson*, Joseph E. Stiglitz (ed.), (Cambridge, Mass.: MIT Press, 1966), p.1647. Italics supplied. Other volumes in this series have various editors.

5 'The Economist and the State', *American Economic Review* vol. 55 (March 1965), p.17.

6 Cf. *Essays in Positive Economics* (Chicago: University of Chicago Press, 1953), p.5; 'Have Monetary Policies Failed?', *American Economic Review* vol. 62 (May 1972), p.17.

7 For a balanced survey of the literature see Bruce Caldwell, *Beyond Positivism, Economic Methodology in the Twentieth Century* (London: Allen and Unwin, 1982). For contrasting views see Donald N. McCloskey, 'The Rhetoric of Economics', *Journal of Economic Literature* vol. 21 (June 1983), pp.481–517, and the reply by Caldwell and Coats, ibid., vol. 22 (June, 1984), pp.575–8. (The state of economic methodology in the early 1990s will be appraised in an extended essay in vol. III of this series.)

8 AEA membership records; also Dael Wolfe, 'Growth and Diversity in the Organization of American Learning', unpublished typescript, p.18.

9 See A.W. Coats, 'The American Economic Association, 1904–1929', *American Economic Review* vol. 54 (June 1964), pp.261–85. To be reprinted in vol.II of this series.

10 Cf. A. Tolles *et al.*, 'The Structure of Economists Employment and Salaries', *American Economic Review* vol. 55 (December 1965), especially pp.13–16, produced by a Committee of the National Science Foundation Report on the Profession; also Nancy D. Ruggles (ed.), *Economics* (Englewood Cliffs, NJ: Prentice Hall, 1970), p.13. This study was compiled as part of a more general behavioural and social sciences survey.

11 During the 1930s in particular, there were various proposals to restrict AEA membership, or at least voting membership, to those properly qualified. However there was no general agreement as to the appropriate criteria to be adopted, and the matter was never pressed vigorously.

12 Data derived from Lindsey R. Harmon, *A Century of Doctorates: Data Analysis of Growth and Change* (Washington, DC: National Academy of Sciences, 1978). Calculated from Appendix A, p.120.

13 There are, however, some data for 1968 referring to economists with advanced degrees:

Employment of economists by education (percentage distribution)

Type of employment	MAs	Ph.D.s
Educational institutions	46	76
Federal government	17	8
State and local government	5	4
Military	2	*
Non-profit organizations	5	4
Business and industry	22	7
Self-employed	2	1
Other employers	1	*

* = less than 1 per cent.

Source: *The Behavioural and Social Sciences: Outlook and Needs* (Englewood Cliffs, NJ: Prentice Hall, 1969), table 9.4. Also in Ruggles, op. cit., p.14.

14 Harmon, calculated from Table 32.

15 ibid., calculated from table 31.

16 ibid., calculated from table 45B. As econometrics is not listed separately I have assumed that it is included under economics. On the implications of this concentration see *infra*, pp.440.

17 William A. Arrowsmith's Preface in W. Patrick Dolan, *The Ranking Game: The Power of the Academic Elite* (Lincoln: Nebraska, 1976), p.ix; cited in L.V. Jones, G. Lindzey and P.E. Coggeshall (eds.), *An Assessment of Research-Doctoral Programs in the United States: Engineering* (Washington, DC: National Academy Press, 1982), p.2. The Dolan study is a powerful critique of the whole business of ranking.

18 The first (1925) report by Raymond Hughes, which covered sixty-five institutions, was reprinted in the first edition of *American Universities and Colleges* (1928), and a follow-up report appeared in the *Educational Record* (April 1934), pp.192–234. The 1957 (Keniston) survey queried department chairmen in twenty-five universities. The 1964 (Cartter) survey collected data from 4,000 faculty members in thirty disciplines at 106 major universities. The 1969 (Roose and Anderson) study used the same methodology as Cartter, but added seven more disciplines and twenty-five institutions. Cf. Kenneth D. Roose and Charles J. Anderson (eds), *A Rating of Graduate Programs* (Washington, DC: American Council on Education, 1970), p.1. The data in the next paragraph are drawn from these sources.

19 Samuelson's achievements and reputation undoubtedly help to explain this rapid change.

20 The post-war ranking for the combined social sciences was: Berkeley, Harvard, Chicago, Michigan, Yale, Wisconsin, Columbia, Standford, UCLA: Princeton – familiar names.

21 See p.440 in this volume.

22 A new periodical, *Economics Letters*, was inaugurated in 1978 'to accelerate the dissemination of new results, models and methods'. However this publication has proved to be far less important than its counterpart in physics. There has

been no systematic investigation of 'multiple discoveries' in twentieth century economics.

23 See Martin Bronfenbrenner, 'Trends, Cycles, and Fads in Economic Writing', *American Economic Review, Papers and Proceedings* vol. 56 (May 1966), pp.538–52; also A.W. Coats, 'The Role of Scholarly Journals in the History of Economics: An Essay', *Journal of Economic Literature* vol. 9 (March 1971), pp.29–44. To be reprinted in vol.II of this series.

24 J.M. Clark, 'Recent Developments in Economics', in Edward Cary Hayes (ed.), *Recent Development in the Social Sciences* (Philadelphia: Lippincott, 1927), p.216.

25 See pp.439–43 in this volume.

26 Ruggles, op. cit., p.14. Note: not all the 'registered economists' are academics.

27 In addition to the classification in Ruggles, ibid., note 13, the chapter titles provide yet another breakdown of subject matter: microeconomic theory; macroeconomics; simulation, modelling, data; survey research and economic behaviour; operations research and economics; economic stabilization and growth; industrial organization; public sector economics; urban economics; labour economics; agricultural economics; economic development; international economics.

28 ibid., pp.27–30.

29 The future laureates who published their first articles in the US before 1940 included Milton Friedman, Simon Kuznets, Wassily Leontief, Paul Samuelson, Theodore W. Schultz, Herbert Simon and George J. Stigler. A roster of immigrants in the same period would include J.A. Schumpeter, F.A. von Hayek, F. Machlup, G. Haberler and O. Morgenstern (Austria); J. Von Neumann (Hungary); A. Wald and N. Georgescu-Roegen (Rumania); T. Koopmans (Netherlands); H. Schultz and O. Lange (Poland); W. Leontief and P. Baran (USSR); K. Boulding (England); J.K. Galbraith (Canada). See also p.431 in this volume.

30 Cf. this volume, pp.413–4.

31 Merle Curti, 'The Setting and the Problem', in Curti (ed.), *American Scholarship in the Twentieth Century* (Cambridge: Harvard University Press, 1953), pp.16–17.

32 According to Clark, op. cit., pp.224, 236, the characteristic mood of thought 'takes nothing for granted, questions everything, and is altogether merciless . . . It is materialistic, skeptical, iconoclastic, irreverent and often undisciplined'. In a concluding chapter on 'The Present Impasse', a younger author, Paul T. Homan, referred to the 'tangled confusion' of diverse and 'antithetical points of view which condition the theoretical thought of contemporary economists'. Yet among orthodox economists he noted the 'restrained amity similar to that which envelops the evangelical churches', by contrast with the vigorous turn of the century controversies. See his *Contemporary Economic Thought* (New York: Harper, 1928), pp.465, 463, 443. Wesley Mitchell concurred.

33 See *The Backward Art of Spending Money and Other Essays* (New York: McGraw Hill, 1937), p.405. Also Clark, op. cit., p.215. Similar observations have often been made in later periods. For example, Kenneth Boulding: 'I have been gradually coming under the conviction, disturbing for a professional theorist, that there is no such thing as economics – only social science applied to social problems. Indeed, there may be no such thing as social science – there may only be general science applied to the problems of society.' *A Reconstruction of Economics* (New York: Wiley, 1950), p.vii.

34 Dorfman, op. cit., vol. V, p.664.

35 Howard Ellis (ed.), *A Survey of Contemporary Economics*, vol. 1 (Homewood, Ill.: Richard D. Irwin, 1948); Bernard F. Haley (ed.), *A Survey of Contemporary Economics*, vol.II (Homewood, Ill.: Richard D.Irwin, 1952). About seventy

economists (editors, authors and critics) contributed to the twenty-three topics covered. Yet distinguished reviewers complained of omissions and an unduly narrow approach to the subject as a whole.

36 Morton D. White, *Social Thought in America. The Revolt Against Formalism*, (New York: Oxford University Press, 1976). This tone was apparent in the stimulating collection of essays edited by Rexford Guy Tugwell, *The Trend of Economics* (New York: Knopf, 1924). It included a powerful essay by Frank H. Knight, a dissenting 'orthodox' economist.

37 J.K Galbraith, *The New Industrial State* (New York, 1967), p.xv. For a more sweeping jeremiad see Joseph J. Spengler, 'Social Science and the Collectivization of Hubris', *Political Science Quarterly* vol. 87 (March 1972), pp.1–21.

38 May, *The End of American Innocence: A Study of the First Years of Our Own Time, 1912–1917* (New York: Knopf, 1959).

39 Cf. Dorfman, *Economic Mind in American Civilization*, vol. III, 1865–1918 (New York: Viking Press, 1949), pp.160–4, 205–12; also A.W. Coats, 'The First Two Decades of the American Economic Association', *American Economic Review* vol. 50 (September 1960), pp.554–74. To be reprinted in vol.II of this series.

40 Mary O. Furner, *Advocacy and Objectivity. A Crisis in the Professionalization of American Social Science, 1865–1905* (Lexington, Ky.: University of Kentucky Press, 1975); also Dorothy Ross, 'The Development of the Social Sciences', in Alexandra Oleson and John Voss, *The Organization of Knowledge in Modern America, 1860–1920* (Baltimore: Johns Hopkins Press, 1979), pp.107–38; and *idem.*, *The Origins of American Social Science* (Cambridge: Cambridge University Press, 1991), which contains valuable material on American economics up to the end of the 1920s.

41 Richard Hofstadter and Walter P. Metzger, *The Development of Academic Freedom in the United States* (New York: Columbia University Press, 1953).

42 Carol S. Gruber, *Mars and Minerva. World War I and the Uses of the Higher Learning in America* (Baton Rouge: Louisiana State University Press, 1975), pp.71–3, 116, 208.

43 Fisher, 'Economists in Public Service', *American Economic Review* vol. 9 (March 1919), pp.5–21. 'During the impending world-reconstruction, economists will have more opportunity to satisfy this impulse [to be of genuine public service] than most students in other departments of human thought; for the great problems of reconstruction are largely economic. . . . A generation ago many economists thought it beneath their dignity to engage at all in practical affairs except to cry "laissez-faire". They believed that a scientist should be simply an observer, compiler, and interpreter of facts, not a guide, counsellor, and friend of humanity. Their attitude of academic aloofness not only failed to give to economic study, in the eyes of the world, that status of a "true science" which they claimed for it, but, on the contrary, brought it into disrepute and provoked a vigorous reaction. . . .
   If we are to succeed [in rendering public service] it will be because we perform our task with wisdom, unselfishness, and impartiality. As economists in public service in a democratic world, we are pledged to serve all humanity throughout the world and throughout future generations.' ibid., pp.5, 21. He believed only one hundred economists had been called to service in Washington as a result of the war. For reservations about this kind of activity expressed by two other Presidents of the AEA see this volume, pp.433–4.

44 Dorfman, op. cit., vol. III, p.494.

45 There is a useful general review of pre-1946 'precedents for economic

advisership' in Edwin G. Nourse, *Economics in the Public Service*, (New York: Harcourt Brace, 1953), chapter 6. According to John R. Commons, *Myself* (New York: Macmillan, 1934), pp.74–6, the first group of economists deliberately brought to Washington for public service was that employed by E. Dana Durand for the United States Industrial Commission, which reported in 1902. The first permanent branch of government to employ a trained staff of economic investigators was the Federal Reserve Board whose Secretary, H. Parker Willis, was an economist. The second was the Department of Agriculture. However, according to Paul B. Cook, *Academicians in Government from Roosevelt to Roosevelt* (New York: Garland, 1982) the Federal Reserve Board was the first permanent agency of the Federal Government to have a trained staff of economic investigators.

For stimulating recent contributions to the large literature on agricultural economics see Harry C. McDean, 'Professionalism, Policy, and Farm Economists in the Early Bureau of Agricultural Economics', *Agricultural History* vol. 37 (January 1983), pp.64–82, and the 'Comment' by Tom G. Hall, ibid., pp.83–9. I owe this reference to Leonard D. Carlson. See also Joseph G. Knapp, *Edwin G. Nourse – Economist for the People* (Danville, Ill., 1979), chapter 7; Richard S. Kirkendall, *Social Scientists and Farm Policies in the Age of Roosevelt* (Columbia, Mo.: University of Missouri Press, 1966); and Ellis W. Hawley, 'Economic Inquiry and the State in New Era America: Antitrust Corporatism and Positive Statism in Uneasy Coexistence' in *The State and Economic Knowledge. The American and British Experiences*, Mary O. Furner and Barry Supple (eds), (Cambridge: Cambridge University Press, 1990), pp.287–324. This volume also contains excellent essays by William J. Barber, Robert M. Collins, Mary O. Furner and W. Elliot Brownlee, which supplement the materials cited in this paper, and contain a wealth of more recent references to secondary sources published since this paper was originally written.

There is a valuable account of the role of economists in government in the 1920s in William J. Barker, *From New Era to New Deal: Herbert Hoover, The Economists and American Economic Policy, 1921–1933* (Cambridge: Cambridge University Press, 1985).

46 This is the description given in Lucy Sprague Mitchell, *Two Lives. The Story of Wesley Clair Mitchell and Myself* (New York: Simon and Schuster, 1953), p.296.
47 ibid., p.301.
48 ibid., pp.303–4. These themes were constantly repeated in later addresses and articles. See, for example, ibid., chapters 19–21; the essays in *The Backward Art of Spending Money*, op. cit.; and Dorfman, vol. III, chapter 20, and vol, IV, especially pp.360–77.
49 Quoted by Dorfman, vol. III, pp.490, 494.
50 Quoted by Dorfman, vol. IV, p.210. As early as 1921 the President of the AEA, Jacob Hollander questioned the wisdom of economists adopting a role as public advisers and active leaders, while A.B. Wolfe (who became President of the AEA in 1943), in sympathy with this view, maintained that the federal government and business corporations had attracted so many economists 'from academic chairs that university research and teaching in economics is temporarily impaired'. Cf. Hollander, 'The Economist's Spiral', *American Economic Review* vol. 12 (March 1922), pp.1–20, and Wolfe, *Conservatism, Radicalism, and Scientific Method, An Essay on Social Attitudes* (New York: Macmillan, 1923), p. 321.

While it would be unwise to generalize from a single instance, there is a striking contrast between Ely's potential martyrdom as an academic radical in the 1890s and complaints of his subservience to business interests in the 1920s, through his Institute for Research in Land Economics and Public Utilities. It is also worth noting that the report of a subcommittee of the AAUP Committee of Ethics saw no objection to the acceptance of payments for government service, but considered that professors should not accept retainers from business, especially where controversial matters were involved. Cf., Dorfman, op. cit., p.209. The general question of professional ethics in economics deserves careful investigation, not only in relation to American economics.

51   Cf. Sidney Fine, *Laissez-faire and the General Welfare State. A Study of Conflict in American Thought, 1865–1901* (Ann Arbor: Michigan University Press, 1956). On the early development of the AEA see Dorfman, vol.III, especially chapter IX, 'The Union of the Economists'; and A.W. Coats, 'The First Two Decades', op. cit.

52   This was a recurrent theme in institutionalist writings.

53   Robert H. Wiebe, *The Search for Order 1877–1920* (New York: Hill and Wang, 1967). Cf. Herbert Hoover, *The Memoirs of Herbert Hoover* (New York: Macmillan, 1952), vol. 2. p.176. See also Ross, *Origins* op. cit., chapter 7, for an extended discussion of the concept of social control; and Guy Alchon, *The Invisible Hand of Planning: Capitalism, Social Science and the State in the 1920s* (Princeton: Princeton University Press, 1985).

54   Cited by David Burner and Thomas R. West in 'A Technocrat's Morality: Conservatism and Hoover the Engineer', in Stanley Elkins and Eric McKitrick, *The Hofstadter Aegis, A Memorial* (New York: Knopf, 1974), p.244. Hoover exemplified Robert Wiebe's concept of the twentieth century reformist belief that the way to social progress is through advanced technical expertise applied to society by continuing administration. He complained that the engineer had been obliged to take a position below the 'parasitic' professions of theology, law and war. Ibid., p.251.

For a stimulating discussion of the cult of efficiency, see Samuel Haber, *Efficiency and Uplift. Scientific Management in the Progressive Era, 1890–1920* (Chicago: University of Chicago Press, 1964).

55   Lucy Sprague Mitchell, op. cit., especially pp.361–72.

56   Cf. Louis Galambos, 'The Emerging Synthesis in Modern American History', *Business History Review* vol. 14 (Autumn 1970), pp.279–90; also Alfred D. Chandler and Louis Galambos, 'The Development of Large Scale Organizations in Modern America', *Journal of Economic History* vol.21 (March 1970), pp.201–17; Otis L. Graham, 'The Planning Ideal and American Reality: the 1930s', in Elkins and McKitrick, op. cit., pp.257–89; *idem, Toward a Planned Society, From Roosevelt to Nixon* (New York: Oxford University Press, 1976), especially pp.3–4: 'careful historical scholarship and a lengthening perspective have brought into new perspective both the basic consistency of his [i.e., Hoover's] approach to questions of political economy, and the reformist thrust of his ideas which was blunted by circumstances. ... His ideas represented the enlightened conservatism of the day, the fostering of economic concentration and modernization through government-business cooperation.'

57   Cf. Dorfman, vol. IV, p.27 for Hoover's testimony before two Senate Committees in 1920, on education and labor, and on reconstruction and production respectively.

58   The participating economists included J.M. Clark, E.A. Goldenweiser, L. Lorwin (of the Brookings Institution), W. Stewart and L. Wolman. Also giving evidence were W.B. Donham, Dean of the Graduate School at Harvard, the author of a popular book *Business Adrift* (1931), and

Eugene Meyer, a Governor of the Federal Reserve Board. During the cross-examination the works of Paul Douglas, J.A. Hobson, J.M. Keynes and the amateurs W.T. Foster and W. Catchings were cited. According to Dorfman, vol. V, pp.743–4, the committee was 'guided' by Isador Lubin, another Brookings Institution economist. Whereas the businessmen's plans envisaged output restriction as a means of achieving economic stability, the La Follette supporters proposed an increase in purchasing power so as to utilize idle productive capacity.

59 Graham, *Toward A Planned Society*, op. cit., pp.14–15.

60 The report is reprinted in John Maurice Clark, *A Preface to Social Economics*, Moses Abramovitz and Eli Ginzberg (eds), (New York: Farrar and Rinehart, 1937), pp.229–69. Three years later, as a consultant to the National Planning Board, Clark published his *Economics of Planning Public Works* (Washington, 1935).

61 Quoted by Bernard F. Haley in 'Some Contemporary Tendencies in Economic Research', *American Economic Review* vol. XLIII (May 1953), p.418. The author of the remark was Richard Ruggles. It should be noted that this assessment entirely depends on the definition of institutional economics. Others have argued that the movement died in the early 1930s. Cf. this volume, pp.435–7.

     For valuable studies of Clark's work see Gruchy, *Modern Economic Thought* op. cit., pp.337–402; and C. Addison Hickman, *J.M. Clark* (New York: Columbia University Press, 1975).

62 The name was changed, successively, from National Planning Board to National Resources Board (1934), National Resources Committee (1935) – after the National Recovery Act was declared unconstitutional – and finally to National Resources Planning Board (1939–43). For an up-to-date comprehensive history see Marion Clawson, *New Deal Planning. The National Resources Planning Board* (Baltimore: Johns Hopkins Press, 1981). Also, more generally, Gene M. Lyons, *The Uneasy Partnership. Social Science and the Federal Government in the Twentieth Century* (New York: Russell Sage Foundation, 1969), chapter 3.

63 'Impressive' is the judgement of Wassily Leontief, who worked for the Board. See his interesting review of Clawson's book in the *Journal of Economic Literature* vol. 21 (March 1983), pp.98–9.

64 See, for example, his essays 'Social Science and National Planning' (1935) and 'Intelligence and the Guidance of Economic Evolution' (1936) in *The Backward Art*, op. cit., pp.83–102, 103–36. Another Columbia economist, R.G. Tugwell, espoused a much more specific and radical view of planning. See his *The Industrial Discipline and the Governmental Arts* (New York: Columbia University Press, 1933).

65 The complex personal connections between Secretary Harold Ickes, Beardsley Ruml and Charles E. Merriam, a Board member and influential social scientist who collaborated frequently with Mitchell, are clearly depicted in Barry D. Karl, *Charles E. Merriam and the Study of Politics* (Chicago: University of Chicago Press, 1974), especially chapter 12.

66 See, especially, Allan G. Gruchy, 'The Concept of National Planning in Institutional Economics', *Southern Economic Journal* vol. 6 (October 1939), pp.121–44; and *idem.*, 'The Economics of the National Resources Committee', *American Economic Review* vol. 29 (March 1939), pp.60–73; also his *Modern Economic Thought*, op. cit., *passim*. He especially emphasizes the role of Mitchell and Gardner C. Means, who was chairman of the industrial subcommittee of the National Resources Committee. The planners aimed to substitute public regulation for 'private regimentation', with the rules determined by public

authority. To Gruchy, the objective was to achieve social efficiency rather than merely economic or engineering efficiency.

67 In addition to Mitchell and J.M. Clark, the roster includes three future Nobel prizewinners (M. Friedman, W. Leontief and P. Samuelson); four future Presidents of the AEA (A. Hansen, G. Ackley, J.K. Galbraith and E.M. Hoover); two future Chairmen of the Council of Economic Advisers (Ackley and L.H. Keyserling); and also E.E. Hagen, P. Sweezy, W. Vickery and the 'spending' economists referred to later, p.427.

68 A noteworthy, but uninfluential offshoot of the National Resources Planning Board was the Fiscal and Monetary Advisory Board which, it is claimed, 'provided the Roosevelt administration with an improvised piece of governmental machinery that came closer than ever before to the Council of Economic Advisers, established in 1946'. Cf. Albert Lepawsky, quoted in Clawson, op. cit., p.145.

69 See, for example, Dorfman, vols.IV and V, especially pp.23–4, 175–8, 341, 385, 640–1, 659–63, 705, 723, 742. Keynes' links with the Stable Money League, later the National Monetary Association, and the heterodox popularizers William Trufant Foster and Wadill Catchings, deserve further investigation. Generally speaking, his views appealed to the younger, less conservative members of the profession.

70 See the careful analysis in J. Ronnie Davis, *The New Economics and the Old Economists* (Ames, Iowa: Iowa State University Press, 1971).

71 Gordon Tullock, Foreword to Davis, op. cit., p.xi. This statement epitomizes the conservative/libertarian interpretation, which underrates Keynes' intellectual achievement and exaggerates his (pernicious) influence on public policy.

72 Paul A. Samuelson, 'The General Theory', in Seymour Harris (ed.), *The New Economics* (New York: Knopf, 1948), pp.145–6. For Kenneth Boulding's similar response see his 'Economics – The Taming of Mammon', in Lynn T. White (ed.), *Frontiers of Knowledge in the Study of Man* (New York: Harper, 1956), p.133. It is worth noting Keynes' success in achieving his primary objective, the conversion of the intellectuals. For effective sketches of Samuelson's and Boulding's life and work see Leonard Silk, *The Economists* (New York: Basic Books, 1976), chapters 1 and 5. The volume also includes studies of Friedman, Galbraith and Leontief. See also William Breit and Roger Ransom, *The Academic Scribblers: American Economists in Collision* (New York: Reinhart and Winston, 1971).

73 There were, however, some converts among the older generation, most notably Alvin Hansen, who joined the Harvard faculty from Minnesota in 1938, and subsequently became the most influential single American propagator of Keynesianism in the 1940s. Hansen had reacted unfavourably to Keynes' *Treatise on Money* (1930) and his initial response to the *General Theory* was unsympathetic.

74 See Galbraith's vividly personal account of 'How Keynes Came to America' in his collection *Economics, Peace and Laughter* (New York: Houghton Mifflin, 1971), pp.43–59. The quotation is from p.44. The essay enumerates most of Keynes' early American supporters, and reflects his own wartime experience, when he was branded as a dangerous radical. An official investigation of the Harvard Departement of Economics, in 1946, concluded that Keynes' influence on its teachings was both excessive and harmful. For an earlier investigation of the department in 1938–9 prompted, curiously enough, by the failure to promote two able radical instructors, see Edward S. Mason, 'The Harvard Department of Economics from the Beginning to World War II', *Quarterly Journal of Economics* vol.97 (August 1982), pp.425–8.

75 For a fascinating and definitive account of the passage of the 1946 Employment
    Act – the term 'full employment' was dropped because of its radical connotations
    – see Stephen J. Bailey, *Congress Makes a Law: The Story Behind the Employment Act
    of 1946* (New York, Columbia University Press, 1950). A prominent economist
    whose bitter criticisms of Keynes' ideas may have exerted an important
    influence on business opinion, was Harold G. Moulton, President of the
    Brookings Institution. See, for example, Donald T. Critchlow, *The Brookings
    Institution, 1916–1952: Expertise and the Public Interest in a Democratic Society* (Dekalb:
    Northern Illinois University Press, 1985). Also Robert M. Collins, *The Business
    Response to Keynes* (Boulder: University of Colorado Press, 1981).

76 There is an excellent account of this whole episode in Herbert Stein, *The Fiscal
    Revolution in America* (Chicago: University of Chicago Press, 1969), especially
    chapter 7. Rexford G. Tugwell, the only economist in Roosevelt's original Brain
    Trust, aptly described Eccles as an 'unconscious Keynesian'. Cf. Stein, op. cit.,
    pp.102, 148, 485. Eccles was prominent among a small group of 'spenders' in
    the administration. He considered that his early unorthodoxy was due partly
    to his experience of the crisis as a country banker, and partly to the fact that 'he
    had never been to college and therefore did not have any orthodox economics
    to unlearn'. The other spenders included government economists Louis Bean,
    Laughlin Currie, Mordecai Ezekiel, Leon Henderson, Isadore Lubin and Harry
    D. White.

77 Stein, op. cit., pp.129, 165–7. The transfer of the Bureau of the Budget from the
    Treasury to the Executive Office and the appointment of a Keynesian, Gerhard
    Colm, as one of its two chief economists, was another significant development.
    There is a revealing account of Currie's career in Roger J. Sandilands, *The
    Life and Political Economy of Lauchlin Currie: New Dealer, Presidential Adviser and
    Development Economist* (Durham and London: Duke University Press, 1990).

78 See Axel Leijonhufud, *On Keynesian Economics and the Economics of Keynes* (New
    York: Oxford University Press, 1968); also T.W. Hutchison, *Keynes versus
    the Keynesians* (London: Institute of Economic Affairs, 1977), with critical
    comments by Lord Kahn and Sir Austin Robinson. Reprinted in Hutchison,
    The Politics and Philosophy of Economics. Marxists, Keynesians and Austrians (Oxford:
    Basil Blackwell, 1981).

79 'Macroeconomics', in Ruggles, op. cit., p.47. In principle Keynes' analysis was
    neutral, for it could be utilized either by advocates of planning and other forms
    of social control, or as a means of preserving the capitalist system, and hence
    staving off the challenge of socialism or communism. As noted elsewhere, only
    a small minority of American professional economists have been doctrinaire
    socialists or communists.

80 Bailey, op. cit., *passim.*

81 For a useful introduction to the burgeoning literature on this subject see Edward
    S. Flash, Jr., *Economic Advice and Presidential Leadership: The Council of Economic
    Advisers* (New York: Columbia University Press, 1965).

82 See, for example, A.W. Coats (ed.), *The Role of Economists in International Agencies*
    (New York: Prager, 1986).

83 For a general survey of this topic see Hugh S. Norton, *The Role of the Economist
    in Government: A Study in Economic Affairs Since 1920* (Berkeley, Calif.: McCutchan
    Publishing Co., 1969); also W. Barber, 'The United States: Economists in a
    Pluralistic Polity', in A.W. Coats (ed.), *The Role of Economists in Government:
    An International Comparative Study* (Durham, NC: Duke University Press, 1981),
    pp.175–205; and *idem.*, 'The Spread of Economic Ideas Between Academia
    and Government: A Two-Way Street', in David C. Colander and A.W. Coats,

The Spread of Economic Ideas (Cambridge: Cambridge University Press, 1989), pp.119–26.

84 The titles were, respectively, *The Theory of Monopolistic Competition*, and *The Economics of Imperfect Competition*. Chamberlin spent much of his subsequent career developing his theory and insisting on its difference from Robinson's.

It should be noted that economists of the Chicago School have not, generally speaking, considered the Chamberlin–Robinson innovations as constructive, and have continued to base their analysis on the earlier theory of perfect competition. Cf. this volume, p.439.

85 For general background see Dorfman, op. cit. vol.V, pp.553–62 and 745ff. Chamberlin's theory owed much to his outstanding teacher Allyn A. Young. For information on Young I am indebted to Charles Blitch's careful researches. See also, Mason 'Harvard Department of Economics', op. cit., pp.411, 419, 423–4.

86 For an extended treatment of Gardner C. Means's work see Gruchy, *Modern Economic Thought*, op. cit., pp.473–539.

87 Cf. Dorfman, op. cit., vol.III, pp.83–7, 357–9, 365–75, and vol.IV, pp.205–6. Also the splendid paper on Moore in George J. Stigler, *Essays in the History of Economics* (Chicago: University of Chicago Press, 1965), pp.343–73.

88 'Economics in a Golden Age: A Personal Memoir', cited in *Paul Samuelson and Modern Economic Theory*, E. Cary Brown and Robert M. Solow (eds), (New York: McGraw Hill, 1983), p.6. This statement, it should be noted, implies that 'analytical equipment' is identified with mathematics, a view that was strongly challenged towards the end of our period. Samuelson has suggested that Keynes probably 'did not truly understand his own analysis' in the *General Theory* until it was translated into mathematics, and contrasted this kind of work with the verbal 'mental gymnastics of a peculiarly depraved type' produced by Keynes' great predecessor, Alfred Marshall, who suppressed his mathematics and relegated it to appendices.

Examples of Samuelson's highly technical contributions to welfare economics, consumption theory, international trade, general equilibrium and stability, monetary and financial economics, capital theory, public goods analysis, macroeconomics and fiscal policy, etc. can be found in the multivolume edition of his *Collected Scientific Papers*, op. cit. See also the essays in George W. Feiwel (ed.), *Paul Samuelson and Neo-Classical Economics* (Boston: Kluwer Nijhoff, 1982), and in Brown and Solow, op. cit.

89 Karl W. Deutsch, John Platt and Dieter Senghaas, 'Conditions Favoring Major Advances in Social Science', *Science*, 5 February 1971, vol.171, pp.450–9. Reproduced on pp.14–21 of Daniel Bell, *The Social Sciences Since the Second World War* (New Brunswick: Transaction Books, 1982). The first two items have proved less amenable to mathematization than the others. I have omitted the names of non-American contributors to these innovations.

90 That is: G. Haberler, F. Machlup, K. Boulding, W. Fellner, W. Leontief. By 1978 there were two further additions to this category, F. Modigliani, and T. Koopmans.

91 Unfortunately there is no chapter on economics in Donald Fleming and Bernard Bailyn (eds), *The Intellectual Migration. Europe and America, 1930–1960* (Cambridge: Harvard University Press, 1969). See also Laura Fermi, *Illustrious Immigrants: The Intellectual Migration From Europe, 1930–41* (Chicago: University of Chicago Press, 1968).

92 See, for example, Erik Lundberg, 'Simon Kuznets's Contribution to Economics', *Swedish Journal of Economics* vol.73 (December 1971), pp.444–61. Also the

Nobel citation, ibid., p.300. It is instructive to compare this account with Kuznets's article on 'National Income' in the *Encyclopedia of the Social Sciences*, vol.11 (New York: Macmillan, 1933), pp.205–24.

93 There were already twenty economic research institutes in 1927. Cf. Mitchell, *Backward Art* op. cit., p.65. For the checkered history of the Harvard Economic Service see Mason, 'Harvard Department', op. cit., pp.414–18, and the critical analysis in Joseph S. Davis, *The World Between the Wars, 1919–39. An Economist's View* (Baltimore: Johns Hopkins, 1975). The US Senate directed the Department of Commerce to prepare estimates of income in the early 1920s. Cf. Carl S. Shoup, 'The Development and Use of National Income Data', in Howard S. Ellis, *Survey of Contemporary Economics*, op. cit., vol.I, pp.288–313; also John W. Kendrick, 'The Historical Development of National Income Accounts', *History of Political Economy* vol.2 (Fall 1970) especially pp.306–15. Also, of course, ever since the later nineteenth century, American economists have played a major role in the development of disaggregated data on specific sectors and aspects of the economy. This cannot be more fully examined here.

94 Ruggles, op. cit., chapter 17. For a balanced, if critical analysis of the Behavioural Sciences Survey see Charles L. Schultze, 'The Reviewers Reviewed', *American Economic Review* vol.61 (May 1972), pp.45–52. A second review by John G. Gurley, 'The State of Political Economics', ibid., pp.53–62, reveals the vast gulf between the orthodox and radical viewpoints. See also the discussion, ibid., pp.63–8.

95 See pp.413ff in this volume.

96 See pp.413–4 in this volume.

97 The periodic reports issued by these institutions constitute the best source of information about their activities. See also NBER, *Half a Century of Economic Research 1920–1970* (New York: National Bureau of Economic Research, 1970), and Charles B. Saunders, Jr., *The Brookings Institution, A Fifty Year History* (Washington, DC: The Brookings Institution, 1966); also Critchlow, op. cit. The Cowles Commission for Economic Research was of considerable scientific importance in the spread of econometrics after 1932, and especially in the 1940s. See, for example, Mary S. Morgan, *The History of Econometric Ideas* (Cambridge: Cambridge University Press, 1990), especially pp.55–6 and sources cited therein.

98 See, for example, Lyons, op. cit., pp.42–6, and Barry D. Karl, *Charles Merriam and the Study of Politics* (Chicago: University of Chicago Press, 1974).

99 For example, George J. Stigler, 'The Foundations and Economics', in Warren Weaver (ed.), *US Philanthropic Foundations, Their History, Structure, Management, and Record* (New York: Harper, 1967), pp.280–2. Stigler emphasized the foundations' contribution to the US lead in large scale statistical work. There is a growing body of research on the role of foundations in economics. See, for example, James A. Smith, *The Idea Brokers. Think Tanks and the Rise of the New Policy Elite* (New York: Free Press, 1991).

100 Milton Friedman, 'Some Contemporary Tendencies in Economic Research – Discussion', *American Economic Review* vol.43 (May 1953), pp.446–7: 'The emphasis on projects and coordination tends to divert able men from the pursuit of their own interests or to deny them resources and to waste the time and energy of the abler men both in dreaming up projects that will be attractive to donors and in supervising the activities of less able people on projects they ought not to be working on.' This is in sharp contrast to Mitchell's optimistic view in 1930. See his 'Institutes for Research in the Social Sciences', in *The Backward Art*, op. cit., pp.58–71.

101 For example, Ralph L. Nelson, 'Economic Research Sponsored by Private Foundations', *American Economic Review, Papers and Proceedings* vol.56 (May 1966), p.520; and Irving Louis Horowitz and James Everett Katz, *Social Science and Public Policy in the United States* (New York: Praeger, 1975), appendix A and B, pp.171–5, from National Science Foundation data.

102 This is argued by Theodore W. Schultz, 'Distortions of Economic Research', in William H. Krusdal (ed.), *The Social Sciences, Their Nature and Uses* (Chicago: University of Chicago Press, 1982), pp.122–33. He considered that economists were 'complacent about their freedom of inquiry, about safeguarding their university functions and about the conditions under which research funds are made available to them by institutions other than the university'. See also, Kenneth E. Boulding, 'The Misallocation of Intellectual Resources in Economics', in Larry D. Singell (ed.), *Kenneth E. Boulding. Collected Papers, Vol.3: Political Economy* (Boulder, Colo.: Colorado Associated University Press, 1973), p.538.

103 Cf. Stigler, op. cit., p.279; Schultz, op. cit., p.213, 131.

104 Edward S. Herman, 'The Institutionalization of Bias in Economics,' *Media, Culture and Society*, vol.4 (July, 1982), p.285: the 'mobilization of bias suggests the possibility that the entire drift of the science . . . may be decisively shaped by market forces.' Also ibid. pp.288–89.

105 Martin Bronfenbrenner, 'Trends, Cycles, and Fads in Economic Writing', op. cit., p.548. Joseph Spengler, 'Was 1922–1972 a Golden Age in the History of Economics?', *Journal of Economic Issues* vol.8 (September 1974), p.524. This is a very useful survey of the period. See also his 'Economics: Its Direct and Indirect Impact in America, 1776–1976', in Charles M. Bonjean, *Social Science in America. The First Two Hundred Years* (Austin: University of Texas Press, 1976), pp.49–76; and *idem*, 'Economics: Its History, Themes, Approaches', *Journal of Economic Issues* vol.2 (March 1968), pp.5–30.

106 This expression is taken from Norbert Elias, Herminio Martins and Richard D. Whitley, *Scientific Establishments and Hierarchies* (Dordrecht, Holland: D. Reidel, 1982), p.ix. See also Richard Whitley, *The Intellectual and Social Organization of the Sciences* (Oxford: Clarendon Press, 1984).

107 This has been a staple topic in methodological controversy in economics during the past century or so, and it figured very prominently in the 'crisis' literature of the late 1960s and 1970s.

108 In addition to the references in note 2, *supra*, see also the general review of the field in Benjamin Ward, *What's Wrong with Economics?* (London: Macmillan, 1972). Arguably the crisis was mainly, but not exclusively, an American phenomenon. It was also evident, for example, in Britain and France. Curiously enough, some Polish economists surveying the scene in the late 1960s referred to the 'progressive decrease in the number of schools and trends in contemporary economics – although this may often mean eclecticism rather than synthesis'. Cf. 'Economics' in *Main Trends of Research in the Social Sciences Part One: Social Sciences* (Paris: Mouton/Unesco, 1970), p.293.

109 See pp.407–8 in this volume.

110 For a time this became a standard feature of presidential addresses and other invited lectures. An especially powerful example was W. Leontief's 'Theoretical Assumptions and Nonobserved Facts', *American Economic Review* vol.61 (March 1971), pp.1–7. Leontief is a Nobel Laureate. For a statement of the opposite view see Walter Heller, 'What's Right with Economics', *American Economic Review* vol.66 (March 1975), pp.1–26.

111 For general sources on institutionalism, see *supra*, note 3.

112 Orthodox economics was no more successful either. As Dorfman has noted, op. cit. vol.V, p.658, the public did not have much confidence in the economists, but they had no one else to turn to. Part II of his study provides a comprehensive review of the impact of the depression on the economics profession. See also William E. Stoneman, *A History of the Economic Analysis of the Great Depression in America* (New York: Garland, 1979).

113 The Association for Evolutionary Economics publishes *The Journal of Economic Issues*.

114 Ayres taught for many years at the University of Texas, at Austin. His followers have been dubbed 'the cactus league of dissenting economists'. For a survey of his work see A.W. Coats, 'Clarence Ayres' Place in the History of American Economics: An Interim Assessment', in *Science and Ceremony: The Institutional Economics of C.E. Ayres* William Breit and William Patton Culbertson, Jr. (eds), (Austin: University of Texas Press, 1976), pp.23–48. Reprinted in this volume pp.386–406.

115 Radical economists argued that the evils they denounced 'are not pathological abnormalities of the system but rather are derived directly from the normal functioning of capitalism'. Cf. Eileen Applebaum, 'Radical Economics' in Sidney Weintraub (ed.), *Modern Economic Thought* (Philadelphia: University of Pennsylvania Press, 1977), p.560. See also, Mark Blaug, 'A Methodological Appraisal of Radical Economics', in *Methodological Controversy in Economics: Historical Essays in Honor of T.W. Hutchison*, A.W. Coats (ed.), (Greenwich, Conn.: JAI Press, Inc., 1983), pp.211–45; and Martin Bronfenbrenner, 'Radical Economics in America, 1970', *Journal of Economic Literature* vol.8 (September 1970), pp.747–66; *idem*, 'Notes on Marxian Economics in the United States', *American Economic Review* vol.54 (December 1964), pp.1019–26, and 'Reply', ibid., vol.55 (September 1965), pp.863–4; *idem*, 'The Vicissitudes of Marxian Economics', *History of Political Economy*, vol.2 (Fall 1970), pp.205–24; Gurley, op. cit. Also more generally, Assar Lindbeck, *The Political Economy of the New Left* (New York: Harper and Row, 1971).

116 For a general survey see A.W. Coats, 'The Revival of Subjectivism in Economics', in *Beyond Positive Economics*, Jack Wiseman (ed.), (London: Macmillan, 1982), pp.87–103, reprinted in this volume pp.472–85; also Israel Kirzner, 'The "Austrian" Perspective', in Bell and Kristol, *The Crisis in Economic Theory*, op. cit., pp.111–22.

117 Cf. James W. Dean's balanced account of 'The Dissolution of the Keynesian Consensus', in Bell and Kristol, *The Crisis in Economic Theory*, op. cit., pp.19–34, in which he distinguishes between 'Revolutionaries, Evolutionaries, and Reactionaries'.

118 The variety of names indicates the state of confusion, e.g. Hicksian-, Neo-, Bastard or Post-Keynesian, with or without a hyphen. With such eminent Nobel prizewinning economists as Sir John Hicks and Paul Samuelson shifting their allegiances it is difficult to keep track of the situation. Representative surveys are: Alfred S. Eichner and J.A. Kregel, 'An Essay on Post-Keynesian Theory: A New Paradigm in Economics', *Journal of Economic Literature* vol.13 (December 1975), pp.1293–314; Paul Davidson, 'Post-Keynesian Economics', in Bell and Kristol, op. cit., pp.151–73; and Geoff Harcourt and Omar Hamouda, 'Post-Keynesianism: From Criticism to Coherence?', *Bulletin of Economic Research* vol.40 (January 1988), reprinted in John Pheby (ed.), *New Directions in Post-Keynesian Economics* (Aldershot: Edwar Elgar, 1989), pp.1–34. There is a *Journal of Post Keynesian Economics* (without a hyphen!).

119 By Karl Brunner. See Allan H. Meltzer, 'Monetarism and the Crisis in Economics', in Bell and Kristol, op. cit., p.43. For reviews of Monetarism

AMERICAN ECONOMICS

see, for example, A. Robert Nobay and Harry G. Johnson, 'Monetarism, A Historic-Theoretic Perspective', *The Journal of Economic Literature* vol.15 (June 1977), pp.470–85; also the series of articles on 'The State of the Monetarist Debate', from the *Review* of the Federal Reserve Bank of St. Louis, 1973, reprinted in Rendigs Fels and John J. Siegfried, *Recent Advances in Economics. A Book of Readings* (Homewood, Ill.: Richard D. Irwin, Inc., 1974), pp.332–46.

120 See the brilliant, if partly tongue-in-cheek review by a Chicago economist in Harry G. Johnson, 'The Keynesian Revolution and the Monetarist Counter-Revolution', *American Economic Review* vol.61 (May 1971), pp.1–14. Johnson perceptively identified the links between intellectual, sociological and environmental factors in the counter-revolutionary movement.

121 See pp.433–4 in this volume.

122 Cf. his 'Chicago Economics: Permanence and Change', *Journal of Economic Literature* vol.20 (March 1982), pp.1–38. For earlier accounts see Henry L. Miller, Jr., 'On the Chicago School of Economics', with replies by George J. Stigler and Martin Bronfenbrenner, *Journal of Political Economy* vol.70 (February 1962), pp.64–75; A.W. Coats, 'The Origins of the "Chicago School(s)"?', in vol. II of this series; and the collection of essays edited by Warren J. Samuels, *The Chicago School of Political Economy* (East Lansing: Michigan State University Graduate School of Business Administration, 1976), especially chapter 1. For an interesting effort to explain the prevalence of 'schools' in Chicago see Milton Friedman, 'Schools at Chicago', *University of Chicago Magazine* (Autumn 1974), pp.11–16.

123 This approach is especially identified with Gary Becker. Other important influences on and figures in this movement have been George Stigler, Ronald Coase and Richard Posner.

124 From a farewell speech on 'The Whence and Whither of Our Science' at Bonn, in 1932, before he moved to Harvard. Quoted in Erich Schneider, *Joseph A. Schumpeter, Life and Work of a Great Social Scientist* (translated by W.E. Kuhn), (Lincoln, Neb.: Bureau of Business Research, 1975), p.40. For emphasis on controversy within consensus, given 'the analytical and empirical ties that bind us' see, for example, Heller, op. cit., p.4; also section II *supra*.

Nevertheless there is still a long way to go when a distinguished economist can refer disparagingly to 'the high positive correlation between the policy views of a researcher (or, what is more, his thesis director) and his empirical findings. I will begin to believe in economics as a science when out of Yale there comes an empirical Ph.D. thesis emphasizing the superiority of monetary policy in some historical episode – and out of Chicago, one demonstrating the superiority of fiscal policy.' Don Patinkin, 'Keynesian Monetary Theory and the Cambridge School', *Banca Nazionale del Lavoro Quarterly Review* (June 1972), p.142, quoted by T.W. Hutchison, *Knowledge and Ignorance in Economics* (Oxford: Blackwell, 1977), p.60. It is not difficult to imagine how an institutionalist, radical or Marxist economist would interpret this observation.

125 For two very different examples from AEA presidential addresses, see J.K. Galbraith, 'Power and the Useful Economist', *American Economic Review* vol. 63 (March 1973), p.2; and Tjalling C. Koopmans, 'Economics Among the Sciences', ibid., vol.69 (March 1979), p.13.

126 Topics considered include: the role of publications and communications networks; career patterns; the reward system; social stratification within the discipline; national 'styles' of research; professional ethics and standards; the regulative and cognitive aspects of methodology etc. Among leading

economists, the late Harry G. Johnson was an unusually perceptive and vigorous contributor to this literature. For a useful recent review of some of the issues see E. Ray Canterbery and Robert J. Burkhardt, 'What Do We Mean By Asking Whether Economics Is a Science?', in Alfred S. Eichner, (ed.), *Why Economics Is Not Yet a Science* (Armonk, New York: M.E. Sharpe Inc.), pp.15–40. Other essays in this volume broadly share the same detached, but critical standpoint.

127 One ingenious author has argued that there are three distinct, consistent and self-contained cosmologies in contemporary economics, each with its professional adherents. See Benjamin Ward, *The Ideal Worlds of Economics. Liberal, Radical, and Conservative Economic World Views* (New York: Basic Books, 1979).

PART V

RECENT, GENERAL ECONOMICS

22

THE CURRENT 'CRISIS' IN ECONOMICS IN HISTORICAL PERSPECTIVE*

I INTRODUCTION AND INTELLECTUAL FRAMEWORK

During the past five years or so, a considerable number of leading American and British economists have publicly voiced their grave concern about the state of their discipline. The terms 'crisis', 'revolution' and 'counter-revolution' have repeatedly been used in books, pamphlets, presidential addresses, essays and scholarly articles in a manner implying that we are currently witnessing a major turning point in the development of the subject.[1]

In an effort to assess the nature and significance of this so-called 'crisis' in economics, it is worth inquiring how far the present situation resembles earlier phases of doubt, uncertainty and intense controversy among economists. What, if any, are its unique or differentiating characteristics?

At the outset it may be tactful to consider whether the historian of economics has any special ability to shed light on the current situation, since he may lack both the technical qualifications of the academic theorist and the experience of the professional economist employed in business or government. In self-defence, it must be noted that, as economics is nowadays such a bewilderingly complex and many-sided subject, no single observer is qualified to discuss more than a limited fraction of the relevant subject matter. Moreover, the ordinary working economist, preoccupied with the cultivation of his own professional patch, may be unable to perceive some of the general features of the intellectual landscape which the historian, with the benefit of his trained hindsight, can more readily recognize. So the experiment is at least worth trying.

In his task of interpreting or recreating the past, the historian requires an intellectual framework or set of criteria by which to select and arrange the available evidence. In the present instance, the most promising model is

459

that contained in T.S. Kuhn's brilliant and fashionable study, *The Structure of Scientific Revolutions*, in which the concept of an intellectual or scientific 'crisis' is fully articulated. Kuhn's theory is, of course, merely suggestive, not definitive. Also, it must be acknowledged that he originally applied his ideas to the natural, not the social, sciences; and even within that sphere his work has been severely criticized by historians and philosophers of science.

According to Kuhn, a scientific 'crisis' occurs as the result of the breakdown of the ruling 'paradigm', or basic theory. In any 'normal' period the majority of scientists in a given discipline work within the generally accepted framework of ideas provided by the ruling paradigm, which provides them not only with 'a map, but also with some of the directions essential for map-making'. He defines paradigms as 'universally recognized scientific achievements that for a time provide model problems and solutions to a community of practitioners', and the paradigm's function is regulative (that is, normative) as well as cognitive, since it enables the scientist to take the foundations of his knowledge for granted and concentrate his attention upon the solution of more concrete problems or 'puzzles'.

Obviously, no paradigm is complete; otherwise normal scientific activity would cease, for there would be no unsolved problems or puzzles. But as normal research proceeds, on lines suggested by the paradigm, unexpected or anomalous results appear. For a time these results can be ignored, or dismissed as irrelevant or accidental, because 'the scientist who pauses to examine every anomaly he notes will seldom get any significant work done'. But as the anomalies increase in number and importance they can no longer be ignored. They become 'critical'; a sense of 'crisis' develops as the inadequacy of the ruling paradigm becomes increasingly obvious, and research will then be diverted from puzzle-solving to paradigm-testing.

In due course the validity of the ruling paradigm will be challenged, but such a challenge will inevitably provoke a reaction. This is both natural and healthy, since the challengers are threatening the established scientific tradition, with its concomitant network of commitments to specific concepts, theories, instruments and standards of scientific performance. In the ensuing debate all the scientific passions are aroused, and if the ruling paradigm is overthrown its defeat will, according to Kuhn, be due to a 'conversion experience', a sudden 'transfer of allegiance' on the part of a significant number of scientists, rather than to 'the logical structure of scientific knowledge'. This is not simply because scientists are irrational, but because the transfer of allegiance which occurs as the result of an intellectual crisis is dependent on the possibilities inherent in the new paradigm, rather than any clearly demonstrable proof of its superiority. Yet, according to Kuhn, the change from one paradigm to another is dramatic and sudden, hence the appropriateness of the term 'revolution'.[2]

This brief outline should be enough to suggest the general applicability of the Kuhnian framework to the current 'crisis' in economics, a state of affairs which, many observers would argue, is largely due to the breakdown of the Keynesian 'paradigm'. According to this view, for about two decades after World War II the majority of professional economists in western capitalist countries accepted the general validity of Keynesian macroeconomic analysis. Moreover, Keynesian ideas (however defined) were dominant not only in academic circles, but also in public policy debates in the mass media, in national governments and in international agencies. Of course, the supremacy of Keynesian ideas was never complete, if only because of time lags in the diffusion and reception of new ideas. Thus, microeconomics retained an important place in university lecture rooms and textbooks, general equilibrium theory gained influential adherents in more advanced circles and there remained a substantial sprinkling – and in some institutions and countries a solid phalanx – of dissenters and heretics, such as institutionalists, Marxists and other radicals. Nevertheless, when all the necessary qualifications have been made, the period from 1945 to about 1965 can properly be viewed as the Age of Keynes.

If this general description is accepted, certain key questions remain to be answered. For example, why did the Keynesian paradigm break down? Is the ensuing crisis comparable to those crisis situations in the natural sciences depicted by Kuhn? How far does the current crisis constitute a novel situation in the history of economics, and what is the outcome likely to be?

According to Kuhn, paradigm breakdowns occur as a result of conditions *internal* to the scientific community, for example, weaknesses inherent in the structure of theory, unexpected or anomalous 'results', or the failure of predictions based on the ruling paradigm. Any of these factors may arise in a well-developed social science like economics, and there has certainly been a growing body of criticism of Keynesian economics. Social scientists, however, are generally less insulated from society than their counterparts in the natural sciences; hence, in explaining a crisis period in economics, due weight must also be given to external, extra-scientific or exogenous influences on the discipline. Historians of economics have long debated the relative importance of internal and external forces on the development of their subject, and, on the whole, in recent decades the consensus of opinion has tended to favour emphasis on the contribution of professional scholarship and what George Stigler has called 'the internal pressures and values of the discipline'.[3] But, wherever the emphasis is placed, both internal and external factors must be taken into account, and it seems clear – as indicated in Section III – that the balance of forces has changed significantly in recent years.

II KEYNESIAN, MONETARIST, INSTITUTIONALIST AND RADICAL APPROACHES

In trying to account for the current 'crisis', no single mono-causal explanation will suffice. But it is convenient to begin with a relatively familiar and simplistic interpretation. In accounting for the strong reaction against Keynesian theory in recent years, many qualified observers have emphasized the profession's failure to provide adequate remedies for the problem of 'stagflation' (the combination of inflation and slow economic growth), a failure which seemed all the more striking to American economists after the well-publicized success of the Kennedy tax cut in the mid-1960s. The phase of professional euphoria and high public esteem at that time was soon followed in the United States by a revival of popular criticism of economists and a corresponding decline of morale within the profession.[4] And it is certainly true that one of the most remarkable features of the current 'crisis' has been the veritable orgy of public self-flagellation provided by some of the economics profession's leading spokesmen. This may, of course, be a healthy sign, as two outstanding ex-government economists have recently claimed,[5] nevertheless, the practice has recently attained almost epidemic proportions.

Undoubtedly the most Kuhnian account of the background to the current crisis in economics is that provided by Harry G. Johnson in his paper, 'The Keynesian Revolution and the Monetarist Counter-Revolution'.[6] This is of special interest in the present context, as Johnson emphasized circumstances endogenous to academic economics up to the mid-1960s, from which point, so he argued, the acceleration of inflation following the escalation of the Vietnam war posed an external problem which the reigning generation of Keynesians was unable to solve. Johnson's analysis of the conditions necessary for a successful counter-revolution embraces methodological, theoretical, empirical, policy and sociological considerations. There are five essential requirements:

(1) an attack, possibly prompted by an obvious social problem, on the central propositions of the ruling orthodoxy – preferably a degenerated, vulgarized version in a simplified form, for example, 'money does not matter';

(2) the production of a new theory which appears to absorb all that was valid in the old theory while emphasizing its novelty by propaganda and by giving new and confusing names to old concepts;

(3) a degree of difficulty of understanding just sufficient to deter the old and to challenge and reward the young (it must not be so difficult as to discourage them from mastering it), and there must be rewards in terms of academic recognition and advancement;

(4) a new and appealing methodology, for example, Friedman's 'positive' economics; and

(5) a new and important empirical relationship which can be 'tested' by the budding econometrician, for example, the demand function for money.

The humorous, tongue-in-cheek tone of Johnson's somewhat cynical account should not be allowed to detract from its genuine interpretative value. In particular, the sociological aspects of his analysis are worth noting, especially in point (3), which is reinforced by his emphasis on the institutional differences between the American and British branches of the economics profession. Johnson himself did not consider that the Monetarists were likely to overthrow the Keynesian hegemony; indeed it appears that they should more properly be regarded as providing a necessary corrective to the earlier degenerated version of Keynesianism which, as Leijonhufvud[7] and others have suggested, involved serious misinterpretations of Keynes' *General Theory*.

In other words, the recent influence of Monetarism may best be regarded as a consequence rather than a cause of the breakdown of the Keynesian paradigm, and much the same is true of the recent revival of interest in Marxian economics. Like Monetarism, this is a minority movement, and it is likely to remain so. But it has gained academic support from several different directions: the reaction against the degenerated versions of Keynesianism, the positive intellectual stimulus provided by Piero Sraffa's *The Production of Commodities by Commodities*,[8] and the current economic difficulties of western capitalist countries which, some radical critics maintain, foreshadow the general crisis and breakdown predicted by Marx and his followers.

Some of the principal Marxian objections to economic orthodoxy in any of its forms stem from the belief that economics is too narrow and technical, and in this respect they have received substantial support from young radical economists, institutionalists and senior intellectual mavericks like Kenneth Boulding, Gunnar Myrdal and J.K. Galbraith. Yet the radicals' objections are by no means novel. Indeed, they are very familiar to historians of economics, and they have been conveniently summarized by Assar Lindbeck as follows:

(a) the failure to explain and give sufficient emphasis to income distribution;
(b) the practice of taking consumers' preferences as given, rather than as a matter for study and analysis;
(c) the preoccupation with quantitative and the neglect of qualitative problems;
(d) the preoccupation with changes at the margin, to the neglect of changes in the total system; and
(e) the failure to take account of the interdependence of economic and political processes, for example, the power structure, and the historical context within which economic forces operate.[9]

Largely under the influence of Kuhn's ideas there has been considerable discussion of the possibility that radical economics, which embraces both Marxist and non-Marxist elements, might conceivably provide a viable alternative paradigm, in opposition to orthodox Keynesianism, Monetarism or general equilibrium theory. However, there seems little likelihood of this eventuality. Radical economics has lacked a coherent intellectual framework and, as one perceptive commentator has suggested, this is largely because it originated in a policy anomaly rather than a scientific anomaly, in Kuhn's sense of the term.[10] With its emphasis on war, racism, pollution and workers' alienation, radical economics was essentially a response by the younger generation to the peculiar strains and stresses of American and Western European society in the 1960s. Seen in historical perspective, the discussion of this movement has, for the most part, consisted of a repetition of criticisms of the limitations of orthodox economics which were expressed in the late nineteenth century and early twentieth century by historicists and institutionalists. Yet even on this issue some impeccably orthodox economists have blamed themselves for its emergence.[11]

III THEORETICAL AND TECHNICAL DEFICIENCIES OF CONTEMPORARY ECONOMICS

The constellations of economic ideas mentioned in the preceding section – Keynesianism, Monetarism, Institutionalism and Radical Economics – constitute doctrinal schools or movements with significant extra-scientific features. While they possess varying degrees of scientific rigor and respectability, they all transcend the conventional boundaries of science as portrayed in Kuhn's model. It is now necessary to consider other, more narrowly technical, scientific and professional misgivings about the current state of economics. The fact that these have been voiced by highly experienced and respected professionals has lent considerable weight to the belief that there now exists a crisis in the discipline.

It is impossible to list all the deficiencies of current economics noted by these critics, but the following sample will suffice to indicate their range and variety. It is said that: the empirical foundations of economics are inadequate (W. Leontief); there has been a scandalous waste of intellectual resources in the overdevelopment of mathematical economics and econometrics (F.A. Hahn); many of the economists' efforts are irrelevant (G.D.N. Worswick) and contribute little or nothing of value to the solution of major practical problems (O. Morgenstern); the profession is in a state of general confusion (P.J. Bauer and A.A. Walters); its members are suffering from a 'collective hubris' (A. Leijonhufvud); an advanced training in economics inculcates a false sense of intellectual values and is therefore actively unhelpful (E.H. Phelps-Brown); and the profession generally maintains a perverse reward system (J.M. Blackman).[12]

Many of these complaints are familiar enough. But their combined impact is remarkable; it is doubtful whether there has ever before been such a powerful chorus of dissatisfaction from qualified observers. This, indeed, is the most distinctive feature of the current 'crisis'. It is not only a crisis of the discipline *per se*, but also a crisis of the economics profession, and it is the result of a historically unique combination of internal and external pressures.

A brief comparison of the state of economics in the early 1970s with that forty years earlier, during the crisis stage immediately prior to the Keynesian revolution, may help to underline the contention. In the intervening period the discipline has grown remarkably in range and technical complexity; there has been a rapid expansion of the numbers of students and trained practitioners, an increasing proportion of whom are employed outside the teaching profession, in business and government; and there has been a significant growth of professional organization and self-consciousness. But while the strength and autonomy of the economics profession has grown, so too have the external pressures. As the result of changing economic and social conditions and policies, a process in which Keynesian economics has played a significant part, the general public has become more aware of economists and economic issues than ever before. Professional and laymen's disagreements about economic ideas, goals and policies have become increasingly publicized and politicized, and the balance of forces within the profession has undoubtedly shifted toward the public domain. After two decades or so in which many economists have been engaged in trying to remake the world according to their own image, they have paused to examine their handiwork and the results have not been pleasing.

In the past economists have often – if not usually – had a bad press, and there has been no lack of self-criticism from within their ranks. During the current crisis, however, self-criticism has risen to a pitch where it has virtually amounted to a collective neurosis, especially in the United States.[13] As already suggested, in the early and mid-1960s there was an exaggerated sense of achievement, and the subsequent reaction and sense of failure has, perhaps, been equally exaggerated. Indeed, as several recent observers have noted, the profession still appears to enjoy a substantial measure of public recognition, despite much popular criticism, and there is no perceptible contraction in the demand for its services. However, this simply makes the crescendo of professional self-denigration all the more remarkable. It is not merely, as Harry Johnson and others have suggested, that the economists have failed to master the problem of inflation – although concern about this matter accounts for a significant proportion of the current malaise. It is a *combination* of theoretical disagreements, policy failures and internal professional dissatisfaction that gives the current crisis its distinctive character and force.

Apart from the sense of crisis resulting from paradigm breakdown, which was mentioned earlier, there have also been certain longer-run causes of dissension and conflict within the discipline which have recently come to a head. The most conspicuous of these results from the growth of mathematical and econometric theory and techniques, itself a direct consequence of the specialization and division of labour inherent in the process of professionalization. The post-war academic boom, with its concomitant abundance of financial resources, research opportunities and academic

465

hardware, has been accompanied by a sharp rise in the level of sophistication of the discipline. This has partly (albeit not very effectively) acted as a barrier to entry into the profession, but also – and more seriously – as an obstacle to communication within its ranks. To some extent the division between mathematical and non-mathematical economists coincides with inter-generational differences,[14] for the older economists have often – though by no means invariably – lacked command of the newer approaches. But beyond this, the elaboration of mathematical theory and techniques has inevitably yielded diminishing returns, and has strengthened long-standing doubts about their scientific value. Disagreement about these matters can be traced back at least as far as the mid-nineteenth century, and in recent years a number of professionally distinguished and technically competent economists have posed searching questions about the philosophical foundations and the scientific value of mathematical methods in economics.[15] Others have expressed concern over the misallocation of intellectual resources in the subject, and especially the tendency to over-value high theory at the expense of less spectacular, but more empirically grounded work. The profession's growing sense of responsibility for and involvement in policy matters has undoubtedly strengthened this feeling.

IV DISTINCTIVE FEATURES OF THE CURRENT CRISIS

It is now time to draw together the main elements in this account and to present a trial balance. How far is the current crisis in economics both novel and significant?

Viewed from a historical standpoint, the recent situation has many familiar features. As in earlier periods of intense controversy, the debate has ranged widely to embrace methodological, doctrinal and policy matters. Thus, complaints about the excessive development of high theory and elaborate mathematical and statistical techniques recall earlier disputes about the proper relationship between economic theory and 'reality'. The conflict between Keynesians and Monetarists resembles earlier disagreements between rival doctrinal schools,[16] and there has recently been much disagreement about the demarcation lines (for example, whether Keynes himself was a Keynesian) and whether some neo-classical or post-Keynesian synthesis is attainable.[17] And the outspoken attacks on economic orthodoxy by so-called neo-institutionalists,[18] Marxists and radicals raise many issues which, either in form or content, can be found in many late nineteenth or early twentieth century economic writings.

The most distinctive features of the present situation stem from longer-run changes, both within the economics profession itself and in its relationship with public affairs – changes which may well be irreversible. The extent and significance of these changes have not been generally appreciated, and for this historians of economics are at least partly to blame. For the most part, they have accepted the conventional academic tradition which values theory as against applications, science rather than practice, and emphasizes the gap between the two. This traditional valuation has become increasingly inappropriate to an epoch in which a growing proportion of trained economists is engaged in non-academic activities.

In its origins economics, like other intellectual disciplines, grew out of practice, and until the late nineteenth century only a minority of individuals recognizable as 'economists' were university teachers. From about that time until the end of World War II the main advances in the subject came increasingly from academics; the attention of economists, subsequent commentators and historians was focused mainly on scientific (that is, academic) achievement, and there was a corresponding tendency to ignore or undervalue practical applications of theory and the contributions of non-academics. During the Age of Keynes, however, the proportion of non-academic economists rose, and the borderlines between academics and non-academics has been blurred, especially as the role of academic economists in policy making has increased, whether as temporary economic advisers, consultants, cabinet members or writers on public policy. There have inevitably been risks for the profession in this process: for example, the likelihood that policy recommendations will prove ineffective or mistaken; the danger that the policy makers' and politicians' failures will be attributed to economists; and the possibility that some economists will abuse their position, whether by tacitly concealing the limitations of their knowledge or openly making claims which they cannot fulfill.[19] Much of the recent epidemic of professional self-criticism stems from these sources, and it is a species of self-criticism that is unlikely to be found in a Kuhnian-type crisis in the natural sciences.

The changing social role and significance of the economics profession is a subject worthy of serious study.[20] The recent sense of crisis stems in part from a realization that economics, as a discipline, has failed to adapt itself to the changing needs of society. There may indeed be two or more economics professions, for example, academic, governmental and business economics, each of which demands special qualities and training, and establishes distinct, if related, criteria of achievement. The current crisis in economics is probably felt more acutely by academics than by government economists, and it is significant that two of the most cogent recent defences of the discipline have come from leading individuals who have had distinguished careers as government advisers – Walter Heller and Sir Donald MacDougall.[21]

One of the most striking features of recent commentaries on the state of economics has been the display of enhanced professional self-consciousness. The critics have been demanding that the profession should 'put its house in order'. Admittedly, most of these commentators have been British and American, but the crisis is by no means confined to those countries, if only because of the international diffusion of American ideas, techniques and conceptions of professionalism. Needless to say, the nature and significance of the crisis varies from place to place depending, among other things, on the influence of the Keynesian paradigm on policy making and the importance assigned to advanced mathematical and econometric techniques in the training of economists. Nevertheless, it seems likely that future historians of economics will regard the crisis as an international phenomenon.

V CONCLUDING THOUGHTS

In the foregoing survey attention has been focused on the applications of economic theory to policy practice and to the sociological dimensions of the contemporary scene. It would be quite wrong, however, to suggest that the current crisis can be resolved merely by successful applications of current economic doctrines or by a resurgence of self-confidence within the profession. In the last analysis – if, indeed, there is such an analysis – such developments will necessarily be transitory unless there is solid progress toward a reconstruction or synthesis at the theoretical level. However, given the profession's value system, which tends to over-value purely theoretical achievements, there is no lack of resources currently being devoted to this end[22].

NOTES

* Based on a lecture delivered in Athens to the Greek Economic Association in March, 1976.

1 These sources are too numerous to be listed here. For an effective brief summary of recent criticisms of the state of economics, and an extended list of references, see Walter W. Heller's presidential address to the American Economic Association, 'What's Right with Economics', *American Economic Review* 65 (March 1975), pp.1–26.

2 The quotations are from T.S. Kuhn, *The Structure of Scientific Revolutions* (Chicago and London: University of Chicago Press, 1970), pp.109, *viii*, 82, 95, 151. Kuhn's ideas have provoked an enormous discussion and exegesis, including many attempts to apply his model to economics. In general, the present writer considers Imre Lakatos' 'Methodology of Scientific Research Programmes' a more promising tool for the historian of economics than Kuhn's theory. However, the concept of scientific 'crisis' plays no significant part in Lakatos' scheme. For relevant background, see Mark Blaug's valuable survey article: 'Kuhn versus Lakatos or Paradigms versus Research Programmes in the History of Economics', *History of Political Economy* 7 (Winter 1975), pp.399–433. This is reprinted, together with other essays applying Lakatos' method to economics, in Spiro Latsis (ed.), *Method and Appraisal in Economics* (Cambridge: Cambridge University Press, 1976).

3 George Stigler, 'The Influence of Events and Policies on Economic Theory', reprinted in his *Essays in the History of Economics* (Chicago and London: University of Chicago Press, 1965), pp.16–30.

4 As Harry Johnson remarked, Monetarism eventually became a public force 'less by its own efforts than as a consequence of the "New Economics" overreaching

itself when it was riding high in the formulation of national economic policy. The "New Economics" was favored by the opportunity to sell Keynesian policies to meet a Keynesian problem; it encountered disaster when it tried to sell reverse Keynesian policies to meet a non-Keynesian problem. And the monetarist counter-revolution has been cashing in on that mistake of intellectual strategy.' 'The Keynesian Revolution and the Monetarist Counter-Revolution', *American Economic Review* 61 (May 1971), p.7.

5 Heller, 'What's Right with Economics'; also D. MacDougall, 'In Praise of Economics', *Economic Journal* 84 (December 1974), pp.773–86.
6 Johnson, 'Keynesian Revolution', op. cit.
7 Axel Leijonhufvud, *On Keynesian Economics and the Economics of Keynes* (New York: Oxford University Press, 1968). Needless to say, Leijonhufvud's views have not been universally approved. See, for example, Richard Jackman, 'Keynes and Leijonhufvud', *Oxford Economic Papers* (July 1974), pp.259–72.

For a recently revised 'authorized' version, see Leijonhufvud's paper, 'Schools, "Revolutions", and Research Programmes in Economic Theory', in Latsis, op. cit., pp.65–108. See also the penetrating review of the current basic interpretations of Keynesian economics in Alan Coddington, 'Keynesian Economics: The Search for First Principles', *The Journal of Economic Literature* 14 (December 1976).
8 (Cambridge: Cambridge University Press, 1960).
9 Assar Lindbeck, *The Political Economy of the New Left* (New York: Harper and Row, 1971).
10 For example, Stephen T. Worland, 'Radical Political Economy as a "Scientific Revolution"', *Southern Economic Journal* 39 (October 1972), p.278. See also the special issue of the *Review of Radical Economics* 3 (July 1971), devoted to 'Radical Paradigms in Economics'; the bitter attack on economic orthodoxy by John Gurley, 'The State of Political Economics', and the reply by Robert Solow, *American Economic Review* 61 (May 1971), pp.53–62 and 63–5, respectively. It is of some interest that Gurley is a former editor of the prestigious *American Economic Review*.
11 According to James Tobin, 'The failure of communication [with young radicals] was in large measure our own fault, perhaps the unintended by-product of scientific progress in economics'. See his review of Lindbeck, *The Political Economy of the New Left*, in *Journal of Economic Literature* 10 (December 1972), pp.1216–18.
12 The papers by Leontief, Hahn, Worswick, Phelps-Brown and Blackman are referred to in Heller, 'What's Right with Economics'. See also O. Morgenstern, 'Thirteen Critical Points in Contemporary Economic Theory: An Interpretation', *Journal of Economic Literature* 10 (December 1972), pp.1163–89; and P.T. Bauer and A.A. Walters, 'The State of Economics', *Journal of Law and Economics* 8 (April 1975), pp.1–25.
13 There are, no doubt, specifically American reasons for this. But while the leadership of the economics profession is no doubt centred in the United States, the 'crisis' is by no means an exclusively American phenomenon.

See, for example, the severe strictures contained in Walter Eltis, 'The Failure of the Keynesian Conventional Wisdom', *Lloyds Bank Review* (October 1976), pp.1–18. This persuasive essay is written by an economist who has made significant contributions both to the history of economics and to contemporary policy debates. For a reply to Eltis, see Lord Kahn, 'Mr Eltis and the Keynesians', *Lloyds Bank Review* (April 1977), pp.1–13; also G.D.N. Worswick, 'The End of Demand Management', *Lloyds Bank Review* (January 1977), pp.17–18.
14 It is doubtful whether there is any precise counterpart in the natural sciences to this division among the economists.

15 For example, K. Arrow, W. Baumol, N. Georgescu-Roegen, K. Menger, O. Morgenstern and G. Shackle. One major issue has been the problem of translation from verbal into mathematical terms and vice versa. On this point the present author is indebted to the unpublished researches of Mr A.G. Llewellyn.

Several recent distinguished critics of the discipline have argued in favour of the reintroduction of economic history into the training of economists as a corrective to the current overemphasis on theory and technique. For a cogent and well-documented presentation of this case by a young and technically expert economic historian, see Donald McCloskey, 'Does the Past Have Useful Economics?', *Journal of Economic Literature* 14 (June 1976), pp.434–61.

16 To use post-Kuhnian language, economics has usually been polyparadigmatic, rather than monoparadigmatic.

17 A prime example of the reappraisal of Keynes' Keynesianism can be found in the lengthy exchanges between Patinkin and Friedman. See, for example, Don Patinkin, 'Friedman on the Quantity Theory and Keynesian Economics', and Milton Friedman, 'Comments on the Critics', *Journal of Political Economy* 80 (1972), pp.883–905 and 906–50, respectively. For a very recent discussion of a possible synthesis of post-Keynesian, as against neo-classical economics, see Alfred S. Eichner and J.A. Kregel, 'An Essay on Post-Keynesian Theory: A New Paradigm in Economics', *Journal of Economic Literature* 13 (December 1975), pp.1291–1314. The authors note that the two paradigms, as in Kuhn's account, are designed to serve quite different purposes. See also the more recent reappraisal of post-Keynesian economics by Harcourt and Harmouda, cited in this volume, p.455, n.118.

18 Allen G. Gruchy, *Contemporary Economic Thought: The Contribution of Neo-Institutional Economics* (New York: Kelly, 1972). For the present author's critical review of this volume, see the *Journal of Economic Issues* 8 (September 1974), pp.597–605. It should be noted that more recently the term neo-institutionalism has been used in a manner incompatible with Gruchy's usage. See for example Richard Langlois, *Economics as a Process. Essays in the New Institutional Economics* (New York: Cambridge University Press 1986).

19 Complaints about professional irresponsibility are especially likely to come from economists unfavourably disposed toward current interventionist policies. See, for example, Milton Friedman's remarks, as quoted by Joan Robinson in 'The Second Crisis of Economic Theory', *American Economic Review* 62 (May 1972), p.11: 'I believe that we economists in recent years have done vast harm – to society at large and to our profession in particular – by claiming more than we can deliver. We have therefore encouraged politicians to make extravagant promises, inculcate unrealistic expectations in the public at large, and promote discontent with reasonably satisfactory results because they fall short of the economists' promised land.'

Some economists have expressed serious concern about the perversion or corruption of scholarly standards in economics. See, for example, T.W. Hutchison, 'On the History and Philosophy of Science and Economics', in Latsis, op. cit., pp.200–3, where he reinforces his views by quotations from H.G. Johnson and Don Patinkin. On the more general issues involved, see also T.W. Hutchison, *Economists and Economic Policy in Britain, 1946–66: Some Aspects of Their Interrelations* (London: Allen and Unwin, 1968).

20 For a preliminary review of the British experience, see A.W. Coats, 'The Development of the Economics Profession in England', in L. Th. Houmanidis (ed) *International Congress of Economic History and History of Economic Theories in Piraeus* (Piraeus: The Piraeus Graduate School of Industrial Studies, 1975),

pp.277–90. Additional essays on the economics profession will appear in vol.II of this series.

21 Cited previously in notes 1 and 5.

22 To be unduly optimistic about the outcome would, however, be foolish. As Leijonhufvud has perceptively remarked ['Schools, "Revolutions", and Research Programmes in Economic Theory', op. cit., pp.103–4], 'On the one hand, it is evident how much more clearly we are now able to define many of the obstacles in the way of a reunification of economic theory than was possible ten or fifteen years ago. On the other hand, the "gap" is thereby seen to yawn wider and the remaining tasks to loom more formidable than they looked – to relatively innocent eyes in any case – in the early sixties. The most helpful contributions in the recent literature have, on balance, been more critical than constructive in nature. Critical assessments, conceptual clarifications, sharper definitions of problem aspects will, of course, mark a natural and required first stage of inquiry, preliminary to constructive solutions of problems of this type. But, in this instance, one may now begin to wonder whether this "first stage" is not threatening to become permanent – or as permanent as the patience of economists will allow before they walk away from the issues in disgust.'

23

THE REVIVAL OF SUBJECTIVISM IN ECONOMICS

INTRODUCTION

Generally speaking, historians are loath to report on current or very recent movements, and the very sound reasons for this disinclination will soon become clear to readers of this chapter. In examining the nature of and reasons for the revival of subjectivism in economics the obvious strategy is to begin by defining the subject and then proceed to trace its origins, development and pre-revival decline; but unfortunately this is much easier said than done. Quite apart from the problem of definition, which will be considered later, the origins of subjectivism in economics go back at least as far as the medieval scholastics, perhaps even to the Greeks, and its subsequent history has been complex as well as protracted. As it is obviously impossible to cover all this ground in the time allotted, an arbitrary choice of starting-point is unavoidable.

Nevertheless, notwithstanding the difficulties involved, the subject is eminently worth tackling. This is a splendid time for historians of economic ideas, for during the so-called 'crisis' in economics of the past decade or so there have been repeated appeals to history as a practical guide to those who have lost their bearings in the welter of current controversy.[1] Even where this is not the case, the historian can find ample justification for his specialism by exposing the pretensions of those controversialists who seek impressive intellectual pedigrees to enhance the respectability of their current notions or nostrums. The subjectivists are no exception in this respect, for they are fond of quoting an assertion by their leading living representative, F.A. Hayek, that:

> it is probably no exaggeration to say that every important advance in economic theory during the last hundred years was a further step in the consistent application of subjectivism.[2]

It is doubtful that many present-day economists would endorse Hayek's contention uncritically, yet it forms a convenient starting-point for this enquiry, for at least two reasons. The first is that Hayek was alluding to one major landmark in the history of subjectivist economics, the so-called 'marginal revolution' of the 1870s, an essential ingredient of which was the reaction against the 'objective' or cost-of-production theory of value that had been prevalent prior to that time. As any decent history of economics text contains an account of this episode it need not be examined further here.[3] The second reason for citing Hayek's claim is that the recent revival of subjectivism extends far beyond value theory – a branch of economics now somewhat undervalued, if the expression is admissible – and this latest phase owes much to Hayek himself and his former teacher, Ludwig von Mises. But at this point the problem of definition can no longer be avoided.

WHAT IS SUBJECTIVIST ECONOMICS?

The crucial difficulty is to identify the outer periphery or limits of subjectivist economics, and to determine the precise relationship between the territory as a whole and the core doctrines of Austrian or neo-Austrian economics, which constitute the most readily identifiable components of the current revival. While these doctrines are primarily attributable to Hayek, Mises and their disciples, their origins are directly traceable to the school's nineteenth century master, Carl Menger. There were in fact significant disagreements between Menger and his leading associates and followers, Eugen von Bohm Bäwerk and Friedrich von Wieser, as indeed there are among current neo-Austrians; but this is not the main source of definitional difficulties. It is significant that the latest review of the field, by Alex Shand, seems to have been originally entitled *Austrian Economics: A Survey*, whereas by the time it was published it had become *Subjectivist Economics: The New Austrian School*.[4] If this implies that the two categories are co-extensive, such an interpretation is clearly incompatible with the views of several contributors to this symposium, including its founding father, Professor Wiseman. But if, on the other hand, they are not, then exactly how are they connected: how far do they overlap?

In confessing my inability to provide satisfactory answers to these questions I am, at least, in distinguished company.[5] The issue is, however, of practical as well as academic importance from both the Austrian and the general subjectivist standpoints. If subjectivism is identified with Austrian or neo-Austrian ideas, it necessarily carries with it a penumbra of intellectual connotations, not all of which will be welcomed by all subjectivists. Under the influence of Hayek and Mises, Austrian economics has become associated with a comprehensive and mutually reinforcing combination of elements, including epistemology, methodology, theory, policy recommendations and political ideology. As represented by the more skilful and dedicated neo-Austrian expositors, these ideas appear to possess a logical coherence and systematic character such that those who find parts of the message appealing are liable to be seduced into acceptance of the entire intellectual creed, or *Weltanschauung*. By contrast, the non-Austrian (or even anti-Austrian) subjectivists possess no such central allegiance or collective identity; and if their views are taken to be typical then subjectivism does not constitute a school or movement capable of effectively mounting a challenge to the reigning orthodoxy.

Reference works in the history of philosophy do not appear to recognize subjectivism as a distinct doctrine or stream of thought, and it was therefore interesting to find Shand's citation from Anthony Quinton's *Fontana Dictionary of Modern Thought*:

> In a general way, subjectivism is defined as any theory which takes private experience to be the sole foundation of factual knowledge, even if it admits that objective knowledge can be derived from this subjective base.[6]

This is, of course, vague, no doubt intentionally so, on the central epistemological question of the relationship between private experience – which is necessarily subjective – and the type of objective (public, or inter-subjective) knowledge required by any discipline claiming scientific status; and this issue has figured prominently in subjectivist writings. An examination of recent neo-Austrian literature reveals considerable, even fundamental, disagreement on the matter. To some neo-Austrians Mises' outspoken and explicit *a priorism* seems to be a distinct embarrassment, and as T.W. Hutchison has shown in a powerful recent paper,[7] Hayek has radically altered his epistemological views since the early 1930s. At that time he whole-heartedly endorsed Mises' position, emphasizing the fundamental differences between the social and the natural sciences, whereas more recently he has moved much closer to Karl Popper, a leading advocate of objective knowledge, acknowledging that the differences between the natural and the social sciences have been 'greatly narrowed'. In his Nobel lecture, Hayek conceded that despite their difficulties the social sciences could 'achieve predictions which can be falsified and which therefore are of empirical significance', and he congratulated Popper on the formulation of the demarcation principle, 'by which we can distinguish between what we may accept as scientific and what not'.[8] These views are very far from the radical subjectivism endorsed by such neo-Austrians as Ludwig Lachmann;[9] and while they fall well short of the naturalistic predictivism espoused by some logical positivists and operationalists in the 1930s, they bear no close resemblance to Mises' position.

This is an issue of considerable importance to subjectivists in general and to neo-Austrians in particular, since most of the latter profess some allegiance to Mises. If the time-honoured Austrian doctrine of methodological dualism is abandoned or severely whittled away, so that the differences between the natural and social sciences appear merely as matters of degree (e.g. complexity) rather than differences of kind, then the basis for a subjectivist separatist movement is seriously undermined. Certain beneficial consequences would, of course, follow from such an interpretation, since it would facilitate a reconciliation between subjectivists and the many mainstream or orthodox economists who have become disenchanted with the exaggerated claims of the 'positive' or 'positivistic' economists, who were in the vanguard of the post-war so-called mathematical and quantitative/economic 'revolution'. However, such a reconciliation may not be entirely welcome to some of the active neo-Austrians who have been so successfully conducting a scholarly and professional struggle for recognition during the past decade or so.

This is not the place to discuss this campaign in detail, which has included the inauguration of undergraduate and graduate programmes in Austrian economics; the holding of special instructional seminars designed to spread the doctrine and to enlist proselytes; the organization of numerous scholarly conferences; the launching of scholarly journals and publication series, including reprints of Austrian economic classics; and the founding of a *Newsletter*.[10] Of course these are some of the customary paraphernalia of modern academic life, and the fruits of this movement have already proved to be of genuine scholarly value.[11] Nor is there necessarily anything sinister in the fact that these activities have been so strikingly varied and vigorous partly, if not largely, because they have been generously subsidized by individuals and groups favourably disposed not only to Austrian economics but also to a wide range of other 'libertarian' causes, including the defence of private enterprise and attacks on government intervention in economic affairs. As with the earlier Mises–Hayek dominated phase of modern Austrian economics, the current neo-Austrian movement possesses epistemological, methodological, theoretical, policy and ideological features, although the last two aspects are much less prominent in the recent scholarly writings than the first three. Moreover, despite the expositors' efforts, these elements are by no means incorporated into a comprehensive and unified whole. Indeed, the prevailing methodological tolerance to which Professor Littlechild referred in his paper might well be regarded by hostile critics as evidence of fundamental confusion and inconsistency.[12]

There is, of course, some justification for the contention that special efforts were required in order to secure scholarly *lebensraum* for proponents of Austrian economics at a time when the major scholarly journals and leading research-funding agencies were dominated by a professional establishment or elite prejudiced against them. Nevertheless, it is probably fair to say that no other among the many contending schools and dissident splinter groups in contemporary economics enjoys such substantial outside resources. And this is directly relevant to the present occasion, when it is important not to exaggerate the significance of the neo-Austrian component in the subjectivist revival simply because it is the most visible and coherent part of that movement.

Any brief attempt to specify the precise differences between contemporary neo-Austrians and other proponents of subjectivist economics is liable to be misleading, given the current diversity of opinions among both groups. In view of his influence, it is tempting to cite Mises as the exemplar of modern Austrianism, especially as he so often expressed himself in clear, forthright and unambiguous terms. Nevertheless, despite their collective loyalty, which sometimes amounts to adulation, few of the younger neo-Austrians would endorse Mises' views *in toto*. Apart from his *a priorism,* referred to earlier, he rejected all attempts at quantification in economics, denying the existence of any constants, and arguing that as all economic statistics refer exclusively to past, non-repeatable historical cases, they therefore provide no basis for reliable predictions of future trends.[13] These contentions are, of course, in marked contrast to the moderate subjectivism expressed in Professor Wiseman's paper, where he acknowledges that 'the development of econometrics is a natural offshoot of the commitment to positivism' and denies any intention of destroying or rejecting 'positive' economics.[14] Without going into the question whether positivism (which Mises and Lachmann explicitly reject) is compatible with subjectivism, which may be partly a semantic issue, it seems clear that few of the younger neo-Austrians wish to cut themselves off entirely from the main stream of the profession. Rather, like many 'orthodox' economists, they complain that disproportionate efforts and resources have been devoted in recent years to econometrics, mathematical modelling and excessively sophisticated static theorizing. Unlike earlier Austrians, such as Mises and Hayek, who were profoundly suspicious of or antagonistic to macroeconomics because it was associated with philosophical 'holism' and collectivist thinking, some neo-Austrians are seeking ways of establishing the connections between macroeconomic aggregates and the underlying microeconomic entities in accordance with the long-established Austrian belief in the principle of methodological individualism.[15] Unfortunately it is too early to say whether this approach is likely to yield fruitful results.

Another significant difference between what might be termed Mises-type Austrians and other subjectivists is their attitude towards psychology. Without necessarily espousing an extreme form of methodological dualism, all subjectivists recognize that the social scientist is necessarily concerned with two distinct levels of 'reality' – the external world of observable phenomena (which also concerns the natural scientist), and the 'inner' world of human motives, purposes and interests (which does not). The precise relationship between economics and psychology has long been a bone of contention. Austrians such as Mises and Lachmann have categorically denied that psychology has any role whatsoever in economics, and they seek to dissociate subjectivism from any so-called 'psychological school' of economists.[16] According to Lachmann the social scientist *'explains* social phenomena by reducing them to acts of the mind',[17] a form of reductionism far too extreme for many subjectivists; but he also maintains that *'Not the psychological causes of human decisions, but their logical consequences form the*

476

subject-matter of the analytical social sciences.[18] This entails no commitment to any specific psychological doctrine, least of all behaviourism, which epitomizes the objectivist fallacy of assuming that human action can be comprehended by studying it exclusively from the outside. Like Mises, he contends that the economist is not concerned with detailed explanations or predictions of human behaviour but with general patterns – with the logic of choice or the general theory of action, for example as set out in Mises' major treatise *Human Action*.[19] This is in complete contrast to Professor Wiseman's paper, which boldly appeals for 'a direct study of human behaviour' and concludes that 'economics as a behavioural science can no longer stand aloof from psychology'.[20] Further examples of contemporary subjectivist efforts to take account of psychology in economics, for example in studying the behaviour of firms and consumers, are provided in Professor Loasby's and Mr Earl's papers.[21]

One of the most frequent criticisms of the logic-of-choice approach to economics adopted by some positivist and behaviourist economists is that it is too abstract, general and lacking in empirical content. As Herbert Simon observed more than a decade ago,

> economics has been moving steadily into areas where the power of the 'classical' model has never been demonstrated and where its adequacy must be considered anew. . . . Classical economics was highly successful in handling small-maze problems without depending on psychology. Labour relations, imperfect competition, uncertainty, and long-run dynamics encase the decision-maker in a much larger maze than those considered in classical short-run static theory. In these areas the economist and the psychologist have numerous common interests in cognitive theory that they have not shared previously.[22]

Most neo-Austrians share the general dissatisfaction with theories that assume stable tastes and preferences, perfect information and predictable mechanistic or probabilistic relations between past, present and future. But unlike some contemporary subjectivists,[23] they do not favour empirical studies designed to reveal the precise links between learning and experience, or the nature of decision-making in organizing or groups. Indeed, in Kirzner's case, which may be untypical yet possibly indicative of a general Austrian tendency, so strong is the emphasis on the diversity of human tastes and abilities, and the unpredictability and indeterminacy of individuals' preferences, explanations and knowledge, that it becomes difficult to see how any empirical science is attainable in practice.[24]

It would be pointless to try to compile a complete inventory of the differences between the neo-Austrians and other subjectivists partly because the distinction between them is blurred, and partly because their intellectual interests do not exactly coincide. Thus, as might be expected, notwithstanding the differences within their ranks, the neo-Austrians naturally tend to reflect the breadth, coherence and systematic quality of the Austrian tradition in economics, whereas other subjectivists usually focus attention on specific problem areas, and consequently remain silent on a number of issues that figure prominently in Austrian writings. These issues include, for example, the concept of a 'spontaneous order' in economic affairs; the difference between 'causal genetic' and 'functional' analysis; the crucial role of the market process; and the inequities and inefficiencies resulting from government interference in economic and social affairs. At the same time, they emphasize the dangers and limitations of equilibrium economics, especially when it is interpreted mechanistically; the problem of uncertainty and information; and the role of time in economic affairs. Some of these problems are, of course, fully acknowledged by many other economists, a fact that further complicates the task of classifying various individuals and groups.

THE REVIVAL OF SUBJECTIVIST ECONOMICS: PROVISIONAL EXPLANATIONS

Although there were premonitory rumblings in the two preceding decades, the revival of subjectivism was not conspicuous until the 1970s. Given the proximity of these events and the definitional difficulties involved, any attempt to explain this movement is bound to be tentative and incomplete. No attempt will be made here to differentiate between neo-Austrian and other species of subjectivism; but any worthwhile account must include developments in at least four distinct but interrelated spheres:

(a) 'autonomous' developments in the subjectivist movement itself – including the emergence of a contingent of neo-Austrians, and the increased recognition of behavioural elements in micro-economic activity;

(b) developments in economics as a whole, especially the breakdown (or at least manifest inadequacy) of the dominant professional consensus (i.e,. Keynesian, neo-classical or positivist). This, of course, provided opportunities for a variety of existing dissident and heterodox groups, in addition to the subjectivists;

(c) developments in other intellectual disciplines, which reacted back on economics – e.g., in the history and philosophy of science; in other cognate social sciences; and even in the natural sciences, to which social scientists have customarily looked for their ideal of 'scientific method'; and, finally,

(d) developments outside the academic world – e.g., in economic policy; in the performance of the economy (the so-called 'crisis of capitalism',); and in the public reputation of the economics profession.

Any such schematic arrangement is necessarily arbitrary, for there was

478

a combination of interacting influences at work, not all of which can be considered in the space available. The following account is therefore selective, and will need to be supplemented and corrected by subsequent research.

Under (a), the most intriguing historical problem is: why did the subjectivist revival of the early and mid-1930s – in the works of Mises, Hayek, the Swedes, the so-called 'LSE cost' theorists,[25] and even Keynes himself – prove so transitory? Why were these innovations so completely submerged in the high tide of Keynesian economics, the mathematical/quantitative 'revolution', and positivism (both in Friedman's 'positive' economics in particular and positivist philosophy in general)? An explanation in terms of purely intellectual, scholarly and scientific factors is obviously inadequate, for there were also more directly practical (i.e., applied and policy-relevant) professional, political and ideological influences. Economists turned from microeconomics, where the subjective aspects of individual actions are more obviously pertinent, to macroeconomics, which seemed at once more exciting and more relevant to contemporary problems. For example, Hayek's attempt to explain the early 1930s depression attracted support only briefly, and his passive approach to policy-making seemed entirely inappropriate to the emergency. By contrast, Keynesian ideas and the concomitant activist policy recommendations gave professional economists unprecedented opportunities to participate in public and private decision making during and after the Second World War. And it was not until serious misgivings arose concerning the adequacy of the Keynesian theoretical apparatus that a number of subjectivists – mainly a handful of distinguished elder Austrians – were again able to secure a hearing.[26] Microeconomics gradually re-emerged as an intellectually challenging field, rather than merely a subordinate part of the curriculum. Recent research has rediscovered and developed earlier pioneering efforts to incorporate uncertainty, expectations and imperfect knowledge into economic theories. So prominent has been the neo-Austrian movement in this connection that there is some danger of overstating the influence of Menger, Mises and Hayek. T.W. Hutchison has provided a valuable corrective in his essay on 'The Keynesian Revolution, Uncertainty, and Deductive General Theory', which draws on a penetrating paper he published as far back as 1937.[27] Indeed, the virtual neglect of Keynes' own writings (with the honourable exception of G.L.S. Shackle)[28] on this topic in the era of Keynesian hegemony is a striking phenomenon.

One lesson subjectivists may learn from this experience is that if they wish their movement to continue and flourish, let alone effect a counter-revolution, they must not rest content with attacks on the ruling orthodoxy and the pursuit of interesting theoretical problems, as the neo-Austrians seem inclined to do. They must also demonstrate the practical relevance of their ideas not only in the policy realm, but also as a means of enhancing their exponents' career prospects within the economics profession.[29]

(b) The second category of developments favouring the subjectivist revival – i.e., those in other branches and approaches to economics – are complex, but familiar to readers of the professional journals. They can be summed up as a reaction, perhaps inevitable, against the excessive claims made on behalf of Keynesian, mathematical and quantitative economics, and the break up of the so-called neo-classical synthesis. There was a growing sense that the returns in terms of new theoretical insights and new empirical relationships were comparatively meagre, given the enormous investment of intellectual and financial resources.[30] Other grounds for dissatisfaction included: the neglect of microeconomics and monetary economics; the inadequacy of the microeconomic foundations of macroeconomics; the failure of repeated, often overambitious, efforts to formulate meaningful and relevant large-scale growth models; the economists' limited success in dealing with the problems of underdeveloped countries – the list is not exhaustive, but it is surely sufficient to establish the general point.

When it came, whether justified or not, the reaction played into the hands of other dissident and heterodox groups as well as the subjectivists – including the institutionalists, Marxists and radical economists, many of whom would have endorsed the subjectivists' criticisms of orthodox or mainstream economics.[31] There has been, in effect, more agreement about *What's Wrong with Economics?*,[32] to cite the title of Benjamin Ward's provocative book, than about appropriate remedies.

(c) The third category of developments favourable to the revival of subjectivism – i.e., those within academic disciplines other than economics – is so large and imprecise that it would take a confident polymath to cover them adequately. As previous papers in this symposium [*Beyond Positive Economics*] have shown, subjectivists do not feel constrained by conventional boundaries of economics. They readily incorporate into their analysis elements from any source – e.g., psychology, anthropology, sociology, organization and decision theory, political science – which help to shed light on economic problems. To attempt to examine these linkages systematically would be an impossible task. But as subjectivist economics is usually, though not invariably, anti-positivist, or at least sceptical of the cruder positivist approach to the social sciences, it is appropriate to note certain compatible trends in the philosophy of science during the past two decades, for example in the works of Michael Polanyi, Norbert Hanson, Stephen Toulmin, Thomas Kuhn, Imre Lakatos and Paul Feyerabend.[33] In this context Karl Popper's role is crucial, for his influence has been virtually all-pervading among British social scientists in the early post-war decades.

Popper strenuously resisted the tendency to take account of psychological and sociological factors in the development of scientific knowledge, a tendency of great interest to historians of economics. He also consistently opposed subjectivist epistemologies – writing an influential essay on 'Epistemology Without a Knowing Subject', in which he insisted that 'scientific knowledge

480

belongs . . . to the world of objective theories, objective problems, and objective arguments'.[34] This was in direct contrast to those continental philosophies that influenced authors such as Menger, Marx, Weber, Mises, Hayek[35] and Fritz Machlup. It is, of course, essential to recognize the difference between the *sources* of knowledge, which may include introspection, and the *nature* of scientific knowledge, which must be either 'objective' in some sense, or at least 'inter-subjective'. If the latter position is adopted the problem arises: whose judgement is to count? Who are the competent authorities? These questions pose significant issues in the sociology of science – such as the sources and criteria of scientific authority; the organization and control of knowledge; and the role of scientific elites – issues that have become more obvious to economists and social scientists generally as a by-product of developments in the natural sciences.[36] Kuhn, for example, may not be a subjectivist, as Professor Littlechild has argued; but his work certainly encouraged a more comprehensive and sensitive appreciation of the nature of scientific development and the processes of testing or validating knowledge within the scientific community.[37] This more flexible, historical and humanistic approach discredited earlier, more rigidly naturalistic and mechanistic views of the growth of scientific knowledge, with their concomitant emphasis on the steady accumulation of new 'truths' and their 'naive falsificationist' conception of empirical testings.[38]

(d) Finally, it must be acknowledged that the revival of subjectivism is at least partly attributable to circumstances outside the academic world, for the development of economics has seldom for long been effectively insulated from societal pressures and inducements.

During the post-war period there has been an unprecedented expansion in the employment of economists in non-academic organizations – in government, business and international agencies; and many leading members of the profession have played a prominent part in public discussion of economic affairs and in key policy-making positions. This was a highly satisfactory state of affairs during the first two post-war decades, when economists seemed to be making constructive contributions to the achievement of such goals as the maintenance of full employment, the promotion of economic growth and the extension of international economic co-operation. But when, in the late 1960s and early 1970s, economic policy making no longer appeared successful and events seemed out of control, there was inevitably a public reaction which contributed directly to the so-called 'crisis' in the discipline, for this was essentially a crisis of professional self-confidence.[39]

This is not the place to assign blame for this state of affairs. The reasons for recent policy failures are complex, and can be explained in a variety of ways. The economists' influence has frequently been exaggerated, both by the economists themselves and by their critics. Admittedly some economists have oversold their product, claiming more than they could deliver, while others have colluded with party politicians seeking re-election or anxious to

481

stay in office.[40] Nevertheless economists have not been primarily responsible for the general tendency to politicize economic affairs or for the consequential public disillusionment at the politicians' failure to fulfil their electoral promises. There has, indeed, been a growing concern about professional ethics, and a novel feature of the situation has been the severe criticism of the academic training of new recruits to the profession by non-academic economists employed in business and government.

Against this background it is easy to see why the combination of public and professional dissatisfaction with the discipline has given aid and comfort to a variety of academic critics of the prevailing economic orthodoxy. Perhaps the best example of a subjectivist reaction is Lachmann's comment that subjectivism appeals to all those who feel that our age has somehow 'gone wrong'[41] – to those who find science, technology and modern materialism distasteful; and who favour individual freedom over large-scale organization. In other words, the revival of subjectivism is, itself, a product of the age.

NOTES

1 Cf. my survey article 'The Current "Crisis" in Economics in Historical Perspective', *Nebraska Journal of Economics and Business* 16 (Summer 1977), reprinted in this volume, pp.459–71. Also the recent special issue of *The Public Interest* (1980) entitled 'The Crisis in Economic Theory', with contributions from a dozen well-known authors. It includes an article on 'The "Austrian" Perspective' by Israel M. Kirzner, a leading neo-Austrian.

2 *The Counter-Revolution of Science* (Glencoe, Ill.; Free Press, 1955) p.38.

3 For a comprehensive survey of the subject see R.D. Collison Black, A.W. Coats, Craufurd D.W. Goodwin, *The Marginal Revolution in Economics. Interpretation and Evaluation* (Durham, NC: Duke University Press, 1973), especially the essay 'To What Extent was the Austrian School Marginalist?' by Erich Streissler.

4 Alex Shand, *Subjectivist Economics. The New Austrian School* (Exeter, Devon: Pica Press, 1980) with a comment by G.L.S. Shackle. For other useful surveys see Edwin G. Dolan (ed.), *The Foundations of Modern Austrian Economics* (Kansas City: Sheed and Ward, 1976); Louis M. Spadaro (ed.), *New Directions in Austrian Economics* (Kansas City: Sheed, Andrews and McMeel, 1978).

5 See, for example, Professor Littlechild's paper in J. Wiseman (ed.), *Beyond Positive Economics?* (London: Macmillan 1983) pp.38–49; also the various meanings of subjectivism referred to in the unpublished paper by Ludwig M. Lachmann, 'Ludwig von Mises and the Extension of Subjectivism', delivered at the New York University Conference in honour of Ludwig von Mises, September 1981. According to the *Austrian Economics Newsletter* there is a division between a 'nihilistic' species of subjectivism associated with Keynes (1937 version) and Shackle, and a more mechanistic strain of Ricardianism in recent Austrian literature.

6 Shand, *Subjectivist Economics*, p.12.

7 'Austrians on The Philosophy and Method of Economics – (since Menger)' in his *The Politics and Philosophy of Economics. Marxists, Keynesians and Austrians* (Oxford: Basil Blackwell, 1981). For a different, less penetrating account of Hayek's shifts of position see Norman P. Barry's *Hayek's Social and Economic Philosophy* (London: Macmillan, 1979) chapter 2; also the recent research of Bruce Caldwell, for example, in his 'Hayek's Transformation', History of Political Economy, vol.20, (Winter, 1988),

pp.513–41.

8 The quotations are from Hayek's *Studies in Philosophy, Politics and Economics* (London: Routledge & Kegan Paul, 1967) p.viii (this volume is dedicated to Karl R. Popper): also his Nobel lecture, 'The Pretence of Knowledge', in his *New Studies in Philosophy, Politics, Economics and the History of Ideas* (London: Routledge & Kegan Paul, 1978) pp.33, 31.

9 See, for example, his collection of essays *Capital, Expectations, and the Market Process. Essays on the Theory of the Market Economy*, Walter E. Grinder (ed.), (Kansas City: Sheed, Andrews and McMeel, 1977). Also his article 'From Mises to Shackle: An Essay', *Journal of Economic Literature* 14 (March 1976), pp.54–62.

10 The neo-Austrian revival has been led from New York University, where Mises conducted an influential seminar until 1969. Two of his students, Israel Kirzner and Murray Rothbard, have been prominent, together with a member of the older generation, Ludwig Lachmann. The resumption of the seminar, in 1975, followed the 'crisis' in orthodox economics and may have been influenced by the centenary of the marginal revolution and renewed interest in Menger's works. See, for example, J.R. Hicks and W. Weber (eds), *Carl Menger and the Austrian School of Economics* (Oxford University Press, 1973). In addition to the *Austrian Economics Newsletter*, from 1977, a new periodical *The Journal of Libertarian Studies* has also appeared. These activities have been supported by the Center for Libertarian Studies, the Liberty Fund, the Institute for Humane Studies, the Cato Institute, the Economic Institute for Research and Education, the Schultz and Koch Foundations.

11 See, for example, the volumes in the Studies in Economics Series referred to above, in notes 4 and 9. Also papers have been given and symposia organized at meetings of the American, Southern and Atlantic Economic Associations, and no doubt others too.

12 Littlechild, chapter 3 in J. Wiseman (ed.), *Beyond Positive Economics*. For additional examples of disagreements among neo-Austrians about such fundamental matters as the predictability of human preferences, expectations and knowledge, testing and falsifiability, and *Wertfreiheit*, see Hutchison, 'Austrians on the Philosophy and Method of Economics'. There are not only basic differences between such leading neo-Austrians as Kirzner and Rothbard, but others can be cited as in fundamental disagreement with Hayek's later views. For example, Mario J. Rizzo in Spadaro, *New Directions*, pp.42–4; Lachmann in *Capital, Expectations*, pp.88–9.

13 See, for example, Rothbard's quotations from Mises in Dolan, *Foundations of Modern Austrian Economics*, pp.33–5. The principal sources are his *Theory and History* (New Haven: Yale University Press, 1957) pp.10–11, and *Human Action. A Treatise in Economics* (New Haven: Yale University Press, 1949) pp.55–6, 345.

14 Wiseman, chapter 1, pp.18, 15.

15 For example, Roger W. Garrison, 'Austrian Macroeconomics: A Diagrammatical Exposition' in Spadaro, *New Directions*, pp.167–204. The author begins, significantly, by apologizing for having focused on aggregates rather than processes, as prescribed by Austrian methodology. For a more conventional Austrian reaction, see Lachmann, 'Toward a Critique of Macroeconomics' in Dolan, *Foundations of Modern Austrian Economics*, pp.152–9. Hayek's *Counterrevolution of Science*, contains an extended attack on 'holism'.

16 Cf. Rothbard, in Dolan, *Foundations of Modern Austrian Economics*, pp.30–2; Lachmann, *Capital, Expectations*, pp.52, 53; Mises, *Human Action*, pp.12, 125, 483–5. The term 'psychological school' has been applied both to the late nineteenth century Austrians and to a group of early twentieth century American economists. For an account of this phase of the debate see A.W. Coats, 'Economics

and Psychology: the Death and Resurrection of a Research Programme', in S.J. Latsis (ed.), *Method and Appraisal in Economics* (Cambridge University Press, 1976) pp.43–64. To be reprinted in vol.III of this series.

17 Lachmann, *Capital Expectations*, p.170 (italics in original). This is an explicit statement of a view that is implicit in many subjectivist writings. It poses obvious problems for the methodology of science. For example, Lachmann (ibid., pp.57–8) virtually excludes the possibility of verification.

18 Lachmann, ibid., p.173 (italics in original). However, according to Kirzner, 'Economics has to make the world intelligible in terms of human *motives*'. Cf. Dolan, *Foundations of Modern Austrian Economics*, p.45 (italics added).

19 Mises, *Human Action*, pp.12, 483–5.

20 Wiseman, op. cit. p.25.

21 Ibid., pp.104–21 and 176–91.

22 'Theories of Decision-making in Economics and Behavioural Science', *The American Economic Review* 49 (1963) pp.709, 711. For more general comments and references on this point see Coats 'Economics and Psychology', pp.57–8. To be reprinted in vol.III of this series.

23 Cf. by contrast Earl's comment on the need 'to engage in fieldwork which investigates consumer perceptions', in Wiseman op.cit., p.189. The subjectivists' willingness to cross conventionally accepted subject boundaries, as noted by Earl, is another reason why it is difficult to define the scope of subjectivist economics.

24 Kirzner, in Dolan, *Foundations of Modern Austrian Economics*, p.42.

25 See J.M. Buchanan and G.F. Thirlby, *LSE Essays on Cost* (London: Weidenfeld and Nicolson, 1973); also J.M. Buchanan, *Cost and Choice* (Chicago: Markham Publishing Co., 1969); and Jack Wiseman, 'Costs and Decisions', in *Contemporary Economic Analysis*, vol.2, David Currie and Will Peters (eds), (London: Croom Helm, 1980).

26 Although there seems to have been little or no significant innovation within Austrian economics during the early post-war years, later subjectivists were able to draw upon important developments taking place outside economics during that period.

27 Included in his volume *On Revolutions and Progress in Economic Knowledge* (Cambridge University Press, 1978) chap.7. On p.211 he quotes, with approval, Herbert Simon's view that 'If economics is to deal with uncertainty, it will have to understand how human beings in fact behave in face of uncertainty, and by what limits of information and computability they are bound. . . . This requires a basic shift in scientific style from an emphasis on subjective reasoning within a tight system of axioms to an emphasis on detailed empirical exploration of complete algorithms of thought.'

28 For example his *Uncertainty in Economics and other Reflections* (Cambridge University Press, 1955); and *The Years of High Theory. Invention and Tradition in Economic Thought 1926–1939* (Cambridge University Press, 1967): 'A recognition and insistence on the role of *uncertainty* are what the *Treatise* lacks and the *General Theory* has' (p.184, italics in original).

29 For penetrating, if somewhat cynical, insights into the professional dimensions of this process see Harry Johnson's 'The Keynesian Revolution and the Monetarist Counter-Revolution', reprinted in Elizabeth S. Johnson and Harry G. Johnson, *The Shadow of Keynes. Understanding Keynes, Cambridge and Keynesian Economics* (University of Chicago Press, 1978) pp.183–202.

30 See, for example, the presidential addresses by F.H. Hahn, 'Some Adjustment Problems', *Econometrica* 38 (January 1970) pp.1–17; and W. Leontief, 'Theoretical Assumptions and Nonobserved Facts', *American Economic Review* 61 (March 1971), pp.1–7.

THE REVIVAL OF SUBJECTIVISM IN ECONOMICS

31 I have benefited from reading an unpublished paper by Warren Samuels, 'Austrian and Institutional Economics: Some Common Elements'.

32 Benjamin Ward, *What's Wrong with Economics?* (London: Macmillan, 1972).

33 To list all the relevant works of these well-known authors would take up too much space. Moreover, it might obscure the parallels between technical works in the history and philosophy of science and the broader, more radical contemporary reaction against objectivist approaches to science and society. For penetrating insights into this wider phenomenological movement see Roger Pool, *Towards Deep Subjectivity* (London: Allen Lane, 1972). 'Without taking the fact of *subjectivity* into account . . . without integrating the ideological factors of the subjective revolt into its analysis, objectivity's considerations are less than objective and its conclusions are no conclusions at all', p.43.

34 See Popper's essay in *Philosophy Today*, Jerry H. Gill (ed.), (New York: Macmillan, 1968) p.228; also his *Objective Knowledge* (Oxford University Press, 1972).

35 For evidence of the recent shifts in Hayek's views see above, p.474 and note 7.

36 On the sociology of science, for example, Joseph Ben-David, *The Scientist's Role in Society: A Comparative Study* (Englewood Cliffs: Prentice Hall, 1971); and Warren O. Hagstrom, *The Scientific Community* (New York: Basic Books, 1965). For a brilliant study of the interrelationships between subjectivity and the organization of science see Michael Polanyi, *Personal Knowledge. Towards a Post-Critical Philosophy* (University of Chicago Press, 1958).

37 Thomas S. Kuhn, *The Structure of Scientific Revolutions*, 2nd edn (University of Chicago Press, 1970); also *The Essential Tension. Selected Studies in Scientific Tradition and Change* (University of Chicago Press, 1971) especially chapters 7,9,11,13.

38 The concepts of 'naive' versus 'sophisticated' falsificationism are especially associated with Imre Lakatos' 'Falsification and the Methodology of Scientific Research Programmes' in *Criticism and the Growth of Knowledge*, I.Lakatos and A. Musgrave (eds), (Cambridge University Press, 1974) pp.91–196. For a valuable brief introduction to the issues see A.F. Chalmers, *What is This Thing Called Science? An Assessment of the Nature and Status of Science and its Methods* (Milton Keynes: Open University Press, 1978) especially chapters 4–6; and, with special reference to economics, Mark Blaug, *The Methodology of Economics or How Economists Explain* (Cambridge University Press, 1980) chapter 4.

39 Cf. the sources cited in note 1.

40 See, for example, the severely criticial analysis by T.W. Hutchison, in his *Economics and Economic Policy in Britain 1946–66: Some Aspects of their Interrelations* (London: Allen and Unwin, 1968); and his *Knowledge and Ignorance in Economics* (Oxford: Basil Blackwell, 1977), Appendix.

41 Lachmann, *Capital, Expectations*, p.181.

INDEX